Library of Congress Cataloging-in-Publication Data

BRYCE, HERRINGTON J.
    Financial and strategic management for nonprofit organizations /
Herrington J. Bryce.—2nd ed.
        p.   cm.
    Includes bibliographical references and index.
    ISBN 0-13-377573-9
    1. Corporation, Nonprofit—Management. I. Title.
HD62.6.B78 1991
658'.048—dc20   91-29025
                                                            CIP

Editorial/production supervision   Copy editor: *William Thomas*
    and interior design: *Laura A. Huber*   Marketing manager: *Alicia Aurichio*
Production assistant: *Jane Bonnell*   Indexer: *Shauna C. Bryce*
Acquisitions editors: *John Willig/Bernard M. Goodwin*
Editorial assistants: *Maureen Diana/Diane Spina*
Prepress buyer: *Mary Elizabeth McCartney*
Manufacturing buyer: *Susan Brunke*

The publisher offers discounts on this book when
ordered in bulk quantities. For more information,
write:
        Special Sales/Professional Marketing
        Prentice Hall
        Professional & Technical Reference Division
        Englewood Cliffs, New Jersey 07632

Printed in the United States of America

10 9 8 7 6 5 4 3 2 1

ISBN   0-13-377573-9

PRENTICE-HALL INTERNATIONAL (UK) LIMITED, *London*
PRENTICE-HALL OF AUSTRALIA PTY. LIMITED, *Sydney*
PRENTICE-HALL CANADA INC., *Toronto*
PRENTICE-HALL HISPANOAMERICANA, S.A., *Mexico*
PRENTICE-HALL OF INDIA PRIVATE LIMITED, *New Delhi*
PRENTICE-HALL OF JAPAN, INC., *Tokyo*
SIMON & SCHUSTER ASIA PTE. LTD., *Singapore*
EDITORA PRENTICE-HALL DO BRASIL, LTDA., *Rio de Janeiro*

Financial and Strategic Management for Nonprofit Organizations

Second Edition

Herrington J. Bryce

Prentice Hall
Englewood Cliffs, New Jersey 07632

To Simón J. Bryce and Myra C. Bryce Laporte
And to the Children of the World

Contents

Preface to the Second Edition

This second edition is organized around what we shall call the Four Ms—Mission, Marketing, Management and Money. The sole purpose for the existence of every nonprofit is its mission. The carrying out of every mission—no matter how charitable—requires money. Good management raises money, marshalls human and other resources and uses them masterfully in meeting the organization's aims. It is by effective marketing that money is raised and the mission is propagated.

The book is intended to be a thorough desk reference, a college and professional level training text and a stimulus toward better nonprofit management which has earned the status of being a highly respected and skill-based profession, not merely an avocation. As such, it requires a commitment to skill development and to awareness of the most advanced and successful strategies being used.

This book, which is addressed to public welfare organizations as well as associations, accomplishes its aim by focusing on the questions: What should a person responsible for the resources, programs and mission of a nonprofit know? What are the facts? What are the successful approaches and practices? What are precautions and the options? Thus, the book is addressed to the chief executive officers, members of the board, managers and students aspiring to be managers in this great sector. It also speaks to donors in its description of pitfalls and approaches to giving.

The overriding intent of this book is to give the reader the perspective and vision needed to participate successfully in the management of a nonprofit organization either as an employed manager, a trustee, or a corporate volunteer. Informed decisions are invariably superior.

This book does **not** mimic business texts. Each chapter begins with a discussion about the specific importance of the topics to be discussed to a nonprofit manager. What are the questions the manager is likely to face that makes this discussion relevant? These introductory statements, models, and principles, many developed specifically for this book are accompanied by several real-world examples.

Furthermore, no topic is treated in a purely mechanical way. For example, the discussion of budgeting explains to the reader how the budget can be used to gain managerial control, flexibility, conformity with the mission and the tax-exempt requirements concerning expenditures and revenue structure, why and how to identify certain costs and to account for them. It then walks the reader through step by step in the development of an operating budget that is more than fictitious or make-believe numbers. Good managers do not permit themselves to be deceived by numbers—even of their own creation. The budget becomes the manager's tool rather than his or her master.

This principle of managerial understanding and ability to ethically manipulate tools for the advantage of the organization is the mold in which this book is formed. Therefore, it does not presume that one is a business or management major—only that one takes the mangerial responsibility for the organization sufficiently seriously to guide in a technically informed manner.

Indeed, the examples in the book are purposefully drawn from a wide scope of nonprofits so that the information will apply whether one is operating a library, hospital, museum, school, nursing home, or theater or one is a business, social work, nursing or education major. Another purposeful strategy in the design of this book is to use a lot of religious examples. The primary reason is to demonstrate that certain managerial and financial principles are important no matter how charitable or benevolent the mission. Perhaps no group has learned this lesson more harshly than the Catholic Church in large urban areas. And as libraries have come to discover, no intellectual pursuit is exempt. They have now become a major competitor for gifts and contributions. Thus, the need is across nonprofit groups and this book is designed to serve this breadth. More specific readings for each type of organization may therefore be used to supplement the foundation formed in this book.

Throughout this book, the primacy of the mission is maintained. It is to serve the public good. Failure to obey this overriding principle can lead to personal penalties on the management and the trustees as well as the removal of tax exempt status from the organization. Consequently, this book religiously warns where danger lurks.

Because issues are not always resolved purely on technical bases, the author demonstrates to the reader ethical issues attendant to the technical topics in this book. The book contains several real-world ethical problems requiring the reader to choose, not necessarily between that which is wrong and that which is right, but between competing logic and duties. For most managers, choosing between right and wrong is not difficult. Sleepless nights come when problems rest at the margin; when courage requires making a choice among deserving clients and programs, penalizing or rewarding an employee, taking or rejecting badly needed money—when written ethical codes are insufficient guides.

HOW THIS BOOK WILL HELP YOU

Part I focuses on mission. The mission of an organization is the sole purpose for its existence. Unlike a firm, a nonprofit cannot veer from its mission without serious legal consequences. A mission is akin to a contract between the organization and society. Thus, it is important to know what constitutes a conforming mission. What are the legal limits and powers with which the nonprofit must conform? What are the important guides to policies and strategies?

Every good mission merits an organization with a firm financial foundation. Hence, in Part I of the book the reader is shown how important certain revenue streams are to the maintenance of tax exempt status, how to improve and manage various income streams and how to control costs. The patterns of revenues and expenditures determine tax exempt and legal statuses; and, simultaneously, staff success and even the survival of the organization itself.

Part I also addresses the role of trustees. They are the overseers. They carry the ultimate responsibility for all of the assets of the organization. The law charges them with the care of these assets and in ensuring that the organization fulfills its mission. Part I also carries an ethical dilemma. When is art obscene? When is it freedom of expression?

Part II of this book deals with marketing. In the nonprofit world, marketing serves multiple functions. It is used to raise money and it is used to market the mission, belief, product or service of the organization. Successful marketing is done within a context. It is important to know the environment in which the organization operates. It is this environment that yields both threats and opportunities. The environment also produces needs that the nonprofit serves as its mission. This book explains and provides a framework for managers to understand their local economies which is a most critical aspect of the environment of all nonprofits.

Strategic planning helps the manager to penetrate an environment and to survive it while meeting a credible mission and raising enough money to finance the mission. Strategic planning can help in making critical choices and in setting direction. But marketing has its limits and dangers. There are pitfalls, prohibitions and personal penalties that all managers should know. The organization is also at risk. Hence we address the question: What must nonprofit managers know about marketing? It goes beyond technique.

Part III of this book deals with money. The principal source of financing in the nonprofit world is tax deductible gifts and contributions. Here, the talent of the manager is how to make a deal; how to satisfy the needs of a potential donor, the restrictions of the law, the proscription of watchdog agencies, and the needs of the organization—all at the very same time. How do trusts, wills, insurance, cash and property mesh into a capital campaign? What are the motives for corporate giving? Why may a corporation say no? What gifts are bombshells?

Business income has attracted many nonprofits as government contracts have become less plentiful and as the competition for gifts and contributions tightens. Many nonprofits cannot receive tax deductible contributions and they rely on dues, fees or business income. Managers who undertake business activities must be clear about the risks, nature and role of business income on the organization. We discuss these topics and eighteen questions managers ought to raise before investing the dollars of nonprofits. Similarly, nonprofits dependent upon dues or fees must develop bases for rate-setting. This book shows how to do this and how various sources of income should be integrated. It also discusses cash management strategies. In its totality, therefore, the book covers money-raising, investing and disbursement. It shows how to create and manage an endowment to handle all of these functions.

Part IV of this book deals with management. Without good management, every organization would eventually collapse in failure. In the nonprofit world, good management is more than interpersonal skill and it is certainly more than commitment. From a financial perspective, the emphasis of this book, management must be able to create budgets, communicate them to staff and to trustees, and use them for cost control and as a marketing and planning tool. This book shows how.

This book also shows the managers how to use a balance sheet, revenue and expense statement, statements of changes in financial position, and how to read the auditor's notes to anticipate trouble and to put the organization on a promising path. In addition, it teaches about debt and asset management. It requires no previous knowledge. It is, as they say, "reader-friendly," and the principles are very applicable to the manager's personal life.

Part IV also deals with cost management and the largest cost to nonprofits—labor. In particular, it focuses on employee benefits. Employee benefits are expensive, but necessary. Employee benefits serve two purposes (a) they compensate workers and thus enable the organization to attract and retain good people; and (b) they are a form of risk management—protecting the organization and particularly its employees against certain risks; i.e., the risk of being ill, injured or dying. What should managers know about employee benefits? How should they be designed to meet employee needs and cost containment?

Part IV also deals with risk management from the perspective of organizational liability. The skyrocketing of liability insurance premiums in the middle 1980s and the increasing number of nonprofits that are being sued as states shed them of absolute immunity, induced a sudden interest in risk management in the nonprofit world. Part IV delineates the different types of risks nonprofits face and shows strategies for dealing with these risks.

USING THE BOOK AS A COLLEGE TEXT AND A PROFESSIONAL REFERENCE

This book is written with an awareness that many readers are best served when information is imparted without the need for working through graphs, equations, and unfamiliar terms. Therefore, this book:

1. Puts technical terms in **bold,** immediately defines them, and places them in a real context,
2. Repeats terms and their definitions so that readers do not need to pause, seek definitions, flip back, and memorize unduly,
3. Gives real-world illustrations using well over fifty organizations with their permission,
4. Allows each chapter to stand alone although each gives references to connecting ideas in other chapters,
5. Gives readers a number of enumerated guides; i.e., "ten steps to implement a . . . policy or program."
6. Gives readers enumerated cautions; i.e., "ten questions to ask . . ."
7. Uses graphs as visual aids—not intellectual puzzles.
8. Avoids excursions into abstruse theory or overly simplistic generalities.

A second edition of any book draws upon the encouragement derived from letters and reviews of the first edition. For this author, it began with Jill Muehrcke's comment in the *Nonprofit World* that: "This book represents a tremendous leap forward across that gap of understanding and beyond." It includes a letter from a complete stranger, Louis F. Gorr, Executive Director of the Museum of the Confederacy who wrote, "It is a valuable reference tool to which I regularly turn." And it includes comments on the use of the text as a teaching and training book by Professor Robert Corbone of the University of Maryland.

THE ORIGIN OF THE BOOK

This book is the outgrowth of 15 years of practical experience as a senior employee, officer, member of the board, and consultant to non-profits and as president of a firm. It also grows out of teaching economics of the firm, both corporate and nonprofit finance, risk and cost management, and as director of a graduate program in budgeting, finance, and legal systems, and endless number of seminars and intellectual interaction with executives who must implement programs and with students who aspire to some day succeed them. It also benefits from my experience as a registered investment advisor, chartered life underwriter (CLU) and chartered life financial consultant (ChFC).

The major source cited in the book is The Internal Revenue Code of 1954 as amended in 1969, 1984 and 1986. I began by reading all of the relevant sections of this law even in its tedious form. To bring this material up to date and to give it perspective, U.S. Treasury regulations, Revenue rulings, private letter rulings, General Counsel Memos, Tax Court rulings, decisions of District and Supreme Courts, and the publications of the IRS were read. The reader will frequently find references to these in the text. Reading these documents was tedious and often frustrating, but comparing the doctrines in these documents with popular notions about nonprofits even among so-called experts revealed how badly nonprofits are understood. Many of the popular notions about nonprofits, for example, the concepts of "charitable," "profits," "foundations," and that the profit and charitable motives are incompatible, have no basis in law, in fact, or in the practice of the most successful and charitable of nonprofits.

This book avoids the common errors of believing that business techniques are readily transferable to nonprofits or that they are totally inapplicable to them. The real opportunity for increasing the efficiency of financial as well as strategic management in nonprofits lies in going beyond some of these popular views. The intellectual challenge is to be creative in a practical manner; i.e., to be useful.

We hope you will find the journey rewarding.

Acknowledgments

I wish to thank John C. Jamison, Director of the Virginia Mariners Museum, for being a good fan of this effort; Phyllis Viands of the College of William and Mary for typing endless drafts of this entire book and being a good friend throughout its revision; the MBA and Executive MBA students and doctoral students in education at the College of William and Mary and at the Graduate School, University College, University of Maryland for enduring long lectures; Drs. Donna and Michael Lenaghan of Campfire Boys and Girls and American Humanics for their insight and enthusiasm; Dr. Ramona Edelin of the National Urban Coalition, Edward Wallace of the Booker T. Washington Foundation, Curtis McClinton of East Coast Community College, and Dr. Dennis Young from the nonprofit program at Case Western Reserve for formative insights. I wish to thank Dean Alfred Page and my colleagues in the Business School of William and Mary for indulging this activity even under severe budget constraints.

The fact is that authors of books such as this frequently are called upon to address groups. In my case, I have benefitted from very thoughtful questions of practicing executives. Those audiences will see their concerns addressed in this book—as in the lectures. It would be unfair not to list some of these groups and the subjects that their inquiries touched. The American Psychological Association's state directors on lobbying, corporate powers, and endowment; The American Humanics on planning and marketing; Dee Brinkley and the YWCA state directors on monitoring, needs assessment and liability; the Pennsylvania Arts Coalition on contributions; the National Association of College Auxiliary Services and the Nonprofit Management Association on commercialism, and QED Communications on budgeting and UBIT; the attendees at the Executive Center seminars at the College of William and Mary on trustees, credit real estate and banking relationships.

I am grateful for the resources in the Professional Resource Center (School of Business Administration) and the library in the School of Law at the College of William and Mary, the library at the Foundation Center, Washington D.C., and the library of the University of Maryland, College Park.

I am most grateful to my family and recognize their newly acquired superiority of knowledge in matters of law.

PART I

Mission

When the face of a suffering child mutely asks,
"Who is my neighbor?" we can only conclude, it is
the one who has mercy.

Source: 1990 Annual Report, World Vision

Chapter 1

The Mission: Financial and Strategic Setting

The principal purpose of a business is to make a profit for the benefit of its owners. The principal purpose of a nonprofit organization is (1) not to make a profit, and (2) not to benefit individuals as owners, but to advance the welfare of society. Put another way, the principal mission of a nonprofit is to advance the welfare of the community in a noncommercial manner.

This definition is not theoretical; it is law. As such, both the law and watchdog agencies use many financial standards to ascertain if a nonprofit is fulfilling its mission ethically and legally. They ask, what are the practices and patterns of revenue-raising and of spending by the nonprofit organization? Without money, no nonprofit, no matter how charitable or controversial, can carry out its mission.

Therefore, it is important that we begin this book by first understanding the way finance permeates the operation of a nonprofit. To put things into perspective, this chapter focuses on the role of the financial management function in nonprofit organizations and compares it to similar functions in government and in for-profit firms. How and why is finance so central to nonprofits—other than providing cash? What is so unique about managing a nonprofit organization? How will this book help you as a manager, a trustee, advisor, or student of this great sector?

THE IMPORTANCE OF THE FINANCIAL FUNCTION IN THE NONPROFIT ORGANIZATION

Unlike the task of upholding the philosophical purpose (the mission) of the organization, the debates over financial matters do not rest principally on differences in beliefs or commitment. The principal focus of the task is to acquire, manage, and allocate dollars so that the philosophical mission of the organization, whatever it may be, can be discharged.

Unlike the task of overseeing the performance of the personnel of the organization, the debate over financial matters does not rest on how personnel should be managed. It does not seek to determine who should be hired, how time should be allocated among projects, or who should supervise whom. Rather, it is concerned with finding and allocating the dollars needed to pay employees, to purchase necessary equipment, to pay the rental for the space in which they work, and to control the costs the personnel generates.

Financial management is not the sole responsibility of the organization's president, controller, treasurer, accountant, or vice-president of finance. Although it is important to designate one person to be in charge of the financial well-being of the organization, ultimately this is the responsibility of the managerial staff, including the chief executive officer, each member of the board of trustees, and any other officer of the organization who has decision-making responsibilities.

The Internal Revenue Service (IRS) regulations that govern nonprofit organizations state that any of the persons mentioned above may be held liable for financial errors as long as there is sufficient evidence to presume that they should have known of such errors and could have acted to avoid them. The regulations do not state that the managers or officers have to participate in the decision or its implementation. All that is required is a reasonable presumption that the decision fell within their area of responsibility; and, as a consequence, that they should have been aware.

In addition to the preservation of self, mastery of the information in this book will enable managers and directors to serve the needs of their organizations. Again, this includes managers in staff positions as well as members of the board of trustees. Persons holding such positions have a responsibility for the organization as a whole and not just for particular programs.

The Financial Function and Fund Raising

The financial management function enables fund raising to be more successful by focusing on the financial techniques for raising large amounts of money from single donors. This can be accomplished through trusts, wills, insurance, annuities, and endowments—instruments that make large and complicated gifts possible. In addition, the financial management function carries out policies that bring high and acceptable rates of return on the investment of these funds. This must be done in a manner that is consistent with the philosophy of the organization and its money needs. Success with these efforts tends to generate additional gifts as fund raisers are able to demonstrate to potential donors that their financial impact on the organization can be several times the size of the original gift.

By answering such questions as how much must be raised in the current period if the organization is to meet its various objectives, the financial management function helps in the setting of fund-raising targets. It also helps in the fund-raising effort by identifying the best instrument to meet a donor's situation. In a fund-raising campaign, it can help to speed up the time that the organization has access to the money pledged to it and, by so doing, earn interest on that money. It can establish relationships with regional banks that collect pledges, debit the accounts of donors, and credit the account of the organization. It can set up a lock box so that pledges are mailed directly to the bank and deposited in the account of the organization.

These types of relationships reduce the time lost in mailing checks from the donor to the organization, for processing the checks in the organization, for the organization to deposit the checks in its own bank, and for the bank to collect payment before crediting it to the account of the organization. The financial function is in a position to perform these services since it has the responsibility for coordinating the organization's banking activities.

The law requires public charities to demonstrate external sources of support, called public support, which we shall explore in Chapter 4. Thus, fund raising and development serve an extremely important function not only in the diversification of the income stream of the organization, but in helping it to maintain its legal and tax status as a nonprofit.

Money raised through fund raising may be unrestricted and can be used at the discretion of the organization in ways that would best advance its mission. But people making large gifts often place restrictions on the use of their money. Proposal writers, grant managers, and program directors focus on grants and contracts for specific tasks. Only a small part of the funds raised in this manner can be used to take care of the financial needs of the organization as a whole. Most, if not all, of the monies must be used to discharge the tasks agreed on in the contract or the grant. In some cases, even shifts of monies from one line item to another within the contract may require approval from the contract source.

The Financial Function and Program Management

The financial management function assists the program officers not only by providing them with funds and the support needed to write proposals, but by assisting them to use these same programs to generate income for individual units, as well as for the organization as a whole. This can be accomplished through assisting these units in determining the full cost of running a project so that these costs may be passed on to the project sponsors, rather than absorbed by the organization.

The charging of a program fee, whether it be for tuition, patient care, or a mark up on a contract, is a business and financial transaction. So, too, is the acceptance of a grant from a foundation. These, unlike a gift, are exchanges of money for the promise of specific performance by the nonprofit. Tuition are fees paid by prospective students based on the promise that the school will educate them. A grant is a payment from the foundation based on the promise that the organization will perform in the manner in which it represented itself to the foundation. A government contract is an agreement that the government will pay the organization based on its promise to perform a specific job.

While it is the duty of the program or operations people in the organization to carry out the specific job and perform as promised, it is the responsibility of those in charge of the financial function to price the job to be done; to manage the collection of payments so as to accelerate the rate that payments are received, recorded, and reported; and to allocate or invest payments received in the best interest of the organization in a manner consistent with the organization's policies and mission.

The Financial Function and Marketing

According to a leading scholar in marketing, "The marketer knows how to research and understand the needs of the other party; to design a valued offering to meet these needs; to communicate the offer effectively; and to present it at the right time and place."[1] From this statement it is clear all management activities, including financial management, involve some marketing.

In the financial function, marketing involves knowing the various ways in which a gift may be made and being able to select the best alternative for each potential donor. The principal marketing function of the financial director is presenting convincingly the right type of instrument and argumentation to make a gift possible. It is a cardinal rule of marketing that the marketer knows the product and the organization.

Marketing and financial functions are distinctly different. The director of marketing is concerned with the intricacies of making the products and services of the organization attractive to clients, in developing client awareness, in disseminating information to stimulate sales and contributions, in studying potential markets, and in designing programs for penetrating these markets successfully. The financial function is concerned with money management. As Kotler points out, in some organizations the marketing function is equal to the finance, personnel, and production functions. In others, it might be subordinate or superior to these other functions.[2]

Although separate and distinct, the financial and marketing functions are related because the former assists in determining the final marketing budget of the latter. It also assists in the pricing of products, services, and proposals to be marketed and can also aid in designing effective strategies and instruments to meet the needs of potential donors.

The Financial Function and Strategic Management

Strategic management refers to the determination of the organization's mission and value system, the setting of long-range targets, the identification of the organization's niche, and the charting of the course that will be followed in fulfilling the organization's mission. No matter how laudable a mission may be, it must be financed in order to be realized. It needs money and financial game plans for the short run (operating budget) and for the long run (capital budgets).

To the financial executive, long-range planning is not visionary. It is dealing with objectives and expectations of future realities. For example, the acquisition of a building is a long-range objective. Once the decision is made to acquire a building, its actual acquisition must respect the conditions of present and future markets for money and real estate. Long-term commitments must be entered into well before the building is occupied. Similarly, the acquisition of a car is a long-term commitment to financing and maintenance costs.

In yet another way, the financial function is intricately tied to strategic management. Recall that strategic management involves considerations of the organization's values and philosophy. This value system influences the sources of support to which the organization may turn. It also influences the kinds of investments the organization makes and the image the organization wishes to portray.

Finally, the financial function and strategic management are intertwined because, as we shall see in this book, bad (although not necessarily illegal) financial decisions can lead to the loss of tax-exempt status and virtually terminate the organization's ability to meet its mission. Certain expenditures and revenue imbalances can also lead to termination.

The Financial Function and the Trustees

The trustees of an organization are responsible for overseeing the assets of the organization and for being sure that the organization sticks to its mission. They can be held personally liable for certain uses of the organization's assets. Thus, it is important to maintain a constant flow of information to them. This book discusses the responsibilities of trustees to the organization, and vice versa. It also suggests forms of presenting budgetary and financial data to the trustees to enable them to carry out their roles.

The Financial Function and Risk Management

There are two aspects of risk management with which this book deals. Nonprofits have employees, and employee benefits are ways of an organization managing risks—protecting against quitting, injury, death, and retirement. In many organizations, like firms, these are the most troubling and rising costs. The second aspect of risk management with which this book deals is related to tort or unintentional negligence; that is, injury which results in personal losses. These risks are associated with volunteers, employees, and other agents and representatives—for example, protecting against child molestation and malpractice by a physician or nurse. Another type deals with risks derived from owning or operating property such as a playground, a swimming pool, or an art gallery. Yet another type of risk nonprofits face derives from their producing and selling a product. These are all parts of risk management that will be discussed in this text.

The Financial Function and the Mission

Without money, no mission, no matter how meritorious, can be achieved. But money has another impact. To obtain tax-exempt status, an organization has to demonstrate that its revenues are received in certain ways and in certain proportions to be discussed in Chapter 4 of this book. In addition, its expenditures must meet an acceptable pattern. Both revenues and expenditures must be reported annually, and on these bases, state and federal authorities make decisions about the nonprofit and whether tax-exempt status is merited. The key determinants of whether an organization keeps its status are (1) the revenue pattern and (2) the expenditure patterns.

The Financial Function and Ethics

It would be improper to write this book without reference to ethics. This is a major problem that runs the full gamut of every nonprofit organization—not just finance. The problem is made more urgent by several types of revelations: a president of a community college rigging the books so as to increase enrollment and state aid; a president of a university convicted of making obscene telephone calls; the finding that less than one-half of all Americans think of fund raisers as trustworthy;[3] a finding by Robert Carbone of the University of Maryland that many fund raisers do not believe that their fellow fund raisers are acquainted with ethical standards;[4] a minister in Virginia raising and then stealing funds; professors holding stock in and testifying on behalf of companies funding their research; organizations getting a pittance out of successful fundraising efforts with considerable gains for hired telemarketers. Such mischief often occurs in the name of God.

It is not that these problems are easily solved. Many ethical problems are not binary—right or wrong. Some are the results of conflicts between the present and the past. Many are the results of true conflict among competing interests or rules. Take the professor at Rutgers University who was dismissed because he used visiting Chinese scholars to do his gardening and household chores. He sued and won. The court ruled that ethical lapses were not grounds for dismissal.[5] Or take the case, discussed in Chapter 5, where a university chose to accept a gift of a work of art displaying female genitalia on dinner plates. Is this in keeping with the openness of the educational institution?

And, finally, take the case of the National Religious Broadcasters. Many of their members resigned "because of new ethics standards requiring that a majority of the board members not be from the same family."[6] And the National Society of Funding Raising Executives caused an uproar when they tried to impose certain rules on the compensation of fund raisers. It turns out, as we shall discuss later in this book, that state laws putting such limits have frequently been found unconstitutional and in opposition to the First Amendment.

Yes, ethical issues are central to the operation of every nonprofit—even those that are honest. As a consequence, ethics is not treated in this book as a specific chapter. It permeates the book, as it does each nonprofit organization. We have selected some real cases and challenge the reader to reveal his or her ethical position. These are not cases where right and wrong are black and white. These are conflicts not unlike those management is paid to resolve.

Finally, the reader's attention is called to the first of six ethical canons in the code of ethics of the National Society of Fund Raising Executives:

> Members shall encourage institutions they serve to conduct their affairs in accordance with accepted principles of sound business management, fiduciary responsibility, and accounting procedures; to use donations only for the donors' intended purposes; and to comply with all applicable local, state, provincial and federal laws.[7]

These issues are constantly played out in this book, which invites the reader to understand the broad range of managerial challenge dealing with **money**—its gathering, use and reporting; **management**—its role in mapping out the future of the organization and in compensating the personnel; **marketing**—its legal and ethical constraints; and **mission**—its legal limits and preservation.

THE FINANCIAL FUNCTION IN THE ORGANIZATION CHART

Figure 1.1. shows one of many ways in which the financial function may be represented in the organizational chart of a nonprofit. Note that at the top of the organizational chart is the public. Nonprofits exist to advance public welfare and are fiduciaries of the public. Unlike a for-profit corporation, they are not owned by stockholders.

The board answers to the public or community, and much of the law that governs nonprofit corporations is intended to assure that decisions made by the board of trustees are aimed at advancing public welfare. The board may be divided into several committees, each having a responsibility to oversee a financial aspect of the organization; for example, there might be a budget committee, an investment committee, an audit committee, and a development committee, with each possibly having several subcommittees. Committee members can be held personally liable for certain financial misdeeds of the organization. We shall say more about the board in Chapter 5.

The chief financial officer may carry the rank of a vice-president or senior vice-president reporting directly to the president or chief executive officer of the organization. On the same rank as the chief financial officer may be vice-presidents for administration, including personnel and purchasing, and a vice-president for programs, who may be responsible for a number of operating programs.

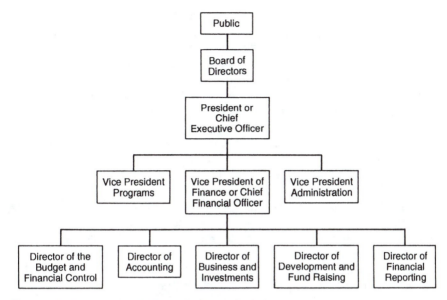

Figure 1.1 Organizational Chart of a Nonprofit Organization.

Directly under the chief financial officer may be the office of budgeting and financial control, which is responsible for preparing the budget for the organization, setting up all financial controls such as procedures for recording receipts and expenditures, scheduling of payments, regularly computing and comparing differences between actual and projected receipts and expenditures, preparing estimates of program costs and revenues for bidding on the contracts, and so on. This office may also keep track of various costs, such as employee benefits, equipment, and rental costs, and compare the products of various benefits and equipment providers.

Also directly under the chief financial officer may be an accounting operation. These people will systematically classify and record the actual income and expenditures of the organization. They keep systematic records of each type of expense, such as payroll, supplies, transportation, and entertainment, as well as records of receipts from fees, gifts and contributions, contracts, and so on. Moreover, this group must keep certain expenditures and receipts segregated from the general accounting of the organization. Certain funds are restricted by covenant, agreement, or contract to specific uses and may not become part of the general funds of the organization. Each building fund and scholarship fund, for example, must be accounted for separately. This is called fund accounting.

Also directly reporting to the chief financial officer may be a director of investments. Some nonprofits have sizable portfolios and businesses that they own and operate. The person who heads this function may not necessarily be the one who makes investment decisions. Investment decisions may be made by the board of directors or through contract with an outside investment advisor. Similarly, each business operated by the organization may have its own manager. All these may, however, report to one person who is responsible for coordinating and overseeing the entire spectrum of investment.

Fund raising is another function that may report directly to the chief financial officer, although it need not. Organizations may have a vice-president for development to whom fund raising is assigned. Even when this is the case, a chief financial officer has some direct responsibility for specific aspects of the fund-raising activity because so much of what is done here requires technical aspects of finance and goes beyond making and perpetuating financial contracts. Fund raising involves contribution campaigns; working with individual, corporate, or foundation donors; working with alumni; and using such technical instruments as wills, trusts, insurance, endowments, and noncash property.

Also reporting to the chief financial officer may be a director of financial reporting. This function covers preparing annual reports on financial matters of the organization and its donors and supporters, filing income tax forms, preparing and making available the public reports that are sometimes required by law, and disseminating these reports.

The nature of the configuration that any single organization may take will depend on the organization's complexity, the level of development, the mission (a hospital compared to a day-care center), the size of the organization, and the management style of its leadership. In some organizations, administrative and financial functions may be combined. Some small organizations may have only one vice-president, and the financial officer may also oversee purchasing and acquisitions. In others, the chief executive officer may carry on the function of chief financial officer. Organizations change structure when confronting new challenges; therefore, it is important to go beyond organizational structure and to focus on the content of certain central financial functions.

While certain configurations and assignments may change, the vice-presidents are always responsible to a president or chief executive officer who is in turn responsible to the board. The board is responsible to the public on whose behalf the legal system acts. To reiterate, in the nonprofit world the financial function is conducted within a set of legal rules that is different from those in the public or for-profit sector. Violation of these rules jeopardizes the organization's existence. The management, including the board of directors, may be held personally liable. Hence, in the nonprofit organization the financial function involves more than the art of investing or politics. It is a specialized aspect of strategic management.

To summarize, the financial management function is a staff function. It assists management in setting realistic financial and performance targets. How much can reasonably be raised and, therefore, how much can reasonably be done? It makes recommendations about ways to increase the inflow of funds into the organization, and it can improve the use of short-term investment techniques to turn idle cash balances into assets earning interest. It can also assist the organization in making long-term investments in such assets as bonds, land, equipment, and buildings and in acquiring and managing its own business. All these involve comparisons of income streams expected from alternative uses of the organization's money and the risks associated with investments, including that of losing the tax-exempt status of the organization.

In addition to assistance in fund raising and development and in the investment of the organization's money, financial management also assists in the assessment of the financial standing of the organization. This is accomplished by interpreting the financial statements prepared by the accountants. Good management must know how to read the three principal financial statements: the balance sheet, the statement of revenues and expense, and the statement of changes in the financial position or of cash flows. Not being accountants, it is not necessary for managers to master the details of fund accounting, which is the accounting method used by nonprofits. However, the financial management function does require the ability to interpret the accounting data in light of the organization's objectives and to work out the alternatives available to management. Stated otherwise, the financial management function converts accounting data into a financial policy consistent with the organization's well being and its mission.

FINANCIAL INFORMATION

In today's highly specialized world, it is not expected that all managers, chief executives, and members of the board of directors of nonprofit organizations be financial wizards. What is important is that management has a working knowledge of the financial management function as it applies specifically to nonprofit organizations. Here is a list of what this necessitates.

The Utility of Financial Information

1. The management has to broaden its perspective about what it means to be a nonprofit from a philosophical to a financial perspective. The mission has to be translated to such terms as how do we raise the money, manage it, and spend it? Recall that the financial management

function does not debate the philosophical merits of a mission. It takes that as a given by the trustees and tries to solve how the mission will be financed. This means talking about money that is measurable. Thus, management's performance can and should be measured.

2. Management has to view its organization as a competitor for scarce dollars. To be financially successful, nonprofits must compete not only among themselves but among the alternative ways that potential donors have to use their money. Giving away money or paying dues are not the only, and frequently are the least attractive, alternatives that a person or corporation has for money. Competition is also involved in recruiting good staff persons and chief executive officers and in being able to retain them by providing good, but affordable benefits.

3. Management has to engage in the planning and the setting of attainable goals and strategies to carry out a mission successfully, including the mission of raising money. From a financial perspective, programs must compete for a limited supply of money. The most profitable program may not always be chosen, but the questions of how much money a certain program can bring the organization or how much the program will cost should never be treated trivially. Except in the cases of mercy and emergency, which are rarities for most nonprofits, a program is not simply an exercise in benevolence. It is a vehicle to directly (through sales) or indirectly (through goodwill) raise money so that even more clients may be served by the organization. Admittedly, money making should not always be the most persuasive reason for choosing one program over the other. Indeed, some money losers may be properly chosen, but the financial impact of such choices on the organization should be known in advance.

4. Management has to understand the major streams of revenues to most nonprofit organizations: gifts and contributions. What are they? From where do they come? When is a gift not a gift? When is a gift likely to be a disguised financial disaster? How are gifts valued and recorded? How do they determine tax exempt status? When might they lead to taxation and reporting requirements?

5. Management has to have a working knowledge of sophisticated tools for raising funds. How can a gift be arranged to provide income for the life of a potential donor or some other person and at the same time provide a handsome contribution to the nonprofit? How can a nonprofit get an annual income from a trust?

6. Management has to understand the legal boundaries placed on the organization and the hidden opportunities available to the imaginative leader. Often, the conclusion that "we can't do it because of our nonprofit status" is incorrect.

7. It is incumbent on management to explore the opportunities to earn the most cherished form of revenues, those self-generating revenues over which the nonprofit management has full discretion. These opportunities lie in making good short- and long-term investments, including the acquisition of profit-making enterprises.

8. Management has to be able to think through an investment decision. This can be done without being trapped by details or formulas that few managers will ever retain or calculate themselves. Yet every manager should be able to understand the thinking and solution to such basic investment questions as how do we know it is a good investment for our organization.

9. Management has to use the budget and the budgetary process as financial planning tools, as tools to coordinate or allocate resources among various programs, and as tools to control spending and the overall direction of the organization.

10. Management has to be able to read certain financial statements. These are the balance sheet, the statement of revenues and expenses, and the statement of changes in the financial conditions or of cash flows. It is the ability to interpret these statements that will give early warning of financial disaster, as well as the financial capacity to grow.

This book deals with all of these topics. It does not presume that the reader has prior knowledge of financial planning. The book tries to make the reader a competent and contributing member of the management staff of a nonprofit organization and of its board of trustees. Such members know their potential liability and are capable of contributing to the growth and financial well-being of the organization. Why? Because such readers will have acquired a firm understanding of the basic blocks of knowledge of the nonprofit financial world and can proceed to institute imaginative and productive programs.

Annual Reporting and Disclosure Requirements

Unless exempted from filing, even those organizations that do not pay taxes must file annual reports with the federal, state, and local governments. These reports are primarily financial—focusing on revenues and expenditures. Unlike an income tax, the objective is not merely to determine gross or net amounts of revenues over expenditures, but to monitor the sources, distributions, and types of revenues and expenditures. Are they appropriate and in keeping with the mission of the organization and with law? This is another reason why this book addresses types of revenues and expenditures.

For the federal government and for some states and local governments, the filing requirements are met by completing Form 990 (and its Schedule A) or Form 990EZ for public organizations and Form 990PF for private foundations. The only exempted nonprofits are those that are churches or church related, those with gross revenues less than $25,000 in that year, federally chartered organizations, agencies of state and local governments, and organizations that are required to file some other reporting form.

These annual reports are the nonprofit's counterpart to the 10Ks that for-profit public corporations file annually. The nonprofit must report major changes in the financing and governance of the organization. Thus, it includes such items as statement of revenues, expenses, and changes in net assets or fund balances; statement of functional expenses; the balance sheet; compensation of trustees and officers; changes in the organizing documents; an analysis of income-producing activities; taxable subsidiaries; and an analysis of the program activities of the organization. All these are subjects of this book.

While the principal purpose of government reporting requirements might be to assess conformity with mission, exemption, and other aspects of the law, a principal purpose of the reporting requirements of the watchdog agencies is to provide clear and relevant information to the public and to assess whether the organization meets certain standards. It is possible to have exemption, carry out the mission, and be very reputable and yet not be in conformity with the standards. And, to the contrary, it is possible to be in conformity with the standards and yet violate the legal requirements for maintenance of exemption. Ethical standards are recommendations; legal standards are law. They both require honesty and disclosure.

In Chapter 2 we shall be looking at legal standards. In the accompanying insert on pages 17–23 we present the standards of the National Charities Information Bureau (NCIB) which along with the Council of Better Business Bureau, Inc. evaluate charities. Note as in the case of government, the emphases on structure, governance, disclosure, and how dollars are received and spent.

UNIQUE CHALLENGES OF FINANCIAL MANAGEMENT IN NONPROFITS

From a financial management point of view, to equate nonprofits with government agencies is devastatingly wrong. Nonprofits are more like businesses. For this reason, increasingly we find statements such as "In its distinguished 88-year history, Goodwill has successfully combined a mission of human service with sound business principles...."[8]

Preamble

The support of philanthropic organizations soliciting funds from the general public is based on public trust. The most reliable evaluation of an organization is a detailed review. Yet the organization's compliance with a basic set of standards can indicate whether it is fulfilling its obligations to contributors, to those who benefit from its programs, and to the general public.

Responsibility for ensuring sound policy guidance and governance and for meeting these basic standards rests with the governing board, which is answerable to the public.

The National Charities Information Bureau recommends and applies the following nine standards as common measures of governance and management.

NCIB Standards

Governance, Policy and Program Fundamentals

1. Board Governance: The board is responsible for policy setting, fiscal guidance, and ongoing governance, and should regularly review the organization's policies, programs, and operations. The board should have

a. an independent, volunteer membership;

b. a minimum of 5 voting members;

c. an individual attendance policy;

d. specific terms of office for its officers and members;

NCIB Interpretations and Applications

Fiscal guidance includes responsibility for investment management decisions, for internal accounting controls, and for short and long-term budgeting decisions.

The ability of individual board members to make independent decisions on behalf of the organization is critical. Existence of relationships that could interfere with this independence compromises the board.

Many organizations need more than five members on the board. Five, however, is seen as the minimum required for adequate governance.

Board membership should be more than honorary, and should involve active participation in board meetings.

e. in-person, face-to-face meetings, at least twice a year, evenly spaced, with a majority of voting members in attendance at each meeting;

Many board responsibilities may be carried out through committee actions, and such additional active board involvement should be encouraged. No level of committee involvement, however, can substitute for the face-to-face interaction of the full board in reviewing the organization's policy-making and program operations. As a rule, the full board should meet to discuss and ratify the organization's decisions and actions at least twice a year. If, however, the organization has an executive committee of at least five voting members, then three meetings of the executive committee, evenly spaced, with a majority in attendance, can substitute for one of the two full board meetings.

f. no fees to members for board service, but payments may be made for costs incurred as a result of board participation;

Organizations should recruit board members most qualified, regardless of their financial status, to join in making policy decisions. Costs related to a board member's participation could include such items as travel and daycare arrangements. Situations where board members derive financial benefits from board service should be avoided.

g. no more than one paid staff person member, usually the chief staff officer, who shall not chair the board or serve as treasurer;

h. policy guidelines to avoid material conflicts of interest involving board or staff;

In all instances where an organization's business or policy decisions can result in direct or indirect financial or personal benefit to a member of the board or staff, the decisions in question must be explicitly reviewed by the board with the members concerned absent.

i. no material conflicts of interest involving board or staff;

j. a policy promoting pluralism and diversity within the organization's board, staff, and constituencies.

Organizations vary widely in their ability to demonstrate pluralism and diversity. Every organization should establish a policy, consistent with its mission statement, that fosters such inclusiveness. An affirmative action program is an example of fulfilling this requirement.

2. Purpose: The organization's purpose, approved by the board, should be formally and specifically stated.

The formal or abridged statement of purpose should appear with some frequency in organization publications and presentations.

3. Programs: The organization's activities should be consistent with its statement of purpose.

4. Information: Promotion, fund raising, and public information should describe accurately the organization's identity, purpose, programs, and financial needs.

Not every communication from an organization need contain all this descriptive information, but each one should include all accurate information relevant to its primary message.

There should be no material omissions, exaggerations of fact, misleading photographs, or any other practice which would tend to create a false impression or misunderstanding.

5. Financial Support and Related Activities: The board is accountable for all authorized activities generating financial support on the organization's behalf:

a. fund-raising practices should encourage voluntary giving and should not apply unwarranted pressure;

b. descriptive and financial information for all substantial income and for all revenue-generating activities conducted by the organization should be disclosed on request;

Such activities include, but are not limited to, fees for service, related and unrelated business ventures, and for-profit subsidiaries.

c. basic descriptive and financial information for income derived from authorized commercial activities, involving the organization's name, which are conducted by for-profit organizations, should be available. All public promotion of such commercial activity should either include this information or indicate that it is available from the organization.

Basic descriptive and financial information may vary depending on the promotional activity involved. Common elements would include, for example, the campaign time frame, the total amount or the percentage to be received by the organization, whether the organization's contributor list is made available to the for-profit company, and the campaign expenses directly incurred by the organization.

6. Use of Funds: The organization's use of funds should reflect consideration of current and future needs and resources in planning for program continuity. The organization should:

a. spend at least 60% of annual expenses for program activities;

b. insure that fund-raising expenses, in relation to fund-raising results, are reasonable over time;

Fund-raising methods available to organizations vary widely and often have very different costs. Overall, an organization's fund-raising expense should be reasonable in relation to the contributions received, which could include indirect contributions (such as federated campaign support), bequests (generally averaged over five years), and government grants.

c. have net assets available for the following fiscal year not usually more than twice the current year's expenses or the next year's budget, whichever is higher;

Reserve Funds

Unless specifically told otherwise, most contributors believe that their contributions are being applied to the current program needs identified by the organization.

Organizations may accumulate reserve funds in the interest of prudent management. Reserve funds in excess of the standard may be justified in special circumstances.

In all cases the needs of the constituency served should be the most important factor in determining and evaluating the appropriate level of available net assets.

d. not have a persistent and/or increasing deficit in the unrestricted fund balance.

Deficits

An organization which incurs a deficit in its unrestricted fund balance should make every attempt to restore the fund balance as soon as possible. Any organization sustaining a substantial and persistent, or an increasing, deficit is at least in demonstrable financial danger, and may even be fiscally irresponsible. In its evaluations, NCIB will take into account evidence of remedial efforts.

Reporting and Fiscal Fundamentals

7. Annual Reporting: An annual report should be available on request, and should include

Where an equivalent package of documentation, identified as such, is available and routinely supplied upon request, it may substitute for an annual report.

a. an explicit narrative description of the organization's major activities, presented in the same major categories and covering the same fiscal period as the audited financial statements;

b. a list of board members;

The listing of board members should include some identifying information on each member.

c. audited financial statements or, at a minimum, a comprehensive financial summary that 1) identifies all revenues in significant categories, 2) reports expenses in the same program, management/general, and fund-raising categories as in the audited financial state-

In particular, financial summaries or extracts presented separately from the audited financial statements should be clearly related to the information in these statements and consistent with them.

ments, and 3) reports all ending balances. (When the annual report does not include the full audited financial statements, it should indicate that they are available on request.)

8. **Accountability:** An organization should supply on request complete financial statements which
   a. are prepared in conformity with generally accepted accounting principles (GAAP), accompanied by a report of an independent certified public accountant, and reviewed by the board;

To be able to make its financial analysis, NCIB may require more detailed information regarding the interpretation, applications and validation of GAAP guidelines used in the audit. Accountants can vary widely in their interpretations of GAAP guidelines, especially regarding such relatively new practices as multi-purpose allocations. NCIB may question some interpretations and applications.

and

   b. fully disclose economic resources and obligations, including transactions with related parties and affiliated organizations, significant events affecting finances, and significant categories of income and expense;

and should also supply

   c. a statement of functional allocation of expenses, in addition to such statements required by generally accepted accounting principles to be included among the financial statements;

   d. combined financial statements for a national organization operating with affiliates prepared in the foregoing manner.

9. Budget: The organization should prepare a detailed annual budget consistent with the major classifications in the audited financial statements, and approved by the board.

Program categories can change from year to year; the budget should still allow meaningful comparison with the previous year's financial statements, recast if necessary.

NCIB believes the spirit of these standards to be universally useful for all nonprofit organizations. However, for organizations less than three years old or with annual budgets of less than $100,000, greater flexibility in applying some of the standards may be appropriate.

National Charities Information Bureau, Inc.
19 Union Square West • New York, NY 10003-3395 • (212) 929-6300
This publication was made possible by a grant from the Exxon Corporation. Reprinted by permission of NCIB.

Management of Nonprofits and of Government Agencies

Government agencies can exist forever under the taxing powers of the state, local, and federal governments. A government can tax the earnings of every entity whether dead (through death taxes) or alive, domestic or foreign. Nonprofits have no such powers. Like businesses, they may go bankrupt and close. Government agencies do not. Governments default (postpone payment of interest) and increase taxes to cover their debt. They do not close down and disappear via bankruptcy. Nonprofits and firms do. The Richmond California school district declared bankruptcy

---

Attendance at the aircraft carrier Intrepid, the floating museum at 46th Street and the Hudson River, has stabilized this summer and organizers say they are confident the three-year-old museum will survive its financial problems.

To provide the museum with breathing room until revenues can be increased, its administrators filed for bankruptcy in late July, just a few days before bondholders were to receive a $1.2 million payment that would have depleted the museum's bank account.

Without the interest payments, the museum's revenues are enough to pay operating expenses. But with the interest, the museum operated at a loss of $4.3 million in the fiscal year ending last April 30, up from $3 million two years earlier.

Source: Michael Quint, "The Intrepid Museum Fighting to Weather a Financial Storm," *New York Times,* Sunday, October 13, 1985, p. 59. Copyright 1985 by The New York Times Company. Reprinted by permission.

in 1990. The court ordered it to remain open and the state to finance it. Would they do the same for your nonprofit? The authority to declare bankruptcy by Bridgeport, Connecticut, was challenged by the state. The city may restructure its debt, or get relief as firms may do in bankruptcy, but it will not go away as firms do when they fail even after using bankruptcy protection. Eastern Airlines disappeared and so too did PTL.

Another error in equating nonprofits with government agencies is the singular importance placed on the budget. In government, the budget is a legal document. When a budget is passed by a legislative body and signed by the executive, it becomes law. This is true on the state, local, and federal levels. In nonprofits, this is not the case. The budget is at best a plan. Nonprofits do not write laws.

To take this argument one step further, most states and local governments have a legal debt limit and a legal taxing limit of some kind and are legally prohibited from running a deficit in their annual budget. All these budgets are subject to public hearings. None of these rules applies to nonprofits. To the contrary, nonprofits run deficits year after year without sanction of any kind—except the possibility of bankruptcy.

In short, by focusing primarily on the budget, which is a financial plan, managers of nonprofit organizations may overlook more critical financial documents that do provide early warnings about the potential financial problems of their organizations.

In another way, the financial function in a nonprofit organization is strikingly different from the same function in most government agencies. There are few chief executive or financial officers of government agencies who worry about raising revenues. The revenues of government agencies are allocated to them through a political process. The revenues of nonprofits are raised through a competitive process and through appealing to donors or supporters, including persons, foundations, and corporations.

All chief executive officers of nonprofits, even those such as the Smithsonian Institution that are funded by the government, must worry about revenues. In government agencies, revenues are allocated by legislative and executive bodies, and they are obtained through taxation. Nonprofit managers cannot tax and do not have legislative allocation of funds. They must raise funds from their public and private sectors. Consequently, their knowledge of money-raising techniques must be extensive and aggressive. They must learn about trusts, wills, and endowments and the use of insurance to magnify small gifts. Neither the manager of a government agency nor the manager of a business has to be concerned with these instruments as ways of raising money.

Few chief executives or senior managers of government agencies need worry about how to invest the agency's dollars. But good managers of nonprofits must choose among various short- and long-term investments. Government executives worry about how to spend, that is, which programs to underwrite and how much to allocate to each, assuming that both the amount and the allocation are not already written into law. On the other hand, chief executives of nonprofits must not only worry about how much to allocate to each program; they must also worry about investing the organization's funds to maintain a desired stream of income. In the case of nonprofits, no program is mandated by law, as in the case of a government agency or a government-created nonprofit.

In a sense, the financial function in government agencies concentrates on financial reporting, on minimizing costs, and on helping to get a budget through the legislative and executive branches. Financial management in the nonprofit sector also concentrates on these factors, but getting a budget accepted by the board of trustees is a substantially less formidable task than getting it through a legislative body or competing with other agencies for the priority of the executive branch. On the other hand, in the nonprofit sector there is greater emphasis on raising revenues. Revenues must come from a variety of sources and cannot be commanded by law as taxes are. Furthermore, the law requires that the revenues of nonprofits be mathematically balanced between sources and types.

Management of For-profit and Nonprofits

The financial functions in nonprofit and for-profit corporations also differ. In the latter, funds for growth and for financing new initiatives can be obtained from earnings retained from past years' profits, from selling stocks or new interests in the business, or from borrowing. Nonprofits cannot sell stocks in themselves because they cannot legally issue them—except as discussed later. Consequently, the nonprofit manager has to rely on borrowing, new gifts and contributions, retained earnings, or assessments of the membership. In short, the inability to issue stocks means that nonprofit managers cannot appeal to the desire of individuals to make monetary gains as a motive for giving. And it means that it is incumbent on those responsible for the financial function of nonprofits to be knowledgeable and imaginative in exploiting the options available to raise money.

A few states, notably Florida and Louisiana, give nonprofits the option of being a stock or a nonstock corporation. Colorado permits the nonprofit to form as a stock corporation only if it is organized to distribute water. California permits stock corporations as nonprofits only if they are mutual benefit corporations. Some nonprofits have stocks because they were previously for-profit corporations. In this case, the stocks discontinue to pay dividends and are not traded.

In the special type of nonprofit created as a cooperative to assist hospitals, stocks may also be issued, but all these stocks are owned by the hospitals that create the cooperative and they too are not traded.

Most states specifically prohibit the issue of stocks by nonprofits. All prohibit the payment of dividends (returns to stockholders). Even in the few states where stocks may be issued, most nonprofits would choose to be nonstock because it is simpler and easier. In any event, the word stock used with nonprofits denotes membership—the right to vote and to enjoy certain privileges and duties—not ownership as in a for-profit firm and not rights to dividends. The stock becomes an alternative to a certificate of membership. For the vast majority of nonprofits, the exceptions being de minimis, our assertion that nonprofits do not issue stocks is correct. Thus, unlike firms, they cannot appeal to the desire of individuals for private monetary gains.

The financial management functions in the for-profit and nonprofit sectors are different in yet another way. In the for-profit sector, the financial function is rarely so constrained that the very existence of the organization is legally threatened by certain types of revenues and expenditures. For example, in the nonprofit sector, large contributors are prohibited from exercising control over the organization. In the for-profit sector, the large investors own the organization and sometimes exercise total control. Therefore, a sense of power as well as of profits becomes a reason for being involved; not so in nonprofits. Large donors are asked to divorce themselves from control of the organization and of the gift once it is made. Failure to do this has dire consequences on the donor, on the organization, and on its management.

All for-profits do not have to maintain a critical balance in the structure of their revenues, as we shall demonstrate in Chapter 4. Nonprofits that are public charities must demonstrate that a high proportion of their revenues comes from public support or that they are owned by an organization that is publicly supported. Violation of the critical balance in revenues by source can lead to loss of tax-exempt status.

Finally, in the nonprofit sector, there are likely to be prohibitions against making certain types of investments or in engaging in certain types of investment strategies. Nonprofits are less likely to be permitted either by state law or by their boards to deal in the commodity markets or in buying and selling options on stocks. These are highly risky.

Contrary to a common belief that has inhibited many nonprofits and once permeated the literature, the law does not prohibit nonprofits from making a profit. The profit might be sizable. We shall point to nonprofits that operate for profit in all kinds of ventures, and we shall cite court and IRS decisions reaffirming that the law does permit nonprofits to make a profit in Chapter 12. We shall also address the question: What should a nonprofit investigate before proceeding on a profit search?

There are those who would challenge the drawing of similarities between for-profits and nonprofits. One common claim is that nonprofits have multiple and complex objectives and for-profits do not. This statement is false. Unlike for-profit firms, nonprofits are legally restricted. The broadest and largest category, 501(c)(3)s, is restricted to certain types of missions discussed in Chapter 2. The principal mission of a university is to educate. The missions of a hospital are health care and, in the case of a teaching hospital, health care and education. The primary mission of a church is religion.

As we shall see later in this book, not only does the law define what it means by education, religion, and the like, but the definitions are short and to the point. There is nothing complicated about them. Indeed, the more complexity or uncertainty a nonprofit uses to define its mission, the less likely it is to be awarded tax-exempt status. Triune (see insert) was not denied tax-exempt status because it was not a religion, but because it could not prove that its operation fit the strict rules set up by the IRS in its definition.

Research as well as the award-winning work by students of U.S. corporations has shown over and over again that for-profit firms do not have singular, easily defined objectives, and often these multiple objectives clash. We should not tolerate claims of multiple objectives as reasons for excusing the failure of the management of a nonprofit to clearly articulate the mission of the organization. This is important because, as we shall show, organizations that rise above these excuses have been very successful.

Another common claim is that nonprofits cannot measure their output as for-profit firms do. This, too, has only a grain of truth. Ask the presidents of a private or a public university—both nonprofits—to compare their institutions. Both will talk about enrollments, student scores, number of undergraduates and graduates, the number of Ph.D.s on their faculties, and their endowments, capital programs, and operating budgets. These are measurable, although not perfectly. They are also both

---

Petitioner is dedicated to the doctrine of the Triune of Life. That doctrine has three components: intelligence, matter, and force. The sole sacrament currently administered by petitioner is that of spinology. The object of spinology is to restore human beings to harmonious unity of mind, spirit, and body for the fulfillment of life. Petitioner's doctrine teaches that, sometimes, when an individual is spiritually inhibited from expressing his or her full life potential, there is a physical manifestation. Spinology seeks to correct this spiritual problem by the physical sacrament of spinology, which involves a gentle laying of the hands on the person by a certified spinologist.

Source: Triune of Life Church, Inc. *Petitioner* v. *Commissioner of Internal Revenue, Respondent*, T.C. 7/1/85.

comparable between a private and public school. The fact that these indicators may not be perfect measures is no reason to accept excuses.

Profits are not perfect measures and they are not the only measures; the same firm can show profits in a given year at several different levels depending on its accounting scheme, no single one of which is perfect. The point is that strategic and financial managements do not surrender to claims of impossibility because measures are imperfect. In the final analysis, every good manager settles on some measurable indicator. It does not always have to be dollars. Yet financial management in for-profit and nonprofit organizations is basically about the same thing—money.

This is not to argue that there are no substantive differences between for-profit and nonprofit corporations and their financial functions. To reiterate, there are differences including *not* whether a profit can be made, but how the profits are used and their centrality to the corporate mission, the role of gifts and contributions, the involvement of the public as a source of financial support as well as in the discharging of the duties of the corporation, the cost of operation because of private and public subsidies such as volunteers and postal rates, the role of owners and donors, and the legal constraints placed on the activities of the organization. These differences are rooted in law and are the critical distinctions that affect the financial function in nonprofits and make this function substantively and legally different in the nonprofit as compared to government agencies or firms.

LEGAL AND ORGANIZATIONAL CONSTRAINTS OF FINANCIAL DECISIONS

As stated earlier, the financial management of nonprofits is about money, and this theme underlies the entire financial management function. It does not mean that the financial function is unaffected by nonmonetary and ideological considerations. It means that those deliberations are done in a larger context and provide the constraints under which the financial planning function operates. Thus, the decision not to invest in South Africa is not a financial planning decision. It is made by the board of trustees of an organization based on its philosophical commitments, and the financial manager is instructed that all relevant financial decisions must obey the basic policy direction set by the board of the organization.

There are also legal constraints on the financial management function. Unlike for-profit firms, nonprofits must obey stringent rules about investments, expenditures, and revenues. Violation of these rules can lead to a loss of tax-exempt status from the IRS and to the termination of the organization by the state. Therefore, it is critical that these rules be understood, and this book focuses on them.

Some major sources for learning new legal constraints are the *Revenue Rulings* (Rev. Rul.) from the IRS, which give an explanation of IRS interpretation and application of the laws, *General Counsels Memorandums* (GCM), which tell how the lawyers in the IRS advised the IRS commissioner to rule on a specific question and the legal reasoning behind their recommendation, a private letter ruling, which is a letter sent to the taxpayer relating the IRS conclusion concerning the legality of a specific question raised by that organization, Tax Court (T.C.) decisions, which tell how the courts responded, and the *Code of Federal Regulations*, which gives details of new regulations. In addition, there is the basic law, the *Internal Revenue Code* (IRC), and decisions made by the Supreme Court.

Finally, there are constraints set by acceptable standards of behavior. Again, all these are reflected in the chapters of this book.

REVENUE STREAMS AND THE PRACTICE OF FINANCIAL MANAGEMENT IN NONPROFIT ORGANIZATIONS

The concepts and strategies that form the core of this book are more than theory and philosophy. They are grounded in decades of legal opinions pronounced by the courts, in the regulatory practices of the IRS, and in the daily practices of the most successful of nonprofit organizations.

Throughout this book we shall, with the permission of these organizations, cite some of their practices. We shall even analyze some of their financial statements, investment strategies, and business operations. Through these approaches we shall have a better understanding of the financial management challenge in the nonprofit world.

To appreciate the scope of this book as well as its practical orientation, the reader is directed to read the following insert taken from the 1990 Annual Report of the Colonial Williamsburg Foundation, which operates Colonial Williamsburg in Williamsburg, Virginia, a historic museum that attracts some 1 million visitors per year.

Note that, unlike a business, this nonprofit cannot carry out its mission merely by relying on revenues from its business income; and, as in the case of many other nonprofits, it cannot rely purely on grants and contributions. Notice also that, contrary to common belief, nonprofits do pay taxes. And, as we shall see when analyzing other nonprofits, the well-run nonprofit strives for a positive fund balance and an operating surplus. It helps to fund future operations. The complexity and breadth of an organization's activities will also be of importance to us. Note that ac-

1989 FINANCIAL REVIEW

The Colonial Williamsburg Foundation continued to enjoy increasing levels of revenue in 1989, despite the adverse weather conditions experienced throughout the year. Two record snowfalls and a record rainfall, the latter resulting in the flooding of the DeWitt Wallace Decorative Arts Gallery in August, are examples of the uncooperative weather that led to a 2.7 percent attendance drop in 1989. Despite the decline in attendance, each of the Foundation's revenue activities generated increases over the prior year. The donor base and unrestricted gift revenue also increased over prior year levels. As a result, the Foundation offered extensive Historic Area programs and made capital expenditures necessary to maintain the buildings and other facilities of the educational and business operations.

OPERATING REVENUE

The Foundation's consolidated operating revenue for 1989 of $119.4 million increased $7.5 million (6.7 percent) compared to 1988. Highlights of the primary revenue generating activities are discussed in the following paragraphs.

ADMISSIONS

Total admissions revenue of $21.6 million increased by 2.4 percent over 1988 revenue of $21.1 million. Admissions revenue comes from ticket sales for general admissions, special events, tours, coach rides, and other Historic Area activities. Approximately 94 percent of the admissions revenue was attributable to general admission ticket sales. A 5 percent increase in average revenue per ticket sold offset the 2.7 percent decrease in attendance. Visitors continue to show a preference for tickets providing unlimited admission to virtually all exhibits, indicating they prefer a full and varied experience at Colonial Williamsburg.

HOTEL AND RESTAURANT OPERATIONS

The Foundation offers visitors the opportunity to partake of the eighteenth-century traveler's experience by providing rooms and meals in its colonial houses and taverns. In addition, a wholly owned taxable subsidiary operates four hotels and seven restaurants surrounding the Historic Area. Hotel and restaurant revenue rose to $65.0 million in 1989, a $3.7 million (6.0 percent) increase compared to the prior year. This increase is primarily attributable to the addition of 128 rooms at the Governor's Inn, which were in operation for all of 1989 compared to seven months in 1988, and an increase in food sales resulting from the January 1989 opening of Shields Tavern.

PRODUCTS

Products revenue of $21.4 million reflects a $.9 million (4.4 percent) increase over 1988. Products activities include the sale of reproductions of items found in the Foundation's collections, and royalties from the sale of Colonial Williamsburg reproductions by licensed manufacturers. Increases were realized from both activities.

GIFTS AND GRANTS FOR OPERATING PURPOSES

The Foundation received $4.8 million in unrestricted gifts during 1989, a $.9 million (23.1 percent) increase over 1988. Of this amount, $4.4 million was contributed to the Colonial Williamsburg Annual Fund. These gifts support the Foundation's general activities and are recognized as revenue in the year received. Gifts restricted for operating purposes increased $1.1 million in 1989 to $2.7 million. These gifts are restricted for specific projects, and revenue is recognized only as expenditures are made on those projects. Gifts restricted for capital purposes are excluded from operating income. A full discussion of gifts, grants, and pledges begins on page 26.

REAL ESTATE OPERATIONS

Real estate operations generated revenue of $3.9 million, a $.4 million (11.4 percent) increase over 1988. Revenue is generated from the rental of commercial and residential real estate properties in and surrounding the Historic Area. The increase primarily arises from commercial rental properties.

OPERATING EXPENSES

The Foundation's consolidated operating expenses for 1989 were $127.7 million and reflect a $10.0 million (8.5 percent) increase over 1988. The Foundation's activities are labor intensive. As a result, approximately 50 percent of the operating expenses are payroll or payroll related. During 1989, payroll and related expenses increased $5.1 million (8.7 percent) over the prior year. Approximately $4.2 million resulted from additions to staff, necessitated by the new hotel and restaurant facilities, and salary rate increases. The remaining $.9 million was a result of increases in the cost of employee benefits and social security tax. The $1.0 million (5.4 percent) increase in cost of sales is primarily related to the increase in food and beverage sales. The $3.1 million (9.2 percent) increase in "Other" expense is due to increases in maintenance, utilities, interest expense, and various other expense categories.

CAPITAL EXPENDITURES

The Foundation invested $16.6 million in land, buildings, equipment, systems, and collections during 1989 compared to $15.9 million in 1988. Significant capital expenditures during 1989 included $6.7 million on hotel and restaurant renovation projects, $.6 million for completion of a new colonial tavern (Shields Tavern), $1.1 million on the construction of the Winthrop Rockefeller Archaeological Museum at Carter's Grove, $.6 million toward the renovation of the Courthouse of 1770, and $1.0 million on the expansion of the Abby Aldrich Rockefeller Folk Art Center. The remaining $6.6 million was spent for numerous Historic Area renewal and replacement projects and for equipment and furnishings. Capital expenditures were funded from operations, debt, or gifts.

ENDOWMENT FUND

The Foundation's endowment fund is comprised of donor restricted and board designated funds that are primarily invested in high-grade stocks, bonds, and short-term securities. The endowment funds are allocated among several independent portfolio managers whose investment strategies stress maximizing returns through long-term investments. The portfolio managers perform under the guidance of the Investment Committee of the Board of Trustees.

The Foundation's policy, designed to preserve the purchasing power of the endowment, is to limit annual withdrawals to 5 percent of the endowment's average market value during the previous three years. The 1989 withdrawal was $8.1 million, compared to $7.6 million in 1988. Of the $8.1 million withdrawal, $6.6 million was designated as available for operations, and $1.5 million was retained in an income stabilization reserve. During favorable securities market conditions, the withdrawal from the endowment should exceed the amount available for operations, and the residual remains in the income stabilization reserve.

The endowment fund experienced annual returns of 21 percent and 17 percent in 1989 and 1988, respectively, on earnings (interest, dividends, and realized gains) of $16.5 million and $9.2 million. Earnings in excess of the amounts withdrawn for operations were reinvested. As the graph shows, the endowment's fair market value on December 31, 1989, increased by 17.6 percent over the prior year.

FINANCIAL RESOURCES

The Foundation maintained its strong financial condition during 1989. Cash reserves increased $.9 million to a total of $27.2 million. This reflects a $.9 million increase in the income stabilization reserve and a $3.2 million increase in the restricted gift reserve. These were offset by a $3.2 million decrease in the capital and operating reserves. The capital program reserve is a reserve established to fund the acquisition of new capital assets and the replacement of capital assets whose useful life has expired. Restricted gift reserves are funds contributed to the

Foundation that are restricted for specific projects. Except for the cash maintained for day-to-day operations, the Foundation's cash reserves are invested in short-term securities managed by professional money managers under the guidance of the Investment Committee of the Board of Trustees. Approximately $9 million of cash, derived from the issuance of museum revenue bonds, is excluded from the cash reserves. These funds are restricted and are being used primarily to fund the Abby Aldrich Rockefeller Folk Art Center expansion and other Historic Area projects.

Working capital requirements of the Foundation depend on the operating needs of its activities. These requirements are seasonal and are influenced by the number of people who visit Colonial Williamsburg. Working capital at December 31, 1989, of $13.3 million declined from $15.7 million at year-end 1988, and the working capital ratio declined to 1.4 from 1.6. During 1989 and 1988, working capital requirements were funded entirely from operations.

The Foundation maintains lines of credit with two major banks. With the exception of the museum revenue bonds, substantially all long-term debt incurred during the past five years financed hotel and restaurant projects that are expected to generate sufficient funds to service the debt.

PENSION PLAN

The Foundation maintains a defined benefit pension plan, in compliance with the Employee Retirement Income Security Act of 1974 (ERISA), for substantially all its employees. Plan assets, with a market value of $62 million, were available to cover a projected benefit obligation of $31 million. Pension plan assets are managed by professional portfolio managers who are regularly evaluated by the Investment Committee of the Board of Trustees.

TAXES

The Colonial Williamsburg Foundation, as a nonprofit educational organization, is exempt (except for the hotel and restaurant subsidiary and certain merchandise sales) from federal income taxes in accordance with Section 501(c)(3) of the Internal Revenue Code. The organization is classified as a publicly supported foundation under the provisions of Section 509(a)(2) of the Code. Gifts and contributions made to the Foundation are tax-deductible.

The Foundation pays real estate taxes to the City of Williamsburg, James City County, and York County on all properties it owns, with the exception of the major exhibition buildings, which, together with the public greens, are exempt from taxation under Virginia law. Exempt properties are, however, subject to a service charge imposed by the City of Williamsburg.

Reprinted with permission of Colonial Williamsburg Foundation.

tivities are put together in order to create a whole: hotels support the large outdoor museums not only financially, but also by attracting visitors who are seeking very close location and an alternative when other hotels are booked. Finally, note the inclusion of employee benefits, particularly a pension plan. Nonprofits compete for workers who must be paid.

Notice also the role of endowments and their use. In this book we shall discuss the role of endowments, capital planning, and gifts.

The report also makes reference to the fact that the books of the Foundation have been audited. Audits are important for a variety of reasons, including the fact that they give confidence to the board of directors and to potential donors that the financial accounting of the organization is in keeping with acceptable accounting procedures. This book will discuss audits and their purposes and characteristics. As a matter of fact, it is a good idea to refer back to this insert every now and again as we work our way through the book. We shall cover all the topics.

SUMMARY AND CONCLUSIONS

There are several similarities between the financial function of the nonprofit and the for-profit firm. From a financial function point of view, both are concerned with money. As we shall see in this book, those nonprofits that appreciate the real differences and similarities between the nonprofit organization and the for-profit firm can explore these in ways that significantly improve the financial well-being of their organizations without sacrificing the conducting of the organization's mission or violating ethical standards, both of which should discipline managerial decisions.

As we saw and shall see again, particularly in Chapter 4, the financial function is crucial for reasons other than raising money. It is the basis on which watchdog agencies measure the ethical performance of nonprofits and on which the IRS confirms and allows organizations to operate under the banner of a tax-exempt organization.

NOTES

1. KOTLER, PHILIP, *Marketing for Nonprofit Organizations* 2nd ed. (Englewood Cliffs, Prentice Hall, 1982) p. 6.
2. JOSEPH, JAMES, *The Charitable Impulse*, (Washington, D.C., The Foundation Center 1990).
3. CARBONE, ROBERT, *Fund Raising as a Profession*, (College Park, Maryland, Clearinghouse for Research in Fund-Raising, 1989).

4. DRUCKER, PETER, *Managing the Nonprofit Organization,: Practices and Principles* (Cambridge, Mass.: Harper Collins, 1990).

5. *The Chronicle of Higher Education*, August 15, 1990, p. A2.

6. JIM CASTELLI, "Some Members of NRB Object to Ethics Rule," *Nonprofit Times*, Mar. 1990, p.3.

7. *The Journal of Contemporary Issues in Fund Raising* (Alexandria, Va.: National Society of Fund Raising Executives, Summer 1990), p. 58.

8. ALBERT S. TRAINA, Chairman of the Board, Goodwill Industries of America, Inc., *1989 Annual Report Goodwill Industries of America, Inc.*, p. 1.

Chapter 2

The Mission and Its Financing

The principal purpose of a nonprofit is to advance public welfare without being substantially commercial. A nonprofit, like a for-profit firm, is a creature of the state. Nonprofits are legal and economic institutions with a mission. The next two chapters will elaborate on the terms (1) legal organization, (2) economic, and (3) mission. It is from these that the organization derives and perpetuates its powers and purpose. They also define its permissible scope of action.

THE IMPORTANCE OF THE LEGAL ENTITY DESIGNATION

To carry out its mission, the nonprofit must organize. It must be an entity, what lawyers call a person. To illustrate, the United Way of America, Inc. is a person or entity that is separate from its founders, member agencies, or trustees as private persons. It was incorporated in the State of New York. It is therefore a New York corporation even though its headquarters are in Virginia and it operates throughout the country. The United Way of America, Inc., in turn, created two other entities. Gifts in Kind, Inc., is a Virginia not-for-profit corporation that coordinates the donations of products and services. It also created Partnership Umbrella, Inc., a nonstock taxable corporation that runs a purchasing program for nonprofits. The key words are "corporation," "nonstock," "taxable," "exempt," and "nonprofit." What do they mean? Why are they germane?

SCOPE OF FINANCIAL ACTIVITIES PERMITTED BY STATE STATUTES

All nonprofits except those created by the U.S. Congress or a foreign government are legal creatures of a state. They are formed and organized according to state laws and must operate within the laws of the states in which they function. The state in which the nonprofit is formed or organized confers certain legal purposes, powers, and obligations on the organization and its officers. In this sense, nonprofits are no different from business firms. As creatures of the state, both may take the corporate form, and when they do, they are called corporations.[1]

All business corporations have the following characteristics:

1. Their principal purpose is to conduct a commercial activity and make a profit.
2. They have centralized management, meaning that management activities are carried out by only a few designated persons rather than having associated persons participate in management decisions.
3. They have continuous life, meaning that the organization does not end due to the death of one of its principals.
4. Ownership is easily transferrable so that one owner can easily transfer or sell his or her ownership interest to another person.
5. There is a limited liability, meaning that the organization is a separate legal entity and the personal assets of the owners and managers cannot be claimed if the organization is in trouble.

In no state does the single word "corporation" distinguish a business organization from a nonprofit. The key differences between the profit and the nonprofit organizations are that the nonprofit may do business but cannot have profit making as its principal purpose—its mission—and cannot have a substantial part of its energies devoted to a commercial activity. Because there are no owners, stocks, or stockholders of a non-

---

DEPARTMENTAL RESPONSIBILITIES

PRIMARY AREAS

As established by the State Constitution, the office of Commissioner of Charities and Corrections is charged with the responsibility of inspecting conditions and management of all state penal, correctional, and charitable institutions at least once a year. The further duty of inspecting all county and city jails on a regular basis has also been assigned to the Commissioner.

COLLATERAL DUTIES

Charitable Organizations, professional fund raisers, and professional solicitors are required to register with the Commissioner of Charities and Corrections by the Oklahoma Solicitation of Charitable Contributions Act, 1959.

This act charges the Commissioner with the responsibility of registering any benevolent, philanthropic, patriotic, eleemosynary, educational, social, civic, recreational, religious, or any other individual group performing acts beneficial to the public.

The Commissioner is further charged with the responsibility of the collection of the annual fees required of these organizations and individuals. Registration information required of each organization is also maintained by the Commissioner and is available as a matter of public record. Each registrant must also file with the Commissioner each year a report of the activities regarding contributions and their solicitation that have occurred during the past year.

SPECIAL INVESTIGATIONS

The Commissioner of Charities and Corrections stands ready to undertake a special investigation regarding any documented complaint concerning care or treatment of patients or inmates in the institutions under his investigative jurisdiction.

Charities and Corrections, Annual Report, Fiscal Year 1972–1973 (Oklahoma City: Charities and Corrections, 1973), p. 7.

---

profit corporation, there can be no transfer of ownership to individuals. For this reason, nonprofits are called nonstock corporations. There are no individual owners of a nonprofit corporation.

A nonprofit or a business corporation is said to be domestic in the state in which it is incorporated. Nonprofit X is a domestic corporation in the state of Maryland if it is incorporated in that state. A nonprofit is called a foreign corporation when reference is being made to a state in which it is operating but is not incorporated. Nonprofit X is foreign to the state of Maryland if it operates in that state but is incorporated in another. A nonprofit is called alien if it is incorporated abroad. Nonprofit X is alien if it is incorporated in Canada but operates in Maryland. A nonprofit does not have to incorporate in each state. It is incorporated in only one, but may need permission from each state in which it wishes to operate.

Both business and nonprofit corporations are governed by the corporate laws of each state. The charter must conform with the charter requirements of the state in which the corporation is formed, and the organization must operate in conformity with the laws of each state in which it is located. Often a group of incorporators (those who form the nonprofit corporation) would purposely incorporate in one state in order to take advantage of some aspect of the law in that state, but operate in another because of a local or some other advantage. Businesses do the same. Many are incorporated in the state of Delaware but operate elsewhere. Many professional and other associations operate and have their headquarters in Washington, D.C., to be close to the center of political and governmental power, but are incorporated elsewhere.

Although it is technically possible for a small nonprofit to operate without being incorporated or being a trust, only an uninformed person would normally take that risk. Most state laws parallel that of Virginia in holding that all individuals acting on behalf of a nonprofit prior to its being incorporated are personally liable to any third party who successfully sues unless that party also knew that the organization was not incorporated. This liability extends to personal property—house, car, jewelry, and the like. Why would any sensible person take that risk? Certainly, not in the name of charity when incorporating is so simple. As a statute of the state of Florida puts it, "lack of a legal organization or capacity is no defense."

The Corporate Charter and Bylaws

The document that describes the purpose, obligations, and character of the corporation is called the charter or the organizing document. The bylaws govern the procedures of the organization. The state awards a certificate of incorporation to a new nonprofit once the state requirements for incorporation are met.

States differ in what they require a nonprofit to include in its charter and bylaws. The state of Maryland, a reasonably typical state, requires that the charter or bylaws of the nonprofit organization include the following:

1. A provision prohibiting the issuing of capital stock
2. A provision that no director's term may be shorter than the period between annual meetings unless such directors are members and the condition of membership is shorter than the period between annual meetings
3. Provisions that describe the rights, duties, privileges, and qualifications of members
4. Provisions that describe the manner of giving notices of meetings
5. Provisions that describe what constitutes a quorum
6. Provisions that deny or limit the rights of members to vote by proxy
7. Provisions that provide for voting by proxy
8. Provisions that provide that any action may be taken by some specified number or proportion of all members entitled to vote

These are merely some of the common provisions. There may be additional ones, including the stipulation that a nonprofit corporation is subject to the same rules of a regular for-profit corporation unless specifically stated otherwise. Note that these specifications are important because they affect how the organization makes decisions, including financial decisions. The latter decisions often must be made by the board of trustees or the membership. The charter or bylaws must state how these issues must be voted on. Even the requirements of announcing meetings can be crucial. For example, the Maryland Section 5.206 provides that, when a meeting is called and a quorum is absent, a new meeting may be called. As long as the meeting has been duly announced in the newspapers of the county where the organization has its principal office stating that decisions other than the ones that were originally being contemplated can be considered, then the persons constituting the new meeting (without regard to their numbers) may form a quorum and may make decisions in addition to those that were originally being considered.

Powers and Purposes of the Nonprofit Corporation

In their creative capacity, states specify the purpose for which a nonprofit must be intended if it is to acquire a nonprofit status in that state. In Washington, D.C., a popular location for both the chartering and location of nonprofits, the Section 29.504 provides that

Corporations may be organized...for any lawful purpose or purposes including but not limited to, one or more of the following purposes: benevolent; charitable; religious; missionary; educational; scientific; research; literary; musical; social; athletic; patriotic; political; civic; professional, commercial, industrial, business, or trade association; mutual improvement....

This broad scope is not unusual. Notice that the intent is not one of being created principally for making a profit. Yet any of these activities can generate revenues. As we shall see later, once the intent is satisfied, it is the relative amount of revenues that comes from the sale of the goods or services and how they are used that matters—rather than the absence of such sales, revenues, or profits or their magnitude.

Just as states admit certain missions to nonprofit status, some states, specifically New York, disallow others. Common disallowances among states are insurance companies or any organization subject to insurance laws of the state. New York (Section 301) lists twenty-four names mostly connoting financial, legal, or insurance that cannot be used. These include such terms as mortgage and investment, state trooper or lawyer, surety and bond.

States also empower nonprofit corporations. The District of Columbia, Section 29.505, lists the following among the powers of nonprofits:

1. To sue and be sued
2. To purchase, take, receive, lease, take by gifts, devise or bequest, or otherwise acquire, own, hold, improve, use, and otherwise deal in and with, real or personal property, or any interest therein, wherever situated
3. To sell, convey, mortgage, pledge, lease, exchange, transfer, and otherwise dispose of all or any part of its property and assets
4. To purchase, take, receive, subscribe for, or otherwise acquire, own, hold, vote, use, employ, sell, mortgage, loan, pledge, or otherwise dispose of, and otherwise use and deal in and with, shares or other interests in, or obligations of, other domestic or foreign corporations, whether for profit or not for profit, associations, partnerships, or individuals, or direct or indirect obligations of the United States, or of any other government, state, territory, governmental district, or municipality or of any instrumentality thereof.
5. To make contracts and incur liabilities, borrow money at such rates of interest as the corporation may determine, issue its notes, bonds, and other obligations, and secure any of its obligations by mortgage or pledge of all or any of its property, franchises, and income
6. To lend money for its corporate purposes, invest and reinvest its funds, and take and hold real and personal property as security for the payment of funds so loaned or invested
7. To conduct its affairs, carry on its operations, hold property, and have offices and exercise the powers granted by this chapter in any part of the world
8. To elect and appoint officers and agents of the corporation, and define their duties and fix their compensation

9. To make and alter bylaws not inconsistent with its articles of incorporation or with the laws of the District of Columbia, for the administration and regulation of the affairs of the corporation

10. Unless otherwise provided in the articles of incorporation, to make donations for the public welfare or for religious, charitable, scientific research, or educational purposes, or for other purposes for which the corporation is organized

11. To indemnify any director or officer or former director or officer of the corporation, or any person who may have served at its request as a director or officer of another corporation, whether for profit or not for profit, against expenses actually and necessarily incurred by him or her in connection with the defense of any action, suit, or proceeding in which he or she is made a party by reason of being or having been such director or officer, except in relation to matters as to which he or she shall be adjudged in such action, suit, or proceeding to be liable for negligence or misconduct in the performance of a duty

Note that these powers give the nonprofit a wide range of financing and operating authority, including the making of loans, issuing of bonds, and selling of goods and services, tangible and intangible. It only prohibits the issuing of stocks and engagement in trade that is ordinarily illegal, such as the sale of marijuana. Thus, in the District of Columbia as in other jurisdictions, the major limits to financing by nonprofits are economic and financial imagination. The District of Columbia also used its powers to issue bonds to raise funds to finance the capital project of some nonprofits. Note also that the general powers include indemnification. Trustees and managers may be held personally liable for the misconduct of their nonprofits.

A Plan of Dissolution

Because nonprofits are legal institutions, states also require that charters contain a plan of dissolution. This plan states the order in which claims against the assets of the nonprofit must be satisfied if the nonprofit is terminating. In the state of Maryland, a typical case, the dissolution plan must provide that:

1. The assets must first be used to meet the outstanding liabilities of the organization, that is, pay off its creditors.

2. The remaining assets must be distributed as is required by the contractual arrangements. For example, some assets are donated with the expressed agreement that the organization will, if necessary, dispose of them in a certain way such as to offer them to a specific other group.

3. The remaining assets not affected by the two previous conditions may be transferred to other charitable organizations (whether domestic or foreign as these terms have been defined earlier) that are connected to the dissolving organization or that have a similar purpose for being.

4. Other assets may be distributed to members as provided for by law.

5. The remainder, if any, may be transferred to other persons as provided in the bylaws.

The plan of dissolution is critical not only because it is required by the state and provides for an orderly and agreed on manner of disposing of the assets of the organization, but because the federal government requires a specific plan before it confers tax-exempt status on the organization. The federal requirement must be met even if it conflicts with what individual states may allow. The federal government prohibits the transfer of assets to individuals if the organization is specifically seeking a 501(c)(3) status. An exception, a charitable lead trust, is described in Chapter 10. In addition to giving the organization exemption from paying federal income taxes, this status permits donors to deduct gifts and contributions. Hence, items 4 and 5 of the preceding list require explanation. The "member" does not necessarily mean a human being; neither does the word "person." These most frequently mean, in this context, another nonprofit organization.

To dissolve an organization is to wind down its business and to terminate it. An organization is a person, and in the same way that its charter becomes its birth certificate, a plan of dissolution becomes its living will telling how its assets are to be disposed of when it terminates. While an individual has a choice of whether to have a will, a nonprofit is required by law to have one. This is called a plan of dissolution, which must be adopted by the board of trustees. Any changes in this plan have to be reported annually on Form 990 to the federal government.

Dissolution, or termination, may be voluntary or involuntary. Voluntary termination can take place either by a vote of trustees, a vote of members, or a combination of the two. Again, the individual state law dictates. In the state of Massachusetts, Section 11A says that the only way one of its nonprofits can dissolve voluntarily is by a majority vote of the board of trustees petitioning the court to dissolve the organization. The court then decides how the assets will be distributed. In Nevada and New Hampshire, the members may elect to dissolve; but in the latter only 25 percent of votes is necessary, while in the former two-thirds is.

Involuntary dissolution can occur for many reasons. In Wisconsin, for example, these include (1) a fraudulent incorporation, (2) abuse of authority and privileges, (3) failure to appoint a registered agent for 90 days, (4) fraudulent acceptance of money or property or the use of them in ways unintended by their donors, (5) failure to comply with court order for records, or (6) if the corporation by its own act or failure to act surrenders its charter, rights, and privileges. Missouri adds another condition, which is a finding by the court that the trustees are deadlocked and unable to act expeditiously on behalf of the organization. Minnesota adds to the Wisconsin reasons by allowing involuntary dissolution by discretion of the attorney general when the liabilities and obligations of the organization exceed its assets. In Missouri, the attorney general dissolved a nonprofit because it operated bingo without a license.

Whether dissolution is voluntary or involuntary, the distribution of the assets of the organization must be in accordance with the dissolution plan. In Minnesota, as long as the organization has substantial assets, such dissolution must also be supervised by the court.

Other Dispositions of Assets

Another item that the states may require in the charter relates to disposing of property through mergers. Generally, like for-profit firms, nonprofits may merge. Nonprofits may only merge, however, with other nonprofits. We shall discuss merger more in Chapter 13.

Dissolution and merger are ways of dealing with financial difficulties. Liquidation, the selling of assets due to the termination of the organization as through bankruptcy, is also a way of dealing with financial difficulties. However, opportunities for asset acquisition by other nonprofits are provided because some state laws stipulate that upon dissolution of a nonprofit the assets must be transferred (unless sold) to a similar nonprofit.

Unlike the creditors of business firms, creditors of nonprofits cannot initiate an act of involuntary bankruptcy against the nonprofit.[2] That is, if a business cannot pay its bills, its creditors may petition the courts to declare that the business is bankrupt. This cannot be done with a nonprofit. There is no involuntary bankruptcy; thus, the museum referred to in Chapter 1 cannot be declared by its creditors to be bankrupt. It must do so itself and then follow the rules of dissolution in determining how to distribute its assets. One possibility is to merge with another museum. A merger is a form of financing. See Chapter 13 for a discussion of mergers.

To summarize this section, the reader should recall that the nonprofit organization is a creation of the state and that in the exercise of its creative powers the state imposes requirements for incorporation. Some typical requirements relate to the way the nonprofit will conduct itself as an organization, how its assets may be disposed of, the kinds of powers that the organization may exercise, and its purpose for being.

SCOPE OF ACTIVITIES PERMITTED BY FEDERAL LAW

Nonprofit is a status conferred by each state according to its laws. The status refers to a corporation or trust that exists to perform one or more functions, such as those enumerated in the District of Columbia's law referred to previously, and without the intent of operating primarily for making a profit. The organization must also commit itself not to distribute its earnings to individuals as if they were owners, for there are no individual owners.

While states may designate those organizations that would be exempt from the state income tax, states may not give exemption from the federal income tax. If there is a dispute between the IRS and the organization, only the IRS or the courts may award federal tax-exempt status. As a rule, states honor the federal decision whether it is made by the IRS or by a court decision that the IRS follows. Thus, the key exemption comes from the IRS or in a dispute by the court.

The Meaning and Privileges of Exemption

On one level, tax exemption means freedom from paying federal, state, and local income taxes unless the income of the nonprofit falls into one of the categories to be described in Chapter 11. On a second level, income tax exemption means that not only is the organization exempt from those income taxes, but that contributions to it are called charitable and so are deductible by the donor in calculating his or her federal and state income tax liabilities. Without this second benefit, many individuals would not have the incentive to give to certain organizations, and these organizations would not then be able to finance their activities.

To be exempt from federal, state, and local income tax, an organization must first be a legally created nonprofit. That is, it must meet the charter and bylaw requirements for nonprofits in the state in which it is created and must show the IRS evidence that it was created according to state law and was granted a nonprofit charter (in the case of a corporation) or a deed (in the case of a trust) by the state in which it is a domestic corporation. The IRS refers to the charter or deed as the organizing document. An example appears on the next page.

To be exempt on both these levels, exemption from paying income tax and the deductibility of gifts and contributions require that the principal mission of the organization be one defined in Section 501(c)(3) of the Internal Revenue Code. This is called the organizational test. This section of the code identifies charitable, religious, educational, scientific, literary, testing for public safety, fostering national or international amateur sports competition (except the provision of athletic facilities or

ARTICLES OF INCORPORATION OF

The undersigned, a majority of whom are citizens of the United States, desiring to form a Non-Profit Corporation under the Non-Profit Corporation Law of ——, do hereby certify:

First: The name of the Corporation shall be ——.

Second: The place in this state where the principal office of the Corporation is to be located is the City of ——, —— County.

Third: Said corporation is organized exclusively for charitable, religious, educational, and scientific purposes, including, for such purposes, the making of distributions to organizations that qualify as exempt organizations under section 501(c)(3) of the Internal Revenue Code of 1954 (or the corresponding provision of any future United States Internal Revenue Law).

Fourth: The names and addresses of the persons who are the initial trustees of the corporation are as follows:

Name   Address

Fifth: No part of the net earnings of the corporation shall inure to the benefit of, or be distributable to its members, trustees, officers, or other private persons, except that the corporation shall be authorized and empowered to pay reasonable compensation for services rendered and to make payments and distributions in furtherance of the purposes set forth in Article Third hereof. No substantial part of the activities of the corporation shall be the carrying on of propaganda, or otherwise attempting to influence legislation, and the corporation shall not participate in, or intervene in (including the publishing or distribution of statements) any political campaign on behalf of any candidate for public office. Notwithstanding any other provision of these articles, the corporation shall not carry on any other activities not permitted to be carried on (a) by a corporation exempt from federal income tax under section 501(c)(3) of the Internal Revenue Code of 1954 (or the corresponding provision of any future United States Internal Revenue Law) or (b) by a corporation, contributions to which are deductible under section 170(c)(2) of the Internal Revenue Code of 1954 (or the corresponding provision of any future United States Internal Revenue Law).

[If reference to federal law in articles of incorporation imposes a limitation that is invalid in your state, as in California, you may wish to substitute the following for the last sentence of the preceding paragraph: "Notwithstanding any other provision of these articles, this corporation shall not, except to an insubstantial degree, engage in any activities or exercise any powers that are not in furtherance of the purposes of this corporation."]

Sixth: Upon the dissolution of the corporation, the Board of Trustees shall, after paying or making provision for the payment of all of the liabilities of the corporation, dispose of all of the assets of the corporation exclusively for the purposes of the corporation in such manner, or to such organization or organizations organized and operated exclusively for charitable, educational, religious, or scientific purposes as shall at the time qualify as an exempt organization or organizations under section 501(c)(3) of the Internal Revenue Code of 1954 (or the corresponding provision of any future United States Internal Revenue Law), as the Board of Trustees shall determine. Any such assets not so disposed of shall be disposed of by the Court of Common Pleas of the county in which the principal office of the corporation is then located, exclusively for such purposes or to such organization or organizations, as said Court shall determine, which are organized and operated exclusively for such purposes.

In witness whereof, we have hereunto subscribed our names this — day of —— 19—.

Source: Internal Revenue Service, *Tax-Exempt Status for Your Organization,* Publication 557, rev. January 1982 (Washington, D.C.: U.S. Government Printing Office, 1982), p. 10.

equipment), or the prevention of cruelty to children or animals as eligible missions. Within these broad categories, the choice of three specific purposes must be made from Table 2.1.

The organizational test is not passed by merely asserting in the organization's application to the IRS that it is a religious, educational, charitable or some other title identified in Section 501(c)(3). The organization must demonstrate that the specific characteristics of its mission are consistent with the description used by the IRS. If a nonprofit applies for tax-exempt status by asserting that it is an educational institution, it should have the characteristics and mission of educational institutions as described under Section 501(c)(3). If it is a charitable organization, it should have the characteristics of charitable organizations as described by the *Code* and so on. These descriptions are set by the U.S. Congress and are subject to the interpretation and enforcement of the IRS. Missions are legally identifiable.

Because these functions could easily be conducted with a motive of making money for the organizers or the managers of the nonprofit organization, the IRS requires that the motive for conducting the mission not be one of advancing the private welfare of individuals. The motive must be charitable, which means that the motive cannot be to make a profit or to benefit individuals as owners or managers. The beneficiaries must be the community or the public. (We shall return to this theme over and over again in this book.) Understanding this is central to how nonprofits can operate and be financed. Unfortunately, it is an often misunderstood concept. For the time being, it is sufficient to know that the exclusive motive of the nonprofit has to be one of advancing community or public welfare; that is, it has be to motivated by public, not private, benefits.

To be tax exempt on both levels, it is also necessary for the nonprofit to pass what is known as the asset test. To pass, the organizing document

TABLE 2.1 Specifically Authorized Missions of Nonprofits

Activity Code Numbers of Exempt Organizations (select up to three codes which best describe or most accurately identify your purposes, activities, operations or type of organization and enter in block 7, page 1, of the application. Enter first the code which most accurately identifies you.)

Code

Religious Activities
001 Church, synagogue, etc.
002 Association or convention of churches
003 Religious order
004 Church auxiliary
005 Mission
006 Missionary activities
007 Evangelism
008 Religious publishing activities
— Book store (use 918)
— Genealogical activities (use 094)
029 Other religious activities

Schools, Colleges and Related Activities
030 School, college, trade school, etc.
031 Special school for the blind, handicapped, etc.
032 Nursery school
— Day care center (use 574)
033 Faculty group
034 Alumni association or group
035 Parent or parent-teachers association
036 Fraternity or sorority
— Key club (use 323)
037 Other student society or group
038 School or college athletic association
039 Scholarships for children of employees
040 Scholarships (other)
041 Student loans
042 Student housing activities
043 Other student aid
044 Student exchange with foreign country
045 Student operated business
— Financial support of schools, colleges, etc. (use 602)
— Achievement prizes or awards (use 914)
— Student book store (use 918)
— Student travel (use 299)
— Scientific research (see Scientific Research Activities)

Code

046 Private school
059 Other school related activities

Cultural, Historical or Other Educational Activities
060 Museum, zoo, planetarium, etc.
061 Library
062 Historical site, records or reenactment
063 Monument
064 Commemorative event (centennial, festival, pageant, etc.)
065 Fair
088 Community theatrical group
089 Singing society or group
090 Cultural performances
091 Art exhibit
092 Literary activities
093 Cultural exchanges with foreign country
094 Genealogical activities
— Achievement prizes or awards (use 914)
— Gifts or grants to individuals (use 561)
— Financial support of cultural organizations (use 602)
119 Other cultural or historical activities

Other Instruction and Training Activities
120 Publishing activities
121 Radio or television broadcasting
122 Producing firms
123 Discussion groups, forums, panels, lectures, etc.
124 Study and research (non-scientific)
125 Giving information or opinion (see also Advocacy)
126 Apprentice training
— Travel tours (use 299)
149 Other instruction and training

Health Services and Related Activities
150 Hospital

(continued)

TABLE 2.1 Specifically Authorized Missions of Nonprofits (*continued*)

Code	Code
151 Hospital auxiliary	— Attracting new industry (use 403)
152 Nursing or convalescent home	— Publishing activities (use 120)
153 Care and housing for the aged (see also 382)	— Insurance or other benefits for members (see Employee or Membership Benefit Organizations)
154 Health clinic	
155 Rural medical facility	211 Underwriting municipal insurance
156 Blood bank	212 Assigned risk insurance activities
157 Cooperative hospital service organization	213 Tourist bureau
	229 Other business or professional group
158 Rescue and emergency service	
159 Nurses' register or bureau	**Farming and Related Activities**
160 Aid to the handicapped (see also 031)	230 Farming
161 Scientific research (diseases)	231 Farm bureau
162 Other medical research	232 Agricultural group
163 Health insurance (medical, dental, optical, etc.)	233 Horticultural group
	234 Farmers' cooperative marketing or purchasing
164 Prepared group health plan	235 Financing crop operations
165 Community health planning	— FFA, FHA, 4-H club, etc. (use 322)
166 Mental health care	— Fair (use 065)
167 Group medical practice association	236 Dairy herd improvement association
168 In-faculty group practice association	237 Breeders association
169 Hospital pharmacy, parking facility, food services, etc.	249 Other farming and related activities
179 Other health services	**Mutual Organizations**
	250 Mutual ditch, irrigation, telephone, electric company or like organization
Scientific Research Activities	
180 Contract or sponsored scientific research for industry	251 Credit union
181 Scientific research for government	252 Reserve funds or insurance for domestic building and loan association, cooperative bank, or mutual savings bank
— Scientific research (diseases) (use 161)	
199 Other scientific research activities	
	253 Mutual insurance company
Business and Professional Organizations	254 Corporation organized under an Act of Congress (see also 904)
200 Business promotion (chamber of commerce, business league, etc.)	— Farmers' cooperative marketing or purchasing (use 234)
201 Real estate association	— Cooperative hospital service organization (use 157)
202 Board of trade	259 Other mutual organization
203 Regulating business	
204 Better Business Bureau	**Employee or Membership Benefit Organizations**
205 Professional association	
206 Professional association auxiliary	260 Fraternal beneficiary society, order, or association
207 Industry trade shows	
208 Convention displays	261 Improvement of conditions of workers
— Testing products of public safety (use 905)	262 Association of municipal employees
209 Research, development and testing	263 Association of employees
210 Professional athletic league	

(*continued*)

TABLE 2.1   Specifically Authorized Missions of Nonprofits (*continued*)

Code

264 Employee or member welfare association
265 Sick, accident, death, or similar benefits
266 Strike benefits
267 Unemployment benefits
268 Pension or retirement benefits
269 Vacation benefits
279 Other services or benefits to members or employees

Sports, Athletic, Recreational and Social Activities
280 Country club
281 Hobby club
282 Dinner club
283 Variety club
284 Dog club
285 Women's club
—   Garden club (use 356)
286 Hunting or fishing club
287 Swimming or tennis club
288 Other sports club
—   Boys Club, Little League, etc. (use 321)
296 Community center
297 Community recreational facilities (park, playground, etc.)
298 Training in sports
299 Travel tours
300 Amateur athletic association
—   School or college athletic association (use 038)
301 Fund raising athletic or sports event
317 Other sports or athletic activities
318 Other recreational activities
319 Other social activities

Youth Activities
320 Boy Scouts, Girl Scouts, etc.
321 Boys Club, Little League, etc.
322 FFA, FHA, 4-H club, etc.
323 Key club
324 YMCA, YWCA, YMHA, etc.
325 Camp
326 Care and housing of children (orphanage, etc.)
327 Prevention of cruelty to children
328 Combat juvenile delinquency
349 Other youth organization or activities

Code

Conservation, Environmental and Beautification Activities
350 Preservation of natural resources (conservation)
351 Combatting or preventing pollution (air, water, etc.)
352 Land acquisition for preservation
353 Soil or water conservation
354 Preservation of scenic beauty
—   Litigation (see Litigation and Legal Aid Activities)
—   Combat community deterioration (use 402)
355 Wildlife sanctuary or refuge
356 Garden club
379 Other conservation, environmental or beautification activities

Housing Activities
380 Low-income housing
381 Low and moderate income housing
382 Housing for the aged (see also 153)
—   Nursing or convalescent home (use 152)
—   Student housing (use 042)
—   Orphanage (use 326)
398 Instruction and guidance on housing
399 Other housing activities

Inner City or Community Activities
400 Area development, re-development or renewal
—   Housing (see Housing Activities)
401 Homeowners association
402 Other activity aimed at combatting community deterioration
403 Attracting new industry or retaining industry in an area
404 Community promotion
—   Community recreational facility (use 297)
—   Community center (use 296)
405 Loans or grants for minority businesses
—   Job training, counseling, or assistance (use 566)
—   Day care center (use 574)
—   Referral service (social agencies) (use 569)

(*continued*)

TABLE 2.1   Specifically Authorized Missions of Nonprofits (*continued*)

Code
— Legal aid to indigents (use 462)
406 Crime prevention
407 Voluntary firemen's organization or auxiliary
— Rescue squad (use 158)
408 Community service organization
429 Other inner city or community benefit activities

Civil Rights Activities
430 Defense of human and civil rights
431 Elimination of prejudice and discrimination (race, religion, sex, national origin, etc.)
432 Lessen neighborhood tensions
449 Other civil rights activities

Litigation and Legal Aid Activities
460 Public interest litigation activities
461 Other litigation or support of litigation
462 Legal aid to indigents
463 Providing bail
465 Plan under IRC section 120

Legislative and Political Activities
480 Propose, support, or oppose legislation
481 Voter information on issues or candidates
482 Voter education (mechanics of registering, voting, etc.)
483 Support, oppose, or rate political candidates
484 Provide facilities or services for political campaign activities
509 Other legislative and political activities

Advocacy
Attempt to influence public opinion concerning:
510 Firearms control
511 Selective Service System
512 National defense policy
513 Weapons systems
514 Government spending
515 Taxes or tax exemption
516 Separation of church and state
517 Government aid to parochial schools
518 U.S. foreign policy

Code
519 U.S. military involvement
520 Pacifism and peace
521 Economic-political system of U.S.
522 Anti-communism
523 Right to work
524 Zoning or rezoning
525 Location of highway or transportation system
526 Rights of criminal defendants
527 Capital punishment
528 Stricter law enforcement
529 Ecology or conservation
530 Protection of consumer interests
531 Medical care service
532 Welfare system
533 Urban renewal
534 Busing students to achieve racial balance
535 Racial integration
536 Use of intoxicating beverage
537 Use of drugs or narcotics
538 Use of tobacco
539 Prohibition of erotica
540 Sex education in public schools
541 Population control
542 Birth control methods
543 Legalized abortion
559 Other matters

Other Activities Directed to Individuals
560 Supplying money, goods or services to the poor
561 Gifts or grants to individuals (other than scholarships)
— Scholarships for children of employees (use 039)
— Scholarships (other) (use 040)
— Student loans (use 041)
562 Other loans to individuals
563 Marriage counseling
564 Family planning
565 Credit counseling and assistance
566 Job training, counseling, or assistance
567 Draft counseling
568 Vocational counseling
569 Referral service (social agencies)
572 Rehabilitating convicts or ex-convicts

(*continued*)

TABLE 2.1   Specifically Authorized Missions of Nonprofits (*continued*)

Code	Code
573 Rehabilitating alcoholics, drug abusers, compulsive gamblers, etc.	907 Veterans activities
574 Day care center	908 Patriotic activities
575 Services for the aged (see also 153 and 382)	909 4947(a)(1) trust
— Training of or aid to the handicapped (see 031 and 160)	910 Domestic organization with activities outside U.S.
	911 Foreign organization
Activities Directed to Other Organizations	912 Title holding corporation
	913 Prevention of cruelty to animals
600 Community Chest, United Way, etc.	914 Achievement prizes or awards
601 Booster club	915 Erection or maintenance of public building or works
602 Gifts, grants, or loans to other organizations	916 Cafeteria, restaurant, snack bar, food services, etc.
603 Non-financial services or facilities to other organizations	917 Thrift shop, retail outlet, etc.
	918 Book, gift or supply store
Other Purposes and Activities	919 Advertising
900 Cemetery or burial activities	921 Loans or credit reporting
901 Perpetual care fund (cemetery, columbarium, etc.)	922 Endowment fund or financial services
902 Emergency or disaster aid fund	923 Indians (tribes, cultures, etc.)
903 Community trust or component	924 Traffic or tariff bureau
904 Government instrumentality or agency (see also 254)	927 Fundraising
	928 4947(a)(2) trust
905 Testing products for public safety	930 Prepaid legal services plan exempt under IRC section 501(c)(20)
906 Consumer interest group	990 Section 501(k) child care organization

Source: U.S. Government Printing Office: 1986—153-054/50004, Form 1023.

must prohibit the nonprofit from distributing any of its assets or income to individuals as owners or as managers except for fair compensation for services rendered. Furthermore, the nonprofit may not be used for the personal benefits of the founders, supporters, and managers or their relatives or personal or business associates. Moreover, the organizing document needs a dissolution plan similar to the one required by the state. However, the IRS insists that to satisfy its requirements the plan should unequivocally prohibit the transfer of assets upon the termination of the organization to any person or entity that is not a tax-exempt nonprofit in the same sense as is the terminating nonprofit. The only exception to this rule is that the assets may be transferred to the state.

Finally, to qualify under Section 501(c)(3), the nonprofit must pass a political test. The organizing document must forbid the nonprofit from participating in any political campaign on behalf of a candidate. Participation is meant to include the preparation and distribution of campaign literature. This test does not prohibit voter education; but because such

The long and the short of the matter is that the [Kneadmore Life Community Church] KLCC was operated for several purposes. We do not doubt that one purpose for which the KLCC was operated was to permit members to explore various religions so that each individual could find God in his own way.

However, other substantial purposes for which the KLCC was operated include to permit experimentation with lifestyles different from the ones community members grew up with, to permit like-minded individuals to live together at little or no cost, and to permit members to grow and eat organic food. While eating organic food may have acquired some religious significance along the way, it is clear that, on the whole, the KLCC was operated, to more than an insubstantial degree, for nonexempt purposes and that it afforded its members benefits which violated the "private inurement" test.

Source: *Canada* v. *Commissioner,* 82 T.C. No. 73, June 1984.

an activity can be broadly interpreted, it is wise to seek specific exemption from the IRS if a nonprofit is planning to be involved in political activities.

Tax-exempt organizations are prohibited from making expenditures for political purposes, defined as spending to affect positively or negatively a candidate for political office. In American Campaign Academy v. Commissioner, the organization was denied 501(c)(3) status because it was training candidates—all of whom turned out to be Republicans. The Association of the Bar of the City of New York was denied status because its rating of judicial appointees was considered to be political and a substantial part of its activities.

Nonprofits are also prohibited from making substantial expenditures for lobbying; because "substantial" is an elastic concept, a nonprofit may elect a more objective test of whether or not it is violating the lobbying law. This test distinguishes between two types of lobbying. One is to influence a particular legislation, that is, by lobbying the law makers, and the other, called grassroot lobbying, is to influence people. Testifying on issues or sending information to members on issues or bills related to the mission of the organization is not lobbying. Telling them how to vote and how to influence their legislators is grassroots lobbying. The numerical limits on each type of lobbying, for those organizations electing the objective test, is calculated on a sliding scale depending on the total annual spending of the organization. Excess lobbying can lead to a 25 percent tax on the excess, penalties on the management, and, in some cases, loss of status.[3]

Once the 501(c)(3) status is awarded, the nonprofit is assigned a foundation status. It is either classified as a private foundation, a private operating foundation, or what is broadly referred to as a public charity. An essential difference between a public charity and the private nonoperating foundation or private operating foundation is that it receives broad public support. Thus, we may say that a public charity is a nonprofit organization that is broadly supported (financially) by the public. Private foundations and private operating foundations are also nonprofits, but they do not have to demonstrate the depth of public support required of public charities. In Chapter 4 we delve more into these distinctions.

Taxation of Nonprofits

Being both nonprofit and tax exempt does not necessarily mean that an organization pays no taxes. Indeed, every nonprofit must have a Federal Employer Identification Number (EIN) for reporting, taxation and other identification purposes. It means simply that (1) the organization pays no taxes on gifts and contributions and income derived from conducting its mission, and (2) persons and corporations that make contributions to the organization may deduct it from their income taxes. Even though tax exempt at all levels, nonprofits must pay taxes on income derived from activities unrelated to their mission and on certain types of expenditures. Penalties may also be levied against the management of the nonprofit, including the board of trustees. We discuss this in Chapters 4 and 5.

Taxation is possible at all three levels of government. Some states require organizations to register with one or more state agencies even if they don't pay taxes. Typically, on the federal level the main tax liability that a nonprofit faces is an income tax on the *profits* of unrelated businesses. On the state and on the local levels, the tax can also be on unrelated business profits. Virginia localities can tax **gross** business receipts of nonprofits. In addition, there may be a sales tax and even a property tax. Federal, state, and local taxes may be applied on all nonprofits, including churches. In California, for example, only nonprofits that distribute food are exempt from sales tax.

In *Jimmy Swaggart Ministries* v. *Board of Equalization of California*, the Supreme Court, through the opinion of Justice Sandra Day O'Connor, affirmed the right of California to impose a 6 percent sales tax on the mail-order and crusade sales of religious items, noting that the tax was so incidental that it did not infringe on the First Amendment rights of freedom of religion; and in the state of Virginia, Reverend Jerry Falwell had to obtain a special exemption from the state legislature to be exempted from local property taxes on his church's Liberty College; and in the state of Pennsylvania, Allegeny County's district attorney seeks to impose taxes on university stadiums, president's houses, and other properties owned by Carnegie-Mellon, University of Pittsburgh, Duquenes, and others, claiming that they engage in unrelated businesses. Again, tax exemption does not mean no taxes.

THE UNIVERSE OF NONPROFITS AND THEIR MISSIONS

There are several types of tax-exempt nonprofit organizations. The most common way of classifying these organizations is according to the section of the *Internal Revenue Code* under which they fall. Each section describes a particular type of organization and its mission and is the basis of the type of tax exemption that the organization has.

Table 2.2 shows that there are twenty-seven types of nonprofit, tax-exempt organizations according to the IRS classification scheme.[4] These range from churches to insurance companies, from fraternal societies to cemeteries, from labor unions to credit unions, from business leagues to civic leagues, and so on.

Table 2.2 also indicates that only seven of these groups of organizations qualify to receive tax-deductible contributions. These include cemeteries; veterans' organizations; nonprofit corporations organized by Congress; day-care; fraternal and beneficiary associations; organizations of past and present members of the armed forces; and that large group of 501(c)(3)s—the largest group. For these seven groups, not only are contributions to them deductible by the donor, but the net revenues these organizations get from conducting their missions are also tax exempt. For the others, donors may not deduct contributions, but the income the organizations get from conducting their missions is tax exempt.

Of all twenty-seven groups, only those that are defined under Section 501(c)(3) are commonly called organizations that aim at advancing public or community welfare. Most of the others tend to advance the welfare of more narrowly defined groups and are generally referred to as social welfare organizations, as differentiated from public or community welfare organizations.[5]

Table 2.2 also shows the number of each type of nonprofit tax-exempt organization that is in existence. In 1985, 886,658 nonprofit tax-exempt organizations were included in the IRS files. By 1989, there were over 1 million. The actual number of these organizations in existence well exceeds this figure because the only organizations that are included in this count are the ones that are required to file an application for tax-exempt status. The footnote to Table 2.2 states which organizations are not included in the figure. Therefore, the actual number of tax-exempt nonprofits, including those omitted from the IRS count, may well exceed the number in the official count.

Table 2.2 also shows that the most numerous of the tax-exempt organizations are the ones falling under Section 501(c)(3) of the code. These include the churches, schools, day-care centers, art and cultural groups, health facilities, research centers, and most of the community and public welfare or service nonprofits groups and foundations, both

TABLE 2.2 The Universe of Nonprofits

Section of 1954 Code	Description of Organization	Number in 1989	General Nature of Activities	Tax Deductible Contributions Allowable
501(c)(1)	Corporations organized under act of Congress (including Federal Credit Unions)	9	Instrumentalities of the United States	Yes, if made for exclusively public purposes
501(c)(2)	Title holding corporation for exempt organization	6090	Holding title to property of an exempt organization	No[1]
501(c)(3)	Religious, educational, charitable, scientific, literary, testing for public safety, to foster certain national or international amateur sports competition, or prevention of cruelty to children or animals organizations	464,138	Activities of nature implied by description of class of organization	Generally yes[1]
501(c)(4)	Civic leagues, social welfare organizations, and local associations of employees	141,238	Promotion of community welfare; charitable, educational, or recreational	Generally no[1]
501(c)(5)	Labor, agricultural, and horticultural organizations	72,689	Educational or instructive, the purpose being to improve conditions of work, and to improve products and efficiency	No[1]
501(c)(6)	Business leagues, chambers of commerce, real estate boards, etc.	63,951	Improvement of business conditions of one or more lines of business	No[1]
501(c)(7)	Social and recreation clubs	61,455	Pleasure, recreation, social activities	No[1]
501(c)(8)	Fraternal beneficiary societies and associations	99,621	Lodge providing for payment of life, sickness, accident, or other benefits to members	Yes, if used for Sec. 501(c)(3) purposes
501(c)(9)	Voluntary employees' beneficiary associations (including federal employees' voluntary beneficiary associations formerly covered by section 501(c)(10)	13,228	Providing for payment of life, sickness, accident or other benefits to members	No[1]

Section	Organization	Number	Description	Deductible
501(c)(10)	Domestic fraternal societies and associations	18,432	Lodge devoting its net earnings to charitable, fraternal, and other specified purposes; no life, sickness, or accident benefits to members	Yes, if used for Sec. 501(c)(3) purposes
501(c)(11)	Teachers' retirement fund associations	11	Teachers' association for payment of retirement benefits	No[1]
501(c)(12)	Benevolent life insurance associations, mutual ditch or irrigation companies, mutual or co-operative telephone companies, etc.	5783	Activities of a mutually beneficial nature similar to those implied by the description of class of organization	No[1]
501(c)(13)	Cemetery companies	8341	Burials and incidental activities	Generally yes
501(c)(14)	State chartered credit unions, mutual reserve funds	6438	Loans to members; exemption as to building and loan associations and cooperative banks repealed by Revenue Act of 1951, affecting all years after 1951	No[1]
501(c)(15)	Mutual insurance companies or associations	1118	Providing insurance to members substantially at cost	No[1]
501(c)(16)	Cooperative organizations to finance crop operations	17	Financing crop operations in conjunction with activities of a marketing or purchasing association	No[1]
501(c)(17)	Supplemental unemployment benefit trusts	674	Provides for payment of supplemental unemployment compensation benefits	No[1]
501(c)(18)	Employee funded pension trust (created before June 25, 1959)	8	Payment of benefits under a pension plan funded by employees	No[1]
501(c)(19)	Post or organization of war veterans	26,495	Activities implied by nature of organization	Yes
501(c)(20)	Group legal services plan organizations	200	Legal services provided exclusively to employees	No
501(c)(21)	Black lung benefit trusts	22	Funded by coal mine operators to satisfy their liability for disability or death due to black lung disease	No
501(c)(22)	Employer liability trusts	0	Established by plan sponsors	No

(continued)

TABLE 2.2 The Universe of Nonprofits (*continued*)

Section of 1954 Code	Description of Organization	Number in 1989	General Nature of Activities	Tax Deductible Contributions Allowable
501(d)	Religious and apostolic associations	94	Regular business activities; communal religious community	No[1]
501(e)	Cooperative hospital service organizations	79	Performs cooperative services for hospitals	Yes
501(f)	Cooperative service organizations of operating educational organizations	1	Performs collective investment services for educational organizations	Yes
501(k)	Treatment of certain organizations providing child care	7	Child care	Yes
512(a)	Farmers' cooperative associations	2279	Cooperative marketing and purchasing for agricultural producers	No
	Taxable farmers' cooperatives	3295		No
	Nonexempt charitable trusts	42,314		No

Source: Adapted from *Tax Exempt Status for Your Organization*, Publication 557 (Washington, D.C.: U.S. Government Printing Office, January 1982), p. 40.

[1] An organization exempt under a Subsection of Code Sec. 501, other than (c)(3), may establish a charitable fund, contributions to which are deductible. Such a fund must itself meet the requirements of section 501(c)(3) and the related notice requirements of section 508(a).

Numbers are taken from Annual Commissioners Report for 1989, Table 20.

large and small. Together they number in excess of 466,000 or over 40 percent of the total number of tax-exempt organizations in existence today. In actuality, there are countless more of these organizations in existence than the IRS is aware of because certain churches and auxiliaries of churches and associations do not have to apply or inform the IRS of their existence.

With the exception of fiscal year 1982 when there was a decline in 501(c)(3) organizations, probably due to a combination of federal budget cuts and the recession, these organizations have grown in number at a healthy rate, thus intensifying the competition for financial support. In fact, they have accounted for the bulk of all the growth in the nonprofit sector as a whole. They grew from 1988 to 1989 from 447,525 to 464,138 or 4 percent. This was about one and two-thirds times the growth of the entire nonprofit sector, which went from 1.01 to 1.04 million. At this pace, they will continue to be the largest type of tax-exempt organizations for the foreseeable future.

Organizations with Community or Public Welfare Missions

Let us focus on the most numerous type of nonprofits, those under Section 501(c)(3). These organizations exist to advance the public or community welfare by undertaking the following broad missions:

1. Religious
2. Education
3. Charitable
4. Scientific
5. Literary
6. Testing for public safety
7. Fostering certain national or international amateur sports competitions
8. Prevention of cruelty to children or animals

One condition that is common to all eight of these purposes is that an organization formed exclusively for one or more of these reasons is not considered tax exempt unless the intent is to serve a public purpose. Thus, in the words of the IRS:

(ii) An organization is not organized or operated exclusively for one or more of the purposes specified in subdivision (i) of this subparagraph unless it serves a public rather than a private interest. Thus, to meet the requirement of this subdivision, it is necessary for an organization to establish that it is not organized or operated for the benefit of private interests such as designated individuals, the creator or his family, shareholders of the organization, or persons controlled, directly or indirectly, by such private interests. *Treasury Regulations, Section 1.50(c) (3)-1 (d) (1) (ii), 1980.*

The serving of a public purpose is equated to a community purpose. Thus, when the IRS writes of the conditions that would qualify an educational institution for exemption, it states:

(3) Educational defined—(i) In general. The term "educational," as used in section 501(c)(3), relates to—

(a) The instruction or training of the individual for the purpose of improving or developing his capabilities; or
(b) The instruction of the public on subjects useful to the individual and beneficial to the community. *Treasury Regulations, Section 1.50(c) (3)-1 (d) (3) (i) 1980.*

And in *Church of the Chosen People v. U.S.,* a group teaching the single tenet that pairings between persons of the same sex (men with men and women with women) are acceptable in the eyes of God was denied exemption because the court held, among other reasons, that this group existed for the benefit of private individuals rather than for a public purpose.[6]

Several shorthand terms have been used in the literature to describe these organizations that fall under Section 501(c)(3). Sometimes they are referred to as nonprofit organizations because they must all be nonprofit. But as we saw earlier in the chapter, all nonprofits do not fall into these eight categories or under this section of the *Internal Revenue Code.* There is a universe of over twenty different types of nonprofits. Sometimes they are referred to as 501(c)(3) organizations, since this is the section of the *Internal Revenue Code* in which they are described. But merely knowing that a nonprofit is classified as a 501(c)(3) is insufficient to determine its foundation status, and therefore, its limits on financing, expenditures, and investment; business relationship to its sponsors, managers, and their relatives and associates; and its corporate relationship to other nonprofits. We must know, for example, if the 501(c)(3) organization is a public charity or a private nonoperating or private operating foundation. Each is subject to different financing rules, which we shall discuss in Chapter 4.

Sometimes they are referred to as charitable organizations; however, this is but one of the eight categories mentioned. Yet, the word charitable is often used by the courts or the IRS as the key word to describe these organizations. Basically, what is meant by charity is that the nonprofit seeks to promote public or community welfare by providing a service that is not otherwise provided by the market and that the principal motive for providing the goods or services is not to make a profit. It includes a wide range of activities, such as housing, neighborhood development, assistance to the poor, advancement of science, and so on. The concept of charitable is so central that we formally return to it in the next chapter.

Sometimes they are referred to as tax-exempt organizations because they are tax exempt on both levels described earlier. Other organizations are also tax exempt, but only in the sense that they do not pay income tax. A good example of this is a mutual fund. It is tax exempt not because it is charitable but because it distributes 95 percent of its earnings. Yet contributions to them cannot be deducted. Like most of the other organizations in Table 2.1, they are tax exempt in a very different way and for a different purpose than the 501(c)(3) organizations.

Sometimes these 501(c)(3) organizations are referred to as public welfare or community welfare organizations, as opposed to social welfare organizations, to highlight that they all must exist to discharge a mission to improve community welfare, rather than the welfare of a select group of individuals. This is their common and distinguishing feature.

In short, the distinguishing characteristic of this group is that, although they are all nonprofits, they are tax exempt on both levels as described earlier and they undertake a mission or purpose that is to advance community or public welfare. Thus, we refer to them as nonprofits with a community or public mission. The single word that best describes community or public welfare is "charitable," even though the word is also used to describe a specific group of tax-exempt nonprofits.

Of all the missions consistent with the 501(c)(3) status, the most numerous is education, followed by religion and the arts. See Table 2.3.

Associations and Their Missions

The word association is often used broadly. It includes social welfare organizations, clubs, leagues, fraternities, and professional organizations. Typically, these are membership organizations that exist to improve the welfare of their members.

Associations do not have to conform to the eight missions for 501(c)(3)s as described in the previous section, although they may include any of these in their mission. As stated earlier, associations exist to promote the welfare of their members, but in a manner that is consistent with public welfare. Associations may be viewed as improving public welfare indirectly through their members.

Thus, the American Medical Association exists to benefit physicians. Its activities, including education, are undertaken with the aim of making physicians better so that, presumably, the public will be better served.

TABLE 2.3   501-(c)(3) Organizations by NTEE Major Code

Major	Freq.	Pct.
Animal-related	3098	0.96
Arts/Culture	34732	10.81
Civil rights	1470	0.46
Community Imprv	13145	4.09
Consumer/Legal	944	0.29
Crime & Delinq	2192	0.68
Disease/Disorder	6163	1.92
Education	58952	18.35
Employment/jobs	3426	1.07
Environment	4111	1.28
Food/Nutrition	2440	0.76
Health—General	21972	6.84
Housing/Shelter	4187	1.30
Human Services	19576	6.09
International	1545	0.48
Mental Health	5028	1.57
Mutual/Member	414	0.13
Philanthropy	38482	11.98
Public Safety	3327	1.04
Public/Soc Bene	5313	1.65
Recreate/Leisure	19685	6.13
Religion	49929	15.54
Science	3479	1.08
Youth Develop	17657	5.50

Source: *The National Taxonomy of Exempt Entities* (The National Center for Charitable, Washington, D.C. 1990) p. 10. Reprinted with permission from The Independent Sector.

On the other hand, a nonprofit hospital is a public welfare organization. It exists to directly administer to the welfare of the public by treating the ill and preventing illness.

Some public welfare organizations [501(c)(3)s] such as the YWCA are also associations in that they have members. Thus, even though it has members, it is public because it is open to any female member of the public and because its mission is public welfare:

The Young Women's Christian Association of the United States....seeks to respond to the barrier-breaking love of God in this day.... The Association draws together into responsible membership women and girls of diverse experiences and faiths, that their lives may be open to new understanding and deeper relationships and that together they may join in the struggle for peace and justice, freedom and dignity for all people and its ONE IMPERATIVE to thrust our collective power toward the elimination of racism wherever it exists and by any means necessary. Source: YWCA *Public Policy*. Reprinted with permission of YWCA.

Notice that the drawing of "women and girls" together is not an end in itself, and their being drawn together is for a larger good, which is value based and humanitarian, both reflecting public welfare.

Frequently, the line between an association and a public welfare organization is very thin, and this is why knowing the section of the IRS code under which the organization falls is important; that is, 501(c)(3) always refers to organizations that have as their mission the advancement of public welfare in one of the eight ways we specified earlier. Put simply, the distinction is not in the name of the organization but in what it does.

There are many associations that are also 501(c)(3)s. Most associations, however, are 501(c)(4)s, (5)s, (6)s, and so on, as listed in Table 2.1. Again, it is not what a group calls itself that distinguishes it, but its mission determines how it is classified.

Because of their different missions, the two groups, associations and public welfare organizations [more accurately, 501(c)(3)s and others] differ in another significant way. The first can obtain tax-deductible gifts and the other (with the exceptions of those pointed out in Table 2.1) cannot. Second, because the first is public, it must demonstrate through its financing that it is publicly supported using a tough standard.

As we return to the main theme below, keep in mind that, regardless of their differences, the nonprofit world has endless similarities so that, unless we make specific reference to the 501(c)(3) status, our discussion applies to all nonprofits. The permissions are greatest and the rules are toughest for this group.

Chapters and Their Missions

Chapters are the nonprofit world's counterpart to franchises in the for-profit world. The local sorority or fraternity legally is to the national roughly what the local Wendy, Burger King, or McDonald's is to their national.

Chapters are founded for a variety of reasons. They permit an organization to extend over the country and to have each chapter respond to unique local needs as long as the response is in keeping with the overall mission and bylaws of the organization. Local chapters may vary in terms of their tax exemption. The American Psychological Association, for ex-

ample, is a 501(c)(3), but many of its local chapters are (501)(c)(6)s and
some are 501(c)(3)s.

Also, chapters are independent corporations, each subject to the specific laws of the state in which it operates and is incorporated. What this
means is that chapters may differ not only because of local needs and
capacity but because of what local and state laws require.

By way of illustration of the chapter–national relationship, take the
Boys and Girls Clubs of America's local chapters,

> each of which is an autonomous corporation organized under the laws of
> the state in which it is located. Each club has its own independent Board
> of Directors which controls the local club, its program and staff.... the na-
> tional organization, does not exercise supervision, direction or control of its
> local member clubs.[7]

Similarly with the YMCA,

> Each YMCA is a charitable nonprofit, qualifying under Section 501(c)(3)
> of the U.S. Tax Code. Each is independent. YMCAs are required by the
> national office to pay annual dues, to refrain from discrimination, and to
> support the YMCA mission. All other decisions are local choices, including
> which programs to offer, staffing, and style of operation. The national office,
> called the YMCA of the USA.... Its purpose is to serve the needs of member
> associations.[8]

Thus, the national YMCA may be excused from suits brought
against individual YMCAs and the results, because of state law, also
differ. In Oregon, the supreme court of that state upheld taxes that were
imposed on the health facilities of that organization. Yet in Kansas and
Illinois, state legislatures passed laws supporting the tax-exempt status
of similar facilities. In South Dakota, county commissioners upheld the
YMCA tax-exempt status, and in Alameda County court the exempt status of a very controversial YMCA in Oakland was upheld.[9] In each of
these cases, the issue has been whether these facilities are competing
unfairly with commercial health clubs. In each case, these YMCAs charge
and do attract people who can pay, arguing that their fees enable others
who cannot pay, but for whom the YMCA operates, to have a facility.

Why do local chapters join a national? Locals are tied to the national
through a common mission, the payment of fees partly in return for services, national recognition, technical assistance, and the like. There are
also benefits from national advertising and media exposure, the lowering
and transfer of certain costs such as the development of pension plans
and benefits, a source of short-term loans—all the benefits of cooperation
discussed in Chapter 6.

The national also speaks on behalf of the organization in front of legislatures and the government. Yet being independent isolates them from liabilities that the national incurs, and vice versa, unless charter arrangements provide differently. For example, there may be a charter provision for assessment of locals by some formula to cover some national liabilities, and vice versa.

The independence of the chapters from the national means, among other things, that they can sue each other. Women have benefited. Take the case of *Board of Directors of Rotary International* v. *Rotary Club of Duarte* and *Roberts* vs. *U.S. Jaycees*. In both of these, the locals sued the national because it revoked their charter for including women. In both cases, the locals went to court and won, opening membership to women. Homosexuals and women may not be so lucky in protesting prohibitions against their being awarded pastoral positions in certain churches. Courts are very reluctant to challenge religious doctrine. See Chapter 16.

The upshot of all this is to call attention to the fact that a chapter is just another nonprofit organization subject to all the rules, opportunities, and challenges discussed in this book plus the linkage effect discussed in Chapter 6.

Federations, Affiliates, Groups, and the Mission

Federations are merely a group of nonprofits that come together with a common purpose and mission. Thus, the National Voluntary Health Agencies is a group of health agencies; the National United Services Agencies is a group of advocacy nonprofits; the United Jewish Appeal and the United Way of America are also federations. Big Brothers/Big Sisters of America is a federation of 488 independent agencies and programs in 49 states. A common purpose is financial support. The organizations that make up these federations are independent corporations.

In this book we shall see various reasons for affiliation and other cooperative arrangements. One reason is purely legal: U.S. taxpayers cannot deduct contributions made to foreign charities and U.S. government aid often may not go directly to a foreign nonprofit. Thus, CARE USA is an independent domestic nonprofit corporation affiliated with CARE International, a cooperative of eleven national CARES such as CARE Australia, CARE Canada, CARE Japan. U.S. citizen contributions to CARE USA are deductible and controlled by CARE USA even though the contributions are used abroad and CARE International coordinates the work of the eleven CARE members.

The basic thing to remember about these and similar arrangements is that each unit is a distinct legal entity subject to the rules of its trustees and the locality in which it operates. Each may disassociate from the larger group (give up certain rights and privileges including the use of a name) without dissolving the organization. Disassociation can sometimes create problems about rights to property and responsibilities for liabilities. We shall see such a case in Chapter 5.

Affiliates are common among church groups. An advantage of affiliates is that each does not have to seek its own exemption. Thus, the Catholic church in the United States, under the bishops, have a master (called a group) list of affiliate organizations, each one of which may be an independent legal entity but is related to the Catholic church's mission. We say more about affiliates in Chapter 13.

Before proceeding, we ought to mention that it is possible for an organization to have exemption without seeking it itself. This is because of the possibility of obtaining that exemption under a group arrangement. Thus, your local scout unit or church may not itself have sought exemption even though it is a separate legal entity. That exemption was obtained by a national body.

SCOPE OF ACTIVITIES PERMITTED BY LOCAL LAWS

While state and federal laws are the basic laws affecting the formation and operation of nonprofits, local laws must also be obeyed. These laws control the local operations of affiliates, chapters, nationals, and independents. Due to local rules, chapters even within a state may be treated dissimilarly. Local zoning laws and building codes affect the physical location of the nonprofit, such as the design and location of its buildings and the physical safety of the building from fire. Local laws also affect solicitation, and local governments may have special rules covering exemptions from property and sales taxes.

Local rules may supplement or be independent of state rules. For example, the City Council of New Orleans had to pass a special ordinance on solicitation even though the state has a law on solicitation. The reason is that the residents of the city were receiving telephone calls from a group selling light bulbs. The calls were made in such a way that the listener would associate them with a nonprofit group, the Lighthouse for the Blind. But the Lighthouse for the Blind does not sell bulbs. It sells brooms, maps, dust cloths, and ironing board covers.[10]

FIVE CHARACTERISTICS OF A MISSION

We have said that the mission must conform to law. What should be its character? This book recommends that the mission of a nonprofit should be seen as having the following properties at a minimum:

1. Social contract: The mission is a promise to the members and to society that for their support the organization will do certain things deemed by the society to be worthy of tax-exempt status. The attorney general of every state and the members of an organization can sue if the organization fails by diverting its resources to activities other than its mission.

2. Permanence: Amendments to the mission require a vote of the board of trustees and must be reported in most states and to the federal government. An amendment could jeopardize the tax-exempt status of the organization if it causes the organization to veer from its mission. A mission is adopted with a spirit of permanence even though it can be amended. Amendments should not be taken lightly.

3. Clarity: A mission should be stated clearly to communicate purpose and yet broadly to give options and to permit the organization to meet new challenges consistent with its mission.

4. Approval: The mission must win the approval of stakeholders. Nonprofits exist to advance community or group welfare—not that of individuals. It must conform to community, not individual, agendas.

5. Proof: A mission should be demonstrable. The key test is finance and resources. How did the organization use its assets? Where did they come from? What has the organization done?

A comment should be made about changing the mission of the organization. It is imperative that the change be consistent with those missions identified as public welfare if the organization expects to maintain tax exemption. Major amendments should not be done without some strategic planning and the ability to answer the issues in Chapters 6 through 8, because a change in mission can have far-reaching financial impact. Wheaton College was sued by nine alumni, alleging that when they made their gifts some years back they were making them to a women's college. Wheaton turned coed. It settled by offering to return $16 million. For the uncontested right to use the name "Boys & Girls Clubs of America," Boys Club of America reached a settlement to pay $740,000 to Girls Clubs of America which is now known as Girls Incorporated.

SUMMARY AND CONCLUSIONS

In Chapter 3 we explore further the definition of charitable and what is meant by referring to these organizations as economic institutions with a community or public welfare mission or, alternatively, economic institutions with a charitable mission.

In Chapter 3 we also explore two other aspects of the definitions of nonprofits with which this chapter opened. These are the nonprofit as an economic institution, and the nonprofit not having profit-making as a principal purpose and not conducting commercial activities as a substantial part of its mission.

In this chapter we established three points:

1. Nonprofits are legal institutions created in the image of state laws that define their responsibilities, purposes, and powers, including the powers of financing.
2. Federal laws interpreted and enforced by the IRS and the courts determine the tax-exempt status of the nonprofit.
3. The common characteristics of the nonprofit organizations that are tax exempt so that the incomes they earn from their missions are not taxed and that the contributions to them are deductible by the donors is that these organizations exist to advance public or community welfare; that is, they are charitable.

In addition, we reviewed state and federal laws related to the creation of nonprofits and the acquisition of tax-exempt status. States create nonprofits and define their powers, including the powers that nonprofits have to finance themselves. State and federal laws also define how the assets and income of the organization may be distributed upon dissolution, bankruptcy, and merger of the organization. An unequivocal rule is that these assets and income may not be distributed to individuals as if they were owners. There are no individual owners of nonprofit corporations. This is consistent with the legal rule that the nonprofit, unlike the business firm, does not exist for the economic benefits of individuals; rather, it exists for advancing the welfare of the community or public.

NOTES

1. See Section 303(a) of the United States Tax Code.
2. The corporate form of organization is not the only possibility. Nonprofits may also organize as trusts, and for-profits may also organize as partnerships or sole proprietorships.
3. These lobbying rules are so important, especially for organizations electing the objective test and large-advocacy nonprofits, that the IRS issued new technical interpretation in 1990. This came after lengthy discussions and dialogue with the nonprofit sector.
4. For a discussion of these various types of nonprofits, see Howard Godfrey, *Handbook on Tax-Exempt Organizations* (Englewood Cliffs, N.J.: Prentice Hall, 1983).
5. "IRS Denial of Charitable Status: A Social Welfare Organization Problem," *Michigan Law Review*, 82, no. 3 (Dec. 1983), 508–36.

6. *Church of the Chosen People* v. *U.S.*, U.S.D.C. Minn, Civil 4:81–311, 10/18/82, 82-2 U.S.T.C., Section 9646.
7. Boys Club of America, 1989 Annual Report.
8. *1989 Annual Financial Report YMCA of the USA*, p. 5.
9. Larry Sterne, "YMCA Loses an Important Tax Case in Oregon Tax Status of Two Portland Health Facilities," *Nonprofit Times*, Feb. 1990, p. 3.
10. Lynn Cunningham, "Charity Law May Put End to False Calls," *Times Picayune*, New Orleans, Louisiana, Tuesday, Aug. 21, 1984, P. E1.

SUGGESTED READINGS

OLECK, HOWARD L. *Nonprofit Corporations, Organizations and Associations,* 4th Edition (Englewood Cliffs, New Jersey: Prentice Hall, 1980).

HOPKINS, BRUCE R. *The Law of Tax-Exempt Organizations,* 5th edition, (New York: John Wiley & Sons, 1991).

Internal Revenue Service, U.S. Department of the Treasury, *Tax Exempt Status for Your Organization,* Publication 557, Revised, October 1988.

——— *Exempt Organization Appeal Procedures,* Publication 892, Revised April 1987.

Chapter 3

Nurturing the Mission in an Economic Institution

In Chapter 2, we defined the nonprofit as a legal organization that does not conduct a substantial commercial activity and that has, as its principal purpose, an objective other than making profits. Rather, its mission is to improve public welfare. A significant difference between the 501(c)(3)s and the others is that the 501(c)(3)s, often known as charities, seek to improve public welfare directly. The others, including associations, do so indirectly through improving the welfare of their members.

Furthermore, we learned the significance of being a legal organization and its relationship to the conduct and definition of the mission. In this chapter, we focus on the concept of the economic institution and its relationship to the definition and conduct of the mission of the nonprofit. Thus, at the end of this chapter we should appreciate why a nonprofit is best viewed as a legal and economic institution that has public welfare as its mission.

Do not lose sight of the reasons for this exploration. Every imaginative and dynamic management of an organization, whether it is a firm, a baseball team, or a nonprofit, needs to know the limits set by rules. A baseball manager can only put nine players on the field. The skill of management is to decide who should play where and when and what plays are most effective and within the rules. They must also know the rules. The challenge to the nonprofit manager is similar; so let's turn to the relationship between being an economic institution and the mission. "Charity" defines the mission; "economic" the organization.

THE IMPORTANCE OF SEEING THE NONPROFIT AS AN ECONOMIC INSTITUTION

In recent years, no other group has learned more harshly than Catholic schools and inner-city churches the importance of running the most charitable mission as an economic institution. Across the country these schools and churches have closed—in Washington, D.C., New York City, Philadelphia, Detroit. Nuns who toiled all their lives end up without retirement security. God does not pay bills.

Today, the orchestra members play backed by an irrevocable bank letter of credit to secure their salaries. The orchestra may have launched a major capital or fund-raising campaign. The orchestra may have become more market oriented and it may also have a business. In all these circumstances, money, not mission, is the missing ingredient. Economics, not philosophy, is the solution. The organization, The Orchestra Association, is the instrument. Libraries have now joined this trend.

THE NONPROFIT AS AN ECONOMIC INSTITUTION

Perhaps, then, the most fundamental change in perspective that is needed to improve the management of nonprofits is to view them as economic institutions with the charitable missions of improving the public or community welfare, rather than as charitable institutions with charitable missions. As an economic institution, revenues must be raised and managed; costs must be identified and constrained. Whatever the mission, the organization has to pay its bills.

As an economic institution, a nonprofit operates within the broader market system and aims at earning revenues to the extent that market conditions, the nonprofit's mission, and the law allow. Nonprofits are legal entities with financial powers and limitations defined by law. Violation of the legal limits can lead to the loss of the tax-exempt status of the organization and to severe penalties on the management, including the board of trustees.

Why Nonprofits Are Economic Institutions

Nonprofits are economic institutions because nonprofits are productive units. Such units acquire inputs of land, labor, and capital and transform them through a productive process into goods and services that have value to society. In the case of a business firm, these values are measured in terms of the market price for which the goods and services are sold. In the case of nonprofits, the value is imputed, a term used by economists to mean approximated. Imputation is required because all the goods and services produced by nonprofits are not sold for a price that truly reflects the value of the good or service to society. Many nonprofits charge no price or charge one that is well below the true market price of the good or service they produce. For others, their output is priceless.

Economists take the view of nonprofits as productive units so seriously that they annually impute the value of goods and services produced by nonprofits and include the imputations in their calculations of the gross national product (GNP) of the country. The gross national product is the sum of goods and services produced by the economy of the country in any given year. It is the most comprehensive indicator of economic production and of the wealth of the nation.

Notice that what is central in the definition of the economic institution is the transformation of inputs into goods and services that have value. A school takes the input of teachers (labor) and capital (buildings and books) and land (the playground) and transforms these into something called an educated student who is valuable to society. Whether or not a price is charged for the good or service produced by the school is not what matters in the definition. The price serves to measure the value of the output of the institution rather than to determine if the institution is an economic entity. What makes the institution an economic entity is that it uses society's scarce resources (land, labor, and capital) to produce a product or service of value. Translated, the nonprofit (1) has operating costs, (2) imposes a cost on the community to the extent that it wastes contributions and voluntary services that could be used by other nonprofits providing superior value to society, and (3) needs a reliable flow of revenues as do all economic institutions.

The Purpose for Producing the Good or Service Must Be to Improve Community or Public Welfare

As an economic institution, the nonprofit's purpose for producing the good or service must be to improve public or community welfare: to be motivated by community welfare rather than by private profits. To repeat, this is only obliquely less true of associations that serve public welfare indirectly through advancing the welfare of their members.

Thus, it is commonly held that nonprofits cannot or should not make profits because they are supposed to be charitable. What does charitable mean? The courts have historically maintained a loose definition of the term. This has been done to accommodate the fact that, over time, the charitable needs of society change; that is, new needs are recognized. [1] In practice, the IRS and the courts use the following criteria to determine if a motive is charitable:[2]

1. The motive of the organization must be to meet a recognized need of the community or some segment thereof in a manner and level that are significantly different to what a for-profit firm would do.

2. The means used to meet the charitable purpose must be integrally related to satisfying the needs that have been identified as charitable.

3. There must be a clear manifestation of providing the service without seeking personal advantages for the providers or for the providing organization.

4. The charitable purpose must be consistent with public policy.

Using these principles, the IRS and the courts have awarded charitable status to nonprofits that specialize in otherwise commercial activities. The IRS has granted charitable status to an organization specializing in making loans to minority businesses that are located in a distressed area and that are unable to get loans from regular commercial

---

(2) *Charitable defined.* The term "charitable" is used in section 501(c)(3) in its generally accepted legal sense and is, therefore, not to be construed as limited by the separate enumeration in section 501(c)(3) of other tax-exempt purposes which may fall within the broad outlines of "charity" as developed by judicial decisions. Such term includes: Relief of the poor and distressed or of the underprivileged; advancement of religion; advancement of education or science; erection or maintenance of public buildings, monuments, or works; lessening of the burdens of Government; and promotion of social welfare by organizations designed to accomplish any of the above purposes, or (i) to lessen neighborhood tensions; (ii) to eliminate prejudice and discrimination; (iii) to defend human and civil rights secured by law; or (iv) to combat community deterioration and juvenile delinquency.

Source: Treasury Regulations Section 1.501(c)(3)-1 (d)(1)(2), 1980.

sources.[3] Similarly, charitable status was awarded to an organization located in a rural area that made development loans to businesses unable to get loans from normal commercial sources and that were located in distressed parts of rural communities.[4]

And, although manufacturing is a for-profit activity, the IRS awarded charitable status to a job-training organization that also ran a toy manufacturing business. The organization hired, trained, gave job counseling, and placed unskilled workers.[5]

In addition, although barber and beauty shops are traditionally for-profit businesses, a beauty and barber shop was given charitable status even though it operated for a profit. The IRS concluded that the shop operated at the convenience of elderly citizens and serving these citizens was a charitable mission.[6]

In the same vein, a medical and dental referral service was designated a charity even though it charges a price and makes a profit. The court held, among other things, that both the profits and salaries were kept reasonably low and that the purpose of the referral system was to improve medical service to the community and not to benefit the medical practitioners. Their benefits were incidental to those of the community.[7]

From these examples it should be clear that a nonprofit is an economic institution with a charitable mission, even if it charges a price and makes a profit. Unfortunately, even when described by their most ardent supporters, nonprofits are too often viewed as purely charitable organizations. A pure charity is defined as an organization that functions to meet benevolent objectives and does not sell its goods or services.[8] Importantly, the law does not restrict nonprofits to operating in this purely charitable mode.

To view nonprofits in this purely charitable mode is to limit them to the detriment of the community. Notice this in the case of the loans mentioned above. These loans are business transactions normally carried out by a bank or other commercial lender. To bar the nonprofit from doing so in this case is to deprive individuals to whom commercial lenders would not lend. To deny them is not to improve social or public well-being.

What distinguishes nonprofits from other economic institutions is not that all nonprofits are pure charities. The fact is that most nonprofits, including churches, could not meet a stringent application of this test of not selling any good or service. Raffles, bargain sales, tuitions, and contributions related to the receipt of a specific good or service by the contributor involve a sale. It is not the inability to sell the good or service that is the distinguishing feature.

The distinguishing feature is that the organization must not have been *created* with the motive of selling its goods and services at a gain; absent this restriction, the organization would merely be a for-profit firm. Recall the discussion in Chapter 2. The word "created" is emphasized because the exclusive motive for creating and operating the nonprofit must be for community welfare or charity as measured by the four criteria previously stated. However, the nonprofit does not have to be a pure charity.

This point is well illustrated in a series of court cases. In *Fraternal Medical Specialist Services, Inc.* v. *Commissioner*,[9] the court stated:

> In determining whether petitioner is operated exclusively for exempt purposes, or whether instead, petitioner is operated in furtherance of a substantial commercial purpose our inquiry must focus upon the purpose or purposes furthered by petitioner's activities, and not on the activities themselves. The fact that an organization's activities may even constitute a trade or business does not, of itself, disqualify it from classification under section 501(c)(3). . . . The determination of whether petitioner is operated for a substantial commercial purpose is primarily a question of fact. . . . . Factors such as the particular manner in which the organization's activities are conducted, the commercial hue of those activities, and the existence and amount of annual or accumulated profits are relevant evidence of a proscribed commercial purpose.

Similarly, the Supreme Court has held that having a trade or business does not disqualify the organization from tax exemption.[10] On the other hand, the existence of a single nonexempt (commercial activity) that is a substantial part of the purpose for the existence of the organization would destroy its qualification as tax exempt regardless of how many tax-exempt purposes it has.[11] In short, the trade or business cannot be a substantial reason for the creation of the organization.

To illustrate, the training or educating of people is a recognized tax-exempt purpose, one that is beneficial to public welfare. But the training of dogs is not a recognized public purpose (although as we see in the next chapter, the neutering of dogs is). Thus, in a well-known case, the courts ruled:

> By contrast, petitioner has not shown that actually training a dog is necessary for teaching an individual how to train a dog. While it is clear that an infant needs custodial care when he or she is learning, it is not plain that an individual cannot be taught to train animals without the animal being present for the entire class time. Essentially, unlike in *San Francisco Infant School*, there are no facts in the administrative record regarding petitioner's curriculum, theories, or methods. While we know that the dogs receive degrees and awards, we do not know whether or how the individual's skills are evaluated.

> We find, therefore, that since the training of dogs is a substantial, if not the primary, purpose of petitioner, petitioner is not operated exclusively for one or more exempt purposes specified in section 501(c)(3). *Ann Arbor Dog Training Club, Inc. Petitioner* v. *Commissioner*, T.C., 1974, pp. 207–212.

The existence of one substantial nonexempt purpose (the training of dogs) led to the denial of the tax-exempt status. Ironically, the status may have been awarded if the training of people were the substantial purpose for which this organization was formed, and the training of dogs only incidental to the training of people. This is what the court meant when it said, "By contrast, petitioner has not shown that actually training a dog is necessary for teaching an individual how to train a dog."

In further illustrating this point of a community welfare or charitable motive, it should be noted that, if the organization was created with the motive of making a gain (a profit) on its activities, the failure to realize this gain does not make the organization a nonprofit. It is merely a for-profit firm that has a loss or is breaking even. Failure does not transform a firm into a charity. Similarly, if the organization was created with a motive of making a profit, its making large charitable contributions does not make it a nonprofit. In this case, it is simply a profit maker with a strong social conscience.

To the for-profit firm, charity may be important, but it is not essential to its existence; the charitable purpose is incidental. Accordingly, many for-profit firms have their own charitable foundations and make sizable charitable gifts to nonprofits. To the nonprofit, charity is the exclusive motive for existing and profits are incidental, although an important means for financing the charitable mission. Thus, as seen from these examples, nonprofits may run profitable businesses that may or may not be related to their mission. Let us explore what this implies.

PROFIT-MAKING AS A SOURCE OF REVENUES

What is the legal history upon which the courts and the IRS have held that nonprofits may make a profit? The seminal case is *Trinidad* v. *Sagrada Orden*.[12] The Supreme Court stated that the law:

> recognizes that a corporation may be organized and operated exclusively for religious, charitable, scientific or educational purposes, and yet have a net income [profits]...it says nothing about the source of the income, but makes the destination the ultimate exemption.

In several cases thereafter, the IRS and the courts have held that organizations dedicated to a charitable, educational, religious, or other tax-exempt purpose could conduct profitable business activities without losing their exempt status and without paying taxes or penalties on these profits. An example is the ruling by the IRS that a tax-exempt museum engaging in the sale of greeting cards displaying printed reproductions of art works contributes importantly to the achievement of the museum's exempt educational purposes by stimulating and enhancing public awareness, interest, and appreciation of art. Moreover, a broader segment of the public may be encouraged to visit the museum itself. . . as a result of the cards. The fact that the cards are promoted and sold in a clearly commercial manner at a profit and in competition with commercial greeting card publishers does not alter the fact of the activity's relatedness to the museum exempt purposes.[13]

Accordingly, the IRS concluded that not only should the engagement in these profitable sales by this museum not result in the loss of tax-exempt status, but the profits should not be taxed. The business earnings were related to, but not the motive for, their mission or existence.

Similarly, in *American College of Physicians* v. *U.S.*, the courts held that revenues from advertising in the *Annals of Internal Medicine* were related to its tax-exempt mission. Therefore, the advertising was not cause for the repeal of its tax-exempt status and the profits from the advertising were not taxable. In the words of the court:[14]

That the primary purpose may have been commercial, however, does not preclude a finding that the activity is substantially related to an exempt function. . . . While the educational function of the advertising may well have been secondary to the purpose of raising revenues, the evidence of record establishes that the advertising in *Annals* fulfilled an important educational function. . . . The evidence of record establishes that the contribution of the advertisements to the exempt purpose is an important one.

Accordingly, the court continued, "We hold that the sales of advertising in *Annals* are substantially related to the exempt purpose of the College to educate internists and, therefore, are not taxable." We shall return to this case. This is not the end of the story.

From these two cases, we see that the two ultimate authorities, the courts and the IRS, both sanction the making of profits by nonprofit organizations. A careful reading of the rulings indicates the separation of two levels of analysis by the courts and by the IRS: (1) Is the tax-exempt mission of the organization threatened or secondary to the for-profit activity? If it is, tax-exempt status is denied or revoked. If it is not, then (2) is the for-profit activity related to the carrying out of the tax-exempt mission? If it is not, the net earnings (profits) from the business are taxed. If it is related, the net earnings are not taxed.

In some cases, both the courts and the IRS rule that the organization may maintain its tax-exempt nonprofit status, but it must pay taxes on the profits. This is so when the business is unrelated to the tax-exempt mission of the organization. Thus, in another case involving a museum, the IRS ruled that an art museum was dealing in an unrelated business when it sold books dealing with science. In the eyes of the IRS, the sale of science books had nothing to do with art. In this case, the museum's tax-exempt status was not threatened, but it had to pay taxes on the profits from the sale of its scientific books, but not on the sale of cards promoting art.[15]

To fully appreciate this point, let us go back to the case of the American College of Physicians. Not satisfied with the lower courts, the IRS appealed the case to the Supreme Court. On April 22, 1986, Justice Thurgood Marshall in *United States, Petitioner* v. *American College of Physicians* rendered the unanimous decision of the Court. It held that the advertising in *Annals of Internal Medicine* was unrelated business and that the American College of Physicians must pay taxes on the earnings from such advertising.

The case against the American College of Physicians turned on whether or not the advertising was conducted in a manner that showed that it was not substantially related to the tax-exempt mission of the organization. The Court pointed to an earlier focus of the Claims Court that:

> The evidence is clear that plaintiff did not use the advertising to provide its readers a comprehensive or systematic presentation of any aspect of the goods or services publicized. Those companies willing to pay for advertising space got it; others did not. Moreover, some of the advertising was for established drugs or devices and was repeated from one month to another, undermining the suggestion that the advertising was principally designed to alert readers of recent developments [citing, as examples, ads for Valium, Insulin, and Maalox]. Some ads even concerned matters that had no conceivable relationship to the College's tax-exempt purposes. 3 Cl. Ct. at 534 (footnotes omitted). *Supreme Court of the United States, United States* v. *American College of Physicians*, No. 84-1737, April 22, 1986, pp. 14–15.

Based on that finding the Supreme Court concluded:

> These facts find adequate support in the record. See, *e.g.*, App. 29a–30a, 59a. Considering them in light of the applicable legal standard, we are bound to conclude that the advertising in Annals does not contribute importantly to the journal's educational purposes. This is not to say that the College could not control its publication of advertisements in such a way as to reflect an intention to contribute importantly to its educational functions. By coordinating the content of the advertisements with the editorial content of the issue, or by publishing only advertisements reflecting new developments in the pharmaceutical market, for example, perhaps the College could satisfy the stringent standards erected by Congress and the

Treasury. In this case, however, we have concluded that the Court of Appeals erroneously focused exclusively upon the information that is invariably conveyed by commercial advertising, and consequently failed to give effect to the governing statute and regulations. Its judgment, accordingly is *Reversed. Supreme Court of the United States, United States v. American College of Physicians*, No. 84-1737, April 22, 1986, p. 15.

Note several points from these quotations. First, the American College of Physicians did not lose its tax-exempt status. Second, it may continue a business of advertising for a profit although it must pay taxes on these profits like any other business. Third, the Court did not ban advertising and did not rule out that this could be a related business of a nonprofit and therefore free of taxes. Fourth, the Court suggested how the American College of Physicians may accomplish this objective. In other words, the specific facts and circumstances surrounding an activity determine whether it is related or unrelated.

It is important to appreciate the purpose of this unrelated business income tax. It is not intended to stop the nonprofit from making a profit. This would be a silly prescription, because it implies (at the extreme) that the nonprofit should aim at making losses or, at the other extreme, commit the organization to breaking even. Planning for such exactitude where costs just equal revenues every year is humanly impossible. Thus, a nonprofit, to be safe if such a prescription were in place, would create a loss every year. It would then go bankrupt and close, serving no useful purpose.

Rather, it is to avoid unfair competition by making sure that, if a nonprofit engages in a business unrelated to the promotion of its mission, the profits on that business are then taxed in the same way as all profit-making firms doing the same kind of business are taxed. A second reason, as we shall see in Chapter 4, is to make sure that, if such a business swamps the activities of the nonprofit, it loses its exemption and is classified as a for-profit firm.

This thinking is revealed in the *Congressional Record* on the legislation leading to the unrelated business tax on nonprofits.[16]

The problem at which the tax on unrelated business income is directed is primarily that of unfair competition. The tax-free status of ... organizations enables them to use their profits tax-free to expand operations, while their competitors can expand only with the profits remaining after taxes. Also, a number of examples have arisen where these organizations have, in effect, used their tax exemptions to buy an ordinary business. That is, they have acquired the business with little or no investment on their own part and paid for it in installments out of subsequent earnings—a procedure which usually could not be followed if the business were taxable

And, the *Congressional Record* continues,

> In neither. . .bill does this provision deny the exemption where the organizations are carrying on unrelated active business enterprises, nor require that they dispose of such businesses. Both provisions merely impose the same tax on income derived from an unrelated trade or business as is borne by their competitors. . . .

In short, a nonprofit may make profits from engaging in a trade or business that is related to its tax-exempt mission without losing its tax-exempt status and without paying taxes on that profit. It may engage in profit-making businesses unrelated to its tax-exempt mission, but it must pay taxes on the profits earned. Neither of these two situations leads to a loss or denial of tax-exempt status.

The status is lost or denied when it appears to the IRS or the courts that the community or public welfare purpose claimed by the organization is nothing but a ruse for carrying on a commercial activity for profit and that the tax-exempt status is intended by the organization simply as a means to evade taxes or to gain a competitive advantage over for-profit firms. Thus, in *Piety, Inc.* v. *Commissioner*, the court held that an organization that did nothing but run bingo games was not tax exempt even though it fed its profits to a tax-exempt organization.[17]

The tax-exempt status is also denied or revoked if the benefits of the organization or the profits of its business inure to private persons. Thus, in *Church of Scientology of California* v. *Commissioner*, the court held that the tax-exempt status was to be revoked because the church was operated for a substantially commercial purpose, and its net earnings privately benefited its founder.[18]

To summarize, this section provides legal evidence that nonprofit organizations are allowed to make a profit (and the very word is used in the law). But if a nonprofit is allowed to make a profit, what distinguishes a for-profit firm from a nonprofit? Under what conditions will an organization that deems itself to be a nonprofit be considered just another for-profit firm in the eyes of the law and consequently be denied its tax-exempt status?

The critical factors, as we learn in this book, in avoiding revocation or denial of tax-exempt status are as follows:

1. The organization must clearly and unequivocally be motivated by a community or public welfare purpose defined by the *Internal Revenue Code* as worthy of tax exemption.
2. The benefits must not inure to private individuals.

3. Commercial activity must not be its primary purpose and must not diminish or rival the ability of the organization to conduct its tax-exempt mission.

4. The activity could not easily be conducted by a commercial firm for a profit.

Note that the community or public welfare purpose to which the organization is exclusively dedicated must also be one that is both defined by law as tax exempt and is contained in the organization's charter as described in Chapter 2. Accordingly, in the example of the second museum, the court held that the sale of scientific books would have been tax exempt to another organization that was scientific in its orientation, but not to an art museum. It is not simply the activity that counts, but the combination of considerations mentioned in the preceding paragraph. Thus, in the case of the American College of Physicians mentioned earlier, the fact that the principal objective of the advertising was to raise money is not separated from whether the purposes served by the advertising are defined as tax exempt. Is it education as defined?

To illustrate further, the community welfare purpose may be stated in the charter of the organization but not be defined as a tax-exempt activity by the law. Thus, in Society of Costa Rica Collectors, both the court and the IRS concluded that tax exemption was not warranted by the philatelic society that primarily engaged in sales that were indistinguishable from commercial sales. Merely the sale of philatelic materials is not by itself defined by law as a tax-exempt purpose.[19] And the training of dogs, as we saw earlier, is not recognized as a community or public welfare purpose (a charity) that is tax exempt.

The Use of the Profits Must Be to Advance Public or Community Welfare

A distinguishing characteristic between a nonprofit and a for-profit firm as an economic institution is that nonprofits may not distribute their assets, profits, or other benefits to individuals as owners. They may not advance private welfare but must only utilize profits to carry on their mission to improve public or community welfare. In this sense, there are the following important differences between a for-profit and a nonprofit.

1. The for-profit obtains revenues strictly from sales of assets, goods, and services; from sale of equity or debt; and from investments. The profits may be distributed to individuals because they are the owners of the assets and earnings of the firm. A stock certificate is evidence of own-

ership, and the payment of dividends to stockholders is a distribution of assets and earnings.

2. In contrast, the nonprofit can obtain revenues from sale of assets, goods, and services; debt and investment; but not equity. There is an alternative source, gifts and contributions. The balance among revenue sources (other than debt) is critical to how a nonprofit is classified and whether it qualifies for tax exemption, as we shall see in Chapter 4. Furthermore, the nonprofit may not distribute its assets, income, or earnings to individuals or to any other entity that is not a similar nonprofit except the state or unless the distribution is compensation for goods or services bought.

Costs and Revenue Perspectives of Being an Economic Institution

As an economic institution, nonprofits have expenses as well as revenues. A firm may seek profits simply to increase the rate of return to its investors. A nonprofit seeks profits and other revenues to secure the attainment of a mission, that is, to finance it now and in the future. Thus, current and future costs are compelling stimuli to fund raising. Major costs are plant, equipment, and labor in the form of salaries and benefits. Salaries in some nonprofit organizations are very high because nonprofits must compete for labor.[20] Rentals may also be high because nonprofits must compete for space. Neither a gift of labor nor space is deductible.

It is sometimes said that the word voluntary best distinguishes the nonprofit from the profit sector but this is not totally accurate. Workers in the nonprofit sector are not all volunteers. Even the most charitable of charities, religious organizations, pay their workers.

The problem with the use of the word voluntary is best described by a long-time and well-respected observer of the nonprofit world. Alan Piper, writing for the Foundation Center, asserts:[21]

> The term itself is elusive. Theoretically, it includes not only all kinds of private enterprise, both nonprofit and for profit, but even the institutions

---

In 1989, more than 200,000 people contributed their time and labor to Catholic Charities service and advocacy efforts. This includes 47,856 paid staff members, 139,348 volunteers, and 14,475 corporate and advisory board members.

Source: Annual Survey, 1989, of Catholic Charities, p. 2. Reprinted by permission.

of a democratic form of government as well—in short any activity by private citizens undertaken in concert and on their own volition.

True, membership in nonprofit associations is voluntary, but most nonprofits are not membership organizations. Moreover, membership in many nonprofits, such as labor, professional, and trade associations, are only nominally voluntary because failure to join is to deprive oneself of employment, advancement opportunities, and information. Indeed, some associations have certifying powers and without being certified a person cannot work in some professional capacities.

True, some participation in a nonprofit is voluntary, but this does not distinguish nonprofits from for-profit organizations or market transactions from transactions in the nonprofit sector. To illustrate, participation in the ownership of corporations is voluntary. All market transactions are voluntary. People are not coerced to buy or sell, as this is illegal. Producers and workers make voluntary decisions about all their activities in a market economy. Indeed, without voluntary initiatives, the market system is an oxymoron. It is precisely the voluntary aspects of the market economy (to be described in Chapter 8) that open opportunities for nonprofits.

From a revenue perspective, nonprofits may charge a price for the assets or goods or services they sell. The range of prices a nonprofit may charge varies from nothing or free to the competitive price that is being charged by for-profit firms. What gives nonprofits this range is that they have one source of income that for-profit firms do not have—gifts and contributions.[22] For-profits do not have gifts and contributions and must sell at a price that absorbs all costs and makes a profit for the owners. In contrast, nonprofits do not have owners and may not distribute profits to anyone.

For-profit firms do frequently charge below going market price (discounted sales) and give products and services away (donations). The difference is that the nonprofit can sustain this behavior as modus operandi, and for-profit firms cannot. But nonprofits may sustain this type of operation only to the extent that they can pay their bills by turning to nonprice support such as gifts and contributions.

IDENTIFYING COST AND OTHER STIMULI TO GENERATING REVENUES

Again, unlike a firm, a nonprofit does not seek to maximize revenues for rewarding investors. A major stimulus for revenue generation is to obtain revenues to expand the ability to carry out the mission. It is also to meet costs, some of which are fixed and must be paid regardless of the level of activity of the organization. Thus, viewing the nonprofit as an economic institution that has costs and needs revenues to meet them should be an objective of management. Let us enumerate.

1. The concept "ability to carry out its mission" means having the required money. It also means having the essentials to do the job conveniently. A university needs a bookstore. What is a university without a bookstore? But there is no need to run a bookstore as if it were a charity. It can be run profitably. Hence, one of the skills of nonprofit management is to isolate those activities that are essential to the mission of the organization, that enhance the ability of the organization to carry out its mission, but that need not be run at a loss. Run them profitably to generate revenues for the mission.

2. Another type of revenue-generating activity comes from observing that there is unused capacity. This capacity may be idle all of the time or just some of the time, for example, the church hall, the fax machine, the computer, the stadium, the classroom. Note that even though these are not being used they generate costs every single day. Lease them.

3. The value of property rights of all kinds are examples of hidden costs that have revenue-generating potential. Take a look at all those sweaters that carry names of colleges and universities. Suppose the university fails. Would you buy the sweater? The university does not fail because millions of dollars are spent every year for it to carry out its mission successfully and therefore the names on those sweaters have a value. Property rights should be sold or leased. Property rights cover royalties, real estate, art, copyright, trademarks, the name of the organization, mailing lists—all of which can generate income.

4. Joint or common costs is another cost stimulus to revenues. Take a journal or magazine produced by a nonprofit. The journal or magazine deals with the mission of the nonprofit, be it wildlife, religion, health, or what have you. It costs. Selling some of the pages of that magazine to an advertiser provides revenues that can help cover the total cost of the magazine. The printing and distribution costs are joint both to the articles and the advertisement. Thus, they can be shared.

5. Every program has costs. Part of these costs can be met by charging a fee to the extent that such fees do not discourage needy clients and diminish the mission. Many goods and services are appropriately distributed free.

All five of the above examples demonstrate a cost situation that is converted into a business revenue stream, which may appropriately be, depending on the circumstance, very small. Yet they help to cover costs. The ability to do this is part of managing the mission of the organization when the organization is viewed as an economic institution with a benevolent mission, that is, conscious of costs and revenues.

Some nonprofits' cost advantages are obvious. Postage is lower and so too are some labor costs because of volunteers. A skilled worker, such as a lawyer, who may charge hundreds of dollars per hour may, as a matter of professional ethics, work pro bono for a nonprofit. Football players through the National Football League promote contributions to the United Way. Business Volunteers for the Arts is a group of approximately 1000 bankers, lawyers, accountants and other business managers who assist over 600 art groups in fifteen cities in marketing, finance, and other management services.

The exploitation of any one or a combination of these cost factors can make the mission more "doable." In Chapter 4, we see how being able to utilize volunteers to lower costs and exploiting a special relationship with the public, as evidenced by hospitals selling tickets to a golf tournament, can turn a needed profit for both the private sector and nonprofit participants in the joint venture, which carries out the mission of the organization.

There are other examples of exploitation of these factors. There are hospitals renting space to physicians, running parking lots and physical fitness centers, giving lessons in yoga, running gift shops and refreshment outlets, and charging fees to profit. As one nonprofit veterinary clinic discovered, the quickest way for a nonprofit to run a profitable business is to charge a fee for some of the services it provides. Because the fee was based on a percentage markup on its costs, the fee not only covered costs but contributed to the organization's mission.

There are other illustrations. *Audubon*, a magazine owned by the National Audubon Society, *National Geographic* owned by the National Geographic Society, and the *Smithsonian* owned by the Smithsonian Institute are magazines that have earned millions of dollars in profits. This is done in part by having a special relationship with the public, including a large membership that purchases the magazines, and through lower postal rates for mailing the magazines; and as in the case of the American College of Physicians, magazines owned by nonprofits are not forbidden from selling advertising space at a profit.

According to one observer, magazine production has been so profitable for nonprofits that when the Minneapolis Star & Tribune Company could not turn a good profit on *Harper's* magazine, it turned it over to two nonprofits. A reverse strategy is for for-profit publishers to enhance their own profits by being associated with a cause.[23] Oxford University Press promises to make donations based on the sale of its version of the Bible.

This book has made reference to a number of other profitable activities carried by nonprofits. Again, it is not profits for the sake of profits.

Some of these activities are an integral part of the mission of the nonprofit, but they need not be run at a loss. We shall discuss more about generating business revenues in Chapters 11 through 13 and distinguish between related and unrelated business income even more than we have done in this chapter. The principal purpose of the preceding discussion is to point out that, when a nonprofit is managed as an economic institution, it has a better chance of fulfilling its mission by remaining financially sound. One strategy is to control costs, as we shall see in Chapter 15; another is to convert cost factors into revenue streams, which has been the topic to this point.

GIFTS AND CONTRIBUTIONS AS SOURCES OF REVENUES

All business firms begin by individuals or firms making an investment. All nonprofit corporations begin by foundations, individuals, government, or firms making a gift or contribution. Unlike for-profit firms, which rely on sales as their principal source of revenues, many nonprofits rely principally on gifts, contributions, and support from their membership. Gifts and contributions are important to nonprofits, even those that generate considerable business income. Generally, as we see in Chapter 4, the law requires that nonprofits demonstrate a relatively high level of financial support from the public or from their membership. For most, their exclusive source of revenues cannot, therefore, be profits from the sale of goods and services, especially from an unrelated business.

Ironically, however, the more successful a nonprofit is in doing business, the more it may have to demonstrate public and membership support. This is true, as shown in Chapter 4, particularly when the business income is unrelated to the mission of the organization. Consequently, for most nonprofits, business income cannot be considered a substitute for obtaining gifts and other forms of financial support from the public. Business income increases the total revenues available to the nonprofit, as an economic institution, to carry out its mission. It does not (and cannot generally) substitute 100 percent for public support. We dedicate Chapter 9 and 10 to gifts and contributions. These distinguish the financing of a nonprofit from a for-profit. But what is the economic motivation behind gifts and contributions? What is a gift? What are the trends upon which nonprofits must rely to finance their missions?

Tax Motivation for Giving

Many books on fund raising focus on public and human relations techniques that work. Sophisticated fund raising goes well beyond that. A major motive for giving is to obtain tax benefits. Even when this is not the motive, the tax consequences are always taken into account by the large or smart donor.

Thus, it is said that the Howard Hughes Medical Institute was created by Howard Hughes to avoid cancellation of a profitable contract made by the Air Force to the Hughes Aircraft Company and to avoid paying taxes. The gift of the stocks of the aircraft company provided Hughes with a huge tax deduction, impressed his workers and lowered their discontent with him, and impressed the public and the Defense Department, which had threatened to cancel his contract. The defense work was now being done by a company that was owned by a nonprofit and the profits would go to serve public welfare. In 1986, the nonprofit sold the Hughes Aircraft Company to General Motors for $5.2 billion dollars.

The tax benefit reduces the cost of the gift to the donor. A person in the 30 percent bracket giving property worth $100,000 to a qualified nonprofit obtains a deduction worth $30,000 from the federal government. A person in the 20 percent bracket gets a deduction worth $20,000 for the same gift. With the first person, the gift of $100,000 only costs $70,000; for the second person it costs $80,000. The savings to the donor is higher as the income bracket of that donor increases. This basic relationship between taxing and giving remains though tax rates are changed. It is for this reason that the lower the tax rate is the less tax incentive there is to give, that is, the less that can be deducted and therefore the more the true cost of the gift to the donor. In Chapter 9 we shall cite some studies that support this conclusion.

Competent management must have a working knowledge of the tax laws as they apply to giving. The ability to work with these laws enhances the chances of getting large commitments. We shall deal with them deeper in the Chapters 9 and 10, but some basic points must be dealt with here.

All gifts and contributions are not deductible. Whether or not a gift is deductible and how much is deductible depends on the item given, to whom it is given, the form in which it is given, and by whom it is given. Gifts of free rent and gifts of labor (volunteering) are never deductible.

Certain gifts may lead to a deduction, but only at a point in the distant future. This is particularly true when the donor wishes to retain some rights or obtain some benefits from the property or to have someone or entity other than a charity benefit from the good. An example of this is one who makes a gift of a large portfolio of securities but wants to share in the income from it. If a deal to satisfy the donor's conditions cannot be worked out, the potential gift may be lost. Such a deal to offer a present deduction can be arranged through the proper creation of a trust or a gift annuity. These strategies were successfully used by a number of North Carolina schools with the leverage buyout of RJR Nabisco.

What's the Gift Worth

Gifts such as artwork require that a qualified professional appraisal be made of the value of the gift. Overvaluation of property can lead to penalties. While the penalty may typically fall on the donor, complicity on the part of the nonprofit will not be tolerated. This abuse was, and probably still is, common. Artwork, automobiles, clothing, even bibles are commonly overvalued. One of the best known examples of overvaluation was a scheme to acquire bibles at a low price and then inflate their value as gifts. This is not allowed.

Some gifts are shams; others are incomplete and really are promissory notes that the nonprofit may never collect. For example, it is reported that many of the pledges made to Hands Across America were never collected. Suffice it to say here that bad checks are not uncommon; neither are proposals for gifts in which the potential donor proposes to retain control.

Some goods are not worth accepting because they lead to the assumption of large liabilities, taxable income, and large operating costs that the nonprofit may not be able to meet. Sometimes it is worth accepting such gifts and operating them under an umbrella that limits the liabilities or exposure of the nonprofit to losses. Creating a separate business or an associated nonprofit is sometimes a workable strategy. By isolating the gift under a separate corporate umbrella, the nonprofit shields itself.

The First Amendment and the Regulation of Solicitation

Giving and receiving are subject to federal and state laws. Recall that the primary purpose for permitting tax exemption to nonprofits is to encourage their work and to encourage citizens to give to them. The purpose of the laws that limit giving and receiving is to defend against the abuse of this exemption. The laws that limit giving generally limit the percent of income an individual or corporation may give in any one year. These are federal laws. The laws that limit receiving and generally limit fund-raising behavior are state laws. It is not uncommon that a nonprofit would obtain 20 percent of the proceeds from a fund-raising activity. Detractors of this type of law argue that this ratio is not unreasonable because of the cost of some fund raisers, because what constitutes "cost" is often arbitrarily determined, and because it limits freedom of expression; that is, it rules out those fund-raising events that are very expensive or that are being conducted not for immediate revenues, but for public relations purposes.

The state of Maryland enacted such a law in 1976 after a religious group was convicted of misuse of funds. The law limited administrative expenses for fund raising to 25 percent. The law provided that the secretary of the state of Maryland could waiver the 25 percent at his or her discretion. It also provided that certain expenses such as feasibility studies, planning, and counseling for fund raising would be excluded in calculating the 25 percent limit.

On June 26, 1984, in *Secretary of State of Maryland* v. *Joseph H. Munson Co., Inc.*, the Supreme Court of the United States in a five to four decision held that the law is unconstitutional on its face. In the majority's view, the Maryland law could not distinguish between those organizations that had legitimately high administrative costs in pursuit of their First Amendment rights and those that did not. The lack of precision of the Maryland law, according to the majority of the Court, meant that its application always risked the suppression of constitutional rights. Whether other state laws placing limitations on fund raising are consequently unconstitutional will depend on the individual state law. In *Riley* v. *National Foundation of the Blind of North Carolina*, 1988, the U.S. Supreme Court concluded that a requirement that nonprofits disclose the percentage of fund-raising receipt they will receive is a violation of the First Amendment.

Trends and Patterns of Giving

If gifts and contributions are important to nonprofits as economic institutions because (1) they provide revenues and (2) they demonstrate public support as evidence on the revenue side that the organization is conducting an activity of public welfare, from what source are the gifts

TABLE 3.1   Total Giving, 1989 (In Billions of Dollars)

Sources	Amount in Dollars	Percent	Uses	Amount in Dollars	Percent
Individuals	96.4	84.1	Religion	54.3	47.4
Foundations	6.70	5.8	Human Services	11.4	9.9
Corporations	5.00	4.4	Education	10.7	9.3
Bequest	6.6	5.7	Arts, Culture, Humanities	7.5	6.5
			Health	10.4	8.8
			Public/Society	3.6	3.2
Total Giving	$114,700,000		Others	17.3	14.0

Source: American Association of Fund-Raising Counsel, Inc., *Giving U.S.A.* (New York, N.Y. 1989–90), 212-354-4799. Adapted by permission.

coming? Table 3.1 shows that, in 1989, 84 percent of all charitable contributions came from individuals. Most, 47 percent, of the donations from all sources went to religion. These figures are similar to previous years. In 1964, individuals accounted for 81 percent of all contributions and religion received the greatest share.

Corporate giving has remained less than 2 percent of net income or profits. Over a third goes to education. Table 3.2 shows the two foundations and corporations making the largest contributions by mission according to the Taft Group. Within the corporate sector, there are distinct patterns. Table 3.3 shows annual patterns within the life and health insurance industry. Notice the sharp rise in the percentage of companies reporting support to AIDS education and treatment between 1986 and 1988.

TABLE 3.2   Types of Community Projects Most Frequently Supported by Life and Health Insurance Companies: Percent of Trend Companies, 1985 and 1989

	1989	1985
Education	95%	84%
Arts and cultural programs	85	90
Local health programs	84	83
Youth activities	79	80
Neighborhood improvement programs	73	76
AIDS education/treatment	65	10
Drug or alcohol abuse programs	63	56
Minority affairs	57	58
Programs for the handicapped	57	59
Programs for hunger/homeless	55	41
Activities for senior citizens and retired persons	50	44
Hard-to-employ programs	44	49
Safety programs	41	44
Housing programs	40	38
Day-care programs	30	28
Environmental programs	26	25
Crime prevention	25	32
Transportation programs	15	26

Source: 1990 Social Report of the Life and Health Insurance Business, p. 4. Reprinted by permission.
Number of Trend Companies (110).

TABLE 3.3 Largest Corporate and Foundation Donors by Mission

Mission	Sources (Rank No. 1)	
	Corporation	Foundation
Arts and Humanities	IBM Corporation[1]	John D. and Catherine T. MacArthur Foundation
Civic & Public Affairs	IBM Corporation	Ford Foundation
Education	Hewlett-Packard Company[2]	Pew Charitable Trusts
Health	IBM Corporation	Robert Wood Johnson Foundation
International	IBM Corporation[3]	Ford Foundation
Religion	MCA	Arthur S. De Moss Foundation
Science	Johnson & Johnson	Kresge Foundation
Social Services	IBM Corporation	Rockefeller Foundation
	(Rank No. 2)	
Arts and Humanities	American Telephone & Telegraph	Pew Charitable Trusts
Civic & Public Affairs	Ford Motor Company	John D. and Catherine T. MacArthur Foundation
Education	IBM Corporation	Lilly Endowment
Health	Johnson & Johnson	W.K. Kellog Foundation
International	Exxon Corporation[3]	Rockefeller Foundation
Religion	Borden	Lilly Endowment
Science	Burroughs Wellcome Company	Pew Charitable Trusts
Social Services	Exxon Corporation	Lilly Endowment

[1] Also ranks highest of all corporations in terms of total nonmonetary support.
[2] Also ranks second highest of all corporations in terms of total nonmonetary support.
[3] Rank transmitted by Fax from Taft Group.
Source: Adapted with permission form *Foundation and Corporate Giving 1991*, © The Taft Group, 12300 Twinbrook Parkway, Suite 450, Rockville, MD 20852.

SUMMARY AND CONCLUSIONS

We should now appreciate that the nonprofit is a corporation with legal limits and powers. Its raison d'etre is its mission, which has the force of a social contract. As a for-profit corporation, it must operate within corporate law as it applied to nonprofits. These laws justify tax exemption whether for income only or both for income and the deductibility that donors receive. Hence, in the same manner that a corporate officer needs to have a basic understanding of corporate law, so too the nonprofit executive does because these define the rules by which he or she manages without causing the organization to lose its tax exemption.

But the nonprofit has costs and needs revenues. Moreover, by being tax exempt and utilizing society's resources, it must also economize. Hence, it is an economic institution.

The definitions of its corporate and tax-exempt status are both tied to this concept of an economic institution, because it is the pattern of expenditures and revenues that ultimately is assessed to determine whether the nonprofit is operating in a manner consistent with its mission. We now turn to the formulas used in this judgment.

NOTES

1. For a review of the literature on this subject, see John P. Persons, John J. Osborn, Jr., and Charles F. Feldman, "Criteria for Exemption under Section 501(c)(3)," *Research Papers: Commission on Philanthropy and Public Needs* (Washington, D.C.: U.S. Treasury, 1979), vol. 4, pp. 1909-2075.

2. Ibid.

3. Revenue Ruling 74-587, 1974-2, Cumulative Bulletin 162, and Revenue Ruling 81-284, 1981-2, Cumulative Bulletin 230.

4. General Consul's Memorandum, 39047, 1/2/83.

5. Revenue Ruling 76-94, 1976-1, Cumulative Bulletin 171.

6. Revenue Ruling 81-62, 1981-1, Cumulative Bulletin 355.

7. *Fraternal Medical Services Incorporated* v. *Commissioner*, Tax Court Memorandum, 84, 644 (12-20-84).

8. *Black's Dictionary of Law*, 5th ed. (St. Paul, Minnesota: West Publishing Company, 1979), p. 212.

9. *Fraternal Medical Specialist Services, Inc.* v. *Commissioner*, Tax Court Memorandum, 84, 644 (12-20-84).

10. *Church in Boston* v. *Commissioner*, 71 Tax Court Memo 102, 106 (1978).

11. *Better Business Bureau* v. *United States*, 326 U.S. 279 (34 after 5) (1945). This is a seminal case.

12. *Trinidad* v. *Sagrada Orden*, 263 U.S. 578, 581, 44 S. Ct. 204, 205, 68 L. Ed. 458 (1924).

13. Revenue Ruling, 73-104, 1973-1, Cumulative Bulletin.

14. *American College of Physicians* v. *United States*, Appeal No. 84-715, Sept. 17, 1984.

15. Revenues Ruling 73-105, 1973-1, Cumulative Bulletin 264. See Alan J. Yanowitz and Elizabeth A. Purcell, "IRS's Recent Approaches to Retail Sales by Exempt Organizations: Analyzing Standards," *Journal of Taxation*, 59, no. 4 (Oct. 1983), 250–255, for a comparison.

16. See Persons et al., Research Papers, for history and citations of congressional debate. At least one economist argues that the law is unfair because it tends to encourage nonprofits to stick to related businesses. The consequence of this is that those for-profit industries that are most likely to be a related business for nonprofits must contend with competition from nonprofits, while other sectors less likely to be a related business do not face the same intervention and competition from non-profits. Competition is healthy for the economy. Susan Rose-Ackerman, "Unfair Competition and Corporate Income Taxation," *Stanford Law Review*, 34, no. 36 (1982), 1017–39.

17. *Piety Inc.* v. *Commissioner, 82 T.C. No. 16*, 1/26/84.

18. *Church of Scientology of California* v. *Commissioner*, U.S. Tax Court Docket. 3352–78.

19. Society of Costa Rica Collectors, T.C.M. 1984-648, 12/13/84.

20. Annual salaries and benefits data for foundations can be obtained from the Council of Foundations and from the Society of Association Executives, both of Washington, D.C.

21. Alan Piper, *Philanthropy in an Age of Transition* (New York: The Foundation Center, 1984), p. 23.

22. Technically, one could make a gift to a for-profit corporation, but this is not a normal source of revenues for such corporation.

23. Patrick Reilly, "Magazines Find Cause Can Help Everyone," *Wall Street Journal*, Tuesday, Sept. 18, 1990, p. B6.

SUGGESTED READINGS

National Center for Charitable Statistics, *The National Taxonomy of Exempt Entities* (Washington, D.C.: The Independent Sector, 1990).

THELIN, JOHN R. AND LAWRENCE L. WISEMAN, "Fiscal Fitness? The Peculiar Economics of Intercollegiate Athletics," *Capital Ideas*, 44, no. 4, February 1990, pp. 1–15.

Chapter 4

Corporate Structure and the Nonprofit Mission

How an organization is classified is affected not only by its mission, but how it is financed. Furthermore, the ability of the organization to carry out its mission depends not only on how it is financed, but on how it is organized. A misunderstanding of these interrelationships not only causes the organization to be less efficient, but it can cause the loss of tax-exempt status.

THE IMPORTANCE OF CORPORATE STRUCTURE

The annual report of the Special Olympics International, Inc. says:

> Special Olympics International (SOI) is a District of Columbia nonprofit corporation, exempt from income tax under Section 501(c)(3) of the U.S.

Internal Revenue Code, and has been designated as a "publicly supported" organization under Sections 509(a)(1) and 170(b)(1)(A)(vi). Special Olympics Productions, Inc., (SOP) is also a District of Columbia nonprofit corporation exempt from federal income tax under Section 501(c)(3), and has been designated as a "supporting" organization under Section 509(a)(3) and 170(b)(1)(A)(vi).

What does this have to do with the mission of the organization, which is:

The mission of Special Olympics is to provide year-round sports training and athletic competition in a variety of Olympic-type sports for all children and adults with mental retardation, giving them continuing opportunities to develop physical fitness, demonstrate courage, experience joy and participate in the sharing of gifts, skills, and friendship with their families, other Special Olympics athletes and the community.[1] Reprinted with permission from *Special Olympics International*, 1989, p. 30.

Do these numbers make a difference in fund-raising? Take a sentence from a Kellogg Foundation program:

To be eligible, the organization must qualify as a 501(c)(3), 509(a)(1), (2) or (3) organization under the Internal Revenue Code.[2]

The second quotation is a clear statement of the mission of Special Olympics. It is very much in keeping with the characteristics of a mission described in Chapters 1 through 3. The first statement says that it is a legal corporation, again in keeping with Chapter 2. But it says more. The numbers are codes for describing the particular type of revenues structure the organization is expected to maintain—its revenue characteristics as an economic institution, as described in Chapter 3.

The phrase "supporting organization" connotes the overall corporate structure and the linkage of independent nonprofit corporations to each other within that structure. Variations of the quotation from Kellogg are to be found in virtually all corporate and private foundation grant and contribution programs. Clearly, it is worth your while to find out what these codes and concepts mean. It is the aim of this chapter to explain.

CORPORATE AND FINANCIAL SIGNIFICANCE OF 501(C)(3) STATUS

As stated in Chapter 2, nonprofit corporations are creations of the laws of individual states. A nonprofit becomes exempt from taxation when it is given a 501(c)(3) status by the Internal Revenue Service (see Figure

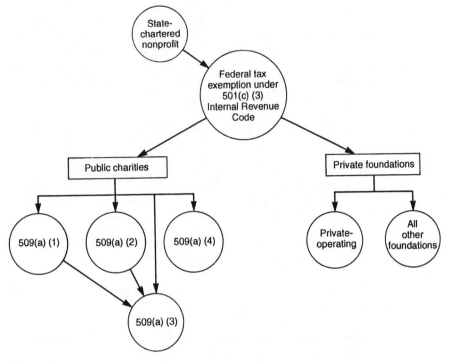

Figure 4.1   Transformation of Organization by Tax-Exempt Status under Section 501(c) (3).

4.1). To qualify under Section 501(c)(3) of the *IRS Code*,[3] the organization must contain in its charter the stipulation that none of the income or assets will be distributed to individuals and, if the organization is dissolved, its income and assets will be distributed to a similarly qualified organization or to the state. Note that this stipulation is required both for state recognition and for IRS exemption. Where it is not required by the state, it is nevertheless required by the IRS. These are not duplicate requirements.

The organizing document, the charter or deed, must also state that the nonprofit exists exclusively for one or more of the following purposes: charitable, religious, educational, scientific, literary, testing for public safety, fostering national or international amateur sports competition (excepting the provision of athletic facilities or equipment), or the prevention of cruelty to children or animals.[4] These are the only missions that would allow an organization to qualify under Section 501(c)(3).[5] Recall from Chapter 2 that they must select a maximum of three purposes that can be described by these broad missions.

Finally, the organizing document must say that the nonprofit will not use a substantial part of its energies or resources for lobbying. Under no condition may 501(c)(3)s be involved in campaigns of candidates for political office. This rule cannot be evaded by setting up a separate account for endorsing or supporting candidates. In short, while some lobbying is permitted, no involvement in a political campaign is tolerated of a 501(c)(3) organization. Violations lead to loss of tax-exempt status.

A nonprofit that meets the conditions as discussed may qualify to be exempt from taxes under Section 501(c)(3), but only a few nonprofits automatically qualify for tax-exempt status. Except for churches and their affiliates, public nonprofits with gross annual receipts of less than $5000 and public nonprofits that are chapters under the tax-exempt umbrella of a national public charity, all other nonprofits must apply and meet certain specific tests before they are exempt.

To be exempt under 501(c)(3), a nonprofit must prove that it is publicly supported and must also pass three tests: organizational, asset, and political. The organizational test determines if the purpose of the nonprofit coincides with the purposes permitted under Section 501(c)(3). The purpose must be one or more of the following: charitable, religious, educational, scientific, literary, testing for public safety, fostering national or international amateur sports competition (excepting the provision of athletic facilities or equipment), or the prevention of cruelty to children or animals.

Because all these functions could be done for profit, it is necessary to demonstrate that the nonprofit organization intends to carry them out in a noncommercial mode. To demonstrate that the mode is charitable is sufficient to distinguish a for-profit from a nonprofit providing the same service, for example, a community clinic from a private clinic. One definition of the word charitable is that the beneficiaries are a class of needy people whose needs are not otherwise met in the marketplace.[6]

To qualify under Section 501(c)(3), a nonprofit must also pass an asset test. To pass, the organizing document must prohibit the nonprofit from distributing any of its assets or income to individuals. Furthermore, the organization may not be used for the personal benefit of the founders, supporters, or managers or their relatives or personal or business associates. Moreover, if the nonprofit is terminated, the assets will be distributed to a qualified public charity or to the state or local government for charitable purposes and not to any individual.

Finally, to qualify under Section 501(c)(3), a political test must be passed. The organizing document must forbid the nonprofit from participating in any political campaign on behalf of a candidate. Participation is meant to include the preparation and distribution of literature. This test does not prohibit voter education; but because such an activity can be broadly interpreted, it is wise to seek specific exemption through an IRS letter ruling if such an activity is contemplated.

Public Charities: Financial and Legal Limits

Once a nonprofit has won classification under Section 501(c)(3), it must, by law, be further classified as shown in Figure 4.1. It must either be classified as a private foundation or a public charity. Public charities enjoy several privileges. Contributions to them receive the most favorable tax treatment in the sense that contributions are deductible by the donors.[7] They do not have to pay an excise tax on their investment income.[8] Unless they fall into the special category, noted as 509(a)(3), they do not have to make annual distributions of their assets to other charities the way private foundations do.

Section 509(a)(1) Organizations

Section 509(a)(1) organizations are nonprofits that are classified as public charities and are known as publicly supported organizations because their common characteristic is that they are supported by the general public. The characteristics required to be classified under this section are given in Section 170(b)(1)(A) of the *Internal Revenue Code*.

The types of organizations that are exempt under Section 170(b)(1)(A) are shown in Table 4.1. These are generally the public charities that provide direct services to the community, but also defined under Subtitle (v) are state and local government agencies. The Constitution of the United States is based on the principle that the federal government is the creation of the state and not vice versa. Therefore, the purpose of Subtitle (v) is not to create states; its principal purpose is to provide for gifts and contributions to be made to state and local government agencies such as school boards and be deductible by the donors. Thus, we can make contributions to reduce the deficit of a jurisdiction, including the federal deficit, and deduct that amount.

TABLE 4.1 Nonprofits Described under Section 170 of the Internal Revenue Code

Section 170(b)(1)(A)	Type of Nonprofit Described
i	Churches
ii	Educational institutions
iii	Hospitals and medical research
iv	Agencies that support government schools
v	Government units that receive gifts for public purposes
vi	Publicly supported charities
vii	Certain private foundations
viii	509(a)(2) and (a)(3) organizations

Note that Subtitle vii includes private nonoperating foundations and private operating foundations. This is to accommodate a special type of private foundation such as a pooled trust, where the individual donors can dictate which charities should be beneficiaries of their gifts and be assured of periodic accounting about the gifts made in their names by the trust and the trust investment performance. Subtitle viii refers to two other sections to be described later in this chapter.

Subtitle vi refers to publicly supported charities, a broad category. This encompasses most of the organizations that we know as public charities and nonprofit organizations. Martha's Table is a public charity, a 501(c)(3) as defined under 509(a)(1) and 170(b)(1)(A)(vi). Martha's Table runs a soup kitchen, a thrift shop, and educational programs for poor children in the District of Columbia.

Similarly, in Figure 4.2 we see in the last sentence that the Joint Center for Political and Economic Studies, a public policy organization, has a similar status. The IRS specifies it is not a private foundation. Both organizations may accept donations, which are deductible by the donors. Neither is subject to the restrictive rules of private foundations. Their missions are distinctly different although both fall under the same broad category. However, importantly, both must demonstrate public support. Both are public charities.

Definition of Public Support: 509(a)(1)

Proof of public support for 509(a)(1) organizations comes in the form of passing two tests: the one-third support test or the 10 percent support and facts and circumstances test. How do these work?

To demonstrate that it "normally" has public support through the one-third test, a nonprofit must show that, over the preceding four years, one-third of its support came from the government or the general public or a combination of the two. The words, "support," "normal," and "public" are specifically defined.

Support includes gifts, contributions, membership fees (excluding the portion that is an assessment for special services), net income from unrelated businesses, gross investment income, revenues from taxes levied by the government for the benefit of the nonprofit, and the value of facilities furnished by the government free of charge if those facilities are usually rented or sold.

There are many aspects of support that deserve to be highlighted. Note that for this group of nonprofits support refers to income from unrelated business rather than to related business.[9] This means that a nonprofit cannot include in its calculation of support any revenues it receives from an activity for which it is tax exempt if the payment benefits the payor. To illustrate, a nonprofit exempt as a day-care center cannot in-

Internal Revenue Service   Department of the Treasury
District Director

Date: 31 Jul 1979   Our Letter Dated:
                                                           June 14, 1976

                                                           Person to Contact:
                                                           F. Buchanan

                                                           Contact Telephone Number:
                                                           (301) 962-4773

The Joint Center for Political Studies, Inc.
c/o Walter Slocombe, Esquire
1101 17th Street, NW
Washington, DC 20036

This modifies our letter of the above date in which we stated that you would be treated as an organization which is not a private foundation until the expiration of your advance ruling period.

Based on the information you submitted, we have determined that you are not a private foundation within the meaning of section 509(a) of the Internal Revenue Code, because you are an organization of the type described in section _____*_____ . Your exempt status under section 501(c) (3) of the code is still in effect.

Grantors and contributors may rely on this determination until the Internal Revenue Service publishes notice to the contrary. However, a grantor or a contributor may not rely on this determination if he or she was in part responsible for, or was aware of, the act or failure to act that resulted in your loss of section _____*_____ status, or acquired knowledge that the Internal Revenue Service had given notice that you would be removed from classification as a section _____*_____ organization.

Because this letter could help resolve any questions about your private foundation status, please keep it in your permanent records.

If you have any questions, please contact the person whose name and telephone number are shown above.
* 509(a) (1) & 170(b) (1) (A) (vi).

                                        Sincerely yours,

                                        Gerald G. Portney

                                        Gerald G. Portney
                                        District Director

31 Hopkins Plaza, Baltimore, Md. 21201   Letter 1050 (DO) (7-77)

Figure 4.2   Joint Center for Political Studies, Washington, D.C., Letter (Reprinted with permission of the Joint Center for Political Studies, Washington, D.C.).

clude as support fees from parents for caring for their children. These payments benefit the payors and are in conjunction with the tax-exempt purpose of the day-care center. If the day-care center owns a fast-food restaurant, an unrelated business catering to the general public, the net income from this business may be included in the calculation of support. If the parents made a contribution for assisting children (other than their own) who are members of the general public, this would be support. If the parents contributed anything such as services that are not deductible contributions, they will not be included in the calculation of support. Do you see the rationale? It does not tempt the organization to penny-pinch poor people to show public support.

Also, membership dues qualify as support only after adjustment is made for the portion of the dues that is a payment for services, such as a magazine. It is only the portion that is for the general support of the organization that counts.

Facilities received by the organization from the government cannot be included as support unless the government usually charges for the use of these facilities or sells them.

By "public" is meant governmental units and the general population. A gift or contribution from a community trust, itself a tax-exempt nonprofit, is a contribution from the public if these trusts receive their funds primarily from contributions from the general public and are based on public participation. Earnings from an endowment created by public funds are also considered a public contribution. Obviously, contributions from individual persons and entities are also public. It is the concentration of contributions in a few areas that creates the problem.

Calculation of Public Support: 509(a)(1)

The word "normally" also has a precise meaning. It spans the experience over the preceding four years. The classification of the nonprofit is determined for a current and the next year based on the performance of the organization over the four preceding years. It is publicly supported in years 1985 and 1986 if it passes the public support test in 1981 to 1984. It is publicly supported in 1986 and 1987 if it passes the test for the period 1982 to 1985, and so on. A nonprofit can have its classification changed depending on how it performed over the preceding four years. Since a classification is not given in perpetuity, a publicly supported organization will lose that favored status when it can no longer prove public support.

For a nonprofit to be classified as a public charity under 509(a)(1) as defined in Section 170(b)(1)(A) by proving it has public support, it must demonstrate that a minimum portion of its total support, as previously defined, is from the general public. How is this proved? One test requires that at least one-third of such support must come from the general public (government and people from the community at large). Alternatively, the nonprofit may show that at least 10 percent of its support comes from the general public, but that the facts and circumstances surrounding the operation of the organization prove that it encourages and involves public participation.

The nonprofit cannot meet either test by merely getting a few large contributions from individuals. Let us demonstrate the test. Based on the definition of support given earlier, assume that nonprofit A has investment income (interest and dividends) of $100,000, contributions from its community chest of $40,000, and from Beverly for $50,000, Audrey for $10,000, and Anhela for $1000. Its total support is $201,000. According to the rule, one-third ($67,000) of the total support must be from the general public. Note, however, that of the $101,000 coming from the public, about half came from one source, Beverly, who contributes $50,000. To defeat this ploy, the rules state that no individual's contribution may be included to an extent that it exceeds 2 percent of the total support (in this case, 2 percent of $201,000 or $4020). Thus, the contributions of Beverly and Audrey are valued for calculation purposes at $4020 each, or a total of $8040. When this $8040 is added to the $1000 and the $40,000 from the community chest, the sum, $49,040, is less than the required $67,000, so the organization fails the one-third support test.

The nonprofit would have made the one-third support test if instead of two large individual contributions by Beverly and Audrey, it had at least fifteen small contributions of no more than $4020 each.[10] Again, the purpose is to avoid defeat of the intent of the law that public support be demonstrated.

Should a nonprofit fail the one-third support test, it may try under the 10 percent and facts and circumstances test. To do this, the nonprofit must show that at least 10 percent of its support is normally (as defined) obtained from government and public sources, and that there is a continuous effort to attract public support, for example, through fund-raising drives.

In the preceding example, the 10 percent of the total support of $201,000 would be $20,100. Since public support is calculated to be $49,040, the 10 percent test is met. But with the lowered requirement of a minimum of 10 percent, the IRS looks deeper into the facts and circumstances surrounding the sources of support of the nonprofit. These tests are more subjective. One focus is on the source of the other 90 percent. Is there some reasonable way to say that the amount came indirectly from the public? For example, is it the earnings on an endowment created by the public? If so, the nonprofit wins or maintains classification as a public charity. In the example just given, the bulk of the support came from investment income. If the interest and dividends are from the investment of funds in a publicly created endowment, the organization will pass, but not if the investment income is from a gift from a single individual.

But the IRS may focus on the 10 percent rather than on the 90 percent. If this came from one or two individuals, the lack of public support may be implied. Because the test is subjective, we cannot be sure how the given example will be interpreted. But observe that the 10 percent came from only four sources: the community chest, Audrey, Anhela, and Beverly. The nonprofit would probably have failed this test without the inclusion of the community chest.[11]

Other considerations in the facts and circumstances test are even more subjective. In one approach the IRS looks into the composition of the governing board of the nonprofit. If the board is a cross section of the community, including elected or appointed public officials, the IRS is likely to conclude that there is evidence of public support.

Public support is also said to exist if the nonprofit makes its facilities and membership open to the public, conducts programs for the public, and is heavily dependent on a public foundation such as the United Way for support.

Section 509(a)(2) Organizations

Return to Chapter 1 and read the section under "Taxes" for the Colonial Williamsburg Foundation. Note the language: "The organization is classified as a publicly supported foundation under the provisions of Section 509(a)(2)...." What is the difference between the (a)(1) and (a)(2)s? What's it all about? The required revenue pattern is the answer.

Definition and Calculation of Public Support: 509(a)(2)

The revenue patterns of 509(a)(2) and (a)(1) organizations are similar in that both are publicly supported organizations. The key difference is that 509(a)(2) includes income from businesses related to conducting their mission as support and the 509(a)(1) includes instead income from unrelated business.[12] The (a)(2)s have clients who can pay for services, and therefore their business income is heavily program related and is considered support. Universities and museums are examples. The (a)(1)s have clients who cannot pay. They depend more heavily on gifts and contributions. All income streams are available to both groups; it is a matter of weight.

In addition, a 509(a)(2) is subject to two tests. The first puts a limit on income from unrelated business and from gross investments. Specifically, such organizations should not normally derive more than one-third of their support from the sum of investment income and the portion of the taxable income from unrelated business that exceeds the amount they paid in taxes on such income. Section 509(a)(1) organizations are not subject to such limitations.

Second, these 509(a)(2) organizations must show that more than one-third of their support comes from gifts, contributions, membership fees, and program-related businesses. The effect of this is to require an emphasis on the public support of the program and to de-emphasize the ability of the organization to gain support through shrewd investments.

Section 509(a)(2) organizations are not conceptually different from 509(a)(1)s. They are alternatives to each other based on the way their public support test is calculated. Many organizations that would satisfy one would satisfy the other.

Diversification and Preservation of Tax Exempt Status

A comparison of the requirements of 509(a)(1) and (a)(2) classifications reveals that it is not simply the source of support that counts, but the composition or structure of support as well. Diversification of funding sources is always wise because it reduces the risk of financial failure. But, as we shall see, diversification has an important implication for how a nonprofit is classified. Furthermore, because one classification tends to favor certain types of support, while other types of support are favored by the other classification, it does not necessarily follow that the favored combinations would lead predictably to either one or the other classification, a Section 509(a)(1) or (a)(2). Exemption may be at risk.

In referring to Figure 4.3, suppose nonprofit A expected to have a large investment income and a large unrelated business income (cell 1). Since both of these are included as support in the calculations for 509(a)(1) status, we may at first conclude that such a status is what nonprofit A would fit. The problem is that this combination only increases the size of support. The rule requires that one-third of the support be public. Thus, the larger the amount associated with cell 1, the greater the amount that has to be obtained from the general public through gifts and contributions in order for the nonprofit to meet either the one-third or the 10 percent support test.

If the organization's fund-raising strategy is represented by cell 1, being a 509(a)(2) may not be the answer either. This is so because the rules stated earlier limit that combination to no more than one-third of the total support. Thus, the higher the amount represented in cell 1, the greater the amount of public support (the other two-thirds) that will be needed to meet the requirements to be a 509(a)(2). For (a)(2) organizations, this implies a larger amount from gifts and donations and from related business income, that is, income from conducting its mission. Both

	Type of business	
	Unrelated	Related
Investment income	1	2
Gifts, grants contributions membership fees	3	4

Other income

Figure 4.3 Hypothetical Major Sources of Funding of Public Charities.

are derived from catering to the public, thus demonstrating greater public support.

Cell 2 is dangerous. While many 509(a)(2)s may seem to fit because of their reliance on fees and the importance of investment income to them, the danger is that this revenue pattern is no different for a firm. A for-profit firm relies on sales of its products or services (a close resemblance to related income) and its earnings from marketable securities or other investments. Consequently, tax exemption is often denied an organization because it "looks" commercial. In short, the more an organization's income stream places it in cell 2, the more the need to demonstrate public support and a strong commitment to a defined tax-exempt mission, as explained in Chapters 1 through 3.

Cell 3 seems safe for a 509(a)(1) organization. The problem may arise from the relative weights of unrelated business income to gifts, grants contributions, membership fees, and the like. Obviously, if a nonprofit falls in cell 3 but with an overwhelming amount of its revenues being unrelated business, then it must resort to providing evidence of a tax-exempt purpose like those in cell 2, because these organizations are also not easily distinguishable from a for-profit firm. They too rely heavily on sales.

Consider cell 4. The rules suggest that a nonprofit that emphasizes gifts and grants and related business as sources of income may be better off selecting Section 509(a)(2) because those two sources of funding are favorably treated. Indeed, the rules would be satisfied if all the funds came from this combination. Suppose, however, 60 percent of the funds fell in cell 4. Then the nonprofit may fail to qualify as 509(a)(2) if more than one-third of the remaining 40 percent falls in cell 1. This is so because a second rule, as described earlier, says that no more than one-third of the support may be a combination of unrelated business income and gross investment income. Again, it is the composition of support that counts.

The key.   All the cells present problems of the same type. The lessons are two: (1) The classifications do not permit escape from the requirement of public support and (2) it is the composition or structure of support rather than the individual source (unless all the funds come exclusively from public sources) that matters. Good management should pay attention to diversification to avoid risk of financial failure and also to meet and maintain the classification requirements.

COMPARISON OF 509(a)(1) AND (a)(2) ORGANIZATIONS

Both the 509(a)(1) and (a)(2) organizations must demonstrate public support, and in this sense they are both publicly supported nonprofits. Both must have a mission to advance public welfare and both may conduct related and unrelated businesses. The basic difference is that the (a)(2) organizations are financed more by business income, particularly related business income, than are the 509(a)(1) organizations. Museums such as the Colonial Williamsburg Foundation cited in Chapter 1 are good examples because their support is heavily weighted in the direction of fees, subscription revenues for magazines, sales of related art products, and other business income and depends less on contributions by individuals or foundations. The backbone of 509(a)(2) organizations is that they are good businesses conducting a public service and generating a substantial amount of their support through sales.

On the other hand, 509(a)(1) organizations cannot rely as heavily on the selling of their goods and services as a means of demonstrating public support. They rely more on gifts and contributions, including contributions from foundations, and may supplement these through conducting a business.

Section 509(a)(3) Organizations

Section 509(a)(3) organizations are nonprofits that exist to support and aid publicly supported nonprofits [Sections (509)(a)(1) and (a)(2)].

Remember SOP in the opening quotation of this chapter? Basically, these supporting organizations, as they are called, could not technically exist without publicly supported organizations. Yet they are not divisions. They have their own organizing documents as corporations or trusts and must obtain their own tax-exempt status. The basis upon which the IRS confers that status on them, however, is that their sole mission will be to support an existing publicly supported organization.

Thus, the annual report of the Special Olympics referred to earlier says that SOP was incorporated on May 22, 1987, as a supporting organization of SOI. SOP's directors and officers are elected by members of SOI. The purpose of SOP is to promote public interest and support for the activities of SOI.

A nonprofit may obtain tax-exempt status as a public charity under Section 509(a)(3) if it is (1) operated, supervised, or controlled by, (2) supervised or controlled in connection with, or (3) operated in connection with a nonprofit that has public charity status as a 509(a)(1) or (a)(2) organization. These concepts provide subtle but important degrees of independence as far as daily management is concerned. In all cases, however, the supporting organization exists to assist the publicly supported organization. Thus, in Figure 4.1 the 509(a)(3) is shown as an independently chartered and exempted organization but subordinate to the 509(a)(1) and (a)(2).

By "operated, supervised, or controlled" is meant that the management and the governing body of the nonprofit are elected or appointed by the governing body of the parent public foundation. They might elect and appoint themselves as trustees of the supporting organization. Thus, the supporting organization is subservient to the parent. The organizing document of 509(a)(3) organizations falling into this category must limit the activities of these organizations to carrying out missions on behalf of the parent organization and furthering the cause of the parent. Thus, it is not enough for a 509(a)(3) organization to serve the same clients as its parents, but it must do so because it is furthering the mission of the parent.

One restriction that is placed on these nonprofits "operated, supervised, or controlled" by a parent 509(a)(1) or (a)(2) is that they cannot be under the influence of a disqualified person other than the manager. For instance, Carlos creates a foundation that gets 509(a)(3) status by being a subsidiary to Carlos's church. Carlos is a disqualified person with respect to the foundation he has created, which means that he is barred from having a business relationship with it. His church cannot circumvent this proscription by making him a member of the board of trustees of the church with responsibility over the foundation he created.

The term "supervised or controlled in connection with" has very much the same meaning as "operated, supervised, or controlled by" except that, instead of the governing body being elected and appointed by the parent organization, the very same persons who form the governing body of the one also form a similar body for the other. This assures subservience, the objective of the law.

By "operated in connection with" is meant that (1) the organization exists in support of the publicly supported organization, (2) is integrally a part of its activities, (3) is guided constantly and regularly by it, (4) conducts only missions that advance its cause, and (5) is not influenced by a disqualified person.

Obviously, the subservience of one nonprofit to another may be stifling, but there are advantages. A supporting foundation such as 509(a)(3) may operate a business, conduct specialized research and technical assistance services, and shield the publicly supported organization from risks and liabilities. While managers of the supporting organizations may complain, the fact is that these organizations could not exist without being subservient.

Section 509(a)(4) Organizations

Section 509(a)(4) organizations will not be discussed in this book because they are highly specialized in testing consumer products for safety. While serving this important function, they do not fall into the general category of the public foundations discussed.

PRIVATE FOUNDATIONS: FINANCIAL AND LEGAL LIMITS

Let us turn now to a discussion of private foundations. A good understanding of these foundations is desirable for several reasons. First, the rules that govern them are good precepts for all nonprofits. Second, they are the primary source of foundation funding that public charities receive. There are some 28,000 such foundations giving well over $4 billion a year to public charities. One out of every $10 contributed to nonprofits comes from private foundations.[13] Appeals to private foundations have a better chance when there is a clear understanding of the framework in which these foundations operate. Third, while private foundations include the Howard Hughes, Ford, Robert Wood Johnson, Andrew Mellon, Rockefeller, MacArthur, and Pew, which are among the seven largest in terms of assets, all public charities [all nonprofits classified as 501(c)(3) organizations] are potentially private foundations. This is how they are classified and treated when the public support test is failed.

This category called private foundations is made up of four types of nonprofits: (1) those that failed the public support tests, (2) those created by individuals as philanthropists (thus the adjective, private) with the intent of financing rather than conducting a charitable mission, (3) endowments, and (4) corporate foundations.

At the end of this discussion, the reader will also appreciate the rationale for the note that appears at the end of the 1989 annual report of the Carnegie Corporation of New York (see Figure 4.4).

Private Foundation Status

The private foundation status is given to any 501(C)(3) organization failing to meet the strict requirements as stipulated for Sections 509(a)(1) or (a)(2). The organization may fail this test upon making its application for 501(c)(3) status. Notice that the Joint Center in the example given earlier did not fail the test and therefore was classified as a public charity, as other public policy and research organizations are.

The letter to the Joint Center is instructive for other reasons. Note that is makes reference to a provisional classification. The IRS initially classifies an organization that qualifies as a 501(c)(3) as a public charity on a provisional basis, pending evidence of how it actually operates and is financed. Thus, if an organization violates the rules concerning financing and operation, it can lose its tax-exempt status. When that hap-

---

The following statements are set forth in accordance with section 6056 of the United States Internal Revenue Code, pursuant to which this annual report has been prepared:

- Carnegie Corporation of New York (employer identification number 13-1628151) is a private foundation within the meaning of section 509(a) of the Internal Revenue Code.
- The names and respective business addresses of the "foundation managers" of the Corporation are set forth in the front section of this annual report.
- No person who is a "foundation manager" with respect to the Corporation has made any contribution to the Corporation in any taxable year.
- At no time during the year did the Corporation (together with other "disqualified persons") own more than 2 percent of the stock of any corporation or corresponding interests in partnerships or other entities.
- Pursuant to section 6104(d) of the Internal Revenue Code, a notice has been published that this annual report and the Corporation's annual return are available for public inspection at the principal office of the Corporation. A copy of this report has been furnished to the Attorney General of the State of New York.

Figure 4.4 Letter, Carnegie Corporation of New York, Annual Report 1990 (Source: Carnegie Corporation of New York, Annual Report, p. 174).

pens, the IRS publishes the name of the organization among those that have lost their status. This information appears regularly in the IRS publication known as the *Revenue Bulletin*. A principal purpose of the announcement is to notify potential donors that they can no longer make contributions to this organization and take the deduction accorded a public charity, which is 50 percent of adjusted gross income. They must take the lower limit (30 percent of adjusted gross income) accorded a private (nonoperating) foundation. This is what the IRS is referring to in paragraph 3 of the letter on page 100. Moreover, it is saying that those individuals who are responsible for an organization's losing its cherished public charity classification cannot be protected by claiming ignorance.

Once the organization has lost its public charity classification, it then becomes a private foundation and is subject to all the stringent rules that apply to such foundations. These rules are discussed later in this chapter.

Finally, the letter states that the Joint Center for Political and Economic Studies is in good standing and may use this letter to assure the public (including potential donors) that it is a public charity, not a private foundation, and therefore, by implication, their contributions will qualify for the maximum deduction of 50 percent of adjusted gross income. It is also eligible for grants from private foundations.

Another reason for our discussion of private foundations is that any public charity that is operating an endowment is operating a private foundation. Endowments and trusts are subject to the same rules as private foundations. Each separate trust and each separate endowment operated by a university, hospital, museum, or any other nonprofit is technically a private foundation and subject to the rules to be described in this chapter.

Except for the fact that private foundations have limited public support, they are also nonprofits with a public welfare or charitable mission. They too must qualify under Section 501(c)(3) of the *Internal Revenue Code* (IRC) and are also economic institutions with a public or community welfare mission. Their mission is to finance the public charities discussed earlier.

If private foundations are 501(c)(3) organizations, why are they treated so differently from public charities? The special treatment is to safeguard against abuse. Since these organizations are not subject to public involvement and because many of them are created by private individuals or their families for personal as well as altruistic reasons, the rules are intended to ensure that these funds are used for public rather than private benefits and to force distribution rather than accumulation of funds, or primarily tax dodging, on the part of the creator of the private foundation.

Contributions to private foundations are less favorably treated than public charities.[14] These foundations are also subject to a 2 percent tax on their investment income, and they are subject to an excise tax on their failure to distribute income. Moreover, a host of penalties can be imposed on both the foundation and its management. The central objective of the regulations and restrictions on these foundations is to prevent their use for the advancement of the private and political aims of their founders and contributors or the business or personal associates of these persons.

Disqualified Persons

The key to understanding this thrust is the term "disqualified person." A disqualified person is a person or entity that is barred from having a business relationship with a private foundation. One such person is a substantial contributor to the private foundation. A substantial contributor is a person or entity that gives a total of $5000 or more if this amounts to 2 percent of all the contributions received by the foundation since its beginning. But the law does not stop here.

The spouse, children, parents, and grandchildren of a substantial contributor are also substantial contributors even if they did not contribute a penny. Based on the legal principle of attribution, the theory is that such close relatives as spouse and children are subject to the control and influence of the contributor. In the eyes of the law, they are all one. Oddly, brothers and sisters are excluded from the taint of attribution.

Attribution also extends to businesses in which the substantial contributor owns 20 percent or more of the voting stocks. And if the business is a substantial contributor, so is the owner. Attribution runs both ways.

Management or anyone who has authority to set policies is also a disqualified person. The attribution rule also applies to the family of the managers of the nonprofit and their businesses and disqualifies them from engaging in certain business transactions with the organization. See "Self-dealing," which follows.

Government officials are also disqualified persons. This includes elected as well as appointed officials and at every level of government and in every branch, whether judicial, legislative, or executive. Again, the attribution rule is applied. Government officials are included among disqualified persons to preclude the use of the private foundation to influence these officials. The conditions under which government officials may receive benefits from private foundations are generally restricted to nonmonetary awards, annuities associated with employee programs during periods that the government official previously worked for the foundation, reimbursement for travel cost if the purpose of the travel was consistent with the tax-exempt purpose of the private foundation, and payment in anticipation of employing the government official if such payment is made within ninety days of termination from government service.

Self-dealing

Direct or indirect business transactions between the private foundation and disqualified persons can lead to penalties imposed by the IRS for self-dealing. What kinds of transactions lead to charges of self-dealing? Hiring, loans, the sale and purchase of assets, the paying of excessive compensation or reimbursement of expenses, the providing of facilities to disqualified persons, and the leasing of space by a disqualified person to the private foundation are all subject to charges of self-dealing.

There are some exceptions worth noting. A lease by a disqualified person to a private foundation is not self-dealing if no rental fees are involved. Self-dealing is not incurred if the transaction is for less than $5000 in one year or if the transaction is generally favorable to the organization. The basic way to avoid issues of self-dealing when a disqualified person must be engaged in a business transaction of any type is to be sure that the transaction is ordinary for such a private foundation, is necessary to discharge its duties, the good or service could not otherwise have been provided more favorably by dealing with a qualified person, and the private foundation was appreciably the net beneficiary of the transaction. We shall return to self-dealing in Chapter 5 as it pertains to trustees.

A penalty for self-dealing may be imposed on the self-dealer as well as the management if it can be shown that the management participated in the action or could reasonably be expected to have known about it, did not try to stop it, engaged in it, or remained silent. The penalty to the self-dealer can rise to 200 percent of the value of the transaction. For the manager, the penalty can rise to 50 percent of that amount.

While these penalties are imposed by the IRS, an individual may bring civil charges. Here is an example of a combination of terms we have used. About half of the space of a building owned by a private foundation is occupied by a for-profit company owned by the foundation manager. The company was a disqualified person with respect to the foundation because of its ownership by the foundation manager. It did not matter that the leasing of the property was done by a property management company with which the manager had no association. The foundation had veto powers over leases, and guess who exercised that veto power on behalf of the foundation? The manager. This was declared self-dealing.[15]

Distribution of Income

Unlike public foundations, private foundations are required to distribute their income annually. Three types of distribution meet the qualification. The private foundation may distribute funds for paying expenses and for making grants to public foundations for conducting those activities for which the private foundation is tax exempt. These may be grants, but they can also be loans that are below the market rate. These loans are called program-related investments.

A second type of distribution that qualifies is set aside to purchase assets to be used in the tax-exempt purpose if those set asides are absolutely necessary (as they are in a building program) and if the funds will be used within sixty months. Set asides or accumulations must be approved by the IRS. A third type of qualifying distribution is the amount spent to purchase assets to be used by the private foundation in its tax-exempt mission or other charitable purpose. These latter amounts, unlike the set asides, do not have to receive prior IRS approval.

The actual dollar amount that a private foundation must distribute is technically determined. Basically, it is substantially all (although 85 percent is acceptable) of the greater of either its minimum investment return or its adjusted net income. Its minimum investment return is the fair market value of its assets not used for tax-exempt purposes, minus the debt associated with those assets multiplied by 5 percent. Its adjusted net income is all income, including those from unrelated businesses, minus the expenses associated with producing that income.

Private foundations must have good accountants and appraisers because the failure to distribute the correct amount can lead to stiff penalties, starting at 15 percent of the amount that should be distributed and rising to 100 percent if the distribution is not made in the time allotted for correction. Fortunately, unlike the self-dealing tax, this tax does not fall on the management but on the private foundation itself. When in doubt, an overpayment is often preferable since any such amounts may be carried over the next five years.

Jeopardy of Investments

Private foundations and their managers are prohibited from making investments that would jeopardize the financial well-being of the organization. Included among the prohibited actions are certain investment strategies, such as buying puts and calls, warrants, buying stocks on margin, selling short, and trading in commodity futures or in futures markets in general.[16] This poses a problem of interpretation since some of these actions, such as buying a put, are viewed in some investment quarters as defensive and conservative in the sense that they may put a limit on losses. Interpretation of the motives for certain transactions is subjective based on the investment intent and strategy, the frequency with which they are used, and so on. States may restrict the type of securities or the companies whose securities may be bought.

Certain investment risks are acceptable and encouraged if they are program related. Offering loans to individuals (or nonprofits) deemed to be among the least preferred risks by a commercial lender is acceptable as long as the making of such loans is within the tax-exempt mission of the nonprofit. Recall the loans to minority and rural businesses referred to in Chapter 3.

If this rule is violated, a 5 percent tax is imposed on the foundation and another 5 percent on the manager who is aware of or participates in the investment decision. In a case such as this, the finance or investment committee of the board of directors, the president, and the investment officers of the organization could all be held responsible.

Excess Business Holdings

In 1985, the Altman Chain was sold.

The Federal Tax Reform Act of 1969 required the foundation to divest "excess" business holdings—about 50 percent of its stock—or face heavy penalties .... The sale of the chain also was pressed by the State Attorney General's office, which wanted to maximize the money made available for local charities.[17]

There is a limit on the business holding of a private foundation. No more than 20 percent of the voting stock or interest of a single business may be owned by a private foundation and all its disqualified persons combined. Some types of businesses are unaffected by this rule. These are program-related businesses and businesses that make their income through dividends, royalties, rents, interest, or so-called passive income, rather than by sale of goods and services. In addition, some foundations such as the Kellogg and the Hershey are exempt from this rule.

A private foundation cannot own a sole proprietorship unless obtained by bequest or prior to 1969. The reader should not confuse a sole proprietorship with sole ownership of a corporation or unrelated business as previously described. The term sole proprietorship simply means that the business is owned by a human and unincorporated. The nonprofit would be totally liable for any failures of the business. If sole proprietorships were allowed, all the assets of the foundation would be exposed to claims by creditors of the business. A large claim against the business that it could not meet by itself would lead to claims against the assets of the foundation.

Should this rule be broken, the penalty is 5 percent of the value of the excess holdings. This penalty is imposed on the foundation, not the management. The penalty could rise to 200 percent if left uncorrected in the time allotted.

(4) EXCESS BUSINESS HOLDINGS:

In accordance with Section 4943 of the Internal Revenue Code, the Foundation was required to dispose (or discontinue the operation) of its excess business holdings as of November 30, 1988. Excess business holdings of the Foundation include principally a public utility company, hotels, golf courses and certain oil and gas interests. The Foundation has complied with the requirement to dispose (or discontinue the operation) of its excess business holdings.

During the fourth quarter of 1988, the Foundation sold Seacoast Utilities, a utility company serving municipalities throughout Palm Beach County, Florida, for $65,000,000 in a purchase money note receivable. During February, 1989, principal and accrued interest on this note were paid in full to the Foundation. On November 28, 1988, the Foundation sold JDM Country Club for $5,225,000 in cash and $71,253,000 in a purchase money note receivable. The Foundation reported the transaction under the installment method as described in Note 1, resulting in the deferral of approximately $36,955,000 of the gain. The terms of these transactions include certain contingent provisions which may result in additional income or expense to the Foundation which is not expected to be material to the financial statements.

Source: John D. and Catherine T. MacArthur Foundation, Report on Activities—1988, p. 104. Reprinted by permission.

Prohibited Expenditures

Some expenditures by private foundations, such as those aimed at influencing legislation, lead to tax penalties. Legislation includes any action by a legislative body at any level of government. School boards, commissions, and authorities such as housing or economic on any level are considered administrative rather than legislative bodies and therefore expenditures to influence them are not prohibited. In addition, expert testimony in response to a written request by a legislative body or nonpartisan studies made public are not construed to be attempts to influence legislation and are not prohibited.

Expenditures to influence the outcome of any election are prohibited. Such expenditures include producing or distributing supporting literature or paying campaign workers or providing facilities for campaigns. Critically, any expenditure such as voter registration is also prohibited if it is centered in a specific geographical area.

This prohibition is not violated if the private foundation makes a contribution:

1. to an organization that is exempt under 501(c)(3)
2. if the activities of that receiving organization are nonpartisan and are conducted over more than one election period and in at least five states
3. the organization spends most (at least 85 percent) of its income on the tax-exempt purposes for which it is organized
4. 85 percent of its support is from the public (government units and the general public)
5. the contributions from the private foundation are not used solely for a specific election or geographic area.

The prohibition against political activities gave way to a strategy used in the presidential elections in the 1980s. Supporters of political candidates would form a nonprofit group under 501(c)(3)—not to support the candidate but to do research and disseminate information on subjects close to the heart of the potential candidate and even to support the potential candidate's travel to speak (not campaign) on these subjects. Some of these foundations even gave money to public charities. Under this guise, the organization did not become involved in politics because its activities were "educational."

There were several advantages to going this route:

1. The contributions to a nonprofit were deductible and did not suffer the same limitations on giving as contributions to a political campaign.
2. The nonprofit organization had several cost advantages, including the lower postal rate.
3. Gifts to foundations are not subject to public disclosure, as are contributions to political campaigns.
4. Many persons who may not otherwise contribute to a candidate may contribute to a foundation.
5. It gave an unannounced candidate a platform and a way of being identified with an issue in a nonpartisan light.
6. It was a source of information and dissemination of information with which the potential candidate could be identified.
7. The foundation could support foundation-related speaking engagements for the candidate that, simultaneously, coincide with the issues with which the candidate seeks identity and in the communities in which the candidate needs exposure.

Another category of prohibited expenditures is grants to individuals. Here the intent is to be certain that grants to individuals are intended to assist them in meeting some measurable objective, such as writing a book or earning a degree, are a bona fide prize or award, are nondiscriminatory (that is, not targeted as a payoff or bribe), or aim at improving skills. Many private foundations shy away from making grants to individuals due to this rule.

Expenditures to carry out missions that are not religious, scientific, charitable, or to foster those activities that permit an organization to qualify under 501(c)(3) as discussed earlier are also prohibited.

Finally, private foundations may not make grants to organizations other than those 509(a)(1)s, (a)(2)s, and (a)(3)s previously discussed unless the foundation takes responsibility for how these funds are used by the donee. The rule means being sure the funds are used only for the purposes for which they are given, keeping proper and thorough records, and reporting expenditures to the IRS. Hence, the policy quoted from Kellogg in the early part of this chapter.

Violation of these rules against prohibited expenditures leads to a 10 percent tax based on the amount involved on both the foundation and its management. An additional tax of 100 percent may be imposed on the foundation and 50 percent on the manager if they fail to correct the situation during the allotted time.

Investment Income

Finally, private foundations may pay a 2 percent tax on net investment income. Net investment income is the total of all income, including rents, royalties, dividends, interest, and business income, plus net capital gains. From this amount are subtracted all ordinary and necessary expenses for producing that income. These include management fees, depreciation, rents, supplies, and the like. Capital losses are deductible only to the extent of capital gains. For example, if the private foundation had $2000 in capital losses and $4000 in capital gains, its net capital gain is $2000 and that becomes part of its net investment income. If, however, it had $2000 in losses and no gains, it would not deduct anything as a capital loss in deriving its net investment income.

PRIVATE OPERATING FOUNDATIONS: FINANCIAL AND LEGAL LIMITS

Note to the reader.   Do not try to remember the details that follow. Try to appreciate the role of the operating foundation and of revenues and expenditure patterns in defining this type of nonprofit as an economic institution. Look at Table 4.2. It shows that the private operating foundation conducts as well as funds charitable missions.

TABLE 4.2 Comparison of Foundations

	Types of 501(c)(3)s		
	Public Charities	Private Foundation (nonoperating)	Private Operating Foundation
Charitable Mission	Conduct	Finance	Conduct and finance

The Operating Foundation

The private operating foundation is a special type of private foundation. It is subject to all the rules governing all other private nonoperating foundations except that contributions to it are treated as favorably as those to public foundations (charities). Operating foundations may receive gifts from private foundations under circumstances previously described, and an operating foundation may own up to 85 percent of the voting interests, not just a combined 20 percent, of a single business that need not be of the special type mentioned earlier. Operating foundations are not subject to the excise tax on undistributed income.

The major distinction between private operating foundations and other private nonoperating foundations is that the first conducts and implements programs. They operate in ways other than the making of grants. The rules that govern these organizations are intended to ensure this distinction. Foundations like the Howard Hughes Foundation, the J. Paul Getty Trust described in the insert and the Twentieth Century Fund are operating foundations carrying on major program activities.

The trust's net income is subject to a 2 percent federal excise tax.

The Getty must spend millions. It doesn't have a choice. It is obliged, by law, to disperse a minimum of 4.25 percent of its appreciated assets three years out of four. And unlike the $3.4 billion Ford Foundation—the only one that's bigger—it does not dispense grants. It is an "operating foundation," and under U.S. law, at least 85 percent of the money it spends must be on programs that it runs.

Source: Paul Richard, "Museum of the Big Bucks," *Washington Post*, Friday, April 13, 1984, p. B1. Reprinted by permission.

The Income Test

For a private foundation to qualify as an operating foundation, it must pass an income test. This test requires that the foundation spend at least 85 percent of its adjusted net income or minimum investment income, whichever is lower, on activities for which it received tax exemption and in which it is a direct participant.[18] Making a grant to a nonprofit that has a similar mission is not enough, but assigning its staff to work with that nonprofit or using its facilities is. Thus, many on the staff of the Howard Hughes Foundation do their research on university campuses. In short, the private operating foundation must do more than contribute money. It must directly participate through staff or facilities or a combination of the two.

Asset, Endowment, and Support Tests

In addition to the income test, a private operating foundation must meet one of three other tests: asset, endowment, or support. The **asset test** is designed to detect how much of the facilities or other assets of the organization are being used directly in activities for which it received exemption. At least 65 percent of the assets of the private foundation must be used directly in the meeting of its tax-exempt mission. If the organization chooses, it may satisfy this condition by running a program-related business using 65 percent of its assets to do so. Or it may control a for-profit corporation by owning 80 percent of all its voting stocks and 80 percent of all other types of stocks issued by the corporation—if all (or 85 percent) of the assets of the corporation are devoted to the same types of activities for which the organization received its exemption.

As an alternative to the asset test, the private operating foundation may elect to demonstrate that its grants are aimed at advancing its charitable cause. This is the essence of the **endowment test.** The basic requirement is that two-thirds of the minimum investment return be expended on qualifying distributions as defined earlier: expenses for conducting the tax-exempt mission, authorized set asides, and expenses for acquiring assets to conduct the mission.

Instead of the asset or endowment test, a private foundation seeking to be an operating foundation may elect to pass the **support test.** Notice that this test is elective, unlike public charities. This can be done by showing that 85 percent of the support of the foundation comes from the broad public and governmental units, or from more than five tax-exempt foundations, or that no more than 25 percent of its support is normally (as defined earlier) received from any one tax-exempt organization, or that not more than 50 percent of its support is normally received from gross investment income.

One problem with public charities that deal with private operating foundations is that the latter constantly interferes. This, as we see, is because of legal requirements to be directly involved. Private nonoperating and public foundations (to the extent that the latter make grants) are not similarly constrained.

POLITICS AND LOBBYING GUIDELINES

Nonprofits, specifically the 501(c)(3) cannot engage in politics, defined as influencing the outcome of an election. They are allowed only limited latitude to lobby. Lobbying may be "substantial" which is defined on the basis of the facts and circumstances, or it may be numeric which is defined in terms of the portion of total organizational expenditures used to (1) affect public opinion and (2) influence legislation. The penalty, as discussed in the previous three chapters, is loss of exemption. Here are some guidelines that may help protect your organization:

1. Assess the risk. The risks are losing the tax exempt status of the organization, penalties on both the organization and the trustees, the possible loss of membership and public support among those who take another view, and a Pyrrhic victory as those who were supported fail to or can't return the favor. The air controllers rushing to support Ronald Reagan and being fired by him as his first notable domestic labor relations act illustrates the point.
2. Stay close to those acts which are acceptable exceptions. These are: (a) nonpartisan information gathering and dissemination, (b) advice or testimony made on written request from the government or legislature, (c) appearing before a legislative body to defend an organization or its mission, (d) communicating with a government or legislative aide in a manner that would not ordinarily be construed as lobbying.
3. If affecting legislation or involvement in political acts are your long-term aim, seek a ruling from the IRS as to how it will affect your status.
4. Remember that the **local** and **state** attorneys general may have equal if not more interest in restricting your political activities than does the IRS because the local parties are likely to be your victims—not the IRS.
5. Weigh the advantages and disadvantages of being judged under the "substantial" or numeric rules. In general, if your lobbying expenses approach 20 to 25 percent of your annual expenditures or $100,000 you are ready to use the IRS dollar or percentage limit.

6. Hiring a third party may not fully free you. Such hiring may have to be reported by you. These lobbyists will also report earnings derived from acting on your behalf. Expenditures are traceable.

7. Consider a corporate reorganization in which political and lobbying activities are segregated and placed in a separate organization. One option is that used by the League of Women Voters—a nonpartisan political, advocacy and lobbying organization. Its affiliate organization is a separate 501(c)(3) corporation, the League of Women Voters Education Fund, which according to its 1989-1990 annual report, "provides a variety of services, research, education, litigation, publications and conferences on current policy issues and on techniques to help citizens take part more effectively in the democratic process." The activities of the League of Women Voters Education Fund is financed through tax deductible contributions. The political arm is not. This does not mean that contributions to the political arm or membership fees are not permitted—just that they are not deductible. Similarly, Common Cause is a nonprofit, nonpartisan political and lobbying group. Contributions to it are not deductible. The Tax Code permits 501(c)(4)s to form tax exempt 501(c)(3)s. But these (c)(3)s must qualify as any other (c)(3)s in order to get tax deductible contributions.

8. Indirect methods such as buying gifts or paying expenses of government employees will get both the employee and the organization in trouble.

9. Private foundations should review pages 115-116.

Let us illustrate an approach. Many nonprofits, including associations, have newsletters and membership lists. They are permitted to analyze issues that relate to them and to their mission, testify before legislative bodies and to communicate with their membership and with the government. Hence one strategy: Do a survey, gather opinions, publish it in the newsletter, send it to members. Another strategy: Testify before a legislative body and publish the testimony. The law attempts to preserve First Amendment rights of freedom of speech while prohibiting the use of tax-deductible privileges to apply political pressure, or to ruin or aid political ambitions.

SUMMARY AND CONCLUSIONS

Section 501(c)(3) permits more than one choice of tax-exempt status. The differences among these choices are to be found in financing rules, the principal objectives of which are as follows:

1. To protect the income and assets of the foundations from the personal use of the founders, donors, and management and their associates

2. To restrict the use of the income and assets to the missions previously selected by each nonprofit and to which it is legally committed in its charter

3. To assure some degree of responsiveness to the general public as participants but surely as beneficiaries of the income and assets of the nonprofit.

Herein lies the significant difference between a nonprofit and a for-profit corporation. Section 501(c)(3) provides alternative ways of satisfying these concerns.

Because the demonstration of such support is critical, particularly to public charities, good management will always be alert not only to sources of financial assistance but to the relative weight of each kind of support in the entire financing effort.

NOTES

1. Fiscal Year 1989, Annual Report, *Special Olympics International, Inc.,* pp. 30–31.

2. W. K. Kellogg Foundation, *1991 Kellogg National Fellowship Program,* p. 1.

3. *The Internal Revenue Code, 1954,* as amended in 1969, created these categories. See the two IRS publications listed in the following Suggested Readings.

4. The charter is to be distinguished from the bylaws. The charter is a legal document analogous to a birth certificate. While the bylaws outline how the organization is to function, the charter states the purpose. The purpose of the organization, regardless of its bylaws, must coincide with the missions included under Section 501(c)(3).

5. Public charity (as defined later) may choose to get a specific dollar and percentage limitation rather than "substantial," and to have lobbying expenditures distinguished from grass-roots expenditures. Lobbying expenditures are aimed to influence legislation, while grass-roots expenditures are aimed at influencing the general public. When the percentage limitation is used, a violation consists of spending 150 percent of the permitted amount. The permitted amount is based on a percentage of the tax-exempt expenditures. Grass-roots expenditures are limited to 25 percent of the expenditures permitted on lobbying. Violation means that the organization loses its status as a 501(c)(3).

6. See discussion of the word charitable in Chapter 2.

7. The differences in the treatment of gifts and contributions will be discussed in Chapter 10.

8. This is discussed later in this chapter.

9. See Chapter 7 for a discussion.

10. Strategies for handling large gifts are discussed in Chapters 10 and 11.

11. We are assuming that the community trust is a publicly supported organization.

Trusts must also pass public support tests. More is said about community trusts in this chapter.

12. The terms related and unrelated are defined in Chapter 7.

13. Margaret Riley, "Private Foundation Information Returns, 1982," in *Statistics of Income Bulletin*, 5, no. 2 (Fall 1985) (Washington, D.C.: U.S. Government Printing Office, 1985), 1–28.

14. See discussion in Chapter 10.

15. Revenue Letter 9047001.

16. On some of these, especially shorts and options, the IRS has given contradictory verdicts. Thus, they are increasingly being used.

17. Kathleen Teltsch, "Stores' Sale Is Bonanza for Altman Foundation," *New York Times*, Sunday, Oct. 20, 1985, p. 52.

18. Note that the income test for private operating foundations requires the lesser of the adjusted net income or minimum investment income. The distribution requirement for private foundations is that the greater of the two be distributed.

SUGGESTED READINGS

Internal Revenue Service, U.S. Department of the Treasury, *Tax Exempt Status for Your Organization,* Publication 557, Revised, October 1988.

——— *Exempt Organization Appeal Procedure*, Publication 892, April 30, 1987. p.1.

Chapter 5

Trustees: Guardians of the Mission

This chapter brings us to the end of Part I, the **mission**. If the mission is so central to the nonprofit, who is its protector? The answer is the trustees.

> The Foundation is governed by an international Board of Trustees....The trustees determine broad policies, set program and management budgets, and review program and grant objectives and accomplishments. *Current Interests of the Ford Foundation,* 1990 and 1991 (New York, Ford Foundation, 1990), p. 38. Reprinted by permission.

This chapter discusses the duties of trustees to a nonprofit organization and the duties of the organization to its trustees. The chapter also describes prohibited transactions, liabilities of trustees, and strategies for dealing with these liabilities. It ends with steps for selecting and appealing to trustee candidates.

THE IMPORTANCE OF TRUSTEES

Trustees or directors of for-profit corporations are charged with setting policies, selecting the chief officers, and monitoring the performance of the corporation so that the wealth of the stockholders who are the owners of the corporation is maximized. In short, in the for-profit world, the trustees represent the economic interests of the stockholders. Because corporate directors are also stockholders, they also represent themselves.

The trustees or directors of a nonprofit organization represent the interest of the public, not the private interests of stockholders. Their principal function is to set policies consistent with the public mission of the organization, to select managers who can carry out the mission, and to monitor the performance of the organization so that public welfare is maximized in a manner consistent with the specific mission of the organization. Their duty, therefore, is to maximize public, not private, welfare.

In between these two extremes is the role of trustees in associations. In these nonprofits, the trustees have a clear responsibility to set policies, select managers, and monitor performance so as to help members. But even here the welfare of the public is important. Professional certification, for example, does give value to practitioners, but it also protects the public against quacks. Similarly, in-service training helps members to learn the most advanced techniques, but it also helps them to serve the public better. Thus, even in a membership association that is nonprofit, trustees have a substantial amount of responsibility to the public.

PUBLIC INTEREST IN THE BOARDS OF NONPROFITS

Because the nonprofit is a creature of the state, states have laws telling how the trustees of a nonprofit organization should operate. In the accompanying insert, note how specific the state of Connecticut is in defining who, how many, and other aspects of the board of mental health nonprofit organizations. It should now be easy to understand why in the paragraphs that follow we shall continuously remind the readers to check their bylaws and statutes of the state. The board of trustees of a nonprofit organization is a legal agency created, as is the organization itself, by state law. Some states are more specific and extensive in their requirements than others, and the requirements may vary according to the mission of the organization.

STATUTE OF THE STATE OF CONNECTICUT

Sec. 33-179g. Management of health care center. Directors. (a) If the health care center is organized as a nonprofit, nonstock corporation, the care, control and disposition of the property and funds of each such corporation and the general management of its affairs shall be vested in a board of directors. Each such corporation shall have the power to adopt bylaws for the governing of its affairs, which bylaws shall prescribe the number of directors, their term of office and the manner of their election, subject to the provisions of this chapter. The bylaws may be adopted and repealed or amended by the affirmative vote of two-thirds of all the directors at any meeting of the board of directors duly held upon at least ten days' notice, provided notice of such meeting shall specify the proposed action concerning the bylaws to be taken at such meeting. The bylaws of the corporation shall provide that the board of directors shall include representation from persons engaged in the healing arts and from persons who are eligible to receive health care from the corporation, subject to the following provisions: (1) One-quarter of the board of directors shall be persons engaged in the different fields in the healing arts at least two of whom shall be a physician and a dentist; (2) one-quarter of the board of directors shall be elected directly at the annual meeting of members of the community, including subscribers who are eligible to receive health care from the health care center, but no such representatives need be elected until the first annual meeting following the approval by the insurance commissioner of the initial agreement or agreements to be offered by the corporation, and there shall be only one representative from any group covered by a group service agreement.

(b) If the health care center is not organized as a nonprofit, nonstock corporation, management of its affairs shall be in accordance with other applicable laws of the state, provided that the health care center shall establish and maintain a mechanism to afford its members an opportunity to participate in matters of policy and operation such as an advisory panel, advisory referenda on major policy decisions or other similar mechanisms.

Public interest is also reflected in the reporting requirements of nonprofits. The federal government, some states and some localities require nonprofits to report annually the names of their trustees and principal officers and whether serving on the board of another organization is a requirement for serving on the board of the reporting organization. We shall discuss interlocking directorates later in this chapter. The compensations, fees, benefits such as retirement and the use of an automobile, severance pay, and loans made by the organization to trustees must also be reported.

For each loan made to a trustee or manager, the name of the borrower, the original amount loaned, the balance, the date of the loan and of its maturity, the terms of repayment, interest rate, the security or collateral provided by the borrower, the purpose of the loan, and what was loaned (cash or property) along with its fair market value must be reported.

Any loan to a trustee, officer, or their personal or business associates should fall within the bylaw provisions for such loans if such loans are permitted by the state in the first place. See the discussion on prohibitions later. If permitted, the loan should occur on a businesslike basis. This means proper collateral, interest, and timely repayments. Loans should also not be repetitive and discriminatory in favor of trustees and officers as compared to other employees.

For the federal government, all the above information must be submitted on Form 990, which, when completed, is available to the public on request. Organizations that fail to provide this information are subject to penalty.

TRUSTEES AS GUARDIANS: AN EXAMPLE

Each side in this dispute was bound by its trustee duties to act.

A long-simmering dispute between the Diocese of Michigan and the Mariner's church on the waterfront in downtown Detroit has erupted into a court battle that challenges ownership of the property and the future direction of the historic parish. In the latest development, Bishop Stewart Wood has filed suit in county circuit court against the parish's board of trustees and the Rev. Richard Ingalls, who has renounced his license as an Episcopal priest, but continues to officiate at the church. The bishop's action seeks to obtain clear title of the 141-year-old riverfront church for the diocese.

"I regret having to take this matter into the civil courts and thereby, of course, into the realm of public scrutiny," Wood said in a letter to his clergy. "Nevertheless, I see it clearly as my duty to proceed."

An opposing suit by the parish trustees seeking ownership of the property has been filed in the Michigan Court of Appeals. The parish contends that the 1848 act which incorporated the church requires that the higher court decide the matter.

Ingalls, rector of the Mariner's Church since 1965, told Wood he wanted to renounce his license, reportedly because of dissatisfaction with the diocese, disapproval of prayer book revision and opposition to women priests. Wood granted the priest's request in June. Wood announced he would appoint a new priest for the parish, but Ingalls has refused to leave the church.

Episcopal Life October 1990, p. 12.

Reprinted by permission.

The true issue between Mariners' and the Diocese of Michigan is the legal right of the trustees of Mariners' Church to retain ownership and control of its property.

When the Episcopal Church General Convention in 1979 amended a canon that intended to take "all real and personal property held by and for the benefit of any Parish, Mission or Congregation" in the event of its disaffiliation from the Episcopal Church, Mariners' trustees approved and sent to officials of the Episcopal Church and Michigan state a legal disclaimer, dated Dec. 11, 1980, rejecting the Episcopal Church's claim of right to Mariners' property on the grounds of Mariners' corporate independence. But the state replied that the disclaimer was "legally redundant" (unnecessary), thus reassuring the trustees of their property rights.

Mariners' is "governed" by its trustees, who at one time sought a limited sacramental union with the diocese. Once the diocese expressed its desire to lay claim to Mariners' property and install a new pastor, the trustees had a legal obligation to defend their rights.

BRITTON L. GORDON JR.

Reprinted by permission of the author from original letter and the adaptation in the *Wall Street Journal*, Thursday, Nov. 29, 1990, p. A13.

In June 1991, Judge Charles Kaufman of The Circuit Court for the County of Wayne, Michigan, ruled in favor of Mariners, saying that the trustees have the duty to obey the will that created the church and to own and operate the property in conformity with the church's mission and that, in this case, the act of affiliating did not transfer any of these rights, duties or powers to the affiliation.

SIZE AND COMPOSITION OF THE BOARD

The charter and bylaws of the organization must state the number of trustees required. The law usually states a minimum and will permit the membership to increase the size in accordance with the bylaws of the organization. Several factors may influence the size of the board other than the state required minimum.

One of these is costs. The larger the board, the more expensive it is to recruit and to operate because of mailing, lodging, transportation, telephone, insurance, printing costs, and honoraria if paid.

Diversity by race, sex, geography, political party, and professional specialty can all be important considerations. Diversity enhances the public image and purpose of the organization and gives it a better chance to accurately reflect its constituency and therefore to meet its public mission. Many national nonprofits try to maintain a balance between Democrats and Republicans on their boards so as to give the appearance of nonpartisanship.

The board should be sufficiently large to involve persons with different skills. For example, the board may choose to have someone who knows about press relations or financial matters. It should always have people who understand the mission and are imaginative about how it may be carried out. Adding a well-known person to a board adds legitimacy.

The size and composition of the board should be determined by considerations of operational efficiency. Large boards can become unwieldy, and a quorum is mathematically more difficult to attain the larger the board is. A paralyzed board is a frustrating, costly, and debilitating experience for trustees, managers, and staff. One way to deal with this is to divide the board into committees. When this is done, there must be an executive committee that can act on behalf of the entire board on certain crucial matters. Another strategy is to permit voting by proxy or phone. Yet another arrangement is to permit some decisions to be made by the majority of those present and voting. In sum, the larger the board, the more it is necessary to create ways in which a smaller group can act on behalf of the entire board.

Finally, the size of the board should reflect convention and certifying requirements, whether these requirements are set by an association for all its members or by a certifying board. The National Charities Information Bureau, which is a watchdog of nonprofits, uses a minimum of five voting members as its standard for assessing the governance structure of a nonprofit.

Organization of the Board

The bylaws of the organization will state the way the board is to be organized. Clearly, the way the board is organized will depend on its size; but it should also depend on the complexity of the mission of the organization. There should almost always be at least one committee that is responsible for overseeing the fiscal integrity of the organization. Money is critical and fungible. The committee or its subcommittees may have responsibility for auditing, fund raising, budgeting, and investments. Other committees may oversee personnel and administrative policies; another may oversee membership and professional practices.

Some committees may be standing as opposed to ad hoc. The latter committees are created for a specific purpose and disband once that purpose is fulfilled. Standing committees are part of the permanent structure of the organization. They are created in the bylaws.

Term of Service

The term of service for each trustee is stated in the bylaws of the organization, which also states how and under what conditions the term of any member may be ended before its due date. In choosing the length of term, consideration ought to be given to the learning curve. How long does it take the average person to learn enough about the organization and its mission and environment in order to participate effectively?

Conversely, how long will it take the average person to become bored and useless? One way to handle this problem is to have staggering terms and also to permit persons to have more than one consecutive term. Hence, each member of a five-person board may have a three-year term, but the term of each may not end in the same year. By also permitting members to succeed themselves, the organization gets continuity, which is important.

The issue is always a trade-off between continuity and fresh blood. This is particularly true in membership organizations that are undergoing rapid change either in size or direction. Thus, limiting the number of persons who may succeed themselves or the number of times a trustee may succeed himself or herself is always advisable. It makes it convenient for tired blood to be replaced and it also stimulates interest in board membership. Some organizations make the turnover palatable by asking replaced board members to serve on an advisory committee or by giving them emeritus status. Yet another strategy is to allow persons to re-qualify for board membership after "sitting out" for a couple of years.

QUALIFICATION AND REMOVAL OF TRUSTEES

The bylaws of the organization should state who is qualified to serve on the board. Qualification may cover years of membership, residence, sex, and the like. Qualification may also be determined by state law, as we saw with the state of Connecticut above. Within the broad parameters of law, organizations may exercise certain discretions.

Disqualified or Interested Persons

A disqualified or interested person may not necessarily be barred from serving on the board. Rather, the law intends to limit the voting power of these individuals so that they do not dominate the activities of the board. Thus, in the state of California, only 49 percent of the board may be made up of interested persons, defined as persons paid by the board in the past twelve months. More broadly, in many states an interested person is one who has a material financial relationship to the organization and includes the close relatives or business associates of such a person. They, too, will be classified as interested persons.

A trustee can also become an interested or disqualified person based on one transaction. Thus, a trustee who has the potential of a material financial gain resulting from a specific transaction becomes an interested person for purposes of that transaction and should be disqualified from influencing the organization on that specific or closely related transaction. The person's business and close relatives should also be disqualified.

Because all trustees who permit such a person to vote, knowing the nature of the relationship can be held liable, disclosure of trustee interest is advisable.

Removal of Trustees

Generally, the board of trustees or the membership can vote to reduce the size of the board as long as in so doing they do not cause the removal of a trustee whose term is not expired. In addition, members, trustees, the court, and the attorney general of some states may act to have a board member removed.

There are several reasons for removing a board member. Section 224 of the code of Louisiana gives an example of commonly held reasons:

1. death
2. resignation
3. incompetence
4. bankruptcy
5. incapacitation for at least six months
6. failure to attend meetings
7. failure to accept the board appointment in writing in sixty days.

Being an interested party where such interest does not violate state law is not in itself justification for removal unless disclosure is fraudulent. Being an interested person is more a restriction on participation. Obviously, at some point interest prohibits total participation. Thus, a major supplier of an organization, its landlord, or the spouse of its chief executive officer may be so intertwined as to prohibit their participation on the board. In sum, a board member does not have to be removed once he or she becomes an interested person.

INTERLOCKING DIRECTORATES

An interlocking directorate is one in which one or more persons serve on two or more boards, thus linking them. With a limited pool from which organizations choose, it is not uncommon to find two or more persons serving on the same board. The issue of interlocking directorates is less concerned with these incidental occurrences than it is in the questions of control, loyalty, and taxation. The basic question is: Does the degree of interlocking imply that one organization is really controlled by the other?

Two organizations, though different in name and mission, may for purposes of policy, control, and taxation, be considered related or essentially one entity if they have the same board members or if the majority of their trustees are the same people. In addition to causing possibilities of conflict of loyalty, there can be tax consequences. Thus, the choice of an interlocking directorate should be strategic and purposeful.

In Chapter 4 we saw that in a supporting organization, 509(a)(3)s, an interlocking directorate may be very wise and legally encouraged. The subservience of one organization to the mission of the other is intended and may be effectively accomplished by interlocking the directorates.

In the case of two related nonprofits each carrying out a different mission, an interlocking board of trustees would imply that one is controlled by the other. Thus, the receipt of income from the controlled organization by the organization that is in control would expose that income to taxation. We shall make much of this point in Chapters 11 through 13.

PROHIBITIONS ON TRUSTEES

Three basic principles describe the duties of trustees. Remembering these is important and they are described in the next section. But, first, let us look at some prohibited acts.

Personal Loans Prohibited

Many states bar trustees from using their organization's assets for guaranteeing or making loans to themselves other than as advances for expenses. Section 719 of the laws of the state of New York is an example. Not only do these statutes prohibit trustees from receiving loans, but they go one step further by making a trustee who attends a meeting in which such a loan was approved personally liable for repayment even though he or she may have abstained in the vote.

To be free of such liability, the trustee must take one of the following steps: (1) record dissent in the minutes of the meeting, (2) submit a dissent to the secretary in writing before the adjournment of the meeting, or (3) if the trustee is absent, send a registered letter informing the secretary of the organization of the dissent to the loan shortly after the meeting. The trustee who obtained the loan can hold all abstaining trustees and those who voted in favor of the loan liable for repaying it.

Self-dealing Prohibited

California's Section 5233 clearly defines self-dealing as any transaction involving the organization and in which one or more trustees or officers have a material financial benefit unless (1) the attorney general gave approval, (2) the organization entered into the transaction for its own benefit, (3) the transaction was fair and reasonable for the organization, (4) it was favorably voted for by the majority of the board not including the affected members, and (5) the board had information that more reasonable terms were not available; (6) if the action was taken in an emergency, the board must approve it in its next meeting. The penalty for the infraction of self-dealing may include the return of the property with interest, payment of the amount by which the property appreciated, and a fee for the use of the property. It may also include a disciplinary penalty for the fraudulent use of the assets of the organization. We shall be saying more about self-dealing later.

But the following examples should remind us what it is all about: The president of a college forms a partnership to lease land for 99 years. The partnership constructs a building to the specification of the college and leases it to the college at fair market price. In the future, the college will purchase the building and the land at the fair market price. The IRS ruled that this was not self-dealing and the college did not lose its exemption.[1] Again, self-dealing does not bar an honest, arm's length transaction that benefits the nonprofit and does not unduly favor the trustee or officer over others. These types of transactions should always be approached with very careful legal and ethical scrutiny.

Here is an example of self-dealing. A trustee of Kermit Fischer Foundation receives irregular compensation ranging from $200 to $8300, sometimes days apart. The foundation purchased a truck used exclusively by him. It made investments with his brother. It never reported him to be an employee in its IRS report. The court ruled that irregularity was suspicious and, using a formula for trustee compensation of $4 to $5 per $1000 of assets plus 50 percent of foundation earnings, that his payments were excessive and self-dealing. The 501(c)(3) status was revoked and an excise tax imposed on both the organization and the trustee.

Falsification of Data Prohibited

Both the federal government and states require that records be kept by the trustees, that they be made available to the public, and that they be accurate. Section 6215 of the California code, for example, holds all the trustees of an organization responsible for the accurate reporting of the following records: (1) membership roles, (2) financial statements, including major changes in the assets or liabilities of the organization or in the distribution of assets, (3) minutes of the board, and (4) any indemnification (actual or promised payments for legal expenses due to suits).

These reporting rules go beyond satisfying government needs and monitoring of the organization. The trustees are liable to any third party who uses falsified information for the purpose of making decisions, for example, a creditor. Thus, many states, such as New York, require the organization not only to provide this information accurately to creditors, but they must also provide creditors with the names and addresses of the trustees when these are requested.

STANDARDS OF ACTION OF TRUSTEES

State laws require trustees to perform certain specific duties. These include approving a plan of dissolution (mentioned in Chapter 2), approving the compensation of officers, voting, and overseeing any merger or consolidation and any distribution of the assets of the organization. The YWCA reminds its trustees that they serve as (1) representatives of a membership, (2) trustees of a corporation, (3) stewards of an idea, and (4) leaders of a movement.

From a legal perspective, each trustee has three standards of action: loyalty, care, and obedience. A trustee who behaves in conformity with these standards escapes personal liability for his or her action on behalf of the organization even if the result is an error so serious as to cause the organization to lose its status. The standards guide actions. They do not judge their brilliance or consequences.

These standards recognize the possibility of error, so they judge only unintentional negligence—not whether the decision was fruitful or intelligent. The application of these principles in a court of law prohibits second guessing as long as the trustees made their decisions in good faith. This is called the business judgment rule.

Together, the terms loyalty, care, and obedience define the fiduciary responsibility of the trustees as well as the officers of the nonprofit, both of whom can be held personally liable for monetary damages for breaching these duties. Let us see what each of these principles mean.

Duty of Loyalty

The duty of loyalty means that, while acting in the capacity of a trustee or manager of a nonprofit, the person ought to be motivated not by personal, business or private interest, but by what is good for the organization. The use of the assets or goodwill of the organization to promote a private interest at the expense of the nonprofit is an example of disloyalty; in such cases, an individual places the nonprofit in a subordinate position relative to his or her own interest. The nonprofit is being used. One purpose of the annual reporting referred to above is to check on self-dealing.

Self-dealing is a form of disloyalty. Again, self-dealing means using the organization to advance personal benefits when it is clear that the personal gains outweigh the benefits to the organization. Thus, a trustee is not prohibited from engaging in an economic or commercial activity with the organization; but such a transaction can be construed as self-dealing if it can be shown that the trustee gained at the expense of the nonprofit, that the trustee offered the nonprofit a deal inferior to what is offered to others or what the nonprofit could acquire on the open market, or that the nonprofit was put in a position of assuming risks on behalf of the trustee. A numerical amount, $5000, or more, makes the self-dealing an illegal—not just an ethical—infraction.

Another form of self-dealing can occur when two or more nonprofits merge assets or transfer assets one to the other and they have the same trustees. Here the issue is whether a good purpose is being served. Thus, before consummating a merger, it is wise to check to see if charges of self-dealing can be alleged. The State Board of Regency for the university system in California asked its members to make public their land holdings in California so as to avoid self-dealing, that is, voting to expand the university system in areas where, as a result of their decisions, the value of their landholdings would rise.

As we stated earlier, self-dealing is punishable by law. Moreover, whether or not a trustee is self-dealing does not rest on his or her personal involvement. Self-dealing embraces the trustee, his or her family, and his or her business associates. Thus, the president of a bank is subject to charges of self-dealing if his or her bank, spouse, or child is engaged in the types of disadvantageous transactions described. One common way in which the board of trustees must defend the nonprofit organization against self-dealing is not in cases of corporate officers abusing their trustee status for the benefit of their firms; rather, it is against the founders of these organizations. It is not unusual to find that, after years of personal sacrifice in calling the public's attention to a good cause, founders of organizations confuse the assets of the nonprofit with their own, confuse the interest of the organization with their own and begin to take dominion over these assets, or install themselves or relatives into highly favorable tenured positions. Operating under the burden of loyalty, boards must separate these persons from the organization.

Duty of Care

The duty of care requires trustees of nonprofits to act in a manner of someone who truly cares. This means that meetings must be attended, the trustees should be informed and take appropriate action, and the decisions must be prudent.

The test of prudence depends on state law. In many states, the trustees of nonprofits are held under the same rules that govern trustees of for-profit corporations. In these states, prudence can be construed to mean making decisions not unlike those expected of any other group of trustees faced with relatively the same "business" facts and circumstances. In other states, nonprofit trustees are held to a higher standard. Thus, prudence means using the same wisdom and judgment that one would if his or her personal assets were at stake. The first is called the corporate model, and the second is called the trust model.

The duty of care can deny defenses of ignorance. Thus, it is inconsistent with this responsibility to allege that a trustee or manager does not hold any responsibility merely because he or she does not know. To know is the duty. It is this duty that makes many compassionate but busy people reluctant to serve on nonprofit boards. In a real sense, they can't care enough—not in the legal sense.

An example of the breach of this duty of care is a suit brought against a nonprofit organization by the state of Minnesota, allegedly because the nonprofit failed to exercise due care of neighborhood facilities for which it was trustee. It implies that the community has invested some confidence in the trustees. Thus, the betrayal of this confidence is both illegal and unacceptable.

Duty of Obedience

The duty of obedience holds the trustee responsible for keeping the organization on course. The organization must be made to stick to its mission. We are reminded throughout this book that the mission of a nonprofit is unlike the mission of a firm. The mission is the basis upon which the nonprofit and tax-exempt status are conferred. Thus, unlike a firm, a nonprofit cannot simply change its mission without the threat of losing either its nonprofit or tax-exempt status or both.

SPECIFIC DUTIES OF TRUSTEES

These principles form the basis for the YWCA's pamphlet to its trustees as shown in the accompanying insert.

TRUSTEE OF A CORPORATION

By the act of incorporating, a YWCA establishes itself as a legal entity subject to laws applicable to not-for-profit corporations. Boards of Directors are responsible for seeing that corporate duties defined by law and by its own corporate charter ("Articles of Incorporation" or "Articles of Association") are discharged, a responsibility shared with boards of trustees in states where the latter are required.

The standard for meeting this responsibility is that the Board member or trustee must discharge her/his duties in good faith and with the degree of diligence that an ordinarily prudent person would exercise in like circumstances. Failure to maintain this diligence may result in personal liability.

To meet her legal responsibilities a Board member should:

- Review and understand the Association's corporate charter
- Attend Board meetings regularly

  The power of a Board of Directors or Trustees rests in the group, acting together. No one Board member has the authority to control or make decisions for the Association, and members may not vote by proxy.

  If it is necessary for her to miss a meeting, she should take reasonable steps to learn of decisions made in her absence and, if necessary, register any opposing view at the first suitable opportunity.

  Bring informed and objective judgment to the decisions the Board must make—

  seeing that the power of the Board is employed for the greatest benefit to the program and to all of the members of the Association:

  putting the Association's needs ahead of her own aspirations.

It is particularly important that the individual Board member avoid a conflict of interests. Preferably, she should have no personal interest in the business transactions of the Association. If this becomes necessary, statutory and charter limitations should be reviewed before action is taken, her interest should be made known to the Board, and she should not participate in the vote.

- Safeguard the Association's property and other assets—

  seeing that decisions concerning property reflect the Association's long-range program plans

  studying and making thoughtful judgments concerning the adequacy and type of the Association's funding

  protecting its tax-exempt status

  seeing that its tax obligations (employee income, FICA, etc.) are met.
- Monitor employer responsibilities, including implementation of an affirmative action plan
- See that written records of Board meetings are kept

- Seek expert advice before taking any action which the directors lack reasonable competence to handle.

Source: *A YWCA Board Member Is* © National Board, YWCA, New York, p. 4. Reprinted by permission.

Each organization determines within the broad guidelines above the specific duties of its board, which are expected to be conducted based on the principles and standards of loyalty, care, and obedience. The law requires the board to approve the mission of the organization and adopt a dissolution plan, and it charges it with protecting and accounting for the collection and use of the assets, choosing the executive officer, and voting on significant changes in the organization such as mergers or changes in the mission.

The board should have responsibility for policy setting, fiscal guidance, and overall governance and should regularly review the organization's policies, programs, and operations. Trustees have accountability for all authorized activities generating financial support on the organization's behalf.

The YWCA states that the specific responsibilities of its board include planning, membership development, executive recruitment and personnel policies, volunteer leadership, developing and overseeing budgets and finance, overseeing the acquisition and maintenance and safety of buildings and equipment, and public relations.

Here are ten specific duties that trustees have in safeguarding the financial function of a nonprofit organization with the chapters in this book that cover the duty. The trustees must approve:

1. Compensation and benefits liability (5, 14, 16)
2. Budgets, programs, policies (6–8, 15, 18)
3. Auditors and lawyers and receive their reports (17)
4. Capital campaigns and certain gifts (6, 9, 10)
5. Dissolution and reorganization plans (2, 13)
6. Loans, accumulations, and restricted accounts (5, 17, 18)
7. Investment advisors and endowments (12, 17, 18)
8. Sales, joint ventures, and businesses (4, 7, 8, 11, 12)
9. Conformity with mission and law (1–4, 6)
10. Establishment of bank accounts (18)

ILLUSTRATION: TRIALS AND TRIBULATIONS OF TRUSTEES

In recent years, the duties of a trustee have not been easy. The public relations and the liability questions have been tough. Nowhere in 1990 was this problem greater than in the arts and in religion where the issue was the same—sex.

So much of what trustees in the arts continue to confront during the 1990s, are conflicts of duties relating to freedom of speech, sex and obscenity. Indeed, the question that Kristol poses in the following box is legitimate. Is it art? What should trustees do?

We are reminded that the courts exonerated the trustees of the Cincinnati museum which displayed Mapplethorpe and that many in Congress reacted sharply and negatively to the Washington museum which showed his work. Indeed, the use of federal funds to finance this kind of work became a cause célèbre.

The University of the District of Columbia (UDC) had a similar well-publicized problem. Judy Chicago made it a gift of the "Dinner Party."

It is very difficult to convey to people who do not follow the weird goings-on in our culture an appreciation of the animating agenda of the "arts community" today. An ordinary American reads about a woman "performing artist" who prances nude across the stage, with chocolate smeared over her body, and though he may lament the waste of chocolate or nudity, it does not occur to him that she is "making a statement," one that the "arts community" takes seriously indeed.

Even museum trustees in Washington, D.C., or Cincinnati—an elite, educated, and affluent group of arts philanthropists—had no idea what Mapplethorpe was up to in his photograph of a man with a bullwhip handle inserted into his rectum. All they knew is that Mapplethorpe was a very talented photographer (which he was), that no such talent could ever create an obscene work (which is false) and that any discriminating judgment on their part was a form of censorship that verged on the sacrilegious. Those trustees are there to raise money and watch the museum's balance sheet. They may or may not know what they like, but they would never presume to assert what is, or is not, "art." To qualify to become a museum trustee these days one must first suffer aesthetic castration.

To reach our current condition, it took a century of "permanent revolution" in the arts, made possible, ironically, by a capitalist economy which created affluent art collectors and entrepreneurial art dealers. "Patrons" of the arts were replaced by "consumers" of the arts, giving the artist an intoxicating freedom.

Source: Irving Kristol, "Its Obscene but Is It Art," *Wall Street Journal,* August 7, 1990, p. A16. Reprinted by permission of author.

The piece is of 39 female genatalia each decorously placed in a seating arrangement on a dinner table. This, it is said, depicted the struggle of women. As is common, the artist-donor made some display stipulations which required expensive renovation of a building and the trustees voted $80,000 for moving and insuring the piece. The work was valued at $2 million. Previously, the piece had been shown and was well received in a number of prestigious settings—some religious. The art promised badly needed revenues from displays as well as from replicas' sales. Moreover, it was argued by some trustees, as a university, UDC has a responsibility to respect freedom of speech and to recognize that art is always controversial. Remember David? The art had to be returned because of Congressional and journalistic outcry.

DUTY OF ORGANIZATION TO TRUSTEES

Trustees have the right to expect that the nonprofit has exactly the same duty to them as they to the organization. They should expect obedience to their policies that are consistent with the mission of the organization. Trustees share liability for infractions; thus, they should expect that their directions will be obeyed. It is they, rather than the employees, who represent the public interest.

Similarly, they should expect a duty of care directed toward them. As their duty of care toward the organization means that they need to be informed and to act prudently on behalf of the organization, so too they should expect that they will be kept informed about those things that matter. These include being kept up to date on major changes in the organization's direction or assets, annual budgets and financial statements, changes in key employees, new risks to which the organization is exposed, employee compensation packages, and an evaluation of the organization's performance.

The duty to the trustees also encompasses loyalty. This concept implies a protection of the trustees. Thus, trustees have a right to presume that the relationship between them and the organization is above board (so to speak), at reasonable arm's length, and that the organization does not expose any trustee to personal or professional risks—even if it forewarned him or her that such risks might be present. Put simply, they have a right to expect that they are not being used or "set up" and that the information given them to form the basis of their decisions is as clear, complete, and relevant as possible, and that the organization will not act imprudently.

Consistent with the exercise of prudence, trustees may rely on information they obtain from appropriately assigned employees, accountants, lawyers, engineers, and other experts. Relying on the expertise of such persons is an act of prudence and not necessarily a skirting or shifting of responsibility.

VOLUNTEER VERSUS PAID BOARDS

Clearly, volunteer boards are less expensive from the point of view of compensation. Their responsibility, however, is no less serious, and they too must operate on the three standards given above. From the individual's point of view, there are no major tax benefits from volunteering since the time worked and the lost income cannot be deducted. Only certain expenses can be deducted, such as transportation and specifically required clothing (for example, protective garments and uniforms).

From the point of view of a corporate officer or the corporation itself, volunteering is not only good citizenship and public relations, but it reduces the nuisance of accounting for inconsequential pay. Furthermore, compensation increases the odds of being an interested person, as described above, and may even expose the person to personal liability (to be discussed later). Most states that limit liability of trustees are more clear in doing so if the trustee is a volunteer than if compensated. This is an advantage of an all-volunteer board. Paid boards are more common with private foundations than with other nonprofits. The word paid includes benefits and other indirect compensation. These must be reasonable.

CONTROLLING TRUSTEE MEETING COSTS

Accomplish as much as possible by mail, fax or phone. Send out detailed agendas in advance. Avoid giving credit cards to trustees to cover their expenses. This is equivalent to giving each trustee the authority to individually decide whenever or for whatever reason, personal or otherwise, to create a debt for the organization. Because credit cards allow cash advances, the trustee can use it just as if it were a personal checkbook.

This practice, is of questionable legality, and definitely a potential nightmare in an audit. Each expense of an organization ought to be traceable to a specific authority, mission-related, and reasonable. Once the debt has been incurred, the organization has a liability no matter how much it may protest. Avoid the problem. Take the following steps:

STEP 1. If the trustees must have a credit card, have them pass a resolution authorizing the issue of the cards, a limit (my preference is $500), and prohibiting cash advances. Each trustee should know that it is possible to be personally liable if any other trustee uses these cards for personal reasons or to make loans to themselves unless they unequivocably prohibit it. Each person who gets a card also gets a copy of the resolution which should, of course, be part of the organization's records if the chief executive officer is not to be personally liable.

STEP 2. Do all billings for trustee meetings through a master account which the organization makes with a local hotel, restaurant and travel agent. Eliminate the need for cash expenditures by the trustees for any reason other than ground transportation. Some trustees may prefer to use their personal credit cards for air travel so as to get the travel insurance or frequent traveler rights. You may be better off buying the insurance, but because of legitimate personal considerations such as these two, you may allow them to purchase their own tickets, but restrict the reimbursement to below first class unless specifically approved.

STEP 3. Require the trustees to submit all bills within 15 to 30 days after the event. This is reasonable and will aid your accounting department.

STEP 4. Have your auditor prepare an expense voucher which you can send to your trustees. This form should conform with the information needed for tax and reporting purposes. Keep a copy and return a copy to the trustee for his or her tax purpose and business purpose.

STEP 5. Make it clear that your policies do not permit paying entertainment expenses. These are the most abused and often the hardest to support as a legitimate organizational expense. Pick up the tab. Have a reception.

STEP 6. Be grateful. Give a holiday present of moderate cost, say $25.00. A birthday card or anniversary present will go a long way.

STEP 7. When meetings are held far from a trustee's office or residence, there may be a concern for telephone billing. Avoid it. Most businesses will accept a collect call and a business call is not an appropriate expense for you. Most certainly a personal call is not. Let them use your telephone or a pay phone.

There is no ethical imperative to be stingy. But trustee costs, as any other costs, must be controlled and accounted for because they have financial, legal and tax implications. They may be considered self-dealing, taxable compensation to the trustee, and inappropriate expenses for the organization. In addition, they may lead a scrupulous auditor to give less than a clean audit opinion of your organization's financial procedures. The use of the credit card to make a personal purchase which the organization pays for is taxable compensation to the trustee. The organization is legally bound to report all compensations, including these.

LIABILITY OF TRUSTEES

The board of trustees of a nonprofit organization may be sued by (1) the members in a so-called derivative suit, where the members are suing the trustee on behalf of the greater good of the organization, (2) a third private party, (3) a government and (4) one of its own members or employees.

Before proceeding, take a look at Table 5.1. Note the forty ways in which a trustee can be held liable. Even though this chart was prepared for corporate directors, it applies to nonprofits, too. Recall that many states use exactly the same rules for for-profit and nonprofit corporate governance, and many nonprofits own for-profit corporations. Either way, the rules apply.

Every trustee and every nonprofit organization has to be concerned with the extent to which trustees and officers can be held personally liable. Liability may arise either for actions taken or for the failure to act. Furthermore, in some instances liability may arise because of the actions of other trustees or officers. For example, a trustee can be held liable for failing to block an inappropriate action by other trustees or by management. Recall that management serves under the stewardship of the trustees and therefore is accountable to them. Also, the duties of care and loyalty mean that a trustee cannot choose to look the other way when any other trustee or officer may be involved in actions that are wrong.

This liability threat would discourage many good people from serving nonprofits. If the trustee can be held personally liable, then he or she faces the possibility of being sued and having to pay monetary damages out of personal resources. Even if monetary damages are not assessed, the trustee faces the unpleasant possibility of having to spend time and resources in a personal defense. In addition, there are the emotional and social costs.

Recognizing this deterrent, many states have taken actions to limit personal liability. Such limitations must be balanced to discourage failure to care, to be loyal, and to be obedient. In Oregon and Maryland among other states, for example, the legislatures passed "expansive" laws, meaning that the legislatures gave the nonprofits considerable power and discretion to exempt their trustees from personal liability.

The Maryland law says that a nonprofit corporation can specify in its bylaws or charter those actions or inactions for which a trustee or an officer of the nonprofit may be held personally liable and the extent of that liability. Thus, at least in Maryland, the nonprofit can choose to impose no personal liability or liability for only certain actions or inactions— and, if so, the amount of personal liability.[2] Recall our discussion above about duty to the trustees?

The Maryland law also says that the personal liability of the trustee or director cannot exceed the amount by which he or she is insured per-

Table 5.1
Potential Claim Areas for Directors, Officers, or Trustees

(1) Acquiescence in conduct of fellow directors engaged in improper self-dealing.

(2) Acts beyond organization powers.

(3) Acts of executive committee.

(4) Approval of organization acquisition with resulting loss of organization assets.

(5) Attendance at directors' meetings and committee meetings.

(6) Conflicts of interest.

(7) Continual absence from meetings.

(8) Disclosure of material facts.

(9) Dissemination of false or misleading information.

(10) Dissent from improper or wrongful acts by board of directors or committee.

(11) Examination of all reports and documents before signing.

(12) Extension of credit where not warranted.

(13) Failure to ascertain whether extension of credit would be warranted.

(14) Failure to detect and stop embezzlement of organization funds.

(15) Failure to file annual report.

(16) Failure to inspect organization books and records in order to keep abreast of its activities.

(17) Failure to require withholding in connection with social security and income tax.

(18) Failure to record dissent from wrongful acts by board of directors whether or not dissenting director attended the meeting at which such action was taken.

(19) Failure to supervise the activities of others in a proper manner.

(20) Failure to verify facts in official documents before signing and filing them.

(21) False or misleading reports.

(22) Fraudulent conduct.

(23) Fraudulent reports, financial statements, or certificates.

(24) Ignorance of organization books and records.

(25) Inducing organization to commit breach of contract.

(26) Inducing or abetting organization in commission of torts.

(27) Inefficient administration resulting in losses.

(28) Loans from officers, directors, or trustees.

(29) Permitting organization to engage in activities prohibited by statute.

(30) Permitting organization to make improper guarantees.

(31) Permitting organization to pay bribes or make other illegal payments.

(32) Preferences at the expense of organization creditors.

(33) Sale of organization assets for unreasonably low price.

(34) Shrinking responsibility.

(35) Transactions with other companies in which officers or directors are personally interested.

(36) Unreasonable accumulations.

(37) Violations of specific provisions of articles or bylaws.

(38) Violations of state statutes.

(39) Wasting of organization assets.

(40) Willful wrongdoing.

Source: Reprinted, with permission, from the *Journal of the American Society of CLU*, Vol. XXXIX, No. 6 (November 1985). Copyright 1985 by the American Society of CLU, 270 Bryn Mawr Avenue, Bryn Mawr, PA 19010.

sonally or by the organization. Some students of the law conclude that if the trustee has no insurance then ipso facto no monetary damage can be assessed against that person. Furthermore, if the organization carries insurance, then the limits of any damages would be the amount available through the organization's insurance coverage. There would be no damages assessed personally on the trustee or director.[3]

Thus, trustees and officers of nonprofits in Maryland and in similar states are protected (1) by the exemption the nonprofit should declare in its bylaws or charter of incorporation, (2) by the insurance carried by the organization, and (3) by the personal insurance carried by the trustees and officers. Presumably, since there has been no test case, items 1 and 2 ought to be sufficient to protect a citizen who serves as a trustee of a Maryland nonprofit corporation—providing that the organization has taken steps to amend its bylaws. This demonstrates one reason why trustees should make sure that bylaws are periodically reviewed.

Before closing this discussion, let us note that even in an "expansionist" state like Maryland the nonprofit cannot shield the trustees from liability for *willful* illegal acts and for acts that lead to improper personal gains or profits on the part of the trustee or director, or *willful* failure to carry out the duties (care, loyalty, or obedience) of the trustee.

Table 5.2 gives a listing of the different special provisions found in states' statutes across the country as far as the liability of trustees is concerned.

Liability Insurance

An organization can elect to cover its trustees and officers by purchasing D&O (directors and officers) insurance. This type of insurance is

TABLE 5.2 Summary of State Laws Offering Liability Protection for Volunteers and Board Members

| | For All Volunteers | | | | | | | | | For Officers and Directors | | | | | | |
| | | Exceptions to Liability Protection | | | | | | | | | Exceptions to Liability Protection | | | | | |
	No Protection	Bad Faith	Willful or Intentional Action	Reckless-ness	Gross Negli-gence	Fraud or Breach of Fiduciary Duty	Use of Motor Vehicle	Knowing Violation of Law	Covers Only Volunteer Officers	Bad Faith	Willful or Intentional Action	Reckless-ness	Gross Negli-gence	Fraud or Breach of Fiduciary Duty	Lawsuit by Organi-zation	Knowing Violation of Law
Alabama	●								●						●	
Alaska	●										●		●	●	●	
Arizona	●	●								●	●		●	●	●	
Arkansas					●		●[2]		●	●	●	●	●	●		
California[1]	●															
Colorado	●	●												●		●
Connecticut	●								●	●	●	●				
Delaware			●		●		●[2]		●	●	●	●	●	●		
D.C.	●															
Florida	●															
Georgia		●	●						●	●	●	●		●		●
Hawaii	●								●		●		●			
Idaho	●		●						●	●	●			●		●
Illinois			●	●					●	●	●	●				
Indiana	●		●						●	●	○	○	○			
Iowa		●	●		●	●		●	●	●	●				●	●
Kansas[1,2]		●	●						●[3]		●	●				
Kentucky		●	●						●[3]		●	●				
Louisiana		●	●						●[3]		●	●			●	
Maine		○	○	○	○				●		○	○	○			
Maryland[1,2]		●	●	●	●				●		●					
Massachusetts	●												●[4]			
Michigan	●								●							
Minnesota		●	●	●		●			●		●	●		●		
Mississippi		●	●	●	●		●		●	●	●	●				
Misso…		○	●	○	○				●		●		●			

146

Montana	●						●	●			
Nebraska	●					●	●				
Nevada	●				●	●	●	●	○	●	●
New Hampshire	●	●			●	●	●	●	●		●
New Jersey	●	●			●	●	●	●	● ●		
New Mexico	●					●	●			●	
New York	●				●	●	●				
North Carolina[2]	●	●	○		●	●	●	●	●	●	
North Dakota	●	●			●	●	●	●			
Ohio	●					●	●				
Oklahoma	●				●	●	●	●	●	●	●
Oregon	●				●	●	●	● ○			
Pennsylvania		○	○		○	●	○	○	○		
Rhode Island	●	●			●	●	●	●			
South Carolina	●				●	●	●				
South Dakota[2]	●	●		●	●	●	●				
Tennessee	●					●	●				
Texas	●	●	●	●[2]	●	●	●	●	●		
Utah[1]	●	●		●		●	●		●		
Vermont	●				●	●	●	●			
Virginia	●				●	●	●	●	●	●	
Washington	●				●	●	●	●	●	●	
West Virginia	●				●	●	● ○	●	○	●	
Wisconsin	●	●	●	●	●	●	●	●	●	●	●
Wyoming	●					●	●			●	

● Indicates that the exception applies in this state.

○ Indicates that the exception has been inferred from the wording of the legislation.

1 For volunteers or officers to be protected, the non-profit organization must carry specified insurance.

2 Liability is limited to the amount covered by insurance.

3 Paid directors and officers of non-profit organizations defined by state law are protected. Directors of other charities are not.

4 Pertains only to acts that result in harm to a person.

Source: Nonprofits' Risk Management & Insurance Institute. Reprinted with permission.

sold by property and casualty insurance agents. It can also be obtained through some insurance pools for nonprofits and through some associations. How does D&O work? Basically, for an annual fee called a premium, an insurance company promises to pay damages arising from certain acts of negligence on the part of the trustee or officer.

In assessing these insurance contracts, it is important to go beyond the premium. It is important to determine what is excluded from coverage. Companies will list specific exclusions for which they will not pay. These should be understood in determining if the contract is suitable. Can the organization live with the stated exclusions? Some common exclusions include libel or slander, governmental penalties, bodily injury, claims covered by other insurance, active and deliberate dishonesty, and actions leading to personal or illegal profits or gains.

Companies pay either on a claims-made or an occurrence basis. These offer significantly different coverages. Strictly speaking, a claims-made policy pays only if the event occurs and is discovered during the contract period—the period of time up to the moment that the contract ends or lapses. Under an occurrence basis, the company will pay if the event occurred while the contract was valid, although the discovery and consequently the claim may have been made long after the contract terminated. Thus, it is important to know how long after cancellation or termination of a contract the company will pay for an event (not necessarily the claim) that occurred during the life of the contract. Let us illustrate.

A nonprofit has a liability insurance contract that terminates in 1991. In 1992 its trustees are sued for an act taken in 1991. Under which one of these claim bases would you prefer your liability insurance coverage? If you said the occurrence basis, you are right. The act of negligence was discovered after the policy had terminated. Under a claims basis, the act, its discovery, and claim would have had to occur prior to January 1, 1992, because the policy terminated on December 31, 1991.[4]

Other concerns in choosing D&O insurance are deductibility and co-insurance. Deductibility means that the company pays only after damages have reached a certain amount. Thus, the company may pay after the nonprofit has already paid the first $10,000 or some other amount agreed to in the contract. Co-insurance means that after a certain amount is reached the company will then ask the nonprofit to share the cost of the damage. To illustrate, the contract may read that if a suit is successful and a judgment, say of $100,000, is awarded, the nonprofit would pay the first $10,000 and 20 percent of any amount over the next $80,000. This would mean that the nonprofit would come up with a total of $12,000, while the insurance company would pay $88,000.

Another concern in choosing among D&O policies is to compare the amount that is covered per claim and the total cap for all claims combined during the policy period. Like all the other considerations above, there is no one good formula for all nonprofits. They must choose among alternatives.

In choosing an insurance policy it is also wise to check to see if there is a right to defend clause.[5] This is important. It means that the insurance company assumes an obligation to defend the trustees or officers so that they would not have to expend personal or organizational funds in their own defense.

Umbrella Policy

It is possible to get extra coverage by buying an umbrella policy. This is an insurance policy that covers all liabilities, both property and personal, beyond the amount covered by each liability policy the organization has. Thus, an umbrella policy would provide protection beyond the automobile, property, and D&O policies. With an umbrella policy, the organization would have an overall policy that would spread dollars around these individual policies when claims are made that are above the limits of the individual policies.

Indemnification

As we saw in Chapter 2, a nonprofit may indemnify its trustees or officers. This means that in the event of a suit the organization will repay the trustee or officer for expenses. In the state of Pennsylvania, under Section 7743, indemnification is obligatory. It is required if the trustee or other agent of the organization is successfully defended in a lawsuit. Virtually every state permits the organization to allow indemnification in its bylaws. What are the limits to indemnification?[6]

First, indemnification usually does not imply a right to defend, Thus, the trustee or officer must pay for his or her own defense and is reimbursed. Furthermore, it is not unusual that indemnification is made only if the trustee or director wins the case. In many states if the damages are punitive, no indemnification can be made since punitive damages are intended to hurt. Out-of-pocket expenses could cause severe personal financial hardship. Even a successful defense could be socially and financially costly, taking a lot of valuable time and energy.

The organization may offer both indemnification and insurance. Under these arrangements, the insurance company pays for the amount in excess of the indemnification paid by the nonprofit. Alternatively, the nonprofit may offer indemnification by purchasing an insurance policy for the amount by which it promises to indemnify the person. This means that the money for the reimbursement does not come from the limited resources of the organization. Thus, indemnification and insurance are composites of an overall strategy to limit the personal liability of the officers and trustees. Hence, when an organization chooses to indemnify its trustees and officers, it can reduce its own financial risk by purchasing an insurance policy to cover the amount by which it promises to indemnify.

There are ethical and legal limits on indemnification. This is particularly true when the cause of damage is the willful violation of appropriate trustee conduct. One way to reduce exposure to these worries is to choose trustees wisely, to educate and inform them, and to recognize the organization's duties to them.

THREE C'S FOR SELECTING TRUSTEES

In congressionally chartered nonprofits, such as the USO, it is customary to have the president of the United States or the first lady, as in the case of the John F. Kennedy Center and the Girl Scouts, as honorary chairpersons of the board of trustees in addition to having cabinet members on the board. In the case of the Kennedy Center, there is a forty-five member board, thirty of whom must be U.S. citizens from the general public and appointed by the president; nine trustees are ex-officio members from the executive branch of the federal government and six are from Congress. Each trustee serves for a period of ten years. Some organizations have almost no discretion over their boards because one is automatically a board member by being an officer of a constituent group. Here is another variation. The General Board of Church and Society of The United Methodist Church has 92 board members. Seventy-four are from the constituent missionary conference—one person from each. Twelve are chosen by the board itself and six are nominated by the Council of Bishops.

A person may be named a trustee because of involvement in the organization and prominence. Steven Spielberg, an Eagle Scout, serves on the board of trustees of the Boy Scouts.

Sometime ago, a white scientist, Albert Barnes, was rebuffed by a number of top-rated Pennsylvania colleges and universities. Their faculties mocked his art collection and his theories about education. The president of a black college, Lincoln University, invited the scientist to speak, but he declined. Subsequently, the mocked scientist named Lincoln University as the trustee of his art collection and gave it the responsibility to name other trustees, except none could come from the schools that mocked him. Today, the collection is worth $1 billion.[7] This true story reminds us that trustees may be chosen for very strong personal reasons.

Whatever the personal or strategic reasons, we recommend that three C's should always guide the selection of trustees:

Character: By this is meant integrity and all that it implies, including good judgment.

Contribution: A trustee should be able to contribute at least time and competence.

Constituency: The trustee should represent more than himself or herself. Trustees need to represent portions of the membership, the community, donors as a group, a philosophy, a region—something other than themselves or an individual donor or the management.

We are reminded by the university chancellor who said, "We need to show the consequences to the public of poor trustee selection."[8] Bad choices can paralyze if not destroy a good organization.

FIVE STEPS TO ATTRACTING GOOD TRUSTEES

Trustees can attract financial and technical resources and attention to an organization. Here are some steps that should be taken to attract good trustees once they have been selected according to the three C's.

1. Sell the mission of the organization, for this is what the trustees must promulgate. Focus on getting an appropriate match between persons, purpose, and organizational mission.

2. Establish a good record of service, management, and finance. Prudent persons shy away from situations that put them at risk.

3. Make sure that your bylaws speak clearly to each of the following: (a) the role of the trustee, (b) time and place of meetings, (c) liability and indemnification protection of the trustees, (d) qualifications necessary to serve on the board, (e) compensation and reimbursement procedures, (f) term of board members and method of removal, (g) disclosure requirements of the management, including trustees, and the organization, (h) commitments such as fund raising, technical assistance, membership enhancement or donation that the organization requires from its board members, and (i) prohibited acts such as making of loans. State laws speak to each of these when the bylaws of the organization are silent.

4. Demonstrate a consciousness and commitment to the trustees as individuals and as a group.

5. Good people attract other good people. Start with the strongest person.

Let us close this chapter by noting that serving on a board of trustees is a good public service. Here are some tips:

QUICK TIPS TO CORPORATE
EXECUTIVES ON BEING A TRUSTEE:

• *Be sure you understand the mission of the nonprofit.* While many nonprofit executives speak of multiple objectives and the complexity of their mission, the mission statement itself should always be simple and direct. Unlike your corporation, which may change its mission by decision of the board of directors acting on behalf of the stockholders, the mission of a non-profit is a legal commitment. It is the basis upon which tax-exempt status is conferred. Violations of the mission may result in the loss of tax-exempt status.

• *Insist that the management of the institution view it as an economic institution.* Public welfare—not the organization's—is the mission. That means producing a product or service that meets a test of social acceptability and therefore warrants support. And concern for financial discipline must be engendered: Full costs have to be covered, no matter how charitable the mission.

• *Encourage the view that the tax-exempt organizations are fundamentally unlike government bureaucracies.* Government agencies are financed by compulsion (taxation) while charity is financed by competition for voluntary gifts, donations and by earned income.

   Further, tax-exempt organizations can go bankrupt and close down. This demands a discipline which makes the tax-exempt more like a business than like a government agency. But unlike a business, the tax-exempt's purpose is to promote public, not private welfare.

• *In a competitive environment, it is important for the management to develop planning skills.* Therefore, nonprofits must be concerned with product life cycles (e.g., the length of an exhibit), changes in technology (e.g., hospital equipment) and changes in production, marketing and financing strategies.

• *If the non-profit enters into a legally permitted business venture, always ascertain if the business activity is related to programs essential to the mission of the organization.* If it is unrelated, any net income may be taxed. Charges of unfair competition or impropriety may also arise. Therefore, subject every investment decision to tests of practicability, propriety and profitability. An art museum can earn considerable revenues by selling art work. These revenues are considered to be related business income, and therefore those revenues are not taxed. If the same art museum earns unrelated business income by selling scientific pieces (e.g., compasses or magnifying glasses) such income is taxed, but it would not be taxed if earned by a science museum.

• *The trustee should avoid focusing on the budget at the expense of balance sheets, income statements, or statements of changes in financial position.* The budget is a plan, a tool for financial control and—perhaps most misunderstood—a marketing aid.

   There is nothing in the law that says a nonprofit must show either a zero or negative fund balance. Often, negative balances are the result of sloppy management rather than deliberate policy. Moreover, a positive balance provides the institution with a source of discretionary funds, as opposed to restrictive funds which can be used only for specific purposes.

> The principal source of finance for many nonprofits is gifts and contributions.
> • *Not all states exempt officers and directors or volunteers from liability.* Trustees serve with the presumption of care and loyalty to the organization and in a fiduciary capacity. Understand the risks to which the organization is exposed and understand that the board may carry the same exposure.
>
> Source: Abbreviated from Herrington J. Bryce. "Answering the President's Call to Public Service." *Wall Street Journal,* July 10, 1989, p. A10. Elaborations of these points can be found in the author's articles appearing in *The Corporate Board* and the *National Association of Corporate Directors.* See Recommended Readings.

The above insert summarizes much that we have said in this chapter and gives a few guidelines, especially to corporate officers who are candidates for service on boards of trustees of nonprofits.

SUMMARY AND CONCLUSIONS

This chapter has reviewed the duties of trustees. The key is that the trustees have as their principal and overriding purpose the selfless care of the assets of the organization and the use of these assets to advance the organization's mission. Failure to abide by these strictures can result in legal sanctions. In later chapters we shall look more closely at some of the tools trustees can use for better financial management.

NOTES

1. IRS Private Letter 8948034.
2. Stewart P. Hoover, "Nonprofit Corporations and Maryland's Director and Officer Liability Statute: A Study of the Mechanics of Maryland's Statutory Corporate Law," *University of Baltimore Law Review,* 18, no. 2 (Winter 1989), pp. 384–402.
3. Ibid. and James J. Hanks, Jr., and Larry P. Scriggins, "Let Stockholders Decide: The Origins of the Maryland Director and Officer Liability Statute of 1988," *University of Baltimore Law Review,* 18, no. 2 (Winter 1989), pp. 235–253.
4. In actuality, there is some leeway even under the claims basis, but it might be very, very short.
5. Julie J. Bisceglia, "Practical Aspects of Director's and Officers' Liability Insurance— Allocating Legal Fees and the Duty to Defend," *UCLA Law Review,* 322, no. 3 (Feb. 1985), 690–718.
6. Michael Gawel, "Directors and Officers Indemnification Insurance: What Is Being Offered?" *Journal of the American Society of CLU,* 39, no. 6 (Nov. 1985), 92–101.
7. *Chronicle of Higher Education.*

8. Blenda Wilson, in *Reports,* Association of Governing Boards of Universities and Colleges, Jan.–Feb. 1990, p. 2.

SUGGESTED READINGS

BAUGHMAN, JAMES, *Trustees, Trusteeships and the Public Good* (New York: Quorum Books, 1987).

BRYCE, HERRINGTON J., "10 Nonprofit Board Guidelines," *Director's Monthly,* July–Aug. 1988.

——, "The Corporate Director on the Nonprofit Board: A Guide to Nonprofit Service," *Director's Monthly,* Apr. 1988.

CHAIT, R. P., AND B.E. TAYLOR, "Charting the Territory of Nonprofit Boards," *Harvard Business Review,* Jan.–Feb. 1989, no. 1, pp. 44–139.

DRUCKER, PETER F., "What Business Can Learn from Nonprofits" *Harvard Business Review,* July–Aug. 1989, no. 4, pp. 88–94.

HERMAN, ROBERT, AND J. VAN TIL, eds., *Nonprofit Boards of Directors* (New Brunswick, N.J.: Transaction Books, 1989).

HOULE, CYRIL, *Governing Boards* (San Francisco: Jossey-Bass, 1989).

KURTZ, DANIEL L., *Board Liability* (Mt. Kisco, N.Y.: Moyer Bell Limited, 1988).

O'CONNELL, BRIAN, *The Board Members Book* (New York: The Foundation Center, 1989).

PART II

Marketing

This we know, the earth does not belong to man; man belongs to the earth. All things are connected like the blood which unites one family. Whatever befalls the earth, befalls the sons of earth. Man did not weave the web of life. He is merely a strand of it. Whatever he does to the earth, he does to himself.

Chief Seattle of the Suquamish people of the Pacific Northwest, in a letter to President Franklin Pierce in 1855.

Source: *1989 McDonald's Annual Report* p. 1.

Chapter 6

Strategic Planning Options and Management Strategies

This chapter opens Part II. The central issue is **marketing**. But strategic planning, the specific topic of this chapter, applies to every function within an organization. Thus, we shall read of it in generic terms with occasional reference to its relationship to marketing. Management strives to make the best decisions within the limits of the mission of the organization. Strategic planning can help management to uncover and make optimal decisions.

Strategic planning cannot be blindly applied because there are significant differences between for-profit and nonprofit organizations. Therefore, this author has developed diagrams and specific discussions of the differences that should be of concern to the nonprofit manager and suggests specific ways for dealing with them.

THE IMPORTANCE OF STRATEGIC PLANNING

The principal purpose of strategic planning is to help the organization systematically arrive at important decisions while involving as many as possible in the deliberations. The following from the National League for Nursing is apropos because it revolves around concepts included in this book: markets, information, feedback, bylaws, trustees and holding company structure.

> The Long Range Planning Committee presented a proposal for a new structure for the League. At that time, information was provided and feedback was sought. In the intervening years, the committee worked diligently at refining the proposal and at educating our members. This year the proposal and the new by-laws were passed. One of the goals of the new structure includes greater flexibility in reaching new and different markets. Another goal was to streamline the board to a workable and cost effective size. Another goal was to take advantage of the benefits incurred by having a holding company structure. *Nursing Health Care*, Vol. 10, No. 7, September 1989, p. 380.

STRATEGIC PLANNING IN PERSPECTIVE

In 1887 a priest, a rabbi, and two ministers founded the first United Way to meet the need of coordinating local services and to conduct a single fund-raising campaign for twenty-two agencies. They recognized a non-commercial need that continues to exist today.

The mission of the United Way of America is "To increase the organized capacity of people to care for one another." This mission is consistent with the definition of organizations defined under Section 501(c)(3) of the code. It is also broad enough to encompass the missions of individual United Way agencies throughout the country.

The strategies of the United Way include community involvement of all segments of the community, a single campaign to raise funds, and a flexible distribution of funds. These strategies do not lead to substantial commercial activities.

The programs of the United Way of America include some 400 information and referral services that link people in need with those with resources; a management assistance program that offers consultation, training, and information sharing; a volunteer leadership development program to enhance the managerial and financial leadership of volunteers; a program that puts those who wish to make gifts of property with those who need them, and a national fund-raising campaign, the proceeds of which are distributed to other nonprofits. The United Way of America cooperates with the National Football League Charities and with employer and employee associations in reaching its goal. It competes with other payroll and combined fund-raising groups. On occasion, it has worked alongside these groups in specific fund-raising efforts; but mostly it is a competition for market share.

STRATEGIC PLANNING AS A WINNOWING TOOL

Let us take a mission:

> The mission of Girls Incorporated is to assist affiliates in effectively meeting the needs of girls in their communities; to help girls and young women overcome the effects of discrimination and to develop their capacity to be self-sufficient, responsible citizens; and to serve as a vigorous advocate for girls, focusing attention on their special needs.   Girls Incorporated Annual Report, 1990, cover. Reprinted with permission.

This is a broad statement but consistent with the criteria of a mission statement discussed in Chapter 1. It admits to an infinite number of possibilities which are common to complex problems. The mission must be met in a basically noncommercial manner. This does not mean that a price cannot be charged, but that profits cannot be the motive and competition with market-oriented firms should be minimized. Choosing programs that are (a) consistent with the mission of the organization, (b) noncommercial, (c) feasible, (d) desirable, and (e) designed to meet the competitive threats of the nonprofit's market (for service to girls) is one use of strategic planning. It is a deductive process through which the organization moves from an infinite number of strategic options to a finite number with the best chances for success.

For another view of how strategic planning can be helpful in winnowing down options, take a look at Table 2.1 which lists the variety of activities that can be conducted under the 501(c)(3) label. Imagine that there are an infinite number of ways of doing each. How many ways can a synagogue or church serve its congregation and its community? Let us recommend a minimum condition for choosing rationally. The choice must be simultaneously, (a) desirable, (b) feasible, (c) effective, and (d) consistent with the mission. How then do we choose? That is the question to which we now turn.

STRATEGIC PLANNING: PURPOSES AND APPROACHES

Strategic planning is a process through which a nonprofit organization may:

1. Identify needs
2. Define its mission
3. Evaluate its capabilities
4. Assess its external environment
5. Set objectives
6. Select strategies
7. Design programs
8. Determine a budget
9. Evaluate performance

At each step in the strategic planning process, it is possible to use the most sophisticated techniques in research, group dynamics, logic, argumentation, program planning, and evaluation. These techniques are discussed in standard texts.[1]

The purpose of this chapter is to illustrate a step-by-step strategic planning process that may be applicable to nonprofits. The litmus test of any strategic planning process is whether it flows logically toward a participatory decision that makes sense and is applicable. Below we recommend a process and explain why it may be best for many nonprofits. The chapter highlights certain concepts upon which nonprofit managers should focus (see Figure 6.1).

The reader will observe the strategic planning process that is briefly outlined begins with an identification of a need consistent with the mission of the nonprofit. This is significant. A for-profit firm is not bound by a mission statement. A nonprofit is. Recall from earlier chapters that a mission is tantamount to a social contract with a nonprofit. It should therefore begin every planning process respecting this constraint. From a marketing as well as from a production perspective, this initial step is equivalent to asking what we should consider producing that is permissible (consistent with our mission). We can make a list of possibilities. Our next step will be to narrow the list.

Logically, the strategic planning process then proceeds to reduce the need to a manageable form for the nonprofit. Only then can realistic programs be designed. This is equivalent to saying that the mission statement, as indicated in Chapter 1, is broad and permits the organization to attack a need from various perspectives. But the organization only has

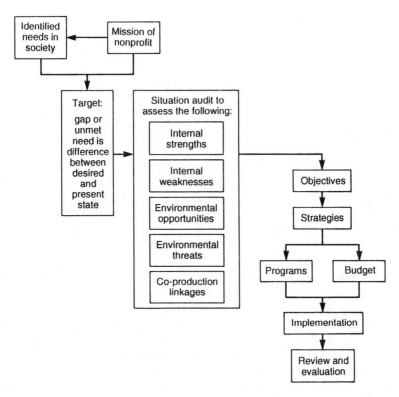

Figure 6.1 Strategic Planning Process.

limited resources. Therefore, which aspect of the need shall it be? At this stage, it is sufficient to narrow the list to include only those needs that are most consistent with the mission and represent a real need in severity or quantity worthy of the organization's attention.

Put another way, because most social needs are complex and stretch well beyond the resources of any one organization, it is important for each nonprofit to identify a specific gap that it may be able to fill. This gap becomes the focus of the planning process. It is the organization's target, for it is the difference between what is being done to meet the need and what is necessary to fully diminish it. The gap is a measure of an unmet need.

Having identified a gap and an unmet need consistent with its mission, the nonprofit must now assess its ability to successfully fill a portion of that gap. This leads to an assessment of the internal weaknesses and strengths of the organization. Does it have the necessary management experience or capacity to fill all or a portion of the gap? What aspect of the gap, from the perspective of its mission and capacity, is it best suited to fill?

Now the management may decide that the current capacity of the organization is inadequate to meet the task. Therefore, it is necessary to identify what is required in addition to existing capacity and how it will be acquired. Is the acquisition of the necessary capacity within the reach of the organization? If not, is there another way? We shall see a strategy of cooperation or joint ventures that permits organizations to go beyond their own capacity to do good.

Similarly, it is necessary to assess the external environment. What opportunities exist in the world at large that are available to the organization so that it may successfully fill the gap it has identified and targeted? What are the external obstacles or threats the organization will face once it has attempted to fill the gap? Are other organizations operating in the same area of unmet need and specifically in the gap targeted by the nonprofit? Is there room for one more nonprofit? Are there licensing laws or political and locational factors that would impede the nonprofit's attempt to fill the gap?

Sometimes these threats and obstacles come in the most oblique and disguised way. Take the case of *Christian Gospel Church Inc.* v. *City and County of San Francisco*.[2] This case is not about religion or meeting a religious need. It is about an environmental obstacle, something external to the church. The court supported local officials, indicating the church had to move from its present location because it created traffic and was noisy and parking was inadequate. These are discoverable in planning. The problems are all external to the organization and led to a costly court case.

Next, the organization must take into account the interaction between itself and a number of external forces. This is particularly important in nonprofit organizations because many of their activities depend upon co-production. Co-production, to be discussed later in this chapter, means that the organization's success or failure in supplying a good or service depends on the participation of others, including the clients, in the production process. Therefore, the nonprofit must be certain about its co-producers as well as the linkage or interaction that brings all factors together to make the production process successful.

An example of this is education. For a school to rank high in the educational performance of its students depends on the quality of the faculty, the facilities, parental support, and the quality and dedication of the students. The students are more than passive clients. They are critical to the production of high scores, for if all the other factors were present and the students were of low intellectual capability or uninspired, high scores would not be possible.

Another example is the resolution of crime. Students of police performance have discovered that the ability of the police to respond quickly and to solve crimes depends heavily on the nature and speed of response and cooperation of the victims. The victims, by virtue of their cooperation with the police, are co-producers of police performance.

This concept of linkage is so important that we need one more illustration. Refer to Table 6.1. Note how many co-producers a typical hospital has. Each has its time to be most important in a decision the hospital makes. Each has its opportunity to determine the success or failure of the hospital. Like the hospital, nonprofits should identify their linkages and co-producers and articulate a policy for dealing with each.

The organization is now prepared to state its objectives. Notice how late in the recommended process this comes. Objectives are statements of intent to meet specified unmet needs or to fill specified gaps. Objectives are meaningful if they reflect the internal and external constraints (opportunities, weaknesses, and threats) to the organization. This is why it is best to state objectives only after the gap is clearly analyzed and iden-

TABLE 6.1 Interdependencies between Organizations in the Health Sector

In the health sector, focal organizations have potential interdependencies with organizations such as:

Accrediting agencies	Insurance companies
Affiliated organizations	Joint venture partners
Alternative health systems	Media
Competitors	Medical staff-hospital joint ventures (MeSHs)
Confederated organizations	
Consortia members	Multiinstitutional systems
Consumer representative (public and private)	Other partners
	Owners
Employee representatives (unions)	Political groups
Fiscal intermediaries	Preferred provider organizations (PPOs)
Financial organizations (bond rating)	Suppliers (including capital, consumables, equipment, and human resources)
Foundations	
Government (all levels)	
Health maintenance organizations (HMOs)	Third party associations (TPAs)
	Trade associations
Independent practice associations (IPAs)	Utilization management companies

Reprinted with permission of Aspen Publishers, Inc. © 1990.

Source: Beaufort B. Longest, Jr., "Interorganizational Linkages in the Health Sector," *Health Care Management Review*, Winter 1990, p. 18.

tified and after a complete assessment of the organization's capacity and environment, including the strength of linkages among co-producers, has been made. To do otherwise is to waste time debating meaningless if not impossible options.

Once the objectives have been specified, the strategic planning process may proceed to develop strategies. Strategies are statements of how the objectives will be accomplished. They are statements of mode or direction. How will the unmet needs be met? Strategies should be broadly stated to provide room for imagination, flexibility, and realism in the design of programs.

Programs activate strategies. Programs are clusters of action that, when implemented in the mode or direction specified by the strategy, enable the organization to meet its objectives.

Programs are of two types. Action programs are clusters of interrelated activities as described. Financial programs are budgets. They tell how much will be needed for what purposes, when and where the money will come from, and in what form. Assuming that the staff of the nonprofit has designed a set of action programs, the next step is to identify the benefits to be derived from each and the feasibility and desirability of each. The challenge for the nonprofit is to select the best program. We show later in the chapter a simple technique for making this choice, and in Chapter 15 we discuss formulating budgets.

Once the preferred programs are chosen, strategic planning moves toward implementation. The length of the implementation process depends on the type of program, but it also depends on decisions concerning the availability of resources, the duration of unmet needs as targeted by the nonprofit, and the effectiveness of the programs. Accordingly, implementation should be accompanied by continuous monitoring and periodic reviews and evaluation. Through this process, the need for adjustments can be detected and the adjustments can be made before resources are wasted. We shall provide helpful steps later in this chapter; for now, let's proceed with the process.

Using the foregoing outline, any manager ought to be able to employ a strategic planning process that is beneficial. More sophisticated processes do require technical assistance and more research on needs assessment, on program planning and evaluation, and on the subject matter (the gap or unmet need) of the planning process.

Whether sophisticated or not, for the nonprofit manager, some basic concepts deserve further elaboration. One is the selection of strategic options because this is what decision making is all about. A second essential concept is co-production because this is central to the operation of most nonprofits. A third basic concept is the life cycle of needs because their fulfillment is the ultimate mission of nonprofits. We discuss each in turn.

MISSION, ETHICAL CODES AND STRATEGIC OPTIONS

Strategic planning decisions should be consistent with the ethical codes of the organization. It is also possible to use strategic planning to develop such a code. The code of ethics adopted in April 1991 by the American Association of Community and Junior Colleges (AACJC) is noteworthy because it manages to be brief, all-encompassing, very clear and yet it recognizes an important fact: an organization's ethical code must be based on shared values. Thus, it begins with the following shared values: trust and respect, honesty, fairness, integrity and reliability, commitment (to community, self, college, intellectual and moral development), openness and diversity.

On these values are founded certain responsibilities to trustees, administrators, staff, faculty, students, other educational institutions, the community at large and the chief executive officer of the college. The Code says all of this in two easily read and enumerated pages. How can an organization develop its own ethical code consistent with its mission and unique character? We recommend:

STEP 1. State the mission

STEP 2. Identify the shared values on which commitment to the mission rests

STEP 3. Identify the principal classes of people and entities (including animals and the environment where these are principals) involved and the principal communities affected

STEP 4. Identify the interaction; i.e., duties and responsibilities each to itself and to each other

STEP 5. Stipulate the ethical norms that should govern these duties and responsibilities

STEP 6. Obtain consensus and commitment

STEP 7. Assign enforcement and overseeing responsibility to a respected authority (even the board of trustees) within the organization

STEP 8. Periodically review and update

The organization's ethical code should guide its strategic options.

STRATEGIC OPTIONS: PROFITS VERSUS MISSION

Before an option is selected, it must be compared with other options along a number of dimensions simultaneously. One dimension is nonmonetary: Is the option feasible, desirable, ethical, and consistent with the mission of the organization? As we saw earlier, veering from its mission can have dire legal and tax consequences on a nonprofit.

Another dimension along which options should be compared is monetary: Do the monetary benefits exceed the monetary costs and, if so, by how much? This does not mean that the managers always have precise measurements of the benefits, costs, feasibility, or other criteria. It means only that they are able to make some reasonable judgment, such as "we believe that the benefits are five times the costs."

But the fact that the benefits may exceed costs is not enough information to make most decisions. Often monetary considerations conflict with the mission and the manageability or feasibility of an option. To appreciate this, let us consider a case where a nonprofit has six options for tending to an unmet need.

Assume that the six, A through F, have the following benefit-to-cost ratios: A = 5, B = 4, C = 3, D = 2, E = 1, and F = 0.1, meaning, for example, that in A the benefits are five times the costs and in D the benefits are only twice the costs. Is A to be chosen over D? To answer this, see Figure 6.2, which shows these options as they fall on a graph that simultaneously considers the feasibility and desirability of the options.

Option A has the highest benefit–cost ratio and, according to Figure 6.2, is very feasible but not desirable. Many options are economically sound but do not comport with the organization's image or value system; moreover, some options not only lead to tax consequences for nonprofits but may even cost them their tax-exempt status. Some options just don't seem right at the time, for example, the decision of the board of trustees of Planned Parenthood not to market condoms.[3]

On the other extreme, while D has the third lowest benefit–cost ratio, it is more desirable and feasible than A. D is superior to A. Although C's benefit–cost ratio is only average, it is more desirable than A. C ranks second to D.

F is both the most feasible and desirable option. However, F has a benefit–cost ratio of less than 1. Its costs exceed its benefits.

Option B is desirable and has the second highest benefit–cost ratio, but the organization is incapable of implementing it. E is infeasible and undesirable; its benefits equal costs, leaving C and D. Both may be chosen because they may be complementary; pursuing one enhances the success of the other. A secondary school could use a primary feeder school.

Both C and D may be chosen if they are independent of each other because this reduces the risk of failure. This is a diversification of options. Both may be chosen because together they will share costs. Finally, both may be chosen even if they are contradictory, because the selection of options is often based on political considerations; that is, "pacifying," or

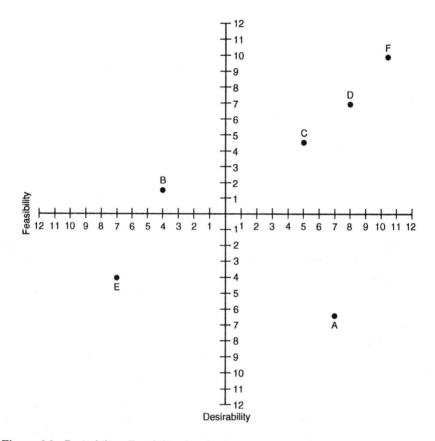

Figure 6.2 Desirability–Feasibility Coordinates.

"satisficing" the opposition or compromising between opposing but legitimate viewpoints.

The lesson for this exercise is that the choice of options is rarely based on the simple calculations of costs and benefits and that sometimes the attractiveness of choices may be influenced by other considerations. This does not mean, as is usually implied, that nonprofits should not be motivated in their decisions by dollar costs and benefits and should not try to maximize the difference between the two so that dollar benefits far outweigh costs. It merely means that often such programs are not within the realm of feasibility or desirability of the organization from the point of view of its mission. We shall discuss ways to deal with necessary infeasibilities or undesirabilities in Chapters 12 and 13.

STRATEGIC OPTIONS: COMPETITORS AND COOPERATORS

One important factor in the selection of options is the role of other organizations. The choice of options is influenced by other organizations, whether they are competitors or allies of the nonprofit. How do other organizations influence the choice of options?

Zero-sum Games among Competitors

While nonprofit managers may at times be oblivious to it, they are often more exposed to competitors than for-profit firms. The capital requirements, technology, licensing, and regulations that affect the rate of entry of new firms in the for-profit market do not exist to the same extent in the nonprofit sector.[4] To see this, list the number of organizations that cater to your different attributes such as age, sex, income, religion, political identification, job, residence ad infinitum.

In many ways, entry of new competitors into the nonprofit market is relatively easy to accomplish. Nonprofits cannot stop the entry of new competitors, and the laws are often not so stringent as to be prohibitive to new organizations.

Aside from the rate of entry of new organizations (both private and nonprofit) over which a nonprofit may have no legal control, there is the task of how to compete with an actual or potential competitor once entry has occurred. The basic question is what the reaction of a competitor will be if the nonprofit should pursue a particular strategy. Suppose, for example, nonprofit A decides to target a specific income group to give drug counseling. Will nonprofit B, in order to justify its funding, intensify its efforts to give drug counseling to the same group? Will it choose a narrower group, such as teen-agers? Would it focus on specific neighborhoods, or drugs, or sex?

Notice that each of these counterstrategies of B chips away at the overall clientele of nonprofit B. If the size of the drug population in the community is relatively fixed, say 1000 people, A can only increase its clients of drug abusers by reducing the number available to B, and vice versa; if A chooses a strategy, any counterstrategy of B that is successful will reduce the extent to which A will increase its clientele.

This is known as a zero-sum game because the overall size of the market is fixed, so one group can only grow at the expense of the other. This is captured in Figure 6.3, which is called a payoff matrix. The rows show the strategies, 1 through 6, that A may choose. The columns show the strategies available to B. The number in each cell is the percentage

Strategies of Nonprofit B

		1	2	3	4	5	6
	1	5	90	48	39	19	27
Strategies of Nonprofit A	2	7	38	75	1	33	79
	3	94	4	88	19	42	39
	4	67	85	22	50	80	0
	5	57	8	37	40	0	10
	6	53	0	69	29	50	40

Figure 6.3 Payoff Matrix of Nonprofits in Highly Competitive Zero-sum Market.

of the market that A will gain when it chooses a specific strategy that is countered by B's choice of one of its six strategies.

The number of cells depends on the number of strategies available. Obviously, the greater the number of strategies under consideration is the greater the number of cells. For this example we assume that each nonprofit has six options. One option may be to do nothing. Options may be active, passive, defensive, or aggressive.

Accordingly, if A chooses strategy 1, it will gain 90 percent of the market only if B chooses strategy 2, but only 5 percent if B also chooses strategy 1. If A chooses strategy 3 and B chooses 1, A gets 94 percent of the market; but if B counters with 2, A only gains 5 percent. Likewise, if A chooses 6 and B counters with 2, A gains nothing; but if B chooses 3, A gets 69 percent. The three cells with zeros indicate that it is important to identify and avoid strategies that can do you no good. They are wasteful.

The central utility of payoff matrices is that they discipline strategy choices so that managers take into account the consequences of counter-strategies by competitors. Hence, the choice of policies 1 through 6 by A will partly depend on what strategy, 1 through 6, it expects B to most likely pursue either in response to its own pressures or because of the threat posed by A. Hence, A will not choose 5 if it believes that B will also undertake 5. In the drug example, A will not focus on teen-agers if B has a competitive advantage working with teen-agers (strategy 5). If, however, A feels that B will counter with 4, A may still pursue 5 and split the market somewhat evenly. A may choose to deal with teen-agers if it believes that B will shift its focus to adult alcoholism.

An Example of Competitive Strategy in a Zero-sum Situation

The Academy of the Holy Name in my home town is proof that theory meets reality. It was a very good Catholic girls' school in the Washington metropolitan area. But Catholic schools in the area were experiencing declining enrollment, which threatened their existence. Within a few miles was a Catholic school for boys beginning to feel the same decline. The priests made the first move. They went co-ed. The Academy of the Holy Name is pleasant history.

Nonzero-sum Games among Cooperators

Nonprofits may have a cooperative relationship so that if A and B undertake supporting strategies they could expand the market for both of them. Suppose that A and B are nonprofits with a mission to eradicate smoking. Suppose that the total number of smokers is 50,000, but A only reaches 5000 and B only 10,000. There are 35,000 more persons to be reached. A and B may decide to cooperate in advertising, in seminars, or by each specializing in a particular subgroup of the 35,000. The situation is depicted in Figure 6.4.

We see that if A chooses strategy 7 and B strategy 3 they are relegated to the small inner circle; that is, the market share of both is small. But if A chooses 4 and B chooses 1, the frontier is expanded and both organizations increase their range. They can reach the entire market if A chooses 1 and B chooses 7. If in a moment of noncooperation A should choose 7 and B chooses 1, then both are hurt relative to where they were when A had chosen 1 and B took 7.

Fortunately for nonprofits, until recently they were not constrained as for-profits firms are through rigid application of law prohibiting collusion in cooperating to expand markets. The law seems increasingly less lenient. Yet cooperation is still possible as long as it does not unfairly defeat competition. The object of the cooperation cannot be to defeat competitors, to restrict the market, or to set prices.[5] By cooperating, they can reach the outer boundaries of their market. Thus, nonprofit A may decide to focus on teen-age smokers if it has a particular advantage in working with youth, and B may focus on adults if this is its comparative advantage.

An Example of Cooperative Strategy

Again, theory meets reality. Data collected by the Council for Aid to Education show two trends. Public schools are getting a larger and larger share of corporate donations. In the mid 1950s, public four-year institutions received about 14 percent of total corporate contributions.

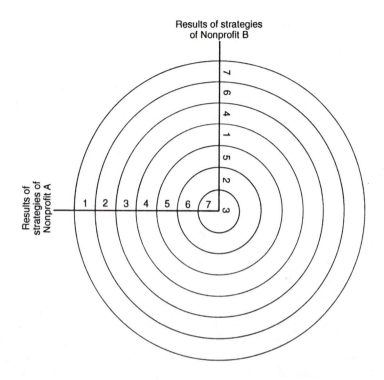

Figure 6.4 Schematic of Nonzero-sum Game among Cooperative Nonprofits.

By 1988, their share was slightly over 50 percent. But during the same period, the total pot available to all institutions more than doubled, from $76 million to over $1.5 billion. Even though the share of the private institutions fell from 86 percent to about 50 percent, their dollars received rose more than ten times to be divided by the same number of schools as in the 1950s. By increasing the size of the pot, everybody was made better off. What accomplishes this? Campaigns that promote "college education" as a worthy cause; not competitive campaigns—public versus private.

Cooperative Strategies When There Is Mistrust

Under certain conditions, the nonprofits may face a "prisoner's dilemma." Suppose nonprofits A and B could benefit by doing nothing once A is at 1 and B is at 7 because they have expanded their market to its maximum. It could occur, as it often does, that both A and B become suspicious of each other so that A believes that B will change its strategy. B may rationally choose to do so because it believes it can exist without A or can outdo A, or because there are pressures for it to shift course. B may harbor the same suspicions about A. Being suspicious, they both act. The consequence of this is that they are both worse off.[6] Any combination of policies other than A taking 1 and B taking 7 is inferior.

The prisoner's dilemma does not have to be so extreme. It is also possible for events to occur in this sequence: A chooses 2 and B chooses 6. Suspicion and discontent arise between the two. A decides to move to 1. What is the probability that B, without knowing that A was going to move to 1, would counter by moving to 7? The probability is small. The chances are that B's countermove would be something other than 7 (if all choices are randomly chosen). The consequence is that both would be worse off.

Strategies for Competitors and Cooperators

In Chapter 7 we shall see more formal cooperative strategies such as joint ventures and partnerships. Another formal alternative is forming a new corporation. For example, 501(e)s are nonprofit corporations created by hospitals for the purpose of carrying out such activities as record-keeping, purchasing, data processing, warehouse, billing, training, printing, and laboratory work for the hospitals that own the corporation. Cooperative efforts by these hospitals help to reduce total cost because volume reduces the cost to each hospital. It also allows the sharing and development of specialization and efficiency. Yet, these hospitals are competitors for clients and medical professionals.

Co-production: Working with Clients and Community

Strategic planning is of particular applicability to nonprofit organizations because it is a method that promotes participation and focuses on a mission.[7] As we saw in Chapter 4, a nonprofit, unlike a for-profit, must justify its existence and tax-exempt status by demonstrating public support and participation and by adhering closely to its mission. One form of public support, under the 10 percent test described to in Chapter 4, is public participation.

Throughout the strategic planning process, a wide level of participation by the public as well as the leadership and staff of the nonprofit is to be encouraged and is easily accommodated by making them part of the strategic planning group. We say more about this later in this chapter as we develop a discussion of needs assessment.

One aspect of participation common to many nonprofits is co-production. Figure 6.5 shows interaction when co-production is absent. A private or public foundation, for example, may provide funding for a nonprofit to produce a newsletter, poetry, a play, a painting—products that the nonprofit can produce without direct involvement of clients in the

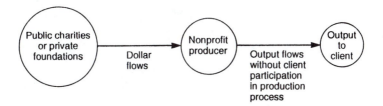

Figure 6.5 Schematic of a Simple Production Relationship in the Nonprofit Sector.

creative process. A newsletter can be produced without its readers writing, printing, or distributing the articles.

Illustration of Co-production

Contrast this simple process with Figure 6.6, which is a depiction of an actual co-production process involving a nonprofit. It is a description of the National Urban Policy Roundtable funded by the Charles F. Kettering Foundation and coordinated by the Academy for Contemporary Problems (ACP) now called the Academy for State and Local Governments.[8] The mission of the Roundtable was to produce policy analyses and recommendations for federal, state, local, and private leaders in a steering committee and in a roundtable. Working papers were prepared, published, and disseminated. Many of the products of the Roundtable were utilized in the annual report of the president of the United States to the U.S. Congress and by the associations of state and local governments that were represented on the governing board of the Academy, the steering committee of the Roundtable, and whose members were frequently a target group of clients. Figure 6.6 traces the complex co-production relationship.

1. The Charles F. Kettering Foundation, a private operating foundation, finances a project. But, as we saw in Chapter 4, the law requires that such foundations directly participate in many of their projects. It is not sufficient to send a check; it is necessary that their assets and staff be directly involved. The consequence of this is intersection A, which shows both the private operating foundation and the nonprofit (ACP) as co-producers.

2. To ensure the policy relevance of the project as well as public participation, both the nonprofit and the private operating foundation encouraged the participation of the clients, which in this case were the public, publicly elected and appointed officials, and private sector leaders.

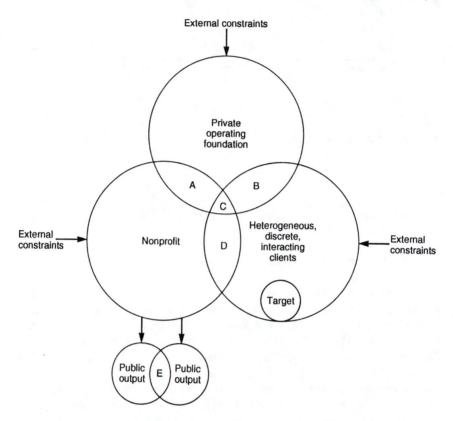

Figure 6.6 Schematic of Complex Co-production in the Nonprofit Sector.

In the parlance of strategic planning, these are called stakeholders because they have a stake in the outcome of the process.

Because the clients were persons from different sectors (public, private, and community) and different groups within each sector (bankers,
builders, governors, state legislators, mayors, citizens), these groups are
referred to as heterogeneous, discrete, and interacting. Indeed, these
groups could also be described as atomistic because they were independent of each other. They sometimes cooperated, but at times had radically
divergent and antagonistic positions on the same issues. No issue was
equally relevant to all groups. Consequently, for each issue a prime target
group was identified.

3. The co-production process also involves direct relationships that
the client group may have with the private foundation, either as a group

or as individual constituencies within the group. This is represented by intersection B. While not directly involving the ACP, the nonprofit, the influences of such relationships were always indirectly felt. For one thing, the co-production activity had to be so defined that it did not infringe on other relationships between the private operating foundation and the clients. In effect, this partly defined the boundaries of the ACP and circumscribed the scope of activity of the Roundtable.

4. Similarly, the clients may have direct relationships with the nonprofit outside the direct co-production relationship. This is represented by intersection D. In the case of the Roundtable, many members of the client group were also members of the board of directors of the ACP and were conducting other joint programs among themselves and with the ACP.

5. Intersection C is the core of the co-production activity. It is the interaction among the client, the private operating foundation, and the nonprofit. In the case of the Roundtable, the ACP (the nonprofit) is the principal producer; the private foundation is both the funding source and a co-producer, and the clients are both consumers and co-producers.

6. As a result of this interaction, a final product, E, is obtained. The final product, the production and dissemination of the policy documents, is not unrelated to other products being produced by the ACP. This is often the case, since one activity of an organization draws on and contributes to other activities in the organization. Note that by the very nature of nonprofits the products, even though targeted to a specific population, may have positive external effects.

A factor that makes co-production difficult is that the actual interaction among all parties, C, may represent a small part of the activities of any one of the organizations. Yet it brings the central producer, the nonprofit, under the influence not only of its external constraints, but under those of all co-producers. One example is worth noting. The Roundtable produced a study listing the cities with greatest potential for fiscal default. One of the cities was vitally related to the client group and the private operating foundation. The morning the study was released, the city announced its intentions to offer a new issue of municipal bonds. Although not required to rescind its results, the nonprofit ACP as coordinator, not just the Roundtable, expended a significant amount of energy explaining its results and the timing of its release. The actions of the Roundtable, though honoring its own constraints for objectivity, affected the external constraints of a key member of its client group to raise badly needed capital at favorable lending rates and involved the entire corporate body of the ACP of which the Roundtable was only a part.

LIFE CYCLE OF NEEDS: TIME TO CHANGE

The level of need (the gap) that a nonprofit addresses can be expected to change over time. (Read the introductory paragraphs to Chapter 8.) It may increase or decrease at a rapid, slow, or constant rate. Some needs may remain constant for a long time, while others may be fleeting. It is important that strategic planning for the nonprofit reflect how the needs it plans to address will change over time. The ability to answer these questions, even in general terms, helps the organization to avert disaster. Imagine investing in meeting an "unmet need" when the need has already been fulfilled or failing to prepare properly for a need that is rapidly escalating. Indeed, the plight of many nonprofits stems from their inability or unwillingness to track the decline in public ranking of the need to which the organization was dedicated or a change in the true level or intensity of the need.

Consequently, it is useful to know the approximate life cycle of the need being addressed by the nonprofit. This involves two separate questions. How long will the need last and how will it change over time? Figure 6.7 shows some possibilities. It is possible that once the program is launched the need for it declines uninterruptedly. The pattern of decline may be as in line a in the first panel or like lines b or c. The decline in line a begins rapidly and then flattens out so that a very low level of need is maintained until the end of the planning period, which, in this example, is the twelfth year of the program.

Alternatively, the decline could be steady but rapid as in line b or steady but slower as in line c. These are not simply geometric expressions. The point is that how rapidly a need disappears has an important bearing on how the organization should plan for it. A nonprofit should not go into debt or assume an obligation for more than five years if the need is likely to have a life cycle such as depicted in line b. Its commitment would outlive the problem. On the other hand, if the life cycle is like line a, a long-term commitment of up to 10 years can be made, and the organization can gradually extricate itself year by year from such commitments.

Alternatively, the need could be increasing over time. Here too the life-cycle pattern in significant. The increase could be at an increasing rate such as line d, a constant rate such as line e or a decreasing rate such as line f. If line d is applicable, then the organization must plan to rapidly increase its capacity over time. This can place great strain on the internal factors, which may now become the major constraints. If, however, the life cycle is as depicted in line f or e, the strain would be less.

Another possibility is that the life cycle is as shown in the third panel, indicating that it remains constant for the planning period. The dot g indicates that the life of the need expires at the end of one year, whichever year the need arises. In this case, the need is anticipated to

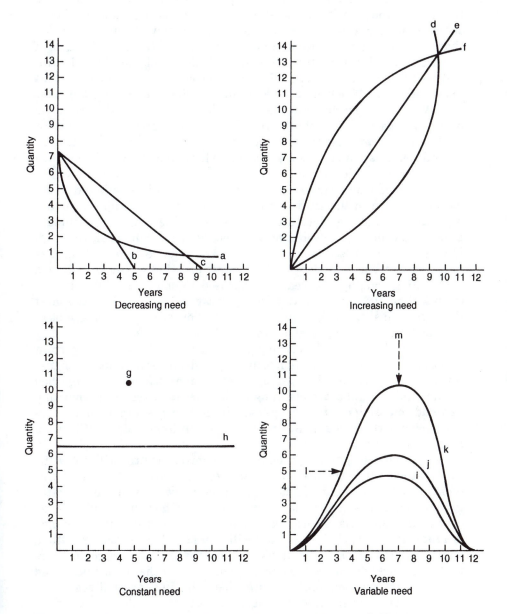

Figure 6.7 Alternative Life-cycle Patterns of Products and Services of a Non-profit.

occur in (not over) five years and will expire in that year. The dot indicates that during the year it may be at only one level. Is this unlikely? Many of the local activities for the Olympics are precisely of this nature. Activities celebrating the bicentennial of the birth of the United States of America were also of this type. They started and ended. They had a known and predictable short life. A profit was made partly because management knew the life cycle of events. Special fund-raising events are often dots!

A constant pattern is represented also in line h. In this case, the need remains fairly constant over the planning period. Planning for schools in a community that is relatively stable is an example. The need for additional facilities may remain stable for a long period of time until affected by dramatic population changes.

The need may be one that varies over time. This is reflected in the patterns shown in the fourth panel. The need may rise rapidly at first up to point l and then increase at a slower rate, eventually reaching a peak m and thereafter declining. The need may reach its peak very rapidly as in line k or less rapidly as in line i or j and be more prolonged as in the case of line i, which gives the lowest peak but the most sustained one, lasting roughly two years, as opposed to one year in line k. The organization would then have to plan its capacity so that it would meet the rapid and short peak as in line k or the slow rise but prolonged peak such as in line i. Can you give examples? Natural disasters?

Being able to spot the turning points such as at l and m is important in the ability of the organization to quickly and efficiently adjust to changing needs. It is possible, for example, that once the peak has been reached the nonprofit would begin planning to shift its resources toward meeting new and emerging needs, perhaps even in the same general field. A drug-abuse center could begin shifting its attention from LSD to PCP, from marijuana to crack.

It is not likely that any nonprofit or for-profit firm will know the exact rate at which the need for its services or products changes. But as economists who estimate demand over time know, it is infinitely better to make plans based on rational expectations of how needs will change over time than to have such changes occur unexpectedly. If the change is a rapid rise in need, the nonprofit will be unable to meet the escalation, which opens the door for dissatisfaction and the entry of new competitors that will quickly displace the existing nonprofit. If the change is a rapid decline, then the nonprofit will find itself having invested scarce resources to meet a need that no longer exists at the levels it once did.

ILLUSTRATION: LIFE-CYCLE AND DISASTERS

Go back to the graphical display of life cycles. It would be tempting to conclude that an event of such short duration that it can be represented by a dot does not lend itself to strategic planning. Planning is justified whenever an event has a probability of occurring, and if it occurs, the cost is significant to the person or entity that bears it. The issue is not if planning should be done, but how.

The Olympics is a short-lived event. But planning is continuous because the event is reasonably certain to occur and the stakes are high. An earthquake, eruption of a volcano, storm, flood, or airplane crash—each can occur and each extracts a high toll. The probability of each is small. We therefore do not plan continuously and not for each separately, but for their common requirements—evacuation and medical assistance—generally applicable to any one of these emergencies; that is, we plan more frequently for disasters as a whole, not specifically for an earthquake.

We can also budget for these short-lived events. The American Red Cross, for example, has a special fund, to be described further in Chapter 17, earmarked exclusively to be used in "disasters." Funds in this account can be used for several types of disasters.

In conclusion, life cycles determine how we plan, the duration of the plan, its contents, and how we budget for it. They do not determine if we should plan. Planning is a form of risk management.

PLANNING PERIOD

This brings us to a more formal treatment of the concept of a "planning period." Every strategic plan should have a predetermined life cycle. Each program in the plan should have its own planning period, which may be coterminous with the program life. But for the organization as whole the planning period should be independent of the life of any one program.

The planning period is the time over which a plan is expected to last before it must be formally reviewed and revised. A strategic plan may be a five-, ten-, or fifteen-year plan.[9] It gives the long-range view. The longer the range, however, the more important that it be divided up into short-range perspectives. Below we shall discuss milestones related to this concept. The point is that a set of targets should be set for each year in a fifteen-year plan. And at the end of each year, actual performance should be measured against these targets and revisions should be made. Each major planning period should involve an assessment of needs consistent with the mission of the organization.

CONDUCTING NEEDS ANALYSIS

To make needs analysis useful, the nonprofit should do a lot of upfront work. Perhaps the following paragraphs will help. Begin with a clear picture of what the mission of the organization is. It makes no sense to discover needs that are outside your mission. You cannot address them unless the mission is changed or the organization is willing to risk losing its exemption.

Select a group of stakeholders. These are people who can be affected by the organization positively or negatively. They include community people, staff, trustees, and members. Brainstorm in a disciplined manner so that the conversation does not flip flop or touch every irrelevant issue. Listen particularly to the members and the community. In the final analysis the organization exists to serve them. Phrase the question that they should address something like the following: This organization, the Paula-Lugardes-Lewis Art Center, exists to advance awareness and appreciation of the arts in the southern states. Can you tell us some specific ways in which we might do precisely that?

Notice that the question is constrained, yet it gives people an opportunity to think and to recommend—but within the framework of the mission of the organization. Think of this question for a moment; there are an infinite number of possible recommendations. "Southern" covers a number of states. One state or a combination might be the new market—perhaps just the largest cities or small towns. "Arts" covers a number of fields—modern, dance, music, Byzantine, vocal, instrumental (and there are numerous types of instruments). Moreover, the target population can be the elderly, the Indians (and there are many tribes), minorities (of any or a combination of descriptions), children (preschool, elementary, high school), or the mentally or physically impaired.

From these "needs," create a list. The list ought to be unpurged. Have this same group and some additional persons representing the same stockholders rank the recommendations after first trying to combine them. Listen to the arguments and record them. Prepare a listing by rank with some of the reasoning under each rank. Get this same group or some other to review and ratify what you have done.

Now have your staff review it. Warning: Staff should not be assumed to be objective and it should not necessarily be viewed as the most informed. To do this is simply to defeat the purpose of having others who have a stake express their points of view. Many of these persons are daily witnesses to the problems and have frontline information. The most precious input of staff is that it can assess what it would take to accomplish any of the needs–objectives gleaned from the steps mentioned previously and highlight the possible impact on the organization of each item on the menu of needs, at least from the operational perspective. This is precious. It is a way of assessing internal capabilities and organizational risks.

With this information, have an executive-level meeting in which all these bits of information are narrowed and made comprehensible for policy-level decision by a board of trustees that cannot possibly handle all the details. This means that the executives must be willing to express their choices—at least to make recommendations or helpful comments, even subjective ones.

The role of the CEO is not to ignore subjective information but to put it into perspective. Why? Because failure to do so is to put inaccurate, incomplete, and sometimes misleading information before a board of trustees so that planning is incomplete.

This is worth a short deviation. Suppose an operational manager opposes a new program. Suppose that the reason she does so is because she knows that the consequence of its adoption would be that resources would be shifted from her program. This view may be disguised in her comments. But can it be ignored just because it is self-serving? No. The point of fact is that part of the judgment that the organization has to make is the opportunity cost. Is it worth shifting those resources in terms of the activities that will be given up by her group? Moreover, is the gap that will remain worth filling? Does it negatively affect other parts of the organization in terms of their ability to perform?

Finally, the material should be put before the board of trustees. They should vote on the needs that the nonprofit will address as part of its mission.

What is accomplished through this process? The organization reduces the risk of straying from its mission. It involves the community and membership that it exists to serve. Surely, this has political and public relations value, but the bigger value is that the organization becomes more relevant and gains wider internal and external support. The staff had an opportunity to assess its capabilities and to express its views. The trustees have met their responsibility, and the organization has met its responsibility to the trustees. Insight is gained.

Now, armed with this information, the organization can do a structured survey if thought necessary. It can focus on asking respondents about the needs that the organization is willing and able to meet. Such a survey, if conducted, should permit the respondents to express orders of preference or strength of needs. For example, which of these do you least (or most) need? Which of these needs are currently being adequately met?

SETTING PRIORITIES: AN ILLUSTRATION

Setting priorities is difficult when there is no framework. Let me share an experience. Many years ago, I was assigned to developing priorities for the educational system of a developing country. A thorough study had been done of the system and a list of over thirty recommendations was made. The Ministry of Education had indicated that it could not respond to all the recommendations because resources were limited. Which should it give priority?

To answer this question, we formed a team of four officials from the ministry who knew the system and understood how it functioned and knew the priorities of the government and the political realities. We proceeded as follows:

1. We spent the first few days discussing how the system works. This provided a common reference for our thinking.

2. We concluded that a working hypothesis is that the overall priority of the educational system was to improve the quality of people and their productivity in the work force—economic development.

3. We designed a simple flow chart of how the system in step 1 works to accomplish the objective in step 2. This is represented in Figure 6.8. Being simple, the flow chart is workable and does not become an issue in itself; rather it becomes a tool. A hammer is a simple tool that does marvelous work. The chart shows both the linear and collateral relationships of how a student flows through the system into the work force. Thus, we identify impact points.

4. We now placed each of the thirty recommendations in the box representing the impact point in which it is most appropriate. Some recommendations belonged in more than one box.

5. We set the order that the recommendations within each box must take in order for the box to fulfill its mission; what is the order necessary for technical schools to produce a better student?

6. Based on step 6, we had the priority for each box. Based on the flow chart, we had the priority for the system. We have solved both si-

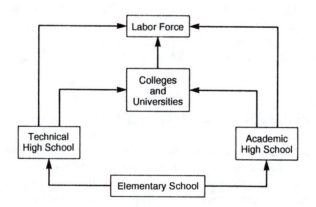

Figure 6.8   Flow Chart for Priority Setting.

multaneously. Because the people who did it were the officials responsible, we had agreement that respects reality. Thus, the final step.

7. Is the result practicable? Is it acceptable? After making any adjustments for the answers to these questions, we wrote our final report. It was the product of a consultant facilitating the decisions of people responsible for turning a plan into priorities, policy, and ultimately practice.

MONITORING FOR PERFORMANCE

We monitor the flow of relevant information in a timely fashion to enable decision making and to provide information that must be incorporated in reports, whether to the trustees, funding agency, or to the government or regulatory body, such as the annual report alluded to in Chapter 1. Through adequate monitoring, the organization can determine when to shift course, intensify, or keep going as is. See the life-cycle discussion in this chapter. It can also take corrective action. Monitoring should be done in the most efficacious way possible, for collecting and processing information is costly.

To appreciate what is involved in monitoring, let us presume an organization such as that shown in Figure 6.9. Every method of monitoring depends on the size and complexity of the organizational structure, the volume and scope of the activities it conducts, the frequency with which it conducts each, the extent to which the information is required for managerial as well as public reporting purposes, and so on. Therefore, there is no one best way. Figure 6.9 helps us to focus on this situation.

A, B, C and D, E, F are on the operating level. Their managers are equivalent, but they supervise distinctly different, but related activities. A, B, C are more like each other than like D, E, F, and therefore they

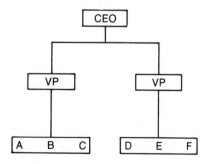

Figure 6.9 Organizational Chart.

are grouped accordingly and report to a different vice-president. The fact that A, B, C are alike does not mean that they do the same thing, have the same external reporting requirements, or are funded in exactly the same way. A, B, C may, for example, be three separate wards in a children's hospital.

The data needed on this operational level are basically information that permits each operation (or each program) to be carried out efficiently. How often these data must be collected and in what form depends partly on the nature of the activity. In a hospital ward, the head nurse needs to take inventory of the medicines, the operating level of each piece of equipment, bed vacancies, turnover of patients, and so on. Furthermore, this level of monitoring occurs at least three times a day, upon the change of each shift. While a considerable amount of these data may be quantitative, some are also qualitative, such as reporting the status of patients and noteworthy turns in their condition. Basically, the data are operational rather than financial. Each of the three wards (A, B, and C) dealing with orthopedic services will report similar types of data, while each of the three wards dealing with cardiac services (D, E, F) will do roughly the same—but differing to the extent that each is specialized.

But the flow is not one way. As each feeds its information up to its supervisor, the vice-president, information must be fed backward. The backward flow should give each manager a trend, an average, and a per unit cost. This information does not have to be daily or even weekly. Monthly may be sufficient. These figures are intended to give the operational manager some picture of performance over time. Is it on par, deteriorating, or improving? The figures are also intended to give these managers some insight as to the cost of their operation. To the extent that there is the possibility of discretion, the manager can contemplate alternatives for reducing the cost of his or her operation.

On the level of the vice-presidents, a different type of information is needed to monitor the activities being overseen. Not only are the numbers generated by the lower levels important, but they must be compared if possible. The manager must also obtain data to monitor the markets for what is being offered by his or her units, how well these units are integrated, whether one has excess capacity and the other is idle, which needs additional persons or machines. In short, the level and kind of information needed tends to be almost equally weighted between physical numbers and dollars. The objective is not simply to determine levels of activities, but to choose among reporting operations, difficult as this might be.

In doing their job, the vice-presidents also need information flowing back from the top. This information should emphasize at least three things: (1) changing legal, marketing, and financial realities of the organization as a whole and their implications for each vice-president's operations; (2) the financial, public relations, and marketing impact on the organization of those activities for which each vice-president is responsible (that is, how they generate overhead cost), and (3) the need to meet the mission of the organization.

The top officer of the organization has the responsibility for keeping the organization relevant. Perhaps the low intake rate for the cardiac service has to do with competition or the narrowness of the service area of the hospital. What changes are appropriate? If the service area is too narrow, is it cost effective to have three or zero wards? Is it cost effective to have to have certain types of specialized but low-volume cardiac services? What is the cost to the overall organization—not just in dollars, but in opportunities lost or, as we shall call it in Chapter 15, opportunity cost? Is the organization properly financed so that there are sufficient funds for the operational-level staff to do their job? And, an often overlooked factor among nonprofit managers, to what risks (including the possible loss of exemption) are the operational, supervisory, and top-level persons exposing the organization?

Thus, the central objective of the monitoring by the top-level persons is to keep the organization alive and well, both financially and legally. It is also to keep it relevant. This completes the flow upward and downward, because the basic source of all such information is the operational-level persons—the nurses, social workers, classroom teachers, and counselors. It is their reports as conformed to organization purpose by the vice-presidents that tell what and how much the organization is doing, how successfully, and the market reaction. They provide frontline intelligence.

The vice-presidents add to this by translating some information to dollars, by showing trends within the organization and comparable organizations, and by recommending through qualitative judgments courses of action or causes for concern.

When a nonprofit fails on the operational level, it is useless, because the basic purpose of a nonprofit, unlike a firm, is not to advance individuals as proprietors or to accumulate wealth through investments, but to advance public welfare. To be useful, it must serve a meaningful public purpose; it must do something of public value. The reader may wish to turn to the discussion of variance analysis in Chapter 15. It is a form of keeping tally and setting off alarms when performance is being monitored.

Monitoring for Planning

Monitoring the activities of A, B, C and E, D, F has planning purposes, some of which were mentioned, for example, the life cycle of activities and the shifting of resources among operational units. But monitoring has other planning dimensions. Imagine, for example, that the organization has a meeting or convention facility. Monitoring helps to determine peak and low levels of use. Therefore, the allocation of personnel, vacation time, special marketing efforts are all more intelligently planned for if data are available that reveal trends and patterns. Monitoring provides data for short- and long-term planning. Monitoring for planning is sometimes equivalent to finding the life-cycle of a product or service. The cable and transportation engineer near your intersection or traffic light are monitoring to plan traffic patterns and the signal cycle. By sitting there all day, they can plot traffic size by time of day; i.e., the shape of the life cycle curves discussed earlier.

Monitoring for Risks and Control

A program should be monitored in order to ascertain whether proper controls are being applied, whether there is conformity with established rules and regulations and whether new ones are needed. Monitoring for risk management helps to uncover potential problems and to develop policies for dealing with them.

When we start a recreational program, build a swimming pool, start a new treatment, have a new exhibit, remove a gate—all of these create and change our risk exposure. Moreover, our risks change as we and others learn more about what we are doing. If we keep records in a hospital, there is a risk of confidentiality just as there is in a school and in the military. Are our procedures adequate? If we are running a museum is the security sufficient? A building inspector, whether it be for asbestos, fire hazard, or building code violations is implementing a risk management policy in no less a critical way than a nurse who monitors the progress of a patient to stabilize his or her condition, or the food inspector who is concerned with the quality of the food we eat. The answers sought through risk management and monitoring are variations on the same theme: What shall we do to avoid a problem? What are new developments in the administration of the organization or program that affect our risk exposure? What shall we do?

Monitoring and Marketing

Monitoring also helps in marketing. Who uses the service of the nonprofit and therefore to whom must it reach out? What time is the service used and by whom and for what purpose? Are they satisfied? Are there improvements to be made? Therefore, what service shall the organization offer to whom? What is its best message in a marketing campaign? We shall say more about marketing in the next two chapters. Let us close this discussion of monitoring by saying that it should be more than collecting data for data's sake.

EVALUATION AND REPORTING

There are several good works on evaluation. We need not repeat the literature here. But evaluation is important, and we have tersely discussed cost–benefit analysis in this chapter and will touch on other techniques when we discuss budgeting in Chapter 15. What we wish to do here is view evaluation from the perspective of the chief executive officer of most nonprofits. Rarely, and for some never, do they have the time or resources to conduct comprehensive textbook evaluations. What then to do?

The simplest way to conduct an evaluation is to set milestones in physical and dollar units and also in terms of customer satisfaction at the very outset of the program. For example, if enrollment declines in a day-care center with no evidence that the population of eligible children has declined, and there is no physical obstacle to the students getting to school, this is indeed an inkling of disapproval by somebody and certainly of a probable problem. The failure of a play to attract an audience or to woo the critics is also a measure of dissatisfaction, no matter how misguided.

At the end (and intermittently as a monitoring objective), compare what actually happened with what was planned. This device may seem too simple to suit some analysts; but the fact is that when CEOs are called forth to justify their programs before their trustees, the public, or their funding agencies, there is no time to do complex analyses. The question is simple: What did you do with the money? The answer cannot be "Wait, let me do a cost–benefit analysis."

Try this technique. At the outset, list a set of benefits or outcomes that are reasonably attainable. These should be separated into direct and indirect. The number of welfare mothers attending a class is a direct outcome of a program aimed at training mothers on welfare. That so many got jobs may be an indirect effect if the program was only to train, not also to place. In setting targets, put the emphasis on the direct benefits because these are the ones the organization can control and for which it is ultimately accountable. Try to report direct and indirect benefits in numbers, not narratives.

Place targets on the costs of running the program and also on required revenues. This should be relatively easy because no funding agency will give you money unless this is forthcoming. These costs should also be classified as direct or indirect. We shall go into these more carefully in Chapter 15 when we discuss budgeting. At this point, let it suffice to think of direct costs as those that the organization would not have had if your program were not adopted. And let us call indirect costs overhead. In short, at the outset you must determine how much the program will cost. At the end of the program, compare these costs, and do so intermittently for monitoring purposes. If the two are way off, you should be concerned.

Finally, prepare a narrative. This is the opportunity to tell your story in words that should not all be apologetic. Part of the narrative is to help the reader and planners for the next round of planning to understand what is behind the numbers. For example, cost might have risen because of the Iraqi invasion of Kuwait and the subsequent embargo. It may be that to enroll one welfare mother is to also incur costs of transportation, baby sitting, and so on, that might have been unplanned for but later authorized with no supplemental budgeting. It may be that because of funding delays the program got off to a slow start. Do not fail to evaluate and report surprises. They form the basis of new programs, directions, and risk avoidance.

Why do we suggest trying to report numbers? Compare the effects of alternative reporting of exactly the same event, which is that 100 families were served three meals a day from January 1 to December 31:

1. We fed 100 families during the year.
2. We served an average of 9000 meals per month.
3. We served 108,000 meals.
4. We served 324,000 meals.
5. We prepare and serve hot meals to needy families.

Alternative 1 is not only the least impressive, but it is the most subject to error. How large is each family? Is it the same family that gets the meal day after day? Are there different families? How about single persons? Alternative 5 has a lot of emotion, but it does not communicate that the organization is doing very much. Alternative 4 may seem large but it is the most informative, impressive, and accurate. Try multiplying 100 × 3 meals a day × 30 average number of days per month × 12 months in a year × 3, the average size of a family. Poor families tend to be larger than the 3 in the formula, but this is offset by single, elderly persons. So 3 is not bad. Put yourself in the position of the funding agency. Having this number affords easy calculation. Let us put a figure of $3 per meal. Now, we have the minimum basis of a grant, $972,000.

The following shows how Volunteers of America, the Salvation Army, and Catholic Charities report their accomplishments. Even for the most charitable organizations, results are quantifiable.

Catholic Charities: Services to Children, Adults, Aging Persons, and Families

Services Provided	Children		Adults		Aging Persons		Total Persons Served	Total Families Served
	Dioceses	Persons Served	Dioceses	Persons Served	Dioceses	Persons Served		
Counseling	113	198,064	120	343,238	103	58,072	599,374	215,436
Pregnancy	108	25,006	108	43,169	—	—	68,175	25,065
Adoption	94	12,859	91	46,547	10	3,275	62,861	41,027
Refugee/immigration	86	41,646	95	158,973	65	13,891	214,500	52,146
Education	72	243,384	84	217,889	48	65,761	527,034	79,707
Socialization	51	316,729	47	75,066	55	354,049	745,884	108,595
Food	65	809,687	74	2,774,885	62	310,768	3,895,340	680,956
Emergency/crisis	91	566,897	98	1,419,861	82	231,462	2,218,220	693,526
Support	62	80,125	75	316,188	69	138,387	534,700	300,259
Housing	48	17,896	61	42,339	50	16,017	76,252	14,905
Out-of-home care	102	518,135	70	159,179	40	114,893	181,207	19,492
Total		2,830,428		5,597,334		1,306,575	9,123,547	2,231,114

Source: Annual Survey, 1989, Catholic Charities, p. 3. Reprinted by permission.

Volunteers of America Services to People

In fiscal year 1988–89, Volunteers of America served 540,566 people.

Program Services	# People	Percentage
Food, Clothing and Shelter	270,283	50.00%
Family Life	133,731	24.73%
Health and Rehabilitation	120,213	22.23%
Corrections	8,846	1.63%
Volunteer Programs	2,679	0.50%
Employment Services	2,607	0.50%
Education	2,207	0.43%
Total	540,566	100%

Source: Annual Report, 1989, Volunteers of America. Reprinted by permission.

The Salvation Army National Corporation

Statistical Highlights for the Year		Spiritual Ministry	
Seasonal assistance (Individuals who received assistance during Thanksgiving and Christmas)	6,475,199	Decisions for Christ	115,325
		Corps (church) membership	445,556
		Officers (ordained clergy)	5,413
		Corps community centers (churches)	1,122
Meals served in Salvation Army programs	57,705,273	Total centers of operation	9,912
Lodging for homeless people	5,611,400		
Correctional services (inmates visited)	196,908	Social Ministry	
		Volunteers	1,152,480
Individuals visited (in institutions)	5,519,558	Hours of service	13,542,070
Rehabilitation center days' care	3,602,932	Job referrals	61,915
Adult and child days' care	1,828,911	Missing persons (number located)	2,984
Religious publication	16,429,175	Community Centers: Boys/girls club participants	18,922,913
Broadcast (radio/TV) minutes	412,798		

Source: Annual Report, 1989, Salvation Army, p. 15. Reprinted by permission.

SUMMARY AND CONCLUSIONS

This chapter has examined strategic planning as a process that can be used by managers of nonprofit organizations to identify unmet needs, to assess the ability of their organizations to meet those needs, given both internal and external constraints, to develop strategies and programs, and to make necessary evaluations and adjustments. Chapter 7 takes us from process to content.

NOTES

1. See the references following this chapter.
2. U.S.C.A., 9th #88-15490, February 27, 1990.
3. William Meyers, "The Nonprofit: Drop the 'Non[1]," *New York Times,* Nov. 24, 1985, Section 1, p. 8.
4. There is no pretense that some sectors of the nonprofit world have barriers to entry. Schools, hospitals, and day-care centers must meet zoning and licensing requirements, for example.
5. These are Sherman antitrust laws that are referred to in other chapters of this book, including Chapter 7.
6. Recall that each of these circles represents a maximum frontier. Each represents a point superior to the receding circle and can only be reached by the combination of policies indicated. The situation is analogous to production frontiers in economic theory of production; those frontiers are technically circles. The "prisoners dilemma" is usually presented in a matrix. The intent in this chapter is not to present a discussion of the dilemma, but to use the principle rather than a theoretical discussion of it.
7. See the references, in particular the work by Mason and Mitroff and the sections dealing with nominal group theory.
8. The Academy for Contemporary Problems, now the Academy for State and Local Governments, was owned and operated on behalf of the Council of State and Local Governments, International City Management Association, National Association of Counties, National Conference of State Legislatures, National League of Cities, and the U.S. Conference of Mayors.
9. I know of no study of planning horizons for nonprofits. Many small cities have twenty-year planning horizons by virtue of local law. These are matched by six-year capital plans and one year operating plans. Herrington J. Bryce, *Planning Smaller Cities* (Lexington, Mass.: Lexington Books, D.C. Heath, 1980), pp. 69–81.

SUGGESTED READINGS

ANTHONY, P. WILLIAM, "Effective Strategic Planning in Nonprofit Organizations," *Nonprofit World Report,* 2, no. 4 (July–Aug. 1984), 12–16.

DeSMIT, J., AND N. L. RADE, "Rational and Non-Rational Planning," *Long-Range Planning,* 13, no. 2 (1980), 82–101.

DOUCETTE, DON, AND BILLIE HUGHES, *Assessing Institutional Effectiveness in Community Colleges,* (Laguna Hills, Calif.: League for Innovation in the Community College, 1990).

MASON, RICHARD O., AND IAN I. MITROFF, *Challenging Strategic Planning Assumptions* (New York: Wiley, 1981).

NUTT, P. C., "A Strategic Planning Network for Nonprofit Organizations," *Strategic Management Journal,* 5, no. 1 (Feb.–Mar. 1984), 57–76.

Public Management Institute, *The Effective Nonprofit Executive Handbook* (Washington, D.C.: Public Management Institute, 1982).

RITTLE, HORST, "Systems Analysis of the First and Second Generations" and "Structure and Usefulness of Planning Information Systems," in Pierre La-Conte, J. Gibson, and A. Rapport, eds., *Human Energy Factors in Urban Planning* (New York: Martinus Nijhoff Publishers, 1982), pp. 35–52 and 53–64.

STEINER, GEORGE A., *Strategic Planning* (New York: Free Press, 1979).

WALKER, J. MALCOLM, "Limits of Strategic Management in Voluntary Organizations," *Journal of Voluntary Action Research,* 12, no. 3, (July–Sept. 1983), 39–55.

WORTMAN, MAX, JR., "A Radical Shift from Bureaucracy to Strategic Management in Voluntary Organizations," *Journal of Voluntary Action Research,* 10, no. 3 (Jan.–Mar. 1983), 62–81.

YOUNG, DENNIS, *Casebook of Management for Nonprofit Organizations* (New York: Haworth Press, 1985).

Chapter 7

The Market: Opportunities and Threats

In Chapter 6, we looked at a procedure for conducting a strategic planning process. We are now concerned with the substance of that process. To do this, we shall use what is called environmental scanning—systematically going through the environment to determine opportunities and threats. We dissect the environment to uncover our relevance and, therefore, our niche.

To be *relevant*, a nonprofit needs to be useful to society. The societal benefits it confers need not be immediate. Therefore, to be operating within its *niche*, the nonprofit must simultaneously (a) have a relevant mission, and (b) run programs that are both feasible and desirable as in our discussion in Chapter 6.

THE IMPORTANCE OF IDENTIFYING NEW NICHES IN OLD MISSIONS

To understand what this chapter is all about, first recall our discussion in the last chapter on life cycles of programs. Then read the following:

> Goodwill's strength lies in its ability to train people to meet **real, identified** labor needs in the community . . . Goodwill's service programs have changed with the changing times, and will continue to do so.   The 1989 Goodwill Industries Annual Report: Reprinted by permission.

> While Goodwill's traditional "client" population has been people with physical, mental or emotional disabilities, the people Goodwill serves today increasingly includes those who face other disadvantaging conditions—illiteracy, a history of substance abuse, advanced age, or a history of welfare dependency and an accompanying lack of work experience. As labor needs change and as the United States continues to face a critical labor shortage, Goodwill will be there to provide training and to help match the work to the job.[1]

Or consider a shorter version from **Public Policy 1988–1989**, a publication that lays out the public policy agenda of the YWCA, the section entitled "Optimum Functioning of the Economy":

> "The interdependent functioning of the economy affects women as workers, consumers and mothers. . . . We therefore support . . . adequate guidance and counseling services, training and retraining opportunities at every level for women and girls confronted with new demands and new opportunities in the work world. . . .[2]

The preceding statements reveal (1) a concern for change and a strategy for adjustment to it by the organization, (2) a relevance of the organization to the larger world of which it is a part, (3) programs that are marketable because they are relevant to a larger changing world, and (4) programs that are consistent with the mission of the organizations. Dynamic organizations adjust to changing environments.

In this text, it is not possible to take apart culture, politics, international relations, and the like. Instead, we choose to focus on the economy because it is so central to the environment in which nonprofits throughout the world function. We shall systematically dissect the economy with the purpose of asking what relevance does each part have for our own nonprofit organization. This is what environmental scanning is all about and the central lesson of this chapter. Please go back to Table 2.1. Note the number of specific purposes that relate to the economy. How does your organization fit? Why is it relevant?

We shall close the chapter showcasing how nonprofits, recognizing their market relevance, enter into joint ventures or other strategic alliances with for-profit firms. This expands the limited capacity of the nonprofits and enables them to discharge their missions.

ECONOMIC PURPOSE OF NONPROFITS

A recent study of 106,449 nonprofits, less than 10 percent of the total nonprofit organizations in the country, found their total assets in 1985 to be $423,544,289,000.[3] This is large. What is the purpose?

Attempting to find a theoretical foundation for the laws on nonprofits, legal scholars have turned to economics. One argument is that nonprofits exist because of "contract failures."[4] This means that there are a number of situations where the purchaser is uncertain of the quality of product or service that a for-profit producer would provide. The producer is seen to be motivated by profits and not necessarily by what is in the best interest of the public. Under these conditions, some contracts with a for-profit firm would fail. In these cases, a nonprofit is said to be superior to a for-profit producer because it has no profit motive, just the single mission or purpose of improving the welfare of the public.

This view is sometimes seen as too narrow. Thus, another legal scholar takes the view that the economic role of a nonprofit is that sometimes it is in the best interest of the customers to own the producers.[5] This view rests on the idea that customers often find among themselves a mutual or common interest that cannot be appropriately satisfied by the market. In such a case, through a nonprofit mode they can join together to produce the product or service themselves. Thus, in the case of a day-care center, a group of working mothers may join together to create a cooperative center responding to their specific needs and desires for the kinds of services they wish for their children. In the normal operation of the market, they cannot control the production process; they can only choose among alternative offerings, none of which may be satisfactory.

Even the view of nonprofits as collectives or voluntary associations to exercise individual beliefs or expressions (the First Amendment) is consistent with economic theory.[6] The economic theory of collectivity argues that people come together in groups or collectives because of interdependencies, or what is known as externalities and economies of scale. An externality in economics means that the action of one person affects another person. For example, a thousand persons of the same religious belief may not only find greater religious satisfaction by worshiping together, but they would find it cheaper to build a house of worship in which they all worship together rather than for each person to build a house of worship.

As a matter of fact, an article appearing in the *Foundation News* suggested that the world of nonprofits be viewed as an economic world of competitive institutions and that, to the extent that some nonprofits view themselves as competitors to each other, the better each would be.[7]

The upshot of these other views is that not only is there justification for viewing the nonprofit as an economic institution, but there is justification for viewing nonprofits as a group of players in a mixed economy. As we shall see, traditional economic theory as well as current practices by the IRS and the courts are supportive.

The reasons for articulating the role that nonprofits play in the economy are more than theoretical. Nonprofits do play a central role in the market economy. Even in its symbolic core, the stock market, nonprofits are major holders of stocks and debt. They were also major sources of funds in leverage buyouts as well as major beneficiaries as the value of endowment portfolios appreciated as raiders bidded for stocks they held. They were also major losers in the October 1987 decline. Furthermore, the National Association of Security Dealers (NASD) regulates security dealers and brokers and carries the most up-to-date and complete price quotations on the over-the-counter stock exchange. NASD is a nonprofit, although not a 501(c)(3). Finally, and our focus in this chapter, the market economy generates endless opportunities and threats (competition) to nonprofits. Let us deal first with opportunities.

SYMBIOTIC RELATIONSHIP

A good starting point of any environmental scanning exercise focusing on the economy is to acknowledge that the economy is mixed. The public sector relies on the private sector. It is the latter that produces the goods and services, creates income, and makes the profits that are taxed as corporate and personal income taxes, which are the two major sources of revenues of the public sector. One way in which the public sector uses its revenues from taxation is to support nonprofits through contracts and grants.

The support that nonprofits get from nongovernmental sources comes from individuals and firms. Individuals can make gifts and contributions because they earn an income from the for-profit sector that pays its own workers and supplies the revenues that government uses to pay its workers. These workers, both in the public and private sectors, make contributions and gifts to the nonprofit sector.

The gifts and contributions made by firms to nonprofits come from their income or profits. Hence, whether the support comes from the public sector or individuals or directly from profit makers, the ultimate source is exactly the same: the for-profit firm.

The reliance on the for-profit sector goes beyond support. It extends to opportunities created by the way for-profit firms operate. Opportunities are also created by the limited effectiveness of government action. To detect the new opportunities for nonprofits requires the ability to appreciate two trends: (1) the dynamics of for-profit firms, that is, of the market economy, and (2) the limited effectiveness of government action. To do this requires dissecting the economy and finding niches and linkages. There is a future for those who can visualize cooperative connections.

NONPROFIT OPPORTUNITIES GENERATED BY THE MARKET ECONOMY

The market system internally generates and satifies many needs. Often, however, capacity and efficiency considerations mean that for-profit firms cannot fully satisfy all market needs, even though there is no lack of ability to pay on the part of those whose needs must be satisfied. Economic growth creates a demand for sudden increases in capacity, information, and other resources often existing in the nonprofit sector. To fully appreciate this, let us look at the economic behavior of each of the major actors in the market economy. We begin each section by specific real-world examples; then we present the basic theory and show how other opportunities may be generated to the discerning and dynamic management of nonprofits. What is our niche?

Consumers

What can the nonprofit do for the consumer? Try Codes 530 and 204 of Table 2.1 or 905 and 906. Do you see others?

There are several real-world examples of nonprofits intervening in the market process to assist consumers. A nonprofit group was given tax exemption as a charity because it gave education on personal financial management to low-income households.[8] Another nonprofit was similarly classified because it provided guidance and information to low-income households on building their own home.[9] These are examples of nonprofits providing information and education to benefit the community. With the rise of concern for health matters, nonprofits, including the American Heart Association (see Chapter 8), choose to inform consumers about the dangers of certain foods, behaviors, and environments that put people at risk. AIDS education is a good example and so too is *Consumer Reports* and the entire Ralph Nader organization.

How does the economy operate to provide these types of opportunities for nonprofits to assist consumers? What are the points of opportunity for a nonprofit? To spot these, we must know how consumers behave and how the private market responds or affects that behavior. From this general framework, each organization can identify and develop its own point of entry. To make this easier, key words are in bold face. Think of the number of permutations and combinations in which these words can form a mission statement! Can you make a purpose in Table 2.1 qualify? This is what creative nonprofit management must do to remain relevant. It must pinpoint a niche.

A consumer can **buy** a good only if he or she has an **income**. The good will be bought only if its **price** does not exceed the dollar value the consumer places on it; that is, its **utility** to the consumer. The money used to make **purchases** is the earnings of the consumer as a worker.

Consumers are **free** to choose how to spend the income they earn as workers. **Low-income consumers** buy fewer **luxuries** and more **low-priced** or inferior goods, but spend just about the same proportion of their income as higher income persons do on **necessities**, such as food, soap, and shelter.

As do other commodities, soap comes in numerous sizes, shapes, brand names, scents, and chemical compositions. Each of these **characteristics** is represented in the price. Similarly, cars come under different **brand** names with different characteristics, which are reflected in differences in price. Yet one can be **substituted** for another. They all provide the same utility or **use**, transportation, but some more comfortably than others. The same thing holds for soap. All can be used for cleaning, but one gives a more favorable scent than the other.

Hence, if the price of one brand of car or soap **rises**, consumers who want basic **transportation** or cleanliness would buy more of the less expensive brand if it has maintained comparable **quality**. They will behave in this way as long as they are **aware** or have **information** on the prices and the brands they want are **available**. In short, consumer **choice** depends on information as well as income, prices, and the availability of substitutes and complements.

Thus, as the for-profit sector grows, producing goods that are **substitutes** for each other, or **complements** to each other, and some of which are unrelated to each other, the opportunities for nonprofits are also increased. The home computer industry is an example. As for-profit firms produce more models that are really varying degrees of substitutes, there is also a rise in the demand for complements (software), which are also varying degrees of substitutes for each other. This has spawned countless opportunities for nonprofits to provide the computer-related complements of information and education. Carnegie-Mellon, for example, owns a subsidiary that develops and licenses the use of its software to for-profit firms.

Education and training even for a fee (as many educational institution charge) are acceptable functions of nonprofits. Education is defined, for tax-exempt purposes, as instruction, information, and training that benefits an individual and the community.[10] It should be evident from the framework just described that the economy generates an endless number of these opportunities. Hence, the basic question for a nonprofit is which of these varying degrees of consumer needs best meet our mission? How will these needs change?

Producers

Codes 180, 200 and 207 in Table 2.1 are real-world examples of nonprofits assisting producers. One type of nonprofit, called an incubator, is credited with spawning nineteen new corporations, creating over 1800 jobs and $80 million income for a depressed Kentucky community.[11] Incubators are nonprofit organizations that finance, assist, and rent space to a cluster of growing firms so that they can interact and nurture each other.

One of the best examples of a cooperative relationship is between McDonald's and the Environmental Defense Fund (EDF). They formed a team which studied ways to reduce trash. After two years of study, the company reduced its volume of packaging by 80 percent by using new wraps, increased use of recycled paper products, and recycled tires for non-skid surfaces for playlands at the more than 1,700 McDonald's restaurants. McDonald's, in its 1990 Annual Report, continues: It does not own or purchase cattle that has been grown on rain forest land—only on corn and grass (alfalfa). What are the gains for McDonald's? Lower costs, higher profits, greater market share—all while advancing public welfare.

On a smaller scale is an organization that was awarded tax exemption for marketing the cooking and sewing of low-income women. On a larger scale is the organization that does research on color science and technology[12] or the society that was formed to do scientific research on air conditioning and ventilating.[13] On even a larger scale are the universities that conduct research that benefits producers. The most rapidly growing and controversial aspects of this relationship are in pharmaceuticals and biogenetics where the ethical issues concerning professors as described in Chapter 1 and of licensing the use of cultured cells have been, to some, bothersome.

What is the basis of missions that aid producers? How about 230 through 249 in Table 2.1? To maximize their **profits**, **producers** create the mix of goods consumers want at the lowest **cost** possible by using the best **technology** and **workers available** and by **selling** the goods at the highest price consumers will pay in a very competitive world market. Nonprofits have contributed in every phase including product development in agriculture.

Research to develop technology **(R&D)** requires **specialized skills**. Research and development are acceptable functions of nonprofits as long as the results are made public, that is, **disseminated**. A very high percentage of the research and development that eventually leads to commercial **applications** is done at universities and other nonprofit laboratories. This is in fields including engineering, crop development and land conservation, medicine and medical procedures, and science in general. A laboratory can be used for teaching and for product development and testing.

Workers

There are numerous real-world examples of nonprofits assisting workers. Goodwill claims to have placed 17,000 disabled workers in jobs in 1989.[14] The National Urban League showcased 4000 new jobs in its Job Opportunity Showcase in 1989.[15] An organization that provided a registry of available nurses was given tax exemption because the registry was seen as assisting the community to find nurses, rather than the nurses to find jobs.[16] The registry was not viewed as self-promotion of the nurses, in which case it would not have been exempt, but as information to the public. Also, an organization formed to transport low-income workers to jobs due to inadequate transportation was also granted exemption.[17] An organization formed to give career counseling and to distribute educational publications was also granted exemption even though it charged a fee.[18] Day-care centers are granted exemptions if nearly all the child-care service is provided to enable parents to work and if the service is available to the general public.

What are the factors that give rise to opportunities to assist workers? An **individual** in the market economy acting **freely** and **knowledgeably** would **choose** the occupation for which he or she is best suited because this would improve the chances of maximizing the **benefits**, including **income**, and minimizing the **unpleasantness** of work. Once in that **occupation** or **job**, the person would seek to work for the highest-paying producer. And, naturally, the higher the pay is the greater the willingness to work.

This economic behavior of workers depends on a number of factors: having adequate **information** about occupations and employment, having **access** to **training** and to jobs, being **compensated** according to **productivity**, having information and access to **leisure**, and being able to make a rational judgment between leisure and **work**. Meeting these training, informational, **search**, and employment needs is an acceptable function of nonprofits. Codes 566, 126, 159, 568 and 031 in Table 2.1 are examples.

This is precisely what job training schools do. They train and help in job search. Some nonprofits aid older workers, the disabled, veterans, women, and the disadvantaged in career development and in finding jobs.

In this regard, they work to help expand the for-profit sector and to improve its efficiency by training and placing workers. Not only do non-profits train the input necessary for growth, but they can also assist in matching input availability (supply) with demand. Organizations such as the National Black Child Development Institute and the National Urban Coalition begin this process of training early.

Investors

A number of large American corporations have subsidiaries in other countries. Some of these countries place a limit on the extent to which profits earned on their soil can be repatriated back to the United States. These are called blocked currencies. Some nonprofits, especially those concerned with the environment, show what imaginative management can do. Here is the anatomy of a transaction. Remember, the currencies are blocked and cannot leave the foreign country. But the organization has a mission in the country that needs money. So, the nonprofit buys the currency from the American corporation at a discount—less than its value. The American corporation is glad to oblige because it cannot move the currency out of the country anyway, and the longer it holds these blocked currencies the lower their value due to inflation and unfavorable exchange rates. In many of these countries, inflation can get to 1000 percent per year and, with little notice, it can take several hundred if not thousands of their currencies to equal one U.S. dollar.

The nonprofit carries out the transaction by delivering a check to the U.S. home office of the corporation. Thus, the block is overcome. The American corporation gets its dollars in the United States; the nonprofit in the foreign country gets additional funds (the foreign currency it needs to operate in that country) at a bargain; and the foreign government takes a fee for the transaction. Everybody gains. The Salvation Army Worldwide Service Office (SWASO) got blocked funds for some of the 93 countries in which it worked but only if the funds were donated. Some conservation groups got countries and companies to swap debt for the groups right to preserve natural habitats like the Amazon.

There are more simple examples of nonprofits assisting investors. Two examples were given in Chapter 6, both of organizations making loans for business purposes. We show in later sections several nonprofits working hand in hand with for-profit corporations.

Economic growth cannot occur without new **net investment** in **plant** and **equipment**. As economic growth occurs, it stimulates more investment as investors begin to expect acceptable **rates** of **return** on their investments. Producers must borrow to invest because the initial cost of most projects is large. They will **borrow** only if the expected rate of return on their investments equals or exceeds the rate of interest they have to **pay** for borrowed funds. It makes no sense, for example, to borrow at 15 percent and get only a 5 percent return on the investments made.

Nonprofits do have a growing opportunity to affect investment decisions. During the 1980s, nonprofit endowment and pensions were major sources of funds for financing corporate takeovers. Economic development corporations and community development corporations are nonprofits that can make investments that are beneficial to the community, but that for-profit firms will not make because the project is too risky or the rate of return too low.

In addition, these nonprofit corporations can lower the cost to the for-profit firm by putting up seed money, making loans at below market rates, packaging and preparing land, and giving **technical** assistance. By lowering costs, these actions increase the profitability of the project and make it more attractive to private investors. A real case will be presented at the end of this chapter.

Savers

Investment dollars come from the savings of workers. To get more savings for investment, consumers must be encouraged to save by having safe vehicles for saving and earning high rates of interest. Encouraging effective saving strategies through education is an acceptable function of nonprofits. Thus, the organization that assisted low-income households to improve their **money management** was granted tax exemption.[19]

By referring again to Table 2.1, we see that there are types of savings-related institutions, Codes 921, 251 and 565 that are nonprofits. Pension trusts, Code 268, have billions of dollars in assets and are nonprofit organizations. TIAA-CREF, a college retirement fund used by educators, has assets in the tens of billions of dollars. It, too, is a nonprofit.

Deposits to these trusts and pension funds are regular, predictable, and dependable. Withdrawals from these trusts are orderly and extend over many years. Therefore, pension trusts are a primary source of dollars for long-term investment. Mutual insurance companies and credit unions are also examples of nonprofits operating to stimulate saving and to provide loans.

These discussions indicate that within the market structure itself there are potential opportunities for nonprofits to assist (1) consumers, (2) workers, (3) producers, (4) investors, and (5) savers. In a growing economy, these opportunities increase, not decrease. Many of these opportunities exist in the shaded area in Figure 7.1. In this area, nonprofits and for-profit firms may be competitors or collaborators, such as joint partners in research, information dissemination, and community development.

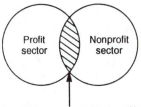

Area of cooperation and competition   **Figure 7.1**   Interaction of Profit and Nonprofit Sectors.

The competition even within the shaded area is limited. It often means that the for-profit and nonprofit corporations divide a market for the same product or service. Constrained by their need to make a profit, the for-profit firms would almost automatically focus on the more profitable segment of the market, while the nonprofit, able to rely on gifts and contributions as supplementary support and being constrained by IRS rules to demonstrate that they are not just another commercial firm but are catering to a clientele that such firms do not reach, will focus on the less profitable segment. Witness the difference between privately owned (for-profit) hospitals and many, admittedly not all, community or nonprofit hospitals. Notice also that this does not necessarily mean economic disaster for the nonprofit. Some nonprofit hospitals do very well compared to for-profit ones.[20]

NONPROFIT OPPORTUNITIES GENERATED BY MARKET FAILURES

Economists use the term externalities to denote the effect that one entity's or person's market behavior has on others.[21] In a market economy, each person or entity acts in a manner to meet his or her economic objectives with only limited regard for its effects on others; that is, the market fails to control the impact that individuals or firms have on society. The existence of these externalities creates a need for nonprofits.

External Diseconomies of Consumption

The use of automobiles (emitting carbon dioxide, making noise, requiring the conversion of open space to roads and highways), flying (noise and air pollution from airplanes), smoking, and the abuse of alcohol and other drugs are said to result in external diseconomies of consumption because they have **harmful** or **deleterious** effects on persons other than the user. When external diseconomies of consumption exist, the obvious reaction is to **curtail** consumption and the negative effects of it. Look at Codes 536 (intoxication), 537 (drugs), 538 (tobacco), 539 (erotica) in Table 2.1.

Governments can impose laws and regulations and may even tax the purchase of the commodity with the hope that the higher price will discourage consumption—the sin taxes. Under certain conditions, such as designating no-smoking areas in public places and in airplanes, the intervention by the public sector may only be partly effective. Experience has shown that public sector actions are not sufficient and often ineffectual. Producers and consumers of products that have strong external diseconomies are usually successful in resisting any truly impeding law or tax, not only by virtue of their political power, but by calling on the constitutional protection of their rights.

Because there are usually **no profits** to be made in restricting consumption resulting in external diseconomies, for-profit firms are usually not attracted to such activities. On the contrary, there are often more profits to be made in the production and sale of commodities and services such as cigarettes, alcohol, and drugs than in curtailing their use. Mothers Against Drunk Driving (MADD) and Alcoholics Anonymous are examples of nonprofits working to solve problems of diseconomies of consumption.

Again, the agreement between the Environmental Defense Fund and McDonald's Corporation alluded to earlier is proof that both nonprofit and for-profits can work together in this area, as well as others. Noting the waste produced by the over 1000 stores, the two agreed to cooperate in formulating conservation strategies. The creation of **waste** (a problem for others) by customers at these and similar stores is a form of external diseconomy of consumption.

If the government taxing and rule-making powers have limited effect, and if the profits to be made in curtailing consumption are also limited, even though curtailing consumption is socially desirable, a natural opportunity then arises for nonprofit organizations. Examples of these are nonprofits using their education and training authority to educate people about the dangers of smoking and drugs, and the organization that received tax-exempt status because it provided funds to owners of cats who could not afford the cost of having the pets spayed or neutered.[22]

The tasks before the management of the nonprofit when external diseconomies exist are (1) to identify the aspect of the external diseconomy which the organization can address, (2) arrive at an appropriate strategy for dealing with it, and (3) use the social merit argument as well as the merits of the organization to justify cooperation and support, as the Environmental Defense Fund did.[23]

External Economies of Consumption

External economies exist when the consumption by any one person of a good or service has a **positive** effect on others. Your use of a deodorant or fragrance is appreciated by others. Vaccinations against communicable diseases benefit both the client and others with whom he or she may come in contact. Many health and educational programs fall into this category; for example, an organization formed to give counseling in employment, citizenship, language, medical information, and housing to immigrants is of this type. The more the immigrants partake of these offerings, the easier their adjustment and the lower the need for social assistance and the possibilities of infractions against the law. Consequently, the entire community is better off.[24] The objective is, therefore, to **increase** such behavior. But who will do it? Perhaps, a nonprofit.

Returning to the case of inoculations, **profits** to be made by inoculating individuals are **limited** by their ability to pay, their awareness of danger, and their willingness or ability to make themselves available for shots. Because it is to the advantage of society to have as many persons as possible inoculated, and because for-profit firms are limited by their need to earn a profit, some needs will remain unmet. One possibility is for the public sector to directly answer these unmet needs. Another is for the public sector to subsidize both for-profit firms and nonprofits so that the unmet needs will be addressed. A third possibility is for the nonprofit to meet these needs by relying on below-market rate fees, using gifts and contributions to make up the difference. Through its normal operation, the economy generates or leaves unanswered a number of consumption externalities or "spillovers," as they are sometimes called, for which fees can be charged by a nonprofit provider.

External Diseconomies of Production

External diseconomies occur when the production process results in **negative** effects on others. Smoke emission from a plant and chemical and industrial wastes dumped in waterways are examples. Economic growth, if only by increasing the rate at which facilities are used, generates diseconomies of production. See Code 351 in Table 2.1, combating air pollution.

One reason external diseconomies of production such as air and water pollution persist is that they bring down the cost of production to the producer. It is cheaper to dump wastes in rivers than to properly dispose of them. In short, producers have limited incentive to **curtail** external diseconomies of production. When such incentive exists, it often is brought about by external forces.

One external force is the government. It can impose fines, taxes, and jail sentences. Another source is for-profit firms that produce substitutes or use substitute methods of production—disposable diapers, biodegradable soap, no-lead paint. The production of substitutes is not enough, as can be seen in the different grades of gasoline. Moreover, the initial force for bringing about change is often a nonprofit movement, as in the fields of environment and energy.

Often there are no profits to be made by discovering these diseconomies, monitoring and reporting them, or even creating solutions to them. Hence, an organization that is **not** constrained by **profit** considerations must often come to the fore. The environmental movement, from monitoring to the development of alternative energy sources, in large measure represents reactions to external diseconomies of production. Thus, when external diseconomies of production exist, a need for nonprofit organizations to reduce them arises perhaps under Codes 350 through 379 or even 203 of Table 2.1 The nonprofit does not have to be in a confrontational position. There are many industry-supported nonprofits that regulate their members. The challenge before the nonprofit management is, again, to answer the three-part question: (1) what is the specific feature of the diseconomy that the nonprofit is capable of addressing, (2) what is the best strategy, and (3) what are the merits upon which funds can be obtained? A specific example of a nonprofit organization that has received tax exemption to meet this challenge is one that was formed to inform the public about the destruction of the environment due to solid-waste disposal and that obtained revenues by collecting and selling solid waste for recycling.[25]

External Economies of Production

External economies arise when the production process of one firm creates **benefits** to other firms. There are benefits that the firm is **incapable of** harnessing and **selling**. Hence, it has very little incentive to produce them at any level greater than what is incidental to its normal production, even though society may benefit from more. As in the case of the consumer, the government could try subsidizing the firm to induce it to do more, but this is expensive. A less expensive way is often to increase the intervention of a nonprofit organization.

As an example, grocery stores always experience spoilage or the need to reduce the price of inventory such as baked goods after they have been on the shelf for some time. A nonprofit, viewing this as an opportunity, entered into an agreement whereby these day-old or damaged foods are distributed by the nonprofit to the poor. Here, what would ordinarily have been a loss is converted to an external economy of production and a social gain. The management of this nonprofit knew (1) where an external economy of production existed or could be created from a potential loss, (2) how the nonprofit and its clients could benefit from it, and (3) how it could raise the very modest support needed. The goods were obtained free and volunteers were used to collect and distribute them. This activity attracted clients to the organization, many of whom purchased commodities received as gifts and sold at bargain prices in its thrift shop, thereby generating revenues.

PURE PUBLIC GOODS AND NONPROFITS

Even though they might be of **inestimable value**, pure public goods are not produced by for-profit firms because the principal characteristic of a pure public good is that, once it is provided, no one can be **excluded** from its enjoyment. Clean air is an example. Once the air is clean, anyone who lives in or visits the vicinity can enjoy it. Because there is no way to exclude anyone, everyone will enjoy it regardless of whether or not he or she is charged or pays a price. Who will voluntarily pay a price for something that can be had without paying? Public goods are sometimes seen as **free** goods to the consumer, even though they are **expensive** to provide.

A corollary characteristic of pure public goods is that they are usually **indivisible**. It is not possible to split them up into units that can be distributed one to an individual. Who will pay for a commodity that cannot be **owned**?

Another corollary of a pure public good is that the consumption by any one individual of that good **does not diminish** the consumption by any other person. When one person breathes fresh air, that does not diminish the amount available to any other person. As a result, there is no bidding because the good does not run out.

These features mean that **pricing** of public goods by a for-profit firm **is impossible**. How can a profit be made on a good that no one is willing to pay a price for? How can a profit be made on a good if ownership cannot be sold? Who will buy it? How can a profit be made if no buyers will bid? Since the pure public good cannot be sold, a profit cannot be made and for-profit firms will not produce them.

Yet there is a cost to producing pure public goods. Clean air is maintained at a cost. Who pays? Generally, the government pays through imposing compulsory taxes and by contracting with or subsidizing for-profit or nonprofit organizations to do the work. Public goods such as clean air are appropriate functions of nonprofits and so too are neighborhood development programs (Codes 400, 401 and 402) and public radio and television (Code 121).

Associations are one type of nonprofits that produce pure public goods on a smaller scale. Associations of employees, employers, counties, and cities are all examples of nonprofits providing public goods. They are listed in Table 2.1. To understand a public good, we only have to see that, once a union wins benefits for workers, those benefits can be enjoyed by workers in the trade or industry regardless of whether or not they are members of the union. This technique is used in automobile and airline negotiations. Unions pick one company to set a pattern. When the American Medical Association fights for and wins a legislative position favorable to doctors, all doctors potentially benefit whether or not they are members of the association.

Associations also provide some private goods. Thus, they can charge a fee for the association's magazine because the magazine is not a public good. As is increasingly the case, members who do not pay a special fee for the magazine will not get it. The magazine is divisible so that many subscribers may be served, each with an individual copy. Members who do not pay conference charges cannot attend; that is, they can be excluded.

On the other hand, the representative effort of the association is a pure public good. No actual or eligible member of the association can be excluded from the representative benefits. Accordingly, associations commonly place a price on some of their activities such as seminars and journals, which are private goods, but not on their representative efforts, which are public goods. These are covered by membership fees.

In the resolutions of the National League of Nursing, we see examples:[26]

A. That the NLN Board of Directors invites . . . in enhancing the image of nurses . . . and in maintaining a climate of respect and dignity for the practicing nurse.

This benefits all nurses, not just members.

B. That NLN, through its education and service membership units, places a priority on supporting . . . underprepared health service employees.

Training and service are individualized.

Both types of goods, public and private, attract members and improve public welfare.

Another example of a nonprofit providing public goods is an organization of physicians that oversees the quality of health care in a particular community.[27] The same is true of an organization created to do improvements on municipally owned property.[28] An organization created to preserve lakes for public recreation is also an example.[29]

In general, public goods offer opportunities for nonprofits because for-profit firms have no price incentive to produce such goods. A price cannot be charged. In this sphere, nonprofits have an advantage because they can charge a general membership fee and also seek additional support in the form of gifts and contributions and special assessments as ways of paying for the public good.

NONPROFIT FINANCING OF PUBLIC GOODS AND RESPONSES TO EXTERNALITIES

Why, it may be asked, would nonprofits be able to find profitable opportunities in externalities and public goods when for-profit firms cannot? The answer is that nonprofits can rely on combined support from individuals, firms, and government and a below-market price to cover costs and produce a surplus. Private firms must rely only on market price.

Does it make sense to speak of reliance on support when such support, at least from the government, is becoming less reliable? This means that nonprofits must increase their persuasion and diversify their revenue base, a major subject of the next section of this book.

Why would an individual give to a nonprofit that produces a public good or responds to an externality when neither may be particularly profitable? The answer is that "giving" is only limitedly related to economic considerations. Moreover, an activity might have too low a return to attract a particular investor. Yet that investor could reap significantly high tax savings and public goodwill by making a contribution to a nonprofit that would make the investment. Indeed, the individual may be a beneficiary of the mission of the nonprofit.

NONPROFITS AND MARKET MONOPOLY

The best way to visualize this subject is to think of medicine, and one of the best examples is AIDS. A company has exclusive rights to produce and to market a medical device or cure. It has monopoly power. It can therefore set prices as high as it wishes. The result is that only a few persons have availability to the product or cure; and many of these for only a short period because their resources will soon be totally depleted. This situation would be described by economists as one in which social benefits exceed the amount that can be satisfied at high monopoly prices.

The government can break up the monopoly. But this is hard to do, expensive, and time-consuming in litigation. It can encourage nonprofits to enter the market either by producing a competitive "generic" product or cure or by taking over one of the logistical functions, such as distribution, which would lower cost. Either way, the role of the nonprofit is to produce social benefits by being an alternative to the monopoly. Many life-saving products will be financed on the strength of this reasoning. The nonprofit is used to reduce monopoly power.

NONECONOMIC CONSEQUENCES OF MARKET BEHAVIOR AND OPPORTUNITIES FOR NONPROFITS

As the market system functions, it produces a number of noneconomic consequences. One is inequity. The market system pays people only if they work. Pay is determined by the value of the contribution of the worker to the value of the final product. Some individuals are unable to work for reasons of disability or age. In a strict market economy, only those who work are able to consume because only they will have income with which to make purchases. Moreover, in a strict market economy, people who are less productive than others would not only be paid less than others but may very well be paid below the amount necessary to afford a socially accepted minimum standard of living. Thus, poverty is consistent with a market economy. There are both working and non-working poor.

The consequence of this is that many persons are not able to afford even basic necessities. The most efficient market economy distributes income according to productivity, not according to need. A producer cannot pay purely by need. A producer can pay according to the value of the product the worker produces, since this is the main source of revenues for the producer. For-profit firms do not get gifts and contributions.

But equity and the needs of individuals cannot be ignored in any humane society. Consequently, there are organizations such as the Samaritan Ministry of Greater Washington, a partnership of thirty-one Episcopal churches with the goal "to provide services to persons in need which enable self-sufficiency, independence and dignity." A mission such as this is clearly noncommercial.

Because revenues place a limit on what firms can pay, a need arises for an entity that is not limited by its earnings. Nonprofits are not so limited. They have other sources of support—gifts and contributions. Therefore, nonprofits are very suited for dealing with issues of equity.

Admittedly, the dimension of the equity problem may be too large for the nonprofit sector alone or for any one specialty within the nonprofit sector. Note the number of codes in Table 2.1 that are reserved for making life fair. This is why understanding these complex problems is important.

SOCIALLY COMPLEX PROBLEMS AND THE NEED FOR NONPROFITS

Whether opportunities appear within or outside the perimeters of the market system, they are likely to present themselves as complex problems. In the view of Horst Rittle, complex does not mean difficult. A complex problem is one that is (1) subject to many definitions, (2) with each definition requiring a unique set of solutions, (3) with each solution creating its own set of side problems, and (4) with each of these side problems (like the original problem) subject to many definitions and solutions and so on in a circular fashion.

Rittle describes these problems in terms of energy and the urban environment. Using a similar approach, we can see that poverty is a complex problem. It has many facets, including health, education, nutrition, employment, legal, and cultural. Each aspect presents a set of specialized challenges; that is, the legal questions are different from the medical and nutritional factors. Each set of specialized solutions represents a role for a special type of nonprofit. Having undertaken the challenges of one solution, a new set of problems arises. For example, setting up a health clinic does not solve the problem of getting people to attend, but it does create the need for a link between their social and health needs.

Moreover, the very definition of poverty is temporal and spatial; that is, the poverty level for an urban family of four is different from that of a similar family in a rural area. The poverty threshold changes every year, and the cash definition of poverty is different from the cash-plus-assistance-received definition.

The point is that a truly complex problem creates a wide range of interrelated needs, with each set of needs requiring a different specialty and with each specialty requiring an organization with a specialized mission. All complex problems are not purely charitable, but even noncharitable complex problems create the need for nonprofits.

The production and use of automobiles, nuclear plants, and a residential development are truly complex problems and create a need for nonprofits, partly because of the externalities as we discussed them and partly because of the creation of pure public goods. An automobile is a private good that creates external diseconomies of consumption through gas emission and reckless driving. It also gives rise to public goods, such as the creation of antidrunk-driving nonprofits. Complex problems, obviously, are also related to the operation and growth of the economy.

Imaginative management of nonprofits requires the ability to detect the existence of a complex problem, to systematically dissect it, and to identify the aspects of the complex problem that the organization can adequately address within its mission and resource capabilities.

OPPORTUNITIES FOR PROFITABLE COOPERATION BETWEEN NONPROFIT AND FOR-PROFIT CORPORATIONS

In the previous section, we showed how nonprofits may intervene in the market process to carry out their charitable missions while at the same time earning revenues and public support because they are relevant. To do this, it is not necessary and often is not advisable for the nonprofit to go it alone or to try to compete with for-profit firms. This section demonstrates several levels of cooperation that can benefit both the for-profit firms and the nonprofits. But why would these for-profit firms and nonprofits have any incentive to cooperate with each other?

Every successful partnership requires the intermeshing of interests among the parties involved. Chapter 3 makes it clear that a nonprofit may make a profit, but it must be used to carry out the charitable purpose of the organization. Thus, the dominant motive is public welfare, not private profits. However, for-profit firms are driven by the profit motive, not public welfare. A profit is a possible shared interest even though its use, once obtained, may vary.

The successful partnership combines the interests of the nonprofit as an economic institution that needs revenues to conduct its mission with that of for-profit firms that need markets from which to derive a profit. The market is composed of the clients and potential clients of the nonprofits. Thus, by serving the clients or mission of the nonprofit, revenues are generated for both the for-profit and nonprofit partners.

What makes these arrangements possible is that neither the for-profits nor nonprofit organization disagrees about the need for revenues. Both are interested in containing costs and in a good public image, and both are economic institutions, but neither maximizes profits.[30] Herbert Simon, a Nobel prize winner, noted that firms engage in "satisficing" rather than in maximizing profits. By this he means that for-profit managers try to accommodate a number of competing constituencies both within and outside the firm, and that this attempt to satisfy rarely leads to maximum performance.

For any partnership to succeed, all parties must contribute something. What the nonprofits contribute is their advantage in meeting certain needs that the regular commercial market cannot profitably satisfy. This advantage derives basically from the following:

1. Nonprofits can sell a product or service at a lower price than for-profit firms can because nonprofits can subsidize their lower price by gifts and contributions.

2. Nonprofits often have a built-in clientele, not only from their membership but from the fact that the relationship that people develop with these organizations is rarely based solely on the quality of product or services they produce or the price at which they sell them.

3. Nonprofits are in a better position to lower costs of production by using volunteers, by obtaining plant and equipment as gifts, by lower postage rates (often challenged by postal authorities), and by not having to pay taxes under certain very circumscribed conditions, even when they run a business for profit.

4. Nonprofits such as research organizations often hold licenses or patents that can be used by for-profit firms to produce a product or service while providing the nonprofits with revenues in the form of nontaxable royalties. We shall say more about this in Chapter 11. A relevant example here is the licensing of use of software by for-profit firms by nonprofits such as universities.

For-profit firms have no such advantages, but they can deduct interest and other operating expenses from their taxes, they can subtract depreciation in calculating their taxes, and, prior to the 1986 tax reform, they could take an investment tax credit on the equipment they bought. The investment tax credit varied from 6 to 10 percent of the purchase of old or new equipment, which could be deducted from their tax bills. Nonprofits could not use these tax credits unless they ran a for-profit business that paid taxes. The net effect of tax breaks like interest, depreciation, and investment tax credit (when it was legal) is to reduce costs and to increase the after-tax rate of return on their investments. In addition, for-profit firms can contribute expertise and capital.

For-profit firms can contribute marketing skills, logistical and transportation capacity to move a product or service across the globe, technological and production capacity, expertise, and capital. By exploiting the main differences between these two sectors, there are endless opportunities for cooperation, sometimes called strategic alliances, between for-profit firms and nonprofits. Let us take a look at three levels of cooperative efforts. Chapter 12 discusses a matrix that helps managers decide when cooperation is advisable.

Transactions

On the transactional level, a for-profit and nonprofit merely engage in a transaction that is mutually beneficial. A nonprofit may use its fundraising advantage to construct a building. It can then sell that building to a for-profit firm and rent space within the same building. The deal involves the nonprofit getting a low rent and getting back the capital it invested in the building and an additional amount of money representing a gain from the sale. The for-profit buyer gets rental income from the building from the nonprofit and other tenants. The taxes on the rental income are reduced by the deduction for interest, depreciation, and investment tax credit, when it applies.[31] If the depreciation is sufficiently high to represent a paper loss for tax purposes, the for-profit investor is also able to shelter income from other sources from taxes. Both parties gain by utilizing their comparative advantages. These sale–leaseback arrangements are profitable for both parties when appropriately structured.

Another example is the agreement between two Washington, D.C., banks and a group of black churches. The churches encourage their members to use the bank and also deposit church monies in the banks, which in turn look more favorably on the credit needs of the churches and their parishioners.

Joint Ventures

On this level, the for-profit and nonprofit organizations work cooperatively toward a common goal. They share authority, risks, costs, and benefits. They do not, however, form a separate legal organization. They merely work together. One study identifies five types of joint ventures between universities and corporations:

1. Research done at universities but sponsored by corporations
2. Corporate use of licenses and patents owned by universities to produce goods for commercial sales and for which the universities get royalty payments
3. Consulting agreements between the corporation and the university faculties for which the university charges a fee
4. Sharing of laboratory space and facilities between the university and corporation
5. Ownership by universities of either the majority or minority share of a for-profit corporation.[32]

The Westchester Golf Classics are examples of joint ventures between nonprofit groups and private firms in a fund-raising event. The Manufacturers Hanover Trust Co. (which has since merged) makes packages of tickets available to its corporate customers who use them to entertain clients. Fourteen hospitals sell tickets and keep the revenues from their ticket sales. The hospitals also get a portion of the tournament proceeds, including revenues from amateur golfers who pay up to $3000 per person to play against the pros. Television pays tens of millions of dollars ($13.2 million in 1984) to carry the classics. To keep costs down, more than 1500 volunteer workers are used.[33] Some tennis tournaments follow a similar model.

Joint ventures are also possible among nonprofits. Hospitals are increasingly entering into joint ventures with nonprofit (or for-profit) corporations owned by physicians. For example, physicians may form firms to collect the fees for services the doctors performed in the hospitals. Joint ventures and partnerships, to be discussed next, are motivated by (1) a desire to share costs and risks, (2) the sharing of assets, technology and management which one party has and the other finds too costly to develop, (3) confidence in each other, and (4) a market for the finished product or service.

Partnerships

One form of working jointly is through a partnership arrangement. In such an arrangement, the nonprofit enters into an agreement with one or more non-profit partners to create a separate legal organization to carry out a trade or business. The partnership is not, however, simply an agreement to work together, such as a joint venture. It is a legal organization with its own identity and staff.

The partnership has one or more general partners. These are organizations or persons who are fully liable for the losses of the business and who manage it cooperatively. General partners also decide how to distribute the earnings and tax benefits among themselves and how to share the responsibility for coming up with the capital required to get the business going. Unlike a general partnership, in a limited partnership the partners cannot participate in the management and are not liable for any losses beyond the amount of money each has invested. If the limited partner invests $1,000,000, it cannot be held liable for any amounts over $1,000,000. In contrast, the general partner's liability may go beyond the investment. For example, a general partner who puts up $1,000,000 is liable for more than that amount if the business is sued or if creditors demand to be paid. One way to protect against this limitless liability is for the general partner to be insured or to be a corporation that has limited liability in the sense that creditors cannot reach the assets of the owners of the corporation. Under ordinary circumstances, the assets of the corporation must do.

This description of a partnership arrangement reveals some of the concerns that the IRS and the courts have about partnership involvements by nonprofits with for-profit firms. The nonprofit's strongest position is in being general partners because they can influence the management. But a general partnership also exposes the nonprofit to limitless losses. Moreover, the motive of the for-profit partner is distinctly different and sometimes in conflict with the assumed motive of the nonprofit. The former seeks profits for private individuals as its primary purpose for engaging in the partnership, while the latter seeks profits as a mean of financing a charitable activity. In the latter case, the profits are only incidental to the charitable goal. Thus, there is an inherent conflict between the two goals. Accordingly, when the facts and circumstances of the partnership arrangement are such that they jeopardize the requirements of a nonprofit organization, the IRS will deny or revoke the tax-exempt status of the organization.

Let us proceed to look at some accepted partnership arrangements in housing and neighborhood development. In one case, a nonprofit and a for-profit firm entered into a partnership to construct and operate a housing project exclusively for the handicapped and the elderly. The nonprofit is responsible for marketing and renting units, lease enforcement, supervising repairs and maintenance, and conducting social programs for the tenants. In ruling favorably on this arrangement, the IRS noted that providing housing for the handicapped and the elderly is a defined charitable goal and is consistent with the charitable purpose of the nonprofit in question. See Codes 380 through 390 in Table 2.1. It also noted that there were sufficient safeguards to protect the nonprofit, because one for-profit general partner had pledged to cover all operating deficits for a specific period of time. The risk of unlimited liability was reduced by the existence of other for-profit general partners who had agreed to share it, and the mortgages were insured by the federal government in case of default by the project.[34]

Partnerships have also been used in the arts. In *Plumstead Theatre Society* v. *Commissioner*, the court ruled in favor of a partnership between a theater that clearly operated as a nonprofit and private individual investors who put up $100,000 in return for a sizable percentage of the profits the theater was expected to make.[35] The court ruled that the theater was not controlled by the private investors, was not required to pay them for losses, and did not depart from its tax-exempt purpose of promoting new and experimental productions and its involvement in the community.

Similarly, the court has ruled in favor of joint ventures in the field of medicine. It ruled that a nonprofit hospital that entered into a joint venture to construct and manage rental office space to its affiliated physicians had not violated its tax-exempt status. The hospital was paid a management fee and its proportionate share of the profits, was protected against losses, and could provide better service to patients by having the doctors around.[36]

It is not simply the activity that counts. The courts and the IRS have also not denied or revoked the tax-exempt status of nonprofits entering into joint ventures in housing, the arts, medicine, and so on. These factors matter:

1. The organization must not depart from its charitable purpose or subvert it to the profit motive of the for-profit partner.
2. The organization must remain free from the control of the for-profit partners.
3. The assets of the organization must not be exposed to cover the liabilities of the venture and its private partners.
4. A significant portion of the activity must be dedicated to the charitable purpose of the organization.
5. There must be a demonstrable advantage to the nonprofit in having a for-profit partner.

Basically, the IRS uses a two-part test to determine the acceptability of an investment partnership to qualify under Section 501(c)(3). First, it must be demonstrated that the organization is legitimately serving a charitable purpose. The housing need of the elderly, for example, is a charitable purpose. But if a housing partnership provides only a token proportion of its housing units to the elderly, this would not qualify.

Second, while recognizing that in a partnership the nonprofit will have some legitimate economic and fiduciary relationship to its partners whose motives are strictly profits, the partnership agreement should insulate the organization from obligations that serve to increase the profits of its for-profit partners or that cause the organization to veer from its charitable purpose. Thus, an arrangement where the nonprofit is placed at risk of guaranteeing profits or covering the losses of the for-profit partners is not acceptable. Neither is it acceptable that the for-profit partners receive a disproportionate share of the profits or losses, that the nonprofit will sell assets such as land and equipment or rent space or make loans to the partnership at below-market rates, or that the profits to either the nonprofit or for-profit partners be excessive. Finally, the IRS looks skeptically on partnerships between the founders and managers of a nonprofit and the nonprofit organization they are supposed to be managing.[37] Remember self-dealing?

ILLUSTRATIONS: COEXISTENCE OF CHARITY AND PROFITS

A nonprofit ballet company has a contract with a for-profit firm. The nonprofit is a major customer, but is having financial problems. The firm does not want to lose a client. So it undertakes to share part of its profits with the nonprofit and induce others to contribute. The firm was allowed to deduct this as a business expense, not as a charitable donation, and the nonprofit got help.[38] The firm's charitable and commercial motives merged. Lets turn to an example in housing:

JOINT VENTURES FOR AFFORDABLE HOUSING: SOLVING A MAJOR PROBLEM
HERRINGTON J. BRYCE

Many cities—large and small—have substantial stocks of abandoned homes which impair the attraction of the city, its communities and neighborhoods, cost millions of dollars to protect and millions more in lost revenues since these abandoned units produce no tax dollars.

Rehabilitation of these housing stocks has been one major approach to bringing these unused houses back on the tax rolls and to answering the quest for affordable housing. Rehabilitation is not as expensive as new housing starts, and rehabilitation that includes the public and nonprofit sectors usually assures that some of the units will be made available to the needy, elderly and the young. Rehabilitation also tends to retain the character of a neighborhood—often an important consideration.

One approach is an agreement that involves the City of New York, the State of New York, Enterprise Foundation (a nonprofit), its subsidiary Social Investment Corporation (a for-profit), the Federal National Mortgage Association (a for-profit) and eligible community development corporations (nonprofits) and their for-profit subsidiaries.

The City of New York has agreed to provide 1,000 rental units which it has in its possession because their owners have failed to pay taxes and which are presently unfit for rental. As is, the City not only loses because these properties are not on the tax roll, but the abandoned properties are havens for crime and fire and are a blight on the City.

The recycling process will begin with a community development organization CDC submitting a proposal to the City and State to get the units rehabilitated, occupied and managed.

The City and the State will make a loan at 1 percent for the initial investment in the rehabilitation project. Because the loans provide that regular payments of the principal do not have to be made, future rent charges can be held comparatively low and yet some cashflow may be provided.

The CDC then submits its proposal to Enterprise Foundation, a nonprofit, for evaluation. Should Enterprise conclude that this project can attract private investor interests, it passes it on to Social Investment Corporation (a for-profit subsidiary of Enterprise) to raise the funds to do the rehabilitation.

The remainder of the costs of rehabilitation (usually a minimum of 25 percent) is obtained from private sources. The Social Investment Corporation will syndicate interests to for-profit corporations. Thus, the Federal National Mortgage Corporation (Fannie Mae) has agreed to invest up to $28,000,000 through the purchase of ownership interests in these properties. The proceeds from the sale of these interests to Fannie Mae by Social Investment Corporation will provide the additional funds needed for rehabilitating these and future units.

There is no gift. Fannie Mae becomes a limited partner. The CDC forms a for-profit subsidiary to be the general partner.

By not making itself, a nonprofit, the general partner, the CDC avoids liability should the project fail. It also avoids mixing the daily task of running a nonprofit with those of running a business.

What are the incentives for each of these partners? Yes, The City gets taxes and so does the State. The neighborhoods and people get better housing. The private developers get jobs and profits. Enterprise Foundation gets to fulfill its mission and may obtain dividends from Social Investment Corporation. The latter gets a fee for syndicating the interests and for putting together the deal. The CDC does not rely on gifts, and it meets its mission.

What does the private investor such as Fannie Mae get? It gets tax credits. It may reduce its total tax liability to the federal government for each of the next nine years by 9 percent of the qualified rehabilitation costs. Almost all of the tax credits generated by the project will go to the private investors.

Let us take another look at this financing structure. It is particularly attractive to corporations or individuals seeking tax credits. The typical private real estate investment offers possibilities of returns through cashflow (monthly net income through rents that exceed operating costs), capital appreciation (or capital gains when the property is sold for a price higher than acquisition and rehabilitation costs), and tax benefits (principally through depreciation and tax credits). Traditionally, low income property offers limited opportunities for cashflow because rents are low relative to expenses and appreciation is limited or nonexistent. These New York properties are no exceptions.

But tax credits are important considerations because they do not rely on charging high rents to low-income persons in order for the private investor to get an attractive return. Investors not heavily dependent upon immediate cashflow can obtain an acceptable return by using the tax credits to increase their income retention after taxes.

I am grateful to Heidi Most of Enterprise for her cooperation. HJB

Source: Bureau of Business Research, School of Business Administration, College of William and Mary, Williamsburg, Virginia, October 1987.

MARKET ACTIVITIES AND THE THREAT TO NONPROFIT STATUS

In this book we give examples of nonprofits operating within the market economy and making a legal profit. In Chapter 3, we discussed some sharp differences between the for-profit firm and the nonprofit. To keep things in perspective, it would be wise to remember that the nonprofit exists to carry out a welfare mission and the profits are incidental to the discharging of that mission.

Thus, in *Copyright Clearance Center* v. *Commissioner*, the court said:[39]

Although an organization might be engaged in a single activity, such activity may be directed toward multiple purposes, both exempt and nonexempt. But, in the case of multiple purposes, it must be kept in mind that qualification for exemption depends upon whether the entity in question is organized and operated "exclusively" for one or more of the exempt purposes in the statue.

The court went on to state that there is no stringent definition of the word "exclusive" and that is may also be interpreted as meaning "primary." Whichever word is used, the legal interpretation is equivalent to substantial. Thus, the nonprofit may be said to exist exclusively for a tax-exempt purpose if it has no substantial activity that is nonexempt; that is, the commercial activities that are undertaken cannot be a substantial part of the activities of the nonprofit.

Finally, be reminded that (1) state laws must be understood, and (2) even simple transactions by a well-meaning group may create unintended problems.

A Salvation Army community center in rural Kansas lost its tax exemption because officials allowed Weight Watchers, a for-profit company that markets a popular weight-loss program, to use part of the building. . .[40]

SUMMARY AND CONCLUSIONS

In most societies, the economy is a dominant sector. By understanding how it operates, nonprofit managers are able to detect new opportunities. These opportunities derive partly from the imperfections of the market— the inability of the economy to fully satisfy important needs of the public or community.

One set of opportunities exists within the market structure itself. These relate to the needs of consumers, producers, investors, workers, and savers. Another set of needs relates to effects that are nonmarket related. Being able to identify specific opportunities within these environments means that the nonprofit can benefit from the dynamic growth of the economy by being relevant.

NOTES

1. Goodwill Industries Annual Report, 1989, p. 3.
2. YWCA, Public Policy 1988–1989, pp. 8–9.

3. Cecelia Hilgert, and Susan J. Mahler, "Nonprofit Charitable Organizations, 1985," *Statistics of Income: SOI Bulletin*, 9, no. 2, pp. 53–65.

4. Henry B. Hansmann, "Reforming Nonprofit Corporation Law," *University of Pennsylvania Law Review*, 129, no. 3 (Jan. 1981), 397–623.

5. Ira Mark Ellmann, "Another Theory of Nonprofit Corporation," *Michigan Law Review*, 80, no. 5 (Apr. 1982), 999–1050.

6. See Tibor Scitovsky, "The Place of Economic Welfare in Human Welfare," *Quarterly Review of Economics and Business*, 13, no. 3 (Autum 1973), 7–19; M. V. Pauly, "Cores and Clubs," *Public Choice*, 9 (Fall 1970), 53–55; Y. K. Ng, "The Economic Theory of Clubs: Pareto Optimality Conditions," *Economica*, 40, no. 159 (Aug. 1973), 291–98; Martin McGuire, "Private Good Clubs and Public Good Clubs: Economic Models of Group Formation," *Swedish Journal of Economics*, 74 (1972), 84–99.

7. Philip S. Broughton, "The Economic Function of Foundations," *Foundation News*, 5, no. 5 (Sept. 1964), 1–4.

8. Revenue Ruling 69–144, 1969-2, Cumulative Bulletin 115.

9. Revenue Ruling 67-138, 1967-1, Cumulative Bulletin 129.

10. Reg. Section 1.501(c) (3)-1(d) (3).

11. Sue Shellenbarger, "Stimulating a Pocket of Appalachia with Venture Funds," *Wall Street Journal*, Friday, Sept. 15, 1989, p. B2.

12. *Munsell Color Foundation, Inc.* v. *U.S.* (DC, Md; 1973), 33 AFTR2d 74-339.

13. Revenue Ruling 71-506, 1971-2, Cumulative Bulletin 233.

14. Goodwill, p. 1.

15. Annual Report, 1989, National Urban League, Inc., New York, 1989, p. 21.

16. Revenue Ruling 55-656, 1955-2, Cumulative Bulletin 262.

17. Revenue Ruling 78-69, 1978-1, Cumulative Bulletin 156.

18. Revenue Ruling 68-71, 1968-1, Cumulative Bulletin 249.

19. Revenue Ruling 69-441, 1969-2, Cumulative Bulletin 115.

20. See Carson W. Bays, "Why Most Private Hospitals Are Nonprofit," *Journal of Policy Analysis and Management*, 2, no. 3 (1983), 366–81; and H. David Sherman, "Interpreting Hospital Performance with Financial Analysis," *Accounting Review*, 61, no. 3 (July 1986), pp. 526–550.

21. Other terms for externalities are indirect effect, neighborhood effect, and spillover.

22. Revenue Ruling 74-194, 1974-1, Cumulative Bulletin 129.

23. Of course, a fee could also be charged. More is said about fees in Chapters 6 and 9.

24. Revenue Ruling 76-205, 1976 Cumulative Bulletin 154.

25. Revenue Ruling 76-204, 1976-1 Cumulative Bulletin 152.

26. *Nursing Health Care*, 10, no. 7 (Sept. 1989), p. 385.

27. Virginia Professional Standards Review Foundation 79-1, United States Tax Court No. 9167.

28. Revenue Ruling 54-296, 1954-2, Cumulative Bulletin 59.

29. Revenue Ruling 70-186, 1970-1, Cumulative Bulletin 128.

30. Herbert A. Simon, "Theories of Decision Making in Economics," *American Economic Review*, 49, no. 3 (June 1959), 253–83; and *Models of Man* (New York: Wiley, 1957), Chapter 14.

31. The Deficit Reduction Act of 1984 placed some limitations on these transactions. The limitations are largely on the private partner. See David Warren, "Leases and Service

Contracts with Tax-exempt Entities after the DRA," *Tax Advisor*, April 1985, pp. 230–34.

32. Kendyl K. Monroe, "Collaboration between Tax-exempt Research Organizations and Commercial Enterprises—Federal Income Tax Limitations," *Taxes—The Tax Magazine*, 62, no. 5 (May 1984), 297–316.

33. Brenton Wellino, "The Westchester Classics: Big Bucks and Good Works," *Business Week*, June 10, 1985, p. 79.

34. General Counsel Memorandum 39005 and Alan J. Yanowitz, "Using the Investment Partnership as a Charitable Activity: A Means/Ends Analysis," *Journal of Taxation*, 60, no. 4, (Apr. 1984), 214–18.

35. *Plumstead Theatre Society* v. *Commissioner*, 74 Tax Court 1324, 1980.

36. IRS Letter Ruling 8201072.

37. For a discussion of these principles, see Michael Schell, "The Participation of Charities in Limited Partnerships," *Yale Law Review*, 93 (1984), 1330–63, and Louise A. Howells, "Community Development under Section 501(c)(3) of the Internal Revenue Code: The Charity in Economic Development," *Taxes—The Tax Magazine*, 62, no. 2 (Feb. 1984), 83–93.

38. International Revenue Letter, 9045015.

39. *Copyright Clearance Center* v. *Commissioner*, T.C., 793–810, (1982).

40. *Chronicle of Philanthropy*, Sept. 5, 1989, p. 25.

SUGGESTED READINGS

DOUGLAS, JAMES, *Why Charity?* (Beverly Hills: Sage Publications, 1983).

JAMES, ESTELLE, AND SUSAN ROSE-ACKERMAN, "The Nonprofit Enterprise in Market Economies," PONPO Working Paper No. 95 and ISPS Working Paper No. 2095, Yale University, New Haven, Conn., 1986.

KRAMER, RALPH M., *Voluntary Agencies in the Welfare State* (Berkeley, Calif.: University of California Press, 1981).

ROSE-ACKERMAN, SUSAN, "Unfair Competition and Corporate Income Taxation," *Stanford Law Review*, 34, no. 5 (May 1982), 1017–39.

YOUNG, DENNIS, *If Not for Profit, for What* (Lexington, Mass.: Lexington Books, 1983).

Chapter 8

Marketing: Warnings and Pitfalls

As indicated in Chapter 7, strategic planning is applicable to all phases of planning and decision making, including marketing. Strategic planning is about making choices. Marketing, including the marketing of an organization's name in fund-raising, is one area where choices are made. In June 1991, the National Easter Seal Society sued the American Lung Association for using a seal in its fund-raising. It claimed that a seal was its trademark and therefore its use by the American Lung Association represented a trademark infringement resulting in confusion and a diversion of donations. Marketing decisions have organization-wide implications. This chapter is concerned with such implications.

What should concern the nonprofit management, including the trustees, about marketing? Every marketing strategy must be evaluated along three dimensions: (1) costs and effectiveness, (2) the mission and image of the organization, and (2) ethics and legalities. Since marketing is an expenditure and an investment, the chapters in this book on strategic planning, budgeting, investment, and expenditures are applicable to point number one. Ethics were discussed in Chapters 1 and 2 and an ethical problem appears at the end of this chapter. Now, let us focus on legalities.

In this chapter, we are less concerned with techniques and strategies than we are with management decisions to meet certain legal standards. Ethical standards were covered in Chapter 1.

In the context of strategic planning, this means exploring the desirability of various marketing decisions. Accordingly, we shall highlight pitfalls that no competent management of a nonprofit can ignore. We begin with the proposition that it is the function of top management, including the trustees, to make sure that the marketing strategies designed by the experts do not jeopardize the organization in any way.

THE ALLURE OF AN EXCHANGE

It is fashionable to view marketing as an exchange of values. Such a concept applies very well to a business and to those activities in a nonprofit organization that are businesses. It does not apply equally well when what is being marketed is an opportunity to give, that is, to make a tax-deductible donation. For this reason, the concept of an exchange needs to be understood by managers of nonprofits and applied differently when the marketing applies to a gift and when it applies to a sale or an exchange of equivalent value. The consequences of error are not trivial.

A tax-deductible gift or donation can involve no exchange of values, whether the values be in a tangible or intangible. Put otherwise, a pure gift is a transfer of property from a donor to a donee with no expectations or actual receipt of benefits by the donor from the donee for that transfer.

In June, 1991, the Sadie Wattley Malcom family makes a gift to St. Gibson's parish for masses said for her and other deceased members of the parish. The IRS ruled that such a gift is tax deductible since the church established that it did not sell or charge for masses and because the donation could be used at the discretion of the parish for its other charitable activities. The donation was not tied to the intangible benefit of a mass.

An exchange is different. It involves a transfer of a property from one person to another with the expectation of something in return from the recipient. When the property expected to be received is cash or something of equivalent or superior value, what we have is a sale. Sales are not gifts. They are not tax deductible. Indeed, the gains on a sale are taxable by federal, state and local governments.

Some exchanges are for properties of like kind and of equivalent values, for example, a rental property for a rental property with the same market value. Such exchanges are also not deductible. They are not taxable because there was no gain and not deductible because there was no measurable economic sacrifice. Each person received an equivalent (no more and no less) of what he or she gave the other. These exchanges are not tax deductible.[1] Thus, a recent exchange of property between the Colonial Williamsburg Foundation (a nonprofit museum) and the local school system for a high school and its surrounding land for real estate of equivalent value produced no tax advantage for either party to the exchange. There is no gift in this transaction.

Some transfers of property are so complex that they involve a sale, an exchange of equivalent value, and also a gift. Such complex transfers are dissected into parts for purposes of identifying each portion, placing a value on it, and determining whether it generates a tax, a deduction, or neither. We shall see such strategies in Chapter 10. For purposes of marketing, it is important to be mindful that there is a distinction with serious consequences both for the organization and the donor.

An error can (1) deprive the "donor" of a deduction or cause the donor to misrepresent facts when filing income tax, (2) cause taxation if the donor received a gain, and (3) cause the nonprofit to be liable for sales and income taxes if in fact it made a sale that is outside its line of work[2] and a violation of law if it fails to make the proper disclosure, to which we now turn.

Exchange of Values and the Law

The distinction between an exchange and a gift is not petty theory. Accordingly, in 1988, the IRS sent 400,000 nonprofits its Publication 1391 informing them that a gift and an exchange are two different things. In a gift, there is no quid pro quo to the donor, but in an exchange one thing is given up for another. In a charitable gift, the donor gives something of value to a nonprofit without the expectation or receipt of anything of value in return.

The publication points out that each nonprofit must determine the fair market value of any property it gives to a donor in connection with his or her gift. The donor must be told by the nonprofit that only the amount of the donation that exceeds the fair market value of such property is a tax-deductible donation because this portion is a gift. The remainder is an exchange of equivalent value or a sale.

A simple example: In a fund-raising dinner, the meal and entertainment are benefits or values received by the attendees. The per person cost of both the food and the entertainment can be ascertained. Only the amount paid by the attendees that exceeds this cost is a tax-deductible gift. The amount that is equal to the per person cost of the food and entertainment represents an exchange of values—dollars for food and fun—and is not deductible. See the insert below. In another example, your nonprofit hospital makes no pretense that its charges to you are anything other than a payment for medical services, a benefit received, and not a gift.

Some exchanges are so insubstantial that they can be ignored.[3] But what is insubstantial is defined by the IRS. For example, Dillan gives as

---

B'NAI B'RITH INTERNATIONAL

Founded in 1843, B'nai B'rith is the world's largest Jewish organization with one-half million members in more than 45 countries. The organization defends human rights, fights discrimination, sponsors inter-faith dialogues, and promotes democracy and world peace. B'nai B'rith has helped instill hundreds of thousands of young adults with moral and ethical values and a sense of identity through the Hillel Foundations on over 400 campuses. Its youth organizations offer leadership training to 35,000 teenagers. B'nai B'rith provides non-sectarian housing for senior citizens. Through community programs, its membership reaches out to those in need and works for the betterments of society.

In tribute to Governor Wilder, and in support of the humanitarian programs of B'nai B'rith International, I (we) will attend the International Great American Traditions Award Dinner on Wednesday, April 17, 1991, at the Richmond Marriott.

☐ **Patron.** Gift of $3,500 ☐ **Contributor.** Gift of $350
(2 tables, 20 reservations) (two reservations)
☐ **Sponsor.** Gift of $1,750 ☐ **Participant.** Gift of $175
(1 table, 10 reservations) (one reservation)

Enclosed is my check for $_____ Place(s) at $175

NAME _____
(Please Print)
FIRM _____

ADDRESS _____

CITY _____ STATE _____ ZIP _____
I cannot attend, but I am pleased to contribute $_____ in honor of Governor Wilder.

Please make your checks payable to *B'nai B'rith Foundation of the U.S.*

Your reservation, excepting dinner costs of $40 per person, is a tax deductible contribution.

P.O. Box 31800   Richmond, VA 23294-1800

part of a campaign and receives a benefit from the nonprofit. The benefit is valued at less than 2 percent of the total amount she gave that nonprofit. Because it was a gift (1) in a campaign and (2) because her benefits were 2 percent or less, the entire amount she gave that nonprofit is tax deductible as long as this benefit does not exceed $50.

The exchange is also insubstantial when the benefits are token items such as mugs, chains, pens, posters, and tee shirts. Thus, a nonprofit can avoid problems for its donors and at the same time do relatively less expensive marketing by offering inexpensive objects of gratitude. Observe this strategy as used by your public radio station.

Newsletters are special. The nonprofit does not have to give the fair market value and the donor does not lose the deduction if the newsletter that is given is not available commercially on newsstands or to nonmembers of the organization through subscription and if the purpose of the newsletter is to inform about the organization. Examples are the books and other literature television ministers send in return for cash contributions. Listen carefully.

Exchange of Values, Accounting and Ethics

Not only the IRS is concerned about exchanges and the need to disclose what values are being exchanged. The standards of ethics of the watchdog agencies do as well. Furthermore, accounting principles call for distinguishing and accounting for gifts differently to exchanges.

Exchange of Values: Churches as Examples

Two religious cases illustrate the legal pitfalls. The first case is about a church that offers full-tuition scholarships to children of its members. It also asks these parents to increase their donations to the church by at least the amount they would have to pay in tuition. The court held that the donations were not tax deductible because they were made in anticipation of a benefit—education and zero tuition.[4]

The second case is about the Church of Scientology. The church offers its members classes designed to increase their spiritual awareness by teaching them church doctrine. As a result of this training, attendees may qualify to teach. The mother church sets fixed tuitions, which vary with the length and sophistication of training. In *Robert L. Hernandez v. Commissioner* and *Katherine Jean Graham et. al, v. Commissioner*, the U.S. Supreme Court denied any deduction for these payments. It argued that the transactions presumed a quid pro quo (exchange of values) and therefore are not deductible, even though what was being exchanged was religious.

Exchange of Values Limitation to Marketing Strategy

The examples given should be sufficient to illustrate a legal pitfall in approaching charitable donations as if they were exchanges of values. There is another problem. Most nonprofits have nothing to exchange with those whose dollars they most need. Therefore, for them, a marketing campaign based on the concept of exchange will fail.

To illustrate, Bill Cosby gives $20 million to Spellman College. True, his daughter attended that college. But paying tuition (an exchange of values—dollars for education) is cheaper than giving $20 million. Certainly, it cannot be suggested that he personally wanted something from the college that was worth $20 million. The same is true of former owner of *T.V. Guide* Walter Annenberg's gift of $50 million to the United Negro College Fund. What could he have been exchanging? It is obvious that if any of these approaches were dependent on an exchange, the gift would never have been made. Neither man needed an exchange—not even recognition. Television provided enough for both men.

A symphony orchestra exchanges music for dollars. It, therefore, sells tickets and admits only those who have tickets and only to the section of the auditorium where the quality of the enjoyment matches the dollars paid. Values are thereby exchanged. But the purchase of a ticket does not provide the purchaser with a deduction. It is a sale because values (dollars for musical entertainment) are exchanged. But gifts to the symphony are philanthropy, not exchanges.

Exchange of Values Applied

We have seen that approaching nonprofit marketing as an exchange of values can be seriously flawed when used outside those activities that are businesslike. We have seen that the consequences could include (1) loss of a tax deduction for the would-be contributor, (2) a possible sales and income tax on the donor if there is a gain and the nonprofit if it gained in an unrelated business, and (3) frustration when the nonprofit has basically little or nothing to exchange with major donors.

On the other hand, some nonprofits can use this approach successfully. These are nonprofits that charge fees in the form of tuition, entrance fees, or prices. They are clear exchanges. It is also applicable when organizations offer meaningful prizes—cars, trips, houses.

One final word. Do not confuse a recognition with an exchange of values. The naming of a building at a university or college, of a room in a hospital, or of a scholarship for a major donor is not an exchange. It is a recognition. If it were an exchange, the person would end up owning the building, room, or scholarship. Recognition is an effective inducement. Few would choose to have that marred by public knowledge that they "sold out."

Similarly, do not confuse opportunity with exchange. Often, especially at the end of the year when preparing for taxes or after some emotional event such as death or joyful event such as winning the lottery, people seek opportunities to give. They are less likely to be interested in what the organization offers them than what it represents and its ability to accommodate their gift. We shall deal with appropriate strategies in Chapter 9 and 10. For these people, the last thing in the world they are seeking is an exchange because this would merely complicate their dilemma.

CHOOSING AN OBJECT OF MARKETING

It is the responsibility of the nonprofit management to make the final decision on what is marketed and how tastefully and accurately. It must choose from a menu of choices offered by the staff persons and their consultants. It must also sign the contracts.

A nonprofit has a choice of marketing its name, its mission, its product or service, or a combination of all of these. "Harvard" is a name that has recognition and therefore value. It can be marketed. The American Red Cross, the American Cancer Society, and the American Heart Association are all marketable names. What's in a name? Money. This is reflected in the large markup on sweat shirts when they carry the name of a school—any school.

Alternatively, a nonprofit may choose to market what it does. "A Mind Is a Terrible Thing to Waste" is a message marketing the educational services of historical black colleges and universities. It is a powerful message, reportedly the most sought-after public service ad of the Advertising Council.[5]

As a group, these black colleges market their mission through a conduit, the United Negro College Fund, which collects and disburses the gifts and donations induced by the message. It is easier for the general public to recognize a single name and mission—if both are attractive.

A nonprofit may also choose to market an individual product or service. Hospitals do this when they send mailings about specific services. Universities do this when they advertise summer and special programs or curricula. Museums do this when they advertise specific exhibits. Many nonprofits have a problem that is analogous to multiproduct firms. They must choose which product or combination of products to push. This decision is based on a number of considerations, but central to any list should be (1) how well they produce the product or service and (2) how

By Joan E. Rigdon
Staff Reporter of THE WALL STREET JOURNAL

CLEVELAND—American Greetings Corp. thinks it has found a new theme to promote greeting card sales: the environment.

The nation's No. 2 purveyor of greetings, behind Hallmark Cards Inc., has signed an agreement with the National Wildlife Federation to launch a new line of nature cards printed on recycled paper. The 70-to-90-card line, to be launched next Father's Day, would be the biggest venture of its kind, analysts say.

The new cards—featuring nature scenes, the National Wildlife Federation logo on the back, and traditional greeting card messages—are designed to appeal to mainstream Americans, who are becoming more aware of the environment.

In return for the right to use National Wildlife's logo, American Greetings would pay undisclosed royalties to the non-profit conservation organization. The greeting card concern would also provide space on the back of each card for National Wildlife to describe the card's nature scenes.

The company says it chose National Wildlife because the organization has few political ties that might offend consumers. Even the cards are designed not to offend.

American Greetings officials insist that profit isn't their only motive. And they say they wouldn't be so crass as to create a separate line for Earth Day. Moreover, while very little of the 70,000 tons of paper they use each year is currently recycled, they say they were planning to recycle a year before they ever crossed paths with National Wildlife. And, they add, they use recycled toilet paper at their world headquarters.

Source: Wall Street Journal, October 9, 1990, p. B6. © Reprinted with permission.

satisfied they are in being identified with the product or service being promoted. See the insert above.

The decision to market a specific product or service carries the pitfall of misrepresentation of the quality or characteristics of these products and services.[6] The decision to market the name of the organization places the image of the organization in jeopardy and should never be done without board approval. The decision to market a mission identifying the organization as capable of carrying out the mission is most desirable for the majority of nonprofits because it carries the least risk and gives the organization the best opportunity of receiving secondary benefits from events. An organization that is solidly identified with disasters is remembered when there is a disaster.

The new Girl Scouts of the U.S.A. ad reflects a combination of these objects of marketing even in its simplicity and brevity. "Girl Scouts . . .

FOLLOW JOSEPH PULITZER'S LEAD
. . . AND YOUR ENDOWMENT GIFT
TO THE NEW YORK PHILHARMONIC
CAN OUTLIVE A CENTURY

Joseph Pulitzer, a lover of orchestral music, supported the New York Philharmonic with generous gifts in the last years of his life. His bequest of $500,000,
used as a permanent endowment, stabilized the future of the Orchestra and
allowed it to embark on its continuing mission. The principal of Mr. Pulitzer's 1911
endowment gift, judiciously managed through the years, supplements the Philharmonic's operating income to this day.

This Philharmonic welcomes your outright gift of cash, securities, real property or other financial interests and will advise you of the substantial tax benefits
and personal recognition these gifts allow.

Source: 1990 Annual Report, New York Philharmonic, p. 36. Reprinted by permission.

As Great as You Want to Make it" capitalizes on the well-known name,
mission, and service.

An Illustration

Virtually every major nonprofit carries on its last page an explanation of how one may give through a bequest. We shall discuss the
structure of this strategy in Chapter 10. But let's look at its marketing
(see the insert above).

Observe that the mission, music, is being marketed. It is coupled
with perpetuity (endowment that can outlive), an association with and
the example of a great name (Pulitzer), an amount that can easily be
reached by a patron's bequest ($500,000), the use to which the gift will
be placed (continuing the mission), and the forms in which the gift can
be made (cash, securities, real estate, and so on). Chapters 10 and 11 will
go deeper into types and amounts of gifts. For the moment, mark the
centrality of mission, method, and means (money) and the promise of
judicious management in this message. There is no suggestion of an exchange.

CHOOSING A TARGET

All marketing efforts should be targeted. Recall from Chapter 2 that
private foundations, corporate donors, and individuals have preferences

and each varies in its willingness and ability to respond positively to any fund-raising campaign. Some, by virtue of their charter or goals, give only to local nonprofits, to the arts, or to certain ethnic, national, or religious causes.

Targeting increases the efficiency and effectiveness of marketing. The United Negro College Fund slogan is targeted to middle-class persons. The Girl Scouts' slogan is targeted to Junior and Cadette Girl Scouts. Obviously, one question managers should raise is to whom is the message being sent? Is the target group large enough and significant enough to the mission of the organization to warrant the effort?

Targeting of the organization's clientele is also implied in the mission of many nonprofits. This is sometimes referred to as market segmentation—isolating a special portion of the overall market for attention. Those nonprofits that serve the needy have, by definition, a defined client group. Those founded to serve the homeless, say in Cleveland or Los Angeles, have an even more specifically defined target clientele. Thus, an essential difference between targeting in a for-profit and in a nonprofit corporation is that the latter often has no choice. It is its mission. Consequently, for each nonprofit, targeting should have at least three facets: (1) targeting donors for fund-raising purposes, (2) targeting volunteers for their assistance, (3) targeting clients for programs, and (4) potential members. Each may demand a different marketing strategy.

It should be obvious that targeting is more endemic to nonprofit organizations than to firms. A hardware store or barbershop is not required to specify its target group in its charter or annual report. Most nonprofits are required to state the persons or locality they exist to serve. Not focusing on their target client group can be construed as a violation of their charter and a misuse of their assets.

Targeting avoids conflict. In many communities nonprofits are accused by small businesses of infringing on their markets. A good deal of public goodwill can be achieved and also taxation of revenues avoided by proper targeting. Thus, a college does not advertise the availability of its dormitories to the general public as a less expensive substitute for local hotels. To do so would not only be bad public relations but, as we shall see in Chapter 11, lead to taxation of the income derived from such advertised activities for they would probably be attacked as unfairly competing.

An organization can target based on a number of dimensions. We have already mentioned geography. Two other dimensions are crucial to most nonprofits. These are income and price, to which we now turn.

Targeting by Income Levels

Appeals also vary according to income. Rich folks give to art more than poor folks do. One study has even shown that there is a sharp distinction between the giving patterns of blacks and whites, the kinds of appeals that are effective with them, and the causes to which they give.[7] Another has studied the giving patterns of physicians by specialty, age, sex, and religious orientation.[8]

A study by the Independent Sector enables us to come up with a profile of the givers. Table 8.1 shows who gave to charity and how much. Running down the columns for 1989, the numbers suggest that the most frequent giver is an upper-income white female, 35 to 44 years of age, married, and working part-time. The largest amount of dollars is given by a white male, aged 55 to 64, who is married, fully employed, and has a family income exceeding $75,000.

In determining a marketing strategy, the organization should bear in mind that some goods, services, and purposes vary in intensity of need and according to income. Income affects the life cycle of a product. The need for most goods changes as income changes. During recessions and when a community is depressed, its needs are more basic and simple. Many inner-city churches in Detroit and other cities experienced a sharp change in their fiscal ability as well as their functions as those communities became poorer. The reverse is also true. Thus, targeting, based on strategic planning as described in Chapter 6 helps the organization to meet changing community needs and, consequently, its mission.

A nonprofit does not necessarily risk its tax-exempt status by serving the rich, because, as we stated in Chapters 2 and 3, not all nonprofits are charities. In fact, many nonprofits, including religious congregations, do target rich populations as their principal clientele. A nonprofit places its status in danger, however, if it was created to serve the needy and fails to do so by shifting resources to attract and serve the rich.

Targeting by Price Levels

With for-profit firms a price is not only a way to recover cost plus make any additional gains, but it works to exclude or deny anyone who cannot pay. You cannot get into the movie theater unless you pay. Indeed, one reason for firms charging high prices is to exclude certain people. Restaurants and apartment buildings that cater to higher-income people do exactly this.

For many nonprofits, the very idea of charging a price that works to exclude is an anathema. This is true of those nonprofits that serve the needy; for surely if the price is set so low that the very poor can afford it, then certainly everyone else can. Thus, while a price can be used de-

TABLE 8.1 Demographic Characteristics of Givers in 1987 and 1989
(Average Contributions of Contributing Households and as Percentage of Income by Groups)

Demographic Characteristic	1989 Contributions			1987 Contributions		
	Percentage of All Respondents	Average	Percentage of Household Income	Percentage of All Respondents	Average	Percentage of Household Income
Total	75.1	978	2.5	71.1	790	1.9
Sex						
Male	71.9	1,294	3.1	68.9	888	2.1
Female	78.1	683	1.8	73.1	700	1.8
Race						
White and other	76.7	1,010	2.5	73.6	816	2.0
Black	60.9	653	2.1	50.5	490	1.6
Hispanic**	62.2	478	1.5	56.2	273	1.0
Age						
18–24	53.9	484	1.2	54.1	219	0.6
25–34	70.0	893	2.1	67.7	625	1.6
35–44	86.3	956	2.2	76.5	825	1.8
45–54	78.6	1,098	2.3	76.3	1,066	2.1
55–64	79.9	1,420	3.6	79.4	1,094	2.6
65–74	78.8	1,070	4.4	72.4	959	3.1
75+	76.7	696	3.2	75.0	737	3.0
Income						
Under $10,000	49.0	379	5.5	48.0	172	2.8
$10,000–$19,999	65.1	485	3.2	67.1	429	2.5
$20,000–$29,999	76.9	728	2.9	73.4	666	2.5
$30,000–$39,999	81.9	894	2.6	77.3	769	2.0
$40,000–$49,999	84.5	831	1.8	72.9	933	1.9
$50,000–$74,999	85.5	1,096	1.8	84.3	1,015	1.5

TABLE 8.1 Demographic Characteristics of Givers in 1987 and 1989
(Average Contributions of Contributing Households and as Percentage of Income by Groups) *(continued)*

Demographic Characteristic	1989			1987		
	Percentage of All Respondents	Contributions Average	Percentage of Household Income	Percentage of All Respondents	Contributions Average	Percentage of Household Income
$75,000–$99,999	92.1	2,793	3.2	75.0	1,602	1.7
$100,000+	86.8	2,893	2.9	79.8	2,225	2.1
Marital Status						
Married	79.7	1,132	2.6	78.6	967	2.1
Single	60.8	654	1.7	55.8	293	0.8
Divorced, separated, or widowed	72.8	592	2.6	60.8	493	1.9
Employment status						
Employed	77.3	1,097	2.4	72.8	797	1.8
Full-time	76.4	1,163	2.5	72.6	788	1.7
Part-time	81.6	806	2.0	73.5	826	2.9
Not employed	70.3	734	2.5	68.0	779	2.4

* Numbers do not add up due to rounding. Estimates exclude those respondents who reported "Not sure or no answer" to particular questions.

** Hispanics may be of any race.

Source: Independent Sector *Giving and Volunteering*, 1990 Edition. Reprinted with permission.

liberately to exclude with for-profit firms, it cannot be similarly used by all nonprofits.

Even among those nonprofits that use exclusionary prices, there is a tendency not to do so completely. Thus, universities, hospitals, museums, and even civic centers find ways to give access to some needy persons. The failure to do so, especially with hospitals, health care centers, and universities, is to risk loss of their nonprofit status and access to government payments. Observe that not all exhibits at a museum require an entrance fee. The Metropolitan Museum of Art in New York City uses a suggested donation that varies by age. This is artful pricing.

The upshot is that price plays a different role in the marketing strategies of nonprofits than it does for for-profit firms. Therefore, nonprofits that rely on the exclusionary aspect of pricing risk the loss of their tax-exempt status as their pricing strategies make the discharge of their mission impossible. Hence, the management of all nonprofits must assess their marketing strategies to see if they are appropriately targeted.

It should be obvious from what has been said that the management of a nonprofit needs to target both its clientele and its sources of funding. Failure to do the former may violate its mission. Failure to do the latter is wasteful.

UNINTENTIONAL CONSEQUENCES OF MARKETING

Management must avoid the pitfall that marketing objectives would be given a disproportionate weight in how the organization carries out its mission. One author writes that a museum that is mission driven emphasizes education and seeks out exhibits for their educational purposes. On the other hand, a museum that is driven by marketing dedicates space to nonart-related activities, such as fancy accommodations and sales, and seeks out exhibits because they draw a lot of people, not necessarily for their educational value.[9]

One observer writes of the danger:

> In a development that gives new meaning to the term "corporate takeover," art museums are increasingly promoting the commercial interests of the companies giving them money . . . by helping to hawk wares ranging from perfume to vodka to credit cards.
>
> The danger is that they may undermine their museum's highest mission— to uphold standards of artistic excellence and scholarly integrity, not to sell their space and prestige to commercial interests.[10]

Another observer writes of the importance of marketing to the creation and sustenance of megachurches—some having tens of thousands of attendees at a single church service. A consequence of marketing that drew these people is the need for more marketing to generate funds and to keep the attendance at a critical minimum.[11] How well can such a church minister to individual needs—its mission? Yet being large yields economies of scale and gives these large congregations access to all types of facilities, including radio and television time, through which they expand their mission.

It is the responsibility of management to assure that marketing does not place the mission at risk. Some directors of corporate foundations are very conscious of this risk. It has been argued in various writings that corporations ought to be motivated in their giving by "doing good" rather than doing "profitably" and have also warned nonprofits about slighting their mission in order to attract a corporate donor.

CONSOLIDATED CHECKLIST OF COMPLIANCE WITH IRS SOLICITATION RULES

1. List the fund-raising activities of the organization.
2. Does it maintain records of (a) names and addresses of donors, (b) solicitation materials, tickets, and receipts used in fund raising, (c) did it state that membership dues are deductible, and (d) what are the benefits of membership received by donors?
3. Did it conduct any fund-raising activities that were part gifts or payments such as for admissions or merchandise? What did it say?
4. When donors received benefits for their donations, (a) what was the nature of the benefit including such things as free tickets, subscriptions, and discounts, (b) did the charity refer to the deductibility of amounts in its solicitations or thank-you communication?
5. Did the charity receive noncash contributions with a fair market value greater than $500?
6. Did the organization sell, exchange, or dispose of any noncash contributions within two years of receipt of the noncash property?
7. Does the charity acknowledge receipt of cash and noncash donations in writing?
8. If the charity accepts noncash donations, (a) does it keep a list of the names and addresses of the donors and fair market value of the gifts when the fair market value exceeds $500, (b) who determines the fair market value, (c) can the organization provide the same information for the noncash gifts exceeding $500 and in addition was there any agreement between donor and donee about the disposition of these latter goods, and (d) did the organization file Form 8283 and give Form 8282 to donors of these latter goods?

9. Was a professional fund raiser hired? If, yes, (a) the name and address, (b) the nature of the contract, including the amount and basis for computing compensation, and (c) if a mailing list was used, its size, cost of mailings, number of donor responses, and the total dollar amount generated by the mailing.

10. If a professional fund raiser was used, was there (a) any business or family relationship between any officer or employee of the fund raiser and the nonprofit, and (b) was the fund raiser the creator of the nonprofit?

11. Did the professional fund raiser have check writing or cashing authority?

12. Did the charity conduct bingo and other games and (a) were these subject to unrelated business income tax, and (b) were the required income tax forms filed?

13. If the charity conducted one or more travel tours, (a) did it do so with a for-profit travel agency, with which it or its officers had a connection, such as sharing the same address or building, personnel, space, officers or other personnel, (b) was there a contract, and (c) did the written promotional material indicate that there were educational, social, or recreational aspects of the tour?

14. If the charity ran a thrift or gift shop, (a) did the charity solicit used clothing or other property from donors for resale by a for-profit firm, (b) did the firm pay the charity and what were the terms of compensation, (c) what is the relationship between the thrift shop and the charity and any for-profit firm, and (d) if the charity received surplus or nonsalable goods from a for-profit firm, what was the fair market value and how were the goods used by the nonprofit?

Source: Prepared by author from Form 9215 (1–90) from the Department of the Treasury-Internal Revenue Service.

UNLAWFUL MARKETING AND SOLICITATION

Solicitation practices have come under more and more scrutiny by the federal, state, and watchdog agencies. The IRS has put nonprofits on notice that it will strengthen its compliance investigations. It expects answers to about 100 questions. These are consolidated above.

States also have specific laws governing solicitation. These vary. Table 8.2 has been prepared to alert the manager to where there may be a specific state provision that ought to be carefully checked before launching a solicitation campaign. A telephone number is also supplied. The table is based on a more complete body of information supplied by the American Association of Fund-raising counsel.

TABLE 8.2 State Laws Regulating Charitable Solicitations

State/Regulatory Agency	Charitable Organizations				Paid Solicitors	Fund-Raising Counsel
	Registration or Licensing Requirements	Reporting Dates and Requirements	Exemptions	Solicitation Disclosure Requirements	Registration/Licensing and Bonding Requirements	Registration/Licensing and Bonding Requirements
Alabama	×	×		×		
Alaska						
Arizona						
Arkansas	×	×	×	×	×	×
California	×	×	×	×	×	
Colorado	×					
Connecticut	×	×	×	×	×	×
Delaware						
District of Columbia	×	×	×	×		
Florida				×		
Georgia	×	×	×	×	×	×
Hawaii	×	×	×	×	×	×
Idaho	×		×			
Illinois	×	×		×	×	×
Indiana	×			×	×	×
Iowa	×					
Kansas	×	×	×	×	×	×
Kentucky	×			×	×	×
Louisiana	×				×	×
Maine	×	×	×	×	×	×
Maryland	×	×	×	×	×	×
Massachusetts	×	×	×	×	×	×
Michigan	×	×	×		×	×

State					
Minnesota	×	×	×	×	×
Mississippi	×				
Missouri	×	×	×	×	
Montana					
Nebraska	×	×			
Nevada	×	×			
New Hampshire	×	×	×	×	×
New Jersey	×	×	×	×	×
New Mexico	×	×	×	×	×
New York	×	×	×	×	×
North Carolina	×	×	×	×	
North Dakota	×	×		×	
Ohio	×	×	×	×	×
Oklahoma	×	×	×	×	×
Oregon	×	×	×		
Pennsylvania	×	×	×	×	×
Rhode Island	×	×	×	×	×
South Carolina	×	×	×		
South Dakota					
Tennessee	×	×	×	×	×
Texas	×	×	×		
Utah	×	×	×	×	
Vermont					
Virginia	×	×	×	×	×
Washington	×	×	×	×	×
West Virginia	×	×	×	×	×
Wisconsin	×	×	×	×	×
Wyoming					

× indicates a regulation exists.

Sources: Adapted with permission by author from complete data published by American Association of Fund-Raising Counsel, Inc. (AAFRC), 25 West 43 Street, New York, N.Y.

Nonprofits are not legally or morally immune from prosecution for violations of laws concerning advertising. They should not misrepresent the facts or give assurances they cannot keep. Such interstate misrepresentation would contravene Federal Trade Commission rules on advertising, in addition to being unethical and perhaps ultimately counterproductive.

Neither should they engage in collusion to set market prices and market conditions; thus, the U.S. Justice Department's investigation of colleges and universities for possible violation of the Clayton and the Sherman antitrust acts. They prohibit collusion in setting prices (in this case tuition and scholarships). They also prohibit the corollary, which is to control market share (in this case enrollment levels). In the same vein, the Federal Trade Commission unleashed an antitrust action against the College Football Association and Capital Cities/ABC for illegally restraining competition by their exclusive broadcast agreement. In 1984, the Supreme Court put an end to the National Collegiate Athletic Association's monopoly over broadcasting of games of college teams.

Other possible violations can arise from marketing techniques that violate Federal Communication Commission rules (see the accompanying insert on page 241).

The U.S. Post Office in some regions has recently tightened their enforcement of postal rates in cases of nonprofits that do joint marketing with for-profit firms. Many of these nonprofits are being charged regular commercial rates on these joint mailings, rather than the lower nonprofits rates. One culprit appears to be envelopes displaying the name of the for-profit firm. This is seen as advertising.

The Omnibus Budget Reconciliation Act (OBRA) of 1987 introduces two new laws concerning advertising by nonprofits. It says that nonprofits to which contributions are not tax deductible (as described in Chapter 2) must state that fact clearly in all advertising. They should not, for example, leave any doubt that the attendance at a dinner, the purchase of an item, and even a contribution would lead to a tax deduction when it would not.

The act also requires that if the tax-exempt nonprofit markets a service or product that is readily obtainable from the federal government to an individual about himself or herself (such as a Social Security number or other personal record) the advertising must contain "an express statement in a conspicuous and recognizable format" that the same product or service can be obtained from the federal government. This rule applies only to a service or product relative to the individual client and only when it can be supplied by the federal government for $2.50, including postage and handling costs. This $2.50 limit will be adjusted upward for inflation.

THE ANNOUNCEMENTS THAT
DREW CRITICISM

Following are the on-air acknowledgments of corporate supporters that prompted the Federal Communications Commission to criticize WVXU-FM, a public radio station in Cincinnati:

"This WVXU traffic-watch update is brought to you by Jiffy Lube, now offering a discount on air-conditioner recharge with a Pennzoil oil change and 14-point lube check."

"'Morning Edition' is brought to you in part by Amatulli & Associates, offering creative services for advertising, marketing, and training."

"The Choice is Yours is pleased to sponsor programming on WVXU. A health-food store and restaurant, The Choice is Yours is located at 831 Delta, on Mount Lookout Square. Fresh and original foods are the specialty."

"'Morning Edition' is made possible in part by a grant from Arthur Andersen & Company and Andersen Consulting, serving accounting and audit, tax, and management-information consulting needs for over 75 years."

"'Morning Edition' is made possible in part by Strauss & Troy, a Cincinnati-based law firm in its 36th year.

Programming on WVXU is made possible in part by the new Maritain Gallery, featuring art expressing timeless traditional truths in contemporary visual vocabulary."

Source: *CHRONICLE OF PHILANTHROPY,* January 23, 1990, p. 23. Reprinted by permission.

MARKETING, LOBBYING, AND LIABILITY

As we discussed in Chapter 4, political expenditures on the part of the nonprofit organization are illegal and there can be no substantial amount spent on lobbying. These rules can be violated when marketing implies or involves endorsement or disapproval of a candidate or the promotion or criticism of a bill. Such statements have to be carefully crafted, or the organization should consider the more objective rule that permits some lobbying based on the aggregate expenditures of the organization, as described in Chapter 4.

To see what we mean, watch the next television commercial of the National Rifle Association. These commercials address the mission of the organization, not necessarily particular bills; they market the organization's purposes and recruit new members. They ask members to express their opinion, not *an* opinion. Which opinion do you think they express?

With regard to liability, discussed in Chapters 5 and 16, a group of doctors called Doctors Ought to Care, sold T-shirts making fun of Miller Lite and its marketing campaign. The T-shirt said, "We're grabbing a potty" and showed a man vomiting in a potty. The doctors argued that beer was detrimental to health and therefore physicians ought to care about reducing or moderating its consumption. They were sued by the beer producer who charged slander, damage to the company's goodwill, and the illegal use of the company's trademark, Miller Lite.[12] While the case was settled, it does show the need to scrutinize marketing campaigns especially for those nonprofits that are advocacy groups. All nonprofits need the same vigilance over their marketing.

UNRELATED BUSINESS INCOME TAX: ADVERTISING

The case of the American College of Physicians, Chapter 3, illustrates the impact that advertising in a newsletter or journal may have. It can lead to taxation through the unrelated business income tax described in that chapter and discussed further in Chapter 11.

It is probably true that for most incidental carrying of advertisements there would be no threat of a taxation. Let us review three cases. Richardson William Charity enters into an agreement with Benjamin's Publishers. The publisher solicits ads, collects fees, and gives the organization a percentage and free copies since these appear in the organization's annual program. The publisher has sole control over ads but makes them conform to the culture of Richardson William's Charity, which gets free copies and a cut in the advertising fees charged by the publisher. The IRS ruled that there were so many ads on a page that not once constituted a significant revenue generator. The amounts were too small to be of any commercial significance.[13]

In another case, The Cesaar-Burns Artists, a nonprofit, enters into a contract with a firm, the Carlogh Corporation. The firm does very much the same thing as above. The nonprofit does not pay overhead, production, or distribution costs, but gets free copies and a share of the total net revenue, including subscriptions, from the publication—not just a share of the advertising income. Here, again, the IRS ruled that this was not unrelated business income.[14]

In a third case, the results were different. An organization leases its mailing list to an insurance company. The company uses the list to actively solicit life insurance among the members of the organization. The organization not only endorsed the company and permitted it to use its logo; it promoted the sale of the policies. The IRS ruled that two aspects of this transaction created unrelated business income—the mailing list rental for commercial purposes and the active promotion of the insurance sales.[15]

Probably one of the most celebrated of these advertisement and taxation cases involves the NCAA, which we will discuss in Chapter 11. All of them point to one fact: before undertaking significant advertising and marketing, consider the tax implication. Again, taxation, by itself, should not defeat a good idea. Pay it.

THE IMPORTANCE OF TRUSTEE POLICY

So much of marketing is based on timing and opportunity that it is judicious for a board of trustees to lay broad policy guidelines. Two events, occurring almost simultaneously in the middle of 1990, are instructive. At the very same time that Volvo was withdrawing a commercial because it falsely "demonstrated" that its car could withstand being driven over by a substantially heavier vehicle, a nonprofit was being sued because an ad in its magazine was allegedly responsible for a boy being shot to death. We need not judge either of these cases here. The message is very similar: marketing is not risk free. Couple this fact with the enforcement of rules governing solicitation and "exchanges" and we see the need for trustees to lay down broad guidelines. The reasons are clear. An ad carried by a magazine or publication owned by a nonprofit can (1) mar its reputation, (2) expose it to unrelated business income tax as discussed in Chapter 3 and 8, (3) expose it to legal action, (4) expose its donors to taxation when an exchange is implied, and (5) probably eventually cause the revocation of its tax-exempt status. The trustees cannot shield themselves from these consequences.

Policy Guidelines for Advertising and Marketing

To assist trustees, here are five topics on marketing and solicitation for which they may have to someday develop a policy:

1. The use of the organization's name, logo, and resources, and the control of prohibited expenditures particularly on politics and lobbying
2. The meeting of legal requirements on disclosures to donors
3. The filing prior to soliciting and the reporting to the governmental authorities as required
4. The avoiding of transactions not at arm's length, and without regard to an ethical and moral code

5. The image the organization wishes to project to whom, and with what purpose

EVALUATION

Every marketing program should be evaluated by management. The evaluation should consider costs, results, and public acceptability. We refer the reader to various marketing texts that discuss the technicalities of evaluating marketing depending on what is being marketed and the strategy being employed. Evaluation methodologies are readily available to any nonprofit. How much was raised? How often are our public announcements sought? How many people respond by requesting more information? What response do we get from a focus group of persons who represent the population to which we are targeting our message? Management needs evaluation of marketing because marketing uses the organization's resources and goodwill.

FIVE MS TO SUCCESSFUL NONPROFIT MARKETING

In the marketing of an organization, begin with the mission. People give to causes in which they believe. Foundations, whether corporate or private, focus on certain missions. One study found that 86 percent of its respondents rated the mission and the programs that support the mission to be extremely important in influencing their decision to give. See Chapters 9 and 10.

Public perception of the management is important. When the public loses confidence in the management, it reduces its gifts. Foundations and corporations do not give to those in whom they have little confidence. Gifts to Covenant House (a very worthy cause) dropped precipitously once negative news about the management hit the streets. The same thing happened to television ministries after the Bakker and the Swaggart episodes. Confidence in the ethics as well as the competence of the management is essential.

Another key factor is the fiscal integrity of the organization. David Rockefeller in his founding address to the Business Committee for the Arts, Inc., 1966, was on target when he said, "Even the most public-spirited corporation has, I think, a right to expect the organization seeking its help to prove that it has competent management, a realistic budget and workable plans to attain immediate objectives as well as long-range goals." The hardest organizations to market are those that have long-lasting deficits. Potential donors view their gifts as going down a drain rather than propelling new initiatives.

A good plan stating the mission of the organization, what and how it intends to do something about it, a competent and trustworthy management, a budget that shows that it is fiscally possible, and financial statements that show the organization is fiscally sound are the sine qua non of marketing a nonprofit. Fancy brochures sometimes draw attention, but they may backfire. They do not hide faults and do not communicate need. Let the organization speak for itself.

Finally, it is important to remember that the essential difference between marketing for a for-profit firm and marketing in a nonprofit is that, in the former, an individual expects to and does have a right to some property or service equal to the value of the money he or she paid. The exchange is based on an assumption of quid pro quo. In nonprofit marketing, the challenge is to have someone give up cash and receive absolutely nothing or something that is noticeably worth less in return. Quid pro quo is not the motivation.

Based on the above, we recommend that successful marketing for a nonprofit organization must depend on 5Ms:

1. **Mission:** The purpose to which people are called should appeal to a meaningful segment of people.
2. **Management:** The ethics and the skills of those who manage the organization and its resources are important assets in marketing.
3. **Money:** Organizations that are broke have a hard time raising money. Money attracts money.
4. **Message:** The message should communicate a name, mission, product, or service, or a combination of these.
5. **Method:** The way the message is communicated should be cost effective and in keeping with legal and ethical standards and yet make it convenient for the audience to respond.

These 5Ms do not describe marketing techniques, which are best discussed in a separate text. These are the principal policy concerns for any nonprofit contemplating a marketing campaign. Bear in mind that a marketing campaign can be ineffective if it does not include opportunities for the target group to respond, and if the resources derived from the response, either through sales or donations, are mismanaged due to a lack of sound management principles or ethical standards. PTL Ministry raised a lot of money and from that perspective was successful. It lost its tax-exempt status, went bankrupt, led many to despair, and a few to jail.

AN ETHICAL DILEMMA IN MARKETING

Aside from general marketing principles, a task that management cannot escape is that of keeping the organization ethical in its marketing and solicitation practices. The state of Virginia and nine others collected a total of $2.1 million in a settlement against a fund raiser and a group of charities for deceptive marketing. Contributors were led to expect large prizes in a sweepstake. Many got 10 cents.

Many difficult ethical issues can arise in any marketing activity, from the sale of mailing lists of members, subscribers, and donors and the associated personal information that these lists may contain, to ethical issues that hit at the heart of the organization's mission. Let us take the following case.

Do Not Eat Your Heart Out

In 1989 the American Heart Association (AHA) announced that it would endorse specific products by brand name based on how healthy these products were. Immediately, the organization was denounced by companies that were to be excluded and questions were raised by the Federal Food and Drug Administration and some state attorneys general about the propriety of this decision. Some of these complaints had to do with the possibility that the AHA's message would lead people to believe that just because some food was not listed it was not as healthy.

Ethical questions were raised about whether this was an appropriate role for a nonprofit to play and whether this would compromise the organization. Companies that were excluded from the approved list complained. Was AHA selling out? Was this ethical? Was this product endorsement? Or, was this just another scheme to raise money if companies were required to pay AHA for the seal of approval? Or, was this just useful information for the public—identifying healthy products? The AHA eventually dropped its plans.

Before you agree with the complaints, consider that the highly regarded and reputable *Consumer Reports* is published by a 501(c)(3) nonprofit, the Consumer Union. What may be the salient differences if any? So-called "seal of approval" labeling is also being considered by other groups. It is not a dead idea yet. What do you think?

Real Angels Fly

Seven former students of the Maharishi Mahesh Yogi are suing their ex-guru because he promised to teach them to fly, but left them sitting on the runway, flapping their knees. They're asking $9 million each. Truly, man is an interesting creature.

The deal was this, complain the earthbound litigants: In exchange for lengthy spells of meditation (and in some cases, it is charged, working for His Holiness at $25 a month), the student would become a "Master of Creation," which meant learning to fly and read minds.

Didn't work, complain the unwilling groundlubbers. They can neither fly nor think straight. "Flying," they discovered, meant hopping around with the legs folded in the lotus position. Moreover, all that time spent meditating, they say, "arrested and retarded the normal process of maturation and development," making it difficult to get a job on the stock exchange or otherwise pursue an ordinary life.

True believers will maintain that the plaintiffs are giving up too soon, that if they just stuck with it a while longer they'd soon be flying circles around Peter Pan. Skeptics, resigning themselves to the dangers of commercial air travel, will say that anyone who thinks he can be taught to fly deserves all he gets, and it is true that, for the right price, someone can be found to teach you almost anything you want to know.

But what is it, do you suppose, that makes grown-ups think they can overcome the law of gravity by shutting their eyes, crossing their legs, and putting their joints in overdrive? Two explanations come to mind. Hope springs eternal is one. The other, a commentary on the backsliding of traditional institutions, suggests that those who stand for nothing will fall for anything.

Source: "Another Air Disaster," *Washington Times,* Wednesday, September 11, 1985, p. 9A. Reprinted with permission of the *Washington Times.*

SUMMARY AND CONCLUSIONS

In Chapter 6 we saw that the strategic planning process is employable in determining general management strategies, as well as some specific tasks such as marketing. In this chapter we focused on caveats that the management of the nonprofit should allow to influence their marketing strategies. We warn of the dangers of the concept of exchange of values. We also elaborated on the role of targeting and the need for management to decide what is to be marketed and to whom. We remind the reader of laws that affect the marketing activities of nonprofits. Keep the mission preeminent.

NOTES

1. The operative word is deductible. Even in exchanges involving property of like kind, such as real estate, there is no deductibility. Such exchanges, called 1035 exchanges, are not taxable.
2. Whether or not these taxes are assessed depends on the transaction being classified as an unrelated or related business income. See Chapters 11 and 12.
3. These rules are explained in Revenue Procedures 90-21.
4. IRS Private Letter Ruling, 9004030, February 5, 1990.
5. Leon E. Wynter, "Edley of United Negro College Fund to Retire after 17 Years in Top Post," *Wall Street Journal*, Wednesday, Aug. 1, 1990, p. B4.
6. We discuss risks in Chapter 16.
7. Emmett D. Carson, *The Charitable Appeals Fact Book: How Blacks and Whites Respond to Different Types of Fund-raising Efforts* (Lanham, Md.: University Press of America, 1989).
8. Ann Bubnic's research on physicians as discussed in "Doctors Are Not Stingy, A New Survey Shows," *Nonprofit Times*, May 1988, p. 3.
9. Peter Ames, "Marketing in Museums: Means or Master of the Mission?" *Curator*, 32, no. 1 (March 1989), pp. 5–15.
10. Lee Rosenbaum, "Art's Cozy Relationship with Business," *New York Times*, Sunday, Sept. 9, 1990.
11. Lyle E. Schaller, "Megachurch," *Christianity Today*, May 5, 1990, pp. 20–24.
12. Wade Lambert and Wayne E. Green, "Law," *Wall Street Journal*, Thursday, Mar. 8, 1990, B8.
13. Based on Internal Revenue Letter 9044071.
14. Based on Internal Revenue Letter 9023003.
15. Internal Revenue Letter 8828011.

SUGGESTED READINGS

Internal Revenue Service Publication #1391, Aug. 1988.

Omnibus Budget Reconciliation Act of 1987, particularly Sections 6711 and 6710.

Philanthropy Monthly, *Survey of State Laws Regulating Charitable Solicitation*, (New Melford, Connecticut: 1991 update).

Revenue Procedure 90-21 in *Internal Revenue Bulletin*, No. 1990-8, Feb. 20, 1990, p. 20.

U.S. Supreme Court, *Robert L. Hernandez* V. *Commissioner*, No. 87-963.

PART III

Money

"Before there was Rio Plaza, there was a vacant
lot, an idea about serving this community, and
hope for what this new housing would mean.
LISC's investment in us—in time, technical
expertise and resources—gave us the confidence to
take on the challenge and see it through. The
difference in East Little Havana is more than
homes. It's the fulfillment of a lifelong dream, and
a step toward our goal of bettering this
community."

Manny Rivero, *Executive Director*
East Little Havana CDC
Miami

Source: *Local Initiative Support Corporation,
Annual Report 1989*, page 1

Chapter 9

Increasing Gifts and Contributions

Nonprofits compete among themselves, and with other uses that corporations and individuals have for money. One responsibility of financial management in a nonprofit is to increase its volume of gifts and contributions. This requires an understanding of the motives that corporations and individuals have for giving, the limitations on giving, and strategies for receiving large gifts. These are the subjects of this chapter which applies to public charities as well as to associations that run foundations.

No nonprofit manager should attempt to give tax or legal advice to a potential donor. Knowing the legal and tax aspects of giving allows the manager to (1) make an effective appeal, (2) avoid problematic gifts and transfers, (3) avoid ethical charges of improper inducement of a donor, and, (4) in general, do the right thing.

THE IMPORTANCE OF CONTRIBUTIONS

As we stated in Chapter 1, the deductibility of contributions distinguishes among 501(c)(3) organizations, from other nonprofits. Even within this category, however, the 509(a)(1)s and the 509(a)(2)s are financed differently with the former, having less business-related income and more contributions than the latter. Consequently, contributions, as a category, is a varying percentage of support and revenues among nonprofit organizations.

Among nonprofits, even religious groups serving the needy, there is also considerable reliance on funding from governments. Gifts and contributions (in cash and in kind) are a significant part of their public support and revenues. Table 9.1 shows the distributions for the Lutheran World Relief as an illustration. Size also makes a difference. Among organizations with assets less than $1,000,000, over 50 percent of their revenues comes from contributions. Among larger institutions, it can be as little as 13 percent—not a negligible amount.

THE COMPETITION FOR GIFTS AND CONTRIBUTIONS

A portion of income earned by a household or a corporation goes to pay current liabilities. These are legal obligations due to be paid within a year and most within thirty days. The obligations include the payment of rent, alimony, child support, food, tuition, credit-card balances, mortgage payments, payment of wages and salaries, current insurance premiums, estimated taxes, and notes and accounts payable. These dollars are not available for giving.

But both corporations and households have discretionary use of some of their dollars after putting away for their own futures. These include saving and planning for retirement and future obligations of the family, investment in new plants or equipment, buying of furniture, buying of automobiles, repayment of long-term debt, paying of dividends to stockholders, research and development, and so on.

It is only after such needs are met that there is a residual that can be donated. We may call this residual donatable funds. This residual is competed for by the approximately 1 million existing nonprofits. Thus, it is a marketing challenge to cause a corporation or household to view a specific nonprofit as more deserving than others, or to obtain a commitment, such as a tithe, so that giving becomes the moral equivalent of a legal obligation.

Foundations too have similar financial obligations that must be met even though their principal purpose is to give. They must pay for office

TABLE 9.1 LWR Condensed Financial Statement for 1989 (subject to audit)

Receipts	
Church body support:	
Evangelical Lutheran Church in America	$ 3,421,296
Lutheran Church–Missouri Synod	1,934,005
Contributions:	
Individuals, congregations	1,062,376
Wisconsin Evangelical Lutheran Synod	15,000
Interfaith Hunger Appeal	60,000
CROP	143,010
Bequests	60,114
Investment income	261,231
U.S. government	
Ocean freight	350,000
Matching grant	557,977
African drought grants	12,608,968
Other receipts	67,297
Total Cash Receipts	20,541,274
Value of gifts-in-kind	16,339,106
	$36,880,380

Source: Reprinted by permission from *Lutheran World Relief* 1989.

space, equipment, and workers. Some foundations also have long-term commitments to support specific nonprofit organizations. Like individuals and corporations, they sometimes experience a decline in their income. It is only after they have met all obligations that donations can be made.

Table 9.2 shows that 47 percent of all donations from all donors (individuals, corporations, and foundations) go to religious groups. The most compelling story of Table 9.2 is that the remaining 50 percent of the contribution pool must be competed for by a variety of missions. Obviously there is competition for funds among and within these large groupings. With such keen competition, an understanding of the motives and methods of giving offers an important edge. What are some of these motives and methods?

INDIVIDUAL AND CORPORATE MOTIVES FOR GIVING

The evidence is very strong that the ability to deduct all or some portion of a gift is a strong impetus for giving.[1] This is so because the deduction means that the cost of the gift is shared by the government. Thus, for a person in the 30 percent bracket, a gift of $3000 means that the gift only

TABLE 9.2   Recipients of Contributions, 1980, 1984, 1989 (in billions of dollars)

Mission	1980		1984		1989	
	Dollars	Percent	Dollars	Percent	Dollars	Percent
Religion	25.05	45.1	35.43	50.2	54.32	47.3
Education	5.77	10.4	7.29	10.3	10.69	9.3
Health	5.79	10.4	6.84	9.7	10.04	8.7
Human service	5.62	10.1	7.88	11.2	11.39	10.0
Arts and culture	3.66	6.6	4.50	6.4	7.49	6.5
Public benefit	1.79	3.2	1.94	2.7	3.62	3.2
All other uses	7.90	14.2	6.67	9.5	17.15	15.0
Total	55.58	100.0	70.55	100.0	114.70	100.0

Source: *Calculated with permission from Giving U.S.A.*, American Association of Fund-Raising Counsel, 1989, p. 15.

costs that person $2100 since income tax liability is reduced by $900. A person in the 20 percent bracket who makes the same gift saves $600 from income tax so that the gift costs only $2400. Thus, the higher the income tax bracket is, the greater the savings and the less the gift costs the donor. For this reason, economists agree that tax reform lowering the income tax rates dampens the tax motive for giving and, by the same token, any increase in the rate strengthens the motive.

The tax motive for giving occurs even when planning one's estate. Thus, economists have found that the ability to deduct 100 percent of all charitable deductions at death is an important reason why wealthy donors pass on property and cash to nonprofits at the time of their death.[2]

There are also nontax reasons for giving that go beyond the emotional appeal. Some people give to express thanks. Thus, alumni make gifts to their alma mater. Gifts are also made to further a mission with

---

HOSIERY MAKERS unite to produce gun covers after soldiers request pantyhose.

The National Association of Hosiery Manufacturers donates 300,000 knitted covers worth about $500,000 to help protect M-16 rifles from sand in Saudi Arabia. The Defense Logistics Agency has also received other items to be used as gun covers including 20,000 plastic bags from Dow Chemical and 1,000 condoms from Safetex Corp., Colonial Heights, Va., says a DLA spokesman.

By Pamela Sebastian, "Business Bulletin," The Wall Street Journal, January 31, 1991, p. 1.

which the donor agrees, such as donations to religious causes. Gifts are made in response to group pressures, objectives, common goals and expectations—payroll deduction or office contribution campaigns in which the office sets or is given a target. People also give simply because they are asked—street corner collections. People give to honor and to memorialize others or special events. Giving sometimes brings attention, influence, and satisfaction. Giving is both altruistic and egotistic.

Sophisticated ways of appealing to a potential donor have been studied. Social psychologists[3] have studied the effect of "foot-in-the-door" approaches.[4] These imply that there can be increased giving if an approach that begins with a plea for a small gift is followed by a plea for a large gift. The thinking here is that a smaller request provides an entry that can be used to get a larger gift once the organization has a foot in the door.

There is also some evidence to support the "door-in-the-face" approach.[5] This approach confronts the potential donor with a very large request, which one does not expect to receive, and then follows with a smaller request. Supposedly, the potential donor after rejecting the larger amount is more receptive to the smaller as a compromise. It appears that the efficacy of these approaches depends on the length of time that passes between the first and second appeal and the probability that the same person in a family or in a corporation receives both appeals.

It has also been shown by social psychologists that "modeling" can influence giving.[6] This means that a potential donor is more likely to make a gift when there is evidence that some other person who has significance to him or her has made a similar or larger gift.

Such phrases as "even a penny" or a "generous family donation" are also considered to be stimuli for giving.[7] The former legitimatizes paltry or small gifts and the latter implies a large gift reflecting well on the family rather than on a single individual. There is even reason to believe that seeking a check is preferred to cash because persons are more accustomed to dealing with larger numbers when writing checks. The gift is, therefore, likely to be larger.[8]

When these techniques are used within a framework that maximizes the tax benefits from giving and that appreciates that most people who give have no legal, tax, or charitable advice on how to give for tax purposes,[9] and that most people give at the time a request is made rather than a long time after,[10] it is evident that a good education in the tax fundamentals of giving could enhance the productivity of fund raising.

Before turning to the fundamentals of giving, however, there are preliminaries to be discussed. Not only do households have reasons for giving, but so, too, do corporations. The evidence is clear that corporations are influenced by the ability to deduct their gifts.[11] However, there are at least four brand nontax reasons.[12] One is the belief by many corporate leaders that they have a social responsibility to respond to the need of the community and that this is a form of expressing corporate citizenship.[13] A second belief held by some corporate leaders is that giving is a form of prudent investment.[14] It stimulates good will with workers, clients, and the community and improves the corporate market. A third view is that giving represents "enlightened self-interest."[15] This view states that the motive for corporate giving is a combination of corporate citizenship, prudent investment, and the desire to take a leadership role in promoting an activity to encourage others to give, permitting each donor to be identified with the success of the project to reap direct and indirect benefits from the gifts. A fourth motive is that giving is an extension of the corporate marketing, sales, and profitability.

These motives for corporate giving are buttressed by responses of corporate leaders about why they give to specific causes. It has been shown that the two most important reasons for corporate giving are a sense of corporate citizenship and to protect and improve the corporate business environment.[16]

As in the case of households, the method of appeal is as important as the motive. Some methods have been identified to stimulate corporate donations.[17] One method is to form a corporate group that pledges a certain percentage of their pretax net income (profits before taxes) and that challenges other corporations to do the same. A second is for the stockholders as a group to instruct the corporation to send perhaps $2 per share owned by the stockholders to a specific organization or to have it set aside for a specific nonprofit mission. A third method is to get the corporation to match employee contributions to qualified nonprofits.

All these methods must be incorporated into a good marketing scheme whether the target is made up of individual donors or corporations or combinations of the two. The marketing scheme will be more successful as more is known about the primary motives for giving—one of which is the tax deductibility of gifts.

Our motives for making these donations are not purely altruistic. Rather, we view them as sound investments in a society that has to cope with illiteracy, poverty, drug abuse and disease. And we believe that they have paid off not only for the communities we serve, but also for our customers, our employees and our shareholders.

Source: Kenneth A. Macke, "... With Some Attendant Risks," *New York Times,* December 30, 1990, p. 11. Macke is chief executive officer and chairman of Dayton Hudson. With permission of the author and the New York Times.

Just as individuals and corporations have motives for giving, so too do governments and foundations. Foundations give to certain causes because this is the purpose of their being. While the government rarely gives, it contracts out government services as a means of promoting social welfare in a manner that is more efficient than if the government itself conducted the activity. As a matter of fact, foundations and governments are similar in the sense that most of what they "give" are contracts requiring specific performance. That is, they typically give with the understanding that only certain activities will be conducted with their funds. Some of these are highly restrictive and are really payments for services and should not be confused with gifts. A gift is an unrequited transfer where nothing of equal value is given in return. We shall say more about this later.

TEN DANGERS IN RECEIVING GIFTS

Some gifts are simply not worth taking. The management of most major nonprofits has had the experience of turning a gift down, wishing they had turned one down, or wishing they had been sufficiently alert so as to have negotiated more favorable terms. Chicago Goodwill, for example, was given a sizable piece of property. Sometime after accepting the gift, but too late to protect themselves, they discovered that the land teemed with hazardous waste. This not only precluded their use of the land, but the value of the land fell, liabilities rose, and the cost of removing the waste became prohibitive. It was too late to return the gift or even have its donor share the liability for the waste removal or any damage that it may do.

In recognition of this tragic event, the following guide is intended to alert managers about some dangers in accepting different types of gifts. Following each is a chapter reference where reading in this book in addition to this chapter may be of help.

Type of Gift and Precaution

1. Land: Beware of easements, restrictions on how all or parts of the land may be used, outstanding debt, hazardous waste and environmental conditions, liabilities, liens held by creditors using the property as security, new restrictions imposed by donor and local zoning laws, unrelated business income tax depending on use, and the cost and risks of holding unimproved land (Chapters 14 and 16).

2. Appreciated property: Beware of being a co-conspirator in a fraudulently inflated appraisal. Art, securities, jewelry, real estate, and historical artifacts are common types of appreciated property (Chapters 7–10).

3. Unappreciated property: Accepting junk leads to disposal costs and potential liability if others are placed at risk (Chapter 16).

4. Real estate: Beware of all considerations in 1 through 3 above. Determine carrying and maintenance costs, depreciation required, income stream to support, proposed use and disposition (Chapters 7–10).

5. Cash: Beware of the impact on the organization, such as changing its character to private foundation, changing its mission, or causing its image or 501(c)(3) status to be lost. Check out the source. Also beware of undue influence of the donor on the organization (Chapters 4 and 10).

6. Short-term gift: The organization must comply with reporting requirements for gifts it disposes of within two years of acquisition (Chapters 1, 8, and 9).

7. Long-term gift: Be sure that maintenance and operating costs are projected and can be met (Chapters 6 and 18).

8. Gift subject to debt: Who will pay off the debt? Beware of unrelated business income tax and valuation problems (Chapters 10 and 11).

9. Insurance: Who owns the policy? Who will collect? Who will pay premiums? The beneficiary status is no assurance (Chapter 10).

10. Testamentary gifts: Be prepared for delay if the will is challenged. Also, the person may change his or her mind prior to death (Chapter 10).

For gifts of **stocks** see the next section.

Some gifts are dangerous because they cause division and controversy. See Chapter 5. Others create expenses. Some gifts come with restrictions as to their use or display. Some are contingent upon matching funds. These challenge grants, as they are called, push the organization on a preconceived course. All of these factors must be taken into account by the trustees. Be cautious about accepting large gifts without a predetermined plan of their use and disposition. How do they fit?

A sensible strategy is to immediately sell properties that are received as donations. This frees the organization of risks and expenses. The cash can be folded into on-going plans already approved by the trustees. Remember there is a reporting requirement. There is also a disclosure required by many corporations. Their deduction may be affected. See discussion later in this chapter.

WHY CORPORATIONS MAY SAY NO

We have discussed the motivations for corporate giving. The objective of this section is to acquaint the reader with certain resistance factors to corporate giving. What do corporations have to give and why may they resist? In short, what must the corporation consider before it makes a specific type of gift? This knowledge should enhance the fund-raising capacity of the nonprofit. Good fund raisers, like good sales people, anticipate points of resistance and prepare for them. The following guide should help you.

1. Stocks: Gifts by the corporation of its own stock are almost certainly illegal and will invite a suit by stockholders. Forget it. A stockholder may make gifts of his or her shares of stocks to the nonprofit. This is how Maccalester College became a major holder of *Readers Digest*, the Hershey Foundation of Hershey stocks, and Kellogg Foundation of Kellogg breakfast stocks. Appeal to the individual as a stockholder—not to the corporation.

To get the controlling share of a stock is also to assume the company's liabilities and problems. One owns the company lock, stock and barrel, so to speak. Check it out before accepting.

Stocks will have to be appraised if they are not publicly traded (that is, on the stock market) and have an estimated value in excess of $10,000. Officers and directors of corporations cannot give stock based on the anticipation that the price of the stock is about to decline so that they can maximize their deductions. This is insider trading, which is illegal. Moreover, they cannot give away stocks just to evade taxes.

2. Real property: This is buildings and land. The corporation would have to consider tax implications, particularly the depreciation and investment tax credit it took on the property or its improvements. It would also have to consider easements—prohibitions about what it can and cannot do with the property, covenants or agreements with creditors who placed restrictions on the disposition of the property, its exposure to environmental hazard liability, future use of the land in corporate long-range plan, resale price, and the donee's use of the land or building, which affects the amount of deduction they can take.

Real property may also be given for conservation purposes. Many times what motivates the company or individual gift is that the value of the property has declined.

3. Bonds: When a corporation issues a bond, it does so to raise capital from creditors. Giving these away would most certainly create legal problems. Again, the best source is a holder of the bond.

4. Equipment: Often the corporation does not own the equipment. It is leased. When the property is owned, it may be possible that the tax benefits to be obtained from selling the equipment at a loss are greater than could be gained from a charitable deduction. Moreover, the equipment has trade-in value. The corporation may also be required to hold the equipment to meet the holding requirements for depreciation and investment tax credit.

5. Inventory: Except for small corporations, small donations, groceries and restaurant food, gifts of inventory may have to be appraised and discounted for spoilage and obsolescence. They must also meet legal quality standards. For many nonperishables, selling at a discount may yield greater gains for the corporation than giving it away. Moreover, the inventory may not be owned by the corporation. Many retailers use trust receipts. This means that the inventory is actually owned by their wholesaler–distributor or by a financing company. Therefore, it is not the retailer's to give.

Work-in-process inventory, which means materials, supplies, and unfinished goods, is not available because it is to be used in the production activities of the firm. Even if such materials are flawed or damaged, it might be better to sell them at a discount or under some other brand name or no brand name at all, as is sometimes done with clothing and bad wine.

6. Employee: Several companies assign employees to nonprofit organizations and encourage others to volunteer. The company gets no charitable deduction but continues to pay wages and benefits to these employees and deducts their salaries and benefits as normal business expenses. Hence, the deduction is not the issue. It is whether the company can afford the loss of services of an individual it continues to pay and whether that individual wishes to do it.

7. Cash: This is the easiest for the company to give. The company considers alternative uses of cash, including paying off debt, the paying of dividends to stockholders, employee benefits and executive bonuses, stock repurchases, increasing cash balances, and reinvestment. Companies have missions to which they commit themselves. Some companies prefer giving in their local or corporate communities. Some prefer the arts, education, or health.

The bottom line is that the corporate assets belong to the shareholders of the corporation, not to the corporate officers. The U.S. Supreme Court gave weight to this when it refused to hear a case concerning a New York public utility. The utility made donations and charged it as an expense that its customers paid. The high court in New York held that this could not be done because the utility was actually giving a property of the shareholders (retained earnings) and that shareholder approval, not customer charge, was the sanction needed.

Shareholder interest is a determining factor. Occidental Petroleum is an example. Its stockholders sued its chairman, Dr. Armand Hammer, for planning to use the assets of the corporation to build a $95 million museum named after him.

In addition, corporate charity is influenced by political and public relations pressures. After 25 years of supporting Planned Parenthood, for example, AT&T stopped in 1990, claiming discontent among its shareholders who oppose abortion. Yet the company continues support of teenage pregnancy prevention programs. It is the second largest corporate donor to arts and the humanities.

DIVERSIFICATION OF GIFTS AND CONTRIBUTIONS

Reliance on any single source for gifts and contributions exposes the organization to the risk of having to terminate its activities should that one source terminate its support. It also leaves the organization open to an IRS challenge of its public charity status, especially if the single donor is an individual or a corporation. In addition, it exposes the organization to the powers and preachment of the single donor. These results are likely even if there are a few donors but one is by far the single most important.

In considering its support base for gifts and contributions, the organization will benefit from an evaluation of the advantages and disadvantages of relying on gifts from individuals, corporations, foundations, or the government. Table 9.3 shows these advantages and disadvantages based on the experiences of managers of nonprofit organizations. These are self-explanatory. However, experiences in the early 1980s with government contracting would suggest that there are disadvantages in addition to the ones listed in Table 9.3. Government contracts can be withdrawn even after the nonprofit has started to fulfill the terms of the contract and has incurred expenses in doing so. Government contractors are subject to audits that could leave the nonprofit liable for returning monies to the government well after the contract has ended. There can be considerable discontinuity in government contracting as priorities and political leadership change.

GOVERNMENT PROMOTION OF GIVING

It is estimated that the deductibility of donations costs the federal government $77 billion in lost revenues.[18] State and local governments also forego revenues in income, sales, and property taxes.

TABLE 9.3 Alternative Source of Funds: Advantages and Disadvantages

The heads of Chicago philanthropic organizations agreed generally on the following "pros" and "cons" of each source of funds.

1. Individuals
    Advantages
        Freedom to use funds without restriction
        Donors have local identification with problem
        Involves volunteers in organization
        Contributions likely to continue in future years
        Large potential of funds available
    Disadvantages
        Great deal of effort required to cultivate; competition increasing
        Gifts are often small
        Capriciousness of some individuals

2. Companies
    Advantages
        Size of gifts
        Support tends to be consistent over time
        Helps develop community understanding
    Disadvantages
        Difficult to approach; requires personal contact
        Frequent turnover of top executives

3. Foundations
    Advantages
        Freedom from political pressure
        Competence of professional staffs
        Willingness to support unusually innovative or unpopular projects
        Ability to act quickly
    Disadvantages
        Unwillingness to support ongoing operating costs
        Occasional interference or too much supervision

4. Government
    Advantages
        Large amount of dollars available
        Competence of Washington personnel at upper levels
    Disadvantages
        Red tape
        Unreliability of congressional action
        Annual time horizon too short for planning
        Lack of local community and volunteer involvement
        Political pressures
        Loss of autonomy

Source: Commission on Foundations and Private Philanthropy, *Foundations, Private Giving, and Public Policy* (Chicago: University of Chicago Press, 1970), p. 237. Copyright © 1970. The University of Chicago Press. All rights reserved.

States promote giving in many ways. Texas allows hunters to deduct $15 in processing fees for the deer they donate to a program that provides meat for the poor. But there are basically two ways in which governments promote giving. One is through ongoing payroll deduction and the other is through the tax system.

Payroll Deduction

One principal way in which federal, state, and local governments assist giving is through payroll deduction. The largest of these is the Combined Federal Campaign (CFC). Through this mechanism, federal employees can have tax-deductible contributions made to charities. They may elect how much to give to each or may leave their contributions undesignated. Eight-two percent of undesignated funds, by formula, end up in local United Ways even though they receive only 29 percent of designated funds.

To qualify to be a recipient of any CFC fund, an organization must be a 501(c)(3) and certify that it is a human health and welfare organization. It must submit proof of activities and achievements in this mission. It must agree to public disclosure of its financing and governance structure. Additionally, it must promise not to release information on CFC contributors. These requirements reconfirm the ethical standards noted throughout this book and the need for engaging in good financial practices and reporting.

An organization has two avenues for joining the CFC assuming that it qualifies. National organizations, those with at least three years of experience serving at least fifteen states or are international, may apply directly to the Office of Personnel Management or, if it is a member of a national federation, through that body. A local organization, one with a local office with regular office hours and providing services to local and adjoining communities, must apply through a local federation (for example, local United Ways).[19]

Tax Deduction and Credit

The federal government coordinates a giving campaign and allows a deduction for charitable contributions. States also allow such a deduction by permitting the taxpayer to include the same contributions in computing their state income tax. In addition, in several states, there is a check-off system. This system allows the taxpayer to check off and to get a deduction for an amount that is to be forwarded by the state to a specific charity as designated by the taxpayer. The most common available check off is for wildlife. In North Carolina, it is the only check-off option. Massachusetts offers checkoffs for AIDS, wildlife and organ trans-

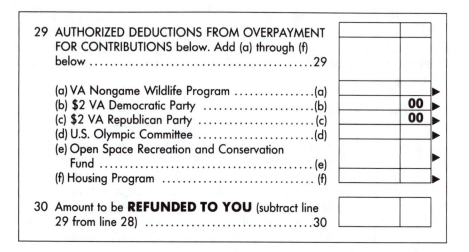

29 AUTHORIZED DEDUCTIONS FROM OVERPAYMENT
FOR CONTRIBUTIONS below. Add (a) through (f)
below 29

   (a) VA Nongame Wildlife Program ....(a)
   (b) $2 VA Democratic Party ....(b)   **00**
   (c) $2 VA Republican Party ....(c)   **00**
   (d) U.S. Olympic Committee ....(d)
   (e) Open Space Recreation and Conservation
      Fund ....(e)
   (f) Housing Program ....(f)

30 Amount to be **REFUNDED TO YOU** (subtract line
29 from line 28) 30

plants. California, Colorado, Delaware, Idaho, Iowa, Kentucky, Rhode Island and Virginia (insert above) use a check-off for the United States Olympics Committee according to the committee's 1989 report. Check-offs are most often used when the taxpayer is expecting a refund, but, may also be added to the tax liability.

A tax credit is more valuable than a deduction because, for each dollar of credit, the taxpayer reduces his or her tax liability by one dollar. With a deduction, the tax liability is reduced by only a fraction of a dollar, which varies with the tax category of the person. To illustrate, if my tax liability is $1000 and I have a credit of $200, my tax bill is reduced to $800. All states give charitable deductions. Among those that give credit, Michigan offers a 50 percent tax credit up to $200 a year for a joint return and up to $5000 on a business return for gifts to community foundations. This, unless extended, is for the period 1989 to 1991. North Carolina gives a credit of 25 percent (but not exceeding $5000) of property given for public access to a beach, wildlife, fishing, trails and waterways.

TAX DEDUCTIBILITY: THREE CASES

Three court decisions highlight some key ingredients in the law to check abuses of the tax deductibility of a donation. In *Venni v. Commissioner*, taxpayers were denied a charitable tax deduction for donations made to a church and for property transferred to the local congregations of the church.[20] The donors could not show that the congregations qualified as a tax-exempt religious group; that the donations were not intended for the personal benefits of the donors, given that the donors maintained

> Petitioners seek to deduct as charitable contributions certain transfers of land and money to the Kneadmore Life Community Church (KLCC). The KLCC's members occupied the land as an "intentional community where [they] could pursue common values of living in harmony with nature." The KLCC provided its members, inter alia, with rent-free accommodations and farmland, use of farm equipment and seed, and food grown in community gardens and orchards. These benefits were not provided as compensation for services performed. *Held*, petitioners' deductions denied because the KLCC was operated for a substantial nonexempt purpose and because its net earnings inured to the benefit of its members. Sec. 170(c)(2), I.R.C. 1954.
>
> Source: *Canada* v. *Commissioner*, 82 T.C., No. 73, June 1984, p. 973.

control over the gifts; or that the gifts were not made because the donors expected something in return. Similarly, in *Davis* v. *Commissioner*, the donation made by a couple to a church was not deductible because the wife maintained sole control over the accounts.[21] In *Magin* v. *Commissioner*, the court held that the contribution made by the taxpayer was not deductible because the recipient was not qualified and because the contribution inured to the private benefit of the donor.[22]

With these and other cases to be illustrated in mind, we can appreciate some of the constraints placed on the deduction of contributions. This knowledge helps in designing effective contribution campaigns. Let us begin with the definition of a gift. First, we give a broad definition and then we define each term.

LEGAL CHARACTERISTICS OF A GIFT

A deductible gift is an irrevocable transfer of property or cash from a qualified donor to a qualified donee for less than full consideration. The property or cash must be accepted by the donee without any retained, remainder, or partial rights belonging to the donor. The donor must not maintain control or influence over the property and may not continue to receive economic benefits from it.

Cash or Property

Deductible gifts must be in the form of property or cash, not services or free rent. While services are not gifts, expenses such as unreimbursed meals or transportation costs that are necessary for providing the service may be deductible.

Likewise, free rent is not deductible. A donor would be better off to rent the space and then donate the rental to the nonprofit. Alternatively, the building might be donated.

If the nonprofit sells a property that it received as a donation and that has a value of $500 or more within two years after it was received, it must report the sale on Form 8282. Exceptions are those properties sold for less than $500 and those that are distributed or consumed without charge and in conducting the nonprofit's mission.

Transfer

Deductible transfers must be voluntary, purposeful, and complete. A transfer of property under duress is not a gift. A transfer that is clearly the result of a misunderstanding is also not a gift. Neither is a transfer a gift when the donor is not mentally or legally competent. A transfer made in expectation of death is not a gift if the person survives. There must be a clear donative motive.

Typically, a transfer that is partial or incomplete is not a gift. Technically speaking, writing a check in the name of a nonprofit is not a gift. To illustrate, Dorotea writes her personal check for $4000 in the name of the Class of '55 to their school, LaBoca High. If she holds the check or destroys it, either action nullifies giving. The situation is only slightly better if she hands the check over to a responsible officer of the nonprofit or if she mails it. Neither of these constitutes a complete gift, for Dorotea could have insufficient funds in the bank, she could call and cancel the check, or the bank could refuse to honor the check. The gift actually takes place when the checks are honored by the bank. In its leniency, tax law treats a check as a donation on the date it was mailed, providing that it is not postdated, which would then be the date, and that it does not bounce. If the check has a condition, the gift is not completed until the nonprofit has accepted the conditions.

A nonprofit needs to keep in mind that it does not have the same recourse as a for-profit when a check bounces. A check made out to a firm represents payment for a service or goods bought. It is a legal obligation. A promise of a gift constitutes no such legal obligation. The nonprofit cannot enforce payment.

State and local laws specify how some properties are to be legally transferred. Suppose instead of $400 in cash that Celestina gave the nonprofit her automobile. This act by itself does not constitute a gift. She must also sign, date, and complete the information required on the car title and hand the title over to the nonprofit.

Real property, land and buildings, is transferred in a similar manner. A proper title must be completed, conveyed, and the transaction recorded. A person who holds stock certificates must endorse and deliver them to the nonprofit or its agents if the gift is to be complete. Gifts of U.S. Savings Bonds must follow rules prescribed by the federal government. These rules might require changes in registration. In some cases, the bond may have to be cashed. Gifts of art must be accompanied by gifts of their copyrights. Gifts to help low-income persons pay their energy bills are deductible, but the amount of the gift should be indicated as a specific part of the total paid the utility company: that is, it must be possible to distinguish the gift from the consumer's own bill.

Irrevocable

A transfer must be irrevocable to constitute a gift, meaning that there is no way in which the donor may repossess the property other than by arm's-length purchase. Any transfer with the intent or with conditions to permit repossession even by purchase is not a gift.

To illustrate, suppose Jeanine makes a transfer of her car and attaches conditions to its use. Suppose she requires that the automobile be returned to her if it is abused. This is not a gift. The transfer provides conditions for revoking the "gift." In a similar vein, an option to buy is not a gift until the option is exercised.[23]

Retained Rights

There are times when a potential donor wishes to make a gift of property but also wishes to retain certain rights over it. The rights might simply be to enjoy its use. Let us couple the concept of retained rights with that of irrevocability and see the results. Shauna makes an irrevocable gift of her horse to a riding academy with the stipulation that she has use of it on Saturdays. The gift is irrevocable if there are no conditions by which she may recapture ownership of the horse. However, she has retained rights over its use. The consequence is that the gift is partial from the point of view of the IRS and therefore there is no tax deduction. It is, however, legally irretrievable. The horse belongs to the academy.

Here is another case:

> United Artists gave old movie negatives to the Library of Congress in 1969 and took a $10 million charitable deduction. But the Claims Court has denied any deduction: Because United Artists, then owned by Transamerica Corp., kept all commercial rights, the negatives had no value.[24]

Remainder Rights

Sometimes potential donors would consider making a transfer to a nonprofit with the condition that, after some event or passage of time, all or some portion of the property be returned. These are remainder rights.

To illustrate, assume that the academy needs the horse to prepare for a show. Shauna might make a transfer with the condition that the horse be returned at the end of the show. This is not a gift. She has maintained remainder interests. No deduction is allowed and the nonprofit has no more than a loan. Furthermore, she cannot deduct the rental not charged the academy, since free rents are not deductible gifts.

Present Interests

A donor may choose to make a gift at some time in the future. This is a future-interest gift, which is not deductible. A gift has to be of present interest to be deductible. This means that the nonprofit must acquire immediate and full control and ownership of the property or cash without restrictions. By inference, a future interest gift becomes deductible only at the time that full control becomes effective, that is, when the conditions of future interest no longer exist so that the future interest is now a present interest. Accordingly, an option to buy a property in five years is a future interest and not deductible until the five-year period has passed and the option is exercised.

There is an important exception to the present-interest rule when the gift is of real property, such as a building or house. This exception will be discussed later in the chapter. What is to be remembered is that, as far as tangible personal property (property other than real estate and intangibles) is concerned, future interests are not deductible until all the contingencies of control, either by the donor or someone related to the donor, are removed. Thus, a gift that is to go from Beverly to her son H. Simon, and then to a charity is not a deductible future-interest gift. But if, after her son receives it he passes it on to an unrelated person,[25] the gift at that point becomes deductible even though it has not yet reached its final destination—the nonprofit.

Exceptions to Incomplete Transfers

In general, a transfer must be complete and of present interest to be deductible. This means that the donee must acquire complete and immediate control of the gift. The donor must maintain no retained, revocable, partial, or remainder rights.

There are notable exceptions to the general rule. One exception pertains to a situation where the donor owns less than 100 percent of a property and is therefore unable to give the entire property. Under these conditions, the donor must give an undivided share of his or her total interest in a property if such a gift is to be deducted. To understand this exception, consider the following example. Shauna owns one-half of an interest in a property comprised of a stable and ten horses. Her undivided interest is one-half of the property as it is comprised. Thus, the maximum she can give and take a deduction for is one-half of the property. One-half is 100 percent of what she owns of each horse. She may give less than 100 percent, but the amount she gives must be undivided; that is, the property, in this case, is the stable and horses together. She cannot divide the property such that she gives some of the horses and none of the stable.[26] The key is how the property is defined.

A second exception to the general rule refers specifically and only to personal (not necessarily a principal) residence or a farm. A personal residence may include a vacation home or condominium. A person may make a future-interest gift of either of these two types of properties to a qualified nonprofit and get an immediate tax deduction. Accordingly, Marisa could get an immediate tax deduction on a gift of her home to her favorite nonprofit while continuing to live in it.

A third exception to the complete transfer rule relates to gifts of real property for qualified conservation purposes. Qualified conservation purposes include preservation of land area, protection of natural habitat, preservation of open space, and preservation of a historic site. The gift of the property must be accompanied by some easement that will restrict the future use of the land for any purpose other than for conservation. The donor may continue to use the property until some date in the future when it passes to the qualified organization.[27]

The other exceptions to the requirement that gifts be complete and of present interest require the use of a trust. We shall postpone discussion of these other exceptions until Chapter 10.

Qualified Donor

Gifts can only be made by qualified donors who must be of age and of sound mind and must own the property. Ownership occurs in various forms, some of which compromise or defeat the goal of giving.

The most straightforward form of ownership is called fee simple. In this case, the person owns all rights to the property by himself or herself and is free to do with it as desired. H. Simon buys a condominium for cash without a mortgage and is the sole owner. He owns it fee simple and may do with it as he wishes.

Some properties are owned in the form of tenants in the entireties. This is a form of ownership normally used only by spouses. It means that neither party may give the property without the express consent of the other. Many homes are owned in this form and therefore no single spouse may, under normal circumstances, give the property without an affirmative approval of the other.

Other properties may be owned as tenants in common. This means that either party may make a gift, but only of that share of the property that he or she owns. When a percentage of ownership is not specified, it is assumed that each cotenant has an equal share. This might be a little more tricky than tenants in the entirety, where one-half ownership by each spouse over the entire property is presumed. In the case of tenants in common, an unequal share or only a specified piece of the property may be owned by the donor.

Property may also be owned in the form of joint tenants with the rights of survivorship. Many properties are owned in this form. It is a popular form of ownership among people who are trying to avoid probate. The objective is to be sure that upon death the property is passed directly to a designated person. It is impossible to make gifts of property owned in this form at the time of death. Full ownership passes automatically on to the survivor.

In the states of Idaho, Washington, Nebraska, California, Arizona, Louisiana, Texas, and Nevada, there is a form of ownership called community property. It is presumed that any property bought during marriage is owned on an equal basis by both spouses. The laws on the transfer of community property differ by state, but, in general, a person is only free to give the one-half of the property owned.

A person may have ownership that terminated upon death, such as a life estate. This form of ownership is obviously temporary. The owner of the life estate can give only the earnings received during his or her life, but cannot give the property that yields those earnings. That property must be passed on to another beneficiary when the first dies. Furthermore, the person with the life estate is obligated to preserve the property so that it may be transferred.

For example, Marisa may own the earnings of a rental unit through bequest from her mother, who stipulated that the unit should belong to Marisa's sister. Marisa can donate the earnings, but not the property. However, she cannot donate the earnings if by doing so there are no funds to repair and maintain the unit to transfer it to her sister in good condition. In the same vein, Marisa's sister cannot give the rental unit while Marisa is still alive, particularly if her giving it means that Marisa's flow of income would be terminated.[28]

Ownership may be contingent or nonvested. In these cases, ownership takes place only after some condition is fulfilled. Until those conditions are recognized as being satisfied, the "owner" has no legal power to give. A common contingency is the passage of time. If, for example, ten years must pass before ownership of the amounts in a pension account is vested, then prior to that time the person in whose name the account appears has no power to give those funds, even though they appear in his or her name.

Acceptance

For a gift to be complete, it must be accepted by a donee. Acceptance may be affirmatively stated, but it may also occur if the donee fails to properly disclaim the gift. A proper or qualified disclaimer is one that is written within nine months after receiving the property and does not tell the donee how to dispose of the property once it is returned.

A donor who makes a gift that is rejected by a donee in a qualified manner as described may nevertheless get a tax deduction if the property ends up in a nonprofit. This is so even though the transfer of property is governed by state law. Therefore, even though the property ends up with a nonprofit purely by the operation of the state law, a deduction may still be taken.

Qualified Donee

Generally, foreign (except some Canadian) charities are not qualified donees for U.S. tax deduction purposes and therefore donations to them cannot be deducted by U.S. taxpayers. Neither can donations to domestic charities if such charities are serving as conduits for a foreign charity or for American donors. For this reason, a domestic charity that wanted to assist foreigners arranged with a foreign charity to identify a group of several thousand potential recipients from which the domestic charity freely chose twenty-five for its assistance. American donors did not know the twenty-five foreign persons who were to be helped and had no part in choosing them. The "qualified donee" did not deposit nor transfer money to the foreign charity. Consequently, the donations to the American charity were deductible.[29]

Also many organizations form "internationals." These are U.S. nonprofit corporations operating abroad. The U.S. taxpayer can get deductions for donations to them; i.e., World Vision (World Vision International), Salvation Army (Salvation Army World Service Office). Do you know the one for the American Red Cross? The next time there is a disaster abroad check out the places to send money. The names are familiar and are legally separate U.S. corporations from their namesakes operating exclusively within the U.S.

Calling an organization charitable, even though religious, does not make it so in the eyes of the law, as we saw in Chapters 2 through 4, and therefore does not make it qualified for tax-deductible donations. Nowhere is this issue more problematic as in religion, which is protected by the First Amendment. In *Davis, et ux* v. *U.S.*, the Supreme Court said that the parents of Mormon missionaries who sent them money in keeping with their religious prescription and purpose, could not deduct it because their sons (not the church) were not qualified charities.

The IRS has identified several characteristics that make a religious organization a qualified donee. These include a distinct legal existence, recognized creeds and form of worship, an ecclesiastical government, doctrine and discipline codes, religious history, a membership not associated with any other church or denomination, an organization of ordained ministers who have completed a prescribed course of religious studies, and an established place of worship and regular religious services.

Qualified donees are domestic charities, such as the ones described in Chapters 2 and 6. Also included are nonprofit cemetery companies, volunteer fire companies, war veteran organizations, states, territories, and possessions. We are reminded that all nonprofits are not tax exempt, and only tax-exempt nonprofits qualify for tax-deductible contributions.

Less Than Full Consideration

A key concept in defining a gift is that the transfer must be for less than full consideration. Simply, this means that the donation must exceed the value of anything the nonprofit may give the donor as an inducement or in appreciation for the gift. By way of illustration, suppose that the fair market value for Shauna's horse in $4000. That is, the most that she could get from someone who wants to buy her horse is $4000. If she gives it to a nonprofit and receives a check for $4000, this is a sale; it is not a gift.

Suppose, however, that instead of a check for $4000, the nonprofit gave her a check for $2000. The transaction has two parts: a gift of $2000 and a sale of $2000. The gift is the difference between the market price and the amount received by the donor in the transfer.

A gift also occurs when one pays more than the value of a service. Hence, a gift occurs when one buys a banquet or dinner ticket for more than either is worth. Paying $150 for a dinner when the dinner and entertainment are worth $50 results in a contribution of $100. The value of the service is declared by the nonprofit sponsor of the event.

Here is another illustration. A university accepted annual payments from individuals in the amount of $300 each for membership in the university's athletic scholarship program. For an additional $120, each member was permitted to purchase a season ticket to the university's home football games and to have preferred seating between the 40-yard lines. Nonmembers were not allowed to sit in this area. Some 2000 persons were on the waiting list for membership. The IRS ruled that no part of the $300 was deductible because the right to preferred seating was of considerable monetary value to the donee. These were not gifts, but purchases of rights for value.[30]

In a similar ruling, the IRS held that a symphony that obtained $20 contributions from donors to whom it gave season memberships, the privilege of attending cocktail parties and a motion picture premiere, and reserved seats at concerts that were not otherwise available did not get deductible contributions. These were sales.[31]

The 1986 tax law allows full deductions for tickets bought for sporting events if the sponsors turn over the net receipts to the nonprofits and use volunteers. Many sports events, such as tennis and golf tournaments, fall in this category.

BORROWING TO MAKE A DONATION

One can borrow to make a donation and obtain a tax deduction. A recent case suggests that at least three conditions must be met. First, the loan should be from an independent lender; that is, an individual should not borrow from him or herself or from a corporation which he or she controls. Second, the money should meet the conditions of a gift as we described it earlier; and, presumably, the donor should remain responsible for paying off the debt. Third, the charity must benefit from the receipt.[32] These conditions were met by Mr. and Mrs. Joel Goldstein, who purchased art partly through debt and made a gift of them to a nonprofit. Note that they did not borrow the art; rather, they bought it by borrowing the money and remaining responsible for the debt. Their deduction was the amount they paid in cash plus the present discounted value of the note they gave the seller of the art.[33] In short, they deducted the cash plus the value of the note—the fair market value.

When a donor borrows to make a gift, the value of the gift is the sum of any cash the donor puts ups, plus the present discounted value of the note. This term, present discounted value, is easier to understand than it seems. Ask yourself: If I have to pay off a note, say, in five years, how much would I have to put in the bank today, given today's rate of interest, so that at the end of five years enough money would be in the bank to pay off the note? This amount that I have to put in the bank is the present discounted value of the note.

PROBLEMS OF ACCEPTING GIFTS SUBJECT TO DEBT

Many properties are bought on credit. The purchaser borrows to acquire the property so that part of the dollar value of the property represents ownership or equity; the other part is debt. Raymond owns a home subject to a mortgage. The fair market value of the home is $50,000 and the home is subject to a $30,000 mortgage, meaning that Raymond's equity is $20,000 from his income-tax perspective. That is all he can deduct, even though the fair market value of the house is $50,000 and the nonprofit may carry such value on its books and even honor him for making a gift of that amount. But who is going to pay the bank the $30,000 that Raymond owes?

Raymond can only give that which he owns. He owns only $20,000, so the gift is worth $20,000. But who is going to pay the bank? Suppose that the nonprofit decides to assume the mortgage. In that case, Raymond has made a gift for which he gets a tax deduction, but he now has to report income. The relieving of his $30,000 debt is income to him even though he has not received a dime. If he agrees to pay the debt, then this payment is included as part of the deductible gift.[34]

Let us assume that the debt is not paid by Raymond. The nonprofit has obtained a piece of property worth $50,000 for which it has only to pay the $30,000 of outstanding debt over a period of years. In addition to assuming a debt, it must now pay operating costs. If it rents the house, it must pay taxes since the property is subject to debt. If it tries to sell the building, it may be subject to tax for the property is subject to debt.[35] If the building has declined in value, the nonprofit must support an asset with a diminishing market value. Raymond may offer to pay the mortgage. If he defaults, the nonprofit pays the bill or loses the property.

BARGAIN SALES AND LOSSES

Raymond may contemplate a different strategy. He may resort to a bargain sale. Assume that he paid $50,000 cash for the home and owns it fee simple. He has no debts and may do as he wishes with the property. Assume further that the property is in an attractive neighborhood so that, rather than declining in price, it appreciated to $100,000. He may decide to give it to his favorite nonprofit through a bargain sale. Instead of the nonprofit paying $100,000, it pays $50,000. Since he receives less than full consideration, the difference between what he gets and the fair market value ($50,000) is a gift. A gift?

The bargain sale is part gift and part sale. Its effects on the donor can be devastating. It is beyond the scope of this book to illustrate all the potential results, but a simplified approach may be useful. In this example, the gift amounts to $50,000, which is one-half of the fair market value. Thus, Raymond gave away one-half of what he could have gotten had he sold the house. He must now reduce his cost by half. Thus, he is deemed to have paid only $25,000 for the house. Since he received $50,000 from the nonprofit, he is deemed to have made a gain of $25,000 on the deal and he must pay taxes on it. Bargain sales can be very cruel to donors because they can lead to taxes on gains never received. In this case, Raymond reports a gain of $25,000 even though he sold the property for the amount he paid for it, and $50,000 less than its true market value. He would have been better off selling the property, paying the tax, and taking a deduction for the contribution.

A bargain sale may also lead to loss of a deduction because a bargain sale is subject first to the regular rules of gifts and sales and then to the specific rules governing bargain sales. To illustrate, suppose H. Simon bought stocks a month ago for $4000. The stocks rise to $10,000 in two months. The sale of these stocks, held for six months, under any circumstance would lead to an ordinary income tax on the $6000 of gain. Suppose H. Simon decides to donate the stocks. He cannot deduct $10,000. Knowing this, he takes a check from the nonprofit for $4000 to cover his cost and then gives them the stocks. Will he be able to deduct the $6000 difference as a gift? No.

The reasoning is that his cost was $4000 for which he got a check from the nonprofit. The stocks, held for six months, are ordinary income property deductible at cost. The cost is $4000 but he was paid that amount from the nonprofit so there is nothing to deduct. He has lost $10,000 worth of stocks.

Losses

While gains may be implied and taxable even when not actually realized by a taxpayer, the converse is not true. A loss realized by making a contribution cannot be deducted. Thus, stocks that have fallen in price with potential for rising may be attractive to a nonprofit but foolish for a person to give. Losses experienced in giving cannot be deducted, but losses experienced in the sale of the property can be deducted. Hence, it is often wiser for the potential donor to sell the property, deduct the loss, give the proceeds to the nonprofit, and deduct the gift of cash.

VALUE OF GIFTS

In general, the value of a gift for purposes of tax deduction is the fair market value of the property. The fair market value is the price a knowledgeable buyer would willingly pay and an equally knowledgeable seller would willingly accept for the property on a specific date, that is, its valuation date.

Determination of Fair Market Value

The fair market value of a property is the actual price for which it could be sold on the date it was donated. The market must not have changed radically between the date of sale and the date of the valuation. A donor cannot deduct $50,000 for a gift that has declined to $20,000 on the date it was given. The value is $20,000. Used clothing is valued at the price it may be sold for at a thrift shop. Some properties, like art and antique furniture, require a competent appraisal.

Valuation of Real Estate

Real estate may be valued at the price similar properties are being sold for in the same neighborhood at the time. Natural restriction on use such as the soil quality or legal restrictions such as easements must be taken into account. Commercial property may be valued according to the expected future income stream, or at replacement cost.

Valuation of Closely Held Stocks

A closely held corporation is one whose stocks are not publicly traded on the stock market, but are held by a few (even one) person. These stocks may be valued through an appraisal of its assets, liabilities and expected income stream, all of which can be discounted for risks, or through a formula agreed to by the owners at a much earlier date. Some closely held stocks may be discounted either because there is no public market for selling them or because the owner who gives them has such a large quantity that selling them depresses the price.

Valuation of Art

Appraising art is a challenge. There are endless opportunities to be dishonest. One official of a famous museum was once accused of determining the value of an artwork based on the amount of deduction the potential donor needed. Value is in the eyes of the beholder. As one observer noted, the value of an art piece may be affected by the purpose for which it is being valued; that is, to determine an inheritance tax, charitable donation, insurance claim, sale as opposed to display or exchange, gift taxes, security, collateral, or resale royalties, which are payments to the seller in the form of a work of art rather than cash.[36]

There are many factors to be considered in determining the value of any single piece of art. These include the identity of the artist, the date or period of its creation, the physical condition of the piece, the amount of restoration it has undergone, the subject of the art, the medium in which it was done, its physical dimension and authenticity, its rarity, and its artistic and esthetic value.[37] In one very controversial case, to decide on the value of a 70-foot sculpture by Bufano called "Expanding Universe," the weighted average of three separate methods (the replacement cost, cost of comparable pieces by Bufano's contemporaries, and an extrapolation of fair market value) called the French grid system was used. The IRS accepted it with the warning that it cannot always be used.[38] The valuation of art remains tricky but required.

Valuing a property 150 percent higher than its true value is penalized by the IRS on the donor,[39] if the tax liability of the donor is reduced by at least $1000 and if the donor owned the property for at least five years (and therefore presumably knows the true value. Participation in fraudulent appraisals by the nonprofit will result in legal consequences on it and its leadership.

Ordinary Income and Capital Gains Valuations

Some properties must be treated for valuation purposes as ordinary income property. An ordinary income good is one for which the proceeds from the sale are taxed as ordinary income, such as wages and salary. Examples of ordinary income goods that may be given are (1) items from the inventory of a retailer or dealer, (2) a product in the hands of its producer, such as a piece of art in the hands of the artist or a machine in the hands of its manufacturer, (3) a piece of equipment or machinery used in a trade or business, such as a truck in the hands of a construction company, (4) property held for investment purposes but for less than six months, such as stocks in the hands of an investor held for less than six months, and (5) some properties subject to depreciation recapture, such as a real estate using a method of rapid depreciation.[40]

Ordinary income property, even if it has appreciated in price, is valued for purposes of deducting a contribution at cost rather than fair market value. The fair market value of the property is determined. From this, the amount of appreciation over cost that is ordinary income is subtracted. The remainder is the value of the property for tax-deduction purposes. Usually it equals cost.

Jeanine buys stocks for $1000 and holds them for two months. The stocks appreciate to $10,000. The gain of $9000 is short term and is subtracted from the fair market value of $10,000 in determining the amount that can be deducted as a gift. This is equal to $1000 or the cost.

Capital gain properties are ones in which the proceeds from their sale would be taxed as capital gains. Examples are (1) properties held for investment purposes but for a period of greater than six months, and (2) coal and timber by special treatment of the tax law. Generally, capital gain property may be deducted at fair market value. The distinction between capital gains and ordinary income applies to the amount deductible. Since 1986 both are taxed at the same rate but offer different deductible amounts.

It would be useful to see one probable consequence of treating a good as a capital gain or an ordinary income good. Robert is a painter and has produced a masterpiece. The cost of supplies and equipment is $1000. The market values the painting at $920,000. If he sold the property to Yvonne for $920,000 and its value rose to $1,600,000 while in her hands for a year, under the general rule she would be able to deduct its fair market value, which is now $1,600,000, if she donates it. In her hands, held for more than six months, the property is a capital gain property.

Whether Robert or Yvonne makes the contribution may be of consequence to the nonprofit if, for example, the property is subject to debt. If it sold the painting for $2,000,000 after receiving it from Yvonne, it will pay taxes on the appreciation of $1,080,000. This is the difference between its cost to Yvonne ($920,000) and the sale price ($2,000,000) to the nonprofit. If it sold it after receiving it from Robert, it will pay taxes on $1,999,000 (the sale price of $2,000,000 and the cost to Robert of $1000). In this example, the tax base for the nonprofit will be nearly $900,000 greater if it received the property from Robert. This is so because, when a nonprofit accepts a gift, it simultaneously accepts the value of the gift when it was in the hands of the donor.[41]

In general, ordinary goods offer the donor a lower tax deduction and the organization a lower base than capital gains property. The basis for deduction in the former is cost. In the latter it is fair market value, which may be higher or lower than the original price paid by the donor. The distinction applies even in the absence of a lower capital gains tax rate.

Appreciated Property

We are now familiar with the concepts of ordinary income property and capital gains property.[42] While ordinary income property is valued at cost regardless of the appreciation, capital gain property is usually valued at its fair market value—reflecting the appreciation, if any. Accordingly, a property that has appreciated in value, called appreciated property, is not necessarily valued for contribution purposes at its new higher value. It depends. Is the property ordinary income property? Is it capital gains property? Together, the classification and the appreciation determine the amount of deduction.

Nonprofit Can Cause Donor to Lose Appreciated Value

If the property is **tangible personal property** (a property other than real estate or an intangible such as stocks) and if it is given to a public charity, private nonoperating, or private operating foundation to be used in any way that is not related to its tax-exempt purpose, then the deduction must be reduced to cost or basis.

Clive donates an appreciated tangible personal property (an antique car) to a medical school that runs an antique business. The business is unrelated to teaching medicine. Clive bought the car for $10,000 and it is now worth $40,000. He cannot deduct $40,000 but must deduct $10,000. This example makes the point: A nonprofit that induces a donor to give property to be used in an unrelated way may be doing that donor a disservice.

Examples of Valuation Problems: Morgues and Cemeteries

Let us illustrate. An entertainment company gave a newspaper morgue to a nonprofit. The morgue is its file of articles, background materials, photographs, and the like. The entertainment company assumed that the value of these had risen over the years, so it took a level of deduction to reflect this appreciation. The IRS ruled that this was incorrect. This was property that probably did appreciate, but it was not a capital asset subject to treatment as a capital gains property. Rather, because it was produced for and by the newspaper, it was to be treated as an ordinary income property justifying a lower deduction.[43]

Mr. and Mrs. Thornton bought cemetery lots some years ago for about $20,000. They gave the lots to the University of Nevada at Reno and took a deduction on the basis that the dilapidated cemetery is best used for real estate development, which makes its value over $500,000. The court ruled that such a prospect is so far and so remote that it is an improbable basis on which to calculate a charitable deduction.[44]

In another cemetery case, some donors made a gift of cemetery property and proceeded to take a fair market value deduction. The court ruled that there was no proof that the fair market value exceeded cost. The donor was unable to prove this claim.[45]

ALTERNATIVE MINIMUM TAX AND APPRECIATED PROPERTY: 1990

Many years ago, Congress decided that too many wealthy people were escaping taxation by exploiting deductions, including charitable deductions, and by investing in real estate, oil and gas, livestock, and farming that gave them huge paper losses.

To curb this practice, Congress instituted the alternative minimum tax. This law, as amended in 1982, requires taxpayers to compute their taxes two ways: with all the deductions they can legally take, and then, without some specified deductions. The second way, without certain deductions, often yields the higher of the two tax liabilities, which is the amount the taxpayer must pay. In computing the second alternative, charitable deduction cannot reflect the amount by which a property appreciated. This lowers the amount of the deduction. Gifts of appreciated property (art and securities), especially to universities and museums plummeted. In 1990, Congress suspended this law, hoping to revive the giving of appreciated property.

Reporting Requirements and IRS Vigilance

Under the new rules, donors who contribute property with a stated value of over $500 (the old rule was $5000) must file Form IRS 8283. The form requires that the donor give the name of the charity and its addresses, a description of the donated property, the date of the contribution, the date the donor acquired the property, how it was acquired, the cost to the donor adjusted for any improvement, the fair market value of the property, and the method used to determine the fair market value.

If the value of the property exceeds $5000, the donor must also provide an acknowledgment by the charity that it was received. Either the donor or the appraiser must provide information on the donated property, and the appraiser must certify the appraisal given to the property. The reader should refer to Chapter 8 and earlier chapters for additional discussions of reporting requirements, including when property received is sold within two years.

LIMITS ON GIVING

Tax deductions allowed for contributions to nonprofits are limited on a calendar year basis. In this section, we discuss these limits as they apply federally, and in the next we discuss strategies that nonprofits may take for accepting large gifts. Certain large gifts can cause a change in the nonprofit tax status.

Foundations

Unlike individuals and corporations, the law seeks to encourage giving on the part of foundations, primarily private nonoperating foundations. The law seeks to force private foundations to distribute their income. So, instead of having limits on giving, it has limits and penalties on the failure to give. These rules were discussed in Chapter 4. An example of the exercise of these rules is the B. Altman Foundation, which held the great majority of the stocks of the B. Altman stores. As a result of the excess business holding rules and pressure by the state attorney general of New York, this foundation divested itself to increase its giving.[46] Public charities 509(a)(1) and (2), are often not grant making and are not required to give.

Individuals

On the other hand, there are limits to the amount of charitable gifts that an individual or corporation is permitted to deduct in any one calendar year. It is important, therefore, to establish the year a gift is made. The limits are all annual, although excesses may be carried forward to other years.

Conrad signs the certificate of stocks he owns and is donating to a nonprofit. The certificate is to be delivered by an agent of the company or a bank to the nonprofit. The gift occurs when the change in name is recorded on the books of the agent or company. If Conrad makes the gift on December 31, it is unlikely that the recording of the transfer would occur in time for him to unchallengeably take a deduction in that year. The same kind of situation (recording ownership change) occurs in real estate, except there is no way to mail it. A better strategy is to mail the stock to the nonprofit since, like cash, the date of the mailing would be used as the date of the gift.

Assuming that the date of the gift is properly established, the limits depend on whether the donor is a corporation or an individual, the type of foundation, the purpose of the gift, and if the gift is appreciated properly.

A person is permitted to deduct charitable contributions up to 50 percent of adjustable gross income per calendar year if the contribution is made **to** a public or a private operating foundation. A community foundation such as the Gainesville Community Foundation of Georgia qualifies as much as the soup kitchen and the church as a public charity.[47] If the charitable contribution is **to** a private nonoperating foundation, the annual limit is 30 percent of adjusted gross income. If the contribution exceeds the limits, the taxpayer can carry it forward for five years. These are the basic rules. They come into play once the total charitable contribution of the individual for the year is 20 percent of adjusted gross income. Thus, if the total contributions of Conrad is less than 20 percent of his adjusted gross income, he can deduct the entire thing regardless of whether the donee is a private operating foundation or a public charity or a private nonoperating.

Here are some variations from the basic rule. Notice the word **to** that is used above. It is deliberate. If the contribution is **for the use of** any one of the three—public charity, private operating or nonoperating foundation, the limit is 30 percent. So, a contribution **to** and/or **for the use** of a private nonoperating foundation is limited to 30 percent of adjusted gross income. It is also 30 percent if it is **for the use of** a public charity or a private operating foundation. But if it is **to** the public charity or operating foundation, then, the limit is 50 percent. **For the use of** implies an indirect and delayed gift, i.e., through a third party that holds the gift for the eventual use of the nonprofit in its mission. **To** implies an immediate and direct donation from donor to the nonprofit, and therefore to its mission.

There are also reduction rules. Unlike the rules in preceding paragraphs, these do not limit a donor's deductibility based on adjustable gross income. Rather, they reduce the value of the property. Here are three. First, capital gains property must be reduced from its fair market value if it is tangible personal property (a truck, typewriter, computer, furniture) donated to be used in a way unrelated to the mission of the nonprofit. We met this rule before. Next, the value of the gift must be reduced if the taxpayer chooses, for example, to give in one of the ways described above which yields a 30 percent limit, but for tax planning purposes, the taxpayer would rather use a 50 percent limit. Finally, capital gains property given to a private nonoperating foundation must also be reduced unless the property given is a qualified exception. Probably, the most important of these exceptions are stocks that are traded on the stock market and where the donor does not give more than 10 percent of the outstanding shares. Thus, rich people who give publicly traded stocks to form private foundations such as the Edna McConnell Clark Foundation, and the Andrew Mellon Foundation usually are not subject to this reduction rule.

Trust, Endowment and Wills

One strategy for limitless giving that individuals may use is the creation of a trust, or an endowment, which is the subject of Chapter 10. A charitable trust is permitted limitless charitable contributions as long as the trust does not engage in unrelated business, unreasonable accumulation of funds, distribution of funds for noncharitable purposes, or prohibited transactions, and its funds are not used against the best interest of the charitable beneficiaries. If it does any of these, it is subject to the same limitations imposed on individuals. While trusts may have limitless power to give, only liquidating trusts do so because most trusts are intended to last into perpetuity.

Another strategy to avoid the limits on individuals is to make the gift through the individual's estate—contingent on the death of the donor as through a will. These types of gifts will also be discussed in Chapter 10. Through a will, a gift can be made of limitless cash or property as long as there is sufficient assets in the estate to meet the legal obligations of the deceased.

There is a subtle but important difference between a deathtime gift and a trust created and funded during life. The latter may make limitless gifts, but the contributions that create them are limited as described in this chapter and the next. In deathtime gifts through the settlement of an estate, both the amount bequeathed by the donor in the estate and the transfer from the estate to the charity are limitless.

Corporations

Corporations are limited to 10 percent of their taxable income regardless of the type of property and foundation to which they give. Any excess over the 10 percent limit for companies is deductible over five years. Corporations, on the average, do not exceed 2 percent of net income. In 1988, Polaroid reached approximately 12 percent, the highest among all reporting companies, followed by Harris Corporation and Pillsbury with approximately 8 percent.[48]

Corporations are required to reduce the fair market value of property so that often the most they can deduct is their cost (called their basis). In some cases, the deduction is below basis if the market value has declined. However, corporations are permitted to deduct cost plus up to 50 percent of the appreciation on the value of equipment used in their line of business or of their inventory if the nonprofit will use it solely for the caring of the ill, the needy, and infants. These gifts must meet quality tests, of the Food, Drug and Cosmetic Act. Further, the 50 percent is not permitted if the nonprofit will sell the gift once it has been received. To assure compliance with these conditions, the corporation must receive a letter from the nonprofit promising that it will comply with the no-sell restriction and have records as to when the goods were received and dispensed by the organization.

Corporations are also allowed a deduction of cost plus up to half of the appreciation on certain research property that they contribute. The donation must be made to an educational institution.

PROBLEMS AND STRATEGIES OF LARGE GIFTS

Nonprofits do not normally see themselves as being limited to the amount that they may receive from any one source. But gifts and contributions are evidence of public support and public charities must demonstrate a high level of public support. Intuitively, one may think, that getting a large gift or contribution would be evidence of public support, but this is not necessarily so.[49]

First, in calculating the one-third or 10 percent of public support described in Chapter 4, no one contribution may be included at a level that is greater than 2 percent of the entire support level. Thus, if the support level is $200,000 and Anhela gave $88,000, her gift will be treated as if it were only $2000 of the $200,000. If Emeline gave $105,000, hers would be treated as $2000. The effect of this is to cause the organization to tail the one-third support test because $4000 (the 2 percent sum of the two gifts) is less than one-third of $200,000.

Second, large gifts and contributions risk making the nonprofit a private foundation and the donor a disqualified person. The rules do, however, provide some protection against this eventuality. If the large donor is not a disqualified person and is not likely to be disqualified because of death, or if the donor is unable to place any conditions or exercise control over the organization, an unusually large gift that is in response to a public appeal may be omitted in calculating public support.

An individual who makes a large gift to a nonprofit may follow one of several strategies. The excess may be deducted over five years. Or the individual may make the gift at the time of death because there is no limit on charitable deductions made at that point. The process is discussed in Chapter 10. Or, the individual may form a private foundation or a public charity such as a 509(a)(3) and make it a subsidiary to a public 509(a)(1) or (a)(2). These are some of the possibilities described in the accompanying article, first appearing in the *Washington Post* and then in a number of newspapers across the country.

Individuals who make large gifts should always be concerned with the possibility that the gift would be so large that it would convert the organization from a public charity to a private foundation and disqualify that individual. The way individuals may avoid such a taint is to obtain a letter from the organization assuring him or her that the gift would not have a disqualifying effect, or by making the gift as a response to a public appeal without stating any conditions of control over the gift, and by not being in a position to exercise any control over the organization. Being dead is an acceptable position for this purpose. At death, large gifts do not disqualify donors under the assumption that no control can be exercised.

Nonprofits, particularly public charities since they are more vulnerable than private foundations, may take certain defensive measures when large gifts are expected:

1. Be sure that the intent and honor of the donor are consistent with the mission of the organization and that there is no misunderstanding. Having to return a sizable gift may destabilize the organization and create tax problems for the donor. If the gift passes this test, take it.

2. The organization may increase the number of contributions from sources such as the government and the public that are considered public support and, therefore, offset the effects of the large gift.

3. The organization may modify its computation period to include the

MICHAEL JACKSON HAS A TAX DILEMMA LIKE JOE LOUIS, THE MORE HE GIVES AWAY TO CHARITY THE MORE HE HAS TO EARN

By Herrington J. Bryce

Michael Jackson's decision to donate his estimated $5 million in proceeds from his multi-city "Victory" tour is an uncommon act of charity, but it could land him in deep trouble with the Internal Revenue Service.

Wealthy as his work has made him, Jackson would do well to review the bitter experience of heavyweight champion Joe Louis. Louis donated large portions of the proceeds from his fights to his country's war effort. But the manner of his giving left him with enormous tax liabilities that ruined him financially. It took a presidential directive to absolve him of his entanglements with the tax laws.

Commonly, when celebrities perform for charity, they do so by prior agreement not to be paid. They designate organizations or institutions to receive the proceeds, or a share of them. Since no pay is received, no tax liability is created and there is no deduction.

From everything that has been printed and stated about Jackson's financial arrangements, however, his contract calls for him to be paid. From a tax standpoint, this means that it may be too late for him to declare that he is performing without compensation and intends to donate his full share to charity. His services are not deductible. And the tax rules clearly state that income once earned cannot escape taxation by shifting it to another entity, even if it is a charity.

All this means that Jackson's performances will create a sizeable tax liability. At his level, 50 cents of every dollar earned is potentially payable as federal taxes. Hence, his $5 million will create a federal tax liability of approximately $2.5 million, on top of state and local levies.

For Jackson to deduct the full $5 million in the year he donates it, he will have to earn some $10–$16 million. This is because the IRS currently limits charitable deductions to 30 percent or 50 percent of income, depending on whether the recipient is a public or private charity. So the more Jackson gives, the more he must earn in order to get the full tax deduction from his contribution in one year. Yet the more he earns, the larger his total potential tax liability will be.

If he gives the full $5 million to a *public* charity such as his church (he is a Jehovah's Witness), he has to earn only $10 million. The tax laws allow deductions to such charities of up to half an individual's income. If he fails to earn $10 million, he can still apply unused portions of his deductions to public charities to his returns during the subsequent five years.

If he donates to a *private* charity, such as a family foundation, he would only be allowed to deduct up to 30 percent of his adjusted income and would have to earn some $16 million in order to deduct the full $5 million that he plans to donate.

Because giving to a public charity has a substantial tax advantage over giving to a private charity, Jackson, faced with a huge tax liability and wanting to keep his commitment to donate his share to charity, may choose to sprinkle his gifts among a number of worthwhile public charities.

It may be too late for him to completely solve his immediate tax problem. But there is a step he could take to ease future difficulties, deal with other immediate concerns and perpetuate his goodness for many years. This is the creation of a charitable foundation.

Dispensing charity through a foundation rather than by making random personal gifts would benefit Jackson as much as it has benefited other wealthy Americans.

Even the initial disadvantages, including the possibility that all $5 million might not be deductible in one year, can be overcome by distributing the gift over several years and by making the gift while seeking tax sheltering investments to make up the difference.

Moreover, foundations help shield donors from the animosity of disappointed charity seekers. Not every applicant can be satisfied. Foundations deflect criticism and bad publicity.

Foundations can invest their resources and grow. Jackson's contributions would attract donations from others. Invested prudently, these funds could touch the lives of deserving persons for many years.

Foundations have the time and expertise to evaluate options for charity and to nurture causes to which Jackson is committed.

And a foundation must make sure that the assets and earnings are not used for purposes that do not qualify, such as the personal benefit of donors and their relatives.

Jackson won't be able to control the foundation once it is operating. But neither will he be able to control the use of his direct contributions after they are made. In setting up the foundation, he could stipulate its overall mission, choose the board of directors or trustees, and withdraw his support if he became dissatisfied with it.

This is an opportunity that should not be lost. Few blacks who have done well in entertainment or sports have been able to accumulate and preserve great wealth. Few persons white or black, in any walk of life, have created lasting philanthropic memorials to celebrate their struggle and achievement and to perpetuate their generosity. The $5 million Jackson has committed to charity gives him the rare opportunity to be an exception.

Sources: Herrington J. Bryce, "Michael Jackson Has a Tax Dilemma," *Washington Post*, Sunday, August 5, 1984, p. C5.

year of the large gift plus the four preceding years. This tends to dampen the magnitude of the large gift.

4. The organization may shift from attempting to qualify under 509(a)(1) to (a)(2), or vice versa, depending upon the amount ob-

tained from investment income, unrelated business or related business sources. This is a judgment made by IRS.

5. The organization may exclude any extraordinary large contributions both from the calculation that gives the sum of all support and from the portion that is considered public support. This removes it from consideration in the calculation of the one-third or 10 percent test. Such exclusion is only possible, however, if the person is not disqualified and had no reason to believe that the effect of the contribution would have been to jeopardize the public charity classification of the organization.

ETHICAL DILEMMAS IN FUND RAISING

The American Red Cross advertised for donations for the victims of the San Francisco earthquake. It collected nearly $50 million. After the crisis abated, it was revealed that all the donations collected in this campaign would not be spent in San Francisco. Many local officials complained and the American Red Cross reversed itself. What do you think?

One way to view the original action of the American Red Cross is to say that it collected more than was needed for local purposes and that it was ethical to transfer these excess funds to other geographical areas with disaster needs even at a future date. Well before the San Francisco earthquake, the American Red Cross had established a separate fund that it uses to quickly respond to disasters. Presumably, in the initial stage, San Francisco benefited from the existence of this fund.

A rebuttal is that many people who gave did so because of a perceived need in San Francisco and that they would not have given to the American Red Cross if they had remotely thought it would have had excess funds and used them elsewhere. Their gift was purpose and place specific. How do you stand? Is this the best way to serve the public good? What happens at the next disaster? Would a slight change in the wording requesting contributions to the disaster fund of the Red Cross been superior to using the name "San Francisco"?

SUMMARY AND CONCLUSIONS

Gifts and contributions are the two most common forms of support of nonprofit organizations. An underlying reason for giving is the tax deduction. Therefore, understanding the impact of taxes on donors increases the efficiency of the appeal. Many forms of giving expose the nonprofit to high risks once the gifts are received. Thus, it is important that the nonprofit manager understand the pitfalls of giving and receiving.

Many appeals are likely to fail because the contribution works to the financial and tax detriment of the potential donor. Knowledge of these pitfalls avoids resentment, waste of energy, and a disservice to unwitting donors and can be avoided by taking the steps to be discussed in Chapter 10 or the strategies of dealing with large contributions discussed in this chapter. Finally, this chapter guides the reader through some pitfalls associated with the acceptance of certain properties as gifts and reasons why corporations may resist giving certain properties.

NOTES

1. The 1986 tax reform allows only taxpayers who itemize deductions to deduct charitable contributions. The literature showing a close and strong correlation between the deductibility of a gift and giving is extensive. It includes Charles T. Clotfelter, *Federal Tax Policy and Charitable Giving* (Chicago, Illinois: University of Chicago Press, 1985); Martin Feldstein and Charles Clotfelter, "Tax Incentives and Charitable Contributions in the United States," *Journal of Public Economics*, 5 (1976), 1–26; Charles T. Clotfelter and E. Eugene Steuerle, "Charitable Contributions," in Henry Aaron and Joseph Pechman, *How Taxes Affect Economic Behavior* (Washington, D.C.: Brookings Institution, 1981); Michael Taussig, "Economic Aspects of the Personal Income Tax Treatment of Charitable Contributions," *National Tax Journal*, 20, no. 1 (March 1967), 1–19.

2. On the relationship between taxation and the estate tax, see Thomas Barthold and Robert Plotnick, "Estate Taxation and Other Determinants of Charitable Bequests," *National Tax Journal*, 38, no. 2 (June 1984), 225–36; Michael J. Boskin, "Estate Taxation and Charitable Bequests," *Commission on Private Philanthropy and Public Need* (Washington, D.C.: U.S. Treasury, 1977), pp. 1453–83; Martin S. Feldstein, "Charitable Bequests, Estate Taxation, and Intergenerational Wealth Transfer," ibid., pp. 1485–97.

3. For a review of the literature on this topic, see Melvin M. Mark and R. Lance Shotland, "Increasing Charitable Contributions: An Experimental Evaluation of the American Cancer Society's Recommended Solicitation Procedures," *Journal of Voluntary Action Research*, 12, no. 3 (Apr.–June 1983), 8–21.

4. J. L. Freedman and S. C. Fraser, "Compliance without Pressure: The Foot in the Door Technique," *Journal of Personality and Social Psychology*, 31 (1975), 206–15.

5. R. B. Cialdini and others, "Reciprocal Concessions Procedure for Inducing Compliance: The Door-in-the-Face Technique," *Journal of Personality and Social Psychology*, 31 (1975), 206–15.

6. C. Wagner and L. Wheeler, "Model, Need, and Cost Effects in Helping Behavior," *Journal of Personality and Social Psychology*, 12 (1969), 111–16; and J. H. Bryan and M. A. Test, "Models and Helping: Naturalistic Studies in Aiding Behavior," *Journal of Personality and Social Psychology*, 6 (1967), 400–407.

7. R. B. Cialdini and D. A. Schroeder, "Increasing Contributions by Legitimizing Paltry Contributions," *Journal of Personality and Social Psychology*, 34 (1976), 599–604.

8. See Mark and Shotland, "Increasing Charitable Contributions," p. 11 (see note 3).

9. James N. Morgan, Richard F. Dye, and Judith H. Hybels, "Results from Two National Surveys of Philanthropic Activity," *Research Papers: Commission on Philanthropy*

and Public Needs, 1 (Washington, D.C.: U.S. Treasury, 1977), 157–324, especially Table 17.

10. Ibid., p. 201.

11. Charles T. Clotfelter, *Federal Tax Policy and Charitable Giving* (see note 1).

12. R. Palmer Baker, Jr., and J. Edward Schillingburg, "Corporate Charitable Contributions," *Research Papers: Commission on Philanthropy and Public Needs*, 3, 1853–1905 (see note 9).

13. Alfred C. Neal, "A More Rational Basis for Nonprofit Activities," *Conference Board Record*, 5 (Jan. 1968), 5–7.

14. Richard Eells, "A Philosophy for Corporate Giving," *Conference Board Record*, 5 (Jan. 1968), 14–17.

15. W. J. Baumol, "Enlightened Self-interest and Corporate Philanthropy," *Foundations, Private Giving and Public Policy: Report and Recommendations of the Commission on Foundations and Private Philanthropies* (Chicago: University of Chicago Press, 1971), pp. 262–75.

16. James F. Harris and Anne Klepper, "Corporate Philanthropic Public Service Activities," *Research Papers: Commission on Philanthropy and Public Needs*, pp. 1741–88 (see note 9).

17. For a review of these, see Bette Ann Stead, "Corporate Giving: A Look at the Arts," *Journal of Business Ethics*, 4, no. 3 (1985), 215–22, and Frank Koch, "A Primer on Corporate Philosophy," *Business and Society Review*, 38 (1980), 48–52.

18. Congressional Research Service, "Charitable Contributions: Pros and Cons of Deductibility" (Washington, D.C.: Government Printing Office, 1990).

19. The Combined Federal Campaign, *Employee Benefits Review*, Aug. 1990, pp. 1–3. No author.

20. *Venni v. Commissioner*, Tax Court Memo 1984-17, 1/10/84.

21. *Davis v. Commissioner*, 81 Tax Court No. 49, 10/26/83.

22. *Magin v. Commissioner*, Tax Court Memo 1982-383, 7/7/82.

23. The value of the gift is the difference between the exercise price and the fair market value of the property at the time the option is exercised.

24. *Wall Street Journal*, Oct. 12, 1988, p. 1.

25. See the discussion of the attribution rule in Chapter 4.

26. A donation could not be made of the legs of the horse while the owner keeps the body. The property may be made up of a single item or many items.

27. The value of the easement is the difference between the market price before the easement and the price after the easement. The easement tends to reduce the price of the property by restricting its use and market.

28. Properties such as this are best passed on by creating a trust. As we shall see in Chapter 11, these rules are aimed at preserving the property for the person with the remainder interest.

29. *Tax Notes*, May 1, 1989, p. 554. Revenue Ruling 63-252.

30. Revenue Ruling 84-132, 1984-1 Cumulative Bulletin.

31. Revenue Ruling 67-246.

32. *Kenneth Allen and Barbara Allen v. Commissioner*, Tax Court, No. 22877-84, Sept. 5, 1989.

33. *Joel H. Goldstein and Elain P. Goldstein v. Commissioner*, Tax Court Report No. 89, p. 535.

34. The principal on the debt is deductible as a gift, but the interest is not since the interest is otherwise deductible as other interest payments are.
35. See Chapter 6.
36. Peter H. Karlin, "Appraiser's Responsibility for Determining Fair Market Value," *Columbia Journal of Law and the Arts*, 13, no. 2 (Winter 1989), pp. 185–220.
37. Ibid.
38. Allen W. Kaftinow, T. C. Memo 1986-396.
39. The current penalty is 30 percent of the true tax liability.
40. Depreciation is a deductible allowance for the use of capital in production of income. Excess depreciation is the difference between a constant sum taken every year and one that assumes that the rate of use of capital per year is largest in the first years.
41. It is true that most times capital gains are not taxable to nonprofits. However, this example is not unlikely if the gift is to a private foundation holding it as an invest-ment, if the property is acquired by debt as that concept is defined in Chapter 6, and if the property is part of an inventory. Any of these could lead to the results stated.
42. Long-term capital gain property must be held for six or more months.
43. Internal Revenue Letter 9037001.
44. *William Thornton* v. *Commissioner*, No. 89-70147, July 24, 1990.
45. *Alexander Weintrob* v. *Commissioner*, T.C. Memo 1990, p. 513.
46. Kathleen Teltsch, "Stores' Sales Is Bonanza for Altman Foundation" *New York Times*, Sunday, Oct. 20, 1985, p. 52.
47. Adjusted gross income is essentially all one's income except such items as workmen's compensation, insurance proceeds, individual retirement account contributions, and certain expenses, such as moving expenses.
48. Data from the Public Management Institute reported in *Chronicle of Philanthropy*, Jan. 23, 1990, p. 15.
49. "Large" simply means sufficient to affect the classification of the nonprofit. The num-ber of dollars that may be large for one organization may be small for another.

SUGGESTED READINGS

American Association of Fund-raising Counsel, Inc., *Giving in U.S.A.* (New York: American Association of Fund-raising Counsel, issues from 1978–1990).

American Institute of Certified Public Accountants, *Tax Planning Tips* (New York: AICPA, produced annually).

Blum, Steven, "Tax-Free Exchanges of Appreciated Art," *Columbia Journal of Law and the Arts*, Vol. 14, No. 4, pp. 557–70.

Buzbee, William W. and Patricia M. Dineen, "How to Deal with Gifts of Con-taminated Real Estate," *The Philanthropy Monthly*, Vol. XXIV, No. 2, March 1991, pp. 6–14.

Foundation & Corporate Giving 1991, (Rockville, MD: The Taft Group, 1991).

Giving and Volunteering in the United States, 1990 Edition (Washington, D.C.: The Independent Sector, 1990).

Internal Revenue Service, Department of the Treasury, Charitable Contributions, Publication 526, rev. November 1989 (Washington, D.C.: U.S. Government Printing Office, 1989).

Internal Revenue Service, Department of the Treasury, Determining the Value of Donated Property, Publication 561, rev. November 1989, (Washington, D.C.: U.S. Government Printing Office, 1989).

Internal Revenue Service, Department of the Treasury, Federal Estate and Gift Taxes, Publication 448 rev. September 1989 (Washington, D.C.: U.S. Government Printing Office, 1989).

Internal Revenue Service, Department of the Treasury, Tax Information on Corporations, Publication 542, rev. November 1989 (Washington, D.C.: U.S. Government Printing Office, 1989).

SALCOSKI, CAROL J., "Looking a Gift Stock in the Mouth," *Michigan Law Review*, 88, no. 3 (Dec. 1989), pp. 604–634.

Chapter 10

Strategies for Large Gifts: Trusts, Wills, Annuities, Life Insurance, and Endowments

A sophisticated money-raising campaign must do more than appeal for cash or property that the potential donor can immediately surrender. Many donors rightfully wish to make a gift of property that they are totally unwilling to surrender any time in the near future. Trusts, wills, insurance, and annuities are instruments that accommodate such desires. They permit the donor to defer the actual transfer of the gift until some future date while getting an immediate benefit either in the form of tax savings, the continued use of the property, and the satisfaction of having made a charitable commitment. The nonprofit benefits because it does not take the risk that in the future the gift would not be available or that the donor might give it to some other group.

Some donors wish to give larger sums than they can presently afford. An insurance policy is one way in which a small gift may multiply itself several times. It is one of the most intriguing gifts. The American Bar Association Endowment gets gifts from bar members by having them donate the dividends on their insurance policies.[1] This involves no out-of-pocket expense to the members because the dividends are paid by the insurance company.

This chapter is a discussion of techniques that can be used to increase the magnitude of giving. They all involve legal and tax technicalities. No person or manager should attempt to implement any of them without very competent legal and tax advice. The reason is that, while the law is permissive and encouraging of the use of these techniques, it also requires that specific rules be obeyed. This chapter has been prepared so that the manager of the nonprofit will be in a position to (1) identify situations when one of these techniques may be appealing to a donor, (2) recognize the specific reasons why a donor may be attracted to a specific technique and what may be the reasons for being leery about it, and (3) identify the benefits to the organization and the constraints on the organization once a specific technique is adopted. In short, the chapter aims to put the manager in a position to negotiate large and difficult gifts.

THE USES OF TRUSTS: DEFERRED, EXTENDED BENEFITS, AND CASH FLOW

A trust is a legal entity created by one or more persons for the purposes of receiving, accumulating, managing, and distributing wealth according to an agreement between those persons who create the trust and the trustees who manage the trust. All this is done on behalf of one or more persons or institutions that are the beneficiaries named by those who created the trust.

The person who creates a trust is called the grantor, creator, or donor. The trust may have more than one grantor and may be created by the donation of property or cash. This initial contribution is called the principal, corpus, or res of the trust.

The creators select a trustee or trustees to manage the trust according to an agreement signed by the trustee and the creator. This agreement specifies the purpose of the trust, the beneficiaries, the term of the trust, and other conditions required by state law. The trust, like the corporate nonprofit, is a creation of the state.

The trustees may be the nonprofit itself, individuals who may or may not be donors, a bank, or a combination of these. A bank may be the custodian or keeper of the corpus. The creator of the trust may serve as a trustee and, in some cases where the beneficiary is some person other than the creator, the creator may be the sole trustee. This is often unwise, however, because any incidence of ownership or control by the creator over a trust could lead to income as well as estate taxes falling on the creator, nullifying any possibility of a deduction since the donor may be construed not to have made a gift.[2]

Like a corporation, a trust is an independent tax and legal entity. It pays its own taxes and is responsible for its own liabilities. As an independent legal entity, a trust has legal ownership over the property entrusted to it. Its relationship to the beneficiary is said to be one of a fiduciary. This means that the obligation of the trustees is to act in ways to promote the interest of the beneficiaries. Violations of this fiduciary relationship can result in civil and criminal charges.

A trust may be simple or complex. A simple trust is one that cannot make charitable contributions, cannot distribute its corpus, and must make annual distributions. Naturally, such a trust cannot be used as a vehicle to make gifts to nonprofits. A complex trust, on the other hand, may accumulate income, distribute its corpus, and make charitable donations. A simple trust is automatically converted to a complex trust once it makes a charitable donation, accumulates income, or distributes its corpus. For the purpose of giving, trusts ought to be initially designed as complex rather than simple. Arriving at this status by default or accident is poor planning.

Trusts may be revocable or irrevocable. A nonprofit that obtains a transfer in a revocable trust may have no gift at all because the transfer may be revoked. The donor will receive no tax deduction and indeed will have to pay taxes on the earnings of the trust if it is revocable. Recall from Chapter 9 that revocable transfers are not gifts. Thus, from the vantage point of nonprofits, obtaining contributions by way of trusts means using an irrevocable, complex trust.

Trusts may be created to operate during the lifetime of an individual (inter vivos) or upon death (testamentary). The rules and discussions are for the most part the same. Obviously, a revocable trust becomes irrevocable at death.[3]

Trusts as Charitable Organizations

A nonprofit can be organized as a trust rather than as a corporation. As a charitable organization, the trust must abide by the two central restrictions on corporations: the assets and income cannot be used for the benefit of individuals and when the trust is dissolved, the assets and income must be distributed to a qualified tax-exempt nonprofit. At that point, the rules of control and attribution discussed in Chapter 4 apply.

Specifically, the governing document of a trust that is a nonprofit should contain the following if it is to qualify for tax-exemption.

1. The trustees will have the power to accept and dispose of property

according to the terms of the trust, but may not accept property if it requires distribution of the income or principal to organizations that are not charitable.

2. The trustees may accept additional property and distribute such property at their discretion as long as they are for charitable purposes. These distributions may be made through a nonprofit or the trustees may make such expenditures directly. But the donations of a U.S. corporation to a trust, as opposed to a nonprofit corporation, may not be used outside the United States. Further, no distribution shall inure to the benefit of individuals or may be used in political campaigns, and no substantial part may be used to influence legislation.

3. The trust will exist in perpetuity unless the trustees determine otherwise. The donor authorizes them to use the funds to create a nonprofit corporation if the trust is dissolved.

4. The trustees may amend the trust.

5. No less than two trustees are permitted.

6. The trustees have the power to invest, sell, hold, exchange, lease, or borrow any type security, and to execute contracts, to vote, to reorganize, to employ a bank, and to use investment advisors.

7. The powers of trustees are exercisable only in a fiduciary capacity.

8. Any person dealing with trustees may accept their actions as representing that of the trust and need not inquire further about the representation.

9. The declaration of trust is governed by the law of the state in which the trust is created.

This last provision is worthy of additional note because it affects the actual operation of the trust in the interpretation of some of the items previously enumerated. For example, the state may restrict the types of investments a trust may make. Generally, these restrictions are intended to prohibit risky investments or investments in the business of the trustees.

A trust that is a charitable organization is bound by the rules that cover private foundations. This is so even if the trust becomes a public charity. This means that trusts are bound by rules of self-dealing and they have to pay excise taxes and penalties as do private foundations. The purpose is to protect the assets and income of the trust against abuse and invasion for individual benefits. Thus, the trustees are bound not merely by the general rules of trusts and the particular stipulations of trust agreements, but by the rules of a private foundation as well.

A special example of a trust is the community trust. A community trust, unlike the community chest, is a trust normally started by one or two individuals. It may subsequently become a public trust by passing the one-third public support test, by having an organizing document stipulating the conditions mentioned before, or by passing the facts and circumstances test. A community trust may be one single entity, or it might be a composite of individual trusts. Unlike a community chest, it does not have to carry on a campaign to gain a large number of small contributions.

A trust as a nonprofit organization may be created by one or more persons. It may specifically designate one or more charitable beneficiaries and it need not receive additional donations. The task of the trustee is principally to manage the principal so that it grows and to distribute it prudently or according to the trust agreement among the stated beneficiaries. Again, once such a trust is created having only charitable beneficiaries, it immediately becomes a "charitable" trust and is subject to the rules governing private foundations.

Trusts for Future, Remainder, and Partial Interests

In another vein, trusts can be used to make partial, future, and split-interest gifts (gifts that are split between a charitable and a noncharitable beneficiary). Only through a unitrust, annuity trust, or pooled trust can such gifts be deductible.[4] When a trust is used to split interests between a charity and a noncharity, it may operate as a regular trust that is not subject to the special tax-exempt rules of nonprofits until such time that the interests of the noncharity are exhausted. The trust is treated as a private foundation and subject to all the stringent rules discussed in Chapter 4.

A basic characteristic of unitrusts, annuity trusts, and pooled trusts is that it distinguishes between remainder interest (what is left after the occurrence of some event, usually the passage of twenty years or death) and the income interest, the annual earnings, and distribution. One of these interests is kept by the donor or given to someone other than a nonprofit, and the other interest is given to the nonprofit.

In those trust arrangements where the donor or a noncharity receives the income leaving the remainder to the nonprofit, the trust is referred to as a remainder trust. In these cases, the charity is the remainderman; it gets what is left of the principal or corpus of the trust. The charitable lead trust is one where the nonprofit gets the income and the donor or the designated noncharitable beneficiary gets the remainder of the principal or corpus.

Essentially, then, a trust permits a donor to give a property and still enjoy it or to give it to more than one beneficiary (only one of which is a charity) and in both cases get an immediate income-tax deduction. Obviously, the trust is a useful tool.

Recall our discussion of incomplete or partial transfers in Chapter 9. With the exception of a primary residence or farm, transfers that are partial or of future interest do not qualify as gifts and are therefore not deductible. Without the possibility of a tax deduction, the person may prefer not to give the property. How can a tax benefit be arranged?

Moreover, there are times when the donor wishes to continue enjoying the property and would prefer to relinquish it at a time in the distant future. The nonprofit, on the other hand, is eager to obtain the property as a gift. How can a deal be arranged?

A trust can solve these types of problems. It can satisfy both the interests of the potential donor and the interests of the nonprofit. The trust can provide for a gift to be split between a beneficiary that is a charity and one that is not. It can provide for a property to be given but still enjoyed by the donor, and it can do this while getting the donor an immediate tax deduction for a property not fully relinquished. Since trust arrangements of this type make the gifts irrevocable, the nonprofit does not have to wait to own it. It does not risk a change of heart by the donor.

From a tax perspective, a trust does the following for the donor. It provides for an immediate deduction of the present value of the gift. It solves an estate tax problem by removing the property from the donor's estate. At the same time it allows the donor to receive some benefits from the property (even though it has been given away) or to assign some benefits to others, such as a relative or a friend.

To illustrate, Camila wishes to make a gift of $1,000,000 to a nonprofit but knows the needs of her parents. It is possible to arrange to have the money set aside to produce a steady stream of income for her parents and at the end of their lives the remainder could be donated to her favorite nonprofit.

Remainder Trusts

A remainder trust permits the donor to make a contribution to one or more charities, get an immediate tax deduction on that contribution, and still get an annual income from the gift or to provide an annual income for a spouse, children, or some other beneficiary that is not a charity for a period up to twenty years or for the remainder of their lives. Some or all of this income may be free from taxes. Hence, it is possible for the donor not only to get a tax deduction, but also a tax-free income for life or for the life of a beneficiary, including a spouse, children, or pet.

At the termination of the designated period, the remainder that is left in the trust will go to the charity. The donor may even be a trustee of the trust, but this is not advisable because the more influence she exercises, the more she is exposed to being taxed. The trust may carry the donor's name.

There are three types of remainder trusts: an annuity trust, a unitrust, and a pooled income trust. Let us see how each works.

A remainder trust that is in the form of an annuity trust is one that offers the donor or some other designated beneficiary or beneficiaries the income generated by the trust. Remember the donor may designate himself or herself as a beneficiary. They receive the income for a term that cannot exceed twenty years or for the life or lives of the donor and/or one or more beneficiaries alive at the time the trust is made. Accordingly, the donor and the spouse may receive the income from the trust for their lives; or the donor may choose to give the income from the trust to a child for a period not to exceed twenty years or for the life of the child. In short, the donor has a choice of whom and how many beneficiaries. The gift can be made over the life or lives of the individual(s) or for a specific period of time called a term. The beneficiary cannot be unborn and obviously not dead; hence, the word "alive."

All or part of the income received by the donor or beneficiaries might be tax free. This is so if the trust is funded by the use of securities such as municipal bonds that are tax exempt. It is also the case when part of the income is a return of the original investment of the donor. This part of the original investment is not taxed (see the accompanying inserts).

Once the annuity trust is created, no further contributions can be made to it. And at least 5 percent of the value of the assets of the trust at the time it is created must be paid to the income beneficiaries at least once a year.

As long as the trust does not invest in an unrelated business, its income is not taxed. If it does so invest, all its income, not just the portion coming from the unrelated business, is taxed. In any period, when the income of the trust exceeds that which is necessary to make the payments to the beneficiaries, a donation can be made to charity. Thus, it is possible for the charity to also be receiving annual donations from the trust (although this amount is not tax deductible by the donor). The trust deducts it. Moreover, part of this excess income could also go to the income beneficiaries as long as it is to cover a shortfall in the payment they received in a past year.

Because the income that the donor and other income beneficiaries receive is a fixed proportion of the value of the assets at the time the fund is created, they do not participate in the growth of the assets; conversely, if the value of the assets declines, they do not suffer. If the initial value of the assets is $1,000,000, 5 percent is $50,000, and $50,000 is received regardless of whether or not the value of the assets increases. If the assets decline, $50,000 is still owed and any shortfall can be made up in future years.

This brings us to an important point. No tax deduction of the gift is gotten by the donor unless there is a strong (at least 5 percent prob-

Loyal alumnus and long-time University supporter Ben Dyer (ENGR '31) recently made an important move, both for himself and for the University of Maryland Foundation. He gave a planned gift of real estate that is expected to bring more than $1 million to the University of Maryland.

In the tailor-made plan for Mr. and Mrs. Dyer, their Howard County home and farm—Hickory Hill—was given in trust to the UM Foundation and subsequently sold to a third party. To facilitate the sale of the property, the Foundation was able to provide favorable financing to the buyer.

The Dyers might have sold Hickory Hill outright, used the proceeds to buy their new home, and invested the remainder. But federal and state tax liabilities on a direct sale would have been substantial. Mr. Dyer had built the impressive stone house on the 225-acre farm 30 years ago and faced a sizable capital gains tax on the appreciation.

Many years ago, Mr. Dyer arranged for a bequest in his Will to leave a considerable part of his estate to the University of Maryland. By arranging a lifetime gift, he was able to accomplish that objective as well as to gain immediate benefits.

In a "bargain sale" gift arrangement made through the Foundation, Mr. and Mrs. Dyer were able to:

• Receive cash to purchase a new home and to pay moving and other expenses.
• Receive a life income from $1 million in trust funds.
• Reduce capital gains liability.
• Receive a substantial charitable income tax deduction.

The arrangement established two trust funds. Both trusts will pay income for life to the Dyers and then come to the University. Their income will be a fixed percentage of the principal in the trust funds. As the principal grows, the dollar amount of their income will increase, providing a hedge against inflation.

One of the trusts is set up so that the principal can be used, if necessary, during their lifetimes as emergency protection.

For more than a quarter of a century, Hickory Hill has been the site of the annual College of Engineering Alumni Bull Roast. Happily, the new owners have agreed to continue that wonderful tradition.

Source: *Milestones, The University of Maryland Foundation Newsletter,* 2, no. 3 (February 1986), p. 1. Reprinted with permission.

ability as calculated by special IRS tables) that the assets in the charity will not be used up so that, at the end of the term or the lives of the income beneficiaries, nothing will be left for the charity.

In times past, donors would arrange the trust so that they or their relatives who held the income interests would exhaust both the income

Trustee Ralph J. Tyser, president of Globe Distributing Company in Alexandria, VA, has used municipal bonds to fund a trust that will bring $235,000 to UM. He will receive a lifetime, tax free income, in addition to an income tax deduction.

Source: *Milestones, The University of Maryland Foundation Newsletter*, 2, no. 2, (November 1985), p. 4. Reprinted with permission.

and the principal of the trust so that eventually there was nothing left for the charity. Today, this is less likely. For one, both the unitrust and annuity trust require that the amount or percentage to be paid be stated when the trust is created and that this amount be set so as not to deplete the trust. Second, trust agreements often provide that capital gains should not be distributed but added to the principal of the trust. Hence, if a trust included among its holdings a property that was worth $1,000,000 at the time it was received, if that property is later sold for $1,200,000, the $200,000 gain is added to the principal of the trust and not distributed to the person or entities holding the income interests. Third, the fiduciary rules require that the remainder interest always be protected.

Despite this fact, however, the annuity trust does pose a risk for the charity. Because the income is based on the value of the assets at the opening of the trust, some trust assets may have to be sold to keep that promise in years when the earnings of the trust are not sufficient to meet its payments to the beneficiaries and if they are unwilling to wait to make up the difference. Because of this fact, annuity trusts tend to invest in securities that maintain their value or provide a steady stream of income, at least to cover the amount the trust must pay annually to the donor or other designated beneficiaries.

Recall that the income from the annuity trust was based on a predetermined percentage or amount of the value of the assets at the time the trust was created. The unitrust is different on this point. It, too, is a remainder trust with all the characteristics of an annuity trust except that the amount it pays is determined annually. That is, the trust is valued annually, and a fixed amount of that value (as determined each year) is paid to the income beneficiaries. Thus, if the value goes up, the amount they receive goes up. If the value goes down, the amount they receive declines.

In addition, a unitrust provides that the donor may make annual contributions to the trust. Furthermore, unlike the annuity trust, the unitrust can protect the interest of the charity by having a clause written into the trust agreement that says that the donor or the beneficiaries are paid only from the income of the trust. This is not permitted with an annuity trust. This clause is important because it means that the assets of the trust do not have to be sold in order to meet the required annual payments to the beneficiaries.

A third type of remainder trust is a pooled income trust. These trusts are particularly useful when the potential donor does not have sufficient money to justify the cost of setting up and administering a separate trust and investment agreement. How does this work?

The donor makes a gift to the charity and gets a tax deduction for the gift. The donor can also be named or name some other person or persons as beneficiaries. Unlike an annuity or unitrust, this designation cannot be for a term or number of years; it must be for the life or lives of the individuals.

Also, unlike the unitrust or annuity trust, there is no separate identity. The trust cannot carry the name of the donor because the trust is a pool to which many donors have contributed. Their funds are all co-mingled into one trust. Furthermore, neither the donor nor any beneficiary may serve as a trustee of the trust, and the trust may not invest in tax-exempt securities. One disadvantage of this is that all the income that the donors or their designated beneficiaries get regularly from the trust is taxable.

The amount of income the donor or beneficiaries get annually is not based on the value of the assets of the trust but on their pro rata share of the trust. Thus, a donor whose contribution makes up 10 percent of the pooled income trust will get 10 percent of the earnings it distributes.

The pooled income trust can be a good tax shelter. To illustrate, a university recently used a pooled income trust to finance the construction of athletic facilities. Being a tax-exempt organization, some of the tax benefits could not be used by the university. The IRS ruled (GCM 30976) that the depreciation expense and the investment tax credit could be passed on to the contributors of the pool. Depreciation expenses, according to a later ruling, must be matched by reserves so that the pool would not depreciate its original value to zero. These "expenses," although they were not incurred by the donors, could nevertheless be used by them to reduce their taxable incomes. Hence, the donor to a properly structured pooled income trust can get a tax deduction on the original gift, a regular flow of income, and an "expense" to reduce taxable income.

Charitable Lead Trusts

With the remainder trust, the donor or a designated beneficiary got the annual income and the charity got the remainder that was left after the predesignated period. Is there a technique that might reverse this process so that the charity gets the annual income and the donor or beneficiary gets the remainder? Such an approach would provide a steady and regular annual flow of income into the coffers of the nonprofit. But what would it do for the donor? Why should he or she go along with the proposal?

The technique is called a charitable lead trust. Such a trust provides a steady flow of income to the nonprofit. This trust must also be either in an annuity form (the flow being based on a fixed amount or percentage of the value of the initial assets) or the unitrust form (based on an annual appraisal of the value of the assets). In either case, unlike the remainder trust, the payments can be less than 5 percent.

As in the case of a remainder trust, the payments to the charity could cover the life of an individual or individuals (either coterminously or consecutively); but, unlike the remainder trust, there is no limit to the number of years if the donor prefers to make the payments for a term of years rather than for the life of some person or persons.

What is the appeal to the donor? The charitable lead trust offers four distinct approaches, each with its advantages and disadvantages to the donor. In one approach, the trust is set up and the donor can take a one-time deduction for the gift. The size of this deduction is based on calculations of what the present value of the amount the charity will receive over the years will be. The way the special IRS tables for calculating this deduction works, the deduction will generally be larger the greater the amount and frequency of payments to the charity (called the payout rate) and the longer the period over which this payment is to be made (designated either in terms of years or the lives of individuals).

If this first approach is taken, part of this deduction will be recalled (recaptured) if for some reason the donor should cease to honor the trust. On the other hand, every annual payment the charity gets counts against the 50 or 30 percent individual limit for charitable contributions discussed in Chapter 9. Hence, the donor gets a large one-time deduction covering all of the years that the charity is expected to receive annual payments, but takes the risk of recapture and limits the amount of annual contributions thereafter. For most donors, the recapture possibilities are more serious than the annual limitations because few donors ever legitimately approach that annual limit.

A second approach to setting up a charitable lead trust is to forego the one-time large deduction for annual deductions. This will appeal to only a few potential donors because the law requires that if they take an annual deduction they must also report the earnings of the trust as theirs. For most potential donors, this will put them in an adverse position because it will increase their income and therefore their tax liability.

A third approach to a charitable lead trust is to set up a trust in which the donor does not by implication or otherwise act as the owner of the trust. In this case, the donor does not have to report the earnings of the trust as his or her own, but neither can the donor take the deduction.

A fourth alternative way of using the charitable lead trust, which is the most common, is to reduce transfer (estate and gift taxes). For example, a potential donor wishes to make a gift to a charity in the form of an annual payment. The donor can be persuaded to do so by pointing to the fact that a trust can be set up such that at the end of some period, payments to the charity are ended, and the remainder of the trust is turned over to a beneficiary. If the trust is well invested so that the annual income is very high and the payments to the charity are correspondingly high, these payments would constitute a deduction so large that they would wipe out the estate tax upon the death of the donor. The benefit of this is that more of the wealth of the donor would be passed on to his or her heirs rather than to the state and federal governments in the form of death, estate, or inheritance taxes.

To this point we have talked about the charitable lead trust as providing annual income to the charity. But it can simultaneously provide a flow of income to the donor or beneficiary. The price for doing this is that the deduction will be decreased by the amount that all noncharitable beneficiaries get. Furthermore, these latter beneficiaries can get paid only after the charity is paid, even if some of the assets of the trust must be sold to meet the obligations to the charity. The donor gets no deductions for the sale of assets to meet the obligations of the trust.

EXAMPLES OF THE APPLICATION OF TRUST CONCEPTS

We shall take a look at some illustrations of how some of the concepts concerning a trust may be applied. There are infinite variations; therefore, the wise financial officer learns to consult an expert. Always work with a lawyer, accountant and financial planner—all specializing in estate planning and taxation.

Illustration 1

Myra, who turned 44 on April 1, 1991, transfers $100,000 to a pooled income fund and retains a life income interest in the property. The highest rate of return experienced by the fund in the immediately preceding three years is 9.2 percent. What amount of deductions did Myra take on her income tax?

Refer to Table 10.1. The factor in the cell referring to age 44 and 9.2 percent is .12167. By multiplying the fair market value of the gift, $100,000 by .12167, we get $12,167, the amount of her deduction. If she

TABLE 10.1 Table, Single Life, Unisex, Showing the Present Worth of the Remainder Interest in Property Transferred to a Pooled Income Fund Having the Yearly Rate of Return Shown

(1) Age	(2) Yearly Rate of Return 9.2%	9.4%	9.6%	9.8%	10.0%	(1) Age	(2) Yearly Rate of Return 9.2%	9.4%	9.6%	9.8%	10.0%
5	.01283	.01221	.01164	.01111	.01062	58	.25231	.24691	.24170	.23665	.23178
6	.01350	.01284	.01224	.01168	.01116	59	.26418	.25868	.25336	.24822	.24325
7	.01425	.01356	.01292	.01233	.01178	60	.27640	.27081	.26540	.26016	.25509
8	.01512	.01439	.01372	.01309	.01252	61	.28899	.28332	.27782	.27249	.26733
9	.01612	.01535	.01464	.01398	.01337	62	.30197	.29622	.29064	.28523	.27998
10	.01724	.01644	.01569	.01499	.01435	63	.31533	.30950	.30385	.29836	.29304
11	.01851	.01766	.01688	.01615	.01547	64	.32905	.32316	.31743	.31188	.30648
12	.01991	.01902	.01819	.01742	.01671	65	.34311	.33716	.33138	.32576	.32030
13	.02139	.02045	.01958	.01877	.01802	66	.35751	.35151	.34568	.34001	.33449
14	.02288	.02190	.02098	.02013	.01934	67	.37221	.36618	.36030	.35459	.34902
15	.02435	.02331	.02235	.02146	.02063	68	.38723	.38116	.37526	.36950	.36390
16	.02575	.02466	.02366	.02272	.02185	69	.40257	.39649	.39056	.38478	.37914
17	.02709	.02595	.02490	.02391	.02300	70	.41826	.41217	.40623	.40043	.39478
18	.02839	.02721	.02610	.02507	.02410	71	.43435	.42827	.42233	.41652	.41086
19	.02971	.02846	.02730	.02621	.02520	72	.45084	.44478	.43885	.43305	.42739
20	.03108	.02977	.02855	.02741	.02635	73	.46765	.46161	.45571	.44994	.44429
21	.03251	.03114	.02986	.02866	.02755	74	.48460	.47861	.47274	.46700	.46138
22	.03402	.03258	.03123	.02998	.02880	75	.50155	.49561	.48979	.48409	.47851
23	.03562	.03410	.03269	.03137	.03014	76	.51841	.51253	.50677	.50112	.49559
24	.03735	.03577	.03428	.03290	.03159	77	.53514	.52934	.52364	.51806	.51258
25	.03927	.03761	.03605	.03459	.03322	78	.55177	.54605	.54043	.53492	.52951
26	.04141	.03966	.03803	.03649	.03505	79	.56837	.56273	.55720	.55177	.54643
27	.04377	.04194	.04023	.03861	.03710	80	.58497	.57944	.57401	.56866	.56341
28	.04639	.04447	.04267	.04098	.03938	81	.60148	.59606	.59073	.58548	.58033
29	.04922	.04721	.04532	.04354	.04187	82	.61775	.61245	.60723	.60210	.59705
30	.05228	.05017	.04819	.04633	.04457	83	.63381	.62863	.62354	.61852	.61358
31	.05554	.05334	.05126	.04930	.04746	84	.64974	.64470	.63973	.63484	.63002
32	.05904	.05674	.05456	.05251	.05058	85	.66558	.66068	.65586	.65110	.64641
33	.06279	.06038	.05810	.05595	.05392	86	.68096	.67622	.67154	.66692	.66236
34	.06677	.06435	.06187	.05962	.05750	87	.69542	.69082	.68628	.68180	.67738
35	.07102	.06839	.06590	.06355	.06132	88	.70891	.70445	.70005	.69570	.69141
36	.07553	.07278	.07019	.06733	.06540	89	.72172	.71739	.71312	.70891	.70474
37	.08030	.07745	.07474	.07217	.06974	90	.73422	.73004	.72591	.72182	.71779
38	.08534	.08237	.07955	.07687	.07433	91	.74632	.74229	.73829	.73435	.73045
39	.09065	.08755	.08462	.08182	.07917	92	.75763	.75373	.74988	.74606	.74229
40	.09624	.09302	.08996	.08706	.08429	93	.76791	.76414	.76042	.75673	.75308
41	.10212	.09878	.09560	.09258	.08970	94	.77710	.77345	.76983	.76626	.76272
42	.10833	.10486	.10156	.09842	.09543	95	.78510	.78155	.77804	.77457	.77113
43	.11484	.11125	.10783	.10456	.10145	96	.79183	.78837	.78494	.78155	.77819
44	.12167	.11795	.11441	.11102	.10779	97	.79783	.79445	.79110	.78779	.78450
45	.12880	.12495	.12128	.11777	.11442	98	.80306	.79975	.79647	.79322	.79000
46	.13625	.13227	.12847	.12484	.12137	99	.80797	.80471	.80149	.79830	.79514
47	.14402	.13991	.13599	.13223	.12863	100	.81283	.80964	.80648	.80335	.80025
48	.15214	.14791	.14385	.13997	.13626	101	.81708	.81394	.81082	.80774	.80468
49	.16060	.15625	.15207	.14806	.14422	102	.82165	.81856	.81550	.81247	.80946
50	.16944	.16496	.16065	.15653	.15257	103	.82754	.82452	.82153	.81857	.81563
51	.17862	.17401	.16959	.16534	.16126	104	.83312	.83017	.82723	.82433	.82144
52	.18816	.18343	.17888	.17451	.17031	105	.84165	.83880	.83597	.83316	.83038
53	.19805	.19320	.18853	.18404	.17972	106	.85562	.85297	.85034	.84772	.84512
54	.20825	.20328	.19850	.19390	.18946	107	.87523	.87288	.87054	.86822	.86591
55	.21878	.21370	.20881	.20409	.19954	108	.90652	.90471	.90291	.90111	.89932
56	.22963	.22443	.21943	.21460	.20994	109	.95788	.95704	.95620	.95537	.95455
57	.24081	.23551	.23040	.22546	.22069						

Source: Internal Revenue Service, *Code of Federal Regulations*, Vol. 26, Part I, Sec. 1.641 to 1.850, April 1, 1985, p. 40.

is in the 50 percent bracket, she saves $6083 on her income tax (50 percent of $12,167). But she will get an annual income from the trust. Suppose the trust paid her $4000 in income the following year.

To calculate the rate of return, her net investment would be $100,000 minus the $6083 she saved in income taxes. This is $93,917 and the rate of return on her net investment is 4 percent. Thus, she would have made a gift, gotten a deduction, and continued to get a positive rate of return for as long as she lives and as long as the pool earns money. The advantage is even greater if one recognizes that often gifts are made of appreciated property. Thus, she might have made a gift with a market value of $100,000 for which she paid substantially less. Thus, the true rate of return might well exceed 4 percent.

Note that the effects of this transaction depend on the age of the donor; that is, the donor's life expectancy is the number of years the donor may expect to receive annual or monthly income. It also depends on the expected payout rate measured by the highest rate of return to the pool in the preceding three years. The higher the expected payout rate is the lower the deduction because the greater the income that a donor will receive. Also, the younger the donor is the lower the deduction because income may be flowing to him or her for a considerable period of time. The tax savings depend on the tax bracket of the donor; the higher the tax bracket the greater the savings. As will be shown by the following illustration, it also depends on the number of noncharitable beneficiaries and their ages regardless of sex.

Illustration 2

Let us add another complication to the pooled income trust. Assume that Simon decides he would like to make a contribution of $100,000 to a pooled income trust but that the income should go to his two daughters prior to the remainder being turned over to the charity. What will his deduction be?

Assume that his two daughters, Emeline and Celestina, are 35 and 30 years of age, respectively. Then we must take both of these ages into account because we are concerned not only with the life expectancy of one person, but of two persons jointly. Assume also that the highest rate of return experienced by the pooled trust in the preceding three years was 9.2 percent. Turn to Table 10.2, Part 4. The factor is .02043 so his deduction would be $2043. But both of his children will receive annual incomes equaling their share of the earnings of the pooled trust for the remainder of their lives.

Note that in both of these cases the nonprofit gets $100,000 and its payments to the donor or his designees depend on the earnings of the investment made with the $100,000. In a pooled trust, the annuity to the

TABLE 10.2 Two-life Last to Die Pooled Income Trust

Table E(2)—Part 4

Yearly Rate of Return

O	Y	8.2%	8.4%	8.6%	8.8%	9.0%	9.2%	9.4%	9.6%	9.8%	10.0%
34	5	.00890	.00812	.00742	.00679	.00622	.00570	.00523	.00481	.00443	.00408
34	6	.00936	.00855	.00782	.00715	.00656	.00602	.00552	.00508	.00468	.00431
34	7	.00985	.00900	.00824	.00754	.00692	.00635	.00583	.00537	.00494	.00456
34	8	.01037	.00948	.00868	.00796	.00730	.00670	.00616	.00567	.00523	.00482
34	9	.01092	.00999	.00915	.00839	.00771	.00708	.00651	.00600	.00553	.00510
34	10	.01150	.01053	.00965	.00886	.00814	.00748	.00689	.00635	.00585	.00540
34	11	.01210	.01109	.01017	.00934	.00859	.00790	.00728	.00671	.00620	.00572
34	12	.01274	.01168	.01072	.00985	.00907	.00835	.00769	.00710	.00656	.00606
34	13	.01339	.01229	.01129	.01039	.00956	.00881	.00813	.00750	.00693	.00641
34	14	.01407	.01293	.01188	.01094	.01007	.00929	.00857	.00792	.00732	.00678
34	15	.01477	.01358	.01249	.01150	.01060	.00978	.00903	.00835	.00772	.00715
34	16	.01548	.01424	.01311	.01208	.01114	.01028	.00950	.00879	.00813	.00753
34	17	.01622	.01492	.01375	.01268	.01170	.01080	.00999	.00924	.00856	.00793
34	18	.01697	.01563	.01440	.01329	.01227	.01134	.01049	.00971	.00899	.00834
34	19	.01775	.01635	.01508	.01392	.01286	.01189	.01100	.01019	.00945	.00876
34	20	.01855	.01711	.01579	.01458	.01348	.01247	.01154	.01070	.00992	.00921
34	21	.01938	.01789	.01652	.01527	.01412	.01307	.01211	.01122	.01041	.00967
34	22	.02025	.01869	.01728	.01598	.01478	.01369	.01269	.01177	.01093	.01015
34	23	.02114	.01953	.01806	.01671	.01548	.01434	.01330	.01235	.01147	.01066
34	24	.02206	.02040	.01888	.01748	.01620	.01502	.01394	.01294	.01203	.01119
34	25	.02302	.02130	.01972	.01827	.01695	.01572	.01460	.01357	.01262	.01174
34	26	.02401	.02223	.02060	.01910	.01773	.01646	.01530	.01422	.01323	.01232
34	27	.02503	.02320	.02151	.01996	.01854	.01723	.01602	.01490	.01388	.01293
34	28	.02609	.02419	.02245	.02085	.01938	.01802	.01677	.01561	.01455	.01357
34	29	.02717	.02522	.02342	.02177	.02024	.01884	.01754	.01635	.01524	.01422
34	30	.02828	.02627	.02442	.02271	.02114	.01969	.01834	.01711	.01596	.01491
34	31	.02942	.02735	.02544	.02368	.02205	.02055	.01917	.01789	.01670	.01561
34	32	.03057	.02844	.02648	.02467	.02299	.02144	.02001	.01869	.01747	.01633
34	33	.03175	.02956	.02754	.02568	.02395	.02236	.02088	.01952	.01825	.01708
34	34	.03295	.03070	.02863	.02671	.02493	.02329	.02177	.02036	.01906	.01785
35	0	.00871	.00803	.00741	.00685	.00634	.00588	.00546	.00508	.00473	.00442
35	1	.00752	.00686	.00627	.00574	.00526	.00482	.00443	.00407	.00375	.00346
35	2	.00785	.00716	.00654	.00599	.00548	.00503	.00462	.00425	.00391	.00360
35	3	.00823	.00751	.00686	.00628	.00575	.00528	.00485	.00446	.00410	.00378
35	4	.00864	.00789	.00722	.00660	.00605	.00555	.00510	.00469	.00432	.00398
35	5	.00909	.00831	.00760	.00696	.00638	.00585	.00538	.00495	.00456	.00420
35	6	.00957	.00875	.00801	.00733	.00673	.00618	.00568	.00523	.00482	.00444
35	7	.01007	.00921	.00844	.00774	.00710	.00652	.00600	.00552	.00509	.00470
35	8	.01061	.00971	.00890	.00816	.00749	.00689	.00634	.00584	.00539	.00497
35	9	.01117	.01023	.00938	.00861	.00791	.00728	.00670	.00618	.00570	.00527
35	10	.01177	.01079	.00990	.00909	.00836	.00769	.00709	.00654	.00603	.00558
35	11	.01239	.01137	.01044	.00959	.00883	.00813	.00749	.00692	.00639	.00591
35	12	.01305	.01198	.01101	.01012	.00932	.00859	.00792	.00732	.00676	.00626

TABLE 10.2 Two-life Last to Die Pooled Income Trust (*continued*)

Table E(2)—Part 4

Yearly Rate of Return

O	Y	8.2%	8.4%	8.6%	8.8%	9.0%	9.2%	9.4%	9.6%	9.8%	10.0%
35	13	.01373	.01261	.01160	.01067	.00983	.00907	.00837	.00774	.00715	.00662
35	14	.01443	.01327	.01221	.01124	.01037	.00957	.00884	.00817	.00756	.00700
35	15	.01515	.01394	.01283	.01183	.01091	.01008	.00931	.00861	.00798	.00739
35	16	.01589	.01463	.01348	.01243	.01147	.01060	.00980	.00907	.00840	.00779
35	17	.01665	.01533	.01414	.01305	.01205	.01114	.01030	.00954	.00884	.00820
35	18	.01743	.01606	.01482	.01368	.01264	.01169	.01082	.01003	.00930	.00863
35	19	.01823	.01682	.01552	.01434	.01326	.01227	.01136	.01053	.00977	.00907
35	20	.01907	.01760	.01625	.01503	.01390	.01287	.01193	.01106	.01026	.00953
35	21	.01994	.01841	.01701	.01574	.01457	.01350	.01251	.01161	.01078	.01002
35	22	.02083	.01925	.01780	.01648	.01526	.01415	.01312	.01218	.01132	.01052
35	23	.02176	.02012	.01862	.01725	.01598	.01482	.01376	.01278	.01188	.01105
35	24	.02272	.02103	.01947	.01805	.01674	.01553	.01443	.01341	.01247	.01161
35	25	.02372	.02197	.02036	.01888	.01752	.01627	.01512	.01406	.01309	.01219
35	26	.02476	.02295	.02128	.01975	.01834	.01704	.01585	.01475	.01373	.01280
35	27	.02583	.02396	.02223	.02065	.01919	.01785	.01661	.01546	.01441	.01344
35	28	.02694	.02500	.02322	.02158	.02007	.01868	.01740	.01621	.01512	.01411
35	29	.02808	.02608	.02424	.02255	.02098	.01954	.01821	.01698	.01585	.01480
35	30	.02924	.02718	.02529	.02354	.02192	.02043	.01906	.01778	.01661	.01552
35	31	.03044	.02832	.02636	.02456	.02289	.02135	.01993	.01861	.01739	.01626
35	32	.03166	.02947	.02746	.02560	.02388	.02229	.02082	.01946	.01820	.01703
35	33	.03290	.03066	.02858	.02667	.02490	.02326	.02174	.02033	.01903	.01782
35	34	.03416	.03186	.02973	.02776	.02593	.02424	.02268	.02123	.01988	.01863
35	35	.03545	.03308	.03089	.02887	.02699	.02525	.02364	.02214	.02075	.01946
36	0	.00896	.00827	.00764	.00707	.00655	.00609	.00566	.00527	.00492	.00460
36	1	.00769	.00702	.00642	.00588	.00539	.00495	.00455	.00419	.00386	.00357
36	2	.00802	.00732	.00670	.00613	.00562	.00516	.00474	.00437	.00402	.00371
36	3	.00841	.00768	.00702	.00643	.00590	.00542	.00498	.00458	.00422	.00390
36	4	.00883	.00807	.00738	.00677	.00621	.00570	.00524	.00482	.00445	.00410
36	5	.00929	.00849	.00778	.00713	.00654	.00601	.00553	.00509	.00469	.00433
36	6	.00978	.00895	.00820	.00752	.00690	.00634	.00584	.00538	.00496	.00458
36	7	.01030	.00943	.00864	.00793	.00728	.00670	.00617	.00568	.00524	.00484
36	8	.01085	.00994	.00911	.00837	.00769	.00708	.00652	.00601	.00555	.00513
36	9	.01143	.01048	.00961	.00883	.00812	.00748	.00589	.00636	.00587	.00543
36	10	.01204	.01104	.01014	.00932	.00858	.00790	.00729	.00673	.00622	.00575
36	11	.01268	.01164	.01070	.00984	.00907	.00836	.00771	.00712	.00659	.00610
36	12	.01336	.01227	.01129	.01039	.00958	.00883	.00816	.00754	.00698	.00646
36	13	.01406	.01293	.01190	.01096	.01011	.00933	.00862	.00797	.00738	.00684
36	14	.01479	.01361	.01253	.01155	.01066	.00984	.00910	.00842	.00780	.00723
36	15	.01553	.01430	.01318	.01216	.01123	.01037	.00960	.00889	.00823	.00764
36	16	.01630	.01501	.01385	.01278	.01181	.01092	.01010	.00936	.00868	.00805
36	17	.01708	.01575	.01453	.01342	.01240	.01148	.01063	.00985	.00914	.00848
36	18	.01789	.01650	.01523	.01408	.01302	.01205	.01117	.01035	.00961	.00892

(*continued*)

TABLE 10.2 Two-life Last to Die Pooled Income Trust (*continued*)

Table E(2)—Part 4

Yearly Rate of Return

O	Y	8.2%	8.4%	8.6%	8.8%	9.0%	9.2%	9.4%	9.6%	9.8%	10.0%
36	19	.01872	.01728	.01596	.01476	.01366	.01265	.01173	.01088	.01010	.00937
36	20	.01959	.01809	.01672	.01547	.01433	.01327	.01231	.01143	.01061	.00987
36	21	.02049	.01893	.01751	.01621	.01502	.01393	.01292	.01200	.01115	.01037
36	22	.02142	.01981	.01833	.01698	.01574	.01460	.01356	.01260	.01171	.01090
36	23	.02238	.02072	.01919	.01778	.01650	.01531	.01422	.01322	.01230	.01145
36	24	.02339	.02166	.02007	.01862	.01728	.01605	.01492	.01388	.01292	.01203
36	25	.02443	.02264	.02100	.01949	.01810	.01682	.01565	.01456	.01356	.01264
36	26	.02551	.02366	.02196	.02040	.01896	.01763	.01641	.01528	.01424	.01328
36	27	.02663	.02472	.02296	.02134	.01985	.01847	.01720	.01603	.01495	.01395
36	28	.02779	.02582	.02400	.02232	.02077	.01935	.01803	.01682	.01569	.01468
36	29	.02899	.02695	.02507	.02333	.02173	.02026	.01889	.01763	.01647	.01539
36	30	.03021	.02811	.02617	.02437	.02272	.02119	.01978	.01847	.01726	.01615
36	31	.03147	.02930	.02729	.02545	.02374	.02216	.02070	.01934	.01809	.01693
36	32	.03275	.03052	.02845	.02655	.02478	.02315	.02164	.02024	.01894	.01774
36	33	.03406	.03176	.02964	.02767	.02585	.02417	.02261	.02116	.01982	.01857
36	34	.03539	.03303	.03085	.02882	.02695	.02521	.02360	.02211	.02072	.01943
36	35	.03675	.03432	.03208	.03000	.02807	.02628	.02462	.02308	.02165	.02032
36	36	.03813	.03564	.03333	.03119	.02921	.02737	.02566	.02407	.02259	.02122
37	0	.00922	.00852	.00788	.00730	.00678	.00630	.00587	.00547	.00511	.00478
37	1	.00785	.00718	.00657	.00602	.00553	.00508	.00468	.00431	.00398	.00368
37	2	.00819	.00749	.00685	.00628	.00576	.00530	.00487	.00449	.00414	.00382
37	3	.00858	.00785	.00719	.00659	.00605	.00556	.00511	.00471	.00434	.00401
37	4	.00902	.00825	.00755	.00693	.00636	.00585	.00538	.00496	.00457	.00422
37	5	.00949	.00868	.00796	.00730	.00670	.00616	.00568	.00523	.00483	.00446
37	6	.00999	.00915	.00839	.00770	.00707	.00651	.00599	.00553	.00510	.00472
37	7	.01052	.00964	.00884	.00812	.00747	.00687	.00633	.00584	.00540	.00499
37	8	.01108	.01016	.00933	.00857	.00789	.00726	.00670	.00618	.00571	.00528
37	9	.01168	.01072	.00984	.00905	.00833	.00768	.00708	.00654	.00605	.00560
37	10	.01231	.01130	.01039	.00956	.00881	.00812	.00749	.00693	.00641	.00593
37	11	.01297	.01192	.01097	.01010	.00931	.00859	.00793	.00733	.00679	.00629
37	12	.01367	.01257	.01157	.01066	.00983	.00908	.00839	.00776	.00719	.00666
37	13	.01440	.01325	.01220	.01125	.01038	.00959	.00887	.00821	.00761	.00706
37	14	.01514	.01395	.01286	.01186	.01095	.01013	.00937	.00868	.00805	.00747
37	15	.01591	.01466	.01353	.01249	.01154	.01067	.00988	.00916	.00850	.00789
37	16	.01670	.01540	.01421	.01313	.01214	.01124	.01041	.00965	.00896	.00832
37	17	.01751	.01616	.01492	.01379	.01276	.01182	.01095	.01016	.00943	.00876
37	18	.01835	.01694	.01565	.01448	.01340	.01241	.01151	.01068	.00992	.00922
37	19	.01921	.01775	.01641	.01518	.01406	.01303	.01209	.01123	.01043	.00970
37	20	.02011	.01859	.01720	.01592	.01475	.01368	.01270	.01180	.01097	.01020
37	21	.02104	.01946	.01802	.01669	.01548	.01436	.01333	.01239	.01153	.01073
37	22	.02201	.02037	.01887	.01749	.01623	.01507	.01400	.01302	.01211	.01128
37	23	.02301	.02131	.01975	.01832	.01701	.01580	.01469	.01367	.01273	.01186
37	24	.02405	.02229	.02068	.01919	.01783	.01657	.01542	.01435	.01337	.01246

TABLE 10.2 Two-life Last to Die Pooled Income Trust (*continued*)

Table E(2)—Part 4

Yearly Rate of Return

O	Y	8.2%	8.4%	8.6%	8.8%	9.0%	9.2%	9.4%	9.6%	9.8%	10.0%
37	25	.02514	.02332	.02164	.02010	.01868	.01738	.01618	.01507	.01405	.01310
37	26	.02627	.02438	.02265	.02105	.01958	.01822	.01697	.01582	.01476	.01377
37	27	.02744	.02549	.02369	.02204	.02051	.01911	.01781	.01661	.01550	.01448
37	28	.02865	.02664	.02478	.02306	.02148	.02002	.01868	.01743	.01628	.01522
37	29	.02990	.02782	.02590	.02412	.02249	.02098	.01958	.01829	.01709	.01598
37	30	.03119	.02904	.02705	.02522	.02353	.02196	.02051	.01917	.01793	.01678
37	31	.03250	.03029	.02824	.02635	.02460	.02298	.02148	.02009	.01880	.01761
37	32	.03385	.03157	.02946	.02750	.02570	.02402	.02247	.02103	.01970	.01846
37	33	.03523	.03288	.03070	.02869	.02683	.02510	.02349	.02201	.02063	.01935
37	34	.03663	.03422	.03198	.02990	.02798	.02620	.02454	.02301	.02158	.02025
37	35	.03807	.03558	.03328	.03115	.02917	.02733	.02562	.02403	.02256	.02119
37	36	.03952	.03697	.03461	.03241	.03037	.02848	.02672	.02509	.02356	.02215
37	37	.04099	.03838	.03595	.03370	.03160	.02966	.02784	.02616	.02459	.02313
38	0	.00949	.00877	.00813	.00754	.00701	.00652	.00608	.00568	.00531	.00498
38	1	.00802	.00734	.00672	.00617	.00567	.00521	.00480	.00443	.00409	.00379
38	2	.00836	.00765	.00701	.00643	.00590	.00543	.00500	.00461	.00426	.00394
38	3	.00876	.00802	.00735	.00674	.00619	.00570	.00525	.00484	.00447	.00413
38	4	.00920	.00843	.00772	.00709	.00652	.00599	.00552	.00509	.00470	.00435
38	5	.00968	.00887	.00814	.00747	.00687	.00632	.00583	.00537	.00496	.00459
38	6	.01020	.00935	.00858	.00788	.00725	.00667	.00615	.00568	.00525	.00485
38	7	.01074	.00985	.00905	.00832	.00765	.00705	.00650	.00600	.00555	.00514
38	8	.01132	.01039	.00955	.00878	.00808	.00745	.00688	.00635	.00588	.00544

Source: Actuarial Values I: Valuation of Last Survivor Charitable Remainders, Part D: Two-Life Last to Die Pooled-Income Fund Factors, Internal Revenue Service, Publication 723D (9–84), p. 128.

donor or his designees is for life. Recall that the income that noncharitable beneficiaries get will be taxable as ordinary income.

Illustration 3

Let's assume that Roy decides to make a gift of $100,000 to a charitable remainder unitrust. The trust instrument requires that the trustee pay at the end of each taxable year of the trust 5 percent of the fair market value of the trust assets as of the beginning of the trust's taxable year to his son, Rene, for life, and then to his son, Robertino, for life. Robertino is 35 and Rene is 30. What will the deduction be for Roy? The factor in Table 10.3, Part 2 is .09193 so the deduction will be $9193. All the arguments stated above about Myra and Simon apply except that in the case of income flowing to the noncharitable beneficiaries, Rene and Rob-

TABLE 10.3 Two-life Last to Die Unitrust

Table E(2)—Part 2

Adjusted Payout Rate

O	Y	4.2%	4.4%	4.6%	4.8%	5.0%	5.2%	5.4%	5.6%	5.8%	6.0%
34	5	.06343	.05605	.04957	.04388	.03887	.03447	.03059	.02718	.02417	.02151
34	6	.06558	.05803	.05139	.04554	.04040	.03586	.03187	.02834	.02523	.02248
34	7	.06780	.06007	.05326	.04726	.04198	.03731	.03319	.02955	.02634	.02349
34	8	.07008	.06217	.05520	.04905	.04361	.03881	.03457	.03081	.02749	.02455
34	9	.07243	.06434	.05720	.05089	.04531	.04037	.03600	.03212	.02869	.02565
34	10	.07484	.05657	.05926	.05279	.04706	.04198	.03748	.03348	.02994	.02679
34	11	.07731	.05886	.06138	.05474	.04886	.04364	.03901	.03489	.03124	.02798
34	12	.07984	.07121	.06355	.05675	.05062	.04535	.04059	.03635	.03258	.02922
34	13	.08241	.07360	.06577	.05881	.05262	.04711	.04221	.03785	.03396	.03049
34	14	.08502	.07603	.06802	.06090	.05456	.04890	.04387	.03938	.03537	.03179
34	15	.08767	.07849	.07031	.06302	.05652	.05073	.04555	.04093	.03681	.03312
34	16	.09033	.08097	.07262	.06517	.05852	.05258	.04727	.04252	.03827	.03447
34	17	.09303	.08349	.07497	.06735	.06054	.05446	.04901	.04413	.03977	.03585
34	18	.09575	.08603	.07734	.06956	.06260	.05637	.05078	.04578	.04129	.03726
34	19	.09850	.08861	.07974	.07181	.06469	.05831	.05259	.04745	.04284	.03871
34	20	.10129	.09122	.08219	.07409	.06682	.06029	.05443	.04917	.04444	.04018
34	21	.10411	.09387	.08467	.07641	.06899	.06232	.05632	.05092	.04607	.04170
34	22	.10697	.09655	.08719	.07876	.07119	.06437	.05824	.05271	.04774	.04325
34	23	.10985	.09926	.08973	.08115	.07343	.06647	.06019	.05454	.04944	.04484
34	24	.11276	.10201	.09231	.08358	.07570	.06860	.06219	.05640	.05118	.04646
34	25	.11570	.10478	.09493	.08604	.07801	.07076	.06422	.05830	.05296	.04813
34	26	.11866	.10758	.09757	.08853	.08036	.07297	.06629	.06024	.05478	.04983
34	27	.12165	.11041	.10024	.09105	.08273	.07520	.06839	.06222	.05663	.05156
34	28	.12465	.11325	.10293	.09359	.08513	.07747	.07052	.06422	.05851	.05333
34	29	.12765	.11610	.10564	.09615	.08755	.07975	.07267	.06625	.06042	.05513
34	30	.13065	.11895	.10835	.09872	.08998	.08205	.07484	.06830	.06235	.05694
34	31	.13364	.12180	.11105	.10129	.09242	.08436	.07702	.07036	.06430	.05878
34	32	.13661	.12464	.11376	.10386	.09486	.08667	.07922	.07243	.06626	.06063
34	33	.13957	.12747	.11645	.10643	.09730	.08899	.08142	.07452	.06823	.06250
34	34	.14250	.13027	.11913	.10898	.09973	.09130	.08361	.07660	.07021	.06437
35	0	.05746	.05075	.04489	.03977	.03528	.03134	.02789	.02485	.02218	.01983
35	1	.05602	.04929	.04341	.03828	.03378	.02985	.02641	.02339	.02074	.01841
35	2	.05783	.05094	.04492	.03964	.03502	.03098	.02743	.02431	.02157	.01916
35	3	.05977	.05272	.04654	.04112	.03637	.03220	.02854	.02532	.02249	.01999
35	4	.06180	.05458	.04824	.04267	.03779	.03349	.02972	.02639	.02346	.02088
35	5	.06392	.05652	.05002	.04430	.03928	03485	.03096	.02752	.02449	.02182
35	6	.06610	.05853	.05186	.04600	.04083	.03627	.03255	.02871	.02558	.02281
35	7	.06836	.06060	.05377	.04775	.04244	.03775	.03361	.02994	.02671	.02384
35	8	.07068	.06274	.05574	.04956	.04410	.03928	.03501	.03123	.02789	.02492
35	9	.07307	.06495	.05778	.05144	.04583	.04087	.03647	.03257	.02912	.02605
35	10	.07552	.06722	.05988	.05338	.04762	.04251	.03798	.03396	.03039	.02722
35	11	.07804	.06956	.06204	.05538	.04946	.04421	.03955	.03541	.03172	.02844
35	12	.08062	.07195	.06426	.05743	.05136	.04597	.04117	.03690	.03310	.02971

TABLE 10.3 Two-life Last to Die Unitrust (*continued*)

Table E(2)—Part 2

Adjusted Payout Rate

O	Y	4.2%	4.4%	4.6%	4.8%	5.0%	5.2%	5.4%	5.6%	5.8%	6.0%
35	13	.08325	.07440	.06653	.05953	.05331	.04777	.04283	.03843	.03451	.03102
35	14	.08592	.07688	.06884	.06167	.05529	.04960	.04453	.04000	.03596	.03235
35	15	.08862	.07940	.07118	.06385	.05731	.05147	.04626	.04161	.03744	.03372
35	16	.09135	.08195	.07355	.06606	.05936	.05337	.04802	.04324	.03895	.03512
35	17	.09411	.08452	.07595	.06829	.06144	.05530	.04981	.04489	.04049	.03654
35	18	.09690	.08713	.07839	.07056	.06355	.05727	.05164	.04659	.04206	.03799
35	19	.09973	.08978	.08086	.07287	.06570	.05927	.05350	.04832	.04366	.03948
35	20	.10260	.09247	.08338	.07522	.06790	.06132	.05540	.05009	.04531	.04101
35	21	.10550	.09520	.08594	.07761	.07013	.06340	.05735	.05190	.04699	.04257
35	22	.10844	.09796	.08853	.08004	.07241	.06553	.05933	.05375	.04872	.04418
35	23	.11142	.10076	.09116	.08251	.07472	.06769	.06136	.05564	.05048	.04582
35	24	.11443	.10360	.09383	.08502	.07707	.06990	.06342	.05757	.05229	.04751
35	25	.11747	.10647	.09654	.08757	.07947	.07215	.06553	.05955	.05414	.04924
35	26	.12054	.10937	.09928	.09016	.08190	.07444	.06768	.06157	.05603	.05101
35	27	.12363	.11231	.10205	.09278	.08437	.07676	.06987	.06362	.05796	.05282
35	28	.12675	.11526	.10485	.09542	.08687	.07912	.07209	.06571	.05992	.05467
35	29	.12987	.11823	.10767	.09809	.08940	.08150	.07434	.06783	.06192	.05655
35	30	.13300	.12121	.11050	.10077	.09193	.08391	.07661	.06997	.06394	.05845
35	31	.13612	.12418	.11333	.10346	.09448	.08632	.07889	.07213	.06598	.06037
35	32	.13924	.12715	.11616	.10615	.09704	.08875	.08119	.07431	.06804	.06232
35	33	.14233	.13011	.11898	.10884	.09960	.09118	.08350	.07650	.07011	.06428
35	34	.14541	.13306	.12179	.11152	.10216	.09361	.08581	.07869	.07219	.06625
35	35	.14846	.13598	.12459	.11420	.10471	.09604	.08812	.08089	.07428	.06823
36	0	.05797	.05125	.04537	.04023	.03572	.03177	.02829	.02524	.02256	.02019
36	1	.05640	.04966	.04376	.03861	.03411	.03016	.02670	.02367	.02100	.01866
36	2	.05823	.05133	.04528	.03999	.03536	.03129	.02773	.02460	.02184	.01942
36	3	.06020	.05312	.04692	.04149	.03672	.03253	.02886	.02562	.02277	.02062
36	4	.06225	.05501	.04865	.04307	.03816	.03385	.03005	.02671	.02377	.02117
36	5	.06439	.05697	.05045	.04472	.03967	.03523	.03132	.02786	.02482	.02213
36	6	.06661	.05901	.05233	.04644	.04125	.03667	.03264	.02907	.02592	.02313
36	7	.06890	.06112	.05427	.04822	.04289	.03818	.03401	.03033	.02707	.02419
36	8	.07126	.06330	.05627	.05007	.04458	.03974	.03544	.03164	.02828	.02529
36	9	.07369	.06554	.05835	.05198	.04635	.04136	.03693	.03301	.02953	.02644
36	10	.07618	.06786	.06049	.05386	.04817	.04303	.03848	.03443	.03084	.02765
36	11	.07875	.07024	.06269	.05599	.05005	.04477	.04008	.03591	.03220	.02890
36	12	.08138	.07268	.06496	.05809	.05199	.04657	.04174	.03744	.03361	.03020
36	13	.08406	.07518	.06727	.06024	.05398	.04841	.04344	.03901	.03506	.03154
36	14	.08679	.07771	.06963	.06243	.05601	.05029	.04518	.04062	.03655	.03291
36	15	.08955	.08029	.07203	.06466	.05808	.05221	.04696	.04227	.03807	.03432
36	16	.09234	.08290	.07446	.06692	.06018	.05416	.04877	.04394	.03962	.03575
36	17	.09517	.08553	.07692	.06921	.06231	.05614	.05060	.04565	.04120	.03721
36	18	.09803	.08821	.07942	.07154	.06448	.05815	.05248	.04739	.04281	.03871

(*continued*)

TABLE 10.3 Two-life Last to Die Unitrust (*continued*)

Table E(2)—Part 2

						Adjusted Payout Rate					
O	Y	4.2%	4.4%	4.6%	4.8%	5.0%	5.2%	5.4%	5.6%	5.8%	6.0%
36	19	.10093	.09092	.08196	.07391	.06669	.06021	.05439	.04917	.04447	.04024
36	20	.10387	.09369	.08454	.07633	.06895	.06232	.05635	.05099	.04616	.04182
36	21	.10686	.09649	.08717	.07879	.07125	.06447	.05836	.05286	.04790	.04344
36	22	.10988	.09934	.08984	.08130	.07360	.06666	.06041	.05477	.04969	.04510
36	23	.11295	.10222	.09256	.08385	.07599	.06890	.06250	.05673	.05151	.04680
36	24	.11605	.10515	.09532	.08644	.07842	.07118	.06464	.05873	.05338	.04855
36	25	.11919	.10812	.09812	.08908	.08090	.07351	.06683	.06078	.05530	.05035
36	26	.12237	.11113	.10096	.09176	.08343	.07589	.06906	.06287	.05727	.05219
36	27	.12558	.11417	.10383	.09447	.08599	.07830	.07133	.06501	.05928	.05407
36	28	.12881	.11724	.10674	.09723	.08859	.08076	.07365	.06719	.06133	.05600
36	29	.13206	.12032	.10967	.10000	.09122	.08324	.07599	.06940	.06341	.05796
36	30	.13531	.12342	.11262	.10280	.09387	.08575	.07836	.07164	.06552	.05995
36	31	.13857	.12653	.11557	.10560	.09653	.08827	.08075	.07390	.06765	.06196
36	32	.14182	.12963	.11853	.10842	.09920	.09081	.08315	.07617	.06981	.06400
36	33	.14506	.13272	.12148	.11123	.10188	.09336	.08557	.07847	.07198	.06606
36	34	.14827	.13581	.12443	.11405	.10457	.09591	.08800	.08077	.07417	.06813
36	35	.15147	.13887	.12736	.11685	.10724	.09846	.09043	.08308	.07637	.07022
36	36	.15464	.14191	.13028	.11964	.10991	.10101	.09286	.08540	.07857	.07231
37	0	.05848	.05175	.04585	.04069	.03616	.03219	.02870	.02564	.02294	.02055
37	1	.05678	.05002	.04411	.03894	.03442	.03046	.02699	.02394	.02126	.01891
37	2	.05862	.05170	.04564	.04034	.03569	.03161	.02803	.02488	.02211	.01968
37	3	.06061	.05352	.04730	.04185	.03707	.03286	.02917	.02592	.02306	.02053
37	4	.06269	.05542	.04905	.04345	.03853	.03420	.03038	.02703	.02406	.02145
37	5	.06486	.05742	.05088	.04512	.04006	.03560	.03167	.02820	.02513	.02243
37	6	.06711	.05949	.05278	.04687	.04166	.03707	.03301	.02943	.02626	.02345
37	7	.06942	.06163	.05475	.04868	.04333	.03859	.03441	.03071	.02743	.02453
37	8	.07182	.06384	.05679	.05056	.04505	.04018	.03587	.03205	.02866	.02566
37	9	.07429	.06612	.05890	.05251	.04685	.04183	.03739	.03345	.02994	.02683
37	10	.07683	.06847	.06109	.05452	.04870	.04355	.03897	.03490	.03128	.02806
37	11	.07944	.07090	.06332	.05660	.05063	.04532	.04060	.03641	.03267	.02935
37	12	.08212	.07339	.06563	.05874	.05261	.04715	.04230	.03797	.03412	.03068
37	13	.08485	.07593	.06800	.06093	.05464	.04904	.04404	.03958	.03560	.03205
37	14	.08763	.07852	.07041	.06317	.05672	.05096	.04582	.04123	.03713	.03346
37	15	.09045	.08115	.07286	.06545	.05884	.05293	.04764	.04292	.03869	.03490
37	16	.09331	.08382	.07534	.06776	.06099	.05492	.04949	.04463	.04028	.03637
37	17	.09619	.08652	.07786	.07011	.06317	.05695	.05138	.04638	.04190	.03788
37	18	.09912	.08926	.08042	.07250	.06539	.05902	.05331	.04817	.04356	.03942
37	19	.10209	.09205	.08302	.07493	.06766	.06114	.05527	.05000	.04526	.04099
37	20	.10511	.09487	.08568	.07741	.06998	.06330	.05729	.05188	.04701	.04262
37	21	.10817	.09775	.08838	.07994	.07235	.06551	.05936	.05381	.04880	.04429
37	22	.11128	.10068	.09113	.08252	.07477	.06778	.06147	.05578	.05064	.04600
37	23	.11443	.10365	.09392	.08515	.07723	.07008	.06363	.05780	.05253	.04777
37	24	.11763	.10667	.09677	.08783	.07975	.07244	.06584	.05987	.05447	.04958

TABLE 10.3 Two-life Last to Die Unitrust (*continued*)

Table E(2)—Part 2

Adjusted Payout Rate

O	Y	4.2%	4.4%	4.6%	4.8%	5.0%	5.2%	5.4%	5.6%	5.8%	6.0%
37	25	.12087	.10973	.09966	.09055	.08231	.07485	.06810	.06199	.05646	.05144
37	26	.12416	.11284	.10260	.09332	.08492	.07731	.07042	.06417	.05850	.05335
37	27	.12748	.11599	.10558	.09614	.08758	.07982	.07278	.06639	.06058	.05531
37	28	.13083	.11917	.10860	.09900	.09028	.08237	.07518	.06865	.06271	.05732
37	29	.13420	.12238	.11164	.10188	.09301	.08495	.07762	.07095	.06488	.05936
37	30	.13758	.12560	.11470	.10479	.09577	.08756	.08009	.07329	.06709	.06144
37	31	.14097	.12883	.11778	.10772	.09855	.09020	.08258	.07565	.06932	.06355
37	32	.14436	.13207	.12087	.11065	.10134	.09285	.08510	.07803	.07157	.06568
37	33	.14774	.13530	.12395	.11360	.10415	.09552	.08763	.08043	.07385	.06784
37	34	.15110	.13852	.12704	.11654	.10695	.09819	.09018	.08285	.07615	.07001
37	35	.15445	.14174	.13011	.11948	.10976	.10087	.09273	.08528	.07845	.07221
37	36	.15777	.14492	.13317	.12241	.11256	.10354	.09528	.08771	.08077	.07441
37	37	.16105	.14809	.13621	.12533	.11535	.10621	.09783	.09014	.08309	.07662
38	0	.05899	.05224	.04633	.04115	.03661	.03262	.02912	.02603	.02332	.02092
38	1	.05714	.05037	.04445	.03927	.03473	.03076	.02727	.02421	.02152	.01916
38	2	.05900	.05207	.04599	.04067	.03601	.03192	.02832	.02516	.02238	.01993
38	3	.06101	.05390	.04767	.04220	.03740	.03319	.02948	.02621	.02334	.02080
38	4	.06311	.05583	.04944	.04382	.03888	.03454	.03071	.02734	.02436	.02173
38	5	.06531	.05785	.05129	.04552	.04044	.03596	.03201	.02853	.02545	.02273
38	6	.06758	.05995	.05322	.04729	.04207	.03745	.03338	.02978	.02659	.02377
38	7	.06993	.06212	.05522	.04913	.04376	.03900	.03480	.03108	.02779	.02487
38	8	.07236	.06436	.05729	.05104	.04551	.04062	.03629	.03245	.02904	.02602

Source: Actuarial Values I: Valuation of Last Survivor Charitable Remainders, Part C, Two-Life Last to Die Unitrust Factors, Publication 723C (9–84), Internal Revenue Service, p. 46.

ertino, are not necessarily treated as ordinary income. They may be totally or partially tax free.

Illustration 4

Henry decides to create a charitable remainder trust. The trust instrument requires that 10 percent of the market value of its assets on June 30 of each year be paid to Camila for a period of 15 years. The adjusted payout rate is 10 percent. Refer to Table 10.4. The factor for 10 percent for 15 years is .205891 so the deduction will be $20,589. Notice in this case the trust must pay a specific percentage and that the valuation date of the trust, once chosen, is fixed; in this case, June 30 of each year. Thus, the amount that is received depends on the value of the trust on that date. If the trust does exceedingly well, say its market value is $400,000 on that date, Camila would receive $40,000. Henry might only

TABLE 10.4 Table Showing the Present Worth of a Remainder Interest Postponed for a Term of Years in a Charitable Remainder Unitrust Having the Adjusted Payout Rate Shown.

(1) Years	(2) Adjusted Payout Rate				
	9.2%	9.4%	9.6%	9.8%	10.0%
1	.908000	.906000	.904000	.902000	.900000
2	.824464	.820836	.817216	.813604	.810000
3	.748613	.743677	.738763	.733871	.729000
4	.679741	.673772	.667842	.661951	.656100
5	.617205	.610437	.603729	.597080	.590490
6	.560422	.553056	.545771	.538566	.531441
7	.508863	.501069	.493377	.485787	.478297
8	.462048	.453968	.446013	.438180	.430467
9	.419539	.411295	.403196	.395238	.387420
10	.380942	.372634	.364489	.356505	.348678
11	.345895	.337606	.329498	.321567	.313811
12	.314073	.305871	.297866	.290054	.282430
13	.285178	.277119	.269271	.261628	.254187
14	.258942	.251070	.243421	.235989	.228768
15	.235119	.227469	.220053	.212862	.205891
16	.213488	.206087	.198928	.192001	.185302
17	.193847	.186715	.179830	.173185	.166772
18	.176013	.169164	.162567	.156213	.150095
19	.159820	.153262	.146960	.140904	.135085
20	.145117	.138856	.132852	.127096	.121577

Source: Internal Revenue Service, *Code of Federal Regulations*, Vol. 26, Part I, Sec. 1.641 to 1.850, April 1, 1985, p. 119.

have put in a small fraction of the $400,000, which is based on his initial investment, plus the compound rate of growth in the value of the assets. Moreover, only part or possibly all of the $40,000 may be received untaxed.

It should be noted that in this example the income is to flow not for the life of an individual or individuals, but for a specific term. Remainder trusts, unlike pooled trusts, can be set up either for a life or for a specific term. Notice from Table 10.4 that the amount that can be deducted varies inversely both with the length of the term and the rate.

These are four simple examples. How a trust operates depends on the nature of the trust, whether it is a pooled, remainder unitrust or remainder annuity trust, a guarantee trust, or a charitable lead trust and the terms specified in the trust document. For example, a creator of a charitable lead trust could get either a one-time or an annual deduction. The latter will depend on the earnings of the trust and the amount transferred each year to the charity. But to do this, the donor has to report the income of the trust as his or her income. Therefore, the net effect of an improperly constructed trust agreement could be to raise the tax liability of the donor.

Furthermore, each trust has a different set of annuity tables and each annuity table differs according to the age and the number of noncharitable beneficiaries. What is important is for the reader to have a firm grasp of the descriptions and applications of each trust as described in this text. With a good tax and legal consultant specializing in estates and trusts, it is possible to construct trusts that yield a donor a higher rate of return on the gift than he or she was receiving prior to the gift.

Table 10.5 compares and summarizes some of the basic features of the trusts we have discussed. This summary may provide a quick reference to the advantages and disadvantages of these trusts. There are features they have in common. Each provides for a gift to the nonprofit that is deductible by the donor. Some provide for an annuity to the donor or beneficiaries while the remainder goes to the nonprofit. This remainder, depending on the financial and investment management of the gift, can be substantially larger than the initial gift. This is so because only a portion of the income in many cases will go to the donor. The remainder accumulates and grows with the investment experience of the fund, and the gift itself may appreciate several times in value by the time it is turned over to the nonprofit.

THE USES OF WILLS: GIFTS DEFERRED UNTIL DEATH

A gift through a will (a bequest) can be easily arranged. All that is basically necessary is a statement in the will to the effect that "I give, devise, and bequeath to . . . the . . . (amount of dollars or name of property)." It is the execution of the will at the time of death that becomes confounding and this can occur for several reasons. Let us start with the well-known case of Howard Hughes. At least 40 wills have turned up as being allegedly written by him. Most are declared forgeries. Hughes died in 1979, and in 1986, after the Supreme Court of the United States had appointed Wade McCree, former Solicitor General, as special master, settlements were being made but not yet complete.

There was even confusion about where Howard Hughes lived and this had an impact on his will. Thus, the estate of Howard Hughes had to pay inheritance taxes to the states of Texas ($50 million in cash) and California ($119 million in cash and real estate), even though the lawyers for the estate had argued that his residence was in the state of Nevada, which had no inheritance taxes. Hughes had lived four of his last ten years in Nevada, 40 years in California and was born in Texas, leaving when he was 20 years old and had not been in the state for 48 hours in the 50 years before he died. He had, in an attempt to escape California

TABLE 10.5 Comparison of Advantages and Disadvantages of Trusts by Type

	Type of Trust	Advantages	Disadvantages
Income Flow to Donor, Remainder to Charity	Pooled income	Small gifts can be placed in pool for more efficient investment management	Income must flow for life of one or more individuals, not for term; income usually is fully taxed
	Remainder unitrust	Income flows for life of one or more noncharity recipients or for a specified term; some or all of income may be untaxed; income keeps pace with growth of value	Because income is percentage of value year to year, income declines if value declines
	Remainder annuity	Same as above except income is fixed percentage of initial value; income is protected against decline in value	Income does not keep pace with growth
Income Flow to Charity, Remainder to Donor	Guaranteed (Gift or Charitable) annuity	Income is assured	Assets of nonprofit exposed to need to pay donors guaranteed income
	Charitable lead unitrust	Flow of income to nonprofit keeps pace with growth of trust	Exposes recipient to tax liability if annual deduction chosen
	Charitable lead annuity	Flow of income to charity not jeopardized by slow growth	Same as above

state taxes, frequently filed papers indicating that Texas was his state of residence.[5]

In a case before the Chester County Courthouse in Westchester, Pennsylvania, the 33-year old widow of a millionaire was said to have spent her 90-year old deceased husband's $4 million fortune on personal expenses, travel, and gifts. His children and the charities that were named as beneficiaries in his will allegedly lost out because of her spending.[6]

Similarly, upon the death of Ron Hubbard, founder of the Church of Scientology, his will was challenged by a son who was disinherited because he had denounced his father and his church. The will provided a trust for his wife and four other children and a trust for the church.[7]

A will specifies how an individual's estate (all properties in which the decedent had an incidence of ownership) is to be distributed. A will must generally be written, signed, dated, and witnessed. Under some conditions, an oral will may have the force of law. Like a trust and a nonprofit corporation, a will must abide by the laws of the individual state. State laws also determine how property will be treated. For example, some properties are subject to taxation and valuation on the basis of their location (situs), while others are determined on the basis of the domicile of the deceased. State laws vary.

A will names an executor (male) or executrix (female) who is responsible for collecting all properties, paying all taxes and debt, preserving the value of the property, and distributing it according to the desires of the deceased. The executor or executrix, unlike the trustee, is nominated by the deceased but serves at the pleasure and approval of the court.

The court may or may not require that the executor or executrix be bonded. It is customary that the testator (the person to whom the will belongs) would not require bonding. Bonding is insurance to protect the creditors of the estate against the errors of the executor. Executors can be held liable for losses but cannot share in the gains made as a consequence of their actions. Thus, the incentive for most executors is to do the minimum required to expeditiously settle an estate in a reasonable period.[8]

Estates are comprised of probate and nonprobate property. Probate property is distributed according to the terms of a will. Nonprobate property is distributed by the operation of the law or by contract or by agreement. If a property is owned through joint tenancy with the right of survivorship, or through tenancy in the entirety (as these terms were defined in Chapter 9), or subject to claims of the government or creditors, or a spouse, such claims are honored without regard to the instructions in a will.

Wills can lead to disappointments. One source of disappointment is that the property supposedly given by bequest may not be probate property and may pass to another through the operation of the law, some previous agreement, or contract. It may not be the deceased's to give, for example, if the property is owned with rights of survivorship being held by another person.

Disappointment might occur for another reason. Promises in a will are not obligations of the testator. A person might change his or her will at will, so to speak. A nonprofit that was once a beneficiary can be dropped whenever the testator wishes.

Furthermore, the will may be too generous. James LaPorte, who is married, decided to leave all his property to his favorite nonprofit, but this will not work. A spouse, and often children, no matter how disliked, cannot be left with nothing. The spouse may go to court to "take against the will." The court may permit the spouse to take between one-third to one-half of the estate despite the will. The nonprofits might be left out, have a reduced share of the estate and have to wait a long time as legal battles are fought.

Worse yet, the entire will could be invalid. This may result if the will or any codicile (amendment) does not conform with the law; (or if the will was not signed, dated, or prepared by a person mentally competent and acting freely.) There might be a later will. Any of these could cause the will to be invalidated. Even if the will is valid, it may be rescinded if written at the point of death and testator does not die. And even if death occurs, such a will may be rescinded if the cause of death is different than specified as a condition of the gift.

Still other problems could occur. If the amount being given is a residual after all other donees and legal and tax matters are taken care of, there might be nothing left. Here again state laws come into play. These laws, known as abatement laws, govern how an estate is distributed when it is not large enough to cover all distributees. When the amount going to a nonprofit is the residual rather than a specific amount taken off the top, there might be nothing for the nonprofit to receive.

The will of Mary Ethel Pew, which provided for the creation of The Medical Trust, specified that, to the extent there is sufficient income available, annual payments in the following order of priority should be made from the funds of The Medical Trust: for a period of twenty (20) years to Lankenau Hospital, Overbrook, Pennsylvania, the sum of $400,000 for research projects; for a period of ten (10) years to the Institute for Cancer Research, Fox Chase, Pennsylvania, 30 percent of the trust's net income or $150,000, whichever is less; for a period of twenty (20) years to Lankenau Hospital, $600,000 for the general purposes of the hospital.

As of December 31, 1989, the amounts which remain payable under the terms of the will of Mary Ethel Pew are $9,500,000 to Lankenau Hospital.

Source: The Pew Charitable Trusts 1989. Reprinted with permission.

TABLE 10.6   Relative Risk of Bequests Through a Will

Rank	Status of Nonprofit in Estate Settlement
1	Ownership, lifetime or by survivorship: automatic ownership
2	Irrevocable beneficiary: cannot be removed
3	Beneficiary: can be removed without warning
4	Specific amount bequest: gets a specific amount off the top
5	Residue: gets what's left over

Note: 1 is strongest position and 5 is weakest.

Despite these uncertainties, wills are necessary if deathtime gifts are to be made. If a person dies intestate, without a will, no provisions are made by state law for contributions to nonprofits. Distributions are made to a legally married spouse, to children, to parents and to the state. Brothers and sisters may, like nonprofits, get nothing.

Even if the nonprofit is named in the will, it makes a difference how it is named. Table 10.6 summarizes the risks of not getting anything when a nonprofit depends upon transfer of properties at the time of death even though there may be a will. These risks vary by the way the nonprofit is named by the donor. The weakest position is to be included among the residue because the residue is what's left over after all other gifts and liabilities are paid. This may be zero or a very large number. On the other extreme, if one is the owner through survivorship, the property gets passed automatically and is not determined by the will at all.

Also, gifts occurring at death are more favorably treated than gifts made during one's lifetime. The latter is subject to deductible limits as described in Chapter 9, but there are not limits to how much one may give to a charity at time of death.

Hence, if the property has appreciated substantially, a deathtime rather than a lifetime gift may be advantageous to the donor since there are no limits to the amount that can be given at death and still receive a tax deduction. But there are also advantages to the nonprofit. This is particularly true if the nonprofit would be subject to unrelated business income tax on the appreciated value of the property when sold because the property was subject to debt as described in Chapter 11.[9] To illustrate, if James LaPorte purchases a property for $50,000 but paid only $25,000 so that the property is subject to debt and the property appreciated to $200,000, and if he bequeathed the property to his favorite nonprofit, the nonprofit will receive it at the value at the time of his death.[10] This value would be $200,000. On the other hand, if the gift were made just before his death, the appreciation on which the tax would be calculated would be $175,000 ($150,000 in appreciation plus the $25,000 owed).

Finally, deathtime gifts give the donor a lifetime to decide among potential donees and to enjoy the property, secure in the knowledge that he or she will have no use for it after death. Little wonder that the largest single gifts take effect at death.

LIFE INSURANCE: MAGNIFYING THE VALUE OF SMALL GIFTS

Through life insurance policies, it is possible for persons of modest means to make gifts of hundreds of thousands of dollars. Therefore, anyone can give well above his or her means. When the person departs, the policy matures and death benefits received by the nonprofit are many times larger than premiums paid by the donor.

Insurance allows the donor to stretch out a gift. This is the case where the donor makes a gift of a policy that requires periodic premium payments. In this way, the organization gets a regular and long-lasting commitment for an annual donation—the premiums—and it maintains contact, to facilitate additional giving.

If the policy is one that accumulates savings, called cash value, the organization also gets a valuable pool of funds that it can use within years, even though the donor is very much alive. Moreover, regular premium payments shift the burden of fund raising to the insurance company, which sends the donor notices of when the premium is due. It replaces the telephone call and letter from the nonprofit asking for annual donations.

Death and the Collection of Gift

An insurance policy may be used to make a joint gift. Frequently, a husband and wife may want to make a joint gift to a nonprofit. If each bought an insurance policy separately, it would be more expensive than if they bought it jointly. In a joint policy, sometimes called last to die, both persons should agree to take out and to give the policy to the nonprofit. This strategy has some peculiarities that call for caution. One is that joint policies often pay only after the last of the two persons has died. Thus, its nicknames, "last-to-die" and "survivor" policy. Some policies pay only a portion of the face value after the first has died; the balance is paid at the death of the second person.

Even though the death of the first spouse could yield no immediate benefit to the nonprofit, this does not make such a strategy useless. The nonprofit will get some or all of the proceeds eventually; both parties will die. In the meantime, the cash value (if it is provided in the contract) and collateral value of the policy are always available as long as the organization owns the policy.

Alternatively, a policy could be bought on the life of each person separately and the proceeds will be obtained by the nonprofit on each person's death, rather than upon the eventual death of both. These policies are more expensive than joint policies.

Ownership

A gift of insurance must be carefully planned, for an insurance policy that is owned by the donor even if it is being held by the nonprofit is subject to the control of the donor. The owner can cancel the policy or permit it to lapse so that it no longer exists. Nothing bars an owner from dropping the name of the nonprofit as beneficiary. If any of these happens, the nonprofit will not collect even though it may have the policy in its possession. Furthermore, if the policy is owned by the donor, he or she may borrow on it. Should that be done and the loan not be repaid prior to the death of the donor, the proceeds that will go to the nonprofit will be the face value minus the amount of indebtedness. In short, the nonprofit could end up with less than the face value if there is outstanding indebtedness.

The outcome could be worse if the owner used the policy as collateral for a loan. In that case, depending on state law, the creditor of the donor may have first claim. Not only will the amount obtained by the nonprofit be less than the face value, but the nonprofit could get nothing at all if in the process of getting the loan the donor made a permanent assignment of the policy to the creditor. A permanent assignment cannot be reversed; the creditor owns the policy.

Also, an insurance policy that is owned by the donor may be included in his or her estate even though it is in the physical possession of the nonprofit. This could mean that some or all the proceeds may be subject to estate (not income) tax, and some or all the proceeds could be subject to the claims of the creditors of the donor and to claims of the donor's spouse should the latter choose to take against the will. Insurance proceeds, while exempt from income tax, are not automatically exempt from estate tax. The donor must have (1) named the nonprofit or any other qualified charity as a beneficiary of the policy, or (2) designated them as donees of the proceeds as it goes through the estate.

These difficulties as the proceeds go through the estate may not be resolved in favor of the nonprofit even if it could prove that it paid the premiums. Ironically, one possible interpretation of paying the premiums is that the nonprofit in its charitable benevolence made a nondeductible gift to the insured. The point simply is that the nonprofit should own, not merely hold, the policy. It does this by being sure that its name appears on the policy not only as beneficiary but also as owner.

Ownership and possession of the policy give the nonprofit another benefit. The nonprofit does not have to wait for the donor to die; for, as owner, the nonprofit may assign the policy, use it as collateral for loans, or borrow the cash value of the policy. The nonprofit will also be able to avoid the creditors of the donor and legal fights over the instructions in the will. The policy will be nonprobate property, meaning that it will escape the legal hassle, delays, costs, and claims that are likely in the settlement of an estate.

The box on the next page reviews ownership options and outcomes.

Form of Gift

The donor does not have to purchase insurance or use a paid-up policy in order to make a gift. It is possible to make a gift of insurance in the form of the face value in excess of $50,000 in a qualified employee insurance contract, as discussed in Chapter 14. Such a gift is not likely to bring any deduction to the donor, but the excess premium is not taxable as income. The employer who pays the excess may deduct it if it is customary for the firm to give in this fashion. Many corporations are offering a similar option to their officers and directors who choose which charity they wish to be beneficiaries.

A gift of insurance can be made in the form of an outright gift of the contract itself; or the policy could be placed in a trust. The trust should be irrevocable, permitting an immediate tax deduction for the gift and immediate ownership by the nonprofit. The deduction of premiums can be lost, however, if the trust is not properly set up, because an insurance policy in a trust is a future interest, as discussed in Chapter 9, since the gift cannot be obtained until the person dies. To qualify the premium payments for immediate tax deduction, the trust agreement should contain a promise to make the premium available to the nonprofit at the time premiums are paid. The nonprofit need not take the money; it must simply have the option to do so. Lawyers call this amendment a Crummey clause.

If the insurance policy is in a trust, there is a second concern; the policy could be considered to have been acquired by debt and, as discussed earlier, lead to unrelated business income tax. To avoid this, the trust agreement should not permit a person who is a noncharitable beneficiary to have an interest in the income of the trust that exceeds the person's lifetime. That is, all such interests should cease upon the person's death so that the remainder goes to the charitable beneficiary, rather than being bequeathed by the person to some other beneficiary.

Life Insurance Risks by Ownership Option

Risks to which the nonprofit is exposed under various ownership options:

Option 1. The donor owns the policy and names the nonprofit as a beneficiary on the policy. The donor may change beneficiary unless the nonprofit is named an **irrevocable** beneficiary. In either case, the risks are the use of the cash value by the donor and cessation of payments by donor without knowledge of nonprofit and nonownership precludes the nonprofit from picking up payments. This strategy avoids probate and lump-sum proceeds go directly to the nonprofit tax free.

Option 2. The donor owns the policy and makes his or her estate the beneficiary. The nonprofit can collect only if donor's will so specifies. As part of the estate, an additional risk is that the proceeds become exposed to creditors of both the decedent and the estate itself and may be used not only to satisfy such debt but to pay taxes of the estate and to satisfy other beneficiaries, such as spouse and dependent children. Probate and settlement of estate may prolong receiving gift.

Option 3. The nonprofit owns the policy. Upon death, the proceeds go directly to the nonprofit without probate and without exposure to creditors of the decedent or the estate. IRS private ruling 9110016 reminds us to check state law to be sure that insurable interest, defined as at risk of economic loss if person dies, is satisfied. If not, a federal donation may be denied.

Key to all options: To reduce default of nonpayment of premiums, have donor make annual gift of at least premium amount directly to nonprofit which uses it to pay premium.

A gift of insurance may also be made through a will at the time of death. The will might provide for the formation of a trust or for outright gift of the insurance proceeds to the nonprofit. One disadvantage of giving at the time of death is that the proceeds must be included in the donor's estate, albeit that a 100 percent tax deduction is available for charitable donation. It, however, precludes any annual deduction for premiums paid.

As part of the estate, the insurance proceeds are also exposed to the claims of the creditors of the deceased. Also, if the gift is made by a trust that becomes irrevocable at the time of death, the charity is less protected, since there is some passage of time, generally after the federal taxes are paid, before the trust becomes a charitable trust and subject to the rules covering private foundations. These rules protect the corpus of a trust for charitable purposes.

There is no single best strategy for using life insurance as a gift. The "best" strategy depends first on the financial position of the donor and the needs of the organization. Each strategy that has been mentioned should be considered. Each strategy is implemented through an insurance policy, which is a contract. As we shall see next, there are several contract or policy options.

Types of Policies

The **universal life** policies give the donor a considerable amount of flexibility. He or she may vary the amount and timing of premium payments or change the face value of the contract. For example, some years the donor may pay more than the minimum premium required. The excess is used to build up a side account called the cash value, which gains interest. In a year when the donor cannot afford to pay, the cash value may be used to pay the premiums. Alternatively, the donor may reduce the face value of the policy and pay the lower premium or increase the face value (called death benefit) by increasing the premium. A universal life's selling point is that it can be tailored to match the current circumstances of a donor and still provide a benefit during his or her lifetime and also at death.

Some universal plans provide for the policy to be paid up in a specific number of years, often seven. These are usually good for a nonprofit because it can receive a fully paid up policy in seven rather than twenty or even ninety-five years. In addition, like the universal life, these policies provide cash value for the use of the nonprofit while the donor lives and the death benefit (decreased by the amount of cash value used) when the insured dies. In addition, the nonprofit has a shorter period of time to worry about a default by a donor. The deal is completed in seven years. Because the annual payments in these policies are larger (so that they can be fully paid up in seven years), they are very expensive, but they offer a large tax deduction to the donor and a large cash value to the nonprofit.

Unlike universal life policies, **whole life** policies do not provide for variations in premiums or death benefits. Both premiums and benefits are fixed at the time the policy is bought. Now the nonprofit takes a greater risk. If the donor defaults, the policy lapses unless the nonprofit pays or there is enough cash value to pay the premium that is due. When a policy lapses, it terminates. Whole life policies provide certainty of premiums and death benefits, as long as the circumstances of the donor do not change. With a universal life, the death benefit can be reduced to meet a lower ability to pay. With a whole life, that is not possible, although some companies would consider reissuing a completely new policy.

On the other extreme is **single-premium** life insurance. In this case, the donor pays off the policy in one single sum at the time the policy is bought. The paid premium qualifies for a tax deduction. In these policies, as in the case of universal life, the nonprofit has the cash value, which it can borrow. It also has the death benefit that will be paid when the donor dies. The advantages of a single-premium policy are that the nonprofit need not worry about default. There is no need to make continuous payments because the total required sum would have been paid at the outset. The nonprofit also gets the cash value while the insured lives if it owns the policy. It gets the death benefit when the donor dies.

Let me give a specific example; in 1984, Clara Springer, 46 years old, purchased a policy with a face value of $100,000 for $22,100 and gave it to a favorite charity, which is now the owner. She got to deduct $22,100; the church gets the $100,000 when she dies. In the meantime it gets to borrow on the account, which grows at, say, 9 percent tax deferred. In about eight years at 9 percent, this account would have in excess of $40,000 that would be available for use by the church.

A person may have a life insurance policy that has already been paid up. There will be no more annual premiums. Hence, a gift of these policies to a nonprofit means that the donor gets a deduction without ever making an out-of-pocket transfer of cash now or in the future. Upon the death of the donor, the organization gets the face value of the insurance minus any outstanding debt, that is, unrepaid withdrawals made during the life of the donor. Prior to the death of the donor, the organization gets to use the cash value in the policy. For an older person who never took a loan or withdrawal, this could be very large depending on how long ago the policy was taken out and the untaxed interest it earned.

Even **term** policies, those that do not accumulate cash values, are suitable gifts because they are inexpensive. In dealing with term policies, the organization would want to know the term; is it 1, 7, 10, 20, 30, or 100 years? Is it level or decreasing? A one-year term means that if the donor does not die within that year the institution gets nothing. The same principle corresponds to 7, 10, 15, 20, 30, or 100 or any other term. Since most people will not live to be 100, such a term policy does assure some benefits to the organization.

The amount of benefits in any term policy depends on whether the face value of the contract is level, increasing, or decreasing. If the term is level, then the death benefit is constant throughout the term of the contract. It is the same whether the person dies in the first or last year of the contract. If it is a decreasing term, then the amount that the organization is due upon the death of the donor decreases the older the donor gets. A decreasing 100-year term policy with an initial death benefit of $100,000 would be worth approximately $10,000 if the person dies at age 65. Yet the person would only have paid about $7000 in premiums during that time.

For this small difference, would it not be better to make a direct annual contribution to the nonprofit, giving it the advantage of having the money on hand to invest rather than waiting? Not necessarily. The advantages of insurance, even term, over regular donations is that it immediately magnifies the gift. In the above case, if the donor paid the annual premium of say $300 and then dies after the first, second, third, or even fifth year, the organization would get approximately $100,000. It would have cost the donor a total of $200, $600, $900, or $1500 in premiums depending on how long he or she lives. The organization would have foregone anywhere from $98,500 to $99,700 if instead of an insurance policy the donor had made a direct gift of cash. A selling attraction of term is it is cheap.

Comparing Characteristics of Contracts

Life insurance, through the death benefits, magnifies a gift many times. This is leverage. All policies except term provide for a cash value, which is the money that accumulates with interest. This money can be borrowed,[11] used as collateral, used to pay premiums, or even used to purchase additional insurance on the donor with the same company.

The dollars that accumulate grow according to the interest being paid and the length of time it is permitted to remain undistributed. The amount borrowed **never** has to be repaid and neither does the interest on the loan, which is generally well below market rate and fixed in the contract at the time the insurance is bought. Any principal and interest owed at the time of death are subtracted from the face value. Thus, a $100,000 face value would lead to a death proceed going to the nonprofit of $90,000 if the sum of the interest and principal due as a result of the loan is $10,000.

It may be useful to compare all we have said in tabular form. How does one type of insurance match the other?

Table 10.7 summarizes four types of policies based on their generic nature. Term policies are the cheapest and single-premium policies are the most expensive; but the amount of leverage is just the reverse. That is, if the donor should die immediately or within a few years after the creation of the gift, the death benefit per dollar of premium paid is highest with a term policy and lowest with a single-premium; thus, the term gets you a lot more dollars per dollar invested.[12] On the other hand, term policies have no loan value and require the longest period of donor commitment since the premiums must be paid every year until either the policy ends or the donor dies.

TABLE 10.7 Insurance Policies by Characteristics

Type	Cost	Leverage[a]	Loan[b]	Flexibility	Length of Commitment Required
Term	1	4	0	1	4
Universal	2	3	2	4	2
Whole life	3	2	3	2	3
Single premium	4	1	4	N/A	1

Key: 1 = lowest.
[a] Death benefits relative to premium costs.
[b] Cash value.

Universal life is the most flexible. Flexibility is not an issue with single premiums because the policy is fully paid up at the inception. Generally, there is no flexibility with whole life or term policies, although some companies will sell term policies in which you may in the future elect a different premium or a face value. On the other extreme is the single premium. It is the most expensive, but it requires the least amount of donor commitment—only long enough to write the check. It also creates the biggest nest egg that can be used by the nonprofit.

Because insurance companies are imaginative in how they configure a policy, Table 10.7 should be considered a guide as to the fundamentals. When working with a potential donor, illustrations of specific and actual policies should be used. The companies will gladly supply them.

ROLE OF INSURANCE IN FUND-RAISING STRATEGY

Insurance policies are morbid. When Boston University launched a campaign to have its alumni buy insurance policies and make it their beneficiary and owner, the announcement was met with cynicism. On the other hand, it is said that when St. Louis University launched its insurance program it was met with enthusiasm and success.[13]

Life insurance should be part of an overall fund-raising package. Instead of launching an insurance campaign, launch a campaign in which insurance is one possibility. This requires the organization to know how insurance can best fit into the ability and taste of potential donors. Then choose the right policy and always try to be the owner and be prepared to explain the benefits to the donor: insurance turns people of moderate income into philanthropists, and when the nonprofit owns the policy, probate and estate taxes are avoided, the nonprofit can make premium payments, and it can also use the cash value for loans and the policy for collateral.

Many nonprofits that have tried insurance policies have run into nonpayments of premiums by donors. This is to be expected as not all pledges are ever paid. This translates into a credit-management problem not unlike those faced by every pledge campaign and every business that extends credit. There are three actions the nonprofit can take to minimize the risk of unpaid premium. First, educate the donor. Second, choose policies that require few premium payments. Many policies can be paid up in one to seven years. This matches short periods of donor enthusiasm and commitment.

Finally, the nonprofit should determine how much of its fund-raising budget it can spend each year to make unpaid premiums so that policies would not lapse. It should pay these premiums only if it owns the policy (otherwise, it would be making a loan or a gift to the owner who may then change the beneficiary). The nonprofit can then collect at a later date from the donor, who will then get a tax deduction for his or her donated premiums. Even if the donor does not reimburse it, the nonprofit will collect if the donor dies. The donor cannot change the beneficiary if the nonprofit owns the policy. The premium payment by the nonprofit becomes an investment in itself.

Mix Strategies

Life insurance can also be part of a mix strategy. For example, suppose an elderly person wishes to put a home in a remainder trust but she has relatives who would possibly be angered. Or suppose that the nonprofit is concerned about having to repair the home. It can get the donor to agree to purchase an annual term insurance policy on her life. The proceeds can be used to make the repairs or to pay off the relatives.[14]

Another example of mix strategy: Percy Pouff promises a gift of $1,000,000 to be delivered in seven years. The nonprofit now has an insurable interest in him. It buys a policy to cover him during this period. When he delivers the million dollars the nonprofit may exchange the policy for it, discontinue its premium payments, or keep the policy alive.[15]

Safety

Insurance policies are reasonably safe even when the company is shaky. Insurance companies are required to carry reserves to cover their potential claims and most insurance companies also engage in reinsurance. This is a process through which companies try not to keep too many high-risk policies on their books. By prior agreement, through reinsurance they sell some of these to other companies. Moreover, in all but six states, the insurance companies guarantee payments through an insurance pool, thus protecting the citizens of that state against the bankruptcy of any company selling in that state. For added protection, make sure the insurance company is financially sound.

Insurance policies and premiums are also calculated and designed based on actuarial calculations (the probability that a person of a certain age, sex, and health condition will die within a given period). The insurance company is not taking a wild gamble when it insures someone; it is taking a calculated risk and protecting against it.

The Deductible Value

From the donor's point of view, when a policy is given makes a considerable amount of difference in the value for tax-deduction purposes and in the cost to the donor. The value of an insurance policy that has just been issued is the gross premium paid. If a policy has just been issued to the donor and the premium on it is $500, all that can be deducted is $500. But $500 can buy over a $100,000 in insurance for a person below 35 years of age. The benefit to the nonprofit is therefore $100,000. What leverage! In addition, regular contributions to the organization that can be used to pay annual premiums qualify as taxable deductions.

The tax-deductible value of a policy that is fully paid up is its replacement cost at the donor's age at the time the gift is made. Giving a paid-up policy might be a superior strategy for an older person than a younger one, particularly if the policy is one that was taken out many years before and is no longer needed. A newly paid up policy, called a single premium, is expensive—ordinarily a minimum of $5000.

In between these two extremes is a permanent policy that is presently being paid for and the value of such a policy is roughly its cash value. It is the amount accumulated as savings up to the point the gift was made. This is the approximate (not the exact) amount that can be deducted. The cash value is shown in the policy.

ANNUITIES: PROVIDING INCOME FLOWS

Annuities are merely payments that must be made over a period of time. Unitrust, annuity trusts, and pooled trusts all pay annuities. Sometimes the annuity is paid to the donor or a noncharitable designated beneficiary and sometimes it is paid to a charity, as in charitable lead trusts.

In Chapter 14, we discuss the possibilities of a worker giving his or her pension annuity to a nonprofit. Let us anticipate that discussion briefly. In the giving or receiving of annuities, care must be taken that the potential donor actually owns the annuity. Most pension annuities have a period that must lapse before the accounts are vested and fully owned by the future annuitant. Until that time has elapsed, the person does not own the balance in the account and is not legally able to donate it, even though the account may be in his or her name. Also, the surviving spouse may have a legal claim on the annuity.

The value of annuities for tax-deduction purposes is determined by finding its present value after discounting at a rate announced by the IRS quarterly. Basically, this value is the amount that would have to be invested today at a specific interest rate given by the IRS so that the annuity would be worth the amount promised at a time in the future. This formula is used in calculating an annuity provided by an employer. If there is a going market for the type of annuity to be donated, that is, if the annuity is a commercial one, then the value is its replacement cost.

Guaranteed or Charitable Gift Annuities

In the case of gift annuities, the donor gives the nonprofit a large amount of money or property with the understanding that the nonprofit will guarantee a specific annual payment to the donor or to some other person for life or for the joint lives of two or more persons. Gift annuities are not issued for a term less than life.

The payments may be immediate, meaning commencing one year after the gift was made, or they may be deferred to sometime after. The promise to make this payment is backed by all the assets of the nonprofit. Can you see what happens when the earnings of the pool of money given to the nonprofit are too small to make the payments promised? Yes, the assets have to be liquidated in order to meet the payments. This caused many of these annuities to go bankrupt during the Depression.

The way a modern financial planner for a nonprofit should use a gift annuity today is as follows. The donor wishes to make a gift but needs an income flow. Unlike the property that may create a remainder trust, the property in a gift annuity may be unable to do so; or even if it could, the nonprofit wants to protect against defaulting in payments because of a downturn in the cash being generated by the assets. What is the solution? The nonprofit takes the property and then turns to an insurance company and buys an annuity that will generate the income required to meet the guarantee payments to the donor. As an example, Calvin decides to give an art piece with a market value of $1,000,000. He needs an income. The Ellis Malcom Art Center accepts the gift. It then uses $487,000 to buy an annuity to pay Calvin at age 59 an annual sum of $50,000 for the remainder of his life. Part of this payment to him may be tax free if it includes any part of the capital used to purchase the annuity by the nonprofit.

Notice that the risk of payment is shifted from the nonprofit to an insurance company. The nonprofit is no longer at risk. Calvin's deduction would roughly be $1,000,000 minus the $487,000, which is the present value (the amount presently needed) to generate an income of $50,000 for the remainder of his life.

A gift of annuity is unlike a remainder or charitable lead trust because it is not necessarily the same property that passes from the donor to the trust and then to the nonprofit or back to the donor or some other noncharitable persons. Furthermore, in some states, gift annuities are regulated and therefore state law should be consulted. For federal tax purposes a gift annuity must either be in the form of a trust or an insurance contract.

Application of Charitable Gift Annuities

Gift annuities must also be concerned with the unrelated business income tax. Let us illustrate this with one of the most common uses of a gift annuity. Clive makes a gift to a university. It gives him an annuity and names one beneficiary and one alternative, who are his children. The life annuity (annual payments) may be used to pay the beneficiary's tuition at the school or to make other payments to another school or any other person. This is a common nontaxable use of gift annuities, and this specific case is based on Private Letter Ruling 9042043.

What conditions are necessary to avoid the unrelated business income tax?

1. The annuity should be the only thing—called consideration—the donor receives in exchange for the gift.
2. It must be less than 90 percent of the value of the donation.
3. Payment must be scheduled over the life of one or two individuals alive (not unborn) at the time the gift was made.
4. The issuing of annuities must not be a substantial part of the activities of the recipient organization.
5. The contract must not guarantee a minimum payment or payments that vary with changing values of the original gift.[16]

STEPS FOR DETERMINING DEFERRED GIVING INSTRUMENTS

The settlement of the Barron Hilton estates is a good example of some of the principles we have reviewed. He was chairman and president of the Hilton Hotels. It took nine years to settle a dispute over his will. The settlement created a charitable remainder trust in which was placed his sizable gift of Hilton Hotel stocks to the Conrad N. Hilton Foundation. The foundation supports Catholic nuns throughout the world. His son,

Conrad, will be a trustee (if not the sole trustee of the trust). At the end of his life or after twenty years, whichever comes sooner, all of the assets of the trust will be turned over to the foundation. What should guide?

1. Be sure that the financial position, responsibilities, and intent of the prospective donor is understood and that they drive the choice. Sophisticated deferred giving is like making a business deal. It works well when both parties can claim satisfaction.
2. Be sure that you understand the basic properties of each type of trust, insurance, and the risk associated with testamentary gifts. Discuss the options.
3. Have your legal counsel meet with the potential donor and his or her counsel. Your counsel should be guided by what is best for the donor and what is consistent with the objectives of the organization. You cannot leave your lawyer alone to determine these facts. Exercise your opinion about the instrument as well as about its details. Your organization, not the lawyer, is at risk.
4. Think of mix strategies.
5. Be patient. These types of deals take time.

ENDOWMENTS: PERPETUATING A GIFT

Any of the mechanisms discussed in this chapter and in Chapter 9 may be used for funding an endowment. An endowment is an account that is established to have perpetual life and to finance a specified set of activities. The endowment may be a separate nonprofit corporation.

To fund an endowment is merely to put money or other property in it. An endowment can therefore be funded singularly or in combination with outright gifts and contributions, annuities, life insurance, and lifetime or testamentary gifts. Small endowments grow when well managed. A small endowment like Mankato State University's grew from $169,000 to $1,500,000 in ten years in spite of regular disbursements to support scholarships.

Uses of Endowments

An endowment serves several important purposes. One purpose is to provide a pool of funds to which the organization can turn in an emergency. As such, it gives some financial stability and quick-response capability to the organization. In Chapter 18 we shall see how well this works for the Red Cross in responding to disasters and other emergencies.

A closely related use occurs when the endowment is used to cover

The Rotary Foundation of Rotary International links the efforts of Rotarians worldwide. The Rotary Foundation has invested U.S. $250 million on programs for world understanding and peace.

Contributions to The Rotary Foundation are made on a voluntary basis; no part of R.I. per capita dues supports the work of The Foundation. Almost all of The Foundation's programs are made possible through funding from annual *unrestricted contributions*, which are given without the donor specifying a particular use. The major exceptions are *PolioPlus*, which uses donations given specifically for use in polio eradication, and *The Rotary Foundation Endowment* for World Understanding and Peace, from which only the earnings income is used to fund programs. The Endowment Fund will provide monies for Foundation programs in the 21st century and beyond.

Reprinted with permission from *A Sturdy Foundation* The Rotary Foundation of Rotary International 1989, p. 14.

shortfalls between the expenditures and revenues of the organization. Continuous invasion of an endowment for this purpose, however, is not to be encouraged. This problem should be solved by better financial management. These types of "endowments" are usually set up as board-designated restricted funds. Sometimes the trustees will approve an interfund transfer from an endowment to operating funds. The Philadelphia Orchestra Association, for example, set up an income stabilization fund to offset operating deficits. The fund is financed by transfers from general operations.

Endowments provide a source of funds that the organization may use to finance activities that are important to it but for which it cannot readily obtain support from outside sources. Many organizations use endowments to finance activities that are innovative, experimental, and developmental. When used this way, the endowment serves to push the organization forward. It helps the organization to carry out its mission without having to meet the constraints and demands of an outside funding agency.

An endowment might be used to separate out and finance specific charitable missions.

Endowments are sometimes required by funding sources to ensure the organization's financial stability and to reduce its drain.

Endowments provide for accumulating funds to finance long-term and major activities or acquisitions by the organization. In this vein are building funds, scholarships, and so on.

Spending from an Endowment

All these ideal uses of endowments can be defeated, however, if (1) the endowment is unintentionally exhausted, and (2) restrictions are violated. Let's deal with these in turn. In practice, there is something called exhaustible or expendable endowments. These are really restricted funds that may be treated as if they were endowments. So sometimes the term quasi-endowment is used. A true endowment is a perpetuity even though for some purposes, such as life annuities, it may be defined in terms of life expectancy.

A quasi-endowment connotes that the principal—not just the earnings—of the fund may be spent. This implies that the fund could be exhausted or totally expended. Even in these cases, however, unless the conditions specified in the gifts call for total exhaustion, management is wise to treat these funds as true endowments—perpetuities.

Structure of Endowment

An endowment should be organized around four functions or responsibility centers: (1) revenue-raising, (2) investment management, (3) disbursement, (4) guardian or stewardship. Figure 10.1 shows the structure of an endowment. Note that the investment advisor and custodian

---

By Richard F. Shepard

A shortage of money is threatening the Frick Art Reference Library, which for 70 years has served as a major research resource for art scholars, dealers, writers, publishers and collectors. The library is seeking to raise at least $15 million from outside sources to avoid a curtailment in services.

OUT OF THE NEST

"If nothing is done, the city will lose this library," said Charles Ryskamp, director of the Frick Collection, last week. The Collection has until now supplied the operating funds for the library through the Helen Clay Frick Foundation.

The foundation has told the library that it should have its own endowment independent of the Collection, starting next year. The Foundation is contributing $18.75 million toward a $34 million total endowment; the remaining funds must be raised from other sources, Mr. Ryskamp said. . . .

"Frick Reference Library Is Obliged to Seek Funds," © *New York Times*, December 30, 1990, p. 45. Reprinted with permission.

Organization of an Endowment

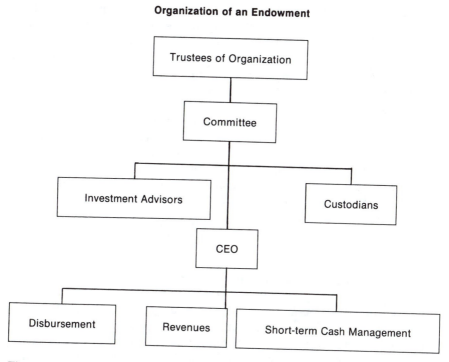

Figure 10.1 Organization of an Endowment.

report to the committee of the trustee of the organization, even though they may do this through the CEO. They, like auditors, are accountable directly to the trustees.

The investment advisors make investment recommendations and invest the funds. In large endowments there may be several advisors competing with the funds assigned them. Advisors may specialize—oil, stock, bonds, real estate, and so on. The custodian's job is to hold the funds or securities. Custodians are often banks.

The revenue function is what fund raising does. It feeds the endowment portfolio with seed money and a continuous flow of fresh funds. Natural lapse of time means that these funds rarely go directly to the investment advisor. During the interim, they should be managed as short-term cash. From there the funds pass to the discretion of the investment advisor, who, given the limits placed on that discretion by the trustees, proceeds to invest.

Annually, the trustees review this performance and make decisions about whether to retain an advisor or change the amount under his or her guidance. They also decide how much to disburse from the endowment. Many endowments operate by simple, fixed rules set by the board of trustees. For example, it may disburse only a fixed percentage of the total endowment or a fixed percentage of its growth. Its growth may be calculated for the most recent year or for the most recent couple of years. For example, the board of trustees may decide that every year they will calculate the amount of earnings (dividends and appreciation) in the portfolio for the most recent five years and disburse only 5 percent of that amount.

One advantage of using a moving average (using the last five years) is that it smoothes out variations. If the organization used only the most recent year, then if that is a good year the disbursement will be high; if it is a very poor year, the disbursement will be very low. The objective should always be to (1) develop a simple rule, and (2) enable the endowment principal or corpus to be preserved and to grow so as to finance future needs.

Endowments as Community Foundations

Community foundations are public charities most of which meet the 10 percent rather than the one-third public support test in Chapter 4. A community foundation is, in reality, a consolidated endowment supporting, as a 509(a)(3), a group of local charities. It is an alternative to a private foundation. It is consolidated because it can consolidate a number of gifts and endowments into one by meeting four conditions: (1) being a legal entity with a name, (2) having one board of directors that oversees all gifts, (3) consolidating all reporting, and (4) having a common governing document over all gifts. Thus, in lieu of setting up a private foundation, a donor may make a named gift to a community foundation and designate the causes or specific local organizations that are to be funded in the name of the donor. All the fiduciary rules apply.

Endowments as Private Foundations

An endowment is subject to the rules of a private foundation. This means that the trustees must be concerned with transactions with disqualified persons, self-dealing, the distribution of income, jeopardy of investments, excess business holdings, prohibited expenditures, unrelated business income—all of which we have discussed in previous chapters. In short, the endowment is a nonprofit organization in its own right. It can even be a 509(a)(3), subject to the strict fiduciary rules that we discussed under private foundations in our discussion of the role of trustees.

FOUR ESSENTIAL STEPS FOR AN ENDOWMENT

1. The board of trustees should pass a resolution that an endowment be started. It should state: (a) the purpose of the endowment and how it fits into the mission of the organization, (b) how and by whom it will be managed, (c) the investment objective and strategy (even as broadly as stating that it will only invest in stocks of blue-chip companies, government securities, and money market accounts), and (d) how disbursements and transfers into and out of the endowment will be determined.

2. Determine how performance will be measured. The most common formula is one that adds all dividends to the amount of appreciation in the value of the portfolio and divides this by the amount invested. This is called the total rate of return.

3. Each year, assess how each responsibility center (revenue generation, investment, custodial, and disbursement) has performed. Chapter 18 will assist you further.

4. From time to time review restrictions. Some may be dated, contrary to policy, and may not provide marketing flexibility to potential donors. Minimize donor-imposed restrictions.

VALUATION OF FUTURE GIFTS

The valuation of deferred gifts (as present gifts discussed in Chapter 9) is of interest to the donor because it determines the amount that can be deducted from federal and state income taxes. It is of interest to the nonprofit financial manager because (1) it may have to be included among the organization's assets at value and among its in-kind contributions. As we shall see in Chapter 17, contributions are assets appearing on the balance sheet of the organization. (2) It may lead to tax and liability consequences if the gift is subject to debt or if it has been so depreciated by the donor that its value in transfer is decreased. For example, a gift that has a market value of $400,000 would be less if the donor owes money on it and the nonprofit assumes the donor's debt. Being a debt-acquired property, it would lead to unrelated business income tax if the property generates income. (3) Its value, as discussed in Chapter 4 and earlier in this chapter, may be used in the calculation of public support, which must be demonstrated in order to retain the tax-exempt status of the organization. (4) Since tax considerations are a major impetus for giving, the amount of deductibility that is directly determined by the value of the gift may be used by the nonprofit to encourage the potential donor to make the gift. In some cases (Chapter 8), the IRS requires that value be known.

A financial manager of a nonprofit would be unwise to try to determine the value of a gift for a potential donor, except as required in Chapter 8. Donations are often part of an overall tax strategy of a person or corporation, and the valuation of specific gifts is a special skill. It is, however, important that the manager understand the key variables that determine the values of gifts and how they interact to determine the level of deduction that a taxpayer may take. Knowing this will help the manager to make a deal by appealing to the tax motive for making the gift. As a general rule, the dollar value of the gift in the hands of the donor is its dollar value to the nonprofit at the time of the transfer to the organization. For accounting and tax purposes, the good does not change values simply because it is now in the hands of a nonprofit, although it may change value later due to market appreciation and depreciation.

The basic rule is that the value of the gift is its fair market value. This is the amount that a knowledgeable buyer would voluntarily pay a knowledgeable seller for the property at the time and under the conditions that the property was transferred from the donor to the nonprofit organization. Note that you cannot presume an extraordinary past or future situation to inflate the value of the gift and you cannot assume laissez faire to mean that the property could be sold to an ignorant buyer or to a buyer acting under duress for more. If the property is one that is usually sold through classified ads, then the value is that appearing in such ads on the day of the transfer. If the property is normally subject to retail sale, then its value is the retail price on that date. Furthermore, the transfer between the nonprofit and the person must represent an arm's-length agreement. That is to say, they cannot conspire or use influence to set an artificially high value.

The simple term "fair market value" can be very complex when the gift is made in a form other than an outright and immediate transfer of cash from the donor to the nonprofit organization. A check written for $1300 by Orvin to his church is a gift valued at $1300. But what if the gift is in some form other than cash? What if the gift is to pass to the nonprofit at a time in the distant future? What if the nonprofit will be permitted to get the income from a gift and then pass the gift on to Orvin's children upon his death? How are deferred gifts valued?

Several factors would affect the answers to these questions: the age of the donor; the term of the gift; the kind of property being transferred; whether the gift is being transferred to the nonprofit first and then to a noncharity or whether the nonprofit gets the gift only after a noncharitable beneficiary has enjoyed it; the payout rate; and the discount or interest rate that is presumed and the kind of trust being used. Let us discuss some of these factors. Our discussion of trusts introduced their importance to us.

Age is a determinant of the value of the gift whenever the transfer of the gift to the nonprofit is keyed to life expectancy. This is so if the gift is to pass to the nonprofit at the death of the donor or some other person or persons before being transferred to the nonprofit, or if the gift must first be used by the nonprofit and then passed on to some other noncharitable entity or person upon the death of the donor. For example, Margaret may elect that a gift be passed on to her church only after her death and her husband's death. This gives both of them the opportunity to enjoy the property during their lifetimes. In this case, the life expectancy of both persons must be taken into account. On the other hand, she may elect to have the church enjoy the benefits of the gift during her lifetime, but require that it be passed on to her husband upon her death since he would need it to sustain life. In this case, only her life expectancy is important.

Life expectancy affects valuation because the longer the noncharitable beneficiary is likely to live, the smaller the contribution that is being made to the charity. If Margaret's gift is to pass to her church at the time of her death and she is only 25 years old, she could live many more years and the contribution to the church, barring a growth in the value of the property, could be very little at the time of her death. Similarly, if Margaret's gift is to pass to the church only after her death and the death of her daughter who is 2 years old, it could be another 60 years before the gift is passed. However, if she is 80 years old and the transfer of the property to the nonprofit will occur at the time of her death, it is conceivable that at her age the transfer could take place in a reasonably short time. Therefore, the value of the gift for purposes of deduction is closer to its current market value.

The term or the specific number of years that must pass before the gift is transferred works similarly to the age variable. Sometimes a donor will make the gift conditional on the passage of a number of years rather than upon death. The donor may require that five, ten, or twelve years must pass before the gift can be transferred to the nonprofit or that the nonprofit may have use of the gift for a specific number of years before it must pass it on to a noncharitable beneficiary. The longer the term that the nonprofit may possess the gift, or the shorter the term it has to wait to receive it, the closer is the present market value to its value for the purposes of deduction.

As in the case of present gifts, the kind of property affects value. Unimproved real property, land that does not have building and developments that increase its value, is valued at the price paid for it or at comparable sales price of similar geographically located and geologically constituted undeveloped land, subject to the same zoning limitations and development rights on the date of the transfer to the nonprofit. Stocks and bonds are valued at the midpoint between their highest and lowest selling price on the stock exchange on the date of the transfer. If the stock exchanges are closed on that date (weekends and holidays), the most recent last date of its opening is used. Unpaid dividends may also be included in the valuation of the security. If the security is a share of a mutual fund, then the valuation price is the redemption price on the date that the funds are transferred. If the stock or interest in a business is not sold on the exchange, then the price is based on such factors as its book value (assets minus liabilities).

If the gift is an annuity regularly sold by a financial company, then the value of the annuity is the price that is usually sold for by the company. But often the value of an annuity, life estate, or remainder of reversionary interests must be calculated by special tables issued by the IRS. An annuity is merely a contract that agrees to pay an annual payment over a number of years. A remainder interest refers to the transfer of the property to the nonprofit after a passage of time either expressed in a specific number of years (term) or the lifetime of one or more persons. A life estate is an interest for payment during the life of an individual.

The way the good is transferred also affects its valuation for purposes of deduction. As stated earlier, a gift of a future interest, a gift that does not take effect until a time in the future, has no deductible value unless the gift is a conservation property or is transferred through a trust. In the case of an annuity, this is handled by an insurance company. But if a trust is used, the value also differs if the transfer is made through a pooled income, a unitrust, or an annuity trust and if it is a charitable lead or charitable remainder trust. The latter usually has very limited deductible value since it often requires that the donor include the income of the trust in his or her own taxable income. These considerations were discussed earlier in this chapter.

Also, as stated earlier in this chapter, the payout rates have a considerable bearing on the value of future gifts. The higher, longer, and more frequent the payout to a noncharitable beneficiary is the lower the deductible value of the gift. While we did not demonstrate it earlier, payout must be at least once a year, but can be monthly, quarterly, or semiannually.

The interest rate or discount rate also affects the value of the property. It is a mathematical fact that the higher the discount rate is the lower the present value of a gift because the value is being discounted by a greater number. The IRS announces quarterly the applicable rate.

To understand how these concepts work or interact to determine value, refer to Table 10.8. Note that the table is based on a 10 percent discount rate (a presumption that the rate of return on an investment is

TABLE 10.8 Table A—10%

1 Age	2 Annuity	3 Life Estate	4 Remainder	1 Age	2 Annuity	3 Life Estate	4 Remainder
0	9.7188	.97188	.02812	55	8.0046	.80046	.19954
1	9.8988	.98988	.01012	56	7.9006	.79006	.20994
2	9.9017	.99017	.00983	57	7.7931	.77931	.22069
3	9.9008	.99008	.00992	58	7.6822	.76822	.23178
4	9.8981	.98981	.01019	59	7.5675	.75675	.24325
5	9.8938	.98938	.01062	60	7.4491	.74491	.25509
6	9.8884	.98884	.01116	61	7.3267	.73267	.26733
7	9.8822	.98822	.01178	62	7.2002	.72002	.27998
8	9.8748	.98748	.01252	63	7.0696	.70696	.29304
9	9.8663	.98663	.01337	64	6.9352	.69352	.30648
10	9.8565	.98565	.01435	65	6.7970	.67970	.32030
11	9.8453	.98453	.01547	66	6.6551	.66551	.33449
12	9.8329	.98329	.01671	67	6.5098	.65098	.34902
13	9.8198	.98198	.01802	68	6.3610	.63610	.36390
14	9.8066	.98066	.01934	69	6.2086	.62086	.37914
15	9.7937	.97937	.02063	70	6.0522	.60522	.39478
16	9.7815	.97815	.02185	71	5.8914	.58914	.41086
17	9.7700	.97700	.02300	72	5.7261	.57261	.42739
18	9.7590	.97590	.02410	73	5.5571	.55571	.44429
19	9.7480	.97480	.02520	74	5.3862	.53862	.46138
20	9.7365	.97365	.02635	75	5.2149	.52149	.47851
21	9.7245	.97245	.02755	76	5.0441	.50441	.49559
22	9.7120	.97120	.02880	77	4.8742	.48742	.51258
23	9.6986	.96986	.03014	78	4.7049	.47049	.52951
24	9.6841	.96841	.03159	79	4.5357	.45357	.54643
25	9.6678	.96678	.03322	80	4.3659	.43659	.56341
26	9.6495	.96495	.03505	81	4.1967	.41967	.58033
27	9.6290	.96290	.03710	82	4.0295	.40295	.59705
28	9.6062	.96062	.03938	83	3.8642	.38642	.61358
29	9.5813	.95813	.04187	84	3.6998	.36998	.63002
30	9.5543	.95543	.04457	85	3.5359	.35359	.64641
31	9.5254	.95254	.04746	86	3.3764	.33764	.66236
32	9.4942	.94942	.05058	87	3.2262	.32262	.67738
33	9.4608	.94608	.05392	88	3.0859	.30859	.69141
34	9.4250	.94250	.05750	89	2.9526	.29526	.70474
35	9.3868	.93868	.06132	90	2.8221	.28221	.71779
36	9.3460	.93460	.06540	91	2.6955	.26955	.73045
37	9.3026	.93026	.06974	92	2.5771	.25771	.74229
38	9.2567	.92567	.07433	93	2.4692	.24692	.75308
39	9.2083	.92083	.07917	94	2.3728	.23728	.76272
40	9.1571	.91571	.08429	95	2.2887	.22887	.77113
41	9.1030	.91030	.08970	96	2.2181	.22181	.77819
42	9.0457	.90457	.09543	97	2.1550	.21550	.78450
43	8.9855	.89855	.10145	98	2.1000	.21000	.79000
44	8.9221	.89221	.10779	99	2.0486	.20486	.79514
45	8.8558	.88558	.11442	100	1.9975	.19975	.80025

TABLE 10.8 Table A—10% (continued)

1 Age	2 Annuity	3 Life Estate	4 Remainder	1 Age	2 Annuity	3 Life Estate	4 Remainder
46	8.7863	.87863	.12137	101	1.9532	.19532	.80468
47	8.7137	.87137	.12863	102	1.9054	.19054	.80946
48	8.6374	.86374	.13626	103	1.8437	.18437	.81563
49	8.5578	.85578	.14422	104	1.7856	.17856	.82144
50	8.4743	.84743	.15257	105	1.6962	.16962	.83038
51	8.3874	.83874	.16126	106	1.5488	.15488	.84512
52	8.2969	.82969	.17031	107	1.3409	.13409	.86591
53	8.2028	.82028	.17972	108	1.0068	.10068	.89932
54	8.1054	.81054	.18946	109	.4545	.04545	.95455

Source: Federal Estate and Gift Taxes, Publication 448, rev. Sept. 1984, Internal Revenue Service, p. 17.

10 percent). Note that the annuity factors (column 2) get smaller the older the age. A person who is 109 years old is not expected to live very long; therefore, an annuity contract promising to pay such a person a specific sum for the remainder of his or her life is not likely to be worth very much. A gift of such a contract would have a very small present value. Hence, a gift of an annuity of $100,000 payable annually over the lifetime of such a person would be valued at ($100,000 × .4545) or $45,540. On the other hand, a similar $100,000 annuity payable each year over the life of a 25-year old person would be valued at ($100,000 × 9.6678) or $966,780. Thus, an annuity may provide either a large or small deduction depending on the age of the donor or the person for whom it is designed.

A life estate given to a nonprofit through a charitable lead trust means that the donor gives the charity the earnings from the property for the duration of a lifetime with the property to revert to a noncharitable donor, such as an heir, at the time of the donor's death. A donor who is 109 years old is not expected to live much longer. Therefore, a gift of a life estate of $100,000 is worth ($100,000 × .04545) or $4545.

The value of remainder interest (column 4 of Table 10.7) is also affected by age. Take a gift appraised at $100,000 that is to be enjoyed by a noncharitable beneficiary who is 25 years of age and then passed on to a charity upon the death of that beneficiary. The present value of that gift ($100,000 × .03322) is $3322 for purposes of tax deduction. The same gift would be worth ($100,000 × .95455) $95,455 if the person is 109 years old. Being that old, the gift would be expected to pass on soon so the deduction and the value of the annuity are higher.

Let us assume that instead of using age, we use a specific term, that is, a number of years. Refer to Table 10.9. First, we see that the upper

TABLE 10.9

Table B—6%

1 Number of Years	2 Annuity	3 Term Certain	4 Remainder	1 Number of Years	2 Annuity	3 Term Certain	4 Remainder
1	0.9434	.056604	.943396	31	13.9291	.835745	.164255
2	1.8334	.110004	.889996	32	14.0840	.845043	.154957
3	2.6730	.160381	.839619	33	14.2302	.853814	.146186
4	3.4651	.207906	.792094	34	14.3681	.862088	.137912
5	4.2124	.252742	.747258	35	14.4982	.869895	.130105
6	4.9173	.295039	.704961	36	14.6210	.877259	.122741
7	5.5824	.334943	.665057	37	14.7368	.884207	.115793
8	6.2098	.372588	.627412	38	14.8460	.890761	.109239
9	6.8017	.408102	.591898	39	14.9491	.896944	.103056
10	7.3601	.441605	.558395	40	15.0463	.902778	.097222
11	7.8869	.473212	.526788	41	15.1380	.908281	.091719
12	8.3838	.503031	.496969	42	15.2245	.913473	.086527
13	8.8527	.531161	.468839	43	15.3062	.918370	.081630
14	9.2950	.557699	.442301	44	15.3832	.922991	.077009
15	9.7122	.582735	.417265	45	15.4558	.927350	.072650
16	10.1059	.606354	.393646	46	15.5244	.931462	.068538
17	10.4773	.628636	.371364	47	15.5890	.935342	.064653
18	10.8276	.649656	.350344	48	15.6500	.939002	.060998
19	11.1581	.669487	.330513	49	15.7076	.942454	.057546
20	11.4699	.688195	.311805	50	15.7619	.945712	.054288
21	11.7641	.705845	.294155	51	15.8131	.948785	.051215
22	12.0416	.722495	.277505	52	15.8614	.951684	.048316
23	12.3034	.738203	.261797	53	15.9070	.954418	.045582
24	12.5504	.753021	.246979	54	15.9500	.956999	.043001
25	12.7834	.767011	.232999	55	15.9905	.959433	.040567
26	13.0032	.780190	.219810	56	16.0288	.961729	.038271
27	13.2105	.792632	.207368	57	16.0649	.963895	.036105
28	13.4062	.804370	.195630	58	16.0990	.965939	.034061
29	13.5907	.815443	.184557	59	16.1311	.967867	.032133
30	13.7648	.825890	.174110	60	16.1614	.969686	.030314

Table B—10%

1	2	3	4	1	2	3	4
1	.9091	.090909	.909091	31	9.4790	.947901	.052099
2	1.7355	.173554	.826446	32	9.5264	.952638	.047362
3	2.4869	.248685	.751315	33	9.5694	.956943	.043057
4	3.1699	.316987	.683013	34	9.6086	.960857	.039143
5	3.7908	.379079	.620921	35	9.6442	.964416	.035584
6	4.3553	.435526	.564474	36	9.6765	.967651	.032349
7	4.8684	.486842	.513158	37	9.7059	.970592	.029408
8	5.3349	.533493	.466507	38	9.7327	.973265	.026735
9	5.7590	.575902	.424098	39	9.7570	.975696	.024304
10	6.1446	.614457	.385543	40	9.7791	.977905	.022095
11	6.4951	.649506	.350494	41	9.7991	.979914	.020086

(continued)

TABLE 10.9 (continued)

Table B—6%

1 Number of Years	2 Annuity	3 Term Certain	4 Remainder	1 Number of Years	2 Annuity	3 Term Certain	4 Remainder
12	6.8137	.681369	.318631	42	9.8174	.981740	.018260
13	7.1034	.710336	.289664	43	9.8340	.983400	.016600
14	7.3667	.736669	.263331	44	9.8491	.984909	.015091
15	7.6061	.760608	.239392	45	9.8628	.986281	.013719
16	7.8237	.782371	.217629	46	9.8753	.987528	.012472
17	8.0216	.802155	.197845	47	9.8866	.988662	.011338
18	8.2014	.820141	.179859	48	9.8969	.989693	.010307
19	8.3649	.836492	.163508	49	9.9063	.990630	.009370
20	8.5136	.851356	.148644	50	9.9148	.991481	.008519
21	8.6487	.864869	.135131	51	9.9226	.992256	.007744
22	8.7715	.877154	.122846	52	9.9296	.992960	.007040
23	8.8832	.888322	.111678	53	9.9360	.993600	.006400
24	8.9847	.898474	.101526	54	9.9418	.994182	.005818
25	9.0770	.907704	.092296	55	9.9471	.994711	.005289
26	9.1609	.916095	.083905	56	9.9519	.995191	.004809
27	9.2372	.923722	.076278	57	9.9563	.995629	.004371
28	9.3066	.930657	.069343	58	9.9603	.996026	.003974
29	9.3696	.936961	.063039	59	9.9639	.996387	.003613
30	9.4269	.942691	.057309	60	9.9672	.996716	.003284

See *Valuation* in both the *Estate Tax* and *Gift Tax* sections of this publication to determine whether you should use the 6% or 10% tables to value these items.

Source: Federal Estate and Gift Taxes, Publication 448, rev. Sept. 1984, Internal Revenue Service, p. 18.

panel of the table presumes a 6 percent discount rate and the lower a 10 percent. We see the difference that a higher discount rate makes by comparing the same cells in both panels. We observe that with a 10 percent discount rate the value of the property is reduced. Thus, for a term of 20 years at 6 percent, the factor is 11.4699 for an annuity, compared to 8.5136 for 10 percent, .688195 for a term certain period (a specific term rather than a lifetime which is an uncertain term) compared to .851356, and .311805 compared to .148644 for a remainder interest.

Also notice that the factors in the 10 percent panel are different from the factors in Table 10.8, which also assume a 10 percent rate of discount. One reason is that the latter has an element of uncertainty. To make a gift contingent on someone's death involves an uncertainty about how long the person may live. The estimates are based on actuarial tables, which are estimates of the life expectancy of persons at specific ages. When a specific term is used, the length of time is for a term certain or a period of time that is certain. A 109-year-old person may live one month, one year, one day. To make a gift after a specific period is to set a specific term regardless of whether or not the person lives.

Rules of Thumb When Using Deductible Value in Appeal for Deferred Gift

Large gifts are often induced by applying the right combinations of factors to bring about a high valuation when a tax motive is important to the potential donor. A couple of simple rules may help: (1) Age works inversely with value when the charity gets a remainder interest and positively with value when the charity gets a life estate (an income interest). (2) The longer the time the nonprofit has the benefits of the property the greater the deductible value. (3) The deductible value must be consistent with the fair market value of the property. (4) The higher the payout rate to the noncharitable beneficiary is the lower the value of the property as a charitable deduction.

This last point suggests trade-offs. A high payout rate may attract a potential donor because it offers a good income to the donor or a loved beneficiary; but it is at the expense of a higher tax deduction. Thus, the tax problem is one of coming up with a trade-off between a present benefit (tax deduction) or a flow of income (the payout) that suits the donor's needs. The loss of an initial part of a tax deduction can be partly offset by investing in securities that lead to tax-free earnings. Always let the lawyers and accountants advise and the donor choose.

SUMMARY AND CONCLUSIONS

This chapter has presented techniques and tools that every manager of a nonprofit organization should know if the organization is to be successful in raising big money. These techniques allow the donor to have a deduction on present income tax, avoid estate taxes on gifts made, have a current income from the earnings of the gift, or make a gift of that current income to someone such as a relative or friend. The techniques also allow the nonprofit to receive annual income from a property only temporarily in its possession or, in the reverse, to finally take possession of a property that was providing an annual income to the donor. Basically, these tools and techniques are ways to strike a deal.

The tools that were discussed were charitable remainder trusts of the unitrust, annuity trust, and pooled trust types. These permit the income interest to go to someone other than the nonprofit. The nonprofit gets the remainder or corpus. The other type of trusts are charitable lead trusts, also of the unitrust or annuity trust types. These permit the nonprofit to get an annual payment, with the principal eventually going to someone else.

Life insurance policies are also instruments for getting large gifts. Insurance policies can magnify the size of the gift thousands of times larger than the actual money outlay of the donor and they shift the burden of periodic reminders of donations to the insurance companies in the form of premium notices. Annuities are yet another tool. These range from gifts of pension plans, including private plans such as individual retirement accounts (IRAs) to gift annuities.

The chapter closes with a discussion of the valuation of future gifts and endowments, a special fund set aside for financing a special program or set of programs. An endowment may be funded by any one or (where permitted by law) any combination of the techniques discussed here and in Chapter 9. We say permitted by law because, once a trust is established, sometimes no further contributions can be made and some trusts must be separate and independent. Indeed, one motive for a donor's setting up a trust or an endowment is to maintain identity. This is why trusts and endowments usually carry the names of persons or corporations. It is their memorial. Regardless of how funded, each endowment requires a separate set of financial records.

APPENDIX 10.1: IRS EXAMPLE OF DECLARATION OF TRUST

In the first part of this chapter and in Chapter 4, it was said that a nonprofit could operate as a trust or as a corporation. Chapter 4 gives an example of an acceptable charter. This appendix is an example of a trust declaration that is acceptable to the IRS.

The _____Charitable Trust. Declaration of Trust made as of the ___day of ___19___, by ___, of ___, and ___of ___, who hereby declare and agree that they have received this day from ___, as Donor, the sum of Ten Dollars ($10) and that they will hold and manage the same, and any additions to it, in trust, as follows:

First: This trust shall be called "The _____Charitable Trust."

Second: The trustees may receive and accept property, whether real, personal, or mixed, by way of gift, bequest, or devise, from any person, firm, trust, or corporation, to be held, administered, and disposed of in accordance with and pursuant to the provisions of this Declaration of Trust; but no gift, bequest or devise of any such property shall be received and accepted if it is conditioned or limited in such manner as to require the disposition of the income or its principal to any person or organization other than a "charitable organization" or for other than "charitable purposes" within the meaning of such terms as defined in Article Third of this Declaration of Trust, or as shall in the opinion of the trustees, jeopardize the federal income tax exemption of this trust pursuant to section 501(c)(3) of the Internal Revenue Code of 1954, as now in force or afterwards amended.

Third: A. The principal and income of all property received and accepted by the trustees to be administered under this Declaration of Trust shall be held in trust by them, and the trustees may make payments or distributions from income or principal, or both, to or for the use of such charitable organizations, within the meaning of that term as defined in paragraph C, in such amounts and for such charitable purposes of the trust as the trustees shall from time to time select and determine; and the trustees may make payments or distributions from income or principal, or both, directly for such charitable purposes, within the meaning of that term as defined in paragraph D, in such amounts as the trustees shall from time to time select and determine without making use of any other charitable organization. The trustees may also make payments or distributions of all or any part of the income or principal to states, territories, or possessions of the United States, any political subdivision of any of the foregoing, or to the United States or the District of Columbia but only for charitable purposes within the meaning of that term as defined in paragraph D. Income or principal derived from contributions by corporations shall be distributed by the trustees for use solely within the United States or its possessions. No part of the net earnings of this trust shall inure or be payable to or for the benefit of any private shareholder or individual, and no substantial part of the activities of this trust shall be the carrying on of propaganda, or otherwise attempting, to influence legislation. No part of the activities of this trust shall be the participation in, or intervention in (including the publishing or distributing of statements), any political campaign on behalf of any candidate for public office.

B. The trust shall continue forever unless the trustees terminate it and distribute all of the principal and income, which action may be taken by the trustees in their discretion at any time. On such termination, the trust fund as then constituted shall be distributed to or for the use of such charitable organizations, in such amounts and for such charitable purposes as the trustees shall then select and determine. The donor authorizes and empowers the trustees to form and organize a nonprofit corporation limited to the uses and purposes provided for in this Declaration of Trust, such corporation to be organized under the laws of any state or under the laws of the United States as may be determined by the trustees; such corporation when organized to have power to administer and control the affairs and property and to carry out the uses, objects, and purposes of this trust. Upon the creation and organization of such corporation, the trustees are authorized and empowered to convey, transfer, and deliver to such corporation all the property and assets to which this trust may be or become entitled. The charter, bylaws, and other provisions for the organization and management of such corporation and its affairs and property shall be such as the trustees shall determine, consistent with the provisions of this paragraph.

C. In this Declaration of Trust and in any amendments to it, references to "charitable organizations" or "charitable organization" mean corporations, trusts,

funds, foundations, or community chests created or organized in the United States
or in any of its possessions, whether under the laws of the United States, any state
or territory, the District of Columbia, or any possession of the United States, organized and operated exclusively for charitable purposes, no part of the net
earnings of which inures or is payable to or for the benefit of any private shareholder or individual, and no substantial part of the activities of which is carrying
on propaganda, or otherwise attempting, to influence legislation, and which do
not participate in or intervene in (including the publishing or distributing of statements), any political campaign on behalf of any candidate for public office. It is
intended that the organization described in this paragraph C shall be entitled to
exemption from federal income tax under section 501(c)(3) of the Internal Revenue Code of 1954, as now in force or afterwards amended.

D. In this Declaration of Trust and in any amendments to it, the term "charitable purposes" shall be limited to and shall include only religious, charitable,
scientific, literary, or educational purposes within the meaning of those terms as
used in section 501(c)(3) of the Internal Revenue Code of 1954 but only such
purposes as also constitute public charitable purposes under the law of trusts of
the State of _____.

Fourth: This Declaration of Trust may be amended at any time or times by
written instrument or instruments signed and sealed by the trustees, and acknowledged by any of the trustees, provided that no amendment shall authorize the
trustees to conduct the affairs of this trust in any manner or for any purpose
contrary to the provisions of section 501(c)(3) of the Internal Revenue Code of
1954 as now in force or afterwards amended. An amendment of the provisions
of this Article Fourth (or any amendment to it) shall be valid only if and to the
extent that such amendment further restricts the trustees' amending power. All
instruments amending this Declaration of Trust shall be noted upon or kept attached to the executed original of this Declaration of Trust held by the trustees.

Fifth: Any trustee under this Declaration of Trust may, by written instrument,
signed and acknowledged, resign his office. The number of trustees shall be at
all times not less than two, and whenever for any reason the number is reduced
to one, there shall be, and at any other time there may be, appointed one or
more additional trustees. Appointments shall be made by the trustee or trustees
for the time in office by written instruments signed and acknowledged. Any suc-
ceeding or additional trustee shall, upon his acceptance of the office by written
instrument signed and acknowledged, have the same powers, rights and duties,
and the same title to the trust estate jointly with the surviving or remaining trustee
or trustees as if originally appointed.

None of the trustees shall be required to furnish any bond or surety. None
of them shall be responsible or liable for the acts of omissions of any other of
the trustees or of any predecessor or of a custodian, agent, depositary or counsel
selected with reasonable care.

The one or more trustees, whether original or successor, for the time being
in office, shall have full authority to act even though one or more vacancies may
exist. A trustee may, by appropriate written instrument, delegate all or any part
of his powers to another or others of the trustees for such periods and subject
to such conditions as such delegating trustee may determine.

The trustees serving under this Declaration of Trust are authorized to pay to themselves amounts for reasonable expenses incurred and reasonable compensation for services rendered in the administration of this trust, but in no event shall any trustee who has made a contribution to this trust ever receive any compensation thereafter.

Sixth: In extension and not in limitation of the common law and statutory powers of trustees and other powers granted in this Declaration of Trust, the trustees shall have the following discretionary powers:

a) To invest and reinvest the principal and income of the trust in such property, real, personal, or mixed, and in such manner as they shall deem proper, and from time to time to change investments as they shall deem advisable; to invest in or retain any stocks, shares, bonds, notes, obligations, or personal or real property (including without limitation any interests in or obligations of any corporation, association, business trust, investment trust, common trust fund, or investment company) although some or all of the property so acquired or retained is of a kind or size which but for this express authority would not be considered proper and although all of the trust funds are invested in the securities of one company. No principal or income, however, shall be loaned, directly or indirectly, to any trustee or to anyone else, corporate or otherwise, who has at any time made a contribution to this trust, nor to anyone except on the basis of an adequate interest charge and with adequate security.

b) To sell, lease, or exchange any personal, mixed, or real property, at public auction or by private contract, for such consideration and on such terms as to credit or otherwise, and to make such contracts and enter into such undertakings relating to the trust property, as they consider advisable, whether or not such leases or contracts may extend beyond the duration of the trust.

c) To borrow money for such periods, at such rates of interest, and upon such terms as the trustees consider advisable, and as security for such loans to mortgage or pledge any real or personal property with or without power of sale; to acquire or hold any real or personal property, subject to any mortgage or pledge on or of property acquired or held by this trust.

d) To execute and deliver deeds, assignments, transfers, mortgages, pledges, leases, convenants, contracts, promissory notes, releases, and other instruments, sealed or unsealed, incident to any transaction in which they engage.

e) To vote, to give proxies, to participate in the reorganization, merger or consolidation of any concern, or in the sale, lease, disposition, or distribution of its assets; to join with other security holders in acting through a committee, depository, voting trustees, or otherwise, and in this connection to delegate authority to such committee, depositary, or trustees and to deposit securities with them or transfer securities to them; to pay assessments levied on securities or to exercise subscription rights in respect of securities.

f) To employ a bank or trust company as custodian of any funds or securities and to delegate to it such powers as they deem appropriate; to hold trust property without indication of fiduciary capacity but only in the name of a registered nominee, provided the trust property is at all times identified as such on the books of the trust; to keep any or all of the trust property or funds in any place or places in the United States of America; to employ clerks, accountants, investment counsel, investment agents, and any special services, and to pay the reasonable compensation and expenses of all such services in addition to the compensation of the trustees.

Seventh: The trustees' powers are exercisable solely in the fiduciary capacity consistent with and in furtherance of the charitable purposes of this trust as specified in Article Third and not otherwise.

Eighth: In this Declaration of Trust and in any amendment to it, references to "trustees" mean the one or more trustees, whether original or successor, for the time being in office.

Ninth: Any person may rely on a copy, certified by a notary public, of the executed original of this Declaration of Trust held by the trustees, and of any of the notations on it and writings attached to it, as fully as he might rely on the original documents themselves. Any such person may rely fully on any statements of fact certified by anyone who appears from such original documents or from such certified copy to be a trustee under this Declaration of Trust. No one dealing with the trustees need inquire concerning the validity of anything the trustees purport to do. No one dealing with the trustees need see to the application of anything paid or transferred to or upon the order of the trustees of the trust.

Tenth: This Declaration of Trust is to be governed in all respects by the laws of the State of _____.

Trustee—

Trustee—

Declaration of Trust. Source: Internal Revenue Service, Tax Exempt Status of Your Organization, Publication 557 (revised January 1982), U.S. Government Printing Office, 1982, p. 10.

NOTES

1. *American Bar Endowment* v. *U.S.*, 56 AFTR 2d 85-5005 (5-10-85), aff'g and rev'g, in part, 53 AFTR 2d 84-942. The Claims Court also concluded that the income derived by the American Bar Association was not taxable to them; that is, it was not unrelated business income. But on April 28, 1986, the Supreme Court ruled that this was an unrelated business and was taxable. (*Supreme Court of the United States, United States* v. *American Bar Endowment*, No. 85-599, April 28, 1986.)

2. The laws on income, estate and gift taxes state that if the creator of a trust has any incidence of ownership in the property that is in the trust, that person is deemed to derive economic benefits from it and therefore must pay both income and estate taxes on the earnings and value of the property. This rule, as we shall see, is relaxed in the case of charitable trusts.

3. There are some differences in the treatment of irrevocable and revocable trusts at the time of death. If, for example, a trust is revocable and becomes irrevocable at the time of death through the estate, then a "reasonable" period is granted to transform

the trust to a charitable one. The basic point to keep in mind is that a revocable transfer even through a trust is not a gift.

4. The reader should recall the discussion in Chapter 9 on the treatment of real property and other partial gifts.

5. Paul Taylor, "Hughes Settlement," *Washington Post*, Thursday, August 30, 1984, p. C18.

6. See the Ellsworth B. Warner Estate, file 15-81-1118, in the office of the Register of Wills, Chester County Courthouse, Westchester, Pennsylvania.

7. Associated Press story appearing *Washington Post*, February 8, 1986, page A2.

8. A "reasonable period" is that period required for the trustees to perform the ordinary duties of the trust. This includes the collection of assets, the payment of debt, the payment of taxes, and the determination of the rights of the subsequent beneficiaries.

9. Chapter 9 discusses capital gains and charitable contributions and organizations.

10. Normally, a property is valued on the date of death. An alternate date is six months after that period or anytime within the first six months that the property is first distributed. If the value of the property is affected by the mere lapse of time, such as a savings account or an annuity because it increases in value over time, then the property is valued as of the time of death.

11. Loans from the policy to purchase income-producing assets will lead to an unrelated business income tax because the assets would have been acquired through debt. *Mose & Garrison Sisken Memorial Foundation, Inc. v. U.S.*, 55 AFTR 2d 85-1024, (12-4-84). See also Chapter 7 of this book. Loans taken within the first seven years of a policy can create an income-tax liability. Check with your tax advisor before taking loans in the first seven years of the contract.

12. We say immediately or within a few years because with a term policy one pays every year as long as the term lasts. Thus, one could conceivably pay every year for 70 years or more, in which case some single premiums or universal life policies would have afforded greater leverage.

13. See J. Barry McGannon, "The Endowment Builders of Saint Louis University," *Fund Raising Management*, January 1988, p. 24.

14. I am grateful to Barrett Carson at William and Mary for the example.

15. This strategy, which I have concocted, may be less simple from a tax perspective than it appears. A tax attorney should check the following: the unrelated business income tax, exchange of value treatment of insurance contracts, and bargain sale implications.

16. GEM 39826.

SUGGESTED READINGS

BAETZ, TIMOTHY W., "Tax Planning for Sophisticated Charitable Transfers: The Divide between Downright Doable and Dangerous," *Taxes—The Tax Magazine*, 62, no. 12 (Dec. 1984), 997–1009.

Internal Revenue Service, Department of the Treasury, Federal Estate and Gift Taxes, Publication 448, rev. September 1989 (Washington, D.C.: U.S. Government Printing Office, 1989).

Internal Revenue Service, Department of Treasury, Tax Information for Private

Foundations and Foundation Managers, Publication 578, rev. January 1989 (Washington, D.C.: U.S. Government Printing Office, 1989).

Internal Revenue Service, U.S. Department of the Treasury, *Federal Estate and Gift Taxes*, Publication 448, revised September 1989.

SCHMOLHA, LEO L., "Income Taxation of Charitable Remainder Trusts and Decedents' Estates: Sixty-Six Years of Astigmatism," *Tax Law Review*, 40, no. 1 (Fall 1984), New York University School of Law (Warren Gortham and Lamont, Inc., Fall 1984), pp. 1–350.

VERES, JOSEPH A., "Using Pooled Income Funds to Pass ITC and Depreciation through to Life-income Donors," *Journal of Taxation*, 61, no. 1 (July 1984), pp. 28–33.

Chapter 11

Financing through the Operation of a Business

This chapter discusses both related and unrelated businesses. It shows how these businesses may be integrated into a simple or conglomerate structure. Nonprofit businesses enable the organization to perform its public welfare mission by providing a stream of income over which the nonprofit has total control. But it does far more than that.

THE IMPORTANCE OF BUSINESS IN THE NONPROFIT CORPORATE STRUCTURE

To some, the discussion of business and charities would seem to be irreconcilably inconsistent. This is wrong. Three critical differences between a charity and a commercial business are that (1) the charity can tolerate a lower than competitive rate of return, (2) it cannot distribute gains or assets to shareholders and (3) it may not have a substantial or primary commercial motive. It must use its resources to further public rather than private welfare.

But this does not imply (1) that the nonprofit should not seek a positive rate of return on its activities and investments or that (2) there are no claimants on its assets and earnings. The interests of these claimants are a dominant force. Nonprofits, like firms, must have earnings targets and cost discipline. These are imposed internally by staff and directors and indirectly by external claimants. There are two groups of claimants, who place constraints and pressures on the performance of nonprofits. One group of claimants has a legal claim. The other, an ethical or moral expectation.

First the legal. Any nonprofit that has tried to borrow a significant amount of funds either through the sale of bonds or from a bank will testify to the fact that lenders are no more generous simply because one is a charity. They charge competitive rates and expect to be paid on time. Therefore, any nonprofit that has a significant loan must have some way of financing it, either through gifts and contributions or through earned revenues. In short, while the rate of return (financial performance) does not have to satisfy shareholders, it must be good enough to pay all creditors—landlords and lenders, managers and workers, vendors and fee collectors, all of whom are legal claimants.

Second, the nonprofit by its very existence and previous operations cultivates an expectation and a clientele. This group does not have a legal claim on the assets or financial performance (income) of the organization. They have a moral claim, which might, in the case of the needy, be stronger than the legal claim. In short, as a business, a nonprofit has to see that its income (revenue and support) is sufficient to satisfy creditors and clients as claimants.

A businesslike perspective is even more clearly applicable in nonprofits which are 509(a)(2)s. For, as we saw in Chapter 4, running as a business is what they do. If it were not a contradiction in terms, they could have been described as businesses with public welfare missions. What would this mean? It means that they are organizations that have public missions, a substantial part of which can be covered by a price. Therefore, it makes sense to encourage these organizations to finance themselves principally by charging. Museums charge fees; universities, tuition; orchestras, prices.

Admittedly, this argument is less true of 509(a)(1)s, but even among these organizations, there are those better able to support themselves by prices than by gifts and donations. "Better" means that they can depend less, not rely exclusively. As we shall demonstrate in Chapter 17, short of running its blood service as a business, the Red Cross would have had to close it down a long time ago. Gifts and donations do not come close to covering costs. Can you imagine how inefficient this service would have been if it had to depend on the federal budget and bureaucracy?

Some 90 percent of the total revenues of Consumer Union publishers of the *Consumer Report* is business income from sales of that publication. Does this offend you? Now, ask yourself if Consumer Union were relying on contributions, how free would it be to confront, rate, and reject products? With what credibility? Business income has its place. It buys objectivity, continuity, growth and freedom.

Some 43 percent of the total revenue and support of the Salvation Army is from sales of its publications to its members. Sales of supplies to its members accounts for 44 percent of the revenues and support of the Girl Scouts, and 41 percent of the revenues and support of Father Flanagan's Boys Home is investment income primarily in its endowment fund.[1]

Suffice it to say that this and the next chapter are not intended to induce nonprofits to plunge willy nilly into commercial activities. It deals with a reality—earned income is a necessary ingredient for nonprofits no matter how charitable their missions. Both chapters, consistent with this entire book, are about managing costs and revenues in the context of furthering the mission of nonprofits. We begin our journey by looking at organization because managing costs and revenues may mean operating certain activities as if they were a separate business. Where do these fit in the nonprofit organization?

DEFINITION OF RELATED AND UNRELATED NONPROFIT BUSINESSES

Does it fit? A related business is one that fits integrally as part of the mission of the organization. That is, the income it generates is directly a result of the organization's conducting its community or public welfare mission. Appropriately, the income from this kind of business is not taxed and it is also categorized as public support for 509(a)(2) organizations.

An unrelated business is one that is not integrally related to the mission of the organization. Its principal purpose is to generate income. As stated in Chapter, 3 net income (profits) generated from an unrelated business is taxed. Income from an unrelated business is classified as support in 509(a)(1) organizations.

An unrelated business is a trade or business regularly conducted by a nonprofit for the purpose of making a profit. The unrelated business makes little or no substantive or programmatic contribution to the exempt mission of the organization. Its primary contribution is money. A program-related business, on the other hand, is directly and integrally related to the programmatic and substantive goals of the nonprofit. Thus, program-related business would be carried on even if it were not profitable. An unrelated business is pursued because it is profitable. Interest earned on loans by a nonprofit that has lending as its mission is related business income. It is related to the mission.

There are three keys to determining if an activity is an unrelated business. First, it is a trade or a business conducted to generate a profit. There must be a clear profit motive. It is the source, intent, and use, not the size of the profits, that matters.

Second, an unrelated business is a regular activity, not a one-time or occasional event where the event normally will occur with greater frequency. It is regular if it is conducted by the nonprofit with the same frequency as would a for-profit firm. A one-time bake sale is not an unrelated business. "Regularity," what does it mean? An example will help.

Once a year the National Collegiate Athletic Association (NCAA) holds a basketball tournament culminating in the Final Four. It arranges with a for-profit corporation to advertise in its program for the Final Four. This advertisement was ruled an unrelated business even though the Final Four is held but once a year. It is regular, it happens every year. In all sports, a tournament once a year is regular. The World Series and Super Bowl are once a year. Finally, the NCAA regularly has tournaments, one for every sport. The NCAA won its case on appeal. The judge ruled that the "duration" of the advertising was not long enough to constitute regularity and that this practice by the NCAA was not significant enough to constitute unfair competition with publications such as *Sports Illustrated*.[2]

Regularity is measured by the norm for that activity reflecting frequency and duration. Regularity does not mean everyday. It means the frequency and duration that is customary among for-profit firms in the same trade or business.

Third, an unrelated business is not substantially related to the tax-exempt mission of the nonprofit. It may raise money but is not programmatically integral or related to the tax-exempt mission. Some examples will help clarify this point.

A halfway house organized to provide room, board, therapy, and counseling for persons discharged from alcoholic treatment centers also operates a furniture shop to provide full-time employment for its residents. The profits are applied to the operating costs of the halfway house. The income from this venture is not unrelated trade or business income.

An exempt organization, organized and operated for the prevention of cruelty to animals, receives income from providing pet boarding and grooming services for the general public. This is income from an unrelated trade or business.

An exempt organization whose purpose is to provide for the welfare of young people rents rooms primarily to people under age 25. This income is not considered unrelated business income since the source of the income flow is substantially related to the purpose constituting the basis for the organization's exemption.

A hospital with exempt status operates a gift shop patronized by patients, visitors making purchases for patients, and employees and medical staff. It also operates a parking lot for patients and visitors only. Both of these activities are substantially related to the hospital's exempt purpose and do not constitute unrelated trades or businesses.

These four examples offered by the IRS illustrate the differences between a program-related business and an unrelated business. The former is an extension of or part of the tax-exempt function of the organization. The latter is not.

The same activity can be either a related or unrelated business depending on how it is handled.

A service run *exclusively* for *members* of an organization or completely provided *voluntarily* by them is a related business. But the same services provided by the same nonprofit for the public or by paid employees would be an unrelated business.

A service such as a laundry or store operated exclusively for the membership of a tax-exempt organization is not an unrelated business. The rental income to a nonprofit created by a local government to provide public facilities including a police station is not unrelated business income.[3]

3ervices only for the *convenience* of members, for example, dorms for students, are related businesses. Services by members or volunteers, the sale of donated property, trade shows that are educational, and the rental or sale of mailing labels to other nonprofits are also related businesses. The rental of a mailing list for commercial purposes has been an unrelated business, but a recent Tax Court decision, Disabled American v. Commissioner, said, at least in this case, it was to be treated as a royalty which is not taxed. This was reversed on appeal by the IRS.

EXCESS PROFITS: A DISTINCTION BETWEEN RELATED AND UNRELATED INCOME

An IRS regulation announced in the *Internal Revenue Bulletin*[4] is instructive. The case is that of a large metropolitan hospital that provides services such as data processing, food service, and purchasing services to other hospitals. The IRS rules that the earnings would be related income if all of three conditions hold: (1) the hospitals purchasing the service have a maximum capacity for inpatients of 100 persons; (2) the service, if performed by the recipient hospital, would have been a normal service for it; (3) the fee in excess of actual cost is not more than one and one-half times the average rates of interest on public debt obligations issued by the Federal Hospital Insurance Trust Fund.

If all these conditions do not hold, then the earnings are unrelated business income and taxed. This case not only shows the thin line between related and unrelated business income, but that, while an absolute dollar level of profits is not stipulated, any profit above a normal rate of return is likely to be considered unrelated business income. It implies a profit motive.

INTEGRATION OF BUSINESS OPERATIONS INTO A CONGLOMERATE STRUCTURE

Figure 11.1 shows a possible configuration of for-profit unrelated businesses and nonprofit entities in conglomerate structure of a nonprofit corporation under Section 501(c)(3). A nonprofit that is a public charity as defined by Section 509(a)(1) or (a)(2) may not only have its internal

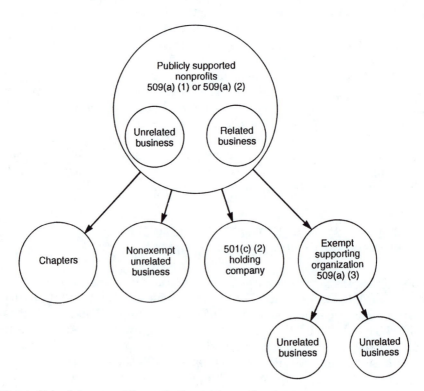

Figure 11.1   Structure of Nonprofit Corporation or Conglomerate.

departments within its corporate corpus but may also house both unrelated and program-related businesses.

In addition, the 509(a)(1) or (a)(2) may have chapters. These are not necessarily separate entities having their own tax-exempt status; rather, they may fall under the umbrella of the parent organization. See Chapter 2. The 509(a)(3) organizations have subsidiaries or corporations wholly beholden to them. Unlike chapters, these are independently chartered and tax–exempt organizations whose existence relies on their relationship with a publicly supported organization. Furthermore, it is acceptable that these 509(a)(3)s run both program-related and unrelated businesses. Picture it this way. An incorporated chapter could break off or be expelled and run programs on its own behalf. A 509(a)(3) cannot. It is beholden to its parent.

The 509(a)(1) or (a)(2) may also run an unrelated business outside of its immediate corporate corpus. For example, an organization may advertise in its journal. The advertisement could be an unrelated business, but the articles could be related to its educational mission. This is best done within the corporate structure of most nonprofits. On the other hand, the same nonprofit may be part or sole owner of an apartment building or hotel. This is best done outside the immediate corporate structure of the organization.

Note that it does not matter if the unrelated business is within the corpus of the organization or if it is a separate corporation owned or controlled by the nonprofit. In either case, it pays taxes. What does matter is that, as independent entities, a corporation outside the structure of the nonprofit shields the latter from liability, provides for separate management and labor contracts, can raise its own capital, shields the nonprofit from unwanted publicity, and provides for the participation of individuals as owners and profit makers.

Figure 11.1 also shows that the 509(a)(1) or (a)(2) may also own a holding company. This company may be exempt or nonexempt. If exempt, it merely serves as a holder of title of property consistent with the tax-exempt function of the parent organization and reports its taxes in combination with the parent. As a nonexempt organization, it may hold title to other properties and report its taxes as a separate corporation. Hence, a nonprofit could have a holding company that is also exempt hold title to all its real estate.

Holding companies are very important to nonprofits, particularly hospitals. Holding companies may be 501(c)(2)s holding real estate. But some holding companies are 509(a)(3)s, which are not holders of real estate but are financial and supporting entities. The likelihood is that the nonprofit hospital in your community is an operating unit of a holding company.

The existence of a holding company is a clue that the nonprofit organization has a far more legally complicated structure than meets the eye. This structure, as we shall more clearly see when we discuss reorganization, mergers, consolidations, and divestitures in Chapter 13, is intended to accomplish a number of objectives, from efficiency in meeting the mission of the organization to protection of the assets of the organization from lawsuits.

Viewing the complete Figure 11.1 and imagining all of the subordinate circles that could be drawn, it is obvious that an imaginative nonprofit could easily create a conglomerate. Some have. In addition to owning *The Washington Times*, the Unification Church has interests in fishing, art, textile, real estate in the U.S., the Soviet Union, China, Japan and Germany, according to Peter Maass writing in the *Washington Post* on July 22, 1990.

Now that we have juxtaposed both a for-profit and a nonprofit, it is worth remembering that the significant difference between the two is that the income and assets of a nonprofit cannot be distributed to individual owners as they can be in the for-profit sector. Accordingly, the nonprofit being one or the sole owner of the for-profit corporation gets annual dividends and also capital gains from the appreciation in the value of the stocks. But unlike other stockholders, nonprofits are given better tax treatment. Nonprofits pay no taxes on dividends or capital gains unless they are generated by property subject to debt as discussed later in this chapter or unless they are a private foundation paying taxes on investment income. Dividends and capital gains are fully taxable to individual taxpayers. Corporations can only exclude from taxation a portion of dividends they receive from other corporations.

An example: your college bookstore. The National Association of College Bookstores is a tax-exempt organization of over 3500 affiliated stores. It provides educational, research and trade shows for its members—all within the nonprofit mission and organization. It owns a for-profit subsidiary which purchases computer software, books, and calendars at a substantial discount because of the size of the orders for the member stores. It also has a computerized resume referral service and joint ventures with Publishers' Clearinghouse in the fulfillment of magazine orders. It also sells Value Packs—a collection of coupons from various vendors. What are some of the advantages of this arrangement?

1. Basically commercial and business activities are separated from educational activities, which allow managerial focus and makes the issue of unrelated business nearly moot. The subsidiary is a business and taxed accordingly.
2. The subsidiary can share its profits (through dividends) with its parents which are the college bookstores.

3. The subsidiary can share costs—paying its share of the rent.
4. The liabilities and losses of the subsidiary do not affect the nonprofit parent.
5. The for-profit can raise funds on its own; and the parent organization could even sell interests in the subsidiary or sell it off without affecting its own nonprofit status.

Organization of an Unrelated Business

In the for-profit world, businesses are organized as corporations, sole proprietorships, or partnerships. Joint ventures may be undertaken between two or more organizations on a specific project. A trust could also be created to hold and exercise the rights of ownership of those who own a business organization. Except for sole proprietorships, these organizations are adaptable to an unrelated business owned and operated by a nonprofit.

A common way of organizing an unrelated business is as a corporation. A corporation, unlike a partnership or a sole proprietorship, is an independent legal and tax entity. Liabilities for failure and error of the corporation do not extend to its owner, as with partnerships and proprietorships. Corporations have centralized management and do not have to share management decisions with all owners, as with general partnerships. Unlike proprietorships, a corporation can raise capital by issuing and selling shares of stocks in itself. A partnership may do so by selling partnership interests, but such interests rarely have as wide a market as a public corporation's stocks. Unlike a general partnership, a corporation does not have to be dissolved in the case of withdrawal of an owner. It has a perpetual life of its own, and ownership can be easily transferred from one person to another. A corporation is easier and safer than other forms of business organizations. Most importantly, even if the nonprofit organized its business as a partnership, it would be taxed as a corporation.

A nonprofit may choose to be a minority, majority, or even sole owner of a for-profit corporation. Its minority ownership may be significantly small or significantly large, but a critical concept of ownership is control. A nonprofit is said to be the controlling owner of a for-profit corporation if it owns at least 80 percent of its voting stocks and 80 percent of all other stocks. How a nonprofit is treated for tax purposes depends not on whether it is a minority or a majority stockholder but on whether it is the controlling organization. In the case of nonstock corporations, which nonprofits are, control means controlling 80 percent or more of the board of directors or trustees.

The way the unrelated business is treated depends on the form of business organization. If it is a corporation or partnership, it will face the same tax rate as other corporations. It will also be subject to a minimum tax.

BENEFITS, CONSEQUENCES, AND OPPORTUNITIES OF UNRELATED BUSINESSES

Obviously, the single most important reason for running an unrelated business is because it is profitable and fits. The income from these enterprises not only finances the activities of the nonprofit but may also satisfy the requirement of demonstrating public support. The reader should recall our earlier discussion in Chapter 4 of the role of unrelated business in defining support and in determining whether or not a nonprofit can demonstrate that it is publicly supported.

Yet another perspective is worth noting. Let's go back to the principles in Chapter 4. Nonprofit A, which receives $100,000 in investment income, $40,000 from a community chest, $50,000 from Beverly, $10,000 from Audrey, and $1,000 from Anhela would fail the one-third support test. Now, assume that it had an unrelated business with a net income of $400,000. Now, its total support is $601,000. One-third of this is $200,333. Each individual donor's contribution is not valued at more than 2 percent of the total support, or $40,066. This means that instead of being valued at $4020 Audrey's contribution is now valued at its full $10,000 and Beverly at $40,060. Now add the contributions of the community chest, $40,000, Beverly at $40,066, Audrey at $10,000, and Clive at $1000. The sum is $91,000 and the organization fails the one-third test and passes the 10 percent test as before. However, there is a subtle difference. Since each individual's contribution can receive a higher true value closer to the actual contribution made by the donor, the organization may be able to pursue a strategy concentrated more toward larger contributions than it could otherwise have done and still demonstrate public support.

Another benefit of an unrelated business other than support is that it enables the organization to carry out some of its programs by subsidizing them. The advertising in a magazine published by a nonprofit for its members subsidizes the magazine. The advertising may be an unrelated business if it is unrelated to the mission of the organization. A pharmacy catering to the general public but located in a hospital is an unrelated business, although without the pharmacy the hospital could not provide its services as well. Tours unrelated to the tax-exempt mission of the organization that are conducted by a nonprofit for its members and others are unrelated businesses, but they help to maintain contact and cohesion and provide a basis for future fund raising.

An unrelated business can also extend the social involvement of a nonprofit while making a profit. An unrelated business corporation can make tax deductible charitable contributions to tax-exempt organizations other than its parents. Similar transfers to its parents are considered dividends. Therefore, they are not deductible by the corporation and not taxable to the charity.

An unrelated business can also be used to hire disadvantaged workers and receive a tax credit for doing so, thereby reducing the tax liability of the unrelated business. The credit also means that the full wages of the worker are not paid by the business but shared with the federal government. They also qualify for a credit for improving access for disabled persons.

Consequences of Unrelated Businesses

Related business profits are not taxed, but unrelated business profits are. For 509(a)(1) organizations, unrelated businesses are considered to be support, whereas related businesses are not. For 509(a)(2) organizations, unrelated business has a limit to the extent to which it is included in support, while unrelated business income is generally included fully. Unrelated businesses take the nonprofit beyond its tax-exempt purpose; related businesses by definition do not.

A nonprofit may simultaneously run related and unrelated businesses. The accounting must be kept separate and time of employees or use of facilities must be properly allocated if they are shared by both types of businesses. The nonprofit may operate several unrelated businesses. The tax is imposed on the net profit of the combined unrelated business income of the organization. The organization cannot subtract from the net income or profit of an unrelated business those losses it incurred in a business in which there was no intent to make a profit.[5]

Thus, the West Virginia State Medical Association and the North Ridge Country Club were stopped from subtracting losses of one business from that of another.[6] In each case, the court ruled that only one of these businesses was operated with a profit motive. An unrelated business must have a profit motive, be regular, and be substantively unrelated to the mission of the organization. The absence of any one of the three means the business is not unrelated.

Benign Origins of Unrelated Businesses

The entry into unrelated business is rarely a deliberate attempt to compete with for-profit firms. Sometimes it is purely defensive to protect one's space or market. See the following insert. Sometimes it is to capture some of the financial benefits from one's large and risky investments and

On a smaller though significant scale, however, development of the District's commercial center and the rebuilding of the old burned-out corridors have been shaped by nonprofit entrepreneurs, primarily churches and institutions of higher education. Driven by different motives, these groups have contributed substantially, nevertheless, to the economic growth of the District.

George Washington University's role as a real estate developer is a prime example. Frequently referred to pejoratively as "Real Estate U," the university has become a developer and owner of commercial real estate properties over the past 17 years. Although not considered a major competitor of for-profit commercial real estate developers, the university, nonetheless, has assumed a prominent role in the development of prime office space bordering its campus in Foggy Bottom.

Although sensitive to criticism of its acquisition and development of property for nonacademic purposes, GWU continues to add to its land bank. Unlike other major developers who are driven by the profit motive, the university, according to officials, is guided by a desire to maintain the integrity of its urban campus.

In the early 1950s, "it became apparent [to university officials] that people had started to build west of 16th Street and that they would move west to Rock Creek Park and wash away property in their path," said Charles E. Diehl, GWU's vice president and treasurer.

The university "started off with 2,000 to 4,000 square feet, and now we have about 4 million square feet of land" in 19 blocks, Diehl noted.

This massive development program, he added, has enabled the university to achieve many of its academic goals. "One building builds another. Since 1968, we have built 2.5 million square feet of academic space."

Much of the academic space was built with federal funds as well as the money that GWU has made as a developer. In addition to buying buildings, aggressive land acquisition and development has enabled GWU to provide resources for its on-campus constituency and to play a significant role in the economic growth of the District.

The university paid $2.8 million in real estate taxes last year on five commercial buildings with net rentable space of 1.7 million square feet.

"We were able to get land off the back of the university and put it in use and create a resource for the city in taxes," Diehl said.

Equally important, he added, the transactions "don't penalize the university's constituency. We don't have to ask students coming here to pay for that land."

Neither does the university want to be compared with Robin Hood, he added, by charging affluent patients in its hospital exorbitant fees to compensate for the inability of the poor to pay full medical expenses.

"We put out pretty close to $10 million a year in uncompensated medical expenses, and only through our real estate assets can we afford to do that," Diehl said.

Although its role in a major downtown office project is not as extensive as that of George Washington University, one of the District's oldest and most prominent black churches is a limited partner with a major developer. In a joint venture headed by Boston Properties, Metropolitan AME Church will own 5 percent of 1615 M St. NW when the project is completed.

Developers of the $30 million project, which is being built on District-owned land, agreed to restore the Sumner School building as a museum and archival center for the school system.

Source: Rudolph A. Pyatt, Jr., "Nonprofit Groups Join Building Boom," *Washington Post,* April 29, 1985, pp. 32–33. Reprinted by permission.

to maintain property rights and control; i.e., universities licensing the products of research. It may also be the result of trying to cover large fixed and overhead costs.

The insert that follows shows 80 auxiliary services operated by universities and colleges throughout the country. They are not all carried out by the same university. Many of the seemingly outlandish examples may be related businesses. Some may be an integral part of the curriculum, such as a bowling alley in a physical education curriculum. A bowling alley may be operated for the convenience of students and staff in a community where an alternative is not readily accessible. They may be open at noncompeting hours of the day. A business run for the convenience of members or part of a curriculum (the mission) is classified as related.

Evidently, (1) there is a thin line between a related and unrelated business and the difference is not in the name but in the relevance, frequency, and motive, and (2) frequently unrelated business ventures can arise from an attempt to extend and serve the mission although the legal or tax judgment is that the relevance is not strong enough to be considered integrally related. Here is an example: the Seventh Day Adventist's, Living Faith, Inc., operates a health food business that is consistent with the doctrines of the religion. The Tax Court ruled that this was a commercial activity, that the connection with religion was not strong enough.[7] Consequently, they must pay unrelated business income tax on the profits. Should they stop? Obviously not.

An unrelated business can arise from a tax-exempt organization using its position, process, goodwill, or reputation to make money in a way that is not directly related to its tax-exempt mission. The IRS gives the examples of exploiting a mission.

An exempt scientific organization enjoys an excellent reputation in the field of biological research. It exploits this reputation regularly by selling endorsements of various items of laboratory equipment to manufacturers. The endorsement of laboratory equipment does not contribute importantly to the accomplishment of any purpose for which exemption

The Scope of Auxiliary Services

Eighty Operational Categories

1. Food Service, Contracted	41. Transportation, Ground Service
2. Food Service, Residence, Self-Op	42. Bus Service
3. Food Service, Cash, Self-Op	43. Motor Pools
4. Cookie Stand	44. Travel Service/Agency
5. Ice Cream Shop	45. Van Rentals
6. Candy Shop	46. Parking Garages, Pay
7. Bakery, Retail Store	47. Parking Lots, Pay
8. Bakery, Production	48. Recreation, Indoor
9. Vending, Contracted	49. Recreation, Outdoor
10. Vending, Self-Op	50. Recreation, Camps
11. Amusement Games, Contracted	51. Bowling
12. Amusement Games, Self-Op	52. Golf Courses
13. Beer Clubs	53. Billiards
14. Night Clubs or Bars (Full Alcohol)	54. Swim Centers
15. Student Unions/Campus Centers	55. Skating Rinks, Ice
16. Faculty Clubs	56. Skating Rinks, Roller
17. Faculty Dining	57. Arenas
18. Laundry, Contracted	58. Bike shop, Sales/Rentals
19. Laundry, Self-Op	59. Sporting Goods Store
20. Laundry Machines, Coin-Op	60. Photo Shops
21. Bookstores, Self-Op	61. Gift Shops
22. Bookstores, Contracted	62. Concessions, Athletic
23. News-Stands	63. Concessions, Other
24. Press, University/College	64. Ski Lodge Operation
25. Print Shops	65. Telecommunications
26. Duplicating Service	66. Computers, Coin-Op
27. Word Processing	67. Computers in Dormitories
28. Copy Machines, Coin-Op	68. Computers, Rentals
29. Typing Service	69. Microcomputers, Food Service
30. Typewriters, Coin-Op	70. Microcomputers, Bookstores
31. Office Machines Repair Service	71. Microcomputers, Housing
32. Housing, Student	72. Radio Station
33. Housing, Faculty	73. TV Station
34. Housing, Married Students	74. Furniture Repair Service
35. Post Office	75. Insurance, Student
36. Mailing Service	76. Central Stores
37. Banks	77. Day Care Centers
38. Check Cashing Service	78. Conferences, Summer
39. Airports	79. Conference Centers
40. Transportation, Air Service	80. Real Estate

Source: Journal of National Association of College Auxiliary Services, June 1987, p. 33. Reprinted by permission of the Association.

is granted to the organization. Accordingly, the income from the sale of endorsements is gross income from an unrelated business.

An unrelated business can arise from wisely trying to cover costs while carrying out a charitable mission. This is evidenced by the opportunity nonprofits have to make dual use of plant and equipment. The same plant or equipment that it uses for conducting its tax-exempt mission can also be used to produce unrelated business income rather than to sit idle, generating costs but no revenues. The university stadium may be used for professional football. When this is done, the nonprofit must separate the two types of income and expenses for reporting purposes. The use of university facilities for professional sports is commonplace. The revenues from these leases help to cover fixed costs.

Advertising and Newsletters

Still another example common to nonprofits is the use of their publications to generate income. This can be done by selling advertising space. The income from the advertising can be unrelated income. But the ads help advertisers to speak to an audience. Let's hear the U.S. Supreme Court.

> There is no merit to the Government's argument that Congress and the Treasury intended to establish a blanket rule requiring the taxation of income from all commercial advertising by tax-exempt professional journals without a specific analysis of the circumstances. There is no support for such a rule in the regulations or in the legislative history of the Internal Revenue Code.*

Furthermore, the publication's income and costs are divided into portions so that, if the readership portion (its tax-exempt purpose) is operating at a loss, all additional costs above that loss level may be deducted from the advertising portion (its unrelated business) as long as such a deduction does not result in the unrelated business showing a loss for tax purposes. In short, the cost of serving the readership may provide a tax deduction to the unrelated business.[8]

There are several variations to this example. The basic rule is that if an unrelated business exploits the activities of a related business the losses from the latter may be deducted from the former if such a deduction does not lead the unrelated business to report a loss. In short, the IRS is willing to reduce the taxes of the unrelated business to the extent that such reduction has a legitimate economic basis.

Accordingly, the tax-exempt mission is subsidized by the unrelated business, and the tax liability of the latter is reduced by the losses of the former.

* Source: Supreme Court of the United States, *United States* vs. *American College of Physicians*, No. 84-1737, April 22, 1986, p. 2.

TAX TREATMENT OF UNRELATED BUSINESS INCOME

Royalties, rents, interests, dividends, and annuities, all passive income, are generally not considered unrelated business incomes and therefore are not taxed. But there are exceptions to this rule.

Dividends are not taxed unless they are received from property subject to debt. This means that a rich source of income for nonprofits is dividends from controlled corporations or profit-making subsidiaries. Certain guidelines may help in setting up these subsidiaries so that the dividends from them will not be taxable to the nonprofit. These guidelines are as follows:

1. While the parent (nonprofit organization) may appoint the board of the subsidiary for-profit corporation, the majority of the members of the board of directors, the employees, and the officers of the for-profit must not be related to or be agents of the nonprofit organization.
2. The parent organization must not participate in the daily activities of the for-profit firm.
3. Any business transaction between the subsidiary and the parent nonprofit organization must conform to strict business principles similar to those governing two organizations that are independent of each other. Transactions must be at arms' length.
4. The subsidiary must be organized for the purpose of conducting a legitimate business that is truly unrelated to the business of the nonprofit organization. Its purpose must be to make a profit through a trade or business unrelated to the mission of the nonprofit parent.

Under the above conditions, expressed in the General Counsel Memorandum 39326, the dividends received by the nonprofit from its for-profit subsidiary are received tax free. The for-profit subsidiary, however, is subject to all taxes of normal corporations.

Interest earnings, royalties, and rents are taxable to the nonprofit if they are payments from an organization that the nonprofit controls, whether or not the organization is itself tax exempt or a for-profit firm. These revenues, like dividends, are also taxable if they are derived from a debt-financed property.

Capital gains from selling property are not subject to tax as unrelated business income unless the property was part of an inventory, acquired by debt, or is sold as an ordinary practice in a trade or business. This again puts a nonprofit corporation in a superior position to most owners of property, including stocks.

The use of property that is contiguous to other property owned by a tax-exempt organization even for an unrelated business purpose may escape being treated as unrelated business if there is a clear intent to use that property within the subsequent ten years for a tax-exempt purpose. The IRS must be convinced of this intent every five years. Churches have fifteen years to use the property to generate income without being taxed.

Some types of activities receive favorable treatment. Income from bingo is not taxed if for-profit firms within the local jurisdiction are barred from holding bingo games to make a profit. If they are permitted, then the nonprofit must pay a tax. The idea is to avoid placing the for-profit firm at a disadvantage.

Speaking of bingo, the city of Spokane, Washington taxed a local chapter of the American Red Cross for income derived from bingo, pull-tab, and punch board games. The unrelated business income tax was overruled by the 9th Circuit Court arguing that the Red Cross, a congressionally chartered nonprofit, was exempt because it was an instrumentality of the federal government.[9]

Income derived by agricultural groups from growing and selling crops contiguously to a retirement home is specifically excluded as unrelated business income if the income provides less than 75 percent of the cost of running the retirement home. Income earned by religious organizations using a federal license is excluded if that income is used for charitable purposes and the prices charged are neither significantly higher nor lower than commercial prices. Research conducted for the U.S. government, its instrumentalities or agencies, or any other level of domestic government is not considered an unrelated business. Furthermore, fundamental research is not an unrelated business, and organizations such as hospitals and educational institutions are not subject to unrelated business tax on the income derived from research whether it be fundamental or applied.[10]

Property Subject to Debt

Certain properties owned by a nonprofit may be subject to acquisition indebtedness. All earnings derived from such properties are considered unrelated income and subject to tax. Acquisition debt is any debt incurred (1) to acquire or improve a property, (2) in anticipation of acquisition or improvement, or (3) because of the acquisition or improvement. For example, if a nonprofit incurred a debt to acquire or improve a property, that is an acquisition debt. Or, if after acquiring a property that might be free of debt the nonprofit enters into debt directly linked to its decision to purchase the property, that is also acquisition indebtedness. In all these cases, the property is said to be debt financed.

Again, the consequence of acquisition indebtedness is that income derived from the property in interest, rent, royalty, dividends, or capital appreciation is, with some exceptions, unrelated business income and taxed. It does not matter if the income is recurrent or nonrecurrent. If during the taxable year the property is subject to debt, all income that it yields during that year is unrelated business income.

There are some modifications to this seemingly harsh rule. One very important one is that property obtained upon death (bequest and devise) is not considered subject to debt for ten years after its acquisition if (1) the donor held the property for at least five years, (2) the debt is at least five years old, and (3) the nonprofit did not agree to be responsible for the debt.

Another exception to the general rule of debt-financed property occurs when the entire property (at least 85 percent) is used for a tax-exempt purpose by the organization itself or by an organization that it controls. In addition, there is a ten-year grace period with mortgages unless the nonprofit, having received real estate from a donor, assumes the mortgage payment. If it does, it is taxed under the debt-financed rule.

Finally, rents from personal property, earnings from thrift shops, and property used in research are not considered debt-financed property and, therefore, are not subject to tax as unrelated business income. Concern should center on rents and proceeds from the sale of real estate, income and proceeds from the ownership and sale of securities, and proceeds from the sale of personal property (as opposed to rents from such property).

The Complexity of Rental Income

Income from renting real estate shows how easy it is for a nonprofit to operate an unrelated business even when it does not intend to do so. Seek advice. It should also alert nonprofit managers to the questions that should be raised before accepting real estate as a gift. Here are some complexities. A simplified view is given at the end of the chapter.

What is rent? If a nonprofit owns a parking lot and operates it, this is rent. If it leases it, then the income is not rent from real property.[11] The IRS has to know the facts and circumstances. It has not had an easy time defining rent.[12]

As stated earlier, generally income from the rental of real estate is not unrelated income. However, if the rental is from a property subject to acquisition indebtedness, then all rental income derived from the property could be unrelated business income after 10 years and immediately if the nonprofit assumes the debt.

If the rental income is from a related organization carrying out its exempt mission, it is not treated as debt financed even if the property is acquired by debt. Yet the income can be taxed if the organization is **controlled** by the nonprofit because, in general, all rents from a **controlled** organizauon are taxed regardless of whether or not the organization that pays it is tax exempt or whether it is subject to debt.

Rental from real estate is also subject to unrelated business income tax if the use of the space is coupled with a service, such as room service in a hotel. Furthermore, if the rental income is combined with a rental fee for the use of personal property such as equipment, the entire income would be subject to tax if the personal property (equipment and machinery) part of the rental exceeds 50 percent of the total. If the personal property part is less than 10 percent of the total, the entire rental is exempt. If it is 10 percent, then only this personal property portion is taxed.

If the rental is from an organization that is **controlled** by the nonprofit, the rental income is unrelated business income regardless of whether the organization that pays is a for-profit or a nonprofit.

If the space is used for both tax-exempt as well as for-profit activities, the amount of the rental must be allocated between the two uses and taxes paid on the part that is for-profit in origin.

If the rentals are from a tax-exempt-related organization and are used for research or for a thrift shop, it is not treated as debt financed and not subject to unrelated business tax under the debt-finance rules. However, it could be considered unrelated business income if the organization paying is controlled by the nonprofit landlord.

If the parent organization uses a debt-financed property (in which case it does not pay rent to itself) exclusively for research or thrift shop, income derived from the use of that property is not necessarily unrelated business income.

If the property was obtained through a bequest or devise and was held by the donor for at least five years, and the debt is at least five years old and the nonprofit does not agree to assume it, then it is not immediately treated as unrelated business income. There is a ten-year grace period.

Rent becomes unrelated business income if it is tied to profits. It can be a fixed percentage of sales or receipts, but not of the profits of the occupant.

Questions to Ask before Renting

There are infinite combinations of these confounding circumstances we have just described. Some of the key questions that must be raised are as follows: Is it debt financed? Is it to be leased along with personal property and, if so, what will be the percentage of the total rental that could be deemed to be derived from the real estate portion of the package? Are the tenants controlled by the nonprofit? Is the rent related to the profits of the tenants? For what purpose is the space being used? How much of the total space is being rented? All of these questions have been answered in this chapter.

SOURCES OF UNRELATED BUSINESS INCOME: A SIMPLIFIED VIEW

There are three main sources of unrelated business income: (1) unrelated business activities, (2) debt-acquired property, and (3) controlled organizations. Some general rules follow.

1. All profits from unrelated business activities are taxable to the non-profit unless they are passive income such as rents, dividends, interest, royalties, and annuities. Profits from unrelated sales, for example, are taxed.

2. Profits from debt-financed properties are usually taxed as unrelated business income unless they are already being taxed under source 1 or 2 or arise from a tax-exempt mission or fall into an exception. (See the Appendix.)

3. All rents, interests, royalties, annuities, and other payments (excluding dividends) to the controlling organization from its subordinates are taxed regardless of whether the subordinate is tax exempt or not.

TEN QUESTIONS TO JUDGE IF BUSINESS WILL BE UNRELATED

Based upon the preceding discussion, we offer ten questions which should be asked in order to get an inkling if an activity is at risk of being declared unrelated business. If the answer is other than the preferred, as indicated next to each question, reread this chapter to see if you are an exception and check it out with a competent attorney and accountant. Remember that the final judgment is based upon the facts and circumstances in each case. Thus, the individual exceptions in the long list shown in the appendix to this chapter get their meaning from the way the activity is actually conducted and by the specific mission of the organization in question. After all, unrelated means unconnected to the carrying out of the organization's mission.

1. If this project had *no* profit expectations or possibilities would you have undertaken it purely and legitimately as a part of your mission? Preferred answer, yes.

2. Do you know of any examples of an organization similar to yours in mission that is conducting that activity as part of its mission? Preferred answer, yes—especially if the organizations can defend the activity on the basis of a Revenue Ruling from the IRS.
3. Can a reasonable person without stretching his or her imagination see the connection between the activity and your mission? Preferred answer, yes.
4. If this activity is being conducted by a local commercial firm or could easily be conducted profitably by one, does yours differ in size, scope, frequency, market, clients, price, and character? Preferred answer, yes.
5. Does the activity involve expending or using the organization's assets, name, goodwill, employees, or space to help a for-profit firm make a profit even if the activity serves your organization? Preferred answer, no.
6. Do you promote or *share* in the profits of a for-profit venture as opposed to recovering costs and charging a flat fee? Preferred answer, no.
7. Is the activity carried on by paid employees? Preferred answer, no.
8. Is the activity one in which persons *other* than those vital to your mission; i.e., employees, volunteers, students, patients, the needy, are beneficiaries? Preferred answer, no.
9. Does the income (other than dividends) flow from a controlled group as defined? Preferred answer, no.
10. Does the income flow from an activity or property subject to debt? Preferred answer, no.

THE FEDERAL TAX

Whenever an exempt nonprofit has **gross** unrelated business income of $1000 or more, it must file an income tax form. While net income or profits determine the tax liability, gross income determines whether or not filing is mandated. Failure to file, to file on time, or to file quarterly estimated income tax may draw penalties and interest charges unless the failure was due to reasonable causes. The tax form (Form 990-T) must be signed by hand by the president, trustee, treasurer, vice president, or some other officer designated by the organization.

If it has more than one unrelated business, even if they are separate for-profit corporations, it may consolidate all into one. This permits the organization to reduce the taxable income of one business by the losses from the others. For-profit corporations can also do this.

If the organization is a corporation, it is taxed at the corporate rates

TABLE 11-1   Tax Rate Schedule for Corporations (Section 11 of the Internal Revenue Code)

If the amount on line 5, page 1 is:		Enter on line 7, page 1:
Over—	but not over—	
0	$50,000	15% of the amount over $0
$50,000	75,000	$7,500 plus 25% of the amount over $50,000
75,000	100,000	$13,750 plus 34% of the amount over $75,000
100,000	335,000	$22,250 plus 39% of the amount over $100,000
335,000	—	34% of the amount on line 5

TABLE 11-2   Tax Rate Schedule for Trusts (Section 1(e) of the Internal Revenue Code)

If the amount on line 5, page 1 is:	Enter on line 8, page 1:
Not over $5,200	15% of the amount over $0
Over $5,200 but not over $13,500	$780, plus 28% of the amount over $5,200
Over $13,500 but not over $27,020	$3,104, plus 33% of the amount over $13,500
Over $27,020	28% of the amount on line 5

shown in Table 11-1 and if a trust, it is taxed at the rates shown in Table 11-2.

Calculating Unrelated Business Income

Taxable net income from the sale of services or products is calculated, as per for-profit corporations.
Gross Sales
  Minus discounts and returns
  Minus cost of goods sold
  Minus general and administrative expenses
  Minus operating expenses
Plus net income from investments
Plus net income from other sources; i.e., capital gains
Total Net Income (taxable income)
Multiplied by tax rate (stepwise as shown in tax table)
Tax Liability before credits
  Minus credits (those available to all corporations)
Unrelated business income tax to be paid by nonprofit.

Taxable Income

What must be included in taxable income? Let's begin with the deductions for business expenses. A nonprofit gets a $1000 deduction called a "specific deduction." But only one specific deduction can be taken no matter how many unrelated businesses the organization runs. However, a religious association; i.e. a diocese, synod, district, and the like, can take one $1000 specific deduction for each of its churches which is not separately incorporated. Those churches that are separately incorporated must file their own tax form and take their own specific deduction.

For all officers and trustees who are paid by the nonprofit and who also work for the unrelated business, their names, the amount of time spent on the unrelated business, and their compensation must be reported to justify their deduction as part of the business expense of the unrelated business. Otherwise, the business could end up subsidizing the nonprofit and also taking a deduction for an expense it did not legally incur.

Now, what is taxable? Unlike a for-profit corporation, a nonprofit, other than a private foundation, does not pay taxes on its investment income. However, there are some important exceptions. Such gains are taxable when they are debt-financed. Thus, capital gains resulting from the sale of a debt financed stock is taxable if the debt was outstanding during the 12 months prior to the sale. Gains from debt-financed properties, in general, are taxable.

Among "other income sources" are some specific treatments. Advertising is treated in the following manner—assuming that it is declared unrelated business income:

CALCULATING INCOME FROM ADVERTISING

Gross advertising income
Deduct all costs **directly** associated with advertising; i.e., salesperson's salary and expenses
Net income from **advertising.**
If this amount is zero, there is no taxable income from advertising. If it is negative, report a loss. However, if it is positive, there is a gain which can possibly be reduced by the next steps.
Gross income from **circulation**; i.e., magazine revenues
Deduct readership costs; i.e., production of articles
Net income from **readership**
If this amount is negative, readership costs exceeding circulation income, then this negative amount can be deducted from the positive net income from advertising; thus reducing the amount that is taxable. This reduction can take place as long as it does not create a net loss.

If an organization has more than one periodical, it may report on a consolidated basis, thereby offsetting the gains of one with losses from the others. This offset is only permitted if all of the periodicals to be consolidated are published with the purpose of making a profit. This is deemed to be the case when gross advertising income is at least 25 percent of the readership costs. If the organization elects to consolidate these profit-oriented periodicals it must include all such profit-oriented periodicals it runs.

Surtax

Those nonprofits with unrelated income tax liability of at least $100,000 must pay an additional 5 percent surtax.

Sharing the Taxes

A nonprofit which operates several for-profit corporations may allot the total tax bill, including the surtax, from its consolidated tax calculations to the various members of the controlled group. To understand this, go back to the tax rates. Notice that they are in brackets. Naturally, it is better to be in the 15 percent bracket. Thus, the regulations limit the group to one $25,000 and one $50,000 bracket use. Assume, for example, that there are two corporations in the controlled group. It could be decided that they would apportion equally. Thus, each would have their first $12,500 (half of $25,000) taxed in the $25,000 bracket and each would have $25,000 (one half of $50,000) taxed in the $50,000 bracket.

It can divide this up by prior signed arrangement among the members of the controlled group. Thus, the group could reduce its taxes by having the one with the largest taxable income taking the entire bracket; i.e., using up the privilege of the group to have its first $50,000 taxed at 15 percent.

SUMMARY AND CONCLUSIONS

This chapter has contrasted program-related and unrelated businesses and showed how they both fit into the corporate structure of a nonprofit to make it a virtual conglomerate. Business operation is important to many nonprofits, even as they carry on their missions. This chapter discusses the impact of both related and unrelated businesses on the nonprofit, how they can be integrated into the corporate structure, and how they develop. It also discussed rental income.

NOTES

1. These numbers are calculated from the 1989 annual reports of these organizations.
2. *NCAA* v. *Commissioner*, no. 89, 9005 (Tenth Circuit 9/20/90).
3. Revenue Letter 9046039.
4. April 28, 1986, No. 1986-17, page 9.
5. "Not-for-profit" does not necessarily imply a charitable or related business, just that there is no motive for a profit, for example, a hobby.
6. *West Virginia State Medical Association* v. *Commissioner*, T.C. 3746-86, 9/20/88, and *North Ridge Country Club* v. *Commissioner*, T.C. 20651-82, 9/15/87.
7. *Living Faith* v. *Commissioner*, T.C. Memo 1990-484.
8. There are special rules governing advertising, and the manager may wish to go over them more carefully than is possible here. For example, circulation costs and revenues must be distinguished from advertising costs and revenues, membership fees must be allocated, and so on.
9. *U.S.* v. *City of Spokane*, No. 90-35118 (9th Circuit, Oct. 31, 1990).
10. Fundamental research is distinguished from applied or commercial research. The latter is done for assisting others to be profitable, and the results need not be published within a reasonable time.
11. GCM 39825.
12. TAM 8445005, GCM 39825 and Sec. 1.512 (b)-1(c)(5) of the Code.

SUGGESTED READINGS

BRYCE, HERRINGTON J. "Joint Ventures: Teaming Up with For-Profits, *Nonprofit World,* Vol 7., No. 1, January/February 1989, pp. 11-13.

DISTELHORST, GARIS, "When Associations Become Entrepreneurs," *Association Management,* February 1985, pp. 109-11.

Internal Revenue Service, U.S. Department of Treasury, *Tax on Unrelated Business Income of Tax Exempt Organizations,* Publication 598, Revised November 1987.

Appendix 11.1 Exclusions to Unrelated Business

Exclusion Codes

General Exceptions

01—Income from an activity that is not regularly carried on (section 512(a)(1))

02—Income from an activity in which labor is a material income-producing factor and substantially all (at least 85%) of the work is performed with unpaid labor (section 513(a)(1))

03—Section 501(c)(3) organization—Income from an activity carried on primarily for the convenience of the organization's members, students, patients, visitors, officers, or employees (hospital parking lot or museum cafeteria, for example) (section 513(a)(2))

04—Section 501(c)(4) local association of employees organized before 5/27/69—Income from the sale of work-related clothes or equipment and items normally sold through vending machines; food dispensing facilities; or snack bars for the convenience of association members at their usual places of employment (section 513(a)(2))

05—Income from the sale of merchandise, substantially all of which (at least 85%) was donated to the organization (section 513(a)(3))

charitable contributions by a section 501(c)(3) organization; by a war veterans' organization; or an auxiliary unit or society of, or trust or foundation for, a war veterans' post or organization (section 513(h))

Modifications and Exclusions

14—Dividends, interest, or payments with respect to securities loans, and annuities excluded by section 512(b)(1)

15—Royalty income excluded by section 512(b)(2)

16—Real property rental income that does not depend on the income or profits derived by the person leasing the property and is excluded by section 512(b)(3)

17—Rent from personal property leased with real property and incidental (10% or less) in relation to the combined income from the real and personal property (section 512(b)(3))

18—Proceeds from the sale of investments and other non-inventory property (capital gains excluded by section 512(b)(5))

Social Clubs and VEBAs

25—Section 501(c)(7), (9), (17), or (20) organization—Non-exempt function income set aside for a charitable, etc., purpose specified in section 170(c)(4) (section 512(a)(3)(B)(i))

26—Section 501(c)(7), (9), (17), or (20) organization—Proceeds from the sale of exempt function property that was or will be timely reinvested in similar property (section 512(a)(3)(D))

27—Section 501(c)(9), (17), or (20) organization—Non-exempt function income set aside for the payment of life, sick, accident, or other benefits (section 512(a)(3)(B)(ii))

Veterans' Organizations

28—Section 501(c)(19) organization—Payments for life, sick, accident, or health insurance for members or their dependents that are set aside for the payment of such insurance benefits or for a charitable, etc., purpose specified in section 170(c)(4) (section 512(a)(4))

29—Section 501(c)(19) organization—Income from an insurance set-aside (see code 28 above) that is set aside for

Specific Exceptions

06—Section 501(c)(3), (4), or (5) organization conducting an agricultural or educational fair or exposition—Qualified public entertainment activity income (section 513(d)(2))

07—Section 501(c)(3), (4), (5), or (6) organization—Qualified convention and trade show activity income (section 513(d)(3))

08—Income from hospital services described in section 513(e)

09—Income from noncommercial bingo games that do not violate state or local law (section 513(f))

10—Income from games of chance conducted by an organization in North Dakota (section 311 of the Deficit Reduction Act of 1984, as amended)

11—Section 501(c)(12) organization—Qualified pole rental income (section 513(g))

12—Income from the distribution of low-cost articles in connection with the solicitation of charitable contributions (section 513(h))

13—Income from the exchange or rental of membership or donor list with an organization eligible to receive

19—Income (gains) from the lapse or termination of options to buy or sell securities (section 512(b)(5))

20—Income from research for the United States; its agencies or instrumentalities; or any state or political subdivision (section 512(b)(7))

21—Income from research conducted by a college, university, or hospital (section 512(b)(8))

22—Income from research conducted by an organization whose primary activity is conducting fundamental research, the results of which are freely available to the general public (section 512(b)(9))

23—Income from services provided under license issued by a federal regulatory agency and conducted by a religious order or school operated by a religious order, but only if the trade or business has been carried on by the organization since before May 27, 1959 (section 512(b)(15))

Foreign Organizations

24—Foreign organizations only—Income from a trade or business NOT conducted in the United States and NOT derived from United States sources (patrons)(section 512(a)(2))

payment of insurance benefits or for a charitable, etc., purpose specified in section 170(c)(4) (Regs. 1.512(a)—4(b)(2))

Debt-financed Income

30—Income exempt from debt-financed (section 514) provisions because at least 85% of the use of the property is for the organization's exempt purposes (**Note:** *This code is only for income from the 15% or less non-exempt purpose use.*) (section 514(b)(1)(A))

31—Gross income from mortgaged property used in research activities described in section 512(b)(7), (8), or (9) (section 514(b)(1)(C))

32—Gross income from mortgaged property used in any activity described in section 513(a)(1), (2), or (3) (section 514(b)(1)(D))

33—Income from mortgaged property (neighborhood land) acquired for exempt purpose use within ten years (section 514(b)(3))

34—Income from mortgaged property acquired by bequest or devise (applies to income received within ten years from the date of acquisition) (section 514(c)(2)(B))

Appendix 11.1 Exclusions to Unrelated Business (continued)

Exclusion Codes

35—Income from mortgaged property acquired by gift where the mortgage was placed on the property more than five years previously and the property was held by the donor for more than five years (applies to income received within ten years from the date of gift (section 514(c)(2)(B))

36—Income from property received in return for the obligation to pay an annuity described in section 514(c)(5)

37—Income from mortgaged property that provides housing to low and moderate income persons, to the extent the mortgage is insured by the Federal Housing Administration (section 514(c)(6) (**Note:** In many cases, this would be exempt function income reportable in column(e). It would not be so in the case of a section 501(c)(5) or (6) organization, for example, that acquired the housing as an investment or as a charitable activity.)

38—Income from mortgaged real property owned by: a school described in section 170(b)(1)(A)(ii); a section 509(a)(3) affiliated support organization of such a school; a section 501(c)(25) organization, or by a partnership in which any of the above organizations owns an interest if the requirements of section 514(c)(9)(B)(vi) are met (section 514(c)(9).

Special Rules

39—Section 501(c)(5) organization—Farm income used to finance the operation and maintenance of a retirement home, hospital, or similar facility operated by the organization for its members on property adjacent to the farm land (section 1951(b)(8)(B) of Public Law 94-455)

Trade or Business

40—Gross income from an unrelated activity that is regularly carried on but, in light of continuous losses sustained over a number of tax periods, cannot be regarded as being conducted with the motive to make a profit (not a trade or business).

Source: U.S. Government Printing Office: Form 990 1990 0-245-133

Chapter **12**

The Suitability of Business Income

This chapter deals with questions that management should ask when contemplating a new related or unrelated business or the continuation of an old one. Should the nonprofit invest in itself? The reader may wish to review the section of Chapter 11 dealing with business revenues and the discussion of eligibility for being a public charity in Chapter 4.

Reference to business is not an invitation to disregard the mission. It is the reality. Most 509(a)(2)s including all museums, universities, orchestras and a good number of (a)(1)s are basically business clones both in fact and in law which recognizes the insufficiency of public support in the form of gifts and contributions. This explains the 10 percent or 33 percent (as opposed to a 50 to 100) percent public support test. The other 66 to 90 percent must be earned. This is more true of nonprofits that are not eligible for tax deductible contributions.

Prepared in a socratic format, the objective of this chapter is to come as close as possible to actual questions the management should ask. The questions are followed by answers or the accepted procedures for working out an answer. The questions are:

1. How will the investment affect the tax-exempt status of the organization?
2. How should a business be acquired?
3. Should the business be related or unrelated?
4. Should the business be incorporated as a for-profit corporation?
5. Where does the money come from to acquire the business?
6. Is the business profitable?
7. Is profitability enough?
8. What will the investment cost?
9. Will the expected benefits exceed the costs?
10. Can the benefit–cost ratio be calculated?
11. When will the organization recapture its investment?
12. What are the risks?
13. What will it take to break even?
14. What can be done with the earnings of the business?
15. How will entry into the business be made?
16. What is the nature of the competition? Is it fair?
17. What do the trustees think of the plan?

HOW WILL THE INVESTMENT AFFECT THE TAX-EXEMPT STATUS OF THE ORGANIZATION?

If this is not the first question to be asked, it surely is the last. As we saw in Chapters 3, 4, 6, and 11, while investment in a business is not barred and is encouraged by the law, income from such investments can seriously affect the tax-exempt status of the nonprofit. The issue in every case is the proportion of revenues of the nonprofit that comes from a business or from investments. The proportion that is permitted without serious consequences on the tax-exempt status depends on the section of the *Internal Revenue Code* under which the organization falls.

The impact is not always negative. A private operating foundation can meet the asset test, for example, if at least 65 percent of its assets are stocks of a corporation that it controls (that is, it owns at least 80 percent of the corporation's voting and other stocks) and if at least 85 percent of the assets of that corporation are devoted to the tax-exempt purpose of the private operating foundation or to a related business.

Also, income from businesses is considered to be part of the support justifying classification of a nonprofit as public foundation, for example, under Section 509(a)(1) or (a)(2). In short, the answer to this question depends on the tax-exempt classification of the nonprofit and the balance between business income and other types of support, such as gifts and contributions. But in no case is business or investment income barred, and in no case is there an absolute limit on the number of dollars that can be earned. It is relative to (1) the ability of the organization to pass the tests shown in Chapter 4, and (2) its ability to carry out its mission with integrity.

HOW SHOULD A BUSINESS BE ACQUIRED?

Ownership or control of a business can be acquired as a gift, by purchase, or by starting it up from scratch. It can also be done by transforming a product or service that is provided free to one that has a price tag. All these involve investment decisions. With a gift, the management has to take into account the tax consequences and costs of operating the business and its development and ultimate disposition. Recall, for example, that a business that is acquired through debt, even if it is a gift, can produce taxable income from activities even though closely related to the tax-exempt mission of the nonprofit.

In starting up a business from scratch, the management has to incorporate, register, certify, and obtain licenses where these are required, hire employees, locate and acquire plant or office space, invest in inventory, establish lines of credit, establish relationships with suppliers and distributors, develop a market and a clientele, and work hard to establish credibility and name recognition. These are expensive and time-consuming activities. Each involves a risk and each delays the flow of revenues into the coffers of the nonprofit.

An alternative is to buy an existing business. In that case, the nonprofit purchaser avoids the difficulties and risks of starting from scratch. The seller of the business will include those start-up costs in the selling price as part of what is known as "goodwill."

If the business is to be bought, the nonprofit may use one of two approaches. It may buy the stocks of the business if it is a corporation, or it may buy the individual assets—plant, equipment, and land. This second approach has the advantage that the purchase does not have to assume the liabilities of the business that are not related specifically to the assets that it is purchasing. For example, if a nonprofit buys all the machines in a business and all the plants, it has to consider only the liabilities (debt) that relate directly to those assets bought.

However, this approach to buying a business does have its disadvantages. First, all the assets have to be individually valued, and the seller may be reluctant to finalize the sale if there are assets that the nonprofit does not want to buy. It is easier and often less expensive to sell the entire enterprise. Second, the nonprofit purchaser does not get the benefit of having a fully operating business in place, that is, one with a clientele, a line of suppliers, distributors, and creditors.

Hence, the option of purchasing the stocks of the corporation and thereby the entire corporation is often used. Buying the entire corporation, however, means assuming all its assets and liabilities. The advantage of this approach for a nonprofit is that it gets a running start by acquiring an operating business. Starting from scratch is best accomplished when the business is related without requiring large investments of capital and when the necessary skills are closely allied to those the nonprofit has or cultivates in satisfying its tax-exempt mission.

SHOULD THE BUSINESS BE RELATED OR UNRELATED?

To begin with, we recognize that this choice is subject to the legal definitions discussed in Chapter 11. Whether a business is related or not is a legal question based on the facts; when in doubt a private letter ruling as described in Chapter 1 should be obtained. It is also evident that when capacity and capital are scarce there is less risk in conducting a related business. Such a business also provides for tax-exempt income, and this income flows directly from the business into the organization.

An unrelated business can be equally simple given that its key difference from a related business is that it is unrelated to the tax-exempt mission of the nonprofit. "Unrelated" has nothing to do with the capacity, capital, or complexity that characterizes the enterprise. It has to do with regularity and relevance. Does it rival the mission for attention and resources? If it does, think twice and incorporate the business as a separate corporation.

SHOULD THE BUSINESS BE SEPARATELY INCORPORATED?

The income from an unincorporated business flows directly to the nonprofit. When, however, a risky and complex business is being contemplated, it might be best to incorporate it to separate it from the nonprofit.

Such action shields the nonprofit from the liabilities and risks of the business. If the business fails, the nonprofit is not in jeopardy. It is not necessary that the new corporation be a for-profit firm. A nonprofit that qualifies under Section 509(a)(3) as discussed in Chapter 4 may conduct a related or unrelated business to benefit its parent nonprofit. It may make a profit, but the profit must be used to support the parent organization and its tax-exempt mission. Unrelated net income (profits) of these corporations is taxable; related income is not.

If a for-profit corporation is acquired, its income is taxable at the level of the for-profit.[1] Dividends to the nonprofits may be received tax free. By creating a separate corporation to do its business rather than doing it itself, the nonprofit interrupts the direct flow of income from the business activity into its coffers. This is because the created corporation must have a board of directors who decide on the dividends the corporation will pay to the nonprofit owner.

The absence of a direct flow is not necessarily a meaningful disadvantage compared to a direct flow of revenues from the business to the nonprofit when the business is unincorporated. First, corporate board members with a sympathetic ear to the nonprofit can be chosen, although their first responsibility is to the for-profit corporation. Second, even if dividends are lower than the revenues in a direct flow, they are likely to be more steady. In a direct flow, the receipts of the nonprofit go up and down, reflecting the net revenues of the business each year. However, dividends can be declared in dollar terms (so many dollars per year) rather than as a proportion of earnings. And dividends can be paid out of past earnings retained by the corporation and even out of new debt. Financial planning is easier when flows are steady and reasonably predictable year to year.

WHERE DOES THE MONEY COME FROM TO ACQUIRE THE BUSINESS?

One deterrent to the purchase of a business is the lack of initial capital, but there are a number of imaginative financing techniques that can be used, including a special fund-raising campaign. Also, a leverage buy out (borrowing) can be arranged. When this is done, the assets of the business are used to make the sale by securing a loan for the purchase. A second approach is to use an installment sale, which may require little or no down payment. The seller receives an annual payment that is comprised of three parts: (1) a return of the capital invested in the company, (2) capital gains or the amount the business increased in value over the seller's basis (initial investment plus improvements and minus depreciation), and (3) interest on the outstanding portion of the payments. An installment sale is attractive to the seller because it constitutes a regular annual payment; the portion that is a return of the capital is not taxable. The return of the owner's investment is not taxable.

In some cases, a business reorganization plan may be used to acquire the enterprise. In this case, the owners give up their common stocks in the business to the nonprofits for preferred stocks that the nonprofit would create and issue in the business. These latter stocks have preference over common stocks in receiving dividends and in protection if the business goes bankrupt; hence, the name preferred stocks. This exchange gives the seller an annual income (the dividends) and gives the buyer (the nonprofit) control. The nonprofit also gets all the capital gains resulting from a future sale of its common stocks. It retains the expertise of the business owner, who will remain interested in the future of the business because the payment of dividends depends on it. Moreover, if the exchange is prepared properly, the seller will not have to pay taxes on the gains received in the swap of stocks at the time that the swap is made, but will be taxed at a future time if and when the preferred stocks are sold.

IS THE BUSINESS PROFITABLE?

The answer is for whom, when, and how much. Imaginative entrepreneurs have been able to turn losing enterprises around, and new businesses often experience losses.

Immediately high levels of profitability might not be a good reason for buying or starting a business. In a market economy, high levels of profitability may be only temporary because they tend to attract other investors. The more investors there are the lower the amount of profits each receives; the large profit eventually disappears.[2]

Similarly, low levels of profits are not necessarily permanent. Profits can be low because of bad management, high costs, and limited markets, all of which can be reversed. Profits can also be affected by the method used to value inventory. In a period of rising costs, a method that values the inventory of a business at the current market price deflates profits. This is because all goods would appear to cost more than they actually did when the business bought or produced the goods sold. A method that values inventory at the original, lower cost inflates the true levels of profits.

Moreover, the earnings of a corporation may be affected by extraordinary nonrecurrent factors. The sale of a piece of land or a plant may result in an extraordinary loss or gain. Such losses and gains are not derived from the operation of the business and will tell us nothing about whether the business is being operated profitably. Also, we must distinguish between after-tax and before-tax earnings of the business.

To illustrate, the gross profit is the difference between the revenues from sales and the cost of the goods sold. Remember that the cost of goods sold is partly determined by the value of those goods in inventory. This gross profit, however, is not the complete story. When other operating costs such as labor, utilities, and insurance are deducted, income before taxes is derived. If the corporation is running an unrelated business, taxes must be paid. Only after these factors are taken into account do we get after-tax net income from operations.

In certain years, the corporation may have extraordinary gains or losses due to damage, the sale of assets such as plants and equipment, and so on. The gains must be added and the losses must be subtracted from income from operations to calculate the net income of the corporation. Hence, in evaluating the income performance of a corporation, its own or one that it wishes to buy, the management ought to focus on income from operations. What the business will have to offer the nonprofit barring an extraordinary event is net income from operations, specifically, income from operations minus expenses and after taxes. This approximates what is sometimes called "free cash flow."

IS PROFITABILITY ENOUGH?

Looking at the income from operations (after taxes if the business is unrelated and pays taxes) of the business in only one year will not suffice. Any one year may be an aberration. Moreover, the nonprofit is interested in the flow of income during the years in which it will remain invested in the business. Based on the information in the income statements over several years and an analysis of future operations and markets through a strategic planning exercise, let us assume the nonprofit may reasonably expect to receive $100,000 per year for the next ten years. Will it be worth the investment of the nonprofit's money? Remember, the nonprofit is not a gambler, and it handles money in public trust for a public purpose. While income is necessary, is it worth the investment of public money?

A good manager faced with this question will quickly consider the fact that the same investment could be placed in a U.S. Treasury bond without default risk, but with ultimate safety and a good rate of return. Why put it in a business and take risks? Obviously, this will be done only if the expected rate of return from the business is higher than the Treasury bond and if the rate is also sufficiently high to compensate the nonprofit for the risk it will be taking. The manager will then say that the investment must yield a rate of return that is higher than the opportunity cost (the amount it will give up by not investing in the Treasury bond) plus a premium for the risk. Thus, in general, the investment is worth it only if it compensates the nonprofit for the opportunity cost plus any risk premium, and the risks can be satisfactorily minimized. Investment is not a synonym for gambling. If the rate is not sufficiently high, the manager might as well invest in U.S. Treasury securities.

The rate of return in any single year of an investment is calculated by dividing the amount of dividends and appreciation after taxes from that investment by the amount of investment made. Obviously, the significance of this ratio is that it gives a measure of how much each dollar that the nonprofit owner has tied up in the business earns for the organization.

Incidentally, this is one reason why perfectly healthy and profitable businesses are often available for sale. It is not because they are unprofitable, but the rate of return might be too low to justify the investment by a particular investor. Again, an advantage for nonprofits is they do not have to compete for investors' dollars by constantly offering higher rates of return to stockholders, as do firms. They have no individual investors to satisfy. For-profit corporations do, so they often will sell a perfectly profitable subsidiary or operation to seek higher rates of return elsewhere.

WHAT WILL THE INVESTMENT COST?

Sometimes the nonprofit will be a price taker. This means that it faces a price that it must pay because it is not in a position to negotiate or to influence the price in any way. Such is the case when the nonprofit purchases stocks or bonds on the stock market. In other cases, such as real estate, the nonprofit is in a position to negotiate a price and can determine what a reasonable price will be by comparing the market price for similar properties in the surrounding area. In yet other cases, a reasonable price may be ascertained by looking at the performance of the business over the past (usually a minimum of five years).

In still other cases, it is possible to ascertain a reasonable price by looking at the book value of the enterprise. The book value is roughly the owner's equity in the business (the net amount the owner of the business has in it), the assets minus the liabilities. But the asking price by the seller will rarely equal the book value. It would invariably be higher, because the book value does not reflect valuable intangibles such as an existing clientele, lines of credit, or a good name. This additional amount, over and above the book value, is called goodwill. The asking price will be the book value plus the goodwill.[3] Whether or not the seller will get the asking price depends on the ability of the nonprofit to negotiate. This ability is enhanced if the nonprofit has an independent professional appraisal made of the business. At the end of this negotiating process, the seller will set an asking price. This is what it will cost the nonprofit to buy the business.

WILL THE EXPECTED BENEFITS EXCEED THE COSTS?

One of the disciplines learned from the previous chapters is that, when a nonprofit enters into an investment or an unrelated business, its main (not necessarily its exclusive) purpose is to earn money. Business is business and the main benefits are measurable in dollars. If at this point the honor of earning a dollar cannot be accepted by the board of the nonprofit, it should drop the idea of making an investment for it will fail.

From a strictly financial perspective, both benefits and costs are measurable in terms of dollars. The benefits are the dollars that are expected to flow into the coffers of the nonprofit over the years. The benefits are the net annual revenues equaling sales price minus operating costs and any taxes, including the unrelated business income tax. The annual operating costs are already reflected in the net revenues, so the concern is with the initial or acquisition cost. These costs are the dollars the organization has to lay out today in order to acquire the investment.

Obviously, the nonprofit should not invest in the business if the amount of money it has to lay out initially is higher than the present value of net benefits it expects to receive over the entire life of the business. But note that the initial investment or cost has to be paid today with today's dollars. The benefits will flow over several years, and while a flow into perpetuity may be desired, given inflation, every dollar that is received several years in the future is worth less than the dollar paid today. What is the future flow of benefits worth today? Is it less than, equal to, or greater than the cost that must be met to acquire and operate the business? In the language of business, what is its present value?

To answer this question, we must discount the future flow of benefits by a factor that reflects the rate at which inflation will lower the value of the dollar over time. This discount rate may also reflect the risk that is involved in the investment; for example, we may take the rate paid on Treasury bonds and add a premium to reflect the risk. In this way we arrive at a discount rate, the rate at which we discount the flow of future earnings from the business to find out what those earnings are worth in today's dollars. This discounted future earnings is called the present value of the expected flow of benefits.

Naturally, if the present value of benefits exceeds the costs of the investment or business, then the investment makes economic sense. If it is less than the cost, the investment makes no economic sense. If it is equal to the costs, the investment is marginal, but still worthwhile. Sometimes the present value of the benefits and the costs is expressed in the benefit–cost ratio. A ratio greater than 1 indicates that the benefits exceed the costs; a ratio of less than 1 implies the reverse; a ratio of 1 indicates that the costs and benefits are equal.

CAN THE BENEFIT–COST RATIO BE CALCULATED?

In principle, yes. To illustrate, let us assume that the seller's asking price after negotiation is $700,000 and the independent professional appraiser agrees with this figure. Let us also assume that we may expect $100,000 per year to flow into the coffers of the nonprofit if it should undertake this investment and that it intends to remain invested in this business for thirty years. Is it worth $100,000 per year for thirty years given an initial cost of $700,000? The answer depends on the discount rate that reflects how risky the investment is compared to a safe one paying high rates, such as the Treasury Bond. It also depends on the expected rate of inflation, which will erode the dollar over time. Suppose we decide that after taking all these factors into account we should discount the future earnings by 15 percent, which is not unusual during periods of high expected inflation. What is the present value of the benefits?[4]

To answer this question, we refer to Table 12.1 and note the number 6.566 in the cell that corresponds to thirty years and 15 percent. If we multiply $100,000 (the annual expected return) by 6.566, we get $656,600, which is the present value of that $100,000 expected over thirty years when discounted at 15 percent. Because this amount of $656,600 is the benefit and the asking price, the cost, is $700,000, the investment is not acceptable to this nonprofit.

Suppose, however, the investment were less risky or that we expected a lower rate of inflation so that our future earnings would not be eroded. In that case, we may use a discount rate of 10 percent, which is not uncommon when inflation is not rampant and investments are not very risky. By referring to Table 12.1, we note that at 10 percent for thirty years the number is 9.427. We multiply $100,000 by 9.427 and get $942,700. In this example, the benefits ($942,700) exceed the costs ($700,000). A good deal!

Try the same example, discounting at 14 percent. Here the present value of the benefits is $700,300 compared to a cost of $700,000. We are at the margin where benefits and costs are about equal and the benefit–cost ratio would be approximately 1. What would you do? It is these marginal cases that are most challenging.

TABLE 12.1 Present Value of an Annuity of $1 a Year

Interest

Years	1	2	4	6	8	10	12	14	15	16	18	20	22	24	25	26	28	30
1	0.990	0.980	0.962	0.943	0.926	0.909	0.893	0.877	0.870	0.862	0.847	0.833	0.820	0.806	0.800	0.794	0.781	0.769
2	1.970	1.942	1.886	1.833	1.783	1.736	1.690	1.647	1.626	1.605	1.566	1.528	1.492	1.457	1.440	1.424	1.392	1.361
3	2.941	2.884	2.775	2.673	2.577	2.487	2.402	2.322	2.283	2.246	2.174	2.106	2.042	1.981	1.952	1.923	1.868	1.816
4	3.902	3.808	3.630	3.465	3.312	3.170	3.037	2.914	2.855	2.798	2.690	2.589	2.494	2.404	2.362	2.320	2.241	2.166
5	4.853	4.713	4.452	4.212	3.993	3.791	3.605	3.433	3.352	3.274	3.127	2.991	2.864	2.745	2.689	2.635	2.532	2.436
6	5.795	5.601	5.242	4.917	4.623	4.355	4.111	3.889	3.784	3.685	3.498	3.326	3.167	3.020	2.951	2.885	2.759	2.643
7	6.728	6.472	6.002	5.582	5.206	4.868	4.564	4.288	4.160	4.039	3.812	3.605	3.416	3.242	3.161	3.083	2.937	2.802
8	7.652	7.325	6.733	6.210	5.747	5.335	4.968	4.639	4.487	4.344	4.078	3.817	3.619	3.421	3.329	3.241	3.076	2.925
9	8.566	8.162	7.435	6.802	6.247	5.759	5.328	4.946	4.772	4.607	4.303	4.031	3.786	3.566	3.463	3.366	3.184	3.019
10	9.471	8.983	8.111	7.360	6.710	6.145	5.630	5.216	5.019	4.833	4.494	4.192	3.923	3.682	3.571	3.465	3.269	3.092
11	10.368	9.787	8.760	7.887	7.139	6.495	5.937	5.453	5.234	5.029	4.656	4.327	4.035	3.776	3.656	3.544	3.335	3.147
12	11.255	10.575	9.385	8.384	7.536	6.814	6.194	5.660	5.421	5.197	4.793	4.439	4.127	3.851	3.725	3.606	3.387	3.190
13	12.134	11.543	9.986	8.853	7.904	7.103	6.424	5.842	5.583	5.342	4.910	4.533	4.203	3.912	3.780	3.656	3.427	3.223
14	13.004	12.106	10.563	9.295	8.244	7.367	6.628	6.002	5.724	5.468	5.008	4.611	4.265	3.962	3.824	3.695	3.459	3.249
15	13.865	12.849	11.118	9.712	8.559	7.606	6.811	6.142	5.847	5.575	5.092	4.675	4.315	4.001	3.859	3.726	3.483	3.268
16	14.718	13.578	11.652	10.106	8.851	7.824	6.974	6.265	5.954	5.669	5.162	4.730	4.357	4.033	3.887	3.751	3.503	3.283
17	15.562	14.292	12.166	10.477	9.122	8.022	7.120	6.373	6.047	5.749	5.222	4.775	4.391	4.059	3.910	3.771	3.518	3.295
18	16.398	14.992	12.659	10.828	9.372	8.201	7.250	6.467	6.128	5.818	5.273	4.812	4.419	4.080	3.928	3.786	3.529	3.304
19	17.226	15.678	13.134	11.158	9.604	8.365	7.566	6.550	6.198	5.877	5.316	4.844	4.442	4.097	3.942	3.799	3.539	3.331
20	18.046	16.351	13.590	11.470	9.818	8.514	7.469	6.623	6.259	5.929	5.353	4.870	4.460	4.110	3.954	3.808	3.546	3.316
21	18.857	17.011	14.029	11.764	10.017	8.649	7.562	6.687	6.312	5.973	5.384	4.891	4.476	4.121	3.963	3.816	3.551	3.320
22	19.660	17.658	14.451	12.042	10.201	8.772	7.645	6.743	6.359	6.011	5.410	4.909	4.488	4.130	3.970	3.822	3.556	3.323
23	20.456	18.292	14.857	12.303	10.371	8.883	7.718	6.792	6.399	6.044	5.432	4.925	4.499	4.137	3.976	3.827	3.559	3.325
24	21.243	18.914	15.247	12.550	10.529	8.985	7.784	6.835	6.434	6.073	5.451	4.937	4.507	4.143	3.981	3.831	3.562	3.327
25	22.023	19.523	15.622	12.783	10.675	9.077	7.843	6.873	6.464	6.097	5.467	4.948	4.514	4.147	3.985	3.834	3.564	3.329
26	22.795	20.121	15.983	13.003	10.810	9.161	7.896	6.906	6.491	6.118	5.480	4.956	4.520	4.151	3.988	3.837	3.566	3.330
27	23.560	20.707	16.330	13.211	10.935	9.237	7.943	6.935	6.514	6.136	5.492	4.964	4.524	4.154	3.990	3.839	3.567	3.331
28	24.316	21.281	16.663	13.406	11.051	9.307	7.984	6.961	6.534	6.152	5.502	4.970	4.528	4.157	3.992	3.840	3.568	3.331
29	25.066	21.844	16.984	13.591	11.158	9.370	8.022	6.983	6.551	6.166	5.510	4.975	4.531	4.159	3.994	3.841	3.569	3.332
30	25.808	22.396	17.292	13.765	11.258	9.427	8.055	7.003	6.566	6.177	5.517	4.979	4.534	4.160	3.995	3.842	3.569	3.332

WHEN WILL THE ORGANIZATION RECAPTURE ITS INVESTMENT?

The benefit–cost ratio and methods of discounting future earnings to determine whether the rate of return on the investment is acceptable are based on the assumption that the nonprofit will remain invested usually for a long period of time or for the expected life of the investment. Some investments, such as in automobiles, may have a life of no more than three to seven years, while others, such as a building, may have a useful life exceeding thirty years. Given the pressures on funds, the need to be prudent, and the need to satisfy a board, the management of the nonprofit may ask another question: How long will it take to get our money out of the investment? Technically, how long is the payback period? For an inexperienced or shy manager or for an organization that takes a conservative approach to investment, it might be ideal to invest only in business projects in which the payback period is short.

It is easy to determine the approximate length of the payback period. Merely divide the investment to be made (the cost or initial outlay) by the amount that can be expected to flow into the coffers of the nonprofit annually. This is the approximate period of time that it would take to retrieve the investment.

To illustrate, assume a project costing $1000 as an initial outlay. The net income (revenues minus operating costs) per year is expected to be $500. In two years, the net income will be enough to recover the initial cost. Notice, however, that these are projections. There is no certainty. Notice also that a low payback period implies a high rate of return on the investment, and recall that high rates are associated with risks. They are the rewards for taking high risks in the market economy.

WHAT ARE THE RISKS?

Every investment is subject to risks. One type of risk is that the investment will go sour, and another is that the earnings from the investment may be eroded by high rates of inflation. A third risk is that the investment may be illiquid, meaning that it cannot be converted to dollars easily without a severe penalty. Another risk may be that the investment is not marketable. Which risk is most important depends on the type of investment. For example, investing in certificates of deposit holds very little risk of total loss of investment compared to investments in hot go-go stocks, as long as the federal guarantee limits are not exceeded. And while stocks are easily marketable, the risk is high because they can fall in price dramatically. Risks have to be compensated for, and the compensation is the rate of return. Would you invest in a high-risk venture if you did not believe that it offered fantastic gains? No, and neither would anybody else. Rational investing is the art involving matching risks and rewards. Would you keep your money in an extremely risky investment for a long period of time? No, and that is why your organization may want to look at a short payback period when risks are high.

Businesses are concerned with two broad types of risks: (1) financial or money-related risks, and (2) business risks which are those that are nonfinancial such as shifts in the market for the product or service. A nonprofit must do the same. But the ultimate risk for a nonprofit is that it would lose its tax-exempt status and that management will be held liable as a result. This risk can only be evaluated by understanding Chapters 1 through 8 and 11.

Holding idle cash balances is not a way to avoid taking risks. Cash invites theft and mishandling. Uninvested cash erodes in value due to inflation. Holding cash is an opportunity cost, the loss of earnings that the nonprofit organization could use.

WHAT WILL IT TAKE TO BREAK EVEN?

Part of judging the suitability of an investment is knowing what is required to break even. It is not enough to know that the recovery period for one's investment may be short or long or that the rate of return might be high enough to compensate for the risk. It might also be important to be able to judge the amount of effort that it might take to at least break even. This means to be able to cover the full cost of operation so that the organization is not dipping into its own pocket or into general support in order to sustain the business. The business is at least supporting itself.

An approximation of a break-even point can be calculated and shown graphically. Recall that the break-even point for a product occurs at the level where the revenues from sales are just enough to cover all costs of producing this product. This is like saying that the difference between the revenues and costs is zero or that revenues equal costs.

Total revenues is the quantity sold multiplied by the price at which each unit is sold. Total cost is the number produced times the cost of producing each unit. In the appendix to this chapter, we demonstrate that once the break-even point is known it is simple to answer a question that should be significant to every nonprofit owner of a business: How much must be produced to meet a target rate of earnings flowing from the business into the nonprofit?

WHAT CAN BE DONE WITH THE EARNINGS OF THE BUSINESS?

To this point, we have been selfish. We see the after-tax earnings of the business as being the property of the nonprofit owner of the business to carry out its mission. This is technically accurate and should be the primary motive. However, the earnings of a business may be retained in it to make further investments to increase its capacity to finance the nonprofit and its mission. It can also be temporarily invested using cash management tools discussed in Chapters 17 and 18.

HOW WILL ENTRY INTO THE BUSINESS BE MADE?

Charles Berry and Edward Roberts recently developed a typological approach to answering this question.[5] While their examples pertain to for-profit firms, with some modification, they can apply to nonprofits as well. See Figure 12.1. A discussion of a few cells is sufficient for our purposes.

The idea is that when an organization chooses to enter into a new business venture, it should begin with an assessment of its familiarity with the market for the goods and services to be produced by the new venture and with its technical competence to produce the goods or services. When the organization is totally unfamiliar with the technology and the market (cell C going left to right), it would be very risky for the organization to go it alone or even to be a working partner in the business. Wiser strategies would be to invest money in the business (venture capital) or acquire the business but keep its present technical staff to run it (educational acquisition). Cells B and F represent the same type of situation. The organization is unfamiliar with the technology and only slightly understands the market. These cells are risky and depend on the learning curve.

Alternatively, the nonprofit may find itself attracted to a business in which it is already involved in both the market and the technology. It has a base in both (cell G). In that case, it would be sensible for the nonprofit to consider going it alone by building internally or by acquiring additional productive resources, even if this meant purchasing the business of a competitor.

Another possibility is that the nonprofit may have a base either in the market or in the technology, but not both (cells A and I). Joint ventures make sense here. The nonprofit enters into an agreement with another organization that takes responsibility for either the technology or market, whichever it does better, and the nonprofit takes responsibility for whichever it does better. Notice that what makes a joint venture practicable is that each party has what the other needs to be successful.

Market Factors	A	B Venture Capital or Venture Nurturing or Educational Acquisitions	C Venture Capital or Venture Nurturing or Educational Acquisitions
New Unfamiliar	Joint Ventures		
New Familiar	D Internal Market Developments or Acquisitions (or Joint Ventures)	E Internal Ventures or Acquisitions or Licensing	F Venture Capital or Venture Nurturing or Educational Acquisitions
Base	G Internal Base Developments (or Acquisitions)	H Internal Product Developments or Acquisitions or Licensing	I "New Style" Joint Ventures
	Base	New Familiar	New Unfamiliar

Technologies or Services Embodied in the Product

Figure 12.1 Optimum entry strategies. Source: Charles A. Berry and Edward B. Roberts, "Entering New Businesses: Selecting Strategies for Success," *Sloan Management Review*, 26, no. 3 (Spring 1985), 13. Reprinted by permission of the Sloan Management Review Association. All rights reserved.

A joint venture is frequently attractive in business deals because each party maintains its own corporate identity. They merely choose to work together on a specific project. To protect themselves, they might form a whole new corporation or partnership simply for the purpose of carrying out that one business deal.

The nonprofit may be attracted to a business opportunity in an area in which it has familiarity both about the market and the technology. While the market and technology are familiar, the business would be risky because the nonprofit has never been actively involved in it (cell E). For protection, the nonprofit may form a separate group or corporation (internal venture) to engage in the business. Or it may acquire an outside firm through purchase that is already in the business. It could also enter the business by acquiring all rights or a license and lease them to a firm

---

By Leigh Johnson

Flat Hat Staff Writer

The College has registered its name, coat of arms, and several other exclusive symbols as trademarks to both protect and promote their use on any merchandise.

This licensing program, which was established in January, allows the College to insist on approval of any merchandise bearing its logos. According to Chuck Lombardo, director of auxiliary services, about 80 manufacturers have been approved by the College to produce licensed goods.

Manufacturers must complete an application and submit a product sample for approval. The main concerns are for product safety and quality, according to Lombardo.

The registered trademark also allows the College to prosecute manufacturers who do not comply with the licensing procedure. The College, however, would most likely warn the offenders first, Lombardo said.

Retailers in the area have been asked to carry only merchandise provided by licensed manufacturers. Lombardo pointed out that many approved products bearing College logos are now labeled with the words "officially licensed product."

Under the licensing program, the College receives a 6.5 percent royalty from licensed items sold, which will go directly to the College's general fund. Revenues in the first six months met the expenses of establishing the program, according to Lombardo.

Source: College Seals Up Merchandise, *Flat Hat*, College of William and Mary, October 19, 1990, p. 3.

---

that can actually do the production. Marketing can be done through a wider network than the nonprofit has. Owning a copyright, permitting manufacturers to use your logo whether on mugs, pens, or shirts amounts to pursuing this type of strategy.

The attraction of this strategy is that production and market risks and costs are shifted from the nonprofit to a commercial enterprise. Unfair competition is avoided, and the nonprofit gets a risk free untaxed flow of income called royalties.

In yet another scenario, the nonprofit may have a good sound footing in the technology, but has never marketed the product, although it has some familiarity with what the market is like. In this case (cell D) the nonprofit may wish to develop an internal marketing department, or it might acquire a firm that specializes in that kind of marketing, or it may establish a joint venture with such a firm to take advantage of its expertise.

In cell H the organization is solidly grounded in the market, but the technology is new. Here the possibilities for internal development of the technology may be considered, although this may be expensive and risky. Better alternatives may be to acquire a firm that is already producing the product or control of the license of such a production. A joint venture may also be possible here, with the nonprofit doing the marketing and the for-profit providing the products. This is precisely what happens when books, insurance, travel plans, and the like are offered through associations. They are actually doing the marketing of a product or service produced by a for-profit firm.

WHAT IS THE COMPETITION? IS IT FAIR?

This question comes in three parts: business, legal and public relations. The business question is strictly, is there a market for this business? Chapter 6 on strategic planning shows how to go about answering that question.

The legal question deals with the Sherman and the Clayton antitrust acts. These laws make it illegal for firms to impede competition either by price fixing or restricting the market. While we are wont to think of these laws as strictly relating to for-profit firms, in recent years we have seen them increasingly applied to nonprofit organizations. This is what happened when the U.S. Justice Department in 1989 declared that it was going to investigate several well-known colleges for fixing tuition by consorting among themselves and sharing tuition and financial aid practices. Such anticompetitive collusion is as illegal for colleges and universities, museums, and hospitals—any organization operating in a competitive environment—as it is for firms such as airlines and automobile companies.

Likewise, setting prices below cost so as to create a restricted, monopolistic market is illegal. Note that it is not just low prices, but prices that are below cost. This is normally not a concern of nonprofits dealing primarily with the poor. It should be to others, since one way to demonstrate public welfare is to set lower than commercial prices. Such low prices may be offset by lower costs, for example, clothing donated to a thrift shop, are also lower than commercial costs. Also, operating costs of nonprofits may be lower by use of volunteers and less attractive facilities.

The antitrust laws can also be infringed on by market share. Using this theory, the court in *U.S.* v. *Rockford Memorial Corporation*, 1989, barred the expansion of this nonprofit hospital by arguing that its expansion would result in its having 90 percent of the market. It would control the market.

Markets can be controlled in other ways. In Virginia, a medical supplier charged a number of nonprofit hospitals with unfair competition. It appears that these hospitals used to refer clients to him. Later, these hospitals concluded that they would set up their own business and service their patients directly.

Can't the hospitals argue that they could better serve their patients in this way? Isn't competition healthy? What was the quality of work being done by the private firm? Is the need for additional revenues by the hospitals so great that they could not have foregone this commercial activity? Was the fray foreseeable?

These questions are not easy and this is why many of these cases end up in court. But they demonstrate why, even for the smallest nonprofit, dealing with the appearance of unfairness is important. Here are 3Ps to guide your decision.

THREE *PS* FOR A DECISION ON A BUSINESS VENTURE

1. **Propriety:** Does it fit the nonprofit's image, its mission, and the law? Is it fair? Does it place the organization and its natural clients at risk?
2. **Profitability:** Does the venture cover all its costs and make a worthwhile monetary and nonmonetary contribution to the nonprofit?
3. **Practicability:** Will the venture survive and for how long?

Of the three Ps, violation of propriety is the most dangerous because it can lead to the loss of exemption—even if the other two Ps are met.

WHAT DO THE TRUSTEES THINK OF THE PLAN?

The trustees have the final word. They must make investment decisions usually with a social conscience and often governed by the "prudent man's rule" stating, in effect, that overly risky use of the organization's resources and energies are to be avoided. The ultimate risk is not financial, although it can be considerable, but the loss of tax-exempt status.

Furthermore, the charter and bylaws of the organization may designate what types of investments are permissible. State and local laws may limit the type of investments the nonprofit may make, and there might be restrictions in the agreements under which trusts, endowments, and gifts were made.

Furthermore, no good manager attempts any meaningful investment without consulting a lawyer, an accountant, and the investment or financial committees of the nonprofit. In short, a business plan containing more than projections of costs revenues, clients and financing needs is advisable. The plan should also answer the questions in this chapter to the critical approval of trustees guided by informed advisors. Once all this has been done, the decision can be made by the trustees.

ETHICAL DILEMMA OF BUSINESS COMPETITION

Unfair competition has been a charge levied by small businesses against nonprofits ever since New York University law school owned Mueller Macaroni Company, which it eventually sold. Spokespersons for coalitions of small businesses charge that nonprofits are able to use their tax-exempt status to acquire capital and their close relationships with their members to create a "halo" effect, and along with their tax-exempt status and nonprofit mailing privileges, they compete unfairly with firms.

The proposals, placed perennially before Congress, go to extremes, including barring nonprofits from entering certain businesses and taking away some of their tax-exempt privileges. Year after year, Congress has delayed action, although in recent years the House Ways and Means Committee of the U.S. House of Representatives has given warning that nonprofits should expect changes in the law. The small business coalition has now moved its fight into the state legislatures, which it has asked to adopt model legislation.

Before new laws are written, certain questions need answering. Basic to any action, as the House committee members have said, is the absence of a clear picture of how extensive this abuse is. The IRS now requires more detailed reporting by nonprofits of their business activities. But there are other serious issues.

Doesn't the enforcement of present law offer a better alternative? Is the issue one of enforcement rather than the need for new legislation? Wouldn't the legislative proposals put forth by some severely, and perhaps unconstitutionally restrict trade? What do we do about small communities in which the nonprofit is really the principal business? Isn't the secondary income stream to a community from a university's running an unrelated business (such as having a pro team use its athletic facilities) something the community is willing to give up? Who in the community would put up facilities to be used a few weeks in a year? Is it ethical to bar an organization from participating in the fruits of an economy it helps to generate and in which (in the case of research and sports) it is also the primary risk taker and cost absorber? What may be the consequence?

Please reread the insert by Pyatt in Chapter 11 and the discussions in Chapter 7.

On the other hand, is it proper that a nonprofit should be selling insurance, given the millions of insurance agents in the country and the fact that these policies sold by nonprofits are often not superior? The same insurance company that produces the policies sold by a nonprofit organization produces competitive policies that their agents sell in the open market. Thus, the insurance company has two sets of agents, nonprofits and their own sales force. Who is responsible for the inequality?

This is not atypical. Companies other than insurance companies do the same thing and usually can justify this arrangement on a cost basis, that is, lower costs of marketing through nonprofits. Therefore, they are in conformity with antitrust laws. Who is creating the advantage, the nonprofit or the company that supplies both the nonprofit and the for-profit firms and therefore gains two marketing channels?

What do you think?

Caution: When I put this before my MBA class, I frequently get answers relating to how profitable some nonprofits are . Remember, what may be profitable for a nonprofit, given the factors discussed in this text that can reduce costs and therefore make them profitable, do not necessarily apply to a for-profit firm. Second, many activities in which nonprofits are engaged are not attractive to for-profit firms. Third, the size of the retained earnings, such as in hospitals, is not the point. They, too, must justify excessive accumulations to the IRS, and they, too, must have sizable funds to finance new buildings, purchase equipment, and pay staff and have strong financial profiles to influence creditors and agencies.

Whatever your arguments, respect case facts and history: Doesn't the insert on page 401 make a lot of sense?

SUMMARY AND CONCLUSIONS

This chapter has asked: Given all our discussions to this point, what are the guidelines for action? The chapter addresses the chain of questions that will arise in making an investment decision.

Investment decisions are influenced primarily by the expected rate of return and the extent to which benefits exceed costs as measured in dollars. But there are other questions that should influence the decision. These include the payback period and the ability to finance the purchase without unduly mortgaging the future of the organization. It should be remembered that, while there are no explicitly stringent rules on investment decisions of public charities, there are on private foundations, as discussed in Chapter 4.

Indeed, there may be legal, social, and organizational considerations

By a Wall Street Journal *Staff Reporter*

PHILADELPHIA—Presbyterian Ministers' Fund, which bills itself as the world's oldest life insurance company and the oldest continuously operated corporation in the U.S., observed its 273 years by changing its name to **Covenant Life Insurance** Co.

The company started in 1717 as a relief fund for Presbyterian ministers and their families who were having financial difficulties.

Presbyterian, incorporated since 1759, said the name Covenant better reflects the diversity of its clientele, which now includes clergy of many denominations, including Baptists and Methodists.

"People wouldn't understand that the company wasn't just for Presbyterians," said a spokeswoman. "We did a lot of biblical research to come up with a name that was more friendly to our customers in the religious community."

The company has offices in 40 states, $471 million in total assets and more than $2 billion of insurance in force.

Source: *Wall Street Journal,* Thursday, December 27, 1990, p. B3. Reprinted by permission.

that prohibit a nonprofit from investing in certain types of enterprises. But such constraints may also apply to for-profit firms, though since the season of deregulation of the 1980s, less frequently and less stringently.

Managers of nonprofits should always consider the short-term or interim investment of cash, which provides a lucrative source of income. We shall return to this theme in Chapter 18. The menu of investments from which to choose is large; there is an opportunity for every nonprofit.

One advantage that nonprofits have over for-profit firms is that the former do not have to seek the highest rate of return within their permissible scope of investments. They have no investor–owners to satisfy. They can also make high-risk investments—lending to the poor, community development, and so on.

Typically, then, nonprofits in their program-related investments take high risks and accept low rates of return, for example, investing in low-income neighborhoods and extending loans to commercially unqualified persons. These risks are underwritten by gifts and contributions.

APPENDIX 12.1: BREAK-EVEN POINT

Recall that point A in Figure 12.1 represents the break-even point where the total revenues from a business owned by the nonprofit equals the total costs. Total revenues (TR) is nothing more than the unit revenue (or average revenue brought in by a unit of product or service sold, that is, the price of that unit) multiplied by the number of units sold. If we sold 200 apples and the average price received per apple was 25 cents, the total revenues (TR) would be equal to the unit revenue (UR) or price multiplied by the quantity (Q) sold.

Total cost (TC) is composed of three parts. First, there is the total fixed cost (TFC), which is the cost to the business for simply existing. It does not vary with the amount of production. Whether the business produces or not it has to pay contractual costs such as rent and mortgages. The bankers and landlord charge for space, and once the organization signs that contract, it pays for the space regardless of how much it uses it. The cost is fixed.

Other costs are variable. They vary with the amount produced. The amount of materials and supplies used and the number of hours per worker vary with the production level. The greater the production is, the more is the total variable cost (TVC). Total variable costs can therefore be divided into two parts: the quantity produced (Q) and the cost per unit produced (UC). Together, TFC + TVC make up total production cost (TC).

Accordingly, the break-even point is where

$$TR = TC$$

or

$$UR \times Q = UC \times Q + TFC$$

If we divide both sides by Q and simplify, we get

$$UR = (TFC/Q) + UC$$

Solving for Q, we get

$$Q = TFC/(UR - UC)$$

This tells us that the break-even point is equal to the total fixed cost divided by the difference between the unit revenue and the unit cost. This difference $(UR - UC)$ is called the unit contribution, or the contribution margin.

Suppose that the nonprofit has a need for $50,000. It decides that this must come from the operation of its business. This business has a fixed cost of $10,000 and a unit contribution of $2.00; that is, the difference between the average price or unit price and the average or unit cost of the item it sells is $2.00. Each unit sold contributes $2.00 to the total operating income of the business. By applying the following formula, it is possible to ascertain the minimum amount of units the business must produce and sell. The formula is:

$$(QR) = TFC + DI/(UR - UC)$$

QR is the quantity required to meet the income target of the organization ($50,000).

TFC is the total cost.

DI is desired income or income target.

UR - UC is the unit contribution.

Accordingly,

QR = $10,000 + ($50,000/2)

The answer is that 30,000 units must be bought and sold to meet the organization's income target of $50,000.

NOTES

1. Nonprofits cannot be shareholders in Subchapter S corporations, which are corporations with special tax advantages. We are therefore referring to a regular corporation.

2. Economic or normal profits are the percentage, over full cost, that represents a return to capital when the capital market is in equilibrium, that is, when no lender wishes to shift funds to some other user. For-profit firms in highly competitive markets that are new and developing often use a price that is so low that potential competitors are kept out because they would not be able to make a profit or pay the interest on the funds they would have to borrow to enter the business. Contrary to popular opinion, a for-profit firm does not always charge the highest price possible.

3. Goodwill is the amount paid for assets that is above the value of the asset. Goodwill reflects a number of intangibles, such as the existence of a clientele, good location, and a good reputation. A seller of a business that has a large clientele would ask more for that business than if the business had no clients at all.

4. When we refer to benefits and present value in this section, we are talking about a net concept. The expected operating costs each year are deducted from the expected operating revenues, and we find the present value of this net. In the income statement, it is represented by the income or revenues from operation.

5. Charles A. Berry and Edward B. Roberts, "Entering New Businesses," *Sloan Management Review*, 26, no. 3 (Spring 1985), 3–15.

6. Wherever there is a controversy, there are several sides to the same story. Rather than list all the articles and books that have come out, each of which is an advocate (even discussed as an academic treatise) of one position or the other, I recommend the reading the hearings of the U.S. House of Representatives, Subcommittee on Oversight of the Committee on Ways and Means, 1987. The testimony of then Deputy Assistant Secretary (Tax Policy) O. Donaldson Chapoton is particularly good because it provides a rich factual background.

SUGGESTED READINGS

Internal Revenue Service, U.S. Department of the Treasury, *Tax on Unrelated Business Income of the Tax Exempt Organization*, Publication 598, Revised November 1987.

——— *Instructions for (Form 990)*, Revised 1989.

——— *1990 U.S. Corporation Income Tax Package*, Package 1120.

Chapter **13**

Reorganizations: Corporate Marriages, Divorces and Adoptions

In this brief chapter, we turn our attention to actions that are ameliorative; i.e. reorganizing a nonprofit corporation. Why do it?

We are describing a legal activity—the creation or dissolution of a legal entity to be approved by the trustees. What we will be discussing are analogous to marriages, divorces and adoptions.

THE IMPORTANCE OF STRUCTURE

We have met the concept of corporate organization in Chapter 2 where we talked about affiliates and chapters. There, the bonding was a common mission. As a consequence, a number of good things such as limited liability and local responsiveness flowed. In Chapter 4, we talked about

BUSINESS COMBINATION

On November 1, 1989, World Vision Relief and Development Inc. (a combined affiliate of World Vision Inc.) acquired Brother to Brother International Inc. (BBI), a nonprofit organization responsible for coordinating the acquisition and distribution of gifts-in-kind, such as food, medical supplies, pharmaceuticals, agricultural products, and other basic commodities. Gifts donated are shipped directly from the donor to other nonprofit organizations. No consideration was paid for BBI, whose net assets at November 1, 1989, and operations for the month then ended were not significant.

Total revenue from BBI included in the results of operations for the 11 months ended September 30, 1990, is $14,330,000, of which $14,325,000 is gifts-in-kind shipped directly from the donor to the recipient. Of this amount $3,299,000 was received by World Vision Relief and Development Inc. Other nonprofit organizations which received significant gifts-in-kind during this period through the coordination efforts of BBI included: World Opportunities International, Cataract Teaching Foundation, World Emergency Relief, Feed the Children, Northwest Medical Teams, Christian Appalachian Project, and Christ for the Nations.

Reprinted with permission from 1990 Annual Report, *World Vision, Inc.*, p. 25.

corporate organization where the purpose was primarily to separate political, lobbying, and advocacy functions from fund-raising and tax-exempt purposes. In Chapters 11 and 12 we looked at organization as a means of accommodating business. Now we shall see corporate organization from the perspective of economics and markets. See the insert above.

Illustration: Riverside Health System

The Riverside Health System is a holding company offering a wide range of health care including acute, long-term, mental health, ambulatory, preventive, education, home care and rehabilitative services. In addition to owning and managing its hospitals and health care centers, Riverside also manages a city owned hospital. It manages the latter through a wholly owned corporation, Riverside Healthcare Services. In addition, it manages a joint venture providing laundry, printing and microfilming services for a group of hospitals. This eliminates the need for each to do its own, with resulting unused capacity and high fixed costs, which would eventually have been reflected in higher prices to patients.

By having several dozen units, the system can cover a large geographic area—market. But these units are in turn grouped under specialties. There are geographically dispersed convalescent centers that form one or more corporations. The board of directors to which this group responds is different from the board of each of the independent hospitals, each a corporation with its own board. This structure permits separate units spreading across several markets or service areas. But the units are grouped according to specialty, thereby gaining both diversity in service and markets as well as managerial efficiency.

One of the ways in which costs are further reduced is through the Riverside Food Production Services, a separate corporation. This is a centralized food production service for the various units. Thus, the capital costs of food storage and preparation in each unit are eliminated. Further, economies are achieved through large procurements and centralized billing.

Illustration: Carilion

Let us look at another example. In Figure 13.1 on pp. 408–09 the separate tax exempt hospitals, each a corporation, under the Carilion Health System, which is a holding company. It is, in other words, the sole member of the individual corporations under it. In for-profit terms, it is the sole owner or stockholder. As the sole member, it has the powers to appoint and remove board members and to approve changes in the articles of incorporation of each of these corporate subsidiaries. We have already seen that different hospitals may serve different areas and specialties. Giles Memorial in Figure 13.1 is an acute care facility; Gill is eye, ear, nose and throat; Burrell is long-term care for the elderly.

Please turn your attention to the three last lines in the chart. Notice that these individual corporations, though specialized, fit into the overall role of running a hospital service. Carilion Transportation Services, Inc. provides nonemergency ambulance service to hospitals which do not have to be part of the Carilion system. Emerald Property Management, Inc. holds title to property, such as apartments, where medical residents and students live. Health East Inc. provides management consulting services and mobile imaging services such as x-rays and scanners to smaller hospitals which cannot afford the equipment. Healthcare Interiors, Inc., provides specialized interior decorating for hospitals and medical facilities. Medical Center Pharmacy, Inc. sells durable medical equipment such as wheelchairs and beds. Providers Allcare Insurance Company, Inc. manages claims of companies that are self-insured. Sterile Concepts, Inc. set up specialized and custom-made surgical trays for hospitals throughout the country. Trays are prepared according to the individual needs of a surgeon, thus reducing the time required for a nurse to put a tray together and waste of sterilized materials. Syndicated Collection Agency, Inc. is a collection agency which removes the chore and onus of forcing payment from the hospital.

Now, turn your attention to another specialized corporation, "The Roanoke Hospital Foundation," which is a supporting organization under 509(a)(3). It too has a separate board which determines how the funds will be used.

Principles Behind Corporate Organizations

By now you may be asking: When do these complex structures make sense?

1. When it is important to separate out liabilities so that the liability of one function does not spill over and ruin other essential parts of the mission; i.e., flying helicopters exposes the organizations to special risks and high operating costs.
2. When specialized management and staff are required and may have to be treated under separate labor-management agreements.
3. When it is necessary or possible for the unit to develop its own financing and have access to capital which the other units may not have; i.e., foundations can get grants and donations while hospitals can charge fees and sell bonds.
4. When the relative size of the organization is too dominant and could change the central core of operation and therefore threaten the carrying out of the principal charitable mission.
5. When there are costs and tax implications; i.e., that by filing a consolidated statement, the loss in one corporation can be covered by the gains in another. Thus, it is possible to carry out an essential service even at a loss as long as it can be partly subsidized by another subsidiary without destroying the profitable one by having it conduct activities that are losers.
6. When there is a fit, but not a direct one; i.e., insurance is a way to secure payments of patients and for self-insuring, but it does not heal illnesses.
7. When there is a perfect fit, but some consideration such as 1 above or 8 below dominates.
8. When the markets are identifiably separate in location, specialty, or clients.
9. When it is anticipated that the service may have to be sold; i.e., it is sometimes easier to dislodge a corporate unit from the rest than it is to dislodge unorganized pieces of a corporation. Thus, in the

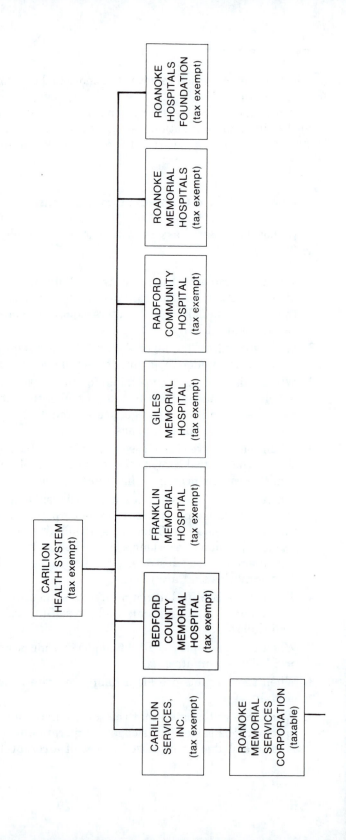

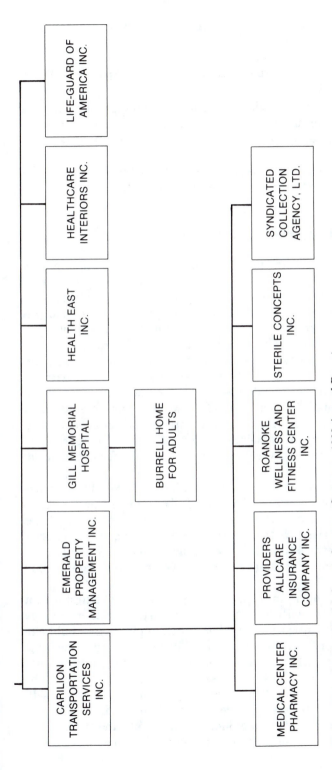

Figure 13.1 *Carilion Health System Corporate Structure*, 1988 Annual Report

for-profit world, a firm takes a service that it wishes to dislodge, turns it into a separate corporation, and sells the corporation. These are called spinoffs.

10. When there is corporate dissonance or an image problem for the parent corporation, isolation of the infant institution is invariably indicated as the treatment of choice; i.e., a collection agency.

Sometimes nonprofit corporations must reorganize. Let us turn to the subject of corporate reorganization in the nonprofit world.

THE IMPORTANCE OF REORGANIZATION

Reorganization was important for hospitals and other nonprofit health providers during the 1980s as they tried to adjust to a number of new laws, including how they were paid. In the 1990s, we are likely to see a lot of reorganization by universities. This is partly because of the tremendous ethical and liability pressures brought on by scientific work.

In the case of Salem University in West Virginia, reorganization took place to avoid a disaster. The university merged with Teyiko University of Japan. As a result, faculty salaries went up over 25 percent. Some $400,000 was added to student scholarships; the university, which was deep in debt, had all its debt paid off. New programs were added. A small West Virginia community was faced with a brighter economic future. The principal purpose of mergers, acquisitions, and corporate reorganization in the nonprofit world is the same as in the for-profit world: economic.

Among the reasons for corporate reorganizations are (1) to increase revenues, (2) to reduce costs, (3) to bring about better performance through consolidation of activities, (4) to separate and isolate liabilities and different types of risks, (5) to create different management structures, and (6) to deal with ethical and public relations problems. We will illustrate many of these points through real cases of corporate reorganization of nonprofits.

There are four dangers in corporate reorganization. The first is that the nonprofit institution will lose its tax-exempt status either entirely or be shifted from one category to another, for example, from a public to a private foundation or from a 509(a)(1) to (a)(3) or something of the kind. A second is that there will be unrelated business income created because of the gains resulting from the shift in assets from one corporation to the other or because of payments from one to the other. The third is self-dealing due partly to interlocking directorates. A fourth is that the organization will end up violating the Sherman Antitrust and the Clayton Antitrust acts prohibiting the restriction of competition. Thus, the courts

> "... we have been negotiating with Valencia Woods Nursing Center (a subsidiary of the Mercy Health System) in order to transfer the control of Valencia Woods to St. Barnabas Health System.
> Valencia Woods is a 75-bed facility, fully approved by Medicare and Medicaid. The missions of St. Barnabas and Valencia Woods have been very similar, although we have cared for the more severely ill and more poor patients. Valencia Woods is situated on 12 acres in Butler County and it has been a participant in Presents For Patients and other cooperative programs for many years.
> Actual transfer of control is not expected for several months due to regulations of the Commonwealth.
>
> Source: Reprinted by permission from memorandum dated 12/12/90 by William V. Day, St. Barnabas Health System.

banned the expansion of Rockford Memorial Hospital because through its acquisition it would have dominated 90 percent of the market share.[1] As a similar case, *United States of America* v. *Carilion Health System and Community Hospital of Roanoke Valley* shows that the definition of the "market" is critical: "When the various hospitals in the market area surrounding Roanoke are included, however, defendants' market share, even adjusted for the six other hospitals in the market that are owned or managed by Carilion, cannot be expected to approach the estimates advanced by the government."[2]

The reader of the following cases should keep three things in mind. The complexity and interconnections of organizations are often the result of growth and change in environments, rather than trickery. This is why strategic planning, as discussed in Chapter 6, is important. It helps organizations to restructure themselves as a consequence of their own internal changes and the changes in their environment.

Second, as we implied above, corporate reorganization is a legal matter requiring changes in the charter of incorporation and bylaws of the organizations involved, even if one organization is under the control of the other. This is not like changing around departments or branches.

Third, the reader should be aware that the cases are based on examples in the IRS files where names are generally not used. All organizations are described in the original by such statements as "M is an organization exempt under section 501(c)(3) of the Internal Revenue Code, and described as not being a private foundation under Sections 509(a)(1) and 170(b)(1)(A)(iii)..." or "...C is...under Section 509(a)(3)." Recall what these numbers mean?

Hint: Do not read the following to memorize the details of what was done to what organization. Read (1) to get a sense of the complexity of structures and (2) to learn what each type of reorganization can accomplish for you.

TYPES OF REORGANIZATION

Case 1: Affiliation

Observe that the organizations keep their independence but gain economies and enter into a formal legal arrangement. This is perhaps the most simple form of restructuring.

In 1985, the World Wildlife Fund entered into an affiliation agreement with the Conservation Foundation, a nonprofit, 501(c)(3) organization. The objective of the affiliation is to provide the ability of doing joint biological and social science activities on key conservation issues and to take advantage of economies resulting from shared management, development, and communication expenses. The two share the same board of directors, but remain separate legal corporations.[3]

A second example is the agreement between the Kennedy Center and the National Symphony Orchestra Association of Washington, D.C. The purpose, among others, was to reduce operating costs, increase fund-raising or development capabilities, and "to add to the artistic lustre and potential of each organization and, thus, improve the Center's and the Association's long-term prospects." Both organizations maintain their separate corporate structure and identity.[4]

Case 2: Restructuring[5]

Observe the repositioning of organizations.

LaPorte Samaritan Hospital has three nonprofit corporations under it. One of these nonprofit corporations, Jason Foundation, controls a for-profit corporation, which is a holding company. That is, this for-profit corporation, called Nia Enterprise, has nine different for-profit corporations under it. It owns 100 percent of their stocks, so it is the sole owner of each of the following:

1. A same-day surgery center
2. A collection agency that collects from patients of physicians at LaPorte Samaritan and other for-profit affiliates of LaPorte
3. A clinical laboratory that performs tests for LaPorte and others
4. A firm that manages industrial medicine for a group of physicians
5. Four corporations that are inactive

In addition to Jason Foundation, the other nonprofit controlled by LaPorte is Enrique Educational Center, which provides health-care education. The third nonprofit it controls is Carla Charity, which is a fund raiser and manager of investments for LaPorte Samaritan and for Jason Foundation.

As a result of the reorganization, Jason will become the parent corporation and LaPorte will be under it and so will be the Carla Charity and the Enrique Educational Center, and it will continue to hold all the stocks of the for-profit corporations. The organizations will continue to have interlocking directors.

The reorganization calls for Jason to carry out certain functions that LaPorte, a hospital, could not do as well. These include strategic planning and financing for the entire group and representing the groups before industry, government, and citizens; and it will act as an intermediary between LaPorte and the for-profits within the system to make sure that LaPorte gets a fair deal.

There will be several commercial transactions between members of the system, such as renting space. Nia Enterprise, which is a for-profit holding company of the nine corporations, will rent space from LaPorte. This, however, needs to be done in an arm's-length transaction, and Jason is responsible for seeing to that. LaPorte's loan to Nia Enterprise must also receive a fair rate of interest and so too must be the charge of the collection agency to LaPorte and its physicians. These were the arguments placed forth for the restructuring:

1. It assured LaPorte's commitment and leadership to its health-care mission.
2. It facilitated compliance with government reporting.
3. It segregated hospital assets from nonhospital assets to limit liability.
4. It segregated regulated from nonregulated activities.
5. It increased investment opportunities.
6. It facilitated long-range planning.
7. It improved recruiting.
8. It increased flexibility in capital expenditure projects.
9. It isolated unrelated from related businesses.
10. It removed the management of nonhospital activities and assets from LaPorte.

Case 3: Mergers[6]

Observe the disappearing of an organization and the creation of one that is composed of two or more preexisting legal organizations. We use letters because names got too confusing.

n is a nonprofit organization. It is the parent holding company of a health-care system that controls acute-care hospitals and other health service organizations. It provides overall management to and direction for the system and conducts certain community health programs. n had another nonprofit p, which was a regional holding company for acute-care hospitals and other health service corporations that were a portion of n. Under p was a nonprofit, m, which operated an acute-care hospital.

The nonprofit n had another affiliate, t, which was formed under the group 501(c)(3) authorization of the U.S. Catholic Conference. Its sole purpose was to be a charitable trust operating solely for the benefit of and in connection with s, which is a nonprofit operating an acute-care hospital serving certain areas served by m. When t became affiliated with m, another nonprofit q was made inactive. This nonprofit q had a nonprofit under it called r, which operated an acute-care hospital serving the same areas as m and s.

s gets its support services from u, which is another nonprofit organization formed under the umbrella of the U.S. Catholic Conference. This nonprofit u owns the real estate around s and a medical clinic e, which is also a nonprofit organization. But s is a nonprofit under p.

Are we clear? Now, the merger.

Three of the nonprofits, p, q, and s, are merged into m. As a result of the merger, all the assets, liabilities, operations, and employees of p, q, and s are transferred to m, and the new entity now takes on the name of p. In addition, r and q will amend their charter to show that they are now under p, and t will amend its to show that it is a supporting organization for p, which will remain under the nonprofit n.

The merger was undertaken for the following reasons:

1. Simplification.
2. The sharing of employees, facilities, and services.
3. To facilitate certain Medicare savings.
4. To improve the availability, efficiency, economy, and effectiveness of delivery of health services in the community previously served by duplicate organizations under the same nonprofit umbrella.

Case 4: Divestiture[7]

Observe that an organization, assets, or business is sold or transferred to someone else. It is no longer the property of its previous owner. Divestiture is exemplified by the sale of excess holdings as described in Chapter 4; it is sometimes required by law.

The Simon Foundation is a nonprofit educational foundation that runs not only educational functions, but a separate nonprofit hospital called the Exalter Memorial. The Simon Foundation proposes to sell its hospital assets (Exalter) to a separate corporate nonprofit entity known as Baxter, which was created by the trustees of the Simon Foundation. Baxter and Simon will be separate entities with distinct boards with no overlaps. Neither does the board of Simon have the power to appoint or remove a member of the board of Baxter, and no board member of Simon works for or acts as an agent of Baxter. (Do you see the avoidance of self-dealing?)

The Simon Foundation will sell (divest itself of, a divestiture) of the following assets to Baxter: an annex, a professional building, a parking garage, radiation therapy buildings, and all associated hospital equipment. The sale will be made at a fair market value. The sale will be made partly by Baxter's signing a note (a loan) for the real estate and equipment. These notes will bear interest at 6 percent per annum, which is payable monthly. The note payments will be for interest only for three to five years. (Do you continue to see the avoidance of self-dealing?)

At the end of this divestiture, Baxter Memorial will be the nonprofit hospital in existence, Exalter Memorial's assets will have been sold to Baxter, and Exalter will be a defunct corporation without assets. Simon Foundation will continue to exist, but only as an educational entity. The divestiture accomplishes the following:

1. Simon can focus on its educational mission without the complexity of running a hospital.
2. Since Baxter will be separate, its medical staff will now be granted a greater voice, even serving on its board of trustees.
3. The management of Baxter will be able to focus on carrying out its medical mission without being burdened with considerations of the educational mission of Simon.
4. Simon Foundation can consider requests for assistance to Baxter in the very same way and under the very same rules it considers such requests from other qualified nonprofits.

Case 5: Acquisition[8]

Observe that an organization, assets, or business is acquired.

The Lorina Conservation Institute promotes interest in and knowledge of a historical community originally established as a social experiment. In carrying out its mission, Lorina operates a building and the grounds around it, all of which are part of the exhibit, lectures, tours, and other activities integral to Lorina's mission.

Jerimiah's enterprise is a for-profit corporation. Lorina proposes to purchase all the stocks of Jerimiah's (which means that Lorina, a nonprofit, will now become the sole owner through acquisition of a for-profit corporation.) When the acquisition is completed, Jerimiah will operate only unrelated businesses. The purchase is paid for by Lorina through the transfer of a portion of the building referred to above to Jerimiah, which will turn it into a multiunit condominium. The other portion of the building will be kept by Lorina and used for its mission.

The majority of the directors of Jerimiah's will not serve on the board of Lorina. The latter's board will control the day-to-day activities of Jerimiah's independently of any relationship with Lorina. All business activities will be conducted on an arm's-length basis and based on fair market values. These business activities include maintaining guest and boarding rooms and meal service.

A board of managers for the condominium units will be created with responsibility for maintenance, insurance, and the management of common elements, but it will not be subjected to day-to-day control by Lorina. Expenses will be allocated among the units on an arm's-length basis.

The acquisition permitted the following:

1. Lorina will be in a better position to carry out its mission and more efficiently. (It does not have to provide guest room services.)
2. There will be separation of the assets and liabilities.

Case 6: Conversion[9]

Observe the change in character of the organization from tax exempt to profitable, or reverse.

In November 1988, the Tybalt Corporation changed its articles of incorporation to indicate that it was from henceforth a nonprofit. Prior to this it was a for-profit corporation.

To implement this change, Tybalt changed the nature of its stock from transferable, proprietary business corporation stock entitling the holder to dividends and a share of the assets upon dissolution to restricted, nontransferable stock that does not entitle the holder to either dividends or a share of the assets upon dissolution. None of the assets of the Tybalt Corporation was distributed to the shareholders because of or in conjunction with the conversion.

At issue was whether the collection of accounts receivables (outstanding amounts owed by customers of what was previously a for-profit firm) constituted unrelated business income. The ruling was that the collection by an exempt organization of its accounts receivable is a necessary day-to-day administrative function and not an unrelated business.

This case involves the conversion of a for-profit into a nonprofit. Admittedly, this is less common than the previous cases. But it is described here to reinforce our understanding of the importance of the ownership of assets in nonprofits. See Chapters 1 through 3. The conversion resulted in the organization getting tax-exempt status.

Conversion also occurs with a nonprofit organization changing from one form of a nonprofit to another. This is exemplified by the private foundation that wanted to go public. It was required to demonstrate public support as discussed in Chapter 4 and file a new application.[10]

SUMMARY AND CONCLUSIONS

We have discussed various forms of corporate reorganization. We have presented the basic ingredients that most corporate managers need be informed about should reorganization fit their purposes. Some forms of reorganization can be very complex. Such complexities are irrelevant for the vast majority of nonprofit managers. What is important is that the manager appreciate the availability of various reorganizations strategies. They may come in handy.

NOTES

1. U.S. Rockford Memorial Corporation, CA 7, No. 1, 89-1900.
2. Transcript of case cited in text, p. 21.
3. *World Wildlife Fund, 1989 Report*, p. 65.
4. *The John F. Kennedy Center for the Performing Arts and National Symphony Orchestra, 1988–89 Annual Report* p.7.
5. IRS Letter Ruling 8913051, Jan. 4, 1989.
6. IRS Letter Ruling 8920021, Feb. 14, 1989.
7. IRS Letter Ruling #9010073.
8. IRS Letter Ruling #8952076, Oct. 5, 1989.
9. IRS Revenue Letter 9005068, Nov. 9, 1989.
10. Private Letter Ruling, 9043028.

SUGGESTED READINGS

BAKER, JOHNATHAN B., "The Antitrust Analysis of Hospital Mergers and the Transformation of the Hospital Industry," *Law and Contemporary Problems*, 51, no. 2 (Spring 1988), pp. 93–164.

COOPERS & LYBRAND, *Corporate Structural Alternative in Higher Education*,

(U.S.A., Coopers & Lybrand, and the National Association of College Stores, 1986).

SINGER, MARK AND JOHN YANKEY, "Organizational Metamorphasis: A Study of Eighteen Nonprofit Mergers, Acquisitions, Consolidations," *Nonprofit Management and Leadership*, Vol. #1, Summer 1991, p. 357–69.

TURK, JAMES C. U.S. America vs. Carilion Health System and Community Hospital of Roanoke Valley, U.S. District Court of Western District of Virginia, Roanoke Division, 2/18/89.

PART IV

Management

I thank the good Lord every day for Father Flanagan's wisdom to begin a Foundation Fund way back in the 1940s. And I thank the good Lord every day for all the people who have contributed to this Foundation Fund. And I thank the Lord every day for the competent, caring money managers that we have, who provide such a remarkable return for our investment. Every day we don't have a new site ready is another day a boy or girl goes without getting better.

Source: Father Val J. Peter, Boys Town Annual Report, 1989, p. 2

Chapter **14**

Benefit Structures for Attracting and Retaining Employees and Minimizing Costs

The financial success of an organization depends on its ability to contain costs, the major and most rapidly growing portion of which are employee salaries and benefits. This chapter describes the types of optional benefits available to attract and retain competent employees in nonprofit organizations. Properly structured, the costs of these optional benefits can be contained and tax advantages can be enjoyed by the employees.

One very important benefit is coverage of both the organization and the management, including the directors, against liability suits. We discussed such coverage in Chapters 5 and 13.

This chapter discusses benefits including life, disability, medical and hospitalization insurance, retirement and pension plans, and other fringe benefits. It shows how some of these can be integrated with Social Security to reduce costs. Prior to January 1, 1984, nonprofits could elect not to be covered by Social Security, but now they must make contributions for employees earning $100 or more in a year. Because of the compulsory participation in Social Security, the wise manager of a nonprofit should know how such participation may be integrated into a benefit package to keep costs down and benefits at a desirable level. This is important because benefits are the most rapidly rising costs and, therefore, a key to understanding the management and financing of nonprofits.

REASONABLE COMPENSATION

The beginning point of any compensation package is reasonableness. For each employee, particularly executives, the entire package taken as a whole should be reasonable. By this is meant that it should be based on considerations of education, duties, experience, and comparability with the earnings of persons similarly situated in the region. For executives, a departure from this norm can lead to penalties for self-dealing. The IRS in its letter 9008001 issued March 5, 1990, ruled that a nonprofit which argued that its unusually high compensations to its trustees hinged on the fact they were doing a lot of staff work, including reviewing of proposals, was really self-dealing in excessive compensation. The IRS could find no similar setup in the area in which the nonprofit operated.

DISABILITY INCOME INSURANCE

We must distinguish between disability income insurance and worker's compensation. The latter is required by law and covers employees for injury sustained on the job regardless of who is at fault. The premiums are paid exclusively by the employer and are based on the type of work done, the occupational composition of the work force, and the past history with respect to the number and seriousness of past claims.

Disability income insurance (sometimes called income continuation plans) is not compulsory. It covers disability whether or not it resulted from work-related activities. One of its purposes is to protect the nonprofit against the cost of paying both the salaries of an incapacitated worker and a replacement. It also assures the worker of continued income during periods of incapacitation.

Because disability income insurance is not compulsory, the nonprofit may elect self-insurance by having a written contractual agreement with its employees to continue the payment of salary to a worker when incapacitated. Unless this is a written plan, all payments received by the worker during periods of incapacity may be fully taxable.[1]

An alternative to self-insurance is for the organization to purchase a disability insurance policy, particularly for its key employees. An insurance policy may be for long- or short-term disability. A short-term disability policy will cover the worker for approximately five months if the worker is unable to conduct normal functions. A long-term policy may cover the worker usually up to age 65, the expected time of retirement.

Cost Control

Cost can be controlled by distinguishing and choosing between long and short coverage and the integration of Social Security. A critical difference between long- and short-term policies is in the definition of disability. Commonly, the short-term definition of disability is the incapacity of the worker to perform normal occupational functions. The long-term definition is most often the incapacity of the worker to perform any occupational function whatsoever, given his or her age, work, and educational experiences. Since these are often subjectively interpreted, a long-term claim could be denied on the grounds that the person can do some type of remunerative work.

In structuring a disability income plan, the nonprofit management may begin by considering the option of not providing it for any employee or only for its key or executive employees. While this may seem inexpensive, it may make it possible to employ certain people. Second, the nonprofit may consider the option of self-insurance, which may be less expensive, depending on the number of employees who have claims and the length of time for which each incident is covered. Self-insurance should only be undertaken if a detailed plan can be written defining disability, what constitutes a new or a continued claim, how many claims each employee may make in a period, what constitutes a benefit period, and so on.

A third option is to provide only a short-run or only a long-run policy. Providing only a long-run policy means that the employee would normally have to wait five months before receiving a check from the insurance company, but during this time the nonprofit may continue full or partial salary payments to the employee.

Social Security Integration

An alternative is to purchase a short-run policy that has a waiting period. This is a period that the employee must wait before receiving the first check. The policy would most likely cover the employee for five months after the waiting period. At the end of this period, Social Security begins payment if the employee is eligible. Social Security disability income payments are long term (up to age 65). Yet another alternative is to provide no short-term coverage and wait until Social Security payments begin in the sixth month of disability.

It is necessary to understand the rules of Social Security disability if it is to be integrated into the benefit package of a nonprofit. Eligibility depends on the age of the worker when the disability occurred and the number of quarters of credits earned prior to the disability. The amount that is paid per these characteristics varies from year to year. For example, to be eligible in 1990, a worker 54 years of age must have thirty-two quarters of coverage, with twenty earned in the ten years prior to the disability.[2] Workers who became disabled before their twenty-fourth birthday need only six quarters of credit in the last three years to be eligible.

The disability must have lasted or be expected to last at least 12 months, be permanent, or result in death. In addition, the worker must be unable to work at any job regardless of age, work experience, and education. Fitness to work is determined by a state agency physician, not by the private physician of the employee. Moreover, the employee must enroll in a state vocational rehabilitation program.

Regardless of which option the nonprofit chooses, it should be aware that other segments of the benefit package may have a disability component. Pension plans and life insurance policies usually provide some disability protection. However, it might not be enough to rely on this simply because it is usually incidental. For example, the most common disability provision in a life insurance policy merely pays the premium on the policy so that it does not lapse. And the most common disability provision in a pension plan is to permit early withdrawals without penalty either by the government or by the company issuing the disability contract.

Disability premiums, as those for workmen's compensation, vary by age of workers, types of occupations, and the location by zip code, reflecting environmental risks. A nonprofit that covers several geographic locations could be faced with a different rate for each, or an average based on all locations, or a rate based on the location where most of its employees are located.

One final word. If an executive wishes a disability contract, it is sometimes wiser to first buy an individual one for him and her alone before creating and enrolling that person in a group policy. The reason for this strategy is that the ceiling (percentage of earnings to be replaced by the disability contract) can be exceeded. If the executive meets the ceiling through a group contract, an insurance company will not sell him or her additional disability. But it would ignore the ceiling reached in the individual contract if he or she subsequently becomes part of a group.

LIFE INSURANCE

Death benefit payments are not compulsory. A nonprofit may or may not choose to make a token gift to the family of a deceased worker.[3] A nonprofit that chooses to be competitive for good workers would also choose the more common alternative, which is to purchase life insurance policies on its workers.

A life insurance policy may be purchased by the nonprofit to protect itself. When a key employee dies, there is work interruption and the need to have an audit and to recruit and train a replacement. A policy bought and owned by the nonprofit on the life of its key employees or on the position held by such a person would, upon the death of the incumbent, provide proceeds that can be used to defray these expenses.

In addition, life insurance may be bought to protect the dependents of the deceased employee against the total loss of income. The life insurance contract may be of two broad types: (1) permanent insurance or (2) term insurance. There may also be an individual or group policy.

Permanent versus Term

A permanent insurance policy is one that does not have to be renewed or converted. It lasts as long as the premiums are paid, and the premiums are usually the same year after year. These policies are expensive. On the other hand, a term policy lasts only for a specifically predesignated term, one, five, ten or fifteen years, and after the predesignated term the policy must be renewed for another term, usually at a higher premium. By agreement with the insurance company, it is possible to convert a term policy to a permanent one.

A disadvantage to the worker of a permanent policy is that the part of the premium that is in excess of what the premium would have been on a term policy is taxable to the worker as income. Therefore, the permanent policy tends to be more expensive to the organization and leads to taxable income on the part of the employee. Yet many employees may prefer a permanent policy because, even with the tax, it is less expensive for the worker to have the organization buy the policy than for the worker to do so. In some instances, a permanent policy for key employees may be an incentive to attract such persons to the organization.

Because of its simplicity and lower costs, the group term policy is best suited for the work force of the nonprofit. The term of the insurance is usually one year. This makes sense because people enter and leave the employ of the organization every year. It is renewed every year, at a higher rate, that the employee remains.

Group versus Individual

The nonprofit may also elect group or individual policies. Group policies are less expensive and often superior in their coverage. They are less expensive because certain administrative costs decline on the average as the group gets larger. Most importantly, group policies protect the insurance company against adverse selection. This refers to the inclination of individuals who are most adversely exposed to the possibilities of death to be the most eager to select life insurance coverage. If only such persons were covered, the insurance company could find itself continuously paying claims. But the larger the group is the more high-risk workers would be balanced by low-risk workers, and therefore the lower the premium the company will charge because the number of claims will be relatively lower.

For important legal purposes, a "large" group is one with ten or more members. For groups of that size, the nonprofit management may exclude certain classes of workers from coverage. A class may be excluded if it is based on such broad definitions as occupational classification, salary, full- or part-time employment, or union status. The class must be defined to avoid individual selection and exclusion. Individuals may be selected or excluded because of their membership in a class within the larger work force of the nonprofit, not because of individual characteristics.

There are important flexibilities with group policies. Upon retirement or separation, the policies may be converted to an individual policy. This conversion is normally possible regardless of the reason for separation, including the demise of the organization.[4] Group policies may have a waiver of premium rider, which waives premiums if the worker becomes permanently disabled so that disability would not cause the policy to lapse.

Cost Control

There may be a probationary period before an employee is covered for life insurance, and employees may also be required to contribute to the premiums. A probationary period often makes sense since it would give benefits to an employee who has made at least a minimal commitment to the organization, even though it could be a hindrance to recruiting workers. Employee contributions are particularly useful if the employee wishes to have the policy cover the life of a dependent or spouse. However, requiring a contribution on the part of the employee to cover his or her own life is a disincentive.[5] Group term is cheaper than permanent.

Death Benefits

The nonprofit is free to choose a policy that would give death benefits that exceed $50,000. For tax purposes, the maximum benefit is $50,000. Any policy that offers a benefit in excess of this amount would create taxable income to the employee. The tax will be levied on the premium paid for the amount in excess of $50,000. Here, again, some executives will gladly pay that tax since any comparable policy bought on the open market is likely to be more expensive even after considering the tax. Of course, the tax can be avoided altogether. If the policy on the life of the employee has a death benefit that exceeds $50,000 and the policy is donated and owned by a nonprofit as a charitable gift, then the excess premiums are not taxable.

Even though a group policy, it is owned by the employee. Thus, the employee is free to name beneficiaries, change them, or even use the policy as collateral for a loan. If the policy is a permanent policy, not only could it be used as collateral for a loan, but it would also have a loan value, that is, a periodic accumulation (called the cash or surrender value) that could be borrowed. Term policies (unless of fifteen years or more) have no such value and, therefore, can at best be used only as security, roughly as credit insurance.

Upon the death of the employee, the beneficiaries may choose one of several settlement options. They may choose to receive the benefits in a lump sum, or over a specific number of payments, or a specific amount per payment; they may guarantee a minimum number or amount of payments; they may take interest, leaving only the principal to another beneficiary; or payments may be made for the life of the beneficiary and terminate upon that beneficiary's death.

Each of these has important tax and financial implications. For example, a lump sum leads to no income taxes to the beneficiary, although it could lead to an estate tax unless the individual gave 100 percent to a spouse or a charity. An interest only leads to a $1000 annual deduction if the beneficiary is a spouse, but a tax on everything above the $1000. Periodic payments are partially taxed. What is important is when organizations increasingly offer financial advice as one of their benefits, there is an awareness of the income, gift, and estate taxes associated with various death benefit options. For example, the naming of a clearly identified beneficiary, by full name and relationship, would enable probate to be avoided.

Social Security Integration

With compulsory participation in Social Security, a nonprofit manager may find it wise to consider survivorship benefits in determining the percentage of the employee's income the nonprofit would wish to replace through its own insurance. Here again it is important to consider the Social Security eligibility criteria.[6] A worker might be eligible in one of two ways. To be currently insured, the worker needs to have earned six quarters of coverage during the thirteen calendar quarters ending with the quarter in which death occurred. To be fully insured, the worker must have quarters of coverage that correspond to his or her age. One who is 54 must have thirty-two quarters; one who is 50, twenty-eight quarters, and so on.

A spouse of at least nine months and the parent of a dependent child, whether natural or adopted, are eligible for survivor's benefits. But there can be no duplication for the same person; a person cannot get payments as a retiree and also as a survivor. One check for the higher of the two benefits is received.

Split-dollar Policies

An organization may wish to recruit or retain a key person through an investment known as split-dollar insurance. In its simplest form, the organization takes out a permanent policy on the life of its executive and pays all or part of the premiums. Upon the death of the executive, his or her beneficiaries receive the death benefit and the organization is repaid the amount it invested in the premiums. This strategy allows the executive to obtain insurance at a very low price, even after paying taxes for the premiums paid by the nonprofit. This is so because the tax is substantially lower than the premium. Another alternative of a split-dollar policy provides for the executive, upon leaving, to take the policy and repay the nonprofit for its contributions by paying it the cash value of the policy. Yet another alternative, called a reverse split-dollar, makes the charity the beneficiary of the death proceeds and the estate (or some other designee) the beneficiary of the cash value upon the death of the executive.

ACCIDENTAL DEATH AND DISMEMBERMENT

A nonprofit may wish to protect its employees who travel or are exposed to risk of injury and death due to accidental causes. Insurance can be bought to protect against losses due to accidental death and dismemberment. This coverage may be bought separately and very inexpensively or as part of the life or health insurance policies.

To some extent, accidental death represents a duplication of coverage. Dismemberment is a real fear in some occupations but not in others; moreover, the disability coverage may well offer sufficient compensation. The full death benefit may be covered on the life insurance policy. If it is not, perhaps it should be. Is it any more expensive to die from an accident than to die from natural causes? Why seek a higher or independent coverage for accidents? One reason for the inexpensiveness of this type of policy is that the probability of collecting is very low.

The conditions under which the beneficiaries or insured may collect under accidental death policies are strict. Death must usually occur within a specific period of time, perhaps 90 days after the accident. Moreover, death must be due exclusively to the accident and not attributed to or the result of another cause.[7] Also, death resulting from certain types of accidents may be excluded from coverage.

If death or dismemberment owing to travel is the risk of concern, consideration should be given to using a credit card to pay for travel. Many include this type of protection.

MEDICAL AND HOSPITALIZATION INSURANCE

Of all elements in the usual benefit package, this is probably the most confusing and difficult because (1) the risk is so high that everybody needs this type of protection, (2) the cost is so high that every employer needs to control it, and (3) every policy is different, with a wide range for comparing seemingly incomparable benefits or costs. Nonprofits that require overseas travel by their employees have the additional problem of being sure that they are covered by an insurer that provides for payment for services rendered abroad, including air evacuation.

Medical and hospitalization costs have been rising dramatically—faster than the rate of inflation. Health and medical benefits are intended to protect the employee against these costs. This protection may be provided through regular commercial or association insurance, Blue Cross/Blue Shield, or through a health maintenance organization (HMO).

Basic versus Major or Comprehensive

Medical and hospitalization insurance policies differ by company, and there may be several different alternative policies from which the nonprofit organization may choose. The most simple and perhaps least expensive insurance plan is the basic plan. The principal characteristic of basic plans is that they emphasize hospital-related benefits. Such plans cover hospital services, some emergency costs, and basic surgical fees. Basic plans may differ from company to company, and one company may have more than one alternative.

Under the basic plan, hospital room and board are covered. The payments may be for a specified amount per day up to some maximum dollar amount or number of days. Other hospital charges such as medicine, drugs, and x-rays are usually paid as a percentage of the benefits being paid for the room and board. Surgical fees may be paid according to a schedule or according to what is usual, customary, and reasonable for similar surgical services in the geographic area.

Major medical insurance policies cover a larger number of medical events, pay a higher maximum, and are more expensive than basic plans. Major medical protects against catastrophic illnesses. A major plan may be a supplement to a basic plan so that it covers illnesses excluded by the basic plan or picks up payments when the basic plan reaches its limits. In this latter case, there may be a deductible before the major plan kicks in. Alternatively, the major plan may be independent of the basic plan or may incorporate it into a comprehensive plan. Again, major plans differ among and within companies.

Tax-Favored Medical Reimbursement Plans

Medical reimbursement plans are an alternative way of financing health care. These plans allow workers to put dollars into an account for paying medical bills. These dollars escape taxation as part of the salary of the employee. The plans work well when the worker has a good estimate of what the annual health bill for the family will be because the amount not used at the end of the year is lost; i.e., "use it or lose it". The amount placed in these plans also counts to reduce the maximum amount the employee can place in a tax sheltered annuity (discussed in this chapter).

Cost-cutting Strategies

Because of the breadth of coverage of major plans, the insurance companies impose cost-sharing devices. The nonprofit may choose how much it wishes to participate in each of these, the net effect of which is to shift costs to the employee. One such device is the deductible and another is co-insurance. A deductible requires the employee to pay the first dollars on a claim, often the first $50 or $100. When the claim exceeds the deductible, the company may share the cost further by paying only a specified percentage of the amount in excess of the deductible, usually 80 percent of that amount. The remaining 20 percent of the claim is paid by the employee. Above the level of co-insurance, the company may pay 100 percent of the claim up to some maximum. The greater the deductible and the co-insurance are the lower the cost to the nonprofit because the lower the exposure of the insurance company.

The insurance company may limit its exposure even further. It may limit the amount it would pay to an employee or a family either per calendar year or per policy year, per medical event, or for all events combined. Similarly, deductibles may be per person, per family, per policy period, and so on. All this is in addition to an overall maximum limit over the life of the employee. Hence, a policy could read that it is limited to $100,000 per calendar year per employee and $400,000 over the life of that person. At this limit the company reserves the right to terminate the policy.

In the same way that the insurance company may wish to limit its exposure, so too should the worker. Therefore, it is wise to seek out a policy that has a stop-loss feature. This means that beyond a certain cost the insurance company takes over 100 percent of payments up to its maximum limit.

In considering medical insurance, the choice is between a basic or a major plan or a combination of the two, either with the major supplementing the basic (which means that the first dollars of payment come from the basic) or a comprehensive plan that contains both the features of a basic and a major plan.

Comprehensive and major plans are expensive. The cost can be lowered is the nonprofit accepts a higher level of co-insurance and deductible and by making the plan contributory (meaning that the employees pay part of the premium, if only for their dependents). Other cost-saving devices include the nonprofit recommending to employees the use of hospitals and physicians who are competent but lower priced and by excluding some routine visits from coverage. The trade-off with cost-saving devices might be the postponement of preventive care.

Partly because of the growth of two-worker families, there is the increased likelihood that each spouse would have independent coverage under the same or different employer plans. This duplication of coverage is costly and wasteful. The rules and practices of health insurance companies require that benefits be coordinated. This means that workers or their dependents can collect from only one policy at a time. While a dependent child must first collect from the father's policy, a child of divorced parents may also have to collect first from the father's policy. The rules of coordination of benefits include considerations of divorce, separation, length of coverage, sex of spouse, and so on. In a nutshell, they simply remove the possibility of collecting from more than one company at the same time and for the same cause.

A closely related principle is the indemnity principle. This says that the insured cannot collect more than the cost of the health and medical service. When this principle is considered with the principle of coordination of benefits, it becomes clear that there is no way to recover from being overinsured as far as medical and health insurance are concerned. Only one company will pay unless the contract says otherwise. The extra premium is wasted.

Outside the insurance itself, many nonprofits, particularly the larger ones, may benefit from using techniques such as providing workers with a list of preferred medical practitioners and encouraging healthy behavior on the part of their employees and families.

Blue Cross and Blue Shield

Blue Cross and Blue Shield were, until the 1986 tax law, nonprofit corporations. They compete with other insurance companies. They were examples of nonprofits operating within the market sphere. As corporations, Blue Cross and Blue Shield are creations of individual states. These organizations differ in coverage, cost, financial strength and charter across states. Do not presume that they are necessarily superior.

Blue Cross is made up of cooperating hospitals within a state and Blue Shield of cooperating physicians. They are separate organizations although they may share facilities and cooperate and offer their coverage as a unit; hence, the familiar term, Blue Cross/Blue Shield.

Blue Cross may have a closer relationship with cooperating hospitals and Blue Shield a closer relationship with physicians than do insurance companies. But the same hospitals and physicians that accept payments from Blue Cross/Blue Shield accept payments from patients covered by insurance policies.

Insurance companies offer a wider range of products (including pensions and life and disability insurance), which make up a complete benefit package. Therefore, it is possible to construct a benefit package with one insurance company but not with Blue Cross or Blue Shield. This is not necessarily advantageous other than for convenience. Finally, both Blue Cross and Blue Shield and individual insurance companies offer options in the design of health and medical benefit contracts with each option being differently priced with different coverage. Cost-cutting under Blue Cross/Blue Shield is roughly the same as discussed for other insurance companies.

Health Maintenance Organizations

Unlike insurance companies and Blue Cross/Blue Shield, health maintenance organizations (HMOs) are direct providers of health and medical services. The employee gets a wide range of services, such as hospital care, outpatient x-ray and laboratory services, physical examinations, eye examinations, routine gynecological examinations, and maternity care, all at no extra cost other than the initial fee called the capitation fee. Many HMOs are also nonprofit.

Often there is no deductible and no co-insurance, although there may be a copayment for prescription drugs. Two misunderstandings about

HMOs should not influence decisions about them. There is the possibility of 24-hour service even if the person is away from the service district of the HMO in which membership is held. Some HMOs may also require that the enrollee pick up some costs. There are exclusions covering such things as cosmetic surgery, some organ transplants, dental care, and custodial services. A new employee with a serious medical history may find that an HMO is less likely to limit his participation because of this prior medical condition.

Because most of the services are provided without extra charge, HMOs are said to be less inclined to prescribe unnecessary treatment and hospitalization. They must absorb all costs. On the other hand, because the enrollees have prepaid for all services, they may be less reluctant to use HMOs and therefore potential problems may be treated early when treatment is likely to be more successful and less expensive.

When a nonprofit employer is considering a health and medical benefit package, it may be required by law to offer its employees the opportunity to select a federally qualified HMO. This is so (1) when the nonprofit employer has and contributes to a health and medical benefit plan for its employees, (2) if the employer has twenty-five or more employees, (3) if it pays at least the minimum wage, and (4) is a federally qualified HMO in the area where the nonprofit has twenty-five or more employees submits a written request to be considered and if those employees are not presently served by an HMO.[8]

Considerations in Choosing

Recognizing that there is a threshold when an HMO option must be offered, a nonprofit employer who is below this threshold may choose among HMOs, Blue Cross/Blue Shield, an insurance company, or an association of nonprofits that form an insurance pool or multiemployer plan. The choice ought to be made based on the cost to the employer and employee, the package of benefits, the competence of the selling agent, and the experience of others with the equivalent quality of service. While it is possible for the nonprofit employer to create its own health and medical benefit package or self-insure, this is not recommended. The antidiscrimination laws that are intended to protect lower-earning workers from being excluded and to prevent management from reaping the major benefits are complicated and stiff and apply to self-insured, not to plans with licensed insurance companies. The law presumes that these antidiscrimination restrictions are satisfied if the insuring responsibility falls on a third party (such as the insurance company) rather than on the employer. Moreover, the organization could experience considerable drain on its resources as employees become ill.

In comparing the HMOs with other medical and health providers, a criticism that is often heard is that the employee does not have a choice of physicians. This is not altogether true. Physicians may form an HMO among themselves as independent providers. The individual may choose among these physicians and still obtain the benefits of an HMO. Such a group of physicians is referred to as an independent practice association or IPA.

COBRA

The Consolidated Omnibus Budget Reconciliation Act of 1985 (COBRA) requires all employers except governments and churches to give employees an extension on health coverage at the point of termination of their employment for any reason, voluntary or involuntary, unless for reasons of gross misconduct. Part or all of the cost of this extension can be shifted to the terminated employee.

The employer is considered to have a health plan if the employer contributes to premium payments, if the plan is maintained for employees, and if the employee's premium is lower than it would have been on the market. The extension must be for eighteen months. It is for thirty-six months for spouses and dependents due to divorce, death, and legal separation; it may also be for thirty-six months for dependents of the worker who lose dependency status because of turning 25.

Social Security Integration

The two points of integration of Social Security is with disability, which we have discussed, and with Medicare. We skip discussion of the details of the latter, but point out that it applies only to workers 65 years of age or older, who have been receiving disability or have kidney defects. Medicare should be considered in the determination of whether the organization wishes to offer postretirement health benefits beyond those required by COBRA.

Nonprofits may be affected by a 1990 change in COBRA. It gives states the right to pay certain employee continuation premiums if they prove lower than Medicare premiums. At this writing, it is not clear how this will affect nonprofits.

PENSIONS

The major objective of a pension plan is to provide support for the employee during retirement years. A properly designed pension plan can provide a number of additional benefits, including the deferring of income taxes and the ability to withdraw cash to meet emergencies.

It is possible for a nonprofit to institute a pension plan that would cost it virtually nothing and still benefit employees. Section 403(b), sometimes called TSA for tax-sheltered annuity, was passed by Congress to give nonprofits a special vehicle. Before discussing Section 403(b) in particular, there are some basic principles about pensions that the nonprofit manager ought to know.

Defined Benefits versus Defined Contribution

Pensions are of basically two types: defined benefits and defined contribution. The defined benefit plans stipulate the amount of benefits an employee will receive upon retirement. This may be a flat number of dollars, a percentage of salary earned over the years the employee worked with the nonprofit, a percentage of the employee's final pay, or an amount adjusted for the number of years of service.[9] What is being defined is the benefit to be received several years from now when the employee retires.

Because the benefits to be received upon retirement are stipulated in a defined benefit plan, the nonprofit must resolve an actuarial problem. It must determine how much it has to deposit in each of the remaining working years of the employee so that the promised amount will be available on the date the employee retires.[10] Furthermore, to ensure that the promise will be kept, the nonprofit may have to comply with several regulations, including the need to put up each year sufficient dollars so that future pension obligations can be met. This is called funding future pension obligations. The amount will vary according to the number, age, and life expectancies of workers covered (including those already retired), the amount the pension plan has and is expected to earn, and the amount that is promised to workers at the time of their retirement.

The defined contribution plan differs from the defined benefit plan because it stipulates the amount of contributions that will be made, rather than the amount of benefits to be paid. It is easier to set up and administer and requires less reporting. The only promise that the nonprofit makes is that it will contribute a specified percentage of the employee's salary or a fixed amount of that salary to his or her retirement account each year. The employee chooses how these contributions are to be invested. And each employee has a separate account, rather than being part of a large pool, such as in the defined benefit plan. The Section 403(b) plan to be discussed later is a defined contribution plan.

Defined contribution plans are of two types. Money purchase plans make a contribution that is fixed in the sense that it does not depend on the performance of the employee or the organization. Thus, the organization may agree to contribute 7 percent or $200 of an employee's salary each month. Alternatively, in profit-sharing or incentive plans, the contribution is based on the fiscal performance of the organization or employees. In addition, the employer may vary the amount contributed each year.

Defined contribution plans that are money purchase plans are usually simpler to administer and therefore more popular. They are not as regulated by the government as are defined benefit plans and do not require annual estimates about how much the organization must contribute in order to meet its pension promises in the distant future. The only promise is to make an annual contribution of a specific percentage of the worker's base pay.

Another approach is called a target plan. This stands between a defined benefit and a defined contribution plan. In this approach the organization sets a target benefit it would like to meet upon the retirement of the worker and defines its contributions in terms of that target. Unlike the defined benefit plan, however, the organization has no legal obligation to achieve the target.

Contributory versus Noncontributory and Fixed versus Variable

Whether a plan is defined contribution, target, or defined benefit, it may be contributory or noncontributory. A contributory plan provides for the employee to make either voluntary (elective) or mandatory contributions. The latter, which have to be set at a low enough level so that all employees may meet it without undue hardship, is simply an amount the employee is required to contribute annually in order to remain in the plan. The voluntary amount is the amount employees may, on their own volition, contribute to build up their accounts.

In a contributory plan, the organization may also make a contribution, but in a noncontributory plan, only the organization makes a contribution. The employees make none. This latter approach is often seen as simpler to administer. The contributory plan, however, may have an advantage in that it could be designed to accommodate the employee's savings and individual retirement account (IRA).[11]

The contributions made to the retirement plan may be deposited into a variable or a fixed account as elected by the employee. Deposits into a variable account are used to purchase common stocks, so the rate at which the contributions grow is determined by the growth in value of the stocks.

Contributions made to the fixed account are invested in securities such as bonds and money market funds where there can be some reasonable assurance of earning no less than some specific rate. Insurance companies are willing to guarantee a rate of return for a specified period, and so too are banks on certificates of deposit.

Settlement Options

The employee can maintain a similar distinction between variable and fixed account earnings upon retirement. The first means that each check will reflect the earnings in the stock market; that is, some checks will be higher than others. The fixed amount means that every check will be the same.

The employees may also choose the manner in which they would like to receive payments upon retiring. The entire retirement benefit can be taken in a lump sum, in periodic payments guaranteed either in terms of the number or amount per payment, or in periodic payments that terminate upon the death of the employee or continue after death to a designated survivor. All plans are required to give married employees the option of payments that continue to the surviving spouse upon the death of the retiree. The employee is not required to accept the option, but if the option is rejected, the employee must supply evidence that the spouse accepts this rejection. The aim is to secure a flow of income to a surviving spouse. One reason why the option may be rejected is that the periodic payments are lower than those the worker would obtain under the life option that terminates payments upon the worker's death.

Each option has income- and estate-tax implications which the employee should seek advise on.

Rules for Retirement Plan

While we have presented the general features of pension plans, there are specific rules that must be followed. One set of rules requires annual reporting to the employees on the developments and earnings in the plan during the year, including any pertinent changes. A second set of rules determines if the plan will be qualified for tax advantages. These rules should be appreciated by managers of nonprofits.

To review the tax benefits, if the plan qualifies, contributions to the retirement plan and earnings of the plan are not taxed to the employee. Taxes are postponed until retirement years when the worker is supposedly in a lower income bracket. For a young worker 21 years of age, taxes could be deferred some forty years until retirement. To be qualified for this tax benefit, the plan must conform to certain rules.

The basic rule is that the plan must not exist only for the benefit of high-salaried workers, directors, managers, trustees, and key supporters (such as disqualified persons discussed earlier). How, then, is eligibility determined?

Aliens, part-time workers, workers who come under a union agreement providing for some other source of coverage, and workers under 21 years of age can be excluded automatically from eligibility without fear of violating the rules against discrimination. The effect of this is to reduce the number of persons the organization has to cover and therefore the cost.[12]

Eligibility might be immediate or after one year of service (defined as 1000 hours of paid employment in a twelve-month period). No more than two years may elapse before the worker becomes eligible. If a two-year waiting period is used, all contributions are 100 percent vested when participation starts, according to the 1986 law. In those cases where a defined benefit plan is utilized, the employer is not required to make an employee eligible if that employee is within less than five years of the normal retirement age, which is usually 65.

The reason for putting an upper limit on the defined benefit plan is to avoid placing a financial burden on organizations. For example, if a new worker has only a short time to work before retiring, an organization would have only a short time in which to accumulate the retirement benefits to which it has obligated itself in a defined manner. The amount required, to begin paying a worker 30 percent of his or her final pay for a lifetime only after two years of service, might be very large. This problem does not exist with a defined contribution plan and such plans do not carry an upper age limit for participation.

The plan must have a vesting schedule. This schedule gives the rate at which the employees acquire ownership over the employer's contributions to their retirement accounts. Note that the vesting schedule refers only to the employer's contributions. All the employees' contributions are 100 percent vested when made. The employees cannot forfeit their contributions.

The 1986 tax law simplified vesting schedules. One provides for 100 percent vesting of all the employer's contributions to the employee's retirement account after five years of service. The other requires vesting of 20 percent after three years, 40 percent at the end of four, 60 percent at the end of five, 80 percent at the end of six, and 100 percent at the end of seven years.[13] This is called the seven-year minimum vesting schedule.

An employee can lose vesting credits or eligibility if there is a break in service, that is, if the employee fails to do paid work for the organization for at least 501 hours in a twelve-month period for reasons other than military and jury duty, pregnancy, vacation time, or layoffs. Federal law now requires that people be given a grace period of five years before all previous credits toward vesting or eligibility be lost because of a break in service. Within the five-year period, the employee ought to be able to buy back into the system, picking up all previously earned credits and all credits that may have been accumulated during the break in service.[14]

A pension plan must be permanent unless termination is the result of economic difficulties. Termination of a plan by the employer leads to 100 percent vesting of all accumulated amounts in the employees.

A Funding Agency

A decision has to be made about the funding agency. For most non-profits, this is done simultaneously with the plan, since they merely accept a prototype plan offered by the company that will manage the funds. These prototype plans permit the organization to fill in certain blanks about eligibility, vesting, and amount of contributions and how the fund is to be invested. In completing these forms, all the above discussions apply. With a defined benefit plan, all the money is placed in one pool and administered by one agency. In a defined contribution plan, each employee has a separate account in his or her name and chooses how that account is managed by the agency. With a 403(b), each employee can choose a different agency (company) to which to have the contributions sent.

There are several alternatives. Banks, mutual funds, and insurance companies are common funding agencies of regular pension plans. With the 403(b), however, banks (unless they sell annuities or mutual funds) are not qualified agents. Insurance companies may offer the widest variations of alternative funding. The best advise to give a manager in selecting among these is to know the services each provides. An insurance company, for example, may have a family of mutual funds and also have a variety of annuities. Nonprofits may also wish to consult association plans. This is a good general rule; the Society for Nonprofit Organizations may be a source of benefit information.

Social Security Integration

Now that nonprofits must participate in the Social Security system, it is wise to integrate the pension plan of the organization with that of the system. Integration of pension plans lowers the organization's costs of providing pension benefits. Basically, what one does in integrating pension systems is to use the Social Security system as a floor. The private plan of the organization provides benefits above that floor. The actual mechanics of accomplishing this depends on whether the plan is a defined benefit or a defined contribution plan. For each, integration is different, but the results are basically the same—using the private system to go beyond the threshold set and paid for by Social Security.

Because participation in the Social Security system was only recently required of nonprofits, workers for these organizations who are 55 years of age on January 1, 1984, or older are allowed to retire with full Social Security benefits with less years of credit than other workers of the same age who are covered outside the nonprofit sector.

Section 403(b)

Section 403(b) is a special retirement plan for 501(c)(3) organizations available through mutual funds, insurance contracts, and some retirement plans for churches. Only 501(c)(3)s, including public schools, may use this defined contribution plan. Section 403(b) permits nonprofit employers to contribute to a pension contract for their full- or part-time employees.

Section 403(b) plans have several advantages. The yearly amount contributed by the employer of employee earnings is not taxed until funds are withdrawn. Thus, employees of nonprofits get to defer some of their income from present taxes. All employees, regardless or part or full-time employment and regardless of age, can be eligible.

Section 403(b) allows withdrawals prior to age 59½ without penalty because of death of the worker, disability, early retirement, or medical expenses that are deductible. All other early withdrawals are subject to income tax and a 10 percent penalty.

One disadvantage of the 403(b) is that if on retiring the worker takes all his or her money in one lump sum, he or she will pay taxes on the entire amount. There is no way to average the income over ten or five years, a device used to lower taxes on lump-sum payments in some pension plans. To avoid this problem, the worker may wish to take the funds in periodic annual payments, in which case part of the payments will be received free of taxes.

The nonprofit can make a 403(b) plan available to its employees at no cost to the institution, and the organization need not contribute any funds of its own. The contributions can be made through salary reductions, where employees agree to reduce their salaries by a specific amount to be used by the employer to make the contributions.[15] The employee's income for tax purposes is lowered by the amount of the contribution, meaning that this amount is not presently subject to tax—except that it is not excluded in the computation of the Social Security tax. The employee can continue to make contributions while employed, all the while sheltering income and the earnings on the accumulated accounts for taxes. Furthermore, all contributions by the employee and all the interest earned on these amounts are immediately vested at 100 percent. It cannot be forfeited. The employee owns it.

Unlike other retirement plans, the amount that can be contributed through a 403(b) depends on the number of years the employee has worked for the nonprofit in question, length being advantageous because contributions can be made even to reflect back years before the plan went into effect. This is called the "catch-up" feature. Obviously, the greater the number of years is the greater the amount that can be contributed. There is a new statutory limit of $9500, an amount subject to revision by Congress in order to adjust for inflation.[16]

A worker who wishes to use the 403(b) plan needs to calculate precisely how much he or she can exclude. The $9500 limit, which is popularly quoted, is the total for all voluntary or elective contributions that the employee makes to all pension plans run by the organization. The fact that this is the elective limit does not mean that any employee may contribute up to that much. For each employee, a specific calculation has to be made to increase contribution the longer the service and to decrease it the greater the amount of tax preferred benefits the employee is already receiving. Publication 571 of the IRS shows how the calculations should be done.

Excess contributions that are not removed before April 15 of the tax year can cause a 15 percent penalty. Church workers have special rules that are especially attractive. For example, even though they may have worked for several churches, they may treat them as one employer, which has the effect of boosting the amount excludable from taxation.

Rabbi Trust

The name derives from the fact that this technique was developed for a rabbi. It is a particular type of retirement plan that is now used widely in corporations (especially where the executives fear an unfriendly takeover), even though it had its legal genesis with a rabbi and his synagogue. Here is how it works. A nonprofit wishes to set up a retirement plan for an executive. If it gives him access to the contributions, he is immediately taxed. If, however, the executive only gets a promise from the nonprofit, then it can be broken or when he is ready to retire he may discover there are no assets. To protect against this, he has the organization make its contributions to a trust that neither he nor the organization controls. This works for tax purposes, however, as long as the creditors of the organization can have access to the funds should the organization go bankrupt. The objective is to protect the executive against changes in the leadership of the organization and at the same time avoid current taxes. The law, however, requires protection for the creditors to be superior to that of the organization or the employee.

CAFETERIA PLANS

Cafeteria or flexible plans are increasingly considered by nonprofits as a way of packaging benefits. Cafeteria plans are based on the premise that no two employees may need exactly the same amount of each type of benefit: One employee would prefer more life insurance and less health and hospitalization. Under a cafeteria plan, the employee may make the trade-off. Each employee can tailor his or her own mix among the benefits included in the plan. Each employee creates his or her own package.

With a cafeteria plan, the employer places all nontaxable benefits, including health and life insurance, retirement plans, cash, disability or others, before the employee. Excluded by law are scholarships and taxable fringe benefits discussed later in this chapter. The employee may choose between cash and nontaxable benefits.[17] As in a cafeteria, the employee is given a meal ticket and chooses from a variety of offerings as much as is wanted (within permissible limits).

PROFIT-SHARING PLAN

In more than one ruling, the IRS has stated that a nonprofit may have a profit-sharing plan.[18] These plans are of two major types: bonus or incentive plans or savings and retirement plans. Basically, the bonus or incentive plans are those that compensate employees on a percentage basis, that is, a percentage of the revenues or cost savings to the organization.

The term profit sharing does not mean that it comes from a profit, although prior to the 1986 changes that was basically true. It means that the employer can have annual discretion about how much to contribute and this may vary from zero to some percentage. It also means that the contribution is based on the performance of the organization. In the other type of defined contribution plan discussed earlier, money purchase, the amount is fixed and must be contributed without regard to the performance of the organization. Thus, profit-sharing plans are ideal for incentive programs.

A study of one plan approved by the IRS suggests that the plan should have the following properties:[19]

1. The bonus should not make the total compensation of the employee (regular salary and benefits combined) unreasonable compared with another person with similar education and experience in a similar position in a comparable nonprofit in the same geographic area.
2. The organization should not deviate from its tax-exempt mission, and benefits should not inure to private persons. Thus, an unrea-

sonable compensation or one that is solely for the benefit of certain managers unrelated to their performance may be construed as a plan to promote their private welfare at the expense of the mission.

3. The plan should be based on some indicator that proffers benefits to others, such as a bonus plan based on cost savings to patients or clients so that they too are beneficiaries.

4. The plan should be so calibrated that if the performance is not achieved, the incentive or bonus payments would not be made.[20]

Two experts caution that the plan should also have the following properties:[21]

1. The organization's management should be omitted from the plan to remove suspicion that the plan is to serve them.

2. The plan should be established as a result of an arm's-length negotiation between the management and workers of the organization.

3. The plan should contain a statement of how it will help the organization advance its tax-exempt status.

4. There should be a limitation on how much each person can receive in a period so that no one would be unreasonably compensated.

5. There should be a formula for calculating the benefits so they would not result in increasing prices and charges to the public.

6. There should be a system of annually comparing the compensation with those in other organizations to maintain reasonableness in compensation and in the quality and quantity of services being provided.

The second type of profit-sharing plan, however, is no longer available to nonprofits. This is a savings or a retirement plan known as a 401(k) that is typically used by for-profit firms to share their profits with their employees. In view of the 1986 tax law, nonprofits can no longer issue these. Those that were in existence were allowed to continue.[22]

FRINGE BENEFITS

There are a number of other benefits that a nonprofit employer might offer. These include loans, to the extent that they are permitted by state law and the bylaws. These loans should require repayment, not be habitual to the same persons, should charge an interest rate comparable to the rate being paid by the federal government for loans of similar term (which would still be better than what the borrower would have to pay commercially), be reported as discussed in Chapters 1 and 5, should require repayment in full by some specific but reasonable date, and should be reasonably small, perhaps less than $10,000. Such loans need to be made on a businesslike basis. Again, beware of self-dealing and prohibited acts as discussed in Chapter 4. Recall that in Chapter 5 we said that personal loans to trustees are prohibited in many states.

Other benefits include discounts such as tuition, child care, and legal assistance. The objective should be to provide these without causing a tax liability for the employee. How can that be done? By being one or more of the following:

1. Employers, the nonprofits, can give services and products to employees, dependents, and retirees without causing them to be taxed as long as there is no additional cost to the nonprofit for doing so and as long as they are made available to all employees on equal basis. The service or product must be in the line in which the employee works. In a nonprofit school, for example, all children and spouses of professors (active and retired) could be given free education without causing that part of the tuition that does not exceed $5000 to be included in the incomes of these professors. This rule does not require that the gift be exercised at the school offering the fringe benefit.

2. The nonprofit can give equal discounts to all present and retired employees, their dependents, and spouses as long as the discount does not exceed 20 percent of the selling price to customers and does not exceed the amount by which it had marked up the goods in order to have a profit. Theoretically, then, a university could give every one of these persons a discount that conforms with these rules without anyone having to report this as income.

3. The nonprofit can offer what is known as working condition fringes, benefits of things that would otherwise be deductible, such as uniforms, had the employee purchased it himself or herself. Again, all employees must be treated alike if any is to avoid being taxed.

4. De minimis: some things are so small that nobody fusses. Try to avoid getting above $25.00.

Two types of assistance are worthy of special mention. Educational assistance that falls into any category mentioned above cannot be for graduate school or for dependent children under 25. Generally, preferential treatment of the cost of dependent (child) care is not available to a one-earner family unless the nondependent employee who is the one-earner is disabled or a student.

ERISA AND IRS RULES

Any employee welfare or pension plan that is operated by an employer whether in the for-profit or nonprofit sector is subject to the rules of the Employee Retirement and Income Security Act of 1974 (ERISA) unless the program is for an employer with less than 100 employees or, if 100 or larger, the program is for a select group of executives or the program is financed through a licensed insurance company; or is based purely on unenforceable promises and not on actual contributions of cash or property; or the employer simply pays the employee directly out of the assets of the organization.

This means that many employee benefit or pension plans run by nonprofits are subject to ERISA rules on disclosure, requiring that specific information be shared with the employees about how the plan operates. ERISA also will subject the organization to annual reporting to the secretary of labor (the Form 5500 for pensions) and also hold the organization, its trustees, and all others involved in administering the plan to fiduciary rules very much as we discussed in Chapter 4 and 5. These later rules also contain prohibited transactions very much as in those chapters.

In addition to its zero cost to employer, 403(b) plans can fall outside of ERISA (which we shall discuss later) requirements for disclosure, reporting, and fiduciary because they need not technically be operated by the nonprofit. By this is meant the following:

1. Participation is voluntary.
2. The employee or his or her designee are the only ones who can control the accounts since each person has a separate account of his or her choosing.
3. The nonprofit is not paid and receives no benefits from having the plan.
4. The employer does not limit which mutual fund or insurance contract an employee may use except for purely administrative reasons.
5. The employer's sole role is to deduct the contributions and transmit the funds to the company chosen by the employee.

Pension and employee welfare plans are tax-exempt organizations operating under private foundation rules. Hence, before undertaking any major employee benefit program, inquire if ERISA applies. The Department of Labor has prepared a list of exceptions to ERISA.

The second set of rules comes from the IRS. Failure to meet them means that the recipients of these benefits are taxed—not the organization, which is not generally taxed anyway. With retirement and pension plans, discrimination (when the plan is top heavy with highly paid employees and underrepresented by nonhighly paid employees) also means that the vesting schedule must provide for 100 percent vesting at the end of three years. This represents a potential cost to the organization, which is the amount that it would have retrieved into the plan for those employees who would normally have left at the end of three years.

An important IRS rule, therefore, has to do with discrimination. This has nothing to do necessarily with race, gender, sexual preference, or religion, although these types of discrimination are illegal for pension-planning purposes. It has to do with whether highly paid persons are preferred in (1) eligibility, (2) contributions, or (3) benefits—any or all three of these. Are lower-paid workers being discriminated against? This is defined differently for each type of benefit. Let us take two of the three most common.

Discrimination in Medical Benefits

Currently, a health insurance program that is through a licensed insurance company is exempt and does not have to meet a discrimination test. A self-insured organization must. Since few nonprofits would be self-insured for medical benefits, let's go to pension plans.

Discrimination in Pension Plans

The general rule for pension plans is that 70 percent of the nonhighly compensated employees must be covered and 70 percent of all those who are covered by the plan must be nonhighly compensated employees. Thus, both the recruiting and enrollment pool must have participation by nonhighly compensated employees.

On the 403(b), the rules are very simple if the contributions are based purely on an agreement to reduce the employee's income. Then the rules say that all employees must be afforded the same opportunity, and all should be able to reduce this contribution by $200 per year. These are easy to meet by having the board pass a resolution instituting the plan and informing all employees by newsletter or employee handbook of their rights to participate and not setting any organizational limits on contributions, except to advise on IRS limits. It can be even easier. The organization honors the request of the employee to reduce his or her salary and sends it to the mutual fund or insurance agency.

For 403(b) plans that permit other contributions, the rules are more difficult. Other contributions (called nonelective contributions) such as matching contributions by the employer or additional (other than income reduction) by the employees are of concern. For example, because the

403(b) is such a good tax-saving device, an employee may wish to periodically add more money to it, that is, after-tax savings, but higher-
paid persons are in a better position to do so. Moreover, if matching is
permitted, then executives can set higher matches for themselves, and
because they can afford to reduce their income more easily than lower-
income employees can, they could reap greater benefit. For these reasons,
the discrimination rules when these types of nonelective contributions
are permitted in the 403(b) plan are tighter. They are described in IRS
Notice 89-23 of February 7, 1989.

Discrimination in Group Term Life

The group term plan is discriminatory unless 70 percent of all employees benefit, 85 percent of all employees participating are not upper
paid, the plan satisfies the rule for a cafeteria plan, and the IRS approves
the classification of employees.

To Discriminate or Not

In deciding on eligibility, contribution, and benefit, the nonprofit
must make the decision based on several factors, including cost, purpose,
employee morale, ethics. In most instances, a nondiscrimination policy
would be preferred by all employees. Yet, in nonprofits as well as for-
profit firms, the overall compensation of key executives should exceed
those of other persons. Some benefits such as permanent insurance, split-
dollar insurance, rabbi trusts, and disability are justifiably used for meeting this objective of higher pay for greater responsibility. When they are
so used, the tax consequence falls on the executive. Yet having that benefit at a very low cost makes the tax worth it.

Avoiding Discrimination

Should the decision be to avoid discrimination, there are certain
broad beginning points. Require everyone to participate once the minimum legal eligibility requirements are met. Make the cost to the employee for his or her coverage zero; that is, make the plan noncontributory,
making the employee's ability to pay irrelevant and therefore not a bar-
rier to participation. The organization pays all.

Use the same contract for all employees. Have contributions based
on a similar percentage of compensation up to legal limits. Accordingly,
the Boys and Girls Clubs of America "has a noncontributory defined contribution pension plan, called a money purchase plan, covering all eligible
employees. Each employee receives the pension purchasable by funds

accumulated from annual contributions based on a percentage of compensation."[23]

TEN STEPS TO SETTING UP THE BENEFIT PACKAGE

1. Create a list of compulsory benefits (workmen's compensation and Social Security) and their costs.
2. Prepare a similar list of optional benefits, discussed in this chapter.
3. Commit the organization to the compulsory benefits.
4. Put priority on a health package and apply the cost control measures discussed.
5. Consider group term life insurance rather than permanent, except as an executive perk.
6. If resources do not permit a contribution by the nonprofit to a pension plan, do a 403(b) based only on salary reduction.
7. Minimize exposure to discrimination (if benefit is not an executive perk or too costly) by making participation compulsory once the legally required age and service requirements are met, by using the same contract for managers and low-paid persons, and also by making it noncontributory so that affordability is not an impediment.
8. Give the employees a choice over the plan to be implemented.
9. Seek outside advice and benefit from the experiences of other organizations. Make the entire package reasonable.
10. Get the vote of the trustees.

CONTRACTING AND CONTRACTORS

The preceding section was about employees. Employment taxes such as Social Security and unemployment, the cost of some liability insurance, and benefits, including worker's compensation, can be avoided by contracting for services in lieu of hiring employees. Note, however, that the organization must file as part of its annual 990 Form a report on the five highest-paid independent contractors who, individually, receive $30,000 or more from the organization.

Whether a person is an independent contractor or an employee depends on the facts and circumstances of the specific case. The IRS, through Revised Ruling 87-41, gives the following guidelines to help in the determination. A person may be presumed to be an employee if the organization:

1. Specifies the time, place, method, and person who is to do the job.
2. Trains the person to do the job.
3. Requires the person to do the job himself or herself.
4. Hires others to assist the person who is doing the job.
5. Integrates a person into its staff.
6. Has a long-standing work relationship with that person even though it may be irregular.
7. Sets the hours of work of the person.
8. Requires the person to work full time.
9. Requires or permits the person to work on its premises.
10. Determines the sequence of work the person does.
11. Requires oral or written reports from the person.
12. Pays the person on a regular and periodic basis, for example, weekly.
13. Pays the person's business or travel expenses.
14. Furnishes the person tools, equipment, or materials.
15. Maintains the right to fire, assign, or discharge the person.
16. Has the right to terminate the contract without liability for breach,

and if the person:

17. Has no other customers.
18. Makes no attempt to get other customers.
19. Makes no profit or losses.
20. Has no investment in himself or herself as a business.

None of these by itself can cause classification as a contractor or employee. It is the weight of the facts and circumstances that matters. Therefore, in contracting for personal services, it is wise to try to keep all these guidelines in mind. Wiser yet, have your attorney draw up a formal contract of a prototype that you can use for all similar situations.

THE TRUSTEES AND EMPLOYEE COMPENSATION

In instituting a compensation package of any kind, except a completely voluntary 403(b), the trustees must pass a resolution consistent with the bylaws and enter it into the minutes which must be available for public disclosure even if ERISA disclosure is not required. Also, set up procedures such that it does not appear that management is pocketing the organization's money. Avoid irregularities. We refer you to self-dealing in Chapter 5.

SUMMARY AND CONCLUSIONS

Nonprofits must compete for competent workers. To do this they must devise benefit packages enabling them to attract and retain such workers while controlling costs. This chapter describes various elements of a benefit package.

NOTES

1. Disability tax liabilities depend on who pays the premiums and the extent to which the payments of disability income may be construed as regular salary payments. If they can be construed as regular salary payments, then they are neither exempt nor eligible for tax credit but are taxable as regular income.
2. The requirements are more lenient when the disability is blindness.
3. Death benefits for any single death that do not exceed a total of $5000 are exempt from income taxes by the recipients.
4. The requirements for conversion may be more difficult if the separation is due to the demise of the organization.
5. Consider the tax effect. When an organization pays the contribution, it is not taxable to the employee as income. However, if the employee receives the same amount as payment, not only will it be taxed as income, but the after-tax income, being smaller, will buy less insurance.
6. Survivors who are themselves recipients of Social Security retirement benefits may elect between their check or the check of the deceased spouse, but two checks cannot be received.
7. Basically, both the event that caused the injury and the injury itself must be accidental.
8. See Section 13-10 of the Public Health Service Act of 1973, and Section 42 of the Code of Federal Regulations, Part 110-801.
9. There are several variations of benefit definitions; for example, it might be the average salary earned in the final ten, five, or three years of the worker's tenure. The years may or may not have to be consecutive. There are numerous variations.
10. The factors that are placed in the actuarial equation to determine the amount that must be contributed include the defined benefit, the annual valuation of the pension fund, the expected mortality rate, the withdrawal rate, and the expected interest earnings.
11. There are Simplified Employee's Pension plans that permit the employer to make deposits into the IRA accounts held by the employee.
12. Actually, there is a strict mathematical rule stating that 70 percent of the workers (excluding those previously mentioned) must be eligible and, if only 70 percent are eligible, then 80 percent must benefit.
13. The IRS disallows vesting schedules that are too restrictive. Variations from the schedules discussed should be attempted with extreme caution.
14. An organization may give a worker a five-year period during which he or she may be away from paid employment with the organization. But at the end of that period, the worker either buys back into the system and becomes a participating employee in the plan, or all previous credits earned toward vesting or eligibility may be for-

feited. Once the employee reenters the plan, he or she may recoup one year of eligibility for every one year worked.

15. It is important that this process be understood. The plan must be the employer's, not the employee's. Even though the contributions come from the employee's pay, the transfer of funds must be made by the employer in accordance with a written agreement. The employee cannot first receive pay and then give money to the employer to place in the fund. This would constitute constructive receipt, and the contribution would be taxed as income to the employee.

16. The actual amount that can be contributed depends on the election of one of three formulas by the employee. There was an upper limit, however, of the lesser of 25 percent of income or $30,000. This limit has been changed to $9500 by the U.S. Congress.

17. Prior to January 1, 1985, the employee could choose among cash, nontaxable and taxable benefits, and property. Now the employee must choose between cash and nontaxable benefits.

18. Revenue Ruling 69-383, 69-2 Cumulative Bulletin 113, General Counsel Memorandum 38283, Internal Revenue Service, Feb. 15, 1980, and prior to that General Counsel Memorandum 35638, Jan. 28, 1974. For a brief history of the IRS position on these plans, see Edward J. Schnee and Walter A. Robbins, "Profit-sharing Plans and Tax-exempt Organizations—A New Benefit for All," *Taxes—The Tax Magazine*, 62, no. 4 (Apr. 1984), 220–23.

19. See General Counsel Memorandum, 35638.

20. Schnee and Robbins, "Profit-sharing Plans and Tax-exempt Organization," pp. 220–23 (see note 19). The 1986 updates are by the author.

21. For a comparison of 403(b) and 401(k) properties, see Labh S. Hira, "Profit-sharing Plans for Nonprofit Entities, "*Taxes—The Tax Magazine*, 62, no. 10 (Oct. 1984), 679–83. See also Robert J. Angell and Joseph E. Johnson, "403(b) Loans: A Money Machine," *Journal of the American Society of CLU*, 39, no. 1. (1985), 56–61.

22. 1989 *Annual Report*, Boys Clubs (now Boys and Girls Clubs) of America, p. 29.

SUGGESTED READINGS

Internal Revenue Service, U.S. Department of the Treasury, *Pension and Annuity Income,* Publication 575, Revised January 1991.

———*Tax Sheltered Annuity Programs for Employees of Public Schools and Certain Tax-Exempt Organizations*, Revised December 1990.

The Nonprofit Times (annual survey of compensation of nonprofit managers)

The Society for Nonprofit Organizations, (Annual Survey of compensation of nonprofit managers)

ROSENBLOOM, JERRY S., AND S. VICTOR HALLMAN, *Employee Benefit Planning* (Englewood Cliffs, N.J.: Prentice Hall, 1981).

SCHNEE, EDWARD J., AND WALTER A. ROBBINS, "Profit-sharing Plans and Tax-exempt Organizations: A New Benefit for All," *Taxes—The Tax Magazine*, 10, no. 4 (Apr. 1984), 221–23.

Chapter **15**

The Budget: Its Role and Formulation

Budgeting is more than balancing expected revenues and expenditures. Chapter 1 noted that one of the functions of management is the determination of how the organization's resources will be allocated among alternative uses. Another function mentioned in that chapter is the raising of money to fund the organization's mission. The budget, a financial plan for the organization, is the document that shows how the management hopes to meet both of these objectives. This chapter discusses central budget concepts and describes how the budget can be used as an aid to management of nonprofit organizations. The first part of the chapter discusses critical concepts in budgeting; second part, the formulation of budgets; and the third part, the presentation of budgets for different users.

THE IMPORTANCE OF BUDGETS

A budget is a projection of costs and revenues approved by the board of trustees. It is the financial game plan for carrying out the mission of the organization. At the end of the year, the financial statements tell how well the organization did in meeting its targets. Reporting on the Chicago Symphony Orchestra, the Chicago Symphony Chorus, and their affiliates, the chairman says:

> ....Earned and contributed revenues totaled $241,306,000, and expenses were $23,950,000 producing the surplus of $350,000. Following a policy established by the Board of Trustees, the excess funds are placed in a special contingency fund to be used in the event of an operating shortfall. This fund now totals $992,000. *The Orchestral Association of Chicago*, 1989 Annual Report, p. 4, reprinted with permission.

THE BUDGET AS A MANAGEMENT TOOL

A budget is also the basis on which actual performance is measured against projections. In addition, the budget is a tool of management control. Once the budget has been adopted, it can be used periodically to compare actual performance with budgeted or planned performance. Variances between actual and planned expenditures or receipts indicate the organization is off course and should sound an early morning alarm to management.

For management, the process of budget formulation is part of the planning process. The budget is the monetary translation of the strategic plan described in Chapter 6. Accordingly, a preliminary budget for each program the organization is considering during the strategic planning process is necessary so that the organization may compare expected benefits and costs before choosing among programs.

Before the chosen programs can be implemented, a final budget must be adopted so that the managers may know the amount of resources that is planned for their programs, the sources of those dollars (from grants, fees, and so on), the way those dollars are expected to be allocated among competing uses within each program, and a schedule of expenditures and receipts over the life of the program. As a planning document, a budget has no legal force.

As a management tool, the budget is a political document. It expresses a policy decision about the priority of some programs over others, and it increases the power of some managers over others. Programs can be dropped or added, weakened or strengthened by using the budget as the rationale, such as "it is not in the budget."

As an instrument for managerial control, actual spending and receipts can be tracked against planned targets. Variances between actual and budgeted performance signal the need to slow spending or increase receipts, or to shift resources from one category to another, or the need to raise more funds.

Variance from budgeted amounts should be of concern to management, even though the variance may be positive.[1] When actual spending is lower than planned amounts, this could be the result of laggard performance in program implementation. But this could also indicate greater than expected cost savings in program implementation. In short, all variances in spending or in revenues that are more than incidental departures from the planned amounts demand management's attention. Variances are often an early warning that something could go or has gone wrong. They can alert managers to the possibilities of cost overruns for which the organization may not be reimbursed. These overruns can create serious financial problems. Much of the deficit nonprofits experience may well represent sloppy financial and operating management, rather than benevolent overspending.

While not audited, the budget as an instrument of control may be used by auditors to judge the extent to which the organization exercises forethought and control over its spending and revenues. Does the organization display reasonable management that plans and sets targets? Does it keep regular and systematic track of its financial performance?

THE BUDGET AS A SUM OF PARTS

For those nonprofits that operate several different programs, endowments, or businesses, the organization's final budget may be a composite of several subbudgets: (1) one for each activity within each program or functional area, (2) one for each program or functional area, and (3) one for the organization as a whole, which is a composite of all functional or program areas plus general administration. A functional or program budget merely refers to one that is set up according to programs or activities, rather than according to objects such as paper, pencil, books, and other items. Thus, each function will have its own detailed budget, and the organization's budget will be a composite of these individual functional budgets.

The nonprofit budget is the sum of restricted and unrestricted amounts. Budgets in nonprofits should distinguish between restricted and unrestricted sources and uses of funds and show any anticipated transfer from one to the other. This is important because the management of the nonprofit has no discretionary use over the restricted funds. These funds must be used for the purposes for which they were received. To use them otherwise is to violate the contract under which the funds were obtained. Therefore, it is imperative that when the amounts of restricted funds are shown as receipts in the budget it is similarly shown that they are restricted; that is, their planned use is predetermined. We shall say more about restricted funds in Chapter 16.

Restricted funds do not always come from outside the organization. Sometimes, as in the case of the Chicago Orchestral Association, the board of directors may choose to set aside a certain portion of the annual revenues of the organization for some special purpose and restrict the management from using it for any other purpose. Here, again, it makes no sense to include such funds as revenues without indicating that their use is restricted. Nonprofits without an independent flow of funds from investments, unrelated or related businesses, or institutional gifts frequently find themselves with relatively little discretionary budgetary power. They function, but with little budgetary discretion.

THE BUDGET AS CONTEMPORARY HISTORY

It is frequently helpful to put the current year's budget into historical perspective. This can be done by showing the budget for the previous five or ten years. By so doing, the board of the organization can get a picture of where the organization has been, how it is growing or declining, and how resources have shifted from one functional use to another. Is the organization changing emphasis or direction? Have some programs been sufficiently funded and emphasized such that now they should be less dependent on the organization's general funds?

She points out that, at a time when reduced government spending on social programs has forced greater competition among private agencies for financial support, the New York league last year increased its budget for special programs by 109 percent, to $2.7 million from about $1.3 million.

A $2 MILLION AID CUT

However, despite the dramatic gain, the New York league still had almost $400,000 less for programs than it did in fiscal 1982–83.

Source: Carlyle C. Douglas, "Urban League Is Rebounding after Cuts in Government Aid," *New York Times,* page 60, Sunday, September 15, 1985. Copyright 1985 by the New York Times Company. Reprinted by permission.

This historical perspective can also provide a basis for forecasting and projecting financial changes in the organization. By comparing how far off last year's planned amounts were from actual, senior management can obtain a picture of how realistic their and their subordinate managers' projections are. Are they consistently overoptimistic or overly cautious and by how much?

To facilitate comparisons over time, budget figures should be shown in current and constant dollars. Constant dollars are current dollars adjusted for inflation. The fact that current budget is 20 percent higher than last year's would not mean that the organization is expanding in real terms if the inflation rate is 20 percent. The organization is standing still. One way to assess this is to show both the dollar and physical amount. Accordingly, rent may be shown as $2500 per month and the number of square feet. Every year, show both the square feet or full-time equivalent for employees and the dollar amounts.

CAPITAL AND OPERATING BUDGETS

Another useful presentation in some nonprofits is between capital and operating budgets. Capital budgets, to be discussed later, relate only to the acquisition or disposition of assets that have a useful life of more than one year. Planned acquisition or disposition of cars, buildings, furniture, and computers will be included in the capital budget. Operating budgets, the subject of this chapter, are prepared annually for showing expected revenues, support, and expenses for the current year. Nonprofits that are on a cash basis with very little capital plans will not need to separate capital from operating budget, but nonprofits with large capital programs must separate these two. Failure to do so would distort the annual operating budget. For example, a building purchased for $1,000,000 is paid for over several years. In an operating budget, this transaction would be shown as a planned expenditure of $1,000,000 in the current year, which is incorrect information.

Now we see a significant difference. To capitalize a cost implies paying for it over several years. To expense it is to pay for it in a year. The budgetary implications, you can now see, are very dissimilar.

BUDGETS AS BASELINE

A budget can commence from the bottom up. Each center gives estimates, which are then aggregated at the top. They may also flow from the top down. The management gives scenarios (reflecting a broader reality of the environment and the responsibilities of the mission of the organization, the constraints and pressures upon it, and the marching orders of the trustees). It is conciliatory within the limits set by the trustees. Managers of responsibility centers tell how they plan to enforce trustee guidelines by how they compose their center's budgets. They are responsible for micromanagement of the budget for their units, given the aggregate limits and policies set by the board. But the board and top management always reserve the right and responsibility over all budgeting. A good budget will be the product of both flows. It reconciles differences.

BUDGETS AS FICTION

Budgets reflect the aim of program managers to occasionally set low expectations so as to avoid the appearance of failure. They also set targets to attract more resources. Budgets are also ficticious in their appearance of accuracy; yet, budgets are imperatives to rational management.

PRINCIPLES UNDERLYING BUDGETS

Budgets of nonprofits should be formed using two distinct principles: policy and efficiency. On the policy level, the trustees should be concerned with what programs will be undertaken in keeping with the organization's mission, how much of the organization's resources will be allocated to each program, and what will be the sources of funds for financing each program. As we saw in Chapter 4, the sources of support and the nature of the programs have implication beyond the budget. They affect the tax-exempt status of the organization and are therefore policy questions.

The other principle that should influence budget formulation in nonprofit organizations is efficiency. Questions here are the following: How much will it cost? How much money must be raised? What will be the schedule of disbursements and expenditures over the life of the program? These questions are not resolvable by policy debates without specific technical estimates.

When capital budgets are being considered, unwarranted accumulations if it overshoots its mark and does not have permission for accumulation, as discussed in Chapter 4.

These two principles, policy and efficiency, undergird all budget formulation processes and techniques.

ZERO-BASED BUDGETING AND PPBS

One technique is zero-based budgeting (ZBB). This technique requires the organization to pretend that it is starting from scratch. Thus, in every budget formulating period, each activity must be ranked in terms of its expected contribution to the organization's mission. Programs that cannot be justified or are of low priority are dropped or their resources are decreased. This ingredient should be present in every budgeting session, whether it is called zero-based or not.

Another technique is program budgeting (planning, programming and budgeting systems, or PPBS). PPBS rests heavily on measures of costs and benefits. One of its main contributions is that it integrates planning, programming, and budgeting. It forces us to see these as related rather than disjointed processes. In PPBS, programs are ranked, and those with the highest ratio of benefits to costs are assumed to be superior.

Regardless of the approach, the ultimate programming and financing decisions are based on policy and efficiency considerations, as described in Chapter 6 and in the preceding paragraphs. Accordingly, it is conceivable that the program with the highest benefit–cost ratio may be rejected because it does not fall within the policy range preferred by the organization. Similarly, the most justified program in a zero-based planning exercise may not be one that the organization can implement with the level of investment or efficiency required.[2]

Furthermore, the essence of both approaches should be present in every decision-making exercise. Programs must be justified and given priority ratings. They should be well integrated, planned for, and efficiently run.

EFFICIENCY: COSTS AND SUPPORT

In earlier chapters we dealt with policy questions. What should the organization's mission be? How should it be funded? What type of tax-exempt status is most appropriate? Let us focus for a moment on the efficiency aspect of the budget. Efficiency may be technological or economic. Technological efficiency refers to the use of the most advanced and appropriate techniques, machines, and tools for getting a job done.

The other type of efficiency, economic efficiency, is concerned not merely with dollar costs, but with additional questions that must be raised. How many dollars must the organization raise today or on a periodic basis if it is to meet a certain target funding level by some specific date in the future?[3]

Other types of capital budgeting questions are the following: How much can a nonprofit extract annually from an endowment that is earning interest at a specific rate before the endowment runs out? How should the capital budget be funded? Should the organization borrow? If so, by note, bond, and of what maturity? Would revenue bonds be wise?[4] How will the loan be amortized? What percentage of the project should be paying for itself? How should the nonprofit invest the funds for the capital project while waiting to start the project?

These are examples of tough questions that pertain to capital planning. They are efficiency and technical in nature and should be resolved first in a technical manner. We shall show how in Chapter 18. From this technical information, a policy choice can be made. To illustrate, some questions require a clear understanding of discounting, present value, and annuity techniques. Without an understanding of these, no sensible policy decision can be made; the objective will not be met and the endowment will be wiped out. Indeed, if the organization is a private foundation, it could be liable for taxes on benefits. Thus, economic efficiency means lowering costs and increasing benefits. Technological efficiency, as opposed to economic efficiency, is concerned only with lowering costs. When constructing its budget, a nonprofit must be concerned with economic efficiency; that is, it wants to provide the greatest amount of help (benefits) at the least cost.

CLASSIFICATION OF COSTS

Let us look at the cost aspect of efficiency. What are the important concepts from the point of view of practical budget making?

Direct and Indirect Costs

Direct costs are those that relate to a specific project or activity. A nonprofit may, for example, hold a concert. The payment to the musicians to perform in that specific concert, aside from all other performances, is a direct cost of that activity.

Indirect costs are costs that do not relate to the specific activity, but to the administration and management of the organization or to the group of activities—not just one. These costs, usually called overhead costs, cut across all activities and would exist even if one or the other activity is discontinued. For example, even without a concert the nonprofit would have to pay salaries and benefits to a core staff (the management of the nonprofit), pay rent, and buy supplies and equipment for the general operation of the organization. Matthew Caron's salary as music director would have to be paid, but his payment as a musician in a specific concert is due solely to that concert. Thus, part of Matt's work is a direct cost of a specific concert in which he performs and part is indirect—that portion as a music director that includes but goes well beyond the specific concert.

Common and Joint Costs

Two types of indirect costs are common and joint. Here is the idea: Basically, by the time we do A we have incurred a substantial part of the cost of producing B. Why not do B and add to our output, especially if the additional cost for completing B (its marginal cost) is small and can generate additional revenues (marginal revenue) equal to or greater than the additional cost? Doing two is slightly more costly than doing one. As a matter of fact, the revenues from B might cover its additional cost plus the common costs it shares with A.

Hence, two products or programs are said to have a common cost when they share an identical cost factor so that the production of one of the programs means incurring part if not most of the costs of producing the other. The same thing is true with joint costs. However, with joint costs, unlike common costs, the ratio of the output of the two products remains the same. To illustrate, the production of beef and hide are joint costs because they have the same cost factors (the production of cattle) and they occur roughly in the same ratio: so many pounds of beef and so much hide in an animal.

The important thing about both common and joint costs is that they provide ways of fulfilling and financing the charitable mission of the nonprofit and for cost sharing of projects. The selling of advertising space in the nonprofit's publication is an example. The advertising (business) and the articles (nonbusiness) activities share common costs: printing, editorial, circulation, material, and space costs.

These costs are important in budgeting. We must determine how much of the common costs is to be allocated among the activities before we can calculate the total cost for each. Obviously, if A and B share a common cost, we need to decide how much of that cost is to be covered by A and how much by B. The more of the common cost we allocate to A the more costly we make it. We may choose to allocate most of the common costs to A if A can be sold and generate revenues to help pay for B.

Here is an example. Reach for your local newspaper. Notice that it has a section that contains only classified ads. Physically separate the ad from the news section. What you have are two different products, news and ads. These products are produced by two different units (called centers) in the newspaper offices, the news and the classified. Each product therefore has direct costs of its own: staff time, the additional paper since news and classified ads are printed on separate pages, and telephone costs traceable directly to ads or to news.

The two products, ads and news, also have certain common or shared costs, most notably distribution; the paper was sent to you in one piece and as a package—not two pieces, ads and news. The common cost is shared, and accountants must use some formula to allocate this joint cost between the news readers and advertisers. In addition to these common and direct costs, the newspaper has indirect costs. These include the personnel department, the publisher, the legal department, and others who would be there if only the ads or the news were published. They serve all products and services of the newspaper—the ads, news, distribution, and so on. These costs also have to be allocated or attributed. The full cost of ads and readership news is then determinable for budgeting.

Fixed and Variable Costs

Costs can also be classified as variable or fixed.[5] These concepts are closely related to direct and indirect costs, but they are not synonymous. A fixed cost is one that does not vary with the number or amount of product or services produced. Thus, if the concert is to be held in Chanel Hall, the cost of Chanel Hall is fixed. If Chanel Hall has a capacity of 590 people, the rental for the hall is the same whether 590, or 400, or zero persons attend the concert. The rental does not vary by the number of attendees. It is also a direct cost to the concert, for without the concert there would be no need to rent the hall. This says that in budgeting a program should be fully charged for its direct cost, part of which could be fixed.

In contrast to fixed costs, there are variable costs. These costs vary with the number or quantity of a product or service produced. The number of tickets printed is a variable cost; usually, the more tickets printed, the higher the total printing bill. It is less expensive, per unit, to print 100 tickets than 500. Thus, in planning the budget for the concert we must add the direct variable costs to the direct fixed costs.

Let's pause to take note. When the decision is made to hold the concert, all costs are variable. The nonprofit has not yet selected a hall; it may choose among many. But once the hall is chosen it is a fixed cost, not simply because it is chosen, but because it holds 590 people and rents for a fixed fee. The nonprofit cannot change the fee or vary the capacity of the hall. It is fixed. But it can certainly affect costs by varying the number of tickets it prints. This reveals two principles: (1) that both direct fixed and direct variable costs should figure in the budgetary plans for an activity, and (2) once the decision has been made, the only discretion is over variable costs.

Rationale for Allocation of Indirect Costs

But who pays for the indirect cost? Who pays the overhead? Someone has to pay the salaries of the nonprofit management and for the office space in which the nonprofit works. Indirect costs are those that exist even in the absence of the particular activity. These costs are not the result of the specific concert. But the concert is being conducted by the nonprofit and the latter needed a staff and offices to function, not only for the concert but for the general mission of the organization. Thus, the indirect costs are allocated (when possible) among all projects of the nonprofit. All projects benefit from the existence, operation, and management of the nonprofit. The concert is charged its share of indirect cost, its full share of direct fixed costs, and its full share of direct variable costs.

Calculating and Reporting Indirect Costs: What Managers Should Know

The arithmetic to allocate indirect and common or joint costs is simple and is basically an accountant's job. It must conform to accounting rules and to IRS rules in the case of a cost relationship between unrelated and related businesses.

Within these rules, managers have discretion and should know that, depending on how overhead and shared costs are computed and allocated, some programs can be subsidized by others. This occurs because the method chosen determines how these costs are divided up among programs—evenly or very unevenly among them. Which program should bear the burden and how much? This is a managerial decision, not the accountant's, whose job it is to find the acceptable allocation procedure to fulfill manager's aim.

Since overhead cost is included in determining the overall cost of a project, it can also determine how successful a nonprofit is when bidding. Therefore, managers need at least the following insight about allocating overhead costs.

One method of allocating indirect cost is the simplified method. It is applicable when every responsibility center or program contributes roughly the same to the overhead costs or according to one simple index. The overhead or indirect cost is divided up evenly.

For accounting and contracting purposes, overhead or indirect costs are usually stated as a percentage of direct labor costs or a percentage of total direct cost (labor, materials, and other costs directly and exclusively caused by an activity). These percentages are referred to as overhead rates. For example, based on the previous year's experience, the organization may find that its indirect cost was $200,000 and its direct labor cost was $100,000. Its overhead rate (sometimes called a burden rate) would be 200 percent of its direct labor costs. If total indirect costs (labor and materials) were used as the base and we presume that it amounted to $150,000, the overhead rate would be 133 percent. This total direct cost would then be used for all projects, even though they use different amounts of materials and labor. In both cases, the heavy user carries the greater burden.

A second method, known as the multiple allocation method, is applicable when there are different pools of indirect costs (depreciation, personnel and administration, utility) and the responsibility centers are unequal in their contribution to each cost pool. Thus, the allocation of overhead should be based on some basis that reflects accurately the different contributions to each pool. Under this method, the organization could allocate one set of indirect costs based on direct labor, another set based on direct materials, and still a third or more sets based on other indexes (for example, time of use in the case of a computer). This simply says that the pool should be allocated to the center and according to the factor (labor, material, time) that causes the cost to rise. These are called cost drivers.

A third type, known as direct allocation, is applicable when the nonprofit divides up its activities into major responsibility centers, such as fund raising and general administration, and requires each to consider its contribution to overhead as part of its own direct cost.[6] This method transforms an indirect to a direct cost by concentrating the activity into an identifiable, manageable, and controllable responsibility center. This is analogous to setting up a fund-raising center, to handle all fund-raising. All fund-raising costs will now become direct costs of the center, hence one consequence of reorganization is to shift costs between direct and indirect.

The nonprofit must choose among these and frequently can do so with the aid of an accountant and the association to which it belongs.[7] Sometimes the task is made easy because it is possible to attribute overhead costs to an activity because there is a clear and reasonably unequivocable cause and effect line between the activity and the indirect cost. Often this facile solution does not present itself, and some arithmetic method of allocation such as those we have discussed is used.

The major conceptual task in calculating the overhead rate is the proper classification of costs between direct and indirect. For this reason an independent judgment, perhaps through an audit, of how the organization classifies costs is necessary before an overhead rate is established. In federal government contracting, agencies may differ among themselves as to what is an appropriate overhead rate for the nonprofit. Even though an agency may accept an overhead rate at the inception of a contract, it may change it if an audit of the organization's books by the agency shows that the classification of direct and indirect costs or the amounts assigned to each were incorrect or inconsistent with the actual cost experience of the organization. Unlike the government, many foundations do not pay overhead when financing specific programs. These programs are financed by restricted funds, and overhead must be covered by unrestricted funds (sometimes called general funds) from other sources.

Illustration of Allocation of Indirect Costs

Now let us see what these terms mean in the world. Notice the two centers in Figure 15.1 taken from World Vision, and notice how the costs for television, direct mail, planned giving, regional offices, and so on are allocated. Read the basis for this allocation. As discussed, allocation is to cover the full direct and indirect cost of operation. The allocation basis must have a clear relationship to reality.

Program Name	Fund-Raising	%	Public Awareness & Education	%	Total
Year Ended September 30, 1990:					
Television Programs	$13,634	60%	$9,089	40%	$22,723
Direct Mail	3,773	90%	419	10%	4,192
Special Programs	369	90%	41	10%	410
World Vision Magazine	118	10%	1,064	90%	1,182
Regional Offices	2,013	70%	863	30%	2,876
Planned Giving	183	70%	79	30%	262
Year Ended September 30, 1989:					
Television Programs	$10,877	60%	$7,251	40%	$18,128
Direct Mail	3,194	90%	355	10%	3,549
Special Programs	526	90%	58	10%	584
World Vision Magazine	110	10%	993	90%	1,103
Regional Offices	1,506	70%	645	30%	2,151
Planned Giving	148	70%	64	30%	212

Note: The costs of providing the various programs and other activities of World Vision have been summarized on a functional basis in the statements of activity. Accordingly, certain costs have been allocated among the ministry and supporting services benefited. The primary costs have been allocated as indicated. Reprinted with permission from 1990 Annual Report, *World Vision*, Inc., p. 25.

Figure 15.1 Functional Cost Allocation (In Thousands of Dollars).

Allocation of Common or Joint Costs

A simple way to allocate common costs is as a corresponding percentage to some measurable unit. If the common cost is, for example, that both programs share a room, the rental is divided up according to the amount of space in the room used or the length of time the room is used, and cost is allocated according to these percentages. Ninety percent of the space, ninety percent of the cost, and so on. The allocation of common costs causes the same concerns about one activity subsidizing another as we learned in the discussion of indirect cost allocation.

Marginal or Incremental Costs

Related to variable costs are marginal or incremental costs. This is the increment in cost due to the production of an additional unit of good or service. By how much does variable cost increase if one more unit of the good is produced? This is marginal or incremental cost. When marginal cost is increasing rapidly, variable cost and total costs are increasing rapidly. In the example of Chanel Hall, the manager knows that once the decision to use Chanel Hall is made costs can only be lessened by reducing variable costs. But how much can he save by printing one less ticket? This is the marginal cost of an additional ticket. In other words, by knowing marginal cost the manager will know how much can be saved by reducing the variable costs (the tickets) one by one and, conversely, how much costs will increase should he increase the number of tickets even slightly.

Marginal cost is important for another reason. It tells the manager how much additional support may be needed as the output of goods or services increases. If a nonprofit produces housing units and the marginal cost of a unit is known to be $4000 (that is, the next unit will add $4000 to total costs), then the minimum amount of support that the nonprofit must raise to fully cover the cost of that additional unit is $4000. By knowing how much variable costs increase as output increases (marginal cost), the manager can tell how much must be raised to cover that cost. Any additional amount above the marginal cost contributes to the reduction of overhead or fixed costs

Average Cost

Marginal costs show only the variation in variable costs as the number of goods and services produced varies. Another concept of costs is average cost. This tells the unit cost of each output. Average cost is the sum of variable and fixed costs or the sum of direct and indirect costs divided by the number of units. For most planning purposes, a nonprofit manager may find it easier to calculate average costs rather than marginal costs. Furthermore, for many reporting purposes, average costs are requested. Often, marginal and average costs are about equal so that one is a good approximation of the other. The astute manager should realize, however, that there is a difference between the two concepts, and a familiarity with both will improve decisions.

Total Costs

The total cost of goods or services produced is the sum of variable and fixed costs, just as the total cost from an earlier perspective is the sum of direct and indirect costs. One perspective shows how cost varies as output varies. The other distinguishes between costs directly and exclusively due to a specific project and, therefore, a direct cost of that project, and those due to the existence and operation of the organization. Both perspectives give important information to the manager.

Opportunity Costs

Another concept of cost is opportunity cost. This is the true economic cost of a project. Because every organization has a limited amount of resources, any decision to undertake one project means that another project has to be reduced or totally sacrificed. Opportunity cost tells the management in monetary or programmatic terms the consequence of its decisions on the ability of the nonprofit to meet all facets of its mission. We saw in Chapter 12 that opportunity cost can be measured in financial terms when choices are being made about alternative investment opportunities.

In a similar manner, when measurement permits, opportunity cost can be measured in terms of the net present value of benefits foregone by choosing one program over another. Even when measurement is not fully possible, the concept of opportunity cost is important in reminding decision makers that the choice of one program over another is not cost-less. This question should be an explicit part of the decision. What are we giving up to pursue this course of action? The answer is the opportunity cost.

Opportunity cost is applicable every time the management thinks, "we could have done X if we didn't have to do Y," or "in order to do X we cannot do Y." Opportunity cost forces management to see the consequence of its decisions on the ability of the organization to fully meet its mission or the targets decided on in the strategic planning process as seen in Chapter 6.

Capital and Operating Costs and Expenses

Costs are not always instantaneous. Some costs flow over several years. This is not simply because the cost is associated with a capital item, the payments of which extend over years, but because once a project has been launched it sets into place a stream of costs from which the organization may not be able to extricate itself. Once a building has been bought, the mortgage must be paid regardless of whether or not the building is used. This is related to an initial capital expenditure, which also sets off the need for various types of operating expenses—insurance, janitorial, utility, security. Similarly, once a journal or newsletter has been launched, the organization must be prepared to carry it through for some time or lose face (a small price to pay compared to bankruptcy.)

In planning, programming, and budgeting, it is important to take into account the operating as well as capital expenditures that flow over time. Often these costs increase rather than decrease as time passes. Inflation and deterioration requiring maintenance are two reasons why these costs increase.

This brings us to another element of costs, **replacement** costs. It is important for the reader to appreciate that the term "cost" could refer to the original cost of the item or the replacement cost at a given period in time. The replacement cost of a machine today would be the price one has to pay to replace it today with at least a comparable machine. The replacement cost tomorrow may be higher. The original cost (what one paid for it in the past) is lower. In capital (*not* operating as in the discussion here) budgeting, replacement cost is sometimes better to consider than original cost because the organization is looking into the future. In accounting, original cost is used because the organization is depreciating or recovering its expenditure on a capital item for which it has already paid. This means that the cost in the balance sheet of an organization may be quite different from the cost in its capital budget for a similarly named property.

Sunk Costs

Another concept is sunk cost. Once an expenditure has been made it represents a sunk cost. It cannot be retrieved or changed. It therefore has no further impact on choice because it has to be paid regardless of the option chosen. Today's choices should not be burdened by yesterday's. Therefore, sunk costs are ignored when choosing among future programs.

Illustration of Costs: Program Termination

As said in Chapter 6, knowing something about the life cycle of a program alerts management to required adjustments, which may be to amend, abolish, or add to the program. Adjustments may be in the form of **incremental** or **total change**. If the decision is to terminate a program, incrementalism implies phasing it out which prolongs both fixed and variable costs.

In both an incremental or total approach, we must know fixed costs; that is, a contract must be honored whether we phase out gradually or end abruptly. Hence, in terminating programs, isolate the fixed costs.

They are sunk. They must be paid regaraless of the approach taken. Focus on direct and variable costs. They can be stopped abruptly or gradually.

All the concepts described are helpful, at least conceptually, even if they cannot be precisely measured and even if in some organizations the activity and budgetary levels are so small and simple that they do not justify expensive calculations.

Cash and Accrual Basis

In many organizations, what appears as costs are really expenditures. It is not what the activity costs, but how much the organization spent on that activity during the year that is reported. To illustrate, on December 1, 1990, Clive III Art Gallery bought a painting for $100,000. It pays for it six months later in June 1991. The accounting records would show an expenditure for 1991, but the actual cost occurred in 1990.

Cash basis also means that the organization spends in every year roughly what it has as revenues from all sources. These organizations are said to be on a cash basis.

Other (perhaps most) nonprofits are on an accrual basis. They record costs when they are incurred, not necessarily when they are paid. Thus, what they would show in their budgets will be the costs they will incur during that period. The actual payment may be made in the future. Similarly, the revenues shown are those to which they have a firm commitment, even though the revenues may not be received until the future. The advantage of this approach to budgeting and accounting is that management can get a more accurate picture of what costs it actually incurred and what revenue commitments is actually had during a period in time. How much did it actually cost to operate in this period even through we do not pay the bills until the next period? What will be the limit on our cost commitments this period? An organization on the accrual basis seeks to avoid financial difficulties by controlling its commitments.

Organizations on a cash basis seek to answer the following questions: How much will we spend and pay for in cash this period? How much will we receive in cash this period? A cash-oriented organization seeks to avoid financial difficulties by controlling its cash flow, cash revenues, and expenditures.

Costs and Responsibility Centers

There is yet another way in which costs are reported for purposes of control and accountability. Many organizations find it wise to set mission or responsibility centers. Accordingly, instead of showing costs simply by function or object, costs are shown by centers of program activity. The center of activity might be a department or a unit that conducts more than one program or project. By doing this, the senior management can hold subordinate managers responsible for cost variations. In very large and complex organizations, this decentralization into centers is often preferred since the central management cannot keep track of all the details of a program or unit. Within each unit, however, there might be a functional and an object budget so that the manager of that unit can keep track of financial and operating details.

The more an organization is divided up into centers and the more transactions among these centers, the more the need for **transfer prices**.

To illustrate, assume that the organization has a reproduction center. Other units in the organization use this center. The reproduction center can recover its costs by charging these other units. These are called transfer prices. One effect of transfer prices is that they turn indirect costs into direct costs. Billing calls to specific phones is an example. They also control use; that is, you can't deny use unless you cheat.

Sometimes a center is assumed to have no control over its costs or revenues. Thus, control is a matter of discretion and these are called **discretionary cost centers**. This should be used only when everything else fails, because it invites arbitrary decisions and unaccountability. Decisions are ruled by negotiation.

In developing transfer price, the price that one department in the organization charges another, think of these 4Cs.

1. **Costs:** What does it cost to produce the service?
2. **Competition:** Is it cheaper to use an outside provider?
3. **Conservation:** Having to pay may reduce wasteful use.
4. **Congruence:** A transfer price should not hinder organizational cohesion and goal attainment.

TEN STEPS TO COST BUDGETING

In what follows, the reader should get an appreciation of the application of the preceding cost concepts to a real situation. Let us assume that our association got direction from its board of trustees to create a new function called membership services. We have done all the background work and now we are prepared to put pencil to paper.

   1. Federal government rules for dealing with costs tell us that functions such as membership services are part of the association's mission and must be considered a **direct** cost. But membership services is a constellation of functions—holding conferences, sending out publications, answering letters, and the like. The way we treat a direct cost that is a

constellation of functions is to create a **cost** or **responsibility center**. Thus, for budgeting purposes membership service is a cost or responsibility center, and those costs exclusively arising from its operations are its direct cost.[8]

2. We must **identify** all the **inputs** necessary to carry out the responsibilities of the membership center. These inputs have a relationship among themselves. Some are complementary, others are substitutes, and others may be independent. An employee who has a desk must also have a chair. The chair and the desk are **complementary**. The simple example is magnified: a school that decides on a chemistry program must also provide the complements of a laboratory and equipment; a museum that decides on certain precious art pieces must also have specific rooms and temperature control; a school that decides on a driver training program must also decide on cars, specialized teachers, and a lane. The failure to detect complementary inputs is a prescription to disaster; dollars can be spent on a project that cannot operate because all the **necessary** inputs are not in place.

Special stationery for the director of membership services may be a **substitute** for regular organizational stationery; one type of desk for another. When we identify substitutes, we identify ways of saving money. Other types of inputs are independent of any other. A training text or desk reference for nonprofit management is **independent** of any other expense. It is also not necessary, although it may be helpful.

3. Once we have identified the **necessary** inputs, we need to **classify** them. The best way to do this is to begin by distinguishing those that are **direct** and those that are **indirect** costs. Recall from our discussion that direct costs relate only to the responsibility (**cost objective**) being carried out. Put another way, if a responsibility center does not have the objective or membership service, then certain costs necessary to carry out a membership service objective would not exist. These costs are therefore directly related to the membership objective (cost objective) and are therefore direct costs to that center. All other costs are indirect.

From a **control** perspective, identifying the direct cost of membership services tells management what costs can be brought down to zero by not having such a service. Since such a service also has indirect costs, not having the service will reduce the indirect cost of the **entire** organization, but only by the amount **traceable** to the membership service. Thus, the sum of the increase in cost of the organization (direct and indirect) is the **marginal** cost of having the membership service. Put another way, we can only reduce the total cost of the organization by this **marginal** amount by not having a membership service center.

4. Now, step back. The sum of direct and indirect costs is the **total** cost of running the responsibility center called membership service. Management's job at this stage is to assess the **opportunity cost.** Do we have better use for that money? What are we giving up by allocating resources to this membership service objective? Is it still worth it?

5. Let's say that the answer is to go forward in establishing the membership service center either because there is no choice or because the opportunity cost is acceptable. The center is both **feasible** and **desirable** (per Chapter 6).

6. We continue our classification. We need to distinguish between **fixed** and **variable** costs. The best way to do this is to go into the category of costs called direct and separate the fixed from the variable costs and then do the very same thing for the indirect-cost category.

How we do this will depend on management's policy, cost-accounting convention, and government regulations. But the manager has tremendous latitude. Here is another point where the smart manager exercises control over a budget and builds in defenses. This is done by recognizing that at the outset all costs are variable, and that it is within the manager's **discretion** to determine which will be fixed. That discretion has to be exercised before commitments are made. An often unrecognized consequence of every commitment is to automatically put a cost factor into either the fixed or variable, direct or indirect cost category.

Let me give you an example and show its implication. The membership service director needs a computer. If the computer is to be bought in the future, it is listed in the **capital budget.** If it is to be paid for in one payment, which is possible with most PCs, it becomes a **capital cost** and it is also a **fixed** cost. If the computer is leased and the lease is year to year and paid in that way, it creates an **operating expense,** which is also **fixed.** This is true even though the computer is a capital item. It is the commitment, not the size or the flow that makes a cost fixed. The implications here are significant. Being fixed by commitment, the cost must be met no matter how much the membership director uses the computer and there is virtually no chance for quick cost cutting.

If it is leased, this fixed cost is part of the monthly **cash out flow.** A monthly payment must be planned for in every year's **operating budget.** Failure to make payments can lead to loss of the computer, a bad credit record, and attorney's fees. But paying for it in a lump sum involves an opportunity cost, roughly the difference between the month's lease payment and the lump sum paid that month. We could have invested that difference. Hence, every purchase needs to be weighed against a lease alternative.

Furthermore, once it has been acquired the computer is a **sunk** cost. It is a done deal. But we cannot allow ourselves to be precluded from thinking of better ways of doing things just because we bought a computer. If it turns out to be too expensive to run our own computer, the fact that we own one should not stop us from contracting for computer services if that proves to be superior. In other words, we cannot be trapped by a sunk cost. The concept of a **sunk** cost is best used to avoid being trapped by the past. It does not rectify a bad decision; it mentally frees us from it; albeit we cannot escape paying for it.

Alternatively, the use of a computer could be made a **variable** cost by contracting to pay on a per use basis rather than purchasing the machine. Which is the better treatment? It depends on the organization and the specific situation. The only point being made is that management has **discretion** over whether a cost is fixed or variable, and how that discretion is exercised has significant financial implications for the organization.

7. Once all costs are identified and classified, we need to **measure** them, to put a dollar value on each. We do this by calculating **standard costs**. The standard labor cost for doing a job is the amount of time that job usually takes multiplied by the hourly wages of the type of personnel needed to do the job. We can do the same for materials costs and computer costs, and so on, in calculating their standard cost. Adding all these, we get an estimate of total direct cost. No magic.

8. Now we have identified, classified, and measured all direct costs. We are not through. Remember membership service? It doesn't exist by itself. It is part of an organization, the nonprofit, which probably has other responsibility centers such as research, publicity, and fund raising. All these responsibility centers are served by the organization and coordinated by the central administration. It also has costs. If these costs are not covered, the whole organization collapses.

The central administration's costs are made up of trustee costs for overseeing the mission, legal fees and payroll services to each of its responsibility centers, ordering of supplies and equipment, providing space, taking care of employee welfare and benefits, and so on. In short, the central administration is an accumulation of the **indirect** costs of all the responsibility centers plus its own **direct** and **indirect** costs.

This combined cost of the central administration (both its direct and indirect) and the indirect costs of each of its responsibility centers, including the membership service, are **pooled** into one or more big, gigantic **indirect cost pools** and divided up among the various responsibility centers; each is **assigned** or **allocated** some percentage of this big indirect cost pool according to one of the three methods discussed earlier. Hence, the final budgeted cost for the membership service center will be its own **direct** and **indirect** costs **plus** its share of the cost for the **total indirect cost pool** of the organization.

Again, various methods are used for allocating or assigning these costs to the individual responsibility centers. From the perspective of management, the method chosen is very important. It provides a means through which some weak but necessary responsibility centers can be supported by others. Let us use the simplified method we introduced earlier in the next step.

9. Calculate an **overhead rate** as a percentage of **direct cost**. A simple way to do this for illustration purposes is to remember that total cost is equal to direct plus indirect cost. So, if we subtracted direct from total cost we should get indirect cost. Thus, we can divide indirect by direct costs and get the overhead rate to be used in subsequent periods to multiply direct cost to get indirect cost. This is a simplified illustration. Recall that in an actual situation direct and indirect costs are first determined by classification and then by division. First, classify costs between direct and indirect. Next, select a ratio that reflects reality and is consistent with the policy aims of the organization.

10. Periodically, this process, particularly the method of allocating **indirect costs (overhead)**, should be reviewed with a good accountant to see if your overhead rate is working to cover full cost. The federal government will accept a provisional rate while the organization determines a more permanent one.

Rates may have to change as the organization grows or changes in complexity. Failure to calculate good rates can mean (1) the organization fails to cover full costs on projects and fails to subsidize some projects, while indirectly subsidizing others; (2) the organization overestimates the cost of every project if the rate is too high, and therefore the organization fails to win programs, or the cost is underestimated, and each time the organization wins a program it loses money; (3) the organization has to reimburse the federal government for mischarges. Usually, this occurs because the indirect cost includes inappropriate costs—misclassified.

HOW TO ESTIMATE COSTS

The cost concepts give us a rational basis for estimating the expenditures to be put in the annual budget:

STEP 1. Begin with fixed cost. The best approximation of this is all the costs we incurred last year that we cannot escape this year. Do this for each item in the budget.

STEP 2. For variable costs, determine a standard quantity that will be used and multiply it by a standard cost. For example, determine how many hours of computer time you will need and multiply it by the cost per unit of time. Do this for each item.

STEP 3. Add steps 1 and 2. This is the total cost.

STEP 4. Separate out the indirect (overhead) from the direct costs for the organization as a whole and allocate them to each program. Ignore those programs which have an uncertain probability of being funded because if they fail to be funded you will have underallocated your indirect costs and therefore not recover the whole amount.

STEP 5. Attribute the remaining direct cost to its program of origin.

STEP 6. Verify that the sum of your direct and indirect costs are equal to the sum of your fixed and variable costs.

KEY TO CONTROLLING COSTS

From the above we should easily discern that to control cost we must first be able to identify and classify it. It is easier to control costs when they are variable than when they are fixed. It is easier to control direct costs since their source is more identifiable. It is easier to control costs when we have a base to estimate what it should be and therefore can compare actual performance against expectations, a topic discussed later in this chapter under the label variance.

Figure 15.2 shows direct costs divided up into fixed and variable portions and the same for indirect costs. It also shows that the easiest costs to control are direct variable costs because you know exactly what program or service is responsible for it and you can increase or decrease it.

The most difficult costs to control are those that are indirect and fixed. These costs appear some distance from individual programs. They

		Total Cost	
		Variable	Fixed
Total Cost	Direct	1	3
	Indirect	2	4

Note: 1 is easiest; 4 hardest.

Figure 15.2 Total Cost Ranked by Ease of Control.

are often administrative. Even though programs are partly responsible, the precise amount each program contributes to the indirect cost may be indeterminable. How much of the cost of the personnel department is attributable to the chemistry department? Because they are fixed, there is nothing you can do about getting rid of them during the relevant period. They are both hard to allocate and to cancel.

LEASING AS A FIXED-COST STRATEGY

Organizations should not presume that purchasing an asset is necessarily better than leasing or vice versa. There are two types of leases—a capital lease and an operating lease. A capital lease is nothing more than an installment or conditional sale. Actually, you bought the asset but are paying for it on an installment basis and will not get full ownership of it until sometime specified in the future. With an operating lease, you never get ownership. The lease may be terminated at an agreeable juncture. It modifies the time over which a cost is fixed. What should management consider in choosing between leasing and purchasing?

1. Does the life of the asset exceed my needs for it? If it does, then a lease is indicated unless the asset appreciates in price and would make a good investment.
2. Does the asset depreciate and how rapidly? A for-profit firm can use depreciation to reduce taxes. A nonprofit, unless it is operating an unrelated business, cannot. Actual depreciation, such as an automobile, results in lower resale price of the asset.
3. Is the asset subject to rapid obsolescence and therefore cannot be sold at a good price; and, worse, incapable of meeting the needs of the organization?
4. Is there a high maintenance cost and possibilities of breakdowns? Assets leased from a reputable dealer can often get repaired and replaced.
5. Is there risk in the design of the asset? Leasing might allow risk-sharing. Who carries the title?
6. Is there a significant cost difference? Bear in mind that the only costs that count are those which are different under one option as compared to the others; i.e., the space needed for the equipment may be the same no matter how it was acquired.
7. How is the asset going to be used? Can you justify cost?
8. What are the cashflow requirements? Operating leases do not include any interest cost which is a significant cost if the property is bought on an installment basis.

9. What is the interest cost? For a firm, this cost is deductible. It is not for the nonprofit except against unrelated business income.

10. Is there reason to use a master lease? Master leases are an umbrella lease contract—a line of credit that covers all properties the organization leases. These may have very stringent terms such as a minimum commitment.

A very special type of leasing arrangement is called tax-exempt leasing.

A supplier would lease more favorably to a nonprofit than to a for-profit firm because the interest earned on the note signed by the nonprofit is not taxable if certain conditions are met. One of these prohibits the supplier from reclaiming the property just because, in the case of government-supported organizations, the legislature did not provide funds to make the monthly payments. These leases, called tax-exempt leases, do permit the nonprofit to eventually own the equipment. These leases are conditional sales.

SUPPORT AND REVENUES

The word support is used intentionally. For nonprofits, the critical revenue data for the organization are sources of support. In Chapter 6 we described what is included in support for different types of tax-exempt qualifications. We now take a budgetary perspective on the same concepts.

In the for-profit sector, firms have only one principal source of revenues and that is from sales. In the public sector, the principal source of revenues is from taxation. In the nonprofit sector, revenues may come from a variety of sources. What is critical is the balance. Good budgeting for a nonprofit means more than showing numbers; it means being alert to the balance required to maintain the nonprofit's classification, as discussed in Chapter 6.

Figure 15.3 shows what this may mean, although it is the consolidated data for Catholic Charities and any one of the 600 agencies making up this group could present a different picture. Note the diversity of revenue and support sources. Budgeting for an organization means being able to have a forecast of each revenue source and maintaining some balance among them.

For the management of the nonprofit, this balance has an important effect not intended by the law. The law intended this balance to assure that the nonprofit was not a sham for a profit or private money-making activity designed to avoid taxes. It turns out that this balance also means that support can be diversified. The more diversified support is the better, because it means that the nonprofit is not overly exposed to the influence

Government Grants and Contracts Total Government	$744,320,545	54.5
Federal	60,342,691	
State/County/City	358,364,226	
Unspecified	325,613,628	

Program Service Fees Total Fees	197,473,284	14.5
Direct Client	67,457,840	
Third Party	23,106,551	
Unspecified	106,908,893	

Church Total Church	157,762,757	11.5
Catholic Charities	58,748,801	(4.3%)
Fund Raising	26,602,687	(1.9)
Other Contributions	50,828,879	(3.7)
Investment Income	21,582,390	(1.6)

Other Total Other	133,422,981	9.9
Unrelated Business	716,337	(0.1%)
Unspecified	36,229,695	(2.7)
Other	96,476,949	(7.1)

United Way	88,568,830	6.5
Foundation Grants	12,350,183	0.9
Total Reported Cash Income	$1,333,898,580	97.8
Total In-Kind Contributions		2.2

Source: 1989 Annual Survey, Catholic Charities. Reprinted with permission.

Figure 15.3 Sources of Revenues and Support for Catholic Charities

of one supporter and to the risk that it would collapse if that supporter declines.

Support falls into several categories. First, there are **fees** from or assessments of the membership. These can be a steady base of support and can be seen as an offset to fixed costs. Fees do not ordinarily go up or down depending on the amount of output of the organization. Obviously, fees relate to the kinds of service the membership gets, but small variations in that quantity do not appreciably affect the number of members. Disputes over particular services do affect membership, and recession does cause a drop in membership as members or the agency or corporation that pays their membership dues fall on hard times. During deep recessions, association membership may decline as it did from 1981 to 1982. Not all nonprofits have membership and therefore not all get membership fees.

Other sources of support are **gifts** and **contributions**. In writing a budget, estimates from past experience should be made concerning amounts of gifts and contributions and their sources. As stated earlier, in dealing with gifts and contributions, it is important to distinguish between those gifts that are made to the general fund of the organization and are unrestricted and those made with restrictions about the uses to which they may be put.

Another source of support is **revenues** from related and unrelated businesses. One advantage of revenues from these sources is that their use is totally at the discretion of the board of trustees of the organization. They are also reasonably predictable in the same sense (and using the same techniques) that for-profit businesses project their earnings. The simplest way for a nonprofit to make these projections is by evaluating past trends and asking if there are any reasons to believe that there would be significant variations from past trends. If there are not, the trend line would be adequate. If variations are expected, then a judgment can be made to adjust the trend line. This is a judgment call. When the issue is more complex than this, then it is up to the management of the business to supply its nonprofit owners with better information. As a matter of fact, this information should always be demanded from the business manager.

Contracts and **grants** are another source of revenues. These may be from the federal, state, or local governments or from a for-profit firm or from another organization. Some grants are unrestricted and are given to enable an organization to get off the ground by having resources that the management needs to build and support the organization. Other grants and all contracts are awards for performing a specific task. The task may be broadly defined, but the money cannot be shifted from that intended by the contract or grant. Even these elements of revenues have a degree of predictability, because many are multiyear grants or contracts.

Investments in securities and **royalties** produce revenue. Many securities have fixed terms and set rates of interest or dividends to be paid over a specified period. Some organizations (such as those in research) get royalties, which are also predictable. The royalties that may be less predictable are production royalties that come from oil, gas, and other materials. Gains and losses in the sale or purchase of securities are unpredictable.

PERMANENT REVENUES AND FIXED COSTS

An implication of the above discussion is that some revenues are more permanent and predictable than others. Previously, we saw that some costs are more fixed than others. Please turn now to Figure 15.4 which combines costs and types of revenues.

Good budgeting and financial planning would argue against financing fixed costs by reliance on transitory or unpredictable revenues (−), but pegging it to a predictable or permanent base (+). It also implies that, when the income stream is transitory, costs are best treated so that they are variable rather than fixed. This strategy gives flexibility. The organization may be in a better position to reduce cost in response to a decline in income. Naturally, in the best of all worlds, one would prefer an abundance of permanent, predictable income. It never is that way.

Total Costs	Type of Income	
	Permanent	Temporary
Fixed	+	−
Variable	−	+

+ = preferred; − = unpreferred.

Figure 15.4 Matching Costs on Revenues

FORECASTING

Implicit in much of the previous discussion is the question of how we know what future revenues and expenditures will be. Answers to this type of question require forecasting or projecting.

The science of revenue and expenditure forecasting can be very complex or very simple. For most nonprofit organizations, simple methods are applicable. One method is to assume that last year's accomplishment will be the same or increase or decrease by a certain percent. This percent can be based on the previous year's performance adjusted by expectations of some unusual event. For example, just by taking a look at how the receipts have grown per year over the past five years is an indication. The simple average of that amount could be used.

Going up the ladder of sophistication one step, the management could look at the weighted average of the past five years. For example, the management may say that we are less likely to perform as we did in the first year, and more likely to perform as we did in the most recent ones. Thus, we may give more credence and weight to the latter than to the former years.

A third level of sophistication may involve some form of an equation. The simplest form is a linear regression model, but we will not discuss that here. However, imagine that the organization has ten years of experience. It may plot its performance each year, as in Figure 15.5. Then it may run or calculate a straight line through these points. The slope of this line is the average rate that the performance may be expected to change over time. This slope can then be used to project the future. Simply move up along the line.

However this is done, it is to be appreciated that forecasting is judgmental. A new organization may simply make a modest guess year after year, and this experience over the years becomes the basis for its projections. Projections should never yield to mathematics even though the latter is important in avoiding wild guesses. Comparing the actual with

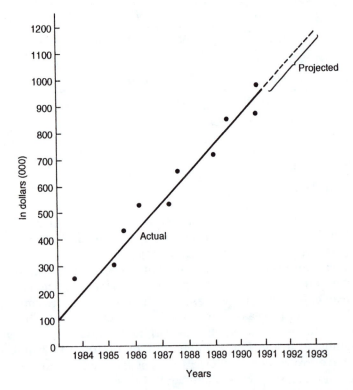

Figure 15.5 Scatter Diagram of Annual Receipts of Expenditures and Projections into future.

the projected, we get a variance that tells us how good our forecasting is. But the past is not necessarily prologue.

For most organizations there is an element of stability. From past experience with commitment, a bottom level of revenues to be received is known. Several grants are multiyear. Some costs are so critical to the organizations that they will never run to zero. If it cannot afford office space, it cannot function. Hence, it is impossible to approach forecasting with the notion "We have no idea." The management may not know it all, but it most surely knows the minimum performance in revenues beyond which it must close down and the minimum performance in expenditures below which it is a useless organization and should close down anyway.

ILLUSTRATION: COSTS AND REVENUES AND THEIR RELATIONSHIP TO THE BUDGET

The final budget disguises the concepts of costs and revenues that we have just discussed. Let us see the relationship.

Budget			
The Budget We See		The Hidden Concepts	
Items		Fixed Costs	Variable Costs
Rental	$45,000	$38,000	$7,000
Telephone	10,000	3,000	7,000
Supplies	3,000	2,700	300
Travel	4,000	0	4,000

The "Items" column is what we generally see in a budget. But this can be broken down into two portions; the fixed and the variable. The fixed portion is the result of past commitments. It is the starting point for today's budget. It has to be met. Thus, most annual budgets are really arguments over the "variable" portion. Start each year's budget by accounting for the fixed portion. The clearer this distinction is made, the more the focus can be on the costs which are manageable and the more unlikely is underbudgeting that is inherently fatal because the fixed cost was ignored.

The importance of this can best be seen with rental income. Many organizations have long-term or capital leases of space. This means that they have to project their rental fees over the term of the lease and account for that schedule and its current portion not only in their budgets but in their financial statements. It is recorded as a liability or a debt in the financial statement. It is a legal obligation, and therefore it must be met.

Similarly, a part of the telephone service is fixed. The telephone company charges a fixed fee no matter how many calls you make. Thus, annual budgeting first involves establishing the fixed cost coverage and then debating about the variable. Many of the supplies budgeted in an annual budget can also be split; for part of the cost is nothing more than accounting for supplies already on the shelf. Only a small amount may, under ordinary circumstances, be variable. Thus, budgeting sunk costs, especially when they are already paid for, is a common although often undetected and unintended way of padding a budget. Travel is almost all variable.

In the same way that costs can be broken down usefully for budgeting, so can revenues.

Budget

The Budget We See		The Hidden Concepts	
Item		Permanent	Transitory
Gifts	$10,000	5,000	5,000
Contracts	45,000	35,000	10,000
Membership fees	7,000	6,000	1,000

Note here that "permanent" means that there is a firm commitment which extends well beyond the current year. The income is reliable. Endowments provide permanent income of gifts. An organization must always take into consideration that some part of their gifts budget is soft money that could disappear by a recession, a change in interest, or the intensity of fund-raising. Contracts may be multi-year and therefore permanent (even though the risk of revocability should be taken into consideration). Some contracts are transitory in that they are for a few days, months, or even revocable upon notice.

Organizations nave a membership base which provides a relatively stable income, but this too may have a soft portion. Good budgeting must take these factors into account. It is risky budgeting to finance permanent projects with transitory income, or to fix costs at levels beyond which the income stream is unreliable. This is a sure invitation to bankruptcy.

Take a look at Figure 15.6. This concept is so important it derives a name. Let us call it Simon's Dilemma: as we get a higher and higher ratio of fixed to *total* costs, we move closer to zero discretionary budgeting and zero organizational initiative at the same time that we increase the intensity of fund-raising, particularly for permanent funds to bail us out. The problem with this dilemma is that few foundations, corporations, or individuals will knowingly make such gifts because the organization is inherently risky. Furthermore, most large gifts are not unrestricted, therefore, they only add to the pressure because they are fixed commitments.

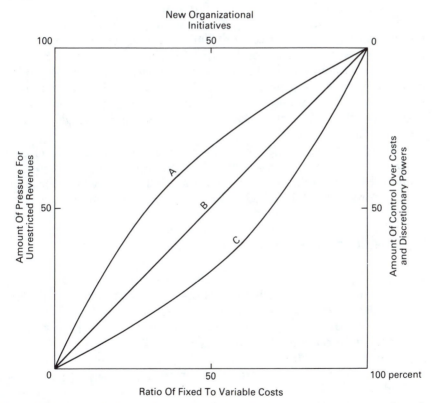

Figure 15.6 Simon's Dilemma. Note: A, B, C, show that organizations may move through dilemma at different rates. The effect is the same.

Let's look behind the numbers from the perspective of direct and indirect costs:

Budget

		The Hidden Concepts			
The Budget We See		Program 1		Program . . . . n	
Items		Direct	Indirect	Direct	Indirect
Rental $45,000		$1000	500	We can break down the	
Telephone 10,000		2000	300	total to the left even	
Supplies 3,000		800	200	further.	
Travel 4,000		90	500		

The direct cost for Program 1 occurs, for example, if this program requires something special, such as a special security that is unrelated to other programs, and its indirect cost of $500 is allocated or attributed to it as part of the entire rental bill of the organization. Supplies and other items can also be broken down. The $800 may be special paper needed by the unit; i.e., photographic, while its allocated share of the total stationery and other general supplies used by it and the rest of the organization is $500. From this we see that individual programs have cost consequences for the entire organization.

Budgeting must recognize this fact lest the consequence of every program is to add to an ever more increasing hidden cost burden and eventually to the collapse of the organization. In sum, behind the simple numbers that appear in a budget are important cost consequences.

ILLUSTRATION OF A BUDGET

The 1990 expense budget for the NCIB is shown in Table 15.1. Note that it is an operating budget showing how the organization expects to operate in the next year, and it was approved by the trustees. This budget is selected for illustrative purposes only and **not** as a guideline. Its use is consistent with the author's aim of using real data.

This budget, published in 1989, does not show how NCIB plans to raise the money. Some organizations with strong underlying seed money to fund basic programs concentrate on expenses because the money is reasonably secured for the coming year.

Others begin with expenses and then set a funding target. Thus, the amount that must be raised is the difference between the secured amount

TABLE 15.1   NCIB's 1990 Operating Budget

	Approved Operating Budget 1990			
	Standards Maintenance and Reporting Services	Management and General	Fund Raising	Total 1990 Budget
Salaries	$271,810	$ 42,360	$ 38,830	$353,000
Payroll taxes and other benefits	63,360	15,840	8,800	88,000
Consulting fees	9,900	9,900	2,700	22,500
Professional fees		29,500	0	29,500
Supplies	5,890	1,710	1,900	9,500
Telephone	7,440	2,160	2,400	12,000
Postage	7,750	2,250	2,500	12,500
Occupancy	63,860	18,540	20,600	103,000
Equipment rental	6,510	1,890	2,100	10,500
Printing	45,600	4,800	9,600	60,000
Travel	0	2,500	7,500	10,000
Conferences and meetings	0	2,280	720	3,000
Mail service	23,400	600	6,000	30,000
Insurance	0	7,500	0	7,500
Interest	0	0	0	0
Miscellaneous	5,580	1,620	1,800	9,000
Total expenses	**$511,100**	**$143,450**	**$105,450**	**$760,000**

Note: This operating budget, approved by NCIB's board of directors, does not include projects that may be funded by special grants. NCIB continues to seek support for its major public outreach effort. The budget does not reflect depreciation, estimated to be $40,000 in 1990.

Source: National Charities Information Bureau, Inc., Annual Report, 1989–90, p. 11. Reprinted with permission.

and the expected expenditures. Expected expenditures may grow every year if for no other reason than inflation reflected in higher salary, supply, rental, and maintenance costs.

Observe that this NCIB budget is the published document. Its principal purpose is public information, not management control. As such, it does not reveal the heavy and arduous thinking behind the numbers, even though such thinking might have taken place; and because the NCIB is not a large or multipurpose nonprofit, it does not reflect the complexity of program and allocation choices. Compared to most nonprofits, this is a simple budget.

BUDGETING BY SCENARIO

An alternative to forecasting as we described it is budgeting through alternative scenarios. We can assume three or four different scenarios. In one the total resources that would be available to each responsibility center would (1) decline by some percentage, say 10, (2) remain the same, or (3) rise by, say, 5 percent.

Let us use the figures in the NCIB budget, (Table 15.1). Let us assume that the organization in 1990 hits its target so that there is no variance. It spent exactly the amounts that it projected in every line. This is an unnecessary assumption; we do it only to avoid having to produce another table of the actual amounts.

Now let us calculate percentages by row and by column. These are shown in Table 15.2. From these we know the composition of costs in each activity area and the distribution of costs across activity areas. Salaries are 53 percent of the cost of maintaining and reporting the standards that are replicated in this text, and salaries in this responsibility center are 77 percent of all salaries paid by NCIB.

TABLE 15.2   Distribution and Composition of NCIB Operating Budget, 1990, by Percent

	Standards Maintenance and Reporting	Management and General	Fund Raising	Total	Standards Maintenance and Reporting	Management and General	Fund Raising	Total
Salaries	53.18	29.53	36.82	46.45	77.00	12.00	11.00	100.00
Payroll taxes and benefits	12.40	11.04	8.35	11.58	72.00	18.00	10.00	100.00
Consultant fees	1.94	6.90	2.56	2.96	44.00	44.00	12.00	100.00
Professional fees	0.00	20.56	0.00	3.88	0.00	100.00	0.00	100.00
Supplies	1.15	1.19	1.80	1.25	62.00	18.00	20.00	100.00
Telephone	1.46	1.51	2.28	1.58	62.00	18.00	20.00	100.00
Postage	1.52	1.57	2.37	1.64	62.00	18.00	20.00	100.00
Occupancy	12.49	12.92	19.54	13.55	62.00	18.00	20.00	100.00
Equipment rental	1.27	1.32	1.99	1.38	62.00	18.00	20.00	100.00
Printing	8.92	3.35	9.10	7.89	76.00	8.00	16.00	100.00
Travel	0.00	1.74	7.11	1.32	0.00	25.00	75.00	100.00
Conferences, meetings	0.00	1.59	0.68	0.39	0.00	76.00	24.00	100.00
Mail	4.58	0.42	5.69	3.95	78.00	2.00	20.00	100.00
Insurance	0.00	5.23	0.00	0.99	0.00	100.00	0.00	100.00
Interest	0.00	0.00	0.00	0.00				
Miscellaneous	1.09	1.13	1.71	1.18				
Total expenses	**100.00**	**100.00**	**100.00**	**100.00**				

Calculated by author.

Armed with these percentages, it is easy to use a spread sheet and calculate what any change in any of the components would do to the budget. We can answer any of these questions: (1) What will be the effect of a change in the size of the overall budget? (2) What would be the effect of a change in any component of the budget, whether that be a program or any of the items such as salaries, postal rates, and so on. By having these percentages, we can postulate various changes or scenarios and see their impact on expenses. Accordingly, not only do we have a baseline for next year's budget, but we have a "living budget" because we can make adjustments throughout the year. Budgeting becomes **flexible**.

Discretionary Forecasting and Budgeting

When forecasting and budgeting by scenarios, computer technology cannot supplant common sense or strategic thinking and decision making. Return to Table 15.2. Some entries have zeros. Take interest expense. A strategic decision to borrow would change that zero to some positive number. Not only will that change the distribution and composition of costs, even slightly, but such a number is reasonable fixed or known. Therefore, for every period a reasonably certain number can be inserted. It is independent of the mechanistic forecast. It is known.

Budgeting and forecasting are discretionary in yet another way. Management has discretionary flexibility over how much of any cost falls into any program, service, or responsibility center. This can be done in a number of ways: (1) reclassifying or relocating a person or activity from one center to another—call it something else; (2) when billings are not exact, management must allocate costs; for example, how much of a long-distance call was really fund raising as opposed to service? At the next budgeting session of your organization, watch how many times and how passionately program managers raise this question: Why should this be charged to my budget?

BUDGET FORMATS: FORM FOLLOWS FUNCTION

No one budget format fits all functions. The purpose of this section is to discuss formats that can be used to set up and analyze budgets for presentation to the trustees. This is not a difficult task once the basic aim, as discussed earlier, is understood.

Combinations of Program and Item Budgets

Table 15.3 shows a combination of a functional or program budget with an object or item budget. Such a display gives management a view

TABLE 15.3 Example of Program or Functional Budget and Object or Item Budget Combined

	Object or Item Budget					
Classification of Program	Salaries and Benefits	Rent and Utility	Supplies and Materials	Travel	Equipment	Totals
Program A						
Program B						
Program C Objective 1 Objective 2 Objective 3						
Program D						
Program E						
Totals						

of how much of the organization's dollars are being spent on each program and their distribution among various items. It enables management to get to the nitty gritty of each program cost, particularly direct costs.

In accounting, each program is referred to as a cost objective. It is the set of actions that generates costs. Each unit that generates these costs or runs a program is called a cost center. Thus, we can see that through a form such as Table 15.3 it is possible to pinpoint which cost center (staff units) is mostly responsible for each type of expenditure.

Each program may have more than one objective. For example, we show that program C has three objectives. Suppose that program C is for operating a new site for a nonprofit organization that runs a chain of day-care centers. Each objective under program C may be a site. Note that other programs are given one objective. Whether or not each should be broken down into objectives is a matter of judgment. In general, a program should not be broken down into multiple objectives if each cannot be clearly defined and if each cannot be clearly and separately evaluated.

Many programs in nonprofit organizations are classical cost centers because they generate no revenues. For such centers a budget format such as the one shown above suffices. Other programs, indeed the organization itself, must consider both costs and revenues. Yet some centers such as fund raising are mostly revenue centers; their aim is to generate revenues. In short, it is useful to look at costs separately and to do the same for revenues before combining the two.

Table 15.4 is an example of a form that may be used to analyze the inflow of expected or budgeted money into the organization. This inflow may be divided between restricted funds such as gifts, contracts, and endowments over which the nonprofit has no discretionary control and unrestricted funds. The latter are inflows from fees, business income, investments, gifts, and contributions that have not been designated exclusively for some specified purpose. The ratio of the two gives an indication of the amount of discretionary authority the management has over

TABLE 15.4 Example of Horizontal and Vertical Presentations of Actual and Budgeted Receipts

Classification of Support	Actual Receipts		Budgeted Receipts 1993	Change in Receipts		Distribution of Dollars by Sources (in percent)	
	1991	1992		1991–1992	1992–1993	1992	1993
Restricted							
Total							
Unrestricted							
Total Unrestricted							
Total						100.0	100.0

its budget. It is possible to have a wealthy nonprofit with minimal discretionary authority if most of its funds are restricted.

The first two columns give a historical backdrop for the budgeted amount in the third column. By doing this, management has some basis for judging the reasonableness of the budgeted amount. Why should we expect this amount of money from gifts and contributions when we have not had anything close to it in the past? Is the staff serious, or do they have something planned? What is it? Is it feasible? Will it generate that much revenue? Is it consistent with the mission of the organization? Will it infringe on the organization's tax-exempt status? Is it desirable?

The next two columns give the rate of growth in past years, as well as the budgeted rate of growth. Rates of growth (occurring across columns) are examples of what accountants refer to as horizontal analysis; that is, one column is divided by another. Again, by setting up the budgeted rate of growth next to the past rate of growth, it is possible to judge the reasonableness of the expectation. By looking down the rows, it is possible to ascertain which sources of support are expected to grow fastest.

The last two columns show the percentage that each source will contribute to the overall expected revenues or the organization during the year for which the budget is made. This is called a vertical analysis because it shows how much each row contributes to the total. Each of these columns will add up to approximately 100 percent. Again, reasonableness can be disclosed by comparing the budgeted amount with the past year's performance. It is important to indicate that once these figures are accepted by the board they become targets. Accordingly, in the next budget cycle, an appropriate question would be why did we not attain our financial objectives? If we outdid our expectations, can we do it again?

A similar type of analysis can be done in Table 15.5 for expenditures. Note that in both the cases of expenditures and revenues we are concerned with the rates and distribution of growth or decline. Variances, discussed next, are concerned with actual performance.

Variances

Variance analysis is a highly technical field and most quantitative approaches would have limited use in nonprofits. Here we present the most basic idea that has the greatest usefulness. Variance analysis can be viewed as a form of record-keeping for the purpose of setting off alarms when the organization's performance is off course. The reader may wish to review the section on monitoring in Chapter 6. Here we present a simple, useful method of flagging performance deviation through the budget and financial statement. Earlier we discussed variances. In this section, we show some forms that may be used. From a policy perspective, management should be concerned with at least three types of variances:

variances in overall program expenditures from the budgeted amount, variances in receipt from the expected amount, and variances from alternatives, especially those that would have been acceptable if the expected expenditures were lower. Operationally, managers may also be interested in variances in actual costs from standard costs, where standard costs may be the list price of an item or the usual and reasonable current cost multiplied by the number of the item used.

Table 15.6 shows a format that may be used to look at variances in expenditures. Note that the advantage of putting all this information on one sheet is that it is easily compared. Each program being implemented (A to E) is assessed at least every six months by comparing the budgeted amount with the actual expenditure. The difference is the variance, which should be shown both in dollars and in percentages. At the end of each year, this is also done so that an annual summary is available.

There is no hard and fast rule saying this analysis must be done every six months. In some cases, it might be wise to do it quarterly or even monthly. The critical factor is that it is done with sufficient frequency that the information needed to generate corrective action is available in time for action to be taken. There is little value in knowing that a program is off target when the program is already ended. The trade-off is interruption in the flow of work and the resistance of many managers to report data accurately and frequently.

At the bottom of the form is room for explanation. This may not be sufficient room. Both positive and negative variances (undershooting or

TABLE 15.5 Example of Horizontal and Vertical Presentation of Actual and Budgeted Expenditures

Classification Programs	Actual Expenditures		Budgeted Expenditures 1993	Change		Distribution of Dollars by Programs (percent)	
	1991	1992		1991 to 1992	1992 to 1993	1992	1993
Program A							
Program B							
Program C							
Program D							
Program E							
Totals						100.0	100.0

TABLE 15.6 Example of Variance between Budgeted (Expected) and Actual Expenditures

Classification of Programs	First Six Months			Second Six Months			Cumulative Year End		
	Budgeted	Actual	Variance	Budgeted	Actual	Variance	Budgeted	Actual	Variance
Program A									
Program B									
Program C									
Program D									
Program E									
Comments: Explanation:									

overshooting targets) need to be explained. As stated earlier, spending less than budgeted may be a sign that the program has been delayed and will not meet its deadline. Overshooting may mean that the program was badly designed and needs revamping and will lead to a deficit. To appreciate this latter point, recall that contracts are often negotiated at a fixed price. This means that if the organization overshoots and ends up in a deficit there is no way to recover the money from the donor or the contracting agency.

A similar type of form can be used for analyzing variances of expected from actual receipts (Table 15.7). In this case, the receipts should be divided into the two basic groups of unrestricted and restricted funds. Restricted funds are from endowments, gifts, or decisions of the board to set aside funds to be used only for specific designated purposes. Unrestricted funds are those that go into the general account of the organization and can be used in the way management chooses. These are discretionary funds. Here, too, the arguments of the previous paragraphs, including the frequency of collecting and reporting these data, pertain. It is obvious that if receipts are lagging behind expenditures the organization is heading for trouble. The purpose of these forms is to give an early warning of what is ahead.

For this reason, a separate summary sheet is necessary for the end of every period to show what the projected deficit or surplus is likely to be based on that period and the past period's performance. An example is Table 15.8. The unrestricted account shows the individual program period and a cumulative deficit or surplus, since all funds in that account may be used for any general purpose. Not so with the restricted account and, therefore, each has its own expected deficit or surplus.

A RECOMMENDED FORMAT FOR USING THE BUDGET AS A CONTROL TOOL

Let us consider the difficulty placed on an executive whose organization conducts many programs. Each responsibility center or mission center in the organization may oversee several cost objectives or programs. If the manager oversees ten mission centers and if each has ten programs, such a manager would either have to look at 100 different budgets or ten summary budgets, one for each responsibility center summarizing all the activities in that center. One hundred budgets are too many to consider in detail and ten summary budgets are, by definition, too broad to grasp the essential details.

From a control point of view, the financial manager needs to identify quickly and flag those programs that are in jeopardy of overspending and those that are moving so laggardly that they are not likely to spend the

TABLE 15.7 Example of Variance between Budgeted (Expected) and Actual Receipts

Classification of Support	First Six Months			Second Six Months			Cumulative		
	Budgeted	Actual	Variance	Budgeted	Actual	Variance	Budgeted	Actual	Variance
Restricted									
Total restricted									
Unrestricted									
Total unrestricted									
Total									
Explanation									

TABLE 15.8   Example of Summary Showing Deficit or Surplus by Program

Classification of Programs	Summary First Six Months		Summary Second Six Months		Summary Cumulative	
	Deficit	Surpluses	Deficit	Surpluses	Deficit	Surpluses
Unrestricted						
Program A						
Program B						
Program C						
Total unrestricted						
Restricted						
Program D						
Program E						
Explanation:						

money committed to them in the time period allotted and may therefore need an extension lest the money allocated to them be lost.

Let me recommend a way in which this can be done for each program and yet not be burdensome. Refer to Table 15.9. It shows a list of over 100 programs according to the responsibility centers under which they fall. Each program has a control number to identify it. The first two digits identify the responsibility center and the other digits identify the specific program within the center; thus, 0110 is a program in the responsibility center designated 01. The number 10 identifies the program. In this display we show each responsibility center having twenty-seven programs. It is not necessary for purposes of financial flagging to deal with specific program names.

The program code is followed by a code such as 2/4/80/70. The first number represents the current year of the program; thus, 2 would mean that the program is in its second year, the year for which the present budget is being submitted. The second number indicates the expected life of the program; 4 means that the program is planned for four years. The third number is the percentage of the total allocation that will be consumed by the end of the year for which the budget is being submitted; 80 means that by the end of this year 80 percent of the budget allotment would have been used up. The fourth number indicates the program manager's assessment of the amount of work that will have been done by the

TABLE 15.9 Format for Flagging Potential Budgetary Problems

Responsibility Center-01			Responsibility Center-02			Responsibility Center-03			Responsibility Center-04		
Program Code	Status	Flag	Program Code	Status	Flag	Program Code	Status	Flag	Program Code	Status	Flag
0100			0200			0300			0400		
0101			0201			0301			0401		
0102			0202			0302			0402		
0103			0203			0303	2/4/80/70		0403		
0104			0204			0304			0404		
0105			0205			0305			0405		
0106			0206	3/4/99/50		0306			0406		
0107			0207			0307			0407		
0108			0208			0308	1/2/110/60		0408	3/5/80/60	
0109			0209			0309			0409		
0110	3/4/10/90		0210			0310			0410		
0111			0211			0311			0411		
0112			0212			0312			0412		

end of the budget year; 70 percent means that by the end of this present budget year only 30 percent of the promised activities will be left to be done.

This technique provides several advantages. First, the financial manager can focus on the possibilities of cost overruns on each program within the organization because the pertinent information is given in simple form. Second, it gives the individual program manager, the manager of the responsibility center in which the program falls, and management of the organization an early warning of trouble. Third, it forces the program manager to assess how much has been accomplished and how much is still left to be done and, consequently, to be accountable as to how the task remaining to be done will get done.

Now, it is not unusual to find program managers who would try to escape this responsibility by saying that it is hard to "measure how much is left to be done." Such a plea is itself often a sign of incompetence. The fact is that you cannot manage a multiyear program under a budget constraint if you cannot see the end of the project and cannot ascertain where you are, where you are going, and roughly what it will take to get there. The judgment does not have to be 100 percent accurate. It has to be reasonable. The users of such information should keep in mind that an objective of all control systems is to be able to flag and avoid potential problems. Control systems do not give answers as much as they flag situations where managerial attention ought to be focused and questions raised.

In addition to reducing the probability of cost overruns, this system also alerts managers to projects that are lagging behind the funding schedule. Some contracts are written such that they terminate at a specific period in time and must be renegotiated at the risk that they will not be extended. Unspent funds may be lost. Thus a program that shows 3/4/10/90 is as much a potential problem as one that shows 3/4/99/50. The first has to find a way to justifiably use 90 percent of the funding in one year when only 10 percent of the job is left to be done. This is not a problem only if the last 10 percent can justifiably use the remaining funds. The latter has to do 50 percent of the work with 1 percent of the funds.

A display such as 1/2/110/60 would raise serious questions about cutting losses. This is a two-year program that at the end of its first year would have overspent its budget by 10 percent and still have 40 percent of the expected work to be completed. A program of 3/5/80/60 is a five-year program that already in its third year shows a sign of a potential need for more funding. This process of seeking additional funding can be started well before the project enters into serious cost overruns.

A Budget Format for the Board

The formats we have discussed are well suited for daily manage-

TABLE 15.10 A Budget Format for the Board of Trustees

	Program Services					Supporting Services			Total Expenses	
	Program 1	Program 2	Program 3	Program 4	Total	Fund Raising	Management and General	Total	1991	1992
Support and revenue:										
Support-contributions and grants and contracts										
Revenue-fees and investment income										
Total support and revenue										
Expenses:										
Salaries										
Employee benefits and payroll taxes										
Fees to consultants and contracted services, including expenses										
Fees to authors and speakers, including expenses										
Rent										
Printing and production										
Postage and mailings										
Office supplies and expenses										
Telephone										
Conference on-site expenses										
Committee meetings										
Travel and other meetings										
Books and periodicals										
Advertising and promotion										
Depreciation										
Other										
Total expenses										

ment. The board of directors needs less detailed information and can request it if it does. The board needs to evaluate the overall direction of the organization.

One format for presenting a budget to trustees is to show simultaneously the revenue, support, and expense expectations and how they are distributed by program and support categories. This is shown in Table 15.10.

This format shows the revenues and support by source and how they are distributed across programs and support activities by the organization at the same time that it shows how the organization plans to allocate its dollars not only by expense category, but simultaneously by program or support category. This budget format may omit considerations of the different objectives of each program. The objectives can be given as part of the supporting document accompanying the budget.

The advantage of this format is that it provides the key information needed by top-level decision makers at a glance. It gives the following information:

1. It shows the total revenues that are expected during the year, how much will be distributed to each of the various programs or responsibility centers, how much will be allocated to support activities, and the composition of revenues by type. For example, it shows how much the organization expects to receive from contributions. Is this reasonable? Does this help the organization maintain its public support requirements? How will these revenues be distributed across programs? Is this consistent with the mission of the organization and the directive of the board? Should some programs be more self-supporting?

2. It shows the major expense categories of the organization and how much the organization plans to allocate to each category by program.

3. It shows annual changes in allocated amounts by type of expenses.

One principal advantage of such a format is that it comes close to the statement of revenues, support, and expenses that records the actual dollars that were received and spent by the organization during the year. Hence, it would be easy to compare actual with planned performance. In Chapter 18 we shall look at statements of revenues and expenses and come back to this discussion.

SUMMARY AND CONCLUSIONS

Our discussion of costs, support, and budgets can be integrated into our discussion of strategic planning in Chapter 6.

Referring to Figure 6.1 and reading it backward, we can say that programming is the process through which programs are designed to execute the strategies to meet objectives, consistent with the mission for which the organization was created.

Any rational choice of programs should be based partly on economic factors. Which program has the greater benefit–cost ratio? Can the organization raise the money to meet the cost? Can it afford the program? Answers to these questions can only be obtained through developing and comparing a standard budget for each alternative. Thus, budgeting and programming are linked, and in the ideal case, when the choice of a program is made, so too is its preliminary budget.

While it is not necessary to go over the entire strategic planning exercise every year, it is necessary to do a budget every year. In those years when a new strategic plan is not developed and the existing plan remains operative, the budgeting exercise implies the continuation of the organization's strategies and objectives.

Any number of factors make annual budgeting imperative. Changes in the prices of labor, materials, and equipment, increases or decreases in revenues, changes in the size and scope of the activity, errors in the previous budget, the requirements of most major sponsors for annual budgets, and the bylaws of the organization are some of the most important forces leading to the pressures for an annual budget.

The concepts learned earlier in this chapter also apply to planning, programming, and budgeting systems (PPBS). We begin by noting that at the point of choosing among programs we also compare their expected costs and revenues. This is what is referred to as a differential analysis. We are comparing the difference between one set of costs and revenues against others. This is how we compared costs and benefits in Chapter 6.

Finally, the student should be instructed by the investigation in 1991 of Stanford, Harvard, and the Massachusetts Institute of Technology among others. In determining overhead, what is included is as important as finding out who will pay for it. All charges are not appropriate. Furthermore, overhead must be allocated between the exempt and nonexempt (including unrelated business) activities of the organization. Thus, a university operating a fieldhouse that is used both for exempt and unrelated business is permitted to allocate the overhead between the two based on the amount of time the facility is used for the two purposes.[9] The effect of this is to reduce the amount of taxes the university pays on unrelated business income because overhead expenses are deducted.[10]

NOTES

1. The reader is referred to any standard text on the mathematics of finance and to Chapter 14 of this book.

2. Some levels of efficiency are required by law. Day-care centers, hospitals, and housing providers are all subject to legal regulations that affect their productivity. Housing providers, for example, must meet housing codes; hospitals and day-care centers must meet health and zoning codes.

3. Ibid.

4. The reader is again referred to the appendix to Chapter 7 and to standard texts in the mathematics of finance.

5. Accountants also refer to semivariable costs. These are costs that are partly fixed and partly variable. They remain fixed over a span, and jump to a higher level where they remain fixed and then jump. Two clerks may handle 1 to 50 people, then another clerk must be added to handle 51 to 100, and then another from 101 to 149, and so on. For most purposes, it is simpler to think of costs as fixed and variable. They are either fixed or variable over a specific range.

6. See *Federal Register*, Vol. 45, No. 132, Tuesday, July 8, 1980, p. A6025, for federal regulations concerning overhead specifically for nonprofits.

7. The Catholic Bishops, United Way of America, and health industry groups may be consulted about what is common and recommended for that group.

8. It is possible to consider a membership center a revenue or profit center as well because it generates revenues and because it is hoped that its revenues are greater than its costs so that it generates an excess for the organization. The issue being discussed, however, is not what the center is called, but how its costs are treated.

9. *Rensselaer Polytechnic Institute* v. *Commissioner*, Docket k#7024-79, 79 Tax Court #60, 12/1/82.

10. Revenue Ruling 79-18 and Revenue Ruling 72-124.

SUGGESTED READINGS

AMERICAN INSTITUTE OF CERTIFIED PUBLIC ACCOUNTANTS, *Accounting Principles and Reporting Practices for Certain Nonprofit Organizations* (New York: The Institute, 1978).

———*Audit of Certain Nonprofit Organizations* (New York: The Institute, 1981).

ANTHONY, ROBERT N., AND REGINA HERZLINGER, *Management Control in Non-Profit Organizations*, rev. ed. (Homewood, Ill.: Irwin, 1980).

CRESS, WILLIAM P., AND JAMES PETTIJOHN, "A Survey of Budget-related Planning and Control Policies and Procedures," *Journal of Accounting Education*, 3, no. 2, (Fall 1985), pp. 61–80.

National Health Council, *Accounting and Financial Reporting for Voluntary Health and Welfare Organizations,* (New York: National Health Council, 1988).

United Ways, *Accounting and Financial Reporting: A Guide for United Ways and Not-for-Profit Human Service Organizations,* (Alexandria, Virginia, 1989).

RAZEK, JOSEPH R. AND SHIRLEY H. PRICE, "Gain Control of Your Organization's Finances: Budgetary Control Reports", *The Nonprofit World*, Vol. 7, Number 1, January-February 1989, pp. 29-33.

Office of Management and Budget (OMB) Circular A-133.

Chapter 16

Managing Risks: Avoiding Trouble

A risk is the probability that an event will occur and will result in losses. In the case of negligence, the subject of this chapter, the relevant loss is personal injury. Nonprofit organizations are exposed to many types of risks leading to personal injury. Some risks relate to actions or inactions of the organization's agents or representatives. These include workers, volunteers, trustees, and officers. Another set of risks of personal injury arises from the organization's owning or leasing property, including furniture, swimming pools, and buildings. Other nonprofits that produce a product are subject to liability resulting from personal injuries that the product may cause.

In recent years, risk management has become a very important topic among nonprofit managers because many have been sued, because of the cost of insurance, and because without a risk management policy some of their facilities are better off closed and trustees and volunteers are harder to get. During the liability insurance crisis of the 1980s, many nonprofits closed swimming pools and other facilities because of the inability to get insurance coverage.

THE BASICS OF RISK MANAGEMENT

Risk management encompasses the following steps:

1. **Identification:** Identify the organizational factors and events that can cause personal injury. In a day-care operation, there are risks of injury to children from failing to properly supervise play, molestation, or defects in facilities. In a building there may be fire, lead paint, and asbestos.
2. **Risk evaluation:** How likely is it to occur and what will it cost the organization if it does?
3. **Decision:** Decide on a policy for dealing with each risk.
4. **Implementation:** Once the policy for dealing with each risk is decided on, implement the policy.
5. **Evaluation:** Finally, periodically evaluate and adjust policy to fit experience and expectations of the future. Experience may teach that the risk is either greater or less than thought, that the policy for dealing with it is inadequate or improperly implemented, or that there are new risks not anticipated.

Now, let's go back to item 3. What are our policy options? The options for dealing with a risk are the following:

1. **Ignore it.** This is a perfectly rational policy if the risk is very unlikely to occur or if it should occur, the cost would be manageable. This is risky because every event has the potential of being worse than anticipated and of inviting a suit even though trivial. Yet this policy makes sense because it is impossible to defend against all conceivable events.
2. **Reduce it.** This policy is always wise. Use of protective garments, doing background checks of school staff, armed guards in a museum—all are ways of reducing risks.
3. **Transfer it.** The risk may be transferred in toto or shared. Obtaining an insurance policy causes the risk to be shared with an insurance company's other policy holders. A school or day-care center that requires parents to provide transportation for their children to and from the school transfers risks associated with busing to the parents.

Another way to transfer risk is to form a separate corporation to conduct the activity that is deemed risky. Review Chapters 11 through 13.

4. **Retain it.** Agree to be totally responsible. To ignore a risk is equivalent to retaining it. But many risks are consciously retained as a matter of policy. Sick leave pay is an example of a risk that the nonprofit consciously retains.

5. **Avoid it.** It is impossible to run an organization and avoid all risks. Some risks, such as the example of the parents bringing and taking the children from school, are ways of avoiding a specific risk. All risks cannot be avoided. Risks are a way of life.

A Simplified Approach to Risk Identification and Intervention

Refer to Figure 16.1. We can divide the performance of an organization into three sets of intervention points. There is an intake of supplies, equipment, personnel, and clients. We could view this initial point as an intake valve. Before turning it on, set quality and flow conditions: accept only supplies, equipment, and clients that minimize risks, and set up rules where high-risk individuals who are accepted are well and properly served but do not exacerbate the risks to themselves or to others.

For many nonprofits, risk taking at the intake point is endemic to the mission. This is obviously true of those that deal with the infirm, the elderly, and the children. Risks are commonly associated with these groups. To have a mission attending the infirm means exposure to certain risks. The handicapped can fall, the ill die, and so on. The theory of **adverse selection** says that people at risk will, disproportionately to others, seek inclusion where that risk gets attention. Accordingly, a nonprofit that has a mission caring to a specific risk will attract a disproportionate number of people with that risk. Clearly, risk avoidance is nearly inconsistent with mission compliance. Under these circumstances, minimization of negligent or careless occurrences is doubly important.

Adverse selection makes insurance expensive for many nonprofits. As a rule, their missions are inherently risky. This is so even in a seemingly benign mission such as economic development.

A second stage in the path of risk taking is the processing point. Here, the organization is doing its thing. Before turning this valve on, set conditions and rules that reduce the probability that the processing will be injurious. The child or senior citizen will fall from a badly kept platform; the nurse will administer a fatal dose—unintentionally.

The final stage is the output. Supposedly, the organization has completed its work or the person is no longer under its aegis. This stage does

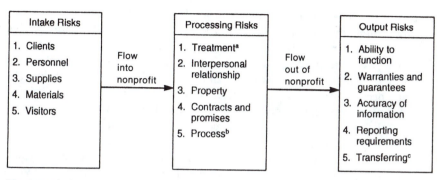

[a]Treatment includes training or anything done to the input.

[b]Process means the method of treatment; the treatment may be proper but the process is not, or vice versa. The excision of a malignant tumor may be indicated, but the procedure used is riskier that others.

[c]An example is transporting a child from school to home.

Figure 16.1   Path of Risk Taking.

not free the organization from risk; for example, a child may contract hepatitis in school and discover it at home. As we shall see, it is not necessarily where the event is discovered that matters, but that there is a cause and effect connection between an event and an injury, making the event what lawyers call a **proximate cause.** Hospitals protect themselves against one type of this risk by using a wheel chair for patients being released, even though they can walk. They escort them to a car— off the premises.

TYPES OF RISKS

Another approach to managing risks is to look at the types as opposed to the specific risks associated with each and every activity. In the following pages we discuss three types of risks of personal injury that are common to nonprofits. These include risks associated with persons who are agents or representatives of the organization, that is, officers, employees, volunteers, and trustees. We shall also discuss risks associated with property and products.

Risks Associated with Agents and Representatives

To understand risks associated with agents or representatives, be they volunteers, officers, employees or trustees, it is necessary to appreciate some rules concerning the concept of agent. An agent is someone who is empowered to act on behalf of another, called the principal. That empowerment may emanate from an apparent, an actual, or an implied authority conferred by the organization (the principal) to the agent.

The words apparent and implied are not synonyms. A hospital that permits an orderly to dress and act like a physician or a nurse takes the risk of a presumption by a patient that the orderly is a nurse or a physician and therefore may act as one. A hospital that hires a physician or nurse implies that he or she is trained to perform certain technical functions.

A hospital in Alabama hired a practical nurse and assigned her the duties of a circulating nurse, which by common hospital practice must be a registered (RN) rather than a practical nurse (LPN). A surgeon gave her (the LPN) duties common to a circulating nurse for a particular patient. The patient died. The hospital was found negligent but the surgeon was not. The court ruled that surgeons do not normally check the credentials of nurses who circulate. Both the surgeon and the patient had the right to assume that the hospital did, for it was its duty to do so.[1]

Agents have actual, apparent, and implied powers to act on behalf of principals, that is, an employee on behalf of the organization. Hence, in identifying risks, the organization (the principal) must look at the apparent, implied, and actual powers it gives all its agents to act on its behalf. The organization would be barred (estopped) from denying that its agents have these powers if it has permitted them to act as though such powers were conferred. In short, the hospital cannot have orderlies act as though they were physicians or nurses and then, when something goes wrong, tell patients that they had no right to presume that these persons had such authority.

Risks Associated with Employees as Agents

There are specific risks to which employees expose a nonprofit. An employee is defined as someone who is under the control and direction of an employer and who works to further the employer's business purpose. Once courts were reluctant to hold nonprofits liable for their employees or volunteers, arguing that neither worked to serve the business purpose of the nonprofit and also because of the fear that damages would destroy nonprofits and discourage volunteerism or employees. This is true no more. In many states, volunteers can be liable. See Table 16.1 for a summary of rules by state.

What kinds of risks do employees create? Employees create a potential liability for a nonprofit because the nonprofit hires, pays, directs, and supervises them. Therefore, it is responsible for their actions when these employees are performing job-related duties and when in the performance of these duties they cause personal injury to others. The most common form of liability for its employees, therefore, is called **respon-**

TABLE 16.1 Liability Limitations for Volunteers Generally

State	Entity	Bad Faith	Willful/ Intentional	Reck-less-ness	Gross Negli-gence	Fraud/ Fidu-ciary	Motor Vehicle	Other	Notes
Alabama									
Alaska									
Arizona									
Arkansas	c3-,gv,oth	◆			◆		◆b	p	b,c,v
California									
Colorado	any	◆							
Connecticut									
Delaware	c-		◆		◆		◆b		
D.C.									
Florida									
Georgia	ch,np,gv	◆	◆						u
Hawaii									
Idaho									
Illinois	c3-		◆						
Indiana									
Iowa	np,gv		◆			◆		q	
	npc	◆	◆			◆		l,q	
Kansas	c		◆					p	a,b,v
Kentucky	c	◆	◆						
Louisiana	np	◆	◆						z
Maine	c3+,c4,np-		■	■	■				v
Maryland	c3,oth		◆		◆			m,p	a
	c3,c4,oth		◆	◆				m	b,v
Massachusetts									
Michigan									
Minnesota	te	◆	◆	◆		◆		o,t	
Mississippi	c3-,gv,oth	◆	◆	◆	◆		◆		c,v
Missouri	c,gv	◆	◆	■	■				c,x
Montana	c,te		◆						
Nebraska									
Nevada	np,oth		◆					s	v
New Hampshire	np,gv	◆	◆		◆		◆	n	k,r,w
New Jersey	np,oth		◆		◆		◆		
New Mexico									
New York									
North Carolina	c3,te-	◆	◆	■	◆		◆	p	b,u,x
North Dakota	np	◆	◆		◆		◆		u
Ohio	np,ch		◆						v
Oklahoma									
Oregon									
Pennsylvania	c3,c4,gv		■	■	■		◆		
Rhode Island	c		◆				◆		

TABLE 16.1   Liability Limitations for Volunteers Generally (*continued*)

State	Entity	Bad Faith	Willful/ Intentional	Reckless-ness	Gross Negligence	Fraud/ Fiduciary	Motor Vehicle	Other	Notes
South Carolina									
South Dakota	c,gv,oth	◆	◆				◆		b
Tennessee									
Texas	c3-,c4-,oth	◆	◆	◆			◆b	l	i
Utah	c-	◆	◆				◆	m,q	a
	gv	◆	◆		◆		◆		
Vermont									
Virginia									
Washington									
West Virginia									
Wisconsin	np		◆				◆	m,q,p,s	
Wyoming									

Nonprofits' Risk Management & Insurance Institute, 1731 Connecticut Avenue, NW, Suite 200, Washington, DC 20009 (202) 462-8190. Reprinted by permission.

deat superior which means that the employee has a servant–master relationship with the employer.

To be liable under respondeat superior, the employer–employee relationship must exist, the employee must cause the injury while performing the duties required by the employer, and the negligence (action or inaction) of the employee must be the connecting cause, called the proximate cause, of the personal injury.

The above examples show that nonprofits have at least one way of minimizing this risk growing out of respondeat superior and that is to contract out activities where the probability of personal injury to anyone is high. Other measures are to make sure that employees are properly trained, that procedures are properly developed and carried out, and that all employees are competently supervised.

Having an independent contractor does not mean that the nonprofit escapes all liability; it may escape it under the theory of respondeat superior and still be liable. A drug dealer was given staff privileges as a physician in a Florida hospital. The "physician" was not an employee but an independent contractor, as many physicians are. They have privileges to hospitalize and treat their patients. A patient under this man's care died. His estate sued and won. The court held that the hospital had a duty to select and retain competent physicians.[2]

Negligent hiring is another risk a nonprofit faces from having employees. Here the risk derives from the hiring practice. Thus, the non-

KEY TO ABBREVIATIONS
AND CODES

■ Exceptions inferred from wording of liability standard

TYPE OF ORGANIZATION

c	Qualifying for tax exemption under any subsection of Internal Revenue Code § 501(c) for nonprofit organizations
c3	Qualifying for tax exemption under Internal Revenue Code § 501(c)(3) for charitable organizations (c4—social welfare organizations)
np	Nonprofit organization as defined by state law
npc	Nonprofit corporation as defined by state law
ch	Charitable organization as defined by state law
gv	Government
te	Exempt from state tax
oth	Other, e.g., homeowners' associations, licensed medical facilities, organizations that would be tax exempt but for legislative or political activities

+	Organizations in addition to the type listed
−	Subset of organizations of the type listed

OTHER

l	Miscellaneous
m	Certain actions by attorney general or other state official
n	Care of premises
o	Contract actions
p	Certain professional services
q	Knowing violation of the law
s	Certain acts of directors, officers, and supervisors
t	Physical injury or wrongful death caused directly by the volunteer

NOTES

a	Organization must carry specified insurance
b	Liability limited to insurance coverage
c	Liability limits apply only to suits by organizations' beneficiaries and participants
j	Less protection for directors and officers against suits by organization
k	Less protection against suits by organization
r	Sports volunteers must have certification or training
u	Does not cover all volunteers, other statutes may apply
v	Greater protection against vicarious liability
w	Volunteer must have prior written authorization to act for organization
x	Liability rule approximates negligence standard
z	Limited to harm arising from policy process or management of organization's affairs

SOCIAL WORKER LIABLE FOR
SEXUAL MISCONDUCT

Both a social worker and his employer—the county—were liable for the social worker's sexual misconduct with a client, the Utah Supreme Court ruled.

The client attended several counseling sessions with the social worker at a county mental health facility. She did not immediately complain about sexual activities with him. In an action against the social worker and the county, she claimed sexual battery and negligence by the social worker and negligent supervision and vicarious liability on the part of the county. The client had a history of sexual abuse from her father as a child and was diagnosed as having multiple personalities.

At the trial, the social worker admitted kissing and fondling the client and that his conduct fell below the required standard of care. There was no contention that the sexual interaction was a part of therapy. The jury found the social worker 50 percent negligent, the county 40 percent negligent, and the client 10 percent negligent. The client was awarded $13,999.83 less 10 percent for her own negligence.

On appeal, the county contended that the trial court should have granted its motion for judgment notwithstanding the verdict because the social worker's sexual misconduct was outside the scope of his employment and therefore the county was not liable under the doctrine of *respondeat superior*. The court agreed. The court said that although the misconduct took place during or in connection with therapy sessions, it was not the kind of activity that a therapist was hired to perform and was not intended to further the employer's interest. Further, it was specifically forbidden by the policy and procedures manual of the county clinic.

As to the claim of negligent supervision of the social worker, the court said that the county could be liable if there were substantial evidence to support the theory. On review of the record, that court found that there was sufficient evidence to support the conclusion.

The appellate court reversed the trial court's judgment that imposed liability on the county for the 50 percent comparative negligence of the social worker, and the court remanded for entry of judgment against the social worker. The court affirmed as to the county's 40 percent comparative negligence liability for negligent supervision of the social worker and the client's 10 percent comparative negligence.—*Birkner v. Salt Lake County,* 771 P.2d 1053 (Utah Sup. Ct., March 22, 1989)

Source: *The Citation,* Vol. 60, No. 2, November 1, 1989. Reprinted with permission.

profit employer may not be negligently at fault for what the employee did, but for having hired that person to carry out the function. Clearly, the best way to protect against this charge is to hire competent people whose relevant backgrounds are checked. Thus, day-care centers face this risk when they hire someone who turns out to be a child molester. In avoiding liability for negligent hiring, it is not necessary, for example, to do a complete check. Rather, it is important that those checks that would unveil facts relevant to foreseeable dangers be done.

Keeping an employee in a position after the lack of qualification is uncovered exposes the nonprofit employer to **negligent retention.** Here the risk derives from the failure to dismiss that person or stop that person from discharging certain functions on behalf of the nonprofit. This risk is easily avoided. Fire the person or stop him from doing that for which he is a misfit.

Finally, nonprofits as employers are exposed to a risk called **negligent entrustment.** This risk does not require that the person be an employee. It has to do with permitting someone to use equipment or a tool for which that person has no skill or competence. Letting a person (stranger or employee) drive a car or use an x-ray or Nautilus machine are possible examples.

In all these types of risks, the evidence must demonstrate a proximate cause. That is, there must be a clear connection between the negligence and the injury. So a common defense against claims of negligence is to suggest that something else caused the injury. When evidence is not clear, however, the nonprofit could be found liable under the principle known as **res ipsa loquitor.** This is Latin for "it could only have happened by negligence."

To illustrate, a patient went to a New York hospital to have foot surgery. The patient entered the hospital with all her natural teeth. She came out of surgery with them missing. I swear this is true. The court ruled negligence under res ipsa loquitor. It concluded that it is not normal for a patient to lose all her natural teeth when having foot surgery, so negligence must have occurred in that operating room.[3] Makes sense to me.

PROTECTING AGAINST LIABILITY OF INDEPENDENT CONTRACTORS

Because nonprofits do so much out sourcing and because the previous paragraphs do connote that an independent contractor could expose the organization to less risk than an employee, we need a little elaboration. An employee is an agent. What is an agent? An *agent* is someone who has the authority (a) to act on behalf of, (b) who is controlled by, and (c) who acts with the mutual consent of the *principal*—the organization or person on whose behalf the agent acts. When these conditions hold, whether expressly or implied by the nature of the relationship, your contractor is really your agent and therefore you are directly liable when that person is acting on your behalf. Not only can you be sued by a third party to whom this person does damage, but you cannot in turn sue the agent to recover your losses.

Furthermore, in some cases you can be held vicariously liable for the actions of an independent contractor. For example, if the work to be done by the contractor is particularly hazardous to others, you must exercise due diligence in selecting that contractor. We saw that rule applied in one of the cases above. You may also be vicariously liable if, given the hazards of the work to be done, you failed to take due precaution to protect others. And there is what the lawyers refer to as "nondelegable duty." This means that the facts show that the danger is endemic in your activity and the resulting damage might have occurred whether it was this contractor or any other competent person doing the work. The responsibility is yours. All said, there are some things which a contract with an independent contractor should include to protect against exposure to liability associated with independent contractors:

1. A limitation on any authority, implied or expressed, beyond that needed to do the job.
2. A limitation on the amount of control the organization exercises over the independent contractor.
3. A careful definition of the job to be done, when, and where, and the responsibility of the independent contractor to choose and compensate the workers.
4. A statement of compensation for the job.
5. A declaration of your right to be held harmless (not responsible) for certain events and to be indemnified (paid) if the contractor does certain harm.
6. A declaration that the contractor is responsible for paying **all** taxes and insurance.
7. A declaration that the person who signs the contract is acting as a dutifully empowered agent of him or herself or the company to do the job.

Risks Associated with Property

Owners or occupiers of property face certain risks. Nonprofits own buildings and run swimming pools, playgrounds, stadiums, dormitories, and so on. What are their risks? Clearly, they take risks of damage and destruction to the building as well as misuse. But they also have certain duties to those who use that property. Hence, a major source of risk is that they would negligently fail to comply with those duties.

Who are the users of property and what duty does the nonprofit have to them? One user is a **trespasser.** While this person is an uninvited guest and comes on the property without permission and for his or her own purpose, the nonprofit still has a duty not to injure that person. The nonprofit does not have a duty to keep the place safe for the use of a trespasser. But it cannot injure or create opportunities for that person to injure himself or herself, that is, as a penalty for trespassing.

The situation is very different with other users. A **licensee** is someone who comes on the property with the expressed or implied consent of the owner but for his or her own purposes. This category of user includes sales people and social guests, such as off-campus students coming to a fraternity party.

The duty of the nonprofit to **licensees** is to warn them of hidden but foreseeable dangers. Three words are important in the preceding sentence. "Warn," "hidden," and "foreseeable." The nonprofit has to warn of (not necessarily correct) the danger; the licensee takes his or her own risk with visible dangers; but the nonprofit must warn of those dangers that are not visible but that are foreseeable—can be reasonably expected.

Most persons who come on to a property, however, do so because they are invited as clients, members, or students, or to provide security and repairs or to attend lectures or an exhibition, and so on. The nonprofit occupier has its strongest duty to these **invitees.** Basically, the invitee has a right to assume that the organization would not invite him to a place that was dangerous without forewarning him. He also has a right to assume that the organization would take all prudent and reasonable steps to remove or correct all dangers.

There are special relationships, each implying a duty of the nonprofit to the invitee. Thus, before the courts decided that students were grown-ups who came to colleges and universities for education rather than in search of parental care, these institutions were said to have had a special relationship known as **loco parentis.** In essence, the college took the place of the parent and had a duty to act as if it were.

Both students and colleges are glad that this duty has all but disappeared. Nevertheless, the college may have a special relationship to students and others even though they cannot invoke loco parentis.[4] Thus, a court found Montana State University liable because a minor in a teenage program got drunk and died in an accident. The court held that the university should have supervised these students because they were minors.[5] In another case of a "special relationship," a court held the University of Kansas liable because a person fell and got injured while visiting a student. The court held that the university had a duty to keep the hallway safe.[6] It had a special duty to the students and their guests.

Nonprofits that have tenants have a duty to them because of the relationship of landlord to tenant. The landlord does not have a duty to the tenant beyond turning the property over and calling the tenant's attention to any latent or hidden but foreseeable danger. Again, foreseeable implies that there are reasons to expect a perilous event or situation. Thus, the State University of New York at Stony Brook was found liable for the repeated rape of a student. The court held that it had a duty to warn students because, in this case, the peril was foreseeable. There were several complaints about strangers roaming through the dormitory prior to the rape.[7]

The occupier of the property also has a duty to children who may be attracted to the property. This is called the **attractive nuisance** doctrine. Basically, this requires that a child be attracted to a danger on a property where the conditions leading to an injury are not purely based on nature and where the occupier, but not the child, could foresee the possibility of injury. This is why people put fences around swimming pools. Note this special duty to children is not restricted to schools.

Risks Associated with Products

Product liability is important to nonprofits because some are manufacturers, distributors, or sellers of products. One does not have to be the producer of a product to be liable for injury caused by its use. Sellers are also liable. Furthermore, liability extends beyond the sale contract. This means that a third party, not necessarily the original purchaser, can sue for personal injury caused by the product. Thus, a worker can sue both his or her employee as well as the manufacturer of a machine that did the employee bodily injury.

What are the different sources of product liability?

1. Product liability may arise out of negligence—the failure to exercise proper care in the manufacture or in the design of a product, that is, recklessness.

2. It may also result from a failure to live up to a warranty—an assurance that a claim made about the product is true—whether that assurance is expressed or implied. A warranty is said to be expressed if it is an affirmation, part of the description, or part of the sample or model used in the sale or bargain. It is implied when the buyer is depending on the seller's knowledge or because the good can be assumed to have certain safe or usable qualities when sold for a specific use unless these qualities are specifically denied. A dealer's sale of a car has an implied warranty that the brakes will work. Cars are not ordinarily sold without working brakes.

3. Product liability may also result from misrepresentation, whether such misrepresentation be purposeful, innocent, or negligent. Lies upon which people base judgments are misrepresentations.

4. Product liability may result from the application of "strict liability" theory. This is the so-called "no fault" liability in which the injured person need not establish fault. The manufacturer is liable because it is in the best position to exercise care or to foot the bill.

Many nonprofits do not face product liability as defendants, but they may be plaintiffs. The American Red Cross and other nonprofits in the blood business faced a serious potential liability question from contaminated blood (hepatitis and AIDS). They were sued, but legal interpretation came to the rescue. The generally acceptable legal solutions today are "blood shield laws," which hold that these organizations do not produce blood and therefore they do not create a product subject to product liability. Furthermore, blood transfusions are services, not sales. Therefore, two criteria, (1) a sale, and (2) a product, are needed to form the basis of product liability suits, were removed by definition.[8]

LEGAL SHIELDS

The case of blood just cited reminds us that nonprofits do enjoy some shield from legal action. But this is a dangerous basis on which to set policy, because shields may be punctured. For example, the blood shield law does not protect against willful misconduct, only against unintentional negligence.

In some cases (see the next chart), the nonprofit may have partial immunity. Thus, some states (Illinois, for example), while not making a hospital totally immune to suit, would protect the hospital against a physician who sues because of being dismissed or sues the hospital or a peer review board. The latter is generally immune from such suits, and the former need only demonstrate that it has followed the procedures laid down in its bylaws.

In Pennsylvania, Section 7107 of the code holds that canon law applicable to a corporation that is a religious organization will hold if such law is in conflict with specific state laws on nonprofit, as long as the law is not inconsistent with the state constitution and the Constitution of the United States of America. Hence, in Pennsylvania a local law is subordinate to a canon law on religious matters if the latter does not violate either the state or national constitutions.

Years ago, nonprofits did not have to worry about suits because most states held them absolutely immune to suits. This is no longer the case in most states. Yet, even when absolute immunity from suit is available by state law, risk management is necessary because of the economic costs; that is, the nonprofit may still have a moral obligation to pay for its damages to others, and to avoid injury.

TABLE 16.2　Charitable Organization Liability

State	General Immunity	Partial Immunity	Limited Liability	No Limitation	No Clear Authority
Alabama		◆			
Alaska				◆	
Arizona				◆	
Arkansas	◆				
California				◆	
Colorado			◆		
Connecticut				◆	
Delaware				◆	
D.C.				◆	
Florida				◆	
Georgia			◆		
Hawaii					◆
Idaho				◆	
Illinois				◆	
Indiana				◆	
Iowa				◆	
Kansas				◆	
Kentucky				◆	
Louisiana				◆	
Maine		◆	◆		
Maryland			◆		
Massachusetts			◆		
Michigan				◆	
Minnesota				◆	
Mississippi				◆	
Missouri				◆	
Montana				◆	
Nebraska				◆	
Nevada				◆	
New Hampshire				◆	
New Jersey		◆			
New Mexico					◆
New York				◆	
North Carolina				◆	
North Dakota				◆	
Ohio				◆	
Oklahoma				◆	
Oregon				◆	
Pennsylvania				◆	
Rhode Island				◆	

TABLE 16.2   Charitable Organization Liability (*continued*)

State	General Immunity	Partial Immunity	Limited Liability	No Limitation	No Clear Authority
South Carolina			◆		
South Dakota					◆
Tennessee			◆		
Texas			◆		
Utah			◆		
Vermont				◆	
Virgnia		◆			
Washington				◆	
West Virginia				◆	
Wisconsin				◆	
Wyoming		◆			

Nonprofits' Risk Management & Insurance Institute, 1731 Connecticut Avenue, NW, Suite 200, Washington, DC 20009 (202) 462-8190. Reprinted by permission.

In addition to partial and absolute immunity, nonprofits are protected by what is called "standing." This is just a legal term to say that the courts do not view the individual who is bringing the suit as being among the injured. Thus, when a pro-choice group brought suit against the Catholic Church, alleging that it had violated the lobbying rules for nonprofits as described earlier, the courts held that the pro-choice group had no standing. It was not injured and it was not prevented from doing the same as the Church did. When their lawyers argued that they were taxpayers and therefore had a right to bring the suit, the court maintained they had no standing here either, because they could not (as individuals apart from the Congress) tell the U.S. government how to spend tax money.

A third way in which nonprofits are shielded from suits is the First Amendment to the U.S. Constitution, which guarantees freedom of speech, association, and religion. As we note in previous and future chapters in this book, State challenges to fund raising are frequently defeated. on the basis of the First Amendment freedoms.

Courts are usually reluctant to judge religious principles or doctrines in civil matters, so they are reluctant to decide whether an individual who is a voluntary member of a church has been wronged by virtue of its doctrine. They are reluctant to go inside the doctrine. Yet, there have been several cases brought against Christian Scientists for failure to seek medical assistance for children. The Amish have been sued for their position on education.

A fourth way in which nonprofits are protected is by limitation on damages. States in recent years have placed limitations on the amount that can be recovered in a successful negligence case against a nonprofit. In the state of Massachusetts, for example, a limit on nonprofit hospitals for malpractice is $20,000.

A fifth way in which nonprofits may be shielded from damages is through a waiver, basically a declarative warning that it will not be responsible and that the person acts at his or her own risk. How good waivers are depends on state law. In New York, for example, waivers (sometimes called releases or hold harmless clauses) are unenforceable as to the use of swimming pools, gyms, and places of recreation. Yet, in a recent California case, a waiver signed as a condition for using the pool at a YMCA was upheld.

A recent ruling in New York is instructive. Arthur Ashe goes to a clinic that charges poor people half price as long as they sign a waiver. When the dentist and his dental students got through, Mr. Ashe's two gold crowns ended up in his lungs. The Appellate Court concluded that to honor the waiver would be to deprive the poor of a protection accorded the rich.[9] How good are waivers? It depends on the state and the circumstances.

Finally, there are specific indemnifications. Take the Arts and Artifacts Indemnity Act of 1975. Through this act, a museum can obtain a certificate that causes the Federal Council of the Arts and Humanities to pledge the full faith and credit of the United States to indemnify lenders for losses of items of educational, cultural, historical, or scientific value. Such indemnification covers international lending. But some states, Florida, Iowa, and Texas, provide coverage for some noninternational lending.[10]

COVERAGE: SHIELDS CAN BE PENETRATED

Wise trustees will not blindly depend on shields, even those state protective laws discussed in Chapter 5 that shield trustees and volunteers from negligence. A case in point: a volunteer for a nonprofit and a boy in his charge had a fatal accident. After considering all the evidence, the estate of the volunteer was assessed by the U.S. Circuit Court in Chicago. Fortunately, the nonprofit had insurance to cover the bill. Little wonder that virtually every major nonprofit's annual report contains language such as "Litigation: . . . is a defendant in a lawsuit. The amount of possible liability has yet to be determined. However, in the opinion of management, there appears to be adequate insurance to cover any eventual judgement."

Therefore, seek shelter, not a shield, and be guided by the adage that an ounce of caution is better than a pound of cure.

MANAGER-IMPOSED OTHER RISKS

By their duties, managers expose the organization to several risks. These include (a) discrimination by sex, race, creed or origin and sexual preference or harassment, (b) libel, slander and flawed dismissal recommendations, (c) failure to report, and (d) failure to exercise supervisory care. A detailed discussion of these should be part of their training.

SUMMARY AND CONCLUSIONS

This chapter has introduced the reader to the basic concepts in risk management. While our examples are drawn principally from mental health, hospitals, higher education, and day care, they apply to all organizations. The key point to remember is that no nonprofit can carry out its mission and avoid all risks. Because this is true, it must identify at least the most serious of these risks and deal with them. This is what the present chapter has been about. Dealing with more specific risks, that of trustees, volunteers, and employee health, welfare, and termination because of death or retirement, are the subjects of Chapter 14.

NOTES

1. *The Citation*, Vol. 60, No. 3, Nov. 15, 1990, p. 84.
2. Ibid., Vol. 60, No. 7, Jan. 15, 1990, p. 84.
3. Ibid., Vol. 60, No. 7, Jan. 15, 1990.
4. Kelly W. Bhirdo, "The Liability and Responsibility of Institutions of Higher Education for the On-campus Victimization of Students," *Journal of College and University Law*, 16 (Summer 1989), pp. 119–135.
5. Fernand N. Dutile, "Higher Education and the Courts: 1988 in Review," *Journal of College and University Law*, 16, no. 2 (Fall 1989), pp. 201–285.
6. Ibid.
7. Susan J. Curry, "Hazing and the Rush," *Journal of College and University Law*, 16 (Summer 1989), Issue 1, pp. 93–118.
8. Terri S. Hall, "Liability for Transfusion—borne Diseases," *Journal of Product Liability*, 12, nos. 1 and 2 (1989), pp. 25–44.
9. Ronald Sullivan, "Liability Waiver Barred at NYU Dental Clinic," *New York Times*, Dec. 30, 1990, p. 27.

10. Nan Morris, "State Art and Artifacts—Indemnity: A Solution Without a Problem," *Comment: Hasting Communications and Entertainment Law Journal*, 12, no. 3 (Spring 1990), pp. 413–422.

SUGGESTED READINGS

Internal Revenue Bulletin 1989-37, September 11, 1989, p. 4.

JACKSON, ANTHONY, "Exclusion of Diocesan Liability for Negligence of Parish Priest," *University of Cincinnati Law Review*, 58, no. 1 (1989), pp. 323–39.

JONES, TONIA PEOLES, "Constitutional Law—Religious Freedom—Forced Disclosure of Church Records Pursuant to State Non-profit Corporation Statute Prohibited," *University of Arkansas Law Review*, 12, no. 1 (1989–90), p. 75–97.

KAHN, JEFFREY, "Organization's Liability for Tools of Volunteers," *University of Pennsylvania Law Review*, 1985, pp. 1433–52.

PETERSON, DONALD J., AND DOUGLAS MASSENGILL, "The Negligent Hiring Doctrine: A Growing Dilemma for Employees," *Employee Relations Law Journal*, 15, no. 3 (Winter 1989/90), pp. 419–432.

TREMPER, CHARLES ROBERT, "Compensation for Harm from Charitable Activity," *Cornell Law Review*, vol. 76, no. 2, January 1991, pp. 401–475.

U.S. Department of Labor, *Employer Centers and Child Care Liability Insurance* (Washington, D.C.: U.S. Government Printing Office, Dec. 1989).

VIRTUE, JULIET, "Tort Liabilities for California Public Facilities," *Santa Clara Law Review*, 29, no. 2 (Spring 1989), pp. 459–487.

WELLINGTON, RALPH C., AND VANCE G. CAMISA, "The Trade Association of Product Safety Standards: Of Good Samaritans and Liability," *Wayne Law Review*, 35, no. 1 (Fall 1988), pp. 37–61.

Chapter 17

Checking the Finances: Interpreting Financial Statements

Budgets are financial plans indicating the level at which the nonprofit plans to operate, how its resources will be allocated among various programs within its mission, and from where those dollar resources are expected to come. Budgets have no legal force in nonprofit organizations and they are usually never audited.

This is not so with the other financial documents that will be studied in this chapter. These documents are audited, they have some legal force and, unlike the budget, they are made up of actual numbers rather than projections or estimates. These documents have legal force in the sense that to propagate them knowing that the numbers are wrong is an act of misrepresentation as we discussed in Chapter 5. It is these documents, not the budget, that creditors and donors to the organization often require. They are also often required by sponsors of single programs within the organization. While sponsors may ask for a budget of the program they expect to support, they usually also ask for a picture of the overall financial condition of the organization to be sure that they are not pouring their donation into a sinking ship. These documents give management an early warning of impending financial disaster and signal the possibilities of financial opportunities. They are the bases for annual financial reporting to governments and evaluation by watchdog agencies. We begin with the balance sheet.

THE BALANCE SHEET

The balance sheet (Figure 17.1) is a statement of the financial position of the nonprofit on a given date, in this case, December 31, 1991. This balance sheet as presented assumes that the nonprofit sells a product in a related business. There are also alternative presentations of a balance sheet.[1] These highlight certain points. As a basic rule, the information in the balance sheet is divided into three major categories: (1) assets, (2) liabilities and (3) fund balances. Assets may be divided into two subgroups: current and fixed or long term.

FIGURE 17.1   Example of a Balance Sheet of a Nonprofit Corporation, 12/31/91

Current Assets		Current Liabilities	
Cash	$ 1,000	Current notes payable	$ 8,000
Pledges of contribution	50,000	Accounts payable	600
(minus allowance for	(5,000)	Wages and salaries	55,500
uncollectibles)		Deferred revenues	700
Marketable securities	5,000	Total current liabilities	64,800
Receivables	400		
(less uncollectibles)	(40)		
Inventory	900		
Supplies	500		
Prepaid items	1,000		
Total current assets	53,760		
Long-lived assets			
Long-term investments	3,000	Long-term debt	1,000
Property and equipment	8,000	Total liabilities	65,800
(less accumulated	(800)		
depreciation)			
Leasehold improvements	3,000	Funds balance; excess	5,260
Deferred charges	1,500	(deficit) of assets over	
Other long-term assets	2,600	liabilities	
Total long-term assets	17,300		
		Total liabilities and fund	$71,060
		balance	

Current assets include:

1. **Cash** and accounts on which checks may be drawn
2. **Marketable securities** (Treasury bills, certificates of deposit, repurchase agreements or any security with a fixed date, usually no more than a year for its redemption)
3. **Pledges** of contributions showing the amount that may not be received as pledges are not kept
4. **Prepaid items** such as insurance when payments are made in advance, usually to cover the current year's costs
5. **Supplies:** paper, pencils, pens, whatever is consumable in the work process
6. **Accounts** receivable: payments expected from others for goods or services rendered minus the uncollectibles
7. **Inventory:** the stock of goods and services the organization has to sell

Since all claims are not collectible because some clients do not pay, the accounts receivable should be adjusted to reflect the uncollectibles. The same is true for pledges. All other assets are listed at fair market value except that marketable securities (stocks and bonds) are either listed at fair market value or cost, whichever is lower.[2] Inventory may be listed according to the latest or earliest price of the item making up the inventory.[3]

Fixed or long-term assets include such items as:

1. **Building and equipment.** These items are listed at cost and the depreciation on them is shown in an accumulation account just below their entry on the balance sheet. The cost (the amount paid for it by the organization) minus the depreciation is known as the book value of the asset.
2. Another long-term asset is **deferred charges,** which are advance payments by the organization for goods and services that will not be delivered to it during the year.
3. Other fixed assets include copyrights and leasehold improvements (long-term leases on real property where the nonprofit maintains the property and remodels it as if it were the owner).

The total assets owned by the organization are the sum of the current and long-lived or fixed assets. In the balance sheet shown in Figure 17.1, this amounts to $71,060. Some balance sheets will separately show **intangible** assets, such as copyrights and trademarks, to be differentiated from physical assets such as land and buildings.

Other major areas of information in a balance sheet are liabilities of the nonprofit and **funds balance.** Liabilities are claims against the nonprofit and may be divided into current and long-term claims. **Current liabilities** include:

1. Current **notes** payable are payments to be made this year. These might be short-term notes or the current portions of long-term debt that are payable in the current year, such as mortgage payments to be made this year.

2. **Accounts payable** are payments due creditors who have extended goods and services to the organization.

3. **Wages** and **salaries** include payments to the employees for services rendered and accrued vacation time.

4. **Deferred revenues** are amounts received but not yet earned by the nonprofit. The nonprofit may receive subscription dollars for a publication not yet produced and distributed. Such revenues are said to be deferred and create a liability or claim of the subscribers against the organization until such time that the goods or services are produced and delivered.

Long-term liabilities include **debt** and other obligations such as long-term leases that must be paid to others in future years. (Note that the current year's amortization of debt is listed as current liability.) Total liabilities are the sum of long-term and current claims. For this organization on December 31, 1991, they are $65,800.

The difference between total liabilities (current and long term) and total assets (current and fixed) is the **fund balance,** which may be an excess or a deficit. This nonprofit has an excess of $5260. Its liabilities are less than its assets. A deficit is easy to spot since it is usually placed within parentheses ($5260).

Interpretation and Use of the Balance Sheet

The balance sheet tells how financially sound the organization is on a specific date. We know from Figure 17.1 that as of December 31, 1991, the assets of this organization exceed its liabilities. For most uninformed observers, this nonprofit is economically sound. If it had to close down tomorrow it could meet all of its liabilities and still have $5260 left over. But there is more to the story.

Liquidity and Cash Management

A balance sheet can give other critical information about a nonprofit. It tells how liquid or solvent the organization is on the date it was prepared. Can it pay its current bills? Does it have enough cash or liquid assets that it can sell easily in order to raise enough cash to pay its current liabilities? In short, is the organization solvent? This organization is not.

There are several ways to use the information in the balance sheet to determine how liquid or solvent the organization is. One test is the size of the **net working capital.** This is the difference between current assets and current liabilities. By definition, the larger the net working capital, the greater the liquidity. The net working capital for this organization is a deficit of $11,040. This is the amount by which its current liabilities exceed its current assets. It cannot pay its bills this year. It must borrow, sell assets, raise more funds, or use a combination of these.

Another way of expressing the same dilemma in which this organization finds itself is to calculate the current or the working capital ratio. This is the current assets divided by the current liabilities for each year in question. Ratios are better than absolute numbers for making comparisons. The ratio for 1991 was 0.286, meaning that the assets were about 83 percent of the liabilities. The organization was 17 percent short of just covering its debts, including paying its employees.

Liquidity is also measured through what is called a **quick ratio** or **acid test.** Instead of using all current assets, as is done in calculating working capital, only cash and assets that are easily converted to money (those that have a fixed redemption date, preferably in the current year) are used. In the balance sheet of Figure 17.1, this would include cash, marketable securities, pledges (minus the expected uncollectibles), and accounts receivable (minus the uncollectibles). The amount, $51,360 in this example, is divided by the current liabilities ($64,800). The ratio is 0.792. It is worse than the working capital ratio. The amount of money or near money the organization has is $51,360, but it is 20 percent short of what it needs to pay its current debt. The amount of cash or near cash the organization has must be viewed in terms of the current claims against it. Can it pay the monthly bills?

Note that we speak of monetary assets—cash and assets easily converted into money—and not just cash. As we have discussed under cash management, a large amount of cash on hand is not necessarily good. The excess cash could be invested in marketable securities, earning interest for the organization. On the other hand, a shortage of cash portends a serious solvency problem if the organization does not have marketable securities that it could readily sell to raise the needed cash. Like the working capital, the quick ratio is a warning signal. There is no magical level that is good or bad. Obviously, however, the lower the cash or working capital relative to the current liabilities is the greater the risk of insolvency.

Here are some illustrations of the use of working capital or quick ratios. Suppose the organization has a current ratio of 2:1 and the assets that yield this ratio are principally receivables, only half of which are collectible. How liquid is this nonprofit? Not very. The true ratio, given the uncollectible receivables, would be closer to 1:1. The lesson: No ratio, no matter how high, is better than the quality of the assets behind it.

Would you be willing to lend a nonprofit money if its quick ratio is less than 1 or its working capital is negative? You probably would not without substantial collateral, because a negative working capital figure or a quick ratio that is less than 1 is a sign of probable insolvency because current liabilities exceed current assets.

As a matter of act, short-term borrowing would not help because it increases current liabilities by the amount of the debt and interest, thus increasing the demand for cash. But long-term borrowing may be helpful. It increases long-term rather than current liabilities and provides cash that increases current assets. The debt ratio of this organization (long-term debt divided by total assets) is .014. Not bad. Over the long run the organization is not overleveraged in excess debt relative to its assets. But would you still want to make the loan? How will the organization pay the interest and the principal? One possibility would be to use the long-term loan to meet its current obligations and begin to restructure its balance sheet so that it will avoid the same dilemma in the future.

One way of restructuring the organization is to increase revenues from its business. Another way is to sell some of its assets and another is to increase gifts and contributions. In all cases, the objective of the organization should be to increase its cash or near-cash items. To illustrate, a gift in the form of a building would not help. It increases fixed assets rather than current assets. Furthermore, if a debt is assumed or if there are current operating costs exceeding current revenues from the building (a negative cash flow), the situation is worsened.

Similarly, a gift that is restricted may not help. To illustrate, suppose that the organization has a cash shortfall. It gets a gift of $1,000,000 from Cita Mathew Landers, but this gift is restricted to the building fund. These dollars, whether received in cash or deferred, cannot be used to meet current expenses unless the restriction can be legally broken.

Bankruptcy: The Donald Trump Threat

A persistent state of current liabilities exceeding current assets could, in the for-profit world, lead to creditors declaring a firm involuntarily bankrupt. This occurs when an important current liability, interest and principal payments due on debt, cannot be paid. This is the threat that Donald Trump continuously faced in 1990. With a nonprofit, such as the one being analyzed, bankruptcy, due to nonpayment of principal and interest, may be declared by the trustees or the state if cash cannot be gotten to pay the creditors. We discuss sources of cash in Chapter 18.

Equity and Debt Management

The balance sheet also tells us something about the claims others have against the organization. Liabilities are claims against the organization. The total liabilities, $65,800, is roughly 60 percent of the total assets, $71,060. This debt ratio may be too high for a nonprofit.

Let us explain. Large nonprofits such as hospitals, universities, and housing, which raise money in the bond market as for-profit firms do, receive credit ratings; and so what is a good debt ratio depends on the rating system's view. Therefore, there is a market discipline to their debt ratio.

With other nonprofits such wide market discipline does not exist; therefore, it is more imperative that it be internally imposed. The amount of debt that can be carried, whether by a household, firm, or nonprofit, depends on several factors: the cost, the use, and, most critically, the level and steadiness of earnings. Debt, short or long, must be paid according to schedule.

Debt that generates income is superior to debt that does not; that is, the difference between debt for a consumer good and debt for an investment. The organization that has a high steady monthly income, after all operating expenses are accounted for, is in a better position to carry debt than one that has an erratic or low net revenue flow. It is precisely these latter organizations that tend to suffer short-term cash flow problems that generate more debt, because their current assets fall below their current liabilities. The need for controlling debt becomes imperative. This should begin by monitoring the debt to equity ratio and keeping it low (below 30 percent). It should also be done by monitoring the revenue, support, and expense statement (which we shall be discussing) to be sure the debt, whatever its size, can very easily be covered because of a large and dependable net cash flow. We refer you to the discussion in Chapter 15 about matching fixed costs with permanent income.

Comparative Balance Sheets

The critical differences between the balance sheets of a for-profit and a nonprofit corporation are in the line items referring to gifts and contributions and in the balancing entry. For-profits do not attract gifts and contributions even when they are insolvent. Nonprofits do not have stockholders and, therefore, there is no stockholder's or owner's equity (net worth) shown on their balance sheets. This is central to the definition of a nonprofit: Its income and assets may not be distributed to individuals. Thus, any excess of assets over liabilities is reflected in fund balances to be used to further the mission, not to increase stockholder's wealth.

However, even this is a matter of degree. Some nonprofits have members who are not owners in the sense of for-profit stockholders. Yet the organization (an association) may be thought of as having earnings that are at the disposal of the membership as a group. Thus, the excess shown in the balance sheet may be labeled "funds balance and membership equity."

STATEMENT OF SUPPORT, REVENUES, AND EXPENSES

Another important financial statement for nonprofits is the statement of activity or statement of expense, revenues and support, as in Figure 17.2. This is an annual statement produced by the nonprofit and is analogous to the income statement of a for-profit firm. The statement is a year-end depiction of the financial operation of the organization during a year.

The **support** and **revenues** of the organization may include:

1. **Fees** from admissions to events
2. Government **contracts,** state, local, or federal
3. **Gifts** and grants from institutions and from individuals
4. **Membership fees** (if applicable)
5. **Investment** income (dividends and interest) on marketable and long-term securities
6. Net realized investment gains or losses from the **sale** of the securities
7. **Royalties;** that is, income from permiting others to use logos, trademarks, and other copyrighted materials
8. **Revenues** from sales of publications and the like

The statement does not show that these revenues and support (except the government contract) are restricted to a specific fund or use, which we shall say more about later. Generally, these revenues and support are available for use by the organization as it sees fit in the conduct of its mission. This nonprofit had unrestricted support and revenues during the year January 1, 1991, to December 31, 1991, of $310,235, minus the $20,000 for government contracts. Contracts are restricted to the performance of a specific task.

There are also **expenses.** For nonprofit organizations, expenses are generally classified by function or program, general administration or

FIGURE 17.2 Statement of Support, Revenues and Expenses of a Nonprofit
Corporation, 1/1/91 to 12/31/91

Support and Revenue		
Admissions	$ 2,235	
Government contracts	20,000	
Gifts and grants	230,000	
Membership	38,000	
Investment income	10,000	
Net realized investment gains (losses)	4,000	
Royalties	1,000	
Revenue from sales	5,000	
Total		$310,235
Expenses		
Programs	290,000	
Supporting services	48,000	
Cost of sales	1,000	
Total		339,000
Excess (Deficit) Revenues and Support over Expenses		(28,765)
Capital additions		
Gifts	300,000	
Net investment income	34,000	
Net realized investment gain (loss)	4,000	
Total		338,000
Excess (deficit) Support and Revenues and Capital Additions		309,235
Fund Balance at Beginning of Period		(30,000)
Fund Balance at End of Period		279,235

supporting services, and the cost of sales (items sold in a business). This
organization had a total operating expense of $339,000. Its operating
expenses exceeded its revenues and support by $28,765. It operated in
the red.

This operating deficit had nothing to do with the related business
that yielded sales of $5000, for the cost of such sales was $1000, giving
a gross profit (defined as the difference between the two) of $4000. As
these businesses become larger, it will be important for the organization
to actually itemize such costs as insurance, wages, rents, and interests
specifically attributed to the business as for-profits do. A more accurate
measure of the profitability of the business can then be obtained.[4]

This organization has two strategies available to it. It can seek to
bring its expenses into line or increase its revenues and support. This
latter approach would work only if the organization increases its unrestricted funds. Restricted funds cannot be applied to general operations,
which is where this organization is in trouble.

A special class of revenues and support is called capital additions. These are receipts, usually in the form of endowments, the use of which are restricted by the donor. The restrictions are expressed in the agreement that leads to the gift, bequest, or contribution. The use of the funds may be restricted in several ways. The restriction may apply to specific purposes, such as the construction of a building. The restriction may require the lapse of time or the occurrence of an event, such as the passage of twenty years or the death of the donor, as in a remainder trust discussed in Chapter 10.

The **capital additions** include:

1. Restricted gifts received during the year
2. Net investment income earned on these gifts and similar ones received earlier
3. Gains or losses realized from the sale of assets related to these restricted gifts

For the organization in this example, the capital additions amounted to $338,000. Taking both operating costs and capital additions into account, the overall performance of the organization during the year is $309,235. This is the amount by which revenues and support exceeded expenses when capital additions were taken into account. This surplus in the restricted fund balance was so high that it was sufficient to make up the deficit ($30,000) with which the organization started the year. Hence, at the end of the year, the fund balance is $279,235.

This balance of $279,235 indicates that the overall performance of the organization led to a surplus. Note, however, that this surplus occurs in the restricted segment. Unless the individual contracts that created these accounts permit, the surplus is not available for the organization to use to stay alive. We shall say more about restricted funds.

Interpretation and Use of the Statement of Support, Revenues, and Expenses

The most basic use of this statement is to determine if the organization operated efficiently during the year. To do this, we must distinguish between operating and capital performance. Each has its bottom line.

This organization operated at a deficit ($28,765). It spent more than it took in for current program and support activities. Its capital account, however, shows just the reverse, a surplus of $338,000, indicating that it accumulated funds for long-run use.

The interpretation of deficits and surpluses depends on the facts and circumstances. Every organization can expect a deficit to occur now and again over its lifetime. The objective should be to have surpluses in both the operating and capital accounts every year, as long as the organization is carrying out its mission satisfactorily. Surpluses provide savings for financing the future and are an indication of the ability to pay off debt.

A nonprofit that conducts many programs may strategically plan for surpluses in one or more of them as a way of financing or subsidizing other programs. A full-blown revenue statement would enable management to distinguish between these two.

It is important to recognize that the statement of activity gives hard facts predicated on reasonable accounting practices, not estimates such as the budget. The data in the statement of activity can therefore be used to compare the actual with the projected figures shown in the budget. Thus, the statement of activity tells whether or not the organization operated efficiently, whether it met its budgetary targets and limits, and how. Moreover, as we can see here, the statement of actual activity if used properly would also form the basis for budgetary targets. This organization needs to review its revenue and expense performance and set new achievable budgetary targets on each if it is to escape the fate now facing it. This organization would benefit from Chapters 15 and 18.

The statement of activities, when compared over several years, gives a picture of the trend toward the diversification of income and support. Is the organization becoming more or less dependent on admissions or fees? Is this a good trend? Is it sustainable? Which expenses are rising fastest, which programs? Why? Is this what we want?

Comparative Statement of Activities

There are differences between the income statement of a for-profit firm and the statement of activity of the nonprofit. The revenues of a firm are earned from the sale of goods or services (called revenues from operation) or from the earnings on investment or the sale of assets (called other or extraordinary or nonrecurring revenues). For-profit firms do not get support from deductible gifts and contributions.[5]

In many nonprofits, this support is the only meaningful form of income. In others, there are both contributions and earned revenues. It is the ability to rely on contributions that permits the nonprofit to operate and sell its goods and services below market price. The price might even be zero, indicating that the nonprofit does not charge at all. It can do this because of its reliance on gifts and other contributions. A for-profit cannot do the same. It must operate at or above market price because it must bear all costs and provide a fair rate of return to its investors.

At the risk of being repetitious, another difference between for-profit and nonprofits is in the bottom line. The income statements of for-profits normally end with an entry that is called net income. This is the bottom line because it shows whether or not the organization operated at a loss or a gain during the course of the year. If there is a gain, that amount can be retained by the firm, distributed to the shareholders in the form of dividends, used to purchase other assets, and used to pay off debt at the discretion of the board of trustees.

A nonprofit has as its bottom line "funds deficit or excess" or a similar phrase. Note that in both the case of a for-profit and nonprofit the possibility of having a positive or negative bottom line exists. Either may have a surplus (called a profit in a for-profit firm) or a deficit (called a loss in a for-profit firm). The major difference is in the use of the surplus or profit. Of all the possible uses, one does not pertain to nonprofits: Nonprofits may not distribute their surplus to individuals or use it other than to foster their mission. Of all the possible ways of dealing with a deficit, the one that cannot be done by nonprofits is that they cannot issue shares of stocks, but they may rely on gifts. Just the reverse is true of a for-profit firm: They may raise additional funds by selling stocks but cannot rely on gifts.

A final difference between the for-profit and nonprofit statement of activity is that the former will have an allowance for taxes while the latter, unless a private foundation or the operator of an unrelated business, would not normally have such a line item.

STATEMENT OF CHANGES IN FINANCIAL POSITION

The principal purpose of the statement of changes in the financial position of the organization is to show how resources were acquired and how they were used during the year and, consequently, why the organization finds itself in either a favorable or unfavorable financial position at the end of the year. Unlike a budget, it is not a projection of the sources and uses of resources. It is an actual accounting of major resource uses and acquisition during the fiscal year of the organization. And, unlike a budget, this statement is subject to audit.

The statement of changes in the financial position of the organization also differs from the balance sheet. The latter describes the financial status of the organization at a point in time. The former shows the flows that contributed to the attainment of that financial status. In short, what are the major financial flows that resulted in the picture portrayed in the balance sheet? Both statements are subject to audit.

The statement of changes in the financial position of the organization differs from the statement of activities just analyzed. The latter shows the dollar expenditures of each set of activities by type of expenditure (salaries, rent, supplies, and so on) and the sources of revenues by type. The latter focuses on broader categories of resource flows.

Sometimes the statement of changes in financial position may be combined with the statement of activities. Instead of a statement of changes in financial position, an organization may report a statement of changes in working capital. This latter statement merely shows the changes in current assets and liabilities that the organization experienced during the year. A statement of changes in financial position is broader than a statement of changes in working capital because it includes all major resource flows, not just those in current assets and liabilities.

Interpretation and Use of Changes in Financial Position

Like all financial statements, the statement of changes in the financial position of the organization contains numbers, and the interpretation of these numbers is an art. Instead of looking at an example of a statement of changes in financial position (we shall see a specific example later), we focus our attention on some of the major resource flows that may appear in the statement. In other words, what are some of the major uses and sources of financial resources for the nonprofit organization during the course of its fiscal year? What resource flows may bring about a change in its financial position? Note the use of the word "resources." It is intended to imply more than the word "cash." Changes in resources may or may not be reflected in the change in cash. This is illustrated below.

Sources of Resources

Here are eight sources of resources for the organization.

1. The operating excesses from the organization's performance during the year arise because the organization's revenues and support from operations exceeded its expenditures. These revenues and support may include sales and contributions that are unrestricted, that is, available to be used for the general operation of the organization. An excess implies that the organization did not spend more than it brought in during the year, so the excess can be used to strengthen its financial position. If the organization operated at a deficit, this too would represent a change in financial position, implying, at least in the short term, a weakening of the financial position of the organization.

2. Decrease in inventories (when the organization runs a related business) implies that sales are made. Therefore, a reduction in inventories implies positive change in the financial position of the organization. An increase in inventories, particularly if such increases were unintended and merely represent the inability to make planned sales, implies a weak-

ening of the financial position of the organization. The organization is less liquid and had to use its resources to build up unintended inventories, which it has been unable to sell.

3. Increases in deferred amounts (such as unfilled orders for the organization's publications) represent changes in the financial position of the organization. By deferring payments or the fulfillment of orders, the organization has more financial resources available to it now. On the other hand, a decrease in these amounts implies that payments were made and, therefore, the organization has less resources available to it.

4. The financial position of the organization is also changed by returns on its investments. These may be from the sales of investments, from interest earned, and from dividends received from corporations in which it owns stocks. This may or may not be a solely owned corporation. Returns on investments represent a positive increase in the financial position of the organization and an improvement in its ability to advance its mission. On the other hand, losses represent a deterioration of the financial position of the organization.

5. Increases in contributions and bequests that are restricted to specific purposes, such as a building fund or a scholarship fund, represent improvements in the financial position of the organization. These are known as capital additions. One aspect of capital additions is that the funds may not be used for operating purposes at the time they are given and that their uses are restricted to those stipulated by the donor. Thus, while capital additions improve the long-term financial position of the organization, they do little to improve its liquidity unless the terms of the gift provide for the transfer of these funds for operating purposes.

6. Sales of the long-term assets of the organization also bring about a change in the financial position of the organization. Such sales bring in cash. This is not to imply that selling the assets of the organization is necessarily good. In some cases it might be a strategy forced by the need to raise cash. But in others, it might be the result of a decision that the assets are no longer needed.

7. Depreciation is another source of resources for the organization. Recall that the organization deducts depreciation every year in determining whether or not it operated at a deficit or a surplus. But unlike other expenses, the organization does not pay out any money to anyone when it incurs a depreciation expense. Technically, it withholds the amount depreciated to be used to finance the replacement of the equipment or property depreciated. Thus, the depreciation is a "source" of resources.

Another way of looking at depreciation as a source of resources is to recall that, when the organization records a depreciation expense, it does not make a payment to anyone such as it does when it incurs a salary or benefit expense. In these latter cases, payments are made. Because no payments are made in depreciation, even though it is deducted as an expense, this deduction represents a source of resources.

8. Another source of financial resources that results in a fundamental change in the financial position of the organization is the acquisition of debt. By borrowing, the organization increases the amount of resources available to it in the short run. At the same time, it increases the claims of others over the future resources of the organization. Debt may be necessary because the organization does not have needed resources. If debt is incurred to purchase an asset that appreciates, then the effect is to increase the total financial resources of the organization by more than the debt.

What are some major uses of resources of the organization that result in a change in its financial position?

Uses of Resources

Now we turn to alternative uses of the organization's resources. They include the following:

1. Resources may be used to purchase new assets such as buildings and equipment. To say that such a transaction represents a change in the financial position of the organization is not to imply that the organization is worse off. The organization is merely less liquid by using its cash to purchase long-term assets; or it may have limited effect on its immediate liquidity position if the purchase is financed totally by long-term debt such as mortgage. Future liquidity will be affected because the interest and principal on the notes will have to be paid. Whatever method is used to finance the purchase, a change in the financial position has occurred.

2. Reductions in short- and long-term debt also represent a change in the financial position of the organization. A reduction in debt implies a payment, that is, a use of the organization's resources.

3. A change in the financial position of the organization is brought about by the purchase of investments such as bonds and certificates of deposit. The change represents the use of cash for the acquisition of an income-producing asset.

4. The resources of the organization are also used to the extent of increasing receivables, including pledges of contributions not received. To understand this, consider that a receivable, whether it is called accounts receivable or pledges due, is really a payment due to the organization. Technically, that payment is due because the organization expended resources either to create and sell a product or service or to create a situation to which a donor wishes to give. The act of creating the product, the service, or the purpose to which the donor wishes to give could only occur by the use of the organization's resources. Put another way, the organization's resources may be used to create a product or service or to create a purpose for giving. If an immediate sale were made or if the donation had been received, then this would have represented an increase (a source) of resources. Since no money is received by the organization, technically all the organization has done is expended its resources in expectation of receiving money. These expectations are receivables. Where there is a sale, collection is legally enforceable; a promise of a gift may not be.

5. Another major flow of resources is the transfer of funds from restricted accounts to the unrestricted operating account (a source of resources), or vice versa (a use or application of resources). This flow is unlike the others because it does not represent bringing in additional resources to the organization or transferring the organization's resources to an outsider. It is a flow of funds between one set of accounts of the organization and another. Thus, the organization changes its financial position without necessarily adding or subtracting from the total amount of resources it commands. These interfund transfers are governed not only by accounting principles but by the legal agreements that set up the funds. For example, the organization may transfer funds from an endowment to the operating fund either because the terms of the endowment provide for such an amount to be transferred at that time or because the organization is borrowing the funds for operating purposes, as long as the terms of the agreement that set up the endowment permit such loans.

Resource Use and Opportunity Costs

Changes in resources are not always cost free. To demonstrate, based on the above discussion, we know that building up inventory is a use of funds; therefore, it has a cost. One cost is an opportunity cost because resources could be used for something else. Inventory has other costs, which we shall discuss later. Building up accounts receivable (while there are claims against others) also has a cost. Take the organization that charges for its newsletters. It can build up readership by building receivables—extending credit making it easier for people to pay. In the meantime, the organization has to pay its bills and foregoes earnings on the interest it could have received had the payments been received and banked.

Rises in inventories and receivable must therefore be monitored. A rise in receivables, for example, could occur because the organization has a bad collection policy. Bills go out late, there is no follow-up, or the organization extends credit to the wrong people. Such laxed management of credit consumes resources. The statement of changes in financial position gives us a clue.

Comparative Statements of Changes in Financial Position

A principal difference between the for-profit firm's statement of changes in financial position and that of a nonprofit is that the former can increase resources by issuing stocks. This produces cash. It can also use resources to pay dividends, which induces some people to purchase and hold the stocks. Neither of these entries will appear on the books of a nonprofit. The nonprofit may not issue stocks to increase its cash and may not pay dividends. It has no individual owners.

GENERAL ASPECTS OF INTERPRETATION

In interpreting financial statements, the management must know whether the accounting is on a cash or an accrual basis. If it is on a cash basis, this means that all accounting entries represent actual cash receipts or outlays. If the organization is on an accrual basis, this means that there is a definite commitment to pay or to receive payment. The transaction may be completed but no cash has been transferred. In this case, the amounts shown as accounting entries represent commitments rather than cash. Small nonprofits tend to operate on a cash basis, while the larger more complex ones, like for-profit firms, operate on an accrual basis.

When interpreting financial statements, managers should also be aware that, as in budgets, vertical and horizontal analyses can be helpful. This is especially true if the data are presented for more than one year. For example, in the support, revenue, and expense statement, a horizontal analysis for more than one year could reveal if the proportion that each line item contributes to expense or revenues has changed. Similarly, a vertical analysis of the same factors over the same number of years could reveal which line items are growing fastest and which are declining. The question for management is, why. Is this in the best interest of the organization? Is this what we planned in our strategic planning process? Do we need to change our plans?

Interpreting financial statements may also involve comparisons with other organizations. This is not necessary, but it is often advisable. In so doing the underlying differences in the organizations ought to be kept in mind. Moreover, when possible, ratios rather than absolute numbers ought to be used to reflect the differences in sizes of the organizations. Because nonprofits tend to be so different from each other and data and accounting procedures are less standardized, comparisons among organizations ought to be done with utmost care.

On the point of standardization of accounting procedures, it should be reiterated that the examples given in this chapter are intended to highlight concepts. All nonprofits do not use exactly the same accounting procedures or reporting format. The mastery of the information as presented in this chapter, however, should be a firm basis for dealing with individual organizations.

FUND ACCOUNTING

Fund accounting refers to a system of financial record keeping and reporting that is common among nonprofit organizations. The basic characteristic of fund accounting is that certain accounts must be kept separate, that funds cannot be comingled except in an approved investment pool or through authorized and documented transfer of funds from one account to another, and that the financial activity in each separate fund is subject to independent accounting. Interfund transfers, the movement of money from one fund to another, must be authorized by the board of trustees.

General Types of Funds

For the purposes of fund accounting, funds may be classified as expendable or nonexpendable. Expendable funds are those that may be totally spent. Unexpendable funds are those where typically only the income to the fund may be spent, but the principal and sometimes the gains from sales of the assets of the funds must be spent so that the fund may have a perpetual life. True endowments are examples of nonexpendable funds.

Endowments, as we discussed earlier, are of several types. A university may have an endowment fund for scholarships, for land acquisition and building construction, for athletic purposes and facilities, for lectureships, and for professorships. Thus, while we may speak of the endowments of Harvard or Columbia universities to be a certain dollar amount, we are actually speaking of the composite of several separate endowments.

Within any category of endowments, there are numerous separate accounts. For example, Syracuse University has a modest endowment of $100 million. This is made up of over 1023 separate restricted accounts.[6] Some are restricted for scholarships, some for academic prizes, and some for financing academic events. Each account represents a specific donor or cause for which a specific endowment has been established, not just a gift but an endowment, that is, a gift that is expected to have a lengthy life whose principal would not generally be spent, but the income of which will be used to support a specific cause specified by the donor or donors.

Each of these separate accounts technically has a balance sheet, an income statement, a financial report, and perhaps a statement of changes in financial position. Each must be kept separate and generally bears the name of the donor. Thus, the Simon and Myra Bryce chair, the Orvin and Sylvia Gaustad chair, and the Mabel and Mary Laporte chair may be in the same university, but each is a separate endowment subject to separate accounting. Each is also subject to a separate agreement between the donor and the donee. It is this separate, written legal document that determines how a fund may be used.

Fund accounting uses another important classification of funds. Funds may be restricted or unrestricted. Restricted funds are those that can be used only for purposes that are specified in the agreement at the time the gift was made or the contract was signed. A grant or payment to a nonprofit to provide research on the topic of AIDS uses its restricted funds. An unrestricted fund is one that can be used to finance activities at the discretion of the board of trustees of the organization. As one Syracuse University official pointed out, unrestricted funds are the backbone of the growth of the university. These unrestricted funds can be used to pay salaries, provide scholarships, make investments, take advantage of unanticipated opportunities, meet emergencies, fund scholarships, begin new programs, and finance general activities.[7]

Sometimes the terms "general funds" or "operating funds" are used to denote unrestricted funds used for general operations and restricted funds used in current operations, but for the specifically restricted purpose for which they are given. Thus, in a current year, a university uses restricted funds to finance scholarships and lectures and also uses unrestricted funds for these and other purposes, including salaries and maintenance.

It should be kept in mind that the terms "restricted" and "unrestricted" are not synonymous with budgeted. An organization may budget $1 million for salaries and benefits. What makes the amount restricted is a legal force. A restricted amount cannot be used for any other purpose than those for which it was given. Variations from this intended purpose legally occur only by an act of the board of trustees, the court, and the donor. Again, a budgeted amount is a planned or anticipated amount. It is not a legal restriction. There are no legal contracts or consequences from their variations. The misuse of a restricted fund is a violation of a contract and can be subject to both civil and criminal penalties.

The fact that the funds are unrestricted does not mean that discretion is absolute. These funds cannot be used for purposes that contravene the mission of the organization or violate the terms discussed in Chapter 4. Unrestricted merely means that the management may use its discretion about how the funds can be used as long as the use is consistent with the mission of the organization and the terms under which it was given legal and tax-exempt status.

Unrestricted funds come from gifts and contributions of donors and the earnings of the nonprofit. Many nonprofits conduct special campaigns to increase the size of their unrestricted funds. Others obtain unrestricted funds almost exclusively through tuitions. They receive limited state aid and have very small endowments.

In addition to giving the organization fiscal discretionary powers, unrestricted funds also have the advantage that there is no legal ratio of unrestricted to restricted funds that it must maintain. Hence, financially skillful nonprofit management can maintain the support ratios discussed in Chapter 4 and still maintain discretion. For example, it is possible to meet the one-third public support test and still have a large percentage, even 100 percent, of the assets of the organization being discretionary. It is possible and customary, for example, to emphasize unrestricted gifts in any contribution campaign the organization conducts.

Many nonprofits do run campaigns for unrestricted gifts at the same time that they seek out funds for restricted purposes. They are two different tracks upon which Chapters 9 and 10 of this book were based. We shall say more about fund accounting in our discussion of the American Red Cross.

The previous discussion on fund restrictions is summarized in Table 17.1 on the next page.

Example of Funds

Each organization's board of trustees sets up its own system of funds. The World Wildlife Fund, Inc., uses the following sets: (1) an unrestricted operating fund used for unrestricted operating purposes; (2) a restricted operating fund used for specific operating purposes or programs as stipulated by the donor; (3) unrestricted board-designated investment fund used to accumulate gifts by bequests and other accumulations designated by the trustees for investment purposes; (4) restricted endowment fund

TABLE 17.1 Summary of Fund Restriction

Type of Fund	Description
Unrestricted	Determined by management via budget
Board restricted	Determined by trustees
Expendable	Both principal and income spendable
Unexpendable	Only part of income spendable
Donor preference	Moral obligation to follow preference
Donor restricted	Determined by legal contract
Expendable	Both principal and income spendable
Unexpendable	Only part of income spendable
Contract and grant	Determined by terms of acceptance

Note: Unexpendable or unexhaustible funds may, by provision of the contract, permit occasional spending of principal. The aim is to avoid this since perpetuity of the fund is the objective.

used to accumulate gifts by bequests that stipulate that the principal be invested in perpetuity.

A restricted endowment fund may be comprised of numerous separate funds (see Figure 17.3). Similarly, the "unrestricted fund" may be comprised of separate funds. Thus, again with the Girl Scouts, "Unrestricted Funds" are the general fund, the capital fund, the properties

FIGURE 17.3 Restricted Funds

Restricted funds are comprised of the following:	1989	1988
Endowment funds:		
DeWitt Wallace Reader's Digest	$1,282,100	$1,273,300
Macy Scholarship	855,600	824,300
Membership Endowment	585,100	518,600
Katharine Packard Crispell	457,200	451,100
Elizabeth A. Bovey	364,300	344,700
Sara Baylis Johnson Memorial	294,500	292,900
Samuel Joseloff	181,900	187,300
Andree Clark Memorial	174,300	172,200
Marie G. Dennett	171,900	164,200
Joseph N. Golding	164,400	155,700
Daniel C. Jackling	146,400	141,600
Other	339,300	266,100
	5,017,000	4,792,000
Other restricted funds	1,453,000	1,283,000
	$6,470,000	$6,075,000

Source: Girl Scouts of the U.S.A., Annual Report, 1989, p 26. Reprinted with permission.

funds, and a special funds that includes board-designated endowment funds and other unrestricted funds. To repeat, the basic function of funds is to keep monies in separate pots for legal and managerial purposes. These are particularly important when organizations have distinctly different activities within their mission, for example, for the American Red Cross, disaster assistance and blood service.

Interfund Transfers

The transfer of money or assets from one fund to another is a formal financial transaction requiring at least three things: (1) a vote or standing permission from the board allowing such a transaction, (2) permission from the donors or broad language in the terms of the gift allowing such transactions or an act by the court or state, and (3) a clear and specific accounting of such transactions in the year-end financial statement.

Interfund transfers occur for several reasons. An expense may be paid from general funds and then recouped from the specific fund to which it belongs. This avoids having to sell securities to make immediate payments. It also allows parking funds in short-term interest earning accounts. Sometimes the maintenance of a separate fund is no longer economical, legally or managerially necessary; i.e. the objective is satisfied or obsolete. Transfers are frequently made into the current accounts to provide cash to carry on current operations consistent with the terms of restriction. There are also interfund loans to cover cash shortfalls.

Example

Figure 17.4 refers to the American Friends Service Committee. At the very top we see three separate funds: (1) land, buildings, and equipment, (2) annuity and life income, and (3) endowment. These are all capital funds as opposed to the operating fund, which appears at the bottom. Capital funds are long term rather than current financing pools. Observe that the accounting is completely separate, under fund accounting.

Let us focus on the middle one, the annuity and life income, which is the deferred giving programs we discussed in Chapter 10. Notice that these capital funds grow on the basis of (1) a constant inflow of contributions and bequests, (2) net income, and (3) any adjustment for actuarial liability. These liabilities are nothing more than statistical estimates based on the payout data we discussed in Chapter 10. The ($789,181) is the amount that would have to be paid as a legal claim by those annuities if the noncharitable beneficiary made the claim today.

Let us illustrate. The remainder trust may be for a term of twenty years and payment is made monthly. To keep its promise to me, the

FIGURE 17.4 Financial Results for Other Funds

	Land, Buildings and Equipment Fund	Annuity and Life Income Funds[1]	Endowment Funds
Beginning Fund Balances, 10/1/88	$2,880,031	$16,561,151	$2,889,755
Income was provided by:			
Contributions and bequests	$26,778	$3,152,840	$290,283
Net investment income	($12,796)	$212,324	$22,810
Miscellaneous	$0	$0	$0
Actuarial liability adjustment	$0	($789,181)	$0
Total Income	$13,982	$2,575,983	$313,093
Expenses were for:			
Total program services	$138,209	$0	$0
General management	$149,557	$0	$0
Fund raising	$20,153	$0	$0
Total Expenses	$307,919	$0	$0
Excess (deficiency) of income over expenses	($293,937)	$2,575,983	$313,093
Other changes in fund balances:			
Matured annuity & income gifts	$0	($1,082,244)	$143,683
Expired term endowments	$0	$0	($57,627)
Property and equipment purchased	$395,910	$0	$0
Total Other Changes	$395,910	($1,082,244)	$86,056
Ending Fund Balances, 9/30/89	$2,982,004	$18,054,890	$3,288,904

Operations Funds Balances

	Beginning Balances 10/1/88	Net Changes	Ending Balances 9/30/89
Restricted Funds:[2]	$3,014,908	($39,947)	$2,974,961
Unrestricted Funds:			
Unsold real estate and other nonmarketable assets	$636,569	$926,385	$1,562,954
Donor-deferred suggestion funds[3]	$1,255,601	$671,826	$1,927,427
Designated pension fund	$784,632	$266,954	$1,051,586
Operating reserves[4]	$2,308,230	$240,841	$3,549,071
Funds functioning as endowments	$1,712,551	$16,464	$1,729,015
Bequests designated for use in future years[5]	$13,788,075	$236,413	$14,024,488
Realized capital gains and other funds[6]	$5,842,345	($477,024)	$5,365,321
	$26,328,003	$1,881,859	$29,209,862

[1] Certain irrevocable gifts which AFSC has received under trust subject to payment of income to one or more beneficiaries for life.

[2] Directed by donors for specific program use.

[3] Special funds created by donors who make suggestions to AFSC regarding grants from their individual fund to appropriate programs and/or other charitable organizations.

[4] AFSC national and regional offices maintain reserves to adjust short-run funding needs and provide for unexpected program opportunities.

[5] Bequest income fluctuates unpredictably. In order to balance this flow of funds, AFSC creates a pool of several years' bequests and allocates 50% of the pool each year for program work. This policy assures program stability and continuity from year to year.

[6] Beginning FY '89, the Committee instituted a policy regarding the use of realized capital gains. $814,000 were used for '89 budget purposes.

Source: American Friends Service Committee, 1989, p. 9. Reprinted with permission.

trustee must plan each year for the amount that is due me that year even though the check is not yet drawn. These are actuarial liabilities, that is, accounting mechanisms for setting money aside to meet known liabilities. They do at least two things: (1) avoid the overstating of the net value of the annuity, and (2) reveal the size of the legal claim against the annuity.

Because funds may have different withdrawal strategies and investment strategies depending on the use and constraints placed on them and may also have different advisors, their year-end results may be very different. This is evidenced by the disparity between ($293,937) and a positive $2,575,983. This disparity may also arise because land, building, and equipment are subject to depreciation.

"Maturity annuity and income gifts" shows a decline, ($1,082,244), for what purpose? Recall from our discussions of trusts and annuities that there is a life estate—a right over the annual flow of income from the trust. This is the annuity income, which in the case of a gift annuity or remainder trust goes to a noncharitable beneficiary. These annuity payments amounted to $1,082,244. Payments are shown as negative numbers.

Let's turn to the operating funds. They are divided into two major groups with which we are familiar: restricted and unrestricted. The note shows that the first is restricted by donors. But look at the unrestricted funds. The bulk is neatly compartmentalized by the trustees into specific trustee-designated uses and is restricted to these uses unless otherwise authorized by the trustees. The parameters of financial management are set by the board and unrestricted does not necessarily imply total and unconstrained discretion, just more discretion.

Even the board may have limits to its discretion. Look at the entry, "Designated pension fund." Here the board is setting aside funds to meet legal claims of workers. The entry "Donor-deferred suggestion funds" implies that the donor expresses a preference, causing the trustees to feel ethically bound to honor it even though the donor does not insist.

AUDIT

The various sectors in the nonprofit world apply different accounting standards. One standard is "Audits of Voluntary Health and Welfare Organizations" of the American Institute of Certified Public Accountants; another is *Accounting Principles and Reporting Practices for Churches and Church Related Organizations* by the Catholic bishops.

General Characteristics of Audits

Audits are done to determine if the accounting procedures used by the organization conform with the general acceptable accounting principles (GAAP). The aim of these principles is to be sure that the accounting of the organization is objective, fair, complete, and accurate. These are the four criteria used to judge the accounting practices of the organization.

In assessing the organization's conformity with these four standards, the auditors look at both expenses and revenues of the organization. In investigating the expenses, the auditors seek clear evidence that the expenses were authorized and approved by a responsible person of the management team, are correctly classified by function (program) or object, are recognized in the correct accounting period, and are justified or supported by documents such as invoices. Auditors are instructed to pay particular attention to the existence of controls over expenditures. These controls include the existence of an organizational chart and a clear line of responsibility for decision making, recording, and monitoring expenses. The auditor may also compare the extent to which actual expenditures deviate from planned or budgeted expenditures. The auditors may also be expected to see if the factors that are included in the overhead of the organization are properly classified as such or whether they should be classified as part of the direct cost of a specific project. Conversely, they will check to see that those items treated as direct costs are properly classified and charged to the correct project. The auditors can be expected to look at business expenses to be sure that they are properly classified as unrelated or related and that there is compliance with the payment of taxes.

On the revenue side, the auditors will be concerned with the accurate recording of the amounts of revenues, in the proper time period and in the proper classification by type such as fees, gifts, and contributions, income from investments, sales, and so on. The auditors will also check to be sure that there are proper controls set over the receiving of revenues, including the persons who are so authorized, and that there is a chain of command within the organization to control the receiving, recording, and accountability for such revenues. Where applicable, as in the case of endowments, the auditors will assure that accounts are segregated and independently recorded.

Where cash is involved, the auditors may want to be sure that there are physical safeguards for keeping cash and that there are procedures that control and limit petty cash to a reasonable amount. Where securities are concerned, the auditor will verify the type and the reasonableness of their reported cost and return.

In carrying out their function, the auditors focus on financial statements, such as the balance sheet, that tell them about the treatment of the assets and liabilities of the organization. They focus on the revenue and expense statements, which tell them about the flow of revenues from various sources and the expenditures of the organization for various purposes. They examine those and other statements that explain how the financial position of the organization has changed over a period that is usually one year. Their only use of the budget is as a standard through which they may judge departures from the organization's commitments, what the organization thought was reasonable, and as evidence that there is some credible attempt to control both the revenues and expenses of the organization.

At the end of the audit, the auditors may render an opinion in writing to the organization. The opinion is divided into a section that describes the scope of the audit, a disclaimer, an explanatory paragraph, and an opinion. The scope tells what financial statements were audited and for what time period; the disclaimer tells what was omitted from the audit and why; the explanatory statement explains departures or peculiar aspects of accounting by the nonprofit and why they may be justified; and the opinion is the judgment of the auditors as to the conformity of the organization with generally acceptable accounting practices. An opinion may be "clean," meaning that the organization conforms with the GAAP, while a "qualified" opinion expresses concern about the practices of the organization.[8]

The Scope

In the scope statement the time period and the specific fund being audited are given, as is the basis for the audit. Note that the scope is limited to a time period, may also be limited to a particular fund and be conducted for a specific purpose.

The Explanation

The explanatory paragraph further defines the scope. In some cases, it emphasizes that the audit is not of the entire organization, which is not unusual. As we recall, endowments are accounted for separately, and often periodic auditing may be called for in the contract. Alternatively, the audit could have been for the organization in general rather than for a specific endowment alone.

The Opinion

Finally, in a clean opinion, there are no qualifying statements. The auditors may state: "In our opinion, the financial statements referred to above fairly present. . . ." Take note that the opinion does not use words that imply that the financial status of the organization is strong or weak or precarious. An audit does not make judgments about the financial strength of the organization. Only those who interpret financial statements make such judgments. Note also that the audit does not say that the numbers used by the accountant or bookkeepers for the nonprofit are right or wrong. Even a clean audit does not verify that the numbers are right. An audit gives an opinion about the soundness and merits of the procedures and practices used.

Audit Trail

In assessing the practices used, the auditors attempt to establish what is known as an audit trail. That is, they try to trail each revenue item and each expense item from its inception. In an audit trail, auditors may discover sloppiness and embezzlement as the perpetrator fails to provide acceptable evidence of the justification, authorization, and disposition of the nonprofit's money. The discussion that follows will illustrate the statements we have just described.

ILLUSTRATION OF INTERPRETATION OF FINANCIAL STATEMENTS: STATUS AND OPERATIONS

The rules provide for affiliated organizations to report a combined financial statement. Thus, the statements to be shown for the American Red Cross combine the financial situation of the entire 2,719 chapters, 54 regional blood services, and the national sector. Because these are consolidated statements, the underlying data for any chapter or the headquarters may be radically different.

As stated in the earlier part of this chapter, there are a variety of ways in which financial statements are presented in the nonprofit world. Each format depends upon the nature of the organization and the requirements of its board and financial needs. There are basic principles to which good financial statements adhere and basic information they all give to management, trustees, creditors, and agencies.

A Role of the Balance Sheet: Asset Management

A balance sheet tells us about the current status of the nonprofit. It also reflects how the organization is managing its debt and assets. Let us turn to three of the financial statements used by the American Red Cross. We begin with the balance sheet for the fiscal year that ended June 30, 1990. Refer to Figure 17.5.

Note that the total **assets** of the organization are greater than the total **liabilities**; i.e., $1,765,331,000 compared to $439,143,000 for **net assets** of $1,326,188,000 which, in a for-profit firm, would be stockholder's equity. The entire $1,326,188,000 would belong to the owners. In a nonprofit this must be maintained for the nonprofit's mission. How are these assets managed?

Relatively little of the organization's monetized assets (**cash and investments**) is in cash. Most of it is invested in **marketable securities** (such as bonds and stocks). They are earning income for the organization in the form of interest, dividends, and capital gains (price appreciation).

These capital gains are **realized** when the securities are sold. Securities, by definition, rise and fall; therefore, accounting convention requires that they be listed at the lower of costs or current market value.[9] The American Red Cross, using this convention, reports its investments at cost. This implies, therefore, that the market value of these securities is higher than the reported book value.

Accounts receivable, amounting to nearly $290,000,000 in 1990, are payments the organization expects from others such as hospitals and the United Way. These include uncollected pledges. It also includes credit extended to others by the Biomedical services which collects, tests and distributes blood, uncollected payments from grants for services performed, and uncollected loans.

The management of accounts receivable by a nonprofit cannot be done merely by looking at the balance sheet. To manage accounts receivable, other information is needed. How long does it take to receive payments, and how many persons never pay? These two questions go together because the longer the bill is unpaid, the greater the cost to the organization. To see this cost, ask: What does the organization lose in interest because it does not have that money in the bank or available to pay its bills thus forcing the organization to owe creditors? What does it cost it to collect outstanding bills?

Accounts receivable have collateral value—they can be used to secure a loan. They can also be sold (called factoring). In either use, their value is discounted. Thus, instead of getting a loan at 100 percent of the value of the receivable it might be at 80 percent. A bank or a broker would be aided in this decision by breaking down accounts receivable by category. "Grants" have good collateral value, especially if they are payments (receivables) for work already done for a federal government agency.

Inventories, amounting to $102,038,000 in 1990, are also important assets of the American Red Cross. In its case, inventory includes an intentional stock of whole blood, its components and plasma derivatives valued at cost or market price.

We normally associate inventories only with businesses. But nonprofits have inventories of a wide variety including publications (magazines and newsletters), uniforms (Girl Scouts and Boy Scouts), blood (Red Cross and hospitals). What should the nonprofit manager know about inventory management?

The composition of the inventory is important. An inventory of perishables loses value; one of Monet's paintings does just the opposite. Some inventories are kept because we expect that they will be processed further (called work-in-process inventory). When inventory builds up it may be for one of two reasons (1) we used or sold less than we projected or (2) we produced or got more than we thought we needed. This latter can occur, for example, when we buy bulk in order to get a better purchase price or produce a lot because it was cheaper or easier to do so. In short, an inventory build-up may be intentional or unintentional. Management needs to know.

Obviously, inventory is expressed in dollars. Imagine a period of inflation. What is the value of the inventory? It is impossible to count each item and determine its exact value. To avoid this accounting impossibility, an organization elects to either use the most recent price to value all similar items in an inventory or it uses the earliest price.[10] Using the most recent price inflates the value of the inventory while the earlier price depresses it. The management should know what method is being used.

In addition, management needs to be aware of the costs of inventory. There are two offsetting costs (1) the ordering cost which includes the acquisition cost minus any discount, and (2) the holding costs. It is possible to get a low purchase price that is completely offset by the inventory holding or carrying costs. These latter costs include the cost of storage space, maintenance and preservation, insurance, obsolescence, and the capital costs of money tied up in inventory. Inventory management must also consider the losses that occur when existing stock is insufficient to meet needs, including emergency needs, and the costs of over-stocking especially of products such as magazines and perishables that have short lives.

The American Red Cross **fixed assets** of land buildings, and equipment has a **book value** of $460,096,000. This value is based on the orig-

FIGURE 17.5 Combined Statement of Net Assets

(in thousands)	Notes	Current Operations Unrestricted	Donor Restricted	Land, Buildings, and Equipment	Endowment	Totals 1990	1989
ASSETS							
Cash and equivalents	1,3,6	$ 54,110	$ 10,234	$ 5,358	$ 643	$ 70,345	$ 61,896
Investments—at cost		469,442	72,772	35,328	174,375	751,917	486,474
Receivables:							
Fund campaign and other pledges	2	124,742		12,266		137,008	140,604
Biomedical services products		100,213				100,213	86,508
Service members' loans		12,951				12,951	11,365
Due from other funds			6,530			6,530	3,673
Grants and other	1	17,269	11,012	3,131	1,033	32,445	28,204
Inventories:							
Biomedical services products and related supplies	2	84,165				84,165	85,071
Program and educational materials, and other supplies		17,873				17,873	18,946
Land, buildings, and equipment—less accumulated depreciation	1,7, 8,10			460,096		460,096	436,019
Prepaid pension costs	4	81,050				81,050	55,854
Other		8,432	988	1,318		10,738	9,180
Total Assets		970,247	101,536	517,497	176,051	1,765,331	1,423,794

LIABILITIES AND DEFERRED PUBLIC SUPPORT

	Notes					Total 1990	Total 1989
Accounts payable and accrued liabilities		127,637	24,595	8,467		160,699	111,424
Long-term debt	7	3,228		122,371		125,599	122,026
Due to other funds		3,681		2,839	10	6,530	3,673
Deferred public support	1,11	136,230	3,215	6,870		146,315	182,323
Total liabilities and deferred public support		270,776	27,810	140,547	10	439,143	419,446
NET ASSETS		$699,471	$ 73,726	$376,950	$176,041	$1,326,188	$1,004,348

NET ASSETS—as follows:

	Notes					Total 1990	Total 1989
Donor restricted for specific services			$ 73,726			$ 73,726	$ 37,931
Land, buildings, and equipment				$376,950		376,950	358,618
Endowment					$176,041	176,041	164,183
Designated by board for:							
Disaster relief	5	$ 28,917				28,917	4,345
Biomedical services operations	2	184,873				184,873	170,733
Retiree health benefits	4	48,191				48,191	
Special projects	4	96,135				96,135	
Replacement and improvements of buildings and equipment		21,863				21,863	19,928
Other specific purposes		102,805				102,805	99,490
Invested in net operating assets		216,687				216,687	149,120
Net assets—as above		$699,471	$ 73,726	$376,950	$176,041	$1,326,188	$1,004,348

(See notes to combined financial statements.)

June 30, 1990, With Comparative Totals for 1989 (Includes the Net Assets of 2,719 Chapters, 54 Regional Blood Services, and National Sector for 1990).

Source: American Red Cross, *Annual Report for 1989–90: A New Face on Old Values* (Washington, D.C., 1990), p. 26. Reprinted with permission.

inal cost of these properties from which an accumulated depreciation of $81,050,000 is to be subtracted. What should the nonprofit manager know about fixed assets in the balance sheet?

The typical building appreciates; hence, the true market value of the buildings is likely to be higher than reported in the balance sheet. On the other hand, equipment does lose value and may become obsolete; therefore, the true value of the equipment is likely to be less than reported. The law frequently does not permit depreciation on land for tax purposes, but land is listed at its original cost even though it usually appreciates. The point is that the book value figure that appears may not reflect the market value of these assets, even when, as in the Red Cross, the accounting is very much in keeping with Generally Acceptable Accounting Principles (GAAP).

Part of asset management is keeping a practicable balance between fixed and current assets. As the real estate market dip in 1990 demonstrated, it can sometimes be very difficult to dispose of fixed assets without discounting them or waiting a long time.

Prepaid Expenses are an asset. These are payments made before they are due. Prepaying insurance premiums and subscription costs are common among nonprofits. For the American Red Cross, the particular prepaid expense of $81,050,000 arises because the pension plan is over funded. This usually occurs when the investment performance of the plan produces more income than would be needed to meet all of the liabilities the plan.

A Role of the Balance Sheet: Debt Management

All borrowing should follow a debt management policy which stipulates the amount of borrowing the trustees will permit. In order to extend a loan, a creditor would ask for financial statements. Let us see how much can be told about the credit-worthiness of an organization from these statements. Management should ask: How well are we managing our debt?

Please return to the balance sheet of the American Red Cross. We focus on "Liabilities and Deferred Public Support." We see that the organization has **debt** in 1990 amounting to $439,143,000. Let us analyze it.

First, recall that this is a consolidated balance sheet, so the debt could be distributed over a number of units. Looking at the **notes** (not displayed in this book) we see that a part of the debt, nearly $37,000,000,[11] is owed by the national and $75,877,000 is owed by the units. The debt is dispersed.

The **short-term** debt (nearly 70 percent of the total debt outstanding) can be divided up into separate pieces. Some $146,315,000 (or more than 25 per cent of the total debt) is in the form of **deferred support.**

This means that the organization owes a product or service for which it has already been paid or received contributions. The debt is not in cash, but performance. In the meantime, the money is in the bank earning interest.

Another $6,530,000 is money the organization owes itself—one fund borrowing from another, **interfund loans.** The remaining $160,699,000 of short-term debt is in the form of **accounts payable** and **accrued liabilities.** These are funds the organization owes outsiders, probably during the year, but not necessarily due today.

Is the organization covered? The organization has well over four times that amount of money in **cash** or in **marketable securities** (securities that it could sell instantly). Furthermore, the organization has over 85 percent of that amount or $137,008,000 in pledges alone.

The **long-term** debt of $125,599,000 is not, by definition, currently due—that is, this year. The notes show that $20,000,000 of this amount is not due until January 1, 2009. Furthermore sinking fund payments (annual deposits into an account to fund the pay off of the bonds as they become due) do not have to start until January 1, 1994.

The notes show that the largest sinking fund deposit between 1991 and 1995 is $8,983,000 for 1991. The income statement of the organization, Figure 17.6, shows that it does produce an excess of revenues over expenses which in the past year was nearly $136,641,000. As long as it continues to do this, then the sinking fund requirements will undoubtedly be met very easily from operations. If not, it can be met in part by selling off investments or restricting charitable campaign contributions to these sinking-fund payments. Fund raising in 1989 yielded $253,404,000 and in 1990 $267,068,000 in unrestricted funds, enough to very comfortably meet the sinking fund requirements. The debt is manageable.

Finally, notice the favorable distribution of assets in the unrestricted accounts. This means that the creditor can assume that there is relatively little encumbrance because those funds in the unrestricted accounts can be used at the discretion of management including the paying of a loan. Creditors would not have to wait on the sale of the property or an act by the board to transfer funds from restricted accounts.

The Red Cross on a consolidated basis is very liquid—very solvent; it can pay its current bills. The total of its **current assets** of cash, investment and receivables is about $1,111,409,000 well exceeding its current external monetary liability of $160,699,000 by nearly 7:1. This is a calculation of the **current ratio.** The ratio says that the Red Cross has nearly seven times as many dollars as it needs to payoff all its debt currently due to external sources.[12]

For a long-term perspective, we turn to its **debt-to-asset ratio.** This is total liabilities divided by total assets ($439,143,000 divided by $1,765,331,000)—roughly 25 percent. The organization owns at least four dollars for each dollar it owes.

A Role of the Balance Sheet: Allocating the Gains

In a complex organization, such as the Red Cross, it is worth going beyond the knowledge that the organization has a positive net asset. It is worth knowing how the net assets of the organization are distributed among its various mission or responsibility centers. This information is given in the bottom of the balance sheet of the American Red Cross. One of the responsibilities of trustees is to allocate these funds in ways that enable the nonprofit to carry out its mission.

OPERATIONS AND ACTIVITIES: THE ROLE OF THE STATEMENT OF REVENUES, SUPPORT AND EXPENSES

Let us look at the income and expense statement for the American Red Cross for the fiscal year ending June 30, 1990, Figure 17.6.

Overall Efficiency of Management

The bottom line, total support and revenues minus total expenses, shows an operating excess of $136,641,000. In the for-profit sector, this is known as profit. In the nonprofit sector, such excesses or surpluses must be used for advancing the mission of the organization.

Efficiency by Fund

Please go to the top of Figure 17.6. The columns are divided into current and capital operations (land, buildings and equipment and endowments). The current operations are divided into those restricted by donors or the trustees and unrestricted funds. For the American Red Cross, the unrestricted support and revenues are nearly ten times as much as the restricted. This gives the organization financial flexibility. It has discretion over the use of unrestricted funds allowing the organization to be responsive to a variety of needs within its mission. Consequently, its expenditures are nearly five times greater in the unrestricted category than in the restricted. The major donor—restricted revenue is for specific performance of grants and contracts.

The major source of revenues is sales of blood products and services. In short, despite its worthy charitable mission, the Red Cross could not survive or conduct that mission as well as it does if it could not generate related business revenues. To appreciate this fact, note that total expenditure for blood services was $741,175,000, which is 40 percent greater than the $520,169,000 in all the gifts and donations, **public support,**

Combined Statement of Public Support, Revenues, and Expenses, and Changes in Net Assets

For the Year Ended June 30, 1990, With Comparative Totals for 1989

(Includes the Operations of 2,719 Chapters, 54 Regional Blood Services, and National Sector for 1990)

(in thousands)	Notes	Current Operations Unrestricted	Current Operations Donor Restricted	Land, Buildings, and Equipment	Endowment	Totals 1990	Totals 1989
PUBLIC SUPPORT AND REVENUES							
Public Support:							
Contributions:							
Fund campaign	1	$ 267,068				$ 267,068	$ 253,404
Disaster relief operations	11		$177,539			177,539	16,166
Other	5	20,712	10,377	$ 12,437	$ 1,103	44,629	40,263
Legacies and bequests	3	21,885	1,151	1,451	6,446	30,933	23,589
Total public support		309,665	189,067	13,888	7,549	520,169	333,422
Revenues:							
Biomedical services	2	706,134				706,134	600,878
Investment income		38,842	1,058	1,630		41,530	30,544
Income from endowment funds	3	11,492	191			11,683	11,042
Contracts and grants		12,376	48,241	1,801		62,418	55,936
Program materials		68,658	1,950			70,608	54,921
Gain on sale of assets and other	4	33,616	10,335	3,682	5,382	53,015	53,452
Total revenues		871,118	61,775	7,113	5,382	945,388	806,773
Total public support and revenues		1,180,783	250,842	21,001	12,931	$1,465,557	$1,140,195
EXPENSES							
Program services:							
Services to members of the armed forces, veterans, and their families	5	68,107	4,906	1,936		$ 74,949	$ 75,216
Disaster	2	70,912	149,456	3,791		224,159	103,974
Biomedical services		697,371	14,281	29,523		741,175	664,492
Health services		98,994	12,972	4,005		115,971	111,264
Community volunteer		35,767	21,958	3,043		60,768	49,035
International		5,960	1,425	98		7,483	6,391

Total program services		977,111	204,998	42,396	—	1,224,505	1,010,372
Supporting services:							
Membership and fund raising		29,372	4,457	1,462	—	35,291	31,172
Management and general		63,953	961	4,206	—	69,120	63,845
Total supporting services		93,325	5,418	5,668	—	104,411	95,017
Total expenses		1,070,436	210,416	48,064	—	$1,328,916	$1,105,389
EXCESS (DEFICIENCY) OF PUBLIC SUPPORT AND REVENUES OVER EXPENSES BEFORE SPECIAL ITEMS	11	110,347	40,426	(27,063)	12,931		
Fund campaign accounting change	4	32,708					
Pension benefit settlement gain		152,491					
EXCESS (DEFICIENCY) OF PUBLIC SUPPORT AND REVENUES OVER EXPENSES BEFORE TRANSFERS	3	295,546	40,426	(27,063)	12,931		
Transfer of realized Endowment Fund appreciation		1,058	15		(1,073)		
Property and equipment purchased with current funds, net of proceeds from sales of property and equipment and other transfers		(40,749)	(4,646)	45,395	—		
EXCESS OF PUBLIC SUPPORT AND REVENUES OVER EXPENSES AND TRANSFERS		255,855	35,795	18,332	11,858		
Unrestricted:							
Increase in balances designated by Board action for:							
Disaster relief	5	$ 24,572					
Biomedical services operations	2	14,140					
Retiree health benefits	4	48,191					
Special projects	4	96,135					
Replacement and improvements of buildings and equipment		1,935					
Other specific purposes		3,315					
Investment in net operating assets		67,567					
NET ASSETS, BEGINNING OF YEAR		443,616	37,931	358,618	164,183		
NET ASSETS, END OF YEAR		$ 699,471	$ 73,726	$376,950	$176,041		

(See notes to combined financial statements.)

the organization received! When we take into account that $177,539,000 of public support was donor designated to disaster, we come to the conclusion that the cost of the blood service in 1990 was nearly twice the amount available through gifts and contributions. This organization could never carry out its blood-related mission if it depended solely on annual benevolence. Related business revenues are necessary.

There is a ($27,063,000) loss in the land, buildings and equipment fund. This loss is not due to property rental activities. Most of the "revenue or support" under this column came from in-kind contribution of property and gains from the sales of property. The expenses are due to depreciation costs allocated to various centers of program services as we discussed in Chapter 15. In short, all funds operated efficiently.

Look a little closer—within services, not funds. Blood services, the major operating and unrestricted center, had total revenues of $706,134,000 and expenses of $741,175,000 for an operating loss. How is this explained? The insert on page 558 shows how a similar deficit was explained in 1989. Remember product liability in Chapter 16?

Finally, a version of the bottom line question: Is the organization better off or worse off financially at the end of the year's operation? Observe that the final two lines show how much the net assets increased by year's end. At the beginning of the year, for example, the unrestricted net assets were $433,616,000 and at the end it increased to $699,471,000. This increase in unrestricted net assets was the result of two factors: (1) efficiency in the operation of the organization that led to surplus; and (2) a decision of the board of trustees about how such excesses are to be allocated. There was a net increase in the bottom lines for all funds. All funds rose sharply. Yes, at the end of the year, the financial position was significantly better.

Interfund Transfers

An organization with segregated funds will usually show interfund transfers. One reason is that transactions may initially be paid from unrestricted funds and later charged to the proper fund. We note the transfer of $1,073,000 from endowment to current unrestricted operations. Part of this transfer, $15,000, is based on prior agreement with donors. So the transfer was made to current operations but restricted to donor stipulated use. The other part was transferred to unrestricted current operation consistent with trustee stipulation. It may be used at the discretion of management to discharge the general mission of the Red Cross.

Transfers also went in the reverse direction. The trustees authorized $40,749,000 to be transferred from unrestricted current operations to the land, building and equipment fund and $4,646,000 by donor stipulation also went into that restricted fund. Interfund transfers go both ways.

In May 1988, the Red Cross placed a hold on certain plasma products pending complete review and release by the Federal Food and Drug Administration (FDA), in keeping with the American Red Cross "zero defects" goal for handling blood products. While the plasma hold had a profound affect on overall Blood Services operations, the Red Cross was able to coordinate and facilitate plasma derivative shipments in order to minimize, to the extent possible, the disruption of service that occurred to hospitals and patients. These events, which lasted for most of fiscal 1988–89, contributed greatly to the $17.7 million deficit incurred to support Blood Services operations, working capital requirements, and fixed asset acquisitions during this difficult period. By the end of the fiscal year, the hold had been lifted and plasma derivative shipments were returning to normal levels.

Red Cross Blood Services is a self-funded, self-sustained program that does not use public support or non-Blood Services revenues to fund operations except for support received and spent by chapters to assist in recruiting donors and other collection activities. During fiscal 1988–89, the increased costs of quality control procedures required Red Cross Blood Services to draw on accumulated reserves to fund operations.

The Red Cross is committed to providing the safest possible blood products to all recipients at the most reasonable cost possible to ensure the quality and availability of the nation's blood supply.

Source: Annual Report, American Red Cross, p. 21.

THE ROLE OF THE STATEMENT OF CHANGES IN FINANCIAL POSITION: WHERE DID THE RESOURCES GO? WHERE DID THEY COME FROM?

Let us look at the statement of changes in the financial position of the American Red Cross for the fiscal year which ended June 30, 1990. See Figure 17.7.

Sources of Resources

The most important source of funds for the Red Cross during 1990 was internal—that is—from operations. The internal sources reflect the excess of $136,641,000 seen earlier in the income statement. The contribution of overall operations increased by nearly four times over the performance in 1989 when it was $34,806,000. This is a major financial change between 1989 and 1990. It also includes adding back in the depreciation ($44,773,000) since it was not paid.

Note that deferred public support declined by nearly $3,301,000. This major financial change says that the organization delivered on that amount of products or services for which it was prepaid. At the same time

FIGURE 17.7 Combined Statement of Changes in Financial Position

(in thousands)	Notes	Current Operations		Land, Buildings, and Equip-ment	Endow-ment	Totals	
		Unre-stricted	Donor Restricted			1990	1989
OPERATIONS:							
Excess (deficiency) of public support and revenues over expenses before special items		$110,347	$40,426	$(27,063)	$12,931	$136,641	$ 34,806
Items not requiring (providing) cash and investments:							
Depreciation of buildings and equipment				44,773		44,773	41,318
Pension credit		(14,750)				(14,750)	(22,149)
Net book value of property disposals				5,471		5,471	2,043
Provisions for doubtful accounts, obsolete inventories, and other allowances		(1,127)				(1,127)	2,113
(Increase) decrease in certain assets:							
Receivables		(6,708)	(7,103)	(4,932)	89	(18,654)	(30,680)
Inventories		2,969				2,969	(4,929)
Other assets		(447)	(305)	(805)		(1,557)	(2,562)

Increase (decrease) in certain liabilities:						
Accounts payable and accrued liabilities	27,368	22,642	4,801	(680)	54,131	14,050
Deferred public support, net	(2,073)	(522)	(706)		(3,301)	10,068
Total operations	115,579	55,138	21,539	12,340	204,596	44,078
PROCEEDS FROM PENSION BENEFIT SETTLEMENT GAIN, NET	142,045				142,045	
INVESTMENTS:						
Purchase of land, buildings, and equipment and other transfers	(40,749)	(4,646)	(28,927)		(74,322)	(69,094)
Transfer of realized endowment fund appreciation 3	1,058	15		(1,073)		
Total investments	(39,691)	(4,631)	(28,927)	(1,073)	(74,322)	(69,094)
FINANCING:						
Increase (decrease) in long-term debt, net	(4,807)		6,380		1,573	14,617
INCREASE (DECREASE) IN CASH AND INVESTMENTS	$213,126	$50,507	$ (1,008)	$11,267	$273,892	$(10,399)

(See notes to combined financial statements.)

For the Year Ended June 30, 1990, With Comparative Totals for 1989 (Includes the Operations of 2,719 Chapters, 54 Regional Blood Services, 54 Chapters, 54 Regional Blood Services, and National Sector for 1990).

Source: American Red Cross, *Annual Report for 1989–90: A New Face on Old Values* (Washington, D.C., 1990), p. 27. Reprinted with permission.

the organization increased by $18,654,000 that which is is owed, i.e., accounts receivable. It is shown in parentheses in the statement because it represents a use of funds to deliver products and services for which it has not yet been paid.

There is a major source of financial change which is in the class of **nonrecurring.** This is the net gain from the pension settlement amounting to $142,045,000. It is important to isolate nonrecurring gains or losses because they distort the financial picture. An **external** source of funding occurred by increasing the liability of the organization. The net increase in debt was only $1,573,000 in 1990 compared to $14,617,000 in 1989. This smaller net increase is composed of two parts. A payoff of $4,807,000 in unrestricted accounts and an increase of $6,380,000 for land, buildings and equipment—or some combination of the three.

Accounts payable increased by $54,131,000. Thus, an increase in accounts payable and accrued liability, as a category, was a very important source of external funding for the American Red Cross. As we said earlier, good cash management always involves some delay in making payments of some accounts. A third source of external funding is gifts and donations which have been received but not for current use.

Uses of Resources

What were funds used to do? Inventories were increased by $2,969,000. Some $4,807,000 in debt was paid down. Some $3,301,000 was used to deliver product and services for which the organization was prepaid. But most of all, $273,892,000 was used to purchase marketable securities or to hold in cash. In 1989, the decrease in cash and marketable securities was $10,399,000.

THE ROLE OF THE COMBINED STATEMENT OF FUNCTIONAL EXPENSES: COMPARATIVE ANALYSIS OF EXPENDITURES

This statement shows expenditures by program, administration and support groups. Conversely, it also shows the distribution of expenses within each group. Figure 17.8 is the statement for the American Red Cross at the end of 1990. Salaries, wages and employee benefits are the single greatest expenses even within the "Community and Volunteer" group.

Blood services is the most expensive program—more than six times the next closest which is health services. It accounts for nearly 60 percent of the entire program expenditure. Clearly, it is the dominant program.

Support services are slightly less than 10 percent of the total expenditures of the organization.

FIGURE 17.8 Combined Statement of Functional Expenses

			Program Services				
(in thousands)	Services to Members of the Armed Forces, Veterans, and Their Families	Disaster	Biomedical Services	Health Services	Community Volunteer	Inter- national	Total Program Services
Salaries and wages	$42,336	$ 35,168	$315,968	$ 52,977	$27,742	$2,018	$ 476,209
Employee benefits	7,163	5,820	53,718	8,453	4,662	306	80,122
Total	49,499	40,988	369,686	61,430	32,404	2,324	556,331
Travel and maintenance	2,595	15,779	17,743	4,379	3,066	459	44,021
Equipment maintenance and rental	1,850	4,424	15,560	2,755	1,628	61	26,278
Supplies and materials	2,666	4,766	151,430	22,260	3,242	386	184,750
Contractual services	9,049	18,484	147,452	18,845	10,128	563	204,521
Financial and material assistance	7,402	135,976	11,576	2,428	7,327	3,593	168,302
Total before depreciation	73,061	220,417	713,447	112,097	57,795	7,386	1,184,203
Depreciation of buildings and Equipment	1,888	3,742	27,728	3,874	2,973	97	40,302
Total expenses	$74,949	$224,159	$741,175	$115,971	$60,768	$7,483	$1,224,505

| | Supporting Services | | | Total Program Services (As Above) | Totals | |
(in thousands)	Membership and Fund Raising	Management and General	Total Supporting Services		1990	1989
Salaries and wages	$12,388	$31,972	$ 44,360	$ 476,209	$ 520,569	$ 472,594
Employee benefits	1,935	5,110	7,045	80,122	87,167	74,027
Total	14,323	37,082	51,405	556,331	607,736	546,621
Travel and maintenance	1,105	3,770	4,875	44,021	48,896	38,251
Equipment maintenance and rental	462	1,758	2,220	26,278	28,498	22,347
Supplies and materials	3,678	4,895	8,573	184,750	193,323	161,282
Contractual services	14,051	16,754	30,805	204,521	235,326	218,991
Financial and material assistance	597	1,465	2,062	168,302	170,364	76,579
Total before depreciation	34,216	65,724	99,940	1,184,203	1,284,143	1,064,071
Depreciation of buildings and equipment	1,075	3,396	4,471	40,302	44,773	41,318
Total expenses	$35,291	$69,120	$104,411	$1,224,505	$1,328,916	$1,105,389
(See notes to combined financial statements.)						

For the Year Ended June 30, 1990, With Comparative Totals for 1989 (Includes the Operations of 2,719 Chapters, 54 Regional Blood Services, and National Sector for 1990).

Source: American Red Cross, *Annual Report for 1989–90: A New Face on Old Values* (Washington, D.C., 1990), p. 25. Reprinted with permission.

HOW MUCH DO FINANCIAL STATEMENTS TELL?

Financial statements show the organization's status at the start and end of a period. They say little about the interim. Financial statements sometimes exclude facts, show them in favorable light, or are dressed to present the best picture of the organization. Sometimes they legitimately give incomplete information. For example, it is not customary for museums to report the value of their collections. Therefore, a museum's balance sheet will frequently underestimate its assets.

Depreciation is now expected of all long-lived assets except rare pieces of art and historical assets. But how a nonprofit chooses to depreciate, whether it considers the asset depreciable, is a matter of discretion. Land may be depreciated if its quality is used up, as in farming. But for a building site, its quality remains reasonably constant once construction is completed. Thus, there may be no depreciation charges shown in the balance sheet.

Similarly, accounts receivables and pledges are not all collectible; how much to report as such and how much to report as uncollectible are matters of judgment based on the history of the organization. Financial statements might be the next best thing to truth. What protects the user and justifies the patience in analyzing them as we have done is not only that they are the best information available, but, as we said in Chapter 5, material misrepresentation of the facts in these accounts is illegal. The threat of the law constrains falsehood. The threat of an unfavorable audit constrains material incompleteness.

To gain greater uniformity and greater reliability in the interpretation of financial statements of nonprofits, the Financial Accounting Standards Board (FASB) has promulgated some changes. These include requiring most nonprofits to report (1) depreciation, (2) gifts when they are deemed to be actually received and free of conditions, and (3) the value of volunteer services when these services can be priced, such as fees for attorneys because even though these services are not deductible, pricing and including them give a truer picture of the cost of running the organization.

Take a simple case. Frances Williams makes a gift to Gertrude and Louisa School for the Handicapped in the form a pledge of a $1,000,000 to be provided through the proceeds of a sale of Frances's mansion. Should the school report this $1,000,000 in its current balance sheet? Should it report it in the year the sale actually takes place? Should it report it in the year the hard cash is received? Each of these projects a different financial picture of the organization.

SUMMARY AND CONCLUSIONS

The budget, as discussed in Chapter 17, and the financial statements are similar in the sense that both are expressed in dollars and cents. The budget, however, is a financial plan and it may or may not be realized. If there are variances from the plan, the manager will wisely ask why. The financial statements discussed in this chapter, on the other hand, are factual representations of what occurred financially in the organization during a given period of time. The budget charts the course, and the financial statements reveal if the course was actually maintained.

Unlike the budget, the financial statements must conform to generally acceptable accounting principles (GAAP). These principles are intended to ensure consistency, objectivity, fairness, and completeness in the reporting of financial data. The purpose of an audit is to ascertain if the practices of the organization conform to good practices. In conducting an audit, auditors seek evidence to confirm that accounting entries are supported by the facts and by authoritative decision making on the part of responsible managers. We have also seen how these statements can be used to assist in the debt and assessment management of the organization.

NOTES

1. The reader is referred to the references in accounting at the end of this text for alternative treatments of the financial statements of nonprofit organizations.

2. Bonds are bought usually at a discount or premium. At maturity the full face value of the bond is paid. During the period between purchase and maturity, the difference between the full face value and the amount paid for the bond is amortized, that is, paid in increments.

3. We refer to the "first-in, first-out" and "last-in, last-out" methods of valuing inventory.

4. The reader may look at a standard accounting text for ratio measures of profitability.

5. While for-profits do not generally receive gifts and contributions, this does not mean that they cannot receive them or be deemed to have received them. But no deduction is allowed. For our purposes, however, it is safe to ignore gifts and contributions to corporations or to their shareholders in the case of closely held corporations.

6. *Syracuse University Leadership Report,* 1., No. 2 (Mar. 1986), p. 7.

7. Ibid., p. 2.

8. The source of this discussion is the American Institute of Certified Public Accountants, *Audits of Certain Nonprofit Organizations* (New York: The Institute, 1981), pp. 53–54.

9. Some organizations report both.

10. FIFO and LIFO.

11. The notes to the statements show a revenue bond through Montgomery County, Maryland, of $17 million and one through the City of Alexandria, Virginia, for $20,000,000. These are both revenue bonds and not loans from either jurisdiction. These bonds are sold on the market. They are explained in Chapter 18.

12. Note that the Red Cross does not separate current from noncurrent liabilities. However, the notes that accompany this balance sheet show that only about half of the notes, capital lease, obligations, and mortgages payable, are current.

APPENDIX TO CHAPTER 17

After reviewing the financial statements of the American Red Cross the auditors rendered their opinions (see Figure 17.9). Note the (1) scope, (2) explanation, (3) opinion, (4) role of audit committee and (5) standards used to conduct the audit.

Independent Auditors' Opinions

Deloitte &
Touche

▲

1900 M Street, N.W.
Washington, D.C. 20036-3564
Telephone: (202) 955-4000

DEPARTMENT OF THE ARMY
Headquarters, U.S. Army Audit Agency
3101 Park Center Drive
Alexandria, Virginia 22302

The American Red Cross:

We have audited the combined statement of net assets of the American Red Cross as of June 30, 1990, and the related combined statements of public support, revenues, and expenses, and changes in net assets, of functional expenses, and of changes in financial position for the year· then ended. These financial statements are the responsibility of management of the American Red Cross. Our responsibility is to express an opinion on these financial statements based on our audit. The financial statements of certain chapters and regional blood services, which statements include 27% of the combined total assets and 37% of the combined public support and revenues, were audited by other auditors whose reports thereon have been furnished to us. Our opinion expressed herein, insofar as it relates to the amounts included for such chapters and regional blood services, is based solely upon the reports of such other auditors. We previously audited the combined financial statements of the American Red Cross as of June 30, 1989 and for the year then ended (not presented herein), from which the accompanying comparative totals for 1989 were derived. Our unqualified opinion, dated October 5, 1989, on such financial statements was based in part on the reports of other auditors.

We conducted our audit in accordance with generally accepted auditing standards. Those standards require that we plan and perform the audit to obtain reasonable assurance about whether the financial statements are free of material misstatement. An audit includes examining, on a test basis, evidence supporting the amounts and disclosures in the financial statements. An audit also includes assessing the accounting principles used and significant estimates made by management, as well as evaluating the overall financial statement presentation. We believe that our audit provides a reasonable basis for our opinion.

In our opinion, based upon our audit and the reports of other auditors referred to above, the 1990 combined financial statements referred to above present fairly, in all material respects, the financial position of the American Red Cross at June 30, 1990 and the results of its operations and the changes in its financial position for the year then ended, in conformity with generally accepted accounting principles.

As discussed in Note 11 to the financial statements, the American Red Cross changed its accounting for fund campaign public support during 1990.

Deloitte & Touche

October 19, 1990

The American Red Cross:

Pursuant to the Act of Congress, January 5, 1905, and Department of Defense Directive Number 1330.5, August 16, 1969, we have audited the Combined Statement of Public Support, Revenues, and Expenses, and Changes in Net Assets; and the Combined Statement of Functional Expenses of the American Red Cross for the year ended June 30, 1990. These statements are the responsibility of the American Red Cross management. Our responsibility is to express an opinion on these financial statements based on our audit. The American Red Cross employs a firm of certified public accountants (principal auditor) to audit its combined financial statements. The financial statements of certain chapters and regional blood services, which statements include 37 percent of the combined public support and revenues, were audited by other auditors whose reports thereon were furnished to the principal auditor. The opinion of the principal auditor as it relates to the amounts included for such chapters and regional blood services was based solely upon the reports of such other auditors. Our opinion expressed herein is based primarily on the report of the principal auditor.

We conducted our audit in accordance with generally accepted auditing standards. Those standards require that we plan and perform the audit to obtain reasonable assurance about whether the financial statements are free of material misstatement. An audit includes examining, on a test basis, evidence supporting the amounts and disclosures in the financial statements. An audit also includes assessing the accounting principles used and significant estimates made by management, as well as evaluating the overall financial statement presentation. We believe that our audit and the reports of other auditors provide a reasonable basis for our opinion.

In our opinion, based on our audit and the reports of other auditors, the Combined Statement of Public Support, Revenues, and Expenses, and Changes in Net Assets; and the Combined Statement of Functional Expenses present fairly, in all material respects, the results of operations of the American Red Cross for the year ended June 30, 1990, in conformity with generally accepted accounting principles.

As discussed in Note 11 to the financial statements, the American Red Cross changed its accounting for fund campaign public support during 1990.

U. S. Army Audit Agency

31 October 1990

Financial Report for Fiscal Year 1989-90

The financial statements in this report show the financial status of the Red Cross network of service units and the cost of delivering all Red Cross services for the fiscal year ended June 30, 1990.

The financial report includes:

- A Combined Statement of Public Support, Revenues, and Expenses, and Changes in Net Assets (page 24).
- A Combined Statement of Functional Expenses (page 25).
- A Combined Statement of Net Assets (page 26).
- A Combined Statement of Changes in Financial Position (page 27).

Red Cross management is responsible for all financial statements in this report. These statements are consistent with financial information in other sections of the report and conform to generally accepted accounting principles prescribed by the Financial Accounting Standards Board.

Federal statutes require that the Red Cross make a report of income and expense to the Department of Defense as soon as is practical after July 1 each year. A copy of this report is then audited under the direction of the Secretary of Defense and forwarded to Congress. The audit is made for the Secretary by the U.S. Army Audit Agency, and the latter's report is presented on the following page.

The audit opinion of Deloitte & Touche, an internationally recognized firm of independent certified public accountants engaged by the Red Cross to audit the combined financial statements, can also be found on the following page.

Red Cross management has adopted an organization-wide system of internal financial controls to provide reasonable assurance that financial records are reliable and that assets are protected. Internal auditors monitor compliance with established policies and procedures. Internal accounting controls—including an appropriate division of responsibilities—are continually evaluated, and accounting standards are disseminated throughout the Organization to assure objectivity and integrity of accounts.

Annually, the Board of Governors appoints an Audit Committee consisting of eight members, plus one representative each from the Board of Trustees of the Retirement System, the Endowment Fund, and the Life and Health Benefits Plan. The Committee reviews matters affecting Red Cross finances, especially those pertaining to internal accounting controls and audits. Auditors have free access to the Committee to discuss the results of their work and give their opinions concerning the adequacy of internal accounting controls and the quality of financial reporting. The Audit Committee Chairman's Letter is presented as part of this financial report.

Sincerely,

George F. Moody
Chairman

John D. Campbell
Vice President, Finance
and Chief Financial Officer

Audit Committee Chairman's Letter

The Audit Committee of the Board of Governors is composed of eight independent directors. The members of the Audit Committee are George T. Rehfeldt, chairman, Burton H. Alden, William F. Andrews, Henry B. Blackwell II, Kerrie Quinn, Sarah A. Schwarz, Louis R. Somers, and John C. VanAken. The Committee held three meetings during the fiscal year ended June 30, 1990.

The Audit Committee oversees the financial reporting process of the American Red Cross on behalf of the Board of Governors. In fulfilling its responsibility, the Committee recommended to the Board of Governors the selection of the Organization's independent public accountants. The Audit Committee discussed with the internal auditor and the independent public accountants the overall scope and specific plans for their respective audits. The Committee also discussed the Organization's consolidated financial statements and the adequacy of its internal controls. The Committee met regularly with the Organization's internal auditor and independent public accountants to discuss the results of their audits and their evaluations of the Organization's financial reporting. Meetings without management present also are held and were designed to facilitate any private communication with the Committee desired by the internal auditor or independent public accountants.

George T. Rehfeldt
Chairman
Audit Committee

22

THE NOTES

The notes to financial statements can provide insight into the meaning of these statements. They give explanations, expand on some accounting, give definitions, and explain procedures. The notes of the American Red Cross are too extensive to replicate here. We use those of the National Multiple Sclerosis Society (Figure 17.10) as an example.

NOTES TO FINANCIAL STATEMENTS

NATIONAL MULTIPLE SCLEROSIS SOCIETY (NATIONAL HEADQUARTERS)
NOTE A—SIGNIFICANT ACCOUNTING POLICIES

The Society's financial statements are prepared on the accrual basis of accounting.

Investments are carried at cost or, if donated, the fair value on the date received.

Investments primarily consist of the following:

	September 30	
	1989	**1988**
Unrestricted:		
Commercial paper	$6,016,421	$5,058,522
Certificates of deposit		1,028,528
Guaranteed interest contracts	582,971	453,554
Other	34,740	33,551
	$6,634,132	$6,574,155
Restricted:		
Certificates of deposit	$ 250,954	$ 228,627
Guaranteed interest contracts	468,724	598,007
	$ 719,678	$ 826,634

Maturities on investments range from less than one month to approximately two years eight months at September 30, 1989.

Campaign materials are carried at the lower of cost (first-in, first-out method) or estimated realizable value.

The Society and its Chapters have agreements under which a portion of contributions received by Chapters is shared with the Society. Amounts received but not remitted by Chapters are recorded by the Society as due from Chapters for national activities. The Chapters' share of contributions solicited by Chapters and received directly by the Society are credited to Chapter receivables.

The Society recognizes income from legacies and bequests when an unassailable right to the gift has been established by the court and the proceeds are measurable in amount.

Figure 17.10

Furniture and fixtures are carried at cost or, if donated, the fair value on the date received. The provision for depreciation is computed on the straight-line method over the estimated useful lives of the assets.

Contributions received are considered to be available for unrestricted use unless specifically restricted by the donor.

The Society records the value of donated goods and services only when the value of these goods and services can be objectively measured.

NOTE B—OTHER RESTRICTED FUNDS

Other restricted funds of the Society at September 30, 1989 and 1988 are as follows:

	September 30	
	1989	**1988**
Ralph I. Straus Award Fund	$249,199	$228,627
Chairman's Fund	329,522	218,865
Ray and Joan Kroc Fund for Research on the Symptomatic Treatment of Multiple Sclerosis	12,890	12,890
John A. Alexander and Elyza C. Alexander Fund	20,000	20,000
Wilfred B. Doner Multiple Sclerosis Student Scholarship Fund	15,500	15,500
	$627,111	$495,882

NOTE C—PENSION

The Society maintains a noncontributory defined contribution retirement plan, which covers all eligible employees of the National Multiple Sclerosis Society and participating chapters. Contributions for the year ended September 30, 1989, as determined by the Society's Board of Directors, were 7 percent of gross annual salary, as defined.

Pension expense for the years ended September 30, 1989 and 1988 was $286,372 and $249,416, respectively.

NOTE D—LEASES

The Society occupies office space under a lease extending to July 31, 1996. Future minimum lease commitments are $438,063 per year. Rent expense, including electricity, for the years ended September 30, 1989 and 1988 was $492,780 and $469,199, respectively.

Figure 17.10 (*Continued*)

The lease agreement includes a provision whereby the owner has the right to terminate this lease and the term thereof effective July 31, 1991. The Society has received written notification from the owner that the lease will terminate on July 31, 1991.

NOTE E—COMMITMENTS FOR RESEARCH GRANTS

Commitments are subject, among other things, to revocation rights by the Society, to the continued qualifications of grantees and to the satisfaction by the grantees of prior conditions before payment. Research and Fellowship projects are scheduled as follows: 1990—$8,474,745; 1991—$5,467,724; 1992—$2,890,475; 1993—$348,227; 1994—$213,660.

NOTE F—PAYMENTS TO CHAPTERS

During 1989 and 1988, the Society made direct payments to its Chapters of $1,528,424 and $2,603,897, respectively. These payments were made under certain agreements regarding the Society's direct mail program ($1,022,051 and $806,607) and receipt of major bequests ($506,373 and $1,797,290) in 1989 and 1988, respectively.

NOTE G—INCOME TAX STATUS

The National Multiple Sclerosis Society (National Headquarters) has been determined by the Internal Revenue Service to be a Section 501(c)(3) publicly-supported charitable organization and is exempt from Federal income taxes under Section 501(a) of the Internal Revenue Code. As a result, all contributions to the National Multiple Sclerosis Society (National Headquarters) entitle the donor to the maximum charitable deduction under the Internal Revenue Laws.

Source: 1989 Annual Report, National Multiple Sclerosis Society.

Figure 17.10   (*Continued*)

SUGGESTED READINGS

AMERICAN INSTITUTE OF CERTIFIED PUBLIC ACCOUNTANTS, *Accounting Principles and Reporting Practices for Certain Nonprofit Organizations* (New York: The Institute, 1978).

———, *Audit of Certain Nonprofit Organizations* (New York: The Institute, 1981).

Financial Accounting Standards Board, *Accounting for Contributions Received and Contributions Made and Capitalization of Works of Art, Historical Treasures, and Similar Assets.* Exposure Draft, No. 096-B, October 31, 1990.

———Statement of Financial Accounting Standards No. 93, *Recognition of Depreciation by Non-for-Profit Organizations,* No. 047, August 1987.

———*Financial Reporting by Non-for-Profit Organizations: Form and Content of Financial Statements,* No. 084-B, August 29, 1989.

Chapter 18

Evaluating, Setting, and Implementing Financial Goals

After the financial statements have been interpreted, decisions have to be made about how the organization will proceed. Should new financial objectives be set? What should be the new targets? With a good system of reporting information, the board of directors and managers of the non-profit should have financial statements at least every six months. On the basis of the information in these statements, financial goals and targets can be modified. These modifications feed right back into the system and, in this sense, financial management is a loop.

Periodic evaluation at mid-year or at the end of the fiscal year leads to the setting of new targets or the affirmation of old ones, which themselves will later be reaffirmed or modified. This chapter is about evaluating old targets and setting new ones and the menu of short-term investment strategies that are available in this process. It is also about capital budgeting and endowment planning, both of which involve setting long-range targets and strategies.

THE IMPORTANCE OF SETTING FINANCIAL TARGETS

The accompanying insert is taken from the J. Paul Getty Trust. Note its reference to short- and long-term investment objectives, investment strategy, diversification of investment, and its reporting.[1] Recall from Chapter 4 that the Getty Trust is a private operating foundation. It must distribute and expend a specific percentage of investment income. For most non-

---

The J. Paul Getty Trust maintains an endowment of high-quality equities and U.S. government securities. These assets are managed by specialized outside investment managers with the objective of generating both current income and long-term growth to fund Trust programs adequately and protect the endowment from the effects of inflation. Recent cyclical and secular trends of inflation and deflation necessitate increased vigilance to protect the long-term purchasing power of the endowment.

The Trust has a minimum investment objective of a 5 percent return plus inflation. Over the past six years, the return has exceeded the objective by 13.7 percent annually, which includes the capital gains resulting from the sale of Getty Oil Company stock in 1984. Since the transfer of assets from J. Paul Getty's estate in March 1982, the Trust's endowment has increased by more than 270 percent.

For the year ending June 30, 1987, the return on the endowment's assets was 12.3 percent. The year ending June 30, 1988, witnessed extremely volatile financial markets, with equities reaching historic highs in August 1987, followed by historic declines in October 1987. The diversification of assets enabled the endowment to provide a return of 2.6 percent over the twelve-month period ending June 30, 1988. The combined return for the two-year period ending June 30, 1988, was 7.3 percent.

Income for the endowment consisted of interest from the fixed-income and short-term investment portfolios and of dividends from the equity portfolio. A report of operating expenses and capital expenditures appears on page 48. The operating expenses in this report have been categorized by the Trust's areas of commitment as described in the Report from the President. Condensed financial statements and the Report of Independent Public Accountants appear on page 49. The totals on pages 48 and 49 differ slightly because of certain required cash-to-accrual adjustment (see footnote on page 48). A complete schedule of investments as of June 30, 1988, is included in the Trust's 990-PF tax return.

Source: Reprinted with permission from *J. Paul Getty Report*, 1986–1988, p. 47.

profits this additional motive does not exist, but they nevertheless need to set targets to meet both capital and operating requirements.

Targets may be set for investment, disbursement, and fund-raising objectives, the subjects of the chapter. Setting targets begins by assessing the status of the organization.

THE QUESTIONS FOR EVALUATING OLD TARGETS

The end of every fiscal period marks the commencement of a new one. Thus, a new fiscal year begins at the very moment that the old one ends, immediately giving an uninterrupted continuity to the financial function. Having the financial data from the closing period means that the managers of the nonprofit organization are now armed with real data indicating the actual financial performance of the organization. They can also assess actual accomplishments as in Chapter 8. The balance sheet will tell the present situation of the organization: What does it have to launch the new year? One way in which these data can be used is to amend or reaffirm old targets. These will be reflected in the new capital and operating budgets. The first step, however, is asking the right questions.

The following are examples of the questions that must be answered in evaluating financial targets:

1. Was the revenue target in the budget met? If not, by how much was it missed and what was the reason? Does it make sense, in light of recent experience, to continue believing that such a target is reasonable? Should it be increased or decreased, or should it remain the same? Why? Are we on course?

2. What form and sources of giving showed the greatest increase? Is this a promising new area of emphasis? Is this where the organization has its best shot? In what form of giving did the organization underachieve? What can be done to get greater support from this form of giving or from this sector? What new strategies shall we try?

3. What is the distribution of support by source? Is there too much dependence on one source or form of giving? Should the organization diversify its base of support? Does the mix of support leave the organization in jeopardy of its tax-exempt status?

4. What are the major cost factors in operating the organization? Can anything be done to contain costs without reducing the productivity and commitment of the organization to its mission?

5. What cost factors are rising and at what rate? Why? Is there a less expensive substitute?
6. What cost centers are exceeding their budgets? Why? Was the budget allocation unreasonable? Should these allocations be re-aligned? Do some centers need less while others need more? What programs should be dropped?
7. Is it time to put some functions on a self-financing basis? Could they survive? Could they provide revenues for the organization?
8. If there is a deficit, how will it be financed? How long can it be sustained before destroying the organization?
9. Is it time to change investment advisors? Is it time to change banks, insurance companies, or the financial committee of the organization?
10. Is there a cash surplus and how can it be used to the best interest of the organization?

These questions feed back into the strategic planning process from the interpretation of the hard facts in the financial statements. Once decisions are made about targets for the new year, renewed efforts must be made to raise money and contain costs, to gather financial data and interpret them and then begin the cycle all over again setting new targets. The process continues as long as the organization lasts.

FIVE CONSIDERATIONS IN SETTING NEW TARGETS

Based on the answers to the preceding questions, the management may set new targets and restrictions.

First, there are policy considerations based on the mission and philosophy of the organization. For example, this organization will not invest in overly risky investments, certain corporations or countries.

Second, there are legal considerations. New targets should not jeopardize the tax-exempt status of the organization or its charter or place it unwittingly at odds with ethical standards.

A third type of consideration is contractual. Do these targets commit the organization unwisely? Do they threaten existing commitments?

A fourth consideration is the capacity or knowledge of the organization. Hopefully, this book has broadened the horizon of management. Yet, some may not have learned, others would fear, and yet others would reject. The point as noted in the strategic planning chapter is that an organization is constrained not only by what occurs externally but by its own internal capacity, imagination, and initiative.

A fifth and realistic type of concern is that the organization may simply not have the financial resources to be flexible. It is common for an organization to receive a high percentage of its support in the form of restrictive gifts, grants, or contracts. Hence, the room for discretionary decision is limited. Ironically, however, it is these very organizations that need to push toward the development of unrestricted money to be used for the general support and development of the organization in the conduct of its growing mission.

Within this broad set of constraints, decisions have to be made and targets set. This chapter gives examples of six common types of financial target-setting problems in nonprofits and shows how they can be resolved.

To set financial targets, the organization has to have a firm vision of what it is and what it can do (Chapters 1 through 4, 7, and 8), because this shapes the range of strategies at its disposal. The management will want to consider these options systematically (Chapters 6 and 15), decide what investments to make (Chapters 11, 12, and 18), or how to strengthen their fund-raising activities (Chapters 9 and 10). Management must also know how to control costs and attract good personnel (Chapter 14). After these managers have had a chance to implement the programs, they must evaluate the fiscal performance of the organization (Chapters 15, 16, and 17) and then reassess targets, set new ones, and make new investment decisions to help meet the targets. The process is continuous and circular and answerable to the trustees (Chapter 5).

A REPORT OF THE TREASURER

Much of what we have discussed about assessment of financial performance can be appreciated by reading the Report of the Treasurer of the Boy Scouts of America reprinted here, and by reviewing the opening insert in Chapter 1 on the Williamsburg Colonial Foundation.

REPORT OF THE TREASURER

1989 IN REVIEW

Led by a record-setting performance by Supply operations, the general operating fund's bottom line for the year was second only to last year's outstanding results. As shown in the highlights above, revenue and expense activity increased by about one-third as a result of the full-year impact of the increased membership fee, which was dedicated to subsidize the general liability insurance program, primarily for the benefit of the local councils. While a positive bottom line is important and affords us the ability to finance special capital needs or unique initiatives, the true measure of our performance is in the "top" lines. We believe we have done well here in expanding our program services, both in development and delivery, and in keeping with the resources available.

Membership registration fees increased by $8,987,000 or 49 percent, primarily due to the increased fee structure, as well as a membership growth, for our 10th consecutive growth year. National service fees from local councils increased $168,000 or 4 percent.

The excellent results of $13,272,000 net income from Supply operations were attributable to many circumstances. Sales volumes were greatly helped by the impact of the national jamboree and a most effective expansion of our retail operations. The mail order business and Scout shops continue to grow, and as a result, margins have benefited from a greater mix of retail business. Supply's operating expenses have been well managed, as reflected in an improvement in the expense have been well managed, as reflected in an improvement in the expense to sales ratio. Interest attached to Supply's working capital increased 44 percent, to $3,383,000, as a result of the added requirements due to the expanded business.

For the third straight year, net income from magazine publications exceeded $2,000,000. This was quite an achievement in view of a somewhat disappointing decline in subscriptions and a static fee structure, while improvement continued in editorial quality. Intensive efforts in adding advertising revenues and effective cost containment have produced positive results.

Fundraising continues to be de-emphasized. Contributions for operations are primarily received from national Executive Board members and from employees.

Investment and other income was $178,000, or 5 percent, ahead of 1988, primarily due to a slightly higher yield from the endowment funds.

As I mentioned at the outset, the significant increase in operating expenses was primarily attributed to the registration fee subsidy to the general liability insurance program, which increased by $8,535,000 to $11,228,000.

This past month the national Executive Board appropriated the 1989 excess of revenues over expenses, the majority of which, $3,603,000, was for capital projects.

Additionally, $1,547,000 was appropriated from the board-designated endowment fund as of December 31, 1989 in support of the general liability insurance program. This amount is included in the $12,585,000 interfund payable/receivable. I am most pleased to report that we have a realistic expectation to initiate in 1990 repayments to the National Council for a part of the prior year fundings to the insurance program.

As our long-term planning related to the general liability insurance program has produced exceptional results under trying conditions, in 1989 we believe we have taken another strong initiative in addressing the need to contain the cost of subsidizing retiree benefits in addition to the retirement plan by establishing the retirement benefit trust.

The national jamboree was a resounding success not only programmatically but in revenues exceeding expenses. This permitted a $1,300,000 appropriation by the national Executive Board for the purpose of funding a major marketing campaign for Boy Scouting.

We can take pride in a number of enhancements of our physical properties. Additions and improvements occurred in the national office, regional service centers, high-adventure bases, and Scout shops. Combined property additions amounted to $8,802,000.

The Boy Scouts of America is better positioned today in facilities and financial resources than at any other time in its history to meet the tremendous challenges and opportunities on the horizon of the 1990s.

Respectfully,

H. L. Hembree III
Treasurer
March 15, 1990

Note: For the complete financial report including the notes and unqualified opinion of Price Waterhouse, Independent Accountants, write: Controller, Boy Scouts of America, 1325 West Walnut Hill Lane, P.O. Box 152079, Irving, TX 75015-2079.

Source: Report of the Treasurer, the Boy Scouts of America, Annual Report, Boy Scouts of America, 1989, p. 20. Reprinted with permission.

CASH MANAGEMENT AND INVESTMENT STRATEGIES: INCREASING CASH

One set of strategies that must be continuously assessed is what to do with the organization's money (cash management) so that it might multiply while waiting to be used to meet the organization's targets. To appreciate the challenges of cash management, it is necessary to revisit the sources and uses of cash. Aside from donations and business income or membership fees, how does the organization get more cash?

Sources of Cash

In Chapter 17 we looked at sources and uses of cash for detecting the changes in the financial condition of the organization. Now we shift from analyzing past actions to the planning of present and future ones.

A source of cash is the operation of the organization. The organization may operate at a deficit or surplus. To this deficit or surplus we add depreciation, since it was an expense charged but no cash was actually spent. Thus, two sources of cash are the surplus (the total revenues and support that exceed expenses) and the depreciation.

A third source of cash is the net decrease in all current noncash assets. A decrease in inventory implies that the organization had sales that yielded cash; a decrease in marketable securities implies they were sold for cash. A decrease in accounts receivable means that cash was received. A decrease in prepaid items and supplies is a source of cash savings and therefore a source of cash. If the organization had increased these current assets instead of decreased them, this would cause a decrease in its cash position. It can only buy more marketable securities or prepay items by spending cash.

A fourth source of cash is the increase in current liabilities. An increase in notes payable implies a loan of cash. An increase in accounts payable means that the organization has increased its cash position by not paying for its purchases. Similarly, an increase in salaries and wages owed implies that the organization has kept cash by postponing the payment of these expenses. If it had paid any of these expenses, its cash position would have decreased. Expenses can only be paid with cash.

A fifth source of cash is the sale of fixed or long-term assets. The sale of the organization's furniture, automobile, and building will all lead to an increase in the organization's cash.

A sixth way to increase cash is to enter into long-term loans. These loans may even be from insurance policies given to the organization or they may be from a lending institution such as a bank. Let us take a deeper look at loans.

Borrowing as a Source of Cash

It is normal for nonprofit organizations, as well as firms, to run into cash flow problems and have to borrow. They also borrow to meet capital projects, such as purchasing a building or equipment or leasehold improvements (improvement in office rental space when the lease runs several years). Loans may be for a short or long term. What are the mechanics and strategies?

Short-term Borrowing

Short-term borrowing refers to loans that are for approximately one year or less. The need for these loans may be indicated when the organization cannot meet current payments, such as for supplies, a month's rent, payroll, and basically payments that are periodic and current. These

LOANS PAYABLE

In November 1989, NCIB received a short-term bank loan of $50,000, secured by forthcoming grants. Such grants were received in December 1989 and were used to repay the short-term loan in 1989.

In December 1988, NCIB received a $25,000 demand bank loan to finance certain projects until receivables were collected. The interest rate on this loan at December 31, 1988 was 12.5 percent. The outstanding principal and accrued interest were repaid in February, 1989.

In October 1984, NCIB received a $125,000 demand bank loan to finance leasehold improvements. This loan was reduced to $95,000 in March 1987. The interest rate at December 31, 1988 was 11.5 percent. In December 1989, NCIB repaid the remaining portion of the outstanding principal balance through the redemption of the $95,000 certificate of deposit which was pledged as collateral.

Source: National Charities Information Bureau, Inc., Notes to Financial Statements for the Year Ended December 31, 1989, p. 15. Reprinted with permission.

loans are sometimes called working capital loans and arise most commonly from cash flow or liquidity problems. That is, the organization is not necessarily broke; it simply is not receiving cash at the same time that it has to pay it out, or wisely chooses not to liquidate assets. At the end of this discussion, you should have a better appreciation for the concepts in the insert.

Calculation of Interest

When negotiating a loan, it is important to determine how the interest rate is calculated. One way is to calculate the interest in dollars based on a nominal rate and then add it on to the amount of the loan. Thus the amount "borrowed" is the amount asked for plus the interest on it. In short, the amount actually borrowed will exceed the amount you wanted.

This is a common way of determining interest on installment loans. When this is done, the annual percentage rate (APR) is the important number to know. It may be higher than the annual interest rate quoted and is required by law to be given.

Sometimes the interest is simple. That is, it is calculated and paid at the end of the term of the loan. Another form of calculation, called discounting, is to determine the interest and subtract it from the loan; therefore, the borrower gets less than requested. Simple interest is the least expensive, but not always available.

It also makes a difference which balance is used. Does the interest apply to the balance at the beginning or end or is it an average of the daily balance during a period? Which will work better for your organization depends on the pattern of borrowing and repayment during the course of the month. See the upcoming discussion on average daily balance.

Sometimes, even though these are unsecured loans (meaning that no collateral is required), the bank may require a compensating balance. This means that the bank requires the organization to keep some total in its checking account at all times receiving no or a lower interest than is being charged for the loan. This plus the add-on procedure mentioned earlier are the two most costly forms of interest calculation.

Lines of Credit

The World Vision, Inc. description of their line of credit reflects many useful concepts; i.e., compensating balances, prime rate plus, and encumbering certain assets as collateral. Most importantly, read: "No debt was outstanding on this line of credit at September 30, 1989 or 1990." Again, establishing a line of credit when the organization is in the strongest financial position is a good strategy. Managing so that the debt does not overwhelm the organization is a necessary strategy.

NOTE D—LINE OF CREDIT

A working capital line of credit is maintained with World Vision's primary banking relationship that allows for borrowing up to $7,000,000 at the interest rate of prime rate plus one-quarter percent (10.25 percent at September 30, 1990). In connection with this agreement, the Organization has agreed not to encumber certain real estate without approval of the bank. In addition, the Organization is to maintain at least $350,000 in net-free demand deposits as a compensating balance. This agreement expires March 31, 1991, and is expected to be renewed. No debt was outstanding on this line of credit at September 30, 1989 or 1990.

Reprinted with permission, 1990 Annual Report, World Vision, Inc. p. 24.

One way to obtain a short-term loan is to request one, called negotiated term loans, when it is needed. One problem with this is that when the organization most needs a loan is when it is also least attractive to a lender and is seen as very risky. Second, the term of the loan may be very unfavorable at that time. Third, the situation may be urgent (for example, to meet a payroll) and there just isn't time. For these reasons, organizations should establish lines of credit when their financial statements and outlook are most favorable.

Because cash flow problems are so common, every organization should consider a line of credit for short-term borrowing. Credit cards are a form of such credit, but these generally have such low limits that they cannot be used for major organizational purposes such as payroll. It is, therefore, good for the organization to negotiate a larger credit line. The question is whether the temptation to use it willy nilly can be contained. To protect against this, lines of credit should probably require the signatures of two authorized persons, just as checks should, when the amount being drawn exceeds, say, $1000.

The bank is a common source of short-term loans whether they be in the form of a credit card or a line of credit. Basically, the bank approves the nonprofit to draw a check on the bank without having to negotiate a loan each time. Lines of credit are good to have as long as they are not abused. Such loans are negotiated well in advance and are formalized by an agreement that is a promissory note. This note lays down the conditions under which the line is established, how the interest and finance charge will be determined, and the rights of both the borrower and the lender:

> This is an agreement between Chanel Bank (the Lender) and Carla Carter Charity, as borrower, for the establishment and use of a line of credit. This agreement constitutes a promissory note executed under seal, and we may enforce it to the full extent allowed by law for the enforcement of promissory notes. The credit line which the lender makes available to you permits you to borrow on a revolving basis up to the maximum indicated in this agreement. The credit line is secured by. . . .

Many types of assets may be used to secure a line, for example, inventory, the income from a contract or a grant already awarded the organization, real estate, or equipment. When an asset is used as security, the lender gets the right to inspect it and to require you to insure and to maintain it so that its value does not fall. The lender also reserves the right to foreclose and to demand that the property be sold when it appears that the loan is not likely to be paid. Under these circumstances, it can also call the loan, demanding full payment. It will demand to receive information if the property is to be sold by you and may prohibit its use as security for other loans without prior approval. Permission may also be required to move or modify the property.

When the organization's property is used to secure a loan, be sure that all legal steps are taken to record and free it once the loan has been repaid. In some cases, for example, on real estate in the District of Columbia, papers releasing the property must be filed. Because of the encumberance, called a lien, placed on the organization's property or future income, loans must be approved by the trustees.

The lender may also retain the right to assign or sell your promissory note. The sale of your note, normally not a problem, may occur without your knowing it because the terms of the loan will not change and because the lender may continue to service the loan, meaning that you will continue to pay the original lender and receive bills from it. The original lender then passes your payments to the institution to which it sold your loan. This is a common and usually harmless procedure.

The interest rate on lines of credit will normally vary according to some index. One commonly used index, the T-bill rate, is the rate that the federal government is paying to borrow money on a three- or six-month basis. Another index is the prime rate of some major bank, the rate that the major bank is charging its best customers. Usually, a credit line will charge a rate at least one and one-half percentage points higher, that is, the prime plus one and one-half.

Because rates may rise while a loan is outstanding, it is smart to choose a credit line that has a maximum by which it can increase per year and a ceiling. Thus, the contract may say that the rate is one and one-half percentage points above prime, but will not rise more than 2 percent per year and will never exceed 21 percent.

But two other concepts are important, partly because they affect your finance charge but also because they are useful information to have in controlling and managing your short-term finances. One of these concepts is the average daily balance. Every day the institution calculates the balance in your line of credit by adding what you borrowed that day from the outstanding balance at the beginning of that day and subtracting the amount it received from you as payment. It does this every day for the billing period—the period that the bill covers. Let us say that the billing period is thirty days. Then it sums up each day's balance over the thirty-day period. Since the billing period is thirty days, it divides the total by thirty and that gives the "average daily balance." It tells the nonprofit what its outstanding debt was per day on average during the period.

The finance charge for the period is obtained by dividing the annual percentage rate by the number of days in a year, 365 or 366. Thus, if the interest rate is 10 percent, dividing by 365 gives a daily rate of .027. This is the amount of "interest" your organization paid every day on its outstanding balance for that day during the billing period. By adding up all these charges for the thirty-day period, the total finance charge for the period is obtained. In short, you can reduce the cost of the loan to your organization by paying early in the billing period. This would reduce the amount outstanding, assuming no further borrowing.

Trade Credit

Another form of short-term loan is trade credit. This occurs, for example, when the organization purchases supplies and has thirty days to pay. If it pays within those thirty days, it pays no finance charge. This is free trade credit.

A variant of this involves discounts, say of 2 percent, if the organization pays in ten days or else it has to pay the full amount due in, say, thirty days. The discount lost by not paying within the ten days is actually an interest charge for a loan for twenty days (the 30 minus the 10). So, delaying beyond the discount period implies paying a finance fee.

Every organization should take advantage of discounts to the extent that by so doing a serious cash flow problem is not created. These discounts may also not be worth it if the organization has to liquidate accounts or assets that are earning higher rates than the organization is being charged by the vendor, or if it has to borrow from the bank at an unfavorable rate. In these cases, it is better to wait thirty days. The cost of a bounced check is usually higher than the implicit cost of foregoing the discount.

Advances

One of the least cumbersome ways of getting a short-term loan is through an advanced payment on a contract or grant. Sometimes it is possible to arrange these before the contract or program period. Other times it is done when money is needed. This is not cumbersome except one should be aware that, when money is advanced, interest can be charged and specific performance may be required. That is, repaying the advance may not free the organization from performance should it decide it does not want to go through with the contract. Consider an advance as a retainer. It is also a debt.

The IRS, Trustees, and Officers Not Lenders

An illegal form of short-term loan is borrowing from the IRS. This occurs when payroll taxes are not paid even though collected by the organization. The penalties on the organization, its management, and trustees can be severe. They are all liable. Do not use payroll and other taxes to meet short-term obligations.

Borrowing from trustees or officers of an organization may be convenient but not always wise. It encourages a merging of identities between persons and the organization they manage. Moreover, when loans are paid back they may give the appearance of self-dealing. Such loans, if they occur, should be documented, should not encumber the organization with any promises or obligations beyond repaying the loan, should be below market rate, should be authorized by the board, and should not violate state law, which may not permit them. Borrowing from trustees or officers should be a very last resort.

Cash Value Insurance

A source of short-term (or long-term) capital can be the cash value of insurance policies donated to the organization. As stated in Chapter 10, these cash values can be borrowed. All that is required is a written request to the insurance company. No collateral is necessary because the security the insurance company has is the insurance contract itself. The rates are usually below the commercial rates, and such loans do not have to be repaid. At the time of death, the total amount owed, including accumulated interest, is deducted from the face value of the insurance before the proceeds are paid to the organization. Policies more than seven years old are generally best for these purposes if a tax on such loans is to be avoided.

Foundations, Government, and Nonprofit Loan Funds

Occasionally, foundations will provide short-term loans to nonprofit organizations. In Minnesota and some other states, nonprofits have another option. The Minnesota Nonprofit Assistance Fund provides loans with terms ranging from thirty days to five years and for amounts ranging from a couple hundred dollars to hundreds of thousand of dollars. The intent is to provide financial stability to nonprofits, particularly 501(c)(3s) in Minnesota. As is similar in some foundation cases, loan recipients can also receive technical assistance.[2]

Long-term Loans

Long-term borrowing occurs principally for long-term reasons, such as the purchase of a building. These are usually secured loans. A common way of securing these loans is by pledging the property owned by the nonprofit, including land, equipment, and building. These can be sold to pay off the creditors or assigned to the creditors if the organization is unable to pay off the loan or meet scheduled interest payments.

Long-term borrowing is also secured by the income stream of the project, rather than the project or property itself. Dormitories, hospital buildings, and low-income housing are good examples of uses of long-term borrowing secured by the income stream of the project. These are called revenue bonds. The loans are made because the lenders believe that the income stream (revenues) from these projects will be high enough to pay the interest and the principal on a timely basis. Income from the project is the only collateral. These bonds are attractive to buyers because they do not have to pay income tax on the interest they earn. Accordingly, the cost of borrowing is lower. These bonds are sold on the capital markets just as every corporate bond is.

Long-term borrowing of this type involves more than can be covered in this book. Suffice it to say that any organization that contemplates this type of borrowing will soon learn how important it is to put together a good financial structure for the organization and a good reporting system. These nonprofits must compete with government agencies and corporations in the capital markets and therefore must be able to demonstrate financial stability. People buy these bonds not because of the mission of the organization but because they expect a competitive rate of return after accounting for the tax-free rates.

Leasing is an alternative to long-term borrowing. Basically, the nonprofit needs to compare the cost and advantages of leasing with the costs and advantages of purchasing. This type of financing is not for small nonprofits, but is of increasing use by housing authorities, hospitals, universities, and other large nonprofits.[3] See Chapter 15.

Borrowing and all the other approaches lead to an increase in the cash position of the organization. Note that the receipt of gifts and contributions is not ignored. As stated in item 1, an excess from operations is a source of cash. This excess is defined as the amount of all revenues and support (including gifts and contributions) minus all expenses. So the organization does increase its cash by increasing its receipt of gifts and contributions and other forms of support, including business income. But the actual amount of cash available at the end of any fiscal year depends on the timing of disbursements and receipts and their volumes. We shall say more about this later. But, first, what are the competing uses of cash?

Uses of Cash

Here are some of the ways the organization may opt to use its cash, whether it is gained from operations or a loan.

It can increase its fixed assets by buying more or better types of plants, equipment, or buildings.

It can increase its current assets by buying more marketable securities, making more prepayments, increasing inventory, buying more supplies, and financing more accounts receivables.

It can decrease its current liabilities by paying off notes, accounts payable, salaries, and wages, and its deferred revenues by spending what it takes to produce and deliver those items for which it has been paid but has not delivered.

It can pay its long-term debt. The organization could also use cash to finance the operating deficit. The fact that an organization has a deficit does not mean that it does not have to pay bills. The deficit may be financed by using previous years' cash accumulations or what would have been this year's cash accumulation.

Alternatively, if there is a surplus, cash could be saved. As we discussed previously under cash management, holding excess idle cash is usually unwise.

Cash management is a skill. It involves increasing the total volume (sources) and the rate (acceleration) at which cash flows into the organization. At the same time the volume (uses) and the rate (deceleration) at which cash flows out must be prudently tempered to meet the obligations and mission of the organization. Unlike government agencies, nonprofits are not "required" to disburse or obligate their funds at the end of the fiscal period. This is even illegal in federal agencies. Some surplus shown in the financial statements of nonprofits results from expenditures lagging behind receipts. This is good management and it provides cash for short-term investment opportunities. The lag might be due to time needed to build the organization's capacity to carry out a program successfully. The gain might be nothing more than interest arbitrage (the interest earned is higher than that due to the delay in paying a bill). Let us look at alternatives for investing excess cash.

LIQUIDITY VERSUS INVESTMENT AND RISK VERSUS SAFETY

The following steps may be taken once cash is available:

The board of trustees of the organization may elect to have a part of the cash placed in a restricted fund. This fund may be restricted so that withdrawals can occur only at the discretion of the board or to finance some specific activity in the future. Accumulation of this type is generally no problem for public charities, as discussed in Chapter 4 except it could affect its meeting watchdog standards. See Chapter 2. For private foundations, any attempt to set aside large amounts of cash should be done only after getting specific authorization from the IRS. Obviously, if accumulation is the choice, holding cash and currency makes no sense. The money ought to be invested.

Second, an amount of cash of approximately six months of the organization's cash need should be kept in a highly liquid asset earning interest with a very low risk of loss. Negotiable order of withdrawals (NOW) and money market accounts available at banks and savings institutions meet these conditions.

Third, beyond this amount, cash should be invested so as to stagger maturity dates. That is, some cash should be placed into instruments that have a 30-, 60-, 90-, and 360-day maturity. Repurchase agreements (as will be explained), certificates of deposit, Treasury bills, and commercial paper (short-term loans to corporations) are examples. These instruments pay higher rates of interest than NOW and money market accounts but are less liquid.

TEN CONSIDERATIONS IN SELECTING AND MAINTAINING A BANK ACCOUNT

The most direct way of dealing with cash is to put it into the bank. The potential losses of deposits by five nonprofits as a result of the demise of the Freedom National Bank in Harlem during the financial debacles of the 1990s is a reminder that banks are not risk free. Here are ten rules that should be helpful:

1. Be sure the bank is insured, preferably by the federal government.
2. Determine dollar limits of the insurance and whether the limit is per depositor, per bank, or per account.
3. Because of items 1 and 2, try to maintain no more than the limit in any one bank—diversify. If more than this amount must be kept, try to have separate accounts and indicate that each account is being held in your capacity as a fiduciary. Thus, it is being held for another entity. Using different branches may not help unless they are separately chartered; i.e., in different states.
4. Balance checks monthly and check each entry.
5. Compare fees, free checking, and interest payments. They differ among banks.
6. Be sure that your bank will be willing to make a short-term loan, or at least provide a line of credit. You may need it.
7. Hold money for investment and retirement in a different bank from holding money for check-writing needs. This relates to items 1 and 2, but it also relates to the fact that the same bank may not be equally good at both.
8. Check the investments of the bank. Some banks are risky.
9. Check the investment and performance of the parent if the bank is a part of a holding company—part of a larger bank family. Children can inherit the problems of their parents.
10. Check to determine if the bank has a social investment policy compatible with your interests. How much does it invest in the local community? Does it cater to nonprofits?

Near-cash Investments

One possible use of cash is to hold it to meet the known cash needs of the organization and to meet emergencies. There is no magic to determine what this amount should be. This depends on the experience of the organization. Aside from putting money in the bank, the organization could buy securities. Bank accounts rise because of the interest earned. A security may earn interest or dividends and rises if buyers bid up their prices and falls if any of these is reversed.

Treasury bills are the lowest-risk securities. They are issued by the U.S. Treasury weekly and carry a three, six, or 12 month maturity. They are sold in $5000 multiples with a $10,000 minimum required. Repurchase agreements have short (overnight) maturity. A borrower gives security to the nonprofit. When the loan is repaid the nonprofit returns the security. The risk of loss of any portion of the investment in commercial paper (a short-term loan to a corporation) can be reduced by buying only the shortest-term papers of the strongest companies. The risk of loss from buying certificates of deposit can be reduced by buying them from institutions covered by federal insurance.

Bonds

U.S. Treasury notes mature in two to five years and are sold in minimums of $1000 to $5000. Bonds may be bought from the Treasury, a government agency, state and local governments, or a corporation. Newly issued bonds mature in twenty to thirty years. This is a long time to commit the organization's money, and while we would like to think of bonds as having little risk, this is not the case. There are risks of default, and there is a risk of inflation, with not only a decline in the real value of the interest earned, but a fall in the bond prices as investors seek to make up for the low interest by lowering the price they will pay for it. Why pay $1000 for a bond that offers 7 percent, when you can get 10 percent on another bond? Thus, if the organization needs to sell before maturity, it will have to take a loss unless interest rates have declined, in which case it might make a gain as the price of the bond rises to reflect the fact that this bond earns more interest than ones issued at a lower coupon (interest) rate.

Low-grade corporate bonds (rated B or under) pay attractive rates but are highly risky not only of default, but of loss of principal if the corporation collapses. These are junk bonds. True, bondholders have a claim on the assets of the corporation, but this claim may be long in exercising and may be worthless.

The most risky of corporate bonds are subordinated debentures that have a below A rating. Subordinated or junior means that claims, in the event of bankruptcy, will be among the last honored. A debenture means that the bond has no collateral behind it. Below A means the firm is not among the financially strongest. These bonds pay high interest rates because of their high risk. They too are junk.

Another risk that bondholders face is that the bond may be called by the issuers. Bonds are called when the issuer sees that it can issue a new bond at a lower rate of interest. Consequently, a bondholder who is getting abnormally high rates of interest may not have that bond for very long as it may be called by the issuer. Unfortunately, it is usually impossible to reinvest the proceeds at similarly high rates and low risks because calls occur when interest rates have fallen. The inability to reinvest at a comparable rate and risk is called reinvestment risk.

Even some state and local government bonds have risks. Not all are backed by the full faith and credit of the issuing government. That is, not all are backed by the full taxing powers of the jurisdiction. Those that are reduce the risk of loss of principal investment or interest because the issuing jurisdiction is required by law to fully utilize its taxing powers to pay bondholders. But the fastest growing type of jurisdictional bonds have no such backing. These are called revenue bonds because they are backed only by the revenues from the project (housing, dormitories, hospitals) they finance. To reduce the exposure to risk, the managers of the nonprofit may obtain information on how the bonds are rated, keep to AAA or AA ratings, and take an additional precaution by being sure that the bond is part of an insured fund.

Stocks

Listed stocks are easily marketable because they can be bought and sold every working day unless some special event causes their trading to be suspended. Stocks are highly volatile. Preferred stocks (stocks that are given preference in the receiving of dividends and in the settlement of claims should the business collapse) are less risky than common stocks. The latter has lowest priority in exercising claims if the firm folds and no preference in the payment of dividends. Usually, the dividends paid are low and may be changed at any time by the board of directors of the corporation. Both types of stocks, but especially the common, offer the possibility of appreciation in their prices as the company's expected earnings are favorably valued by investors. They also have the possibility of decline as they become less favored, and common stocks are more volatile than preferred because, even in a decline, the investor can expect higher dividends from the preferred.

Stocks are dubious investments for some nonprofits because of their long-term perspective, volatility, and the capital needed to diversify among many companies so as to reduce the risk associated with any one doing poorly. Yet stocks have served many others well. One of the country's top twenty holders of stocks is a nonprofit: Teachers Insurance and Annuity Association and College Retirement Equities Fund (TIAA-CREF). Moreover, a number of nonprofits and foundations have sizable ownerships of businesses and indeed were originally founded by gifts of stocks in these businesses. Playing the stock market, however, requires a lot more expertise and involvement than some nonprofits have. For many, their involvement should not go further than accepting gifts of stocks and investing in mutual funds.

Mutual Funds

Mutual funds, other than money market funds, are of all types, There are corporate bond funds, municipal bond funds, energy funds, gold funds, and aggressive common stock funds, to name a few. There is virtually a mutual fund for every investment taste. Mutual funds are marketable in that they can be bought and sold with relative ease. They avoid the need for investment expertise on the part of the organization because they are managed by professional investment advisors.

Mutual funds reduce the risks of losses associated with individual common stocks because they are very large and highly diversified. Even a mutual fund that specializes only in gold will carry the stocks of several firms involved in gold. Mutual funds do not generally invest more than 10 percent of their portfolio in any one company so that the individual investor in one of these funds is not overexposed to the risks of collapse by any one company.

Partnerships

There is also the option of investing in tax-sheltered partnerships, but this serves no useful purpose to most nonprofits except pension funds. These partnership interests cannot be redeemed without considerable penalty and only in the amounts and at the times stated in the contract. Moreover, the need of nonprofits for a shelter is less than it is for tax-paying entities, and the use of such shelters may be challenged by the IRS.

Notice in the above paragraph that we were referring to partnerships for tax purposes. These are very different from the types of partnerships discussed in Chapters 8 and 12, where the partnership is for a productive purpose or for producing rental income, as discussed in Chapter 11. Several nonprofits, including the American Medical Association, engage in the latter types of partnerships. They are common in the non-profit housing and health sectors.

Buying Guide

Ratings can be used as a guide to determine the investment quality of bonds, commercial paper, municipal notes, and stocks. These ratings are not recommendations and they are not forecasts of how well the security will perform in the future. They are evaluations of the financial integrity of the issuer and the issue. In the following, we summarize certain ratings, beginning with the Moody's rating of corporate bonds.

Aaa: These bonds are judged to be of the highest quality. The interests are believed to be protected by exceptionally stable profit margins and the principal is deemed to be secure. The chances that the fundamental financial qualities of the issuer will deteriorate are deemed to be unlikely.

Aa: These bonds, like Aaa bonds, are considered high-grade bonds. They are not graded Aaa because their underlying financial position is subject to wider changes than the Aaa bonds, but they are of high quality.

A: These bonds are backed by the sound financial situation of the issuer, but some of these conditions may be subject to change in the future. These bonds are said to be of medium grade.

Baa: These are also medium-grade bonds but they are more speculative since it is believed that some of the underlying factors that protect principal and interest could deteriorate in the foreseeable future.

Ba: These bonds are characterized as uncertain. They are speculative with very modest protection of principal and interest.

B: These bonds are speculative and there is limited assurance that the principal or interest will be forthcoming in the future or that even the terms of the contract under which the bonds were purchased can be met.

Caa: These bonds may either be in default (interest has not been paid) or there are visible dangers that a default or the inability to pay principal may be imminent.

Ca: These are very speculative. They are either in default or seriously flawed.

C: These bonds have little likelihood of ever being upgraded to investment standing. They are the most speculative.

Sometimes Moody's will show the letter grades and a numerical grade. An Aaa 1 rating means that the security is in the top of the Aaa ratings and a C3 means that it is the lowest of the C-rated bonds.

Standard and Poor's has a similar rating system except that it uses pluses and minuses instead of a numerical grade to indicate the standing of each security within its generic class, and the letter grades are somewhat different. Thus, instead of Aaa, it uses AAA and instead of Ba, it uses BBB. Ratings of securities do change.

Again, the major purpose of these rating systems as far as the financial manager is concerned is as an indication of the investment worthiness of securities. It is often unnecessary, unwise, and sometimes illegal to invest the dollars of a nonprofit organization in a highly risky (below A) security. Another way to reduce risk is to purchase securities that are insured. Even municipal bonds may be insured so that the purchaser's risk is reduced. A good investment strategy is an excellent source of unrestricted income for running an organization. The earnings can generally be used at the discretion of the management to carry out the mission. Table 18.1 displays some typical investments and their risks.

TABLE 18.1 Securities: Their Typical Minimum Maturities and Risks

Securities	Typical Minimum Maturity Period	Comments
Negotiable order of withdrawal*	Immediate	Low risk, especially if institution is federally insured
Money market mutual fund	Immediate	Low risk, especially if portfolio is weighted toward U.S. Treasury paper
Repurchase agreements	1–90 days	Risk depends on security backing agreement
Commercial paper	20 days or more	Risk depends on issuing corporation
Certificate of deposit	90 days	Low risk, especially if institution is federally insured
U.S. Treasury bills	90 days	Low risk
Negotiable certificates of deposit	90 days	Low risk, but requires large initial amount of $100,000
U.S. Treasury notes	3 years	Low risk, but long holding period
U.S. Treasury bonds	30 years	Low risk, but long holding period
State and local government bonds	30 years	Varying risk depending on issuer; long waiting period
Mutual funds (other than money market)	Immediate	Risk depends on investment philosophy of fund
Corporate bonds	20 years	Risk depends on issue
Common stocks	Immediate	Wide fluctuations
Preferred stocks	Immediate	Fluctuate like bonds; risk of dividend default
Tax-sheltering partnerships	Indefinite	Risky and redemption depends on terms set in contract; early redemption will lead to losses
Guaranteed investment contracts	3–5 years	Fixed interest; should be considered long term

* By law, available only to individuals and nonprofits.

INVESTMENT STRATEGIES: ILLUSTRATION OF THREE PORTFOLIOS

Refer to the insert on the investments of the National Trust for Historic Preservation. They demonstrate that investment strategies must comply with cash needs. The distribution of investments is different among its three funds. The National Preservation Loan Fund and the Inner-City Ventures Fund provide low-interest loans as part of the mission of the organization. Consequently, much of their investments are in cash or cash equivalents (such as certificates and bank deposits) to provide liquidity; that is, easy access to the cash needed to make loans. A loan is an investment, noted on the books as "notes receivable." On the other hand, endowments are long term; hence, a greater proportion of this fund is in long-term securities such as corporate stocks, bonds, and U.S. government securities.

Turn back now to the notes (Note A) of the National Multiple Sclerosis Society in Chapter 17. Note A demonstrates an investment strategy

---

Investments

The composition of investments owned by the Trust at September 30, 1989 and 1988 is presented below:

September 30, 1989	National Preservation Loan Fund	Inner-City Ventures Fund	Endowment and Similar Funds	Total
Cash and cash equivalents	$ 1,531,637	1,647,943	2,150,709	5,330,289
Notes receivable	1,219,614	343,446	94,278	1,657,338
Master investment account:				
Cash and cash equivalents	—	—	1,037,693	1,037,693
Corporate stocks and bonds	—	—	25,323,361	25,323,361
U.S. government obligations	—	—	6,144,479	6,144,479
	$ 2,751,251	1,991,389	34,750,520	39,493,160
September 30, 1988				
Cash and cash equivalents	1,869,204	1,874,247	2,150,709	5,894,160
Notes receivable	862,486	317,959	1,064,423	2,244,868
Master investment account:				
Cash and cash equivalents	—	—	639,686	639,686
Corporate stocks and bonds	—	—	24,386,092	24,386,092
U.S. government obligations	—	—	174,710	174,710
	$ 2,731,690	2,192,206	28,415,620	33,339,516

Source: National Trust for Historic Preservation, Annual Report, 1989, p. 46.

that is diversified but conservatively focused on fixed income securities. The Girl Scouts is also diversified, but balanced between growth and fixed income securities. The difference between cost and market is the un- realized (because the securities have not yet been sold) gain from this investment strategy.

Marketable Securities at September 30, 1989 and 1988, Girl Scouts, Inc.				
	1989		1988	
	Cost	Market	Cost	Market
Common stocks	$ 7,235,000	$ 8,927,000	$ 6,912,000	$ 6,950,000
Corporate bonds	1,950,000	1,917,000	3,318,000	3,268,000
U.S. government obligations	3,535,000	3,546,000	2,958,000	2,916,000
Certificates of deposit and other short-term investments	6,482,000	6,482,000	3,142,000	3,142,000
Mutual funds:				
Equity	13,230,000	17,146,000	10,546,000	10,878,000
Fixed income	7,178,000	7,235,000	7,161,000	7,022,000
	$39,610,000	$45,253,000	$34,037,000	$34,176,000

Source: 1989 Annual Report, Girl Scouts, p. 24.

Investment Pools

Managers of small organizations may wonder whether investment strategies such as those used by larger organizations may be available to them. The answer is yes if through an investment pool. Such pools provide for several organizations to invest as a group. By doing this, they share risks, are able to diversify among several investments, are able to hire an investment advisor, and trade at a lower commission rate.

The National Conference of Catholic Bishops, the United States Catholic Conference, the American Board of Catholic Missions, the Campaign for Human Development, the Committee for the Church in Latin America, and the Catholic Communication Campaign, for example, have a short- and long-term investment pool for themselves. This assists them in conducting a wide range of charitable missions here and abroad, including financial support of other charities. Section 501(d) organizations,

Chapter 2, are specifically organized to permit religious organizations to have a common treasury and carry out investments.[4]

CAPITAL BUDGETING AND ENDOWMENT PLANNING: SETTING TARGETS

The operating budget that we described in Chapter 15 is concerned with the annual operation of the organization. It shows planned inflow and outflow of the organization's resources during the course of the coming year. Some organizations, but not many, have a multiyear operating budget. These budgets show the plan for annual operation of the organization for each of the next five years.

A capital budget shows the planned acquisition, disposition, or reconstruction of capital items. A capital item is one that has a useful life of more than one year. Furniture, equipment, buildings, automobiles, and computers are examples of capital items. The launching (not operation) of large, flagship, or sustaining programs that are at the core of the mission of the organization should also be considered a capital expense, especially if such programs are associated with endowments or capital expenditures such as the acquisition of new buildings or equipment.

Expenditures on capital items are called investments or capital expenditures. These are different from expenditures planned in the oper-

---

The Campaign for The Philadelphia Orchestra Association advanced to $25 million, raising $5.7 million in capital gifts during the 1990 fiscal year. This high level of capital fundraising took place side by side with an active Annual Giving Program, which grew by 12%.

The campaign consists of four capital components: the concert hall, the recital/chamber music hall, modernization of the Academy of Music, and augmentation of the Association's endowment funds. During Phase One of the Campaign, the objective is to solicit leadership gifts for the concert hall to reach the threshold of $50 million required before groundbreaking. As of August 31, the end of the 1990 fiscal year, gifts and pledges committed to the concert hall totaled $20.4 million. The end of the fiscal year also marked the early completion of the 1990 requirement to raise $2 million in new gifts and pledges for the concert hall, posed by the William Penn Foundation in order to qualify for their $3 million grant. During Phase Two, the priority will be to raise the remaining funds needed for the concert hall and the other components of the campaign.

Reprinted by permission: 1989–1990 Annual Report, The Philadelphia Orchestra, p. 12.

ating budget, which are operating expenses. An investment is an expenditure on an item that may change in value over time and that is not all consumed or used up in one year. A building is not used up in one year. It has a useful life of decades. But each year, a portion of the building, the computer, or the automobile is used up; that is, there is wear and tear. The dollar approximation of this wear and tear is called depreciation. Because depreciation arises as a result of annual operation, depreciation is shown as an annual expense in the operating budget and financial statements of the organization.

Furthermore, once the capital item is placed in service, it requires maintenance, and the principal and interest on the loan used to purchase the asset (mortgage in the case of a building and car loan in the case of an automobile) must be paid annually. These become annual operating expenses.

Thus, capital planning and budgeting require analyses not only of when and how the capital asset will be obtained, but how it would affect the annual operating budget. Two routes through which this impact occurs are by way of maintenance and amortization costs (payment of principal and interest). Another source is through insurance premiums. Credit and liability insurance premiums must be paid annually; they may increase as capital expenditures increase. An additional building means greater liability and credit risk exposures.

From a financial point of view, several questions arise in capital budgeting. Let us put ourselves in the position of the board of directors of a nonprofit organization considering the acquisition of a building. What are some of the questions that may arise?

Accumulation: Sources of Capital Funds

One question is the source of the required funds. Potential sources are gifts and contributions of money, including a large gift obtained in trust or the running of a special gift campaign, that is, a capital campaign.

A second potential source is through the accumulation and setting aside of part of the annual earnings of the organization. Recall that with private foundations such accumulations must be authorized by the IRS.

A third source of capital acquisition may be the physical gift of a building, which may be used, sold, or leased by the organization. Be reminded, however, that if the building is obtained through a gift and has a mortgage on it, the income from the rental could be subject to an unrelated business income tax and this annual tax payment would affect the organization's operating budget.

A fourth source that provides the basis for systematic accumulation is depreciation. By depreciating existing assets, an expense is written off current operations. But depreciation does not represent the kind of expense that requires the organization to draw a check. It is a paper expense. Therefore, one way to finance new acquisitions is to accumulate these paper expenses—actually setting aside each year the amount of depreciation so that these amounts may be used to purchase new assets as is done to help finance the Shriners Hospitals for Crippled Children.

A fifth source is debt; borrow the money. This source would also have an impact on the organization's operating budget since the principal and interest on the debt must be paid annually.

A sixth "source" is a leasehold arrangement. This is a cross between a lease (a long-term liability) and ownership. Basically, the owner of the property makes physical changes in the building to suit the specific needs of the nonprofit with the commitment from the nonprofit that it would stay for a specific number of years, pay rent according to a specific schedule, and leave a security deposit. In this case, the source of cash for rental payments is a capital fund or the operating revenues of the organization.

As we stated earlier in this book, nonprofits may not sell stocks in themselves. Therefore, this source of financing capital projects is not available to them as it is to for-profit corporations. As Chapter 10 tells, a company they control can issue stocks.

ACCUMULATION AND DISBURSEMENT STRATEGIES

A related set of questions has to do with the schedule of accumulating the funds needed to acquire the building. For example, the organization could collect all the money it needs in one year or it could collect it over a number of years. How much does it need to collect in each year if it chooses the latter course? How much does it need to collect by the end of the first year if it chooses to collect all the money at the end of that year?

Both answers depend on the rate of interest, for the smart financial manager would invest the collected sum in a safe investment paying a relatively predictable fixed rate. By doing this, the amount that has to be collected, borrowed, or taken from the organization's savings or shifted from the monies available for the daily operation of the organization would be lessened.

Let us assume that the rate of interest is 10 percent, the planning horizon, the time over which to accumulate the money, is four years, and the amount needed to acquire the building is $5,000,000. What are some of the alternative targets for accumulating the funds?

Present Value of Single Sum

One option is to have a fund-raising drive that ends at the end of the first year and to put that money into the bank so that, at 10 percent, it will accumulate the money needed to acquire the building over a four-year period. If the organization can be successful in doing this, it will be able to avoid debt, shift its fund-raising efforts to another program, and avoid using any of its operating income or savings from operations to buy the building. How much must it raise in the first and only year of its fund-raising effort in order that this strategy may be successful? What is its target amount?

A strategy such as this obviously depends on the amount of money that must be collected in the first year so that when it is invested at 10 percent over a four-year period it will equal $5,000,000. This is called the present value of a single sum. It is the dollar value of a single amount of money that, if invested, would yield the targeted amount at the end of some specified period (in this case 4 years) when the rate of interest per year is some specific amount (in this case 10 percent).

This problem can be solved by going to a table such as Table 18.2, which can be found in interest rate books. We look under the column called single payment present worth, and the row that applies to four years and we find a factor .6830. We multiply $5,000,000 by this factor and get $3,415,000. This is the amount that must be raised and invested in the beginning of the first year at 10 percent annual rate of return each year if the $5,000,000 target is to be met by the end of the fourth year. Of course, the board could significantly reduce this amount and still not take a greater risk by looking for a higher rate of return if it stretches out the time it has to accumulate the funds. If they chose to wait eight rather than four years, their fund-raising target would be (.4665) × $5,000,000) or $2,332,500.

Future Value of a Single Sum

Alternatively, the organization may already have a large gift that it can invest in the first year. The question that the board of trustees is

TABLE 18.2 Time Value of Money Assuming 10% Interest Factor

n Years	Single Payment Compound Amount — Future Value of $1	Single Payment Present Worth — Present Value of $1	Uniform Series Compound Amount — Future Value of Uniform Series of $1	Sinking-fund Payment — Uniform Series Whose Future Value Is $1	Capital Recovery — Installment to Amortize $1	Uniform Series Present Worth — Present Value of Uniform Series of $1
1	1.100	0.9091	1.000	1.00000	1.10000	0.909
2	1.210	0.8264	2.100	0.47619	0.57619	1.736
3	1.331	0.7513	3.310	0.30211	0.40211	2.487
4	1.464	0.6830	4.641	0.21547	0.31547	3.170
5	1.611	0.6209	6.105	0.16380	0.26380	3.791
6	1.772	0.5645	7.716	0.12961	0.22961	4.355
7	1.949	0.5132	9.487	0.10541	0.20541	4.868
8	2.144	0.4665	11.436	0.08744	0.18744	5.335
9	2.358	0.4241	13.579	0.07364	0.17364	5.759
10	2.594	0.3855	15.937	0.06275	0.16275	6.144
11	2.853	0.3505	18.531	0.05396	0.15396	6.495
12	3.138	0.3186	21.384	0.04676	0.14676	6.814
13	3.452	0.2897	24.523	0.04078	0.14078	7.103
14	3.797	0.2633	27.975	0.03575	0.13575	7.367
15	4.177	0.2394	31.772	0.03147	0.13147	7.606
16	4.595	0.2176	35.950	0.02782	0.12782	7.824
17	5.054	0.1978	40.545	0.02466	0.12466	8.022
18	5.560	0.1799	45.599	0.02193	0.12193	8.201

n						
19	8.365	0.11955	0.01955	51.159	0.1635	6.116
20	8.514	0.11746	0.01746	57.275	0.1486	6.727
21	8.649	0.11562	0.01562	64.002	0.1351	7.400
22	8.772	0.11401	0.01401	71.403	0.1228	8.140
23	8.883	0.11257	0.01257	79.543	0.1117	8.954
24	8.985	0.11130	0.01130	88.497	0.1015	9.850
25	9.077	0.11017	0.01017	98.347	0.0923	10.835
26	9.161	0.10916	0.00916	109.182	0.0839	11.918
27	9.237	0.10826	0.00826	121.100	0.0763	13.110
28	9.307	0.10745	0.00745	134.210	0.0693	14.421
29	9.370	0.10673	0.00673	148.631	0.0630	15.863
30	9.427	0.10608	0.00608	164.494	0.0573	17.449
35	9.644	0.10369	0.00369	271.024	0.0356	28.102
40	9.779	0.10226	0.00226	442.593	0.0221	45.259
45	9.863	0.10139	0.00139	718.905	0.0137	72.890
50	9.915	0.10086	0.00086	1,163.909	0.0085	117.391
55	9.947	0.10053	0.00053	1,880.591	0.0053	189.059
60	9.967	0.10033	0.00033	3,034.816	0.0033	304.482
65	9.980	0.10020	0.00020	4,893.707	0.0020	490.371
70	9.987	0.10013	0.00013	7,887.470	0.0013	789.747
75	9.992	0.10008	0.00008	12,708.954	0.0008	1271.895
80	9.995	0.10005	0.00005	20,474.002	0.0005	2048.400
85	9.997	0.10003	0.00003	32,979.690	0.0003	3298.969
90	9.998	0.10002	0.00002	53,120.226	0.0002	5313.023
95	9.999	0.10001	0.00001	85,556.760	0.0001	8556.676

faced with is will this be sufficient when invested at 10 percent over the four-year period to meet our target? Would we have to raise more money? How much more? This type of problem is called finding the future value of a single sum. That is, how much is a single sum invested today at, say 10 percent, worth in the future, say 4 years? Once we have found the answer to this, we can subtract this amount from our required amount and determine if we are going to meet, exceed, or fall short of the target.

To answer this question, turn to Table 18.2 and look under the single-payment compound amount. Assume that the amount the board of directors has on hand is $2,000,000. What would this amount be worth in four years invested in a manner that yields 10 percent per year? The factor is 1.464. Multiply $2,000,000 by this factor and get $2,928,000. Since $5,000,000 is needed, the board knows that it cannot rely merely on its initial investment. It must raise more money to meet its target.

Future Value of a Uniform Series of Payments

The board of directors may conclude that they prefer not to deal with a single sum. Rather, they would prefer to have a fund-raising campaign that is annual and stretches over a four-year period. This has the advantage of being less pressing on them and on the staff. They can assume, based on past experience and on their contacts, that they could raise a specific amount of money every year, say $800,000 per year. Would they meet their target if they collected that amount every year and put it into an investment paying 10 percent per year? Would they overshoot their target, fall short of it, or just meet it?

This type of problem requires finding the dollar value that a series of uniform payments made at the beginning of every year for a specified number of years would be worth on a specific future date. To solve this we go to Table 18.2 and the column that shows a uniform series compounded amount. We see the factor 4.641. Multiply this by $800,000 and get $3,712,800, which is how much $800,000 raised and invested each of four years will be worth at the end of the fourth year. The board will fail to meet its $5,000,000 target unless it raises more money or stretches out the period of raising and investing funds.

Sinking Fund

The reciprocal of the same uniform series of payments problem stated above is a sinking-fund problem. In this case, the trustees are less interested in whether they will exceed, fall short, or miss their target. They wish to give a clear and specific annual target to the fund-raising manager. "We have a target of $5,000,000 that we must have in four years. We know that the safest rate of return we can get on our money is 10 percent. To accomplish this, we give you a directive to set a fund-raising target of X number of dollars per year." The director of fund-raising retorts, "I shall be happy to follow your orders if you could specify how much must be raised each year under the conditions you have set."

The answer can be found by resorting to Table 18.2. The column entitled "Sinking-fund Payment" tells how much money must be sunk into a fund each year if a specific target is to be met over a specific number of years and when the rate is 10 percent. Multiply the factor shown for four years, .21547, by $5,000,000. The fund-raising team must come up with $1,007,350 per year. Notice that this is substantially lower than the fund-raising target when the money is expected to be raised only in one year (the example given earlier), but to accomplish the objective, the fund-raising campaign must last at the same intensity for four years.

Capital Recovery

The board of directors may follow another option. They may decide that they would rather go out and borrow the money to acquire the building. They know that if they do this they will have to pay principal and interest on the loan each year until the loan is paid off. This is called amortization, the paying off of a debt. They will borrow the entire $5,000,000. How much will be their annual payment in principal and interest? In other words, how much will the lender charge per year so as to recover the full amount loaned plus the interest charged? This is called a capital recovery problem.

To solve this problem, go to Table 18.2 and locate the column showing capital recovery. The factor is .31547, which when multiplied by $5,000,000 gives $1,577,350. This is how much the organization would have to come up with each year if it borrows the funds at 10 percent and pays off the mortgage in four years. More realistically, it may choose a thirty-year mortgage. The factor there is .10608. Multiply it by $5,000,000 and get $530,400, the amount it must come up with each year (its target) to pay off its principal and interest.

Present Value of a Uniform Series

The reciprocal of the capital recovery problem involves finding out how much money the organization could borrow given its capacity to pay a total sum of money each year. Would the amount of money we can afford to pay each year for the next specific number of years be sufficient to pay both principal and interest on our loan so that at the end of that period our loan would be paid off?

In this case, the trustees are willing to commit to a specific annual payment, but only if it would be enough to pay off the principal and interest on the debt. To answer the question, turn to Table 18.2 and the column showing the present worth of a uniform series. Assuming that the organization is willing to come up with $200,000 per year for the next 10 years, what size mortgage could it afford assuming a mortgage rate of 10 percent? The factor is 6.144, which when multiplied by $200,000 gives $1,118,800, the maximum mortgage it can afford.

Perpetual Endowment

Once a building is built it has to be maintained for the remainder of its life. It has to be painted, remodeled, refitted with heating and air conditioning systems, and so on. Good planning will involve the kind of strategy used by the Colonial Williamsburg Foundation. They decided that they would not only raise the funds to construct a building but raise the funds to do the maintenance for the life of the building. Hence, once the building is in service, they do not have to be searching for funds to keep it maintained. It is a farsighted and wise strategy. A precious building will not stand in jeopardy of being ruined, as did the Statue of Liberty, for the lack of money to do maintenance and repairs.

Since a building could conceivably last forever, the board may well ask, assuming that we have a fund of $4,000,000 that we intend to last forever, how much would we have per year to take care of maintenance and repairs if we use just the earnings of the fund for repairs? By using only the earnings, the principal amount we invested in the fund would last forever. It will always be there earning money to pay for the maintenance and repairs. This is the called perpetual endowment problem. Funding scholarships and professorships are of this type. Thus, Chapter 10 refers to endowments as lasting forever.

The answer to this problem is not found in Table 18.2. It is simple. Multiply the principal amount by the rate of interest expected per year and we get the target. Hence, if the rate of return on the invested $4,000,000 is 10 percent, $400,000 would be available each year to maintain and operate the building.

Capitalization

Capitalization is the opposite of a perpetual endowment. In capitalization, the board of trustees is asking, how much must we put up in an endowment if we know that the annual cost of repairs and maintenance or of scholarship awards is $200,000 per year? In other words, how much capital must we put in an endowment if we intend to use only the earnings of the endowment so that the principal will last forever, earning the required amount of money we need to do maintenance and repairs or to award scholarships so that we might never have to undertake (unless in an unusual circumstance) to borrow, use operating funds, or have another fund raiser for this specific purpose.

To answer this question, let us assume that the expected rate of return on the investment is 10 percent. Divide this required amount of $200,000 by 10 percent and get $2,000,000. This is the target amount by which an endowment would have to be capitalized if it is to yield sufficient money annually to pay for the repairs and maintenance of the building.

Disbursement in Practice: Simple Rules and Practices

In practice, trustees are responsible for setting disbursement schedules and procedures for capital and endowment funds. Beginning with the foregoing exercise, they set simple rules. Note one thing about all these rules; they aim to have the endowment last forever. They also assume a 10 percent rate of interest is available every year and inflation does not erode the value of the earnings by causing the cost of the repairs, scholarships, or other reasons for withdrawal to escalate. In actuality, these do happen, and so trustees monitor annual performance and requirements particularly over withdrawals, which, unlike earnings, they control. How do they do it?

The American Red Cross uses what is known as the total return method for withdrawing and disbursing funds from its endowment. At the beginning of each year, the trustees set a spending or withdrawal rate, called a target withdrawal rate, which is a percentage of the market value of the portfolio at the beginning of each year.[5] Under this method, disbursements to meet this target are made first from net investment earnings of that year. If this is insufficient to meet the target, the rest is taken from cumulative realized gains (the amounts accumulated from the past sale of assets and securities). This preserves the original principal, which grows whenever current investment income equals or exceeds withdrawal needs.

A variation of this approach using moving averages is used by many colleges. It works this way. A policy setting a fixed percentage of 5 percent of the earnings of the past five years is the withdrawal target. This means that in 1986 the withdrawal was based on 1980–1985 earnings, in 1987, on 1981–1986, and in 1988 on 1982–1987. This dampens the impact of erratic earnings—when they are in a valley or peak—on how many dollars can be disbursed.

Disbursements conform to contingencies set up by the board or by the grantor of the endowment. To illustrate, the Fund for the New Era is the legal name of an endowment set up by the National Urban League based on a grant from the Ford Foundation. The terms of the grant prohibit disbursement from the principal for five years. Such terms are based on the calculations that we discussed earlier and are intended to give the endowment an opportunity to grow and to last into perpetuity. The League is permitted to expend, for operational purposes, any net realized gains. The basis for calculating this gain is the dollar value of the endowment when it was started. But it is also required to plow into the endowment over a five-year period cash and securities matching the $4,500,000 of the original gift.[6]

Finally, when starting a new endowment, postponing all disbursements may be a good strategy. Accordingly, the board of trustees of Camp Fire Boys and Girls prohibits any disbursements from its endowment until it has reached $750,000.[7]

PRESERVATION OF ENDOWMENTS

The law requires that endowments be prudently administered to preserve the intent of the donor and that the trustees act with loyalty toward the public purpose of the endowment. The list of actions given in Chapter 16 that could be cause for suit applies to endowments.

When we say that endowments must be administered by the terms of the contracts that create them, we are making reference to law. The borrowing of money that is in an endowment, shifting it to some other use, and closing an endowment are all legally prohibited transactions unless allowed in the endowment contract. Otherwise, the management, trustees, or board can be sued by the donors or their public beneficiaries. To make such unspecified transactions legal, the trustees or board may have to get permission from a court. Such permission is usually granted if a financial crisis that cannot be satisfied in some other manner can be demonstrated; if the purpose of the endowment no longer exists or is impracticable, contrary to public policy, or financially infeasible; and when actions required by the endowment would lead to its destruction. Under what the lawyer's call a **cy pres** ruling, the court may give authority for the funds to be used in some manner other than that stipulated in the contract but consistent with the mission of the organization.

To illustrate the need for abiding with public policy, in one case the IRS concluded that a charitable trust, though established and functioning for decades, was no longer qualified for tax exemption and its donors no longer qualified for tax deductions because the fund's mission was to aid "worthy white people."[8]

To avoid these types of problems, attorneys try to eliminate this type of language, which was perfectly acceptable at the time that trust was set up. Of course, the problem can be reduced when the fund is created by the board of trustees of the organization by transferring operating surpluses into a restricted fund. Yet it is not uncommon that universities and other nonprofits run into serious problems with their own restrictions.[9] Time changes.

Some endowments are set up so that they will not commence making awards or cash payments until the passage of some time. Recall deferred giving in Chapter 10. This gives the fund an opportunity to grow, to establish some critical level based on a calculation of the future value of a single payment, and then to make perpetual awards based on some calculation and the capitalized value, that is, the amount that is needed to sustain a perpetual gift at some specific amount.

TIME AND RISKS IN ENDOWMENT PLANNING

It should be obvious from what has been said in this section that capital planning and endowment management are related to sustaining the growth and performance of the organization over several years. It has not only to do with buying buildings, equipment, and machines but in creating funds that can finance the mission of the organization well into the future.

In all capital planning problems, as we saw above, the pressures on the fund-raising campaign can be reduced by stretching out the time required to accumulate a targeted amount of money or investing it in assets that pay a higher rate of return. Let us consider each of these. A higher rate of return always implies a greater risk: the rate may decline, the investment is risky and that is why it must pay a high rate so as to attract money, the issuer may default or go bankrupt because of its inability to meet high expenses, including the high rates it must pay, and so on. Because securities of the federal Treasury are generally considered to be the lowest risk, a rate approximating their prevailing rate is what should be used as a basis for judging the relationship between risk and return. For most legal purposes, the IRS requires the presumption of a rate around 10 percent. It is periodically announced.

Moreover, because the rate has to be presumed to prevail for the length of the planning horizon, in the above case four years, the investment that should be made is one that is likely to keep a relatively fixed rate for that period of time. The accumulated funds should be invested in reasonably safe fixed-rate assets that mature at about the time the money is needed. Notes, bonds, U.S. Treasury securities, securities of government agencies, certificates of deposits, even high-grade zero-coupon bonds and municipal bonds are examples.

Stretching out the time reduces the pressures on the fund-raising efforts and may perhaps make the project more realistic. This has to be weighed against other factors. Stretching out the time increases risk: inflation would cause the cost of the project to rise. If the assets held are fixed rate, then their value will decline or probably will not keep pace with the rise in inflation. Thus, the earnings to finance the project will not keep pace with its rising costs and more, not less, fund raising will be necessary, and common stocks may be a superior alternative to bonds.

Stretching out time also risks loss of interest on the part of donors and, in the case of buildings, changes in zoning or building codes that could increase costs. On the other hand, stretching out time does have an advantage—feasibility.

SETTING TARGET PRICES, FEES, AND DUES

For a nonprofit organization to do well selling its goods and services requires a rational approach to the setting of prices and fees. In this section, we describe some approaches.

Prices and Fees

It is essential to note that all prices are eventually determined by the market, some prices more so than others. In a very competitive market, the price or fee that a nonprofit will be able to charge will depend on the prices or fees being charged by its competitors. Even in a monopoly situation where the nonprofit sets a price and does not have to worry about competition, market forces will determine how much of that good or service will be sold. If there is no demand for the product, it will not sell. If the demand is limited by a very high price, only a few will be purchased. If the price is low enough and consumers are very sensitive to prices, more will be sold. This is the basic law of supply and demand.

Not only does the market set limits on prices, but so too do the laws and regulations from federal, state, or local authorities. For example, where there is rent control, nonprofits may not exceed it unless by special exemption.

In short, whatever the price or fee level set by the nonprofit and whichever of the methods it uses to determine those prices or fees, they must eventually adjust to the realities of the market and the law. Therefore, the methods to be discussed may best be viewed as rational ways to determine target prices or fees.

The rational setting of prices and fees means that they should have some relationship to costs. To simplify matters, let us describe the full costs of producing a good or service as composed (1) of direct costs resulting solely from the production of the good or service, and (2) indirect costs only partly related to the production of the good and service. Put another way, direct costs exist only because the good or service is being produced. Indirect costs would exist whether or not a specific good is being produced because the organization has to incur costs to exist and to carry on its nonprofit mission.

Various price or fee targets can be set depending on the amount of the direct and indirect costs the organization wishes to recover. On one level, the nonprofit may set a fee or price that does not meet even its direct costs. It can do this only to the extent that gifts and contributions make up the difference. This is in fact what many nonprofits do. When they set the price of their goods or service at zero (or no charge), they are totally dependent on gifts and contributions to pay for the cost of the service they provide.

On a second level, the nonprofit may set a price or fee that only recovers its direct costs. When this is done, less pressure is placed on gifts and contributions to support that particular activity. Gifts and contributions would be needed only to cover the indirect costs, a portion of which would exist even if the good or service were not being produced.

On a third level, the price or fee could be set so that the full costs, both direct and indirect, are being covered by the price. In this case, the activity is self-supporting. The gifts and contributions can be used to advance other missions of the organization.

On yet another level, the price or fee may be set so that the organization not only recovers its full costs (direct and indirect) but more. It can do this by adding a percentage to its full costs. In the for-profit world, this percentage reflects a profit or a return on the investment to owners. This margin is also permitted to nonprofits. In the General Council Memorandum 39346, dated March 15, 1985, the IRS concluded that the provision of veterinary service for a fee of cost plus a percent was not in violation of the tax-exempt status of 501(c)(3) organizations formed to provide veterinary services. Moreover, the IRS concluded that, given the facts and circumstances of that organization, the markup did not constitute an unrelated business and therefore it was not taxable.

The significance of this last level of setting a target price or fee is that this extra percentage can be (and virtually must be if it is not to be taxed as an unrelated business) used to support the advancement of the mission of the organization. Hence, the pricing levels described progress from losses that impose a burden on the organization to one that provides a legal surplus helping to support the organization in its mission.

Setting of prices or fees does not necessarily subvert or destroy the charitable character of the organization or its mission. The fees or prices may be set according to some means test. Clients are charged according to their ability to pay. Those who cannot pay are served without charge, and the charge rises as the ability to pay increases. Thus, in setting rental levels in homes for the elderly, the nonprofit must set the prices so that they fall within the financial reach of a significant proportion of the elderly population in the community. Should a resident not be able to pay, the organization should be prepared to make necessary arrangements to continue to provide housing even in a housing project operated by another organization. The organization should also operate at the lowest feasible cost. This does not mean that it does not provide amenities, but that the cost of these plus other necessary costs should not become so high that the subsequent price is out of reach of a large segment of the elderly population.

Prices can be set in a deliberate attempt of the organization to meet its mission and to demonstrate public support. The John F. Kennedy Center for the Performing Arts sells tickets at half-price to seniors, low-income groups, students, military, and handicapped persons. The cost of doing this is considered by the Center as part of its educational and public service mission. The Metropolitan Museum of Art in New York "suggests" an entrance fee (presently $6.00) to its visitors on a sliding scale—lower rates for senior citizens and zero for children.

Dues

Membership dues are prices; the cost to an individual or entity to be a member. For nonprofits that are not social clubs, setting these dues should balance the ability to pay with the benefits received. Partly because of the support rules described in Chapter 4, the rules on deductions, and for marketing purposes, it helps to separate these two considerations.

Accordingly, part of the dues should be based on the average (per person) total cost of running the organization and providing benefits from which people cannot be excluded. This part of the dues should be based on a sliding scale according to the ability to pay. This portion could very well have a value of zero for the least able to pay.

The second component of the dues may reflect benefits received. Thus, we may tilt higher dues to those who receive the greater benefit. For most organizations, this runs counter to the ability to pay, and, unlike a firm, a nonprofit should place more weight on the ability to pay.

One way to reconcile this difference is to structure the dues based on the ability to pay. Then take all those benefits that can be priced and make them available to the membership at a price. Hence, there is an annual dues according to a sliding scale; but if one wishes to attend a conference or receive a publication, a price is charged. The target dues, like the target price, are subject to market considerations. It will be lowered if people do not value the organization's services as highly as it does or cannot pay, in which case the organization will have to return to the point from which we began this book: Whose welfare is it advancing?

SUMMARY AND CONCLUSIONS

The final chapter of this book has shown how the financial function of the nonprofit organization is continuous and feeds back into the planning of the future of the organization and the continuous search for new opportunities.

The successful search rests on the ability of management to expand its view of what the organization can and cannot do legally and the identification of appropriate niches within and outside the boundaries of the marketplace. However, merely identifying these potential niches is not enough. The organization needs to have a well thought out set of financial strategies and targets that is consistent with its mission and capabilities and objectives. This chapter focused on setting targets and the management of cash to meet these financial targets. Best wishes for the mission and future of your organization.

NOTES

1. Form 990-PF, mentioned in the insert, is the form used by private foundations.
2. Susan Kenny Stevens, "Loan Fund Eases Temporary Financial Binds," *Giving Forum*, July 1990, p. 7.
3. Gregory H. Eden, "Tax Exempt Leasing for Colleges and Universities," Richard E. Anderson and Joel W. Meyerson, eds., *Financing Higher Education: Strategies after Tax Reform* (San Francisco: Jossey Bass 1987), pp. 41–52.
4. United States Catholic Conference, *Reports on Examinations of Financial Statements and Additional Information*, 1983 and 1984 (Washington, D.C.: The Conference, April 19, 1985), p. 6.
5. American Red Cross *Annual Report 1989*, p. 31.
6. National Urban League, Inc., Annual Report, 1989, p. 41.
7. Camp Fire Boys and Girls, Annual Report, 1988–89, p. 32.
8. Private Letter Ruling, 8910001.
9. For a summary of this literature, see Edward Johnson and Kent M. Weeks, "To Save a College: Independent Colleges Trustees and Decisions on Financial Exigency, Endowment Use, and Closure," *Journal of College and University Law*, 12, no. 4 (Spring 1986), pp. 455–488.

SUGGESTED READINGS

FABOZZI, FRANK J., AND LESLIE MASON, *Corporate Cash Management* (Homewood, Ill.: Dow-Jones Irwin, 1985).

JOHNSON, EDWARD A., AND KENT M. WEEKS, "To Save a College: Independent College Trustees and Decisions on Financial Exigency, Endowment Use, and Closure," *Journal of College and University Law*, 12, no. 4 (Spring 1986), pp. 455–488.

VIGELAND, CARL A., *Great Good Fortune, How Harvard Makes Its Money* (Boston: Houghton-Mifflin, 1986).

Index